SCOTT: THE CRITICAL HERITAGE

THE CRITICAL HERITAGE SERIES

GENERAL EDITOR: B. C. SOUTHAM, M. A., B.LITT. (OXON.)

Formerly Department of English, Westfield College, University of London

SCOTT

THE CRITICAL HERITAGE

Edited by

JOHN O. HAYDEN

Assistant Professor of English
University of California, Davis

NEW YORK
BARNES & NOBLE, INC.

64116

First published in Great Britain 1970
Published in the United States of America 1970
by Barnes & Noble, Inc., New York, N.Y.

© John O. Hayden 1970

SBN 389 01331 5

Printed in Great Britain

General Editor's Preface

The reception given to a writer by his contemporaries and near-contemporaries is evidence of considerable value to the student of literature. On one side we learn a great deal about the state of criticism at large and in particular about the development of critical attitudes towards a single writer; at the same time, through private comments in letters, journals or marginalia, we gain an insight upon the tastes and literary thought of individual readers of the period. Evidence of this kind helps us to understand the writer's historical situation, the nature of his immediate reading-public, and his response to these pressures.

The separate volumes in the *Critical Heritage Series* present a record of this early criticism. Clearly for many of the highly-productive and lengthily-reviewed nineteenth- and twentieth-century writers, there exists an enormous body of material; and in these cases the volume editors have made a selection of the most important views, significant for their intrinsic critical worth or for their representative quality—perhaps even registering incomprehension!

For earlier writers, notably pre-eighteenth century, the materials are much scarcer and the historical period has been extended, sometimes far beyond the writer's lifetime, in order to show the inception and growth of critical views which were initially slow to appear.

In each volume the documents are headed by an Introduction, discussing the material assembled and relating the early stages of the author's reception to what we have come to identify as the critical tradition. The volumes will make available much material which would otherwise be difficult of access, and it is hoped that the modern reader will be thereby helped towards an informed understanding of the ways in which literature has been read and judged.

B. C. S.

This book is for Mary

Contents

CONTENTS

The Antiquary (1816)

The Black Dwarf and Old Mortality (1816)

Rob Roy (1818)

The Heart of Midlothian (1818)

Ivanhoe (1820)

The Monastery (1820)

Ivanhoe (1820) [cont.]

The Pirate (1821)

CONTENTS

The Fortunes of Nigel (1822)

CONTENTS

Acknowledgments

I would like to thank T. M. Raysor for permission to quote from his edition of *Coleridge's Miscellaneous Criticism* (1936); Oliver and Boyd for permission to quote several passages from Tait and Parker's edition of *The Journal of Sir Walter Scott* (1939-47); A. P. Watt & Son for permission to quote from W. G. Partington's edition of *The Private Letter Books of Sir Walter Scott* (published in the United States by Frederick Stokes Co., copyright 1930 Wilfred George Partington, copyright renewed 1958 by Audrey Mary Ormrod); The Foreign Languages Publishing House, Moscow, for permission to quote from V. G. Belinsky's *Selected Philosophical Works* (1956); the Clarendon Press, Oxford, for permission to quote from E. L. Grigg's edition of the *Collected Letters of Samuel Taylor Coleridge* (1956-59), from Ernest De Selincourt's edition of *The Letters of William and Dorothy Wordsworth: The Middle Years* (1937), from R. W. Chapman's edition of *Jane Austen's Letters*, 2nd ed. (1952), and N. C. Smith's edition of *The Letters of Sydney Smith* (1953); and Charles Scribner's Sons for permission to quote from Sidney Colvin's *Memories and Notes of Persons and Places* (1921); Calder & Boyers Ltd. for permission to reproduce the translation of Stendhal's 'Walter Scott and La Princesse de Clèves' (1959).

James T. Hillhouse's account of the reception of Scott's novels and James C. Corson's annotated bibliography of Scott were of inestimable value, the former especially in composing the introduction, the latter especially in the selection and location of items. A debt of another nature I owe to the Interlibrary Loan Department of the University of California, Davis, Library: Vera Loomis, Susan Moger, Mary Ann Hoffman, Jeri Bone, and Loraine Freidenberger. Their professional competence and expedition were essential to my project; their friendliness obligates me still further. I would also like to express my appreciation to my colleague at Davis, Mr. Elliot Gilbert, and to an old friend, Mr. George Dekker of the University of Essex, both of whom read the introduction and made suggestions for its improvement. A generous grant from the Humanities Institute of the University of California provided me with the free time necessary to put together this edition.

My thanks also to Mr. Stephen Arroyo and Miss Karen Kahl, work-study assistants who have been a great help in preparing the text, and to Mrs. Susan Freitas, my indefatigable typist.

Note on the Text

The materials printed in this volume follow the original texts in all important respects. Lengthy extracts from Scott's poems and novels have been omitted whenever they are quoted merely to illustrate the work in question. These omissions are clearly indicated in the text. Typographical errors in the originals have been silently corrected.

Introduction

I

Intensives and superlatives are the devices of the puffing book-jacket, not the terms of sober literary history. No one, in any case, pays much attention to such extravagant descriptions. How then does one draw attention to the extraordinary popularity of a writer like Sir Walter Scott? Bald statements must suffice: no writer before him had been so well received by his contemporaries—*ever*.

Scott's unprecedented popularity is perhaps best shown in a singular fact about the publication of the Waverley novels. They were printed in Edinburgh and copies for the English market were then shipped from Leith to London on a packet. What the reviewer in the *Literary Museum* had to say in 1823 about one of the occasional delays of the boat makes the point directly:

Rarely, we believe, has the fury of the winds and waves been deprecated by more numerous wishes than were lately put up for the safety of that vessel which sailed from the north, freighted with the impression of *Peveril of the Peak*.

Now, he continued, it is safely docked, and in a few hours the book 'will stand blazoned in immense capitals in the window, or on the doorposts, of every bookseller in the metropolis'.[1] The publication of each Waverley novel was an EVENT, albeit a frequent one, and the weekly literary journals often had copies shipped down at some expense by coach to beat their competitors in reviewing the book.

The number of contemporary reviews of each novel was large; from ten to thirty reviewing periodicals gave attention to each. The popularity of the novels can also be seen in the correspondence and diaries of the time: scarcely any were without some reference to 'the author of *Waverley*' or to his works. In short, there was no lack of materials to select from in compiling this volume.

There is, of course, the reception of Scott's poetry as well as his prose to contend with. His verse romances, such as *Marmion* and *The Lady of the Lake*, have never been as popular as his novels; although they continued to enjoy a considerable sale, when *Waverley* appeared in 1814 the poems were eclipsed. But when they first appeared, they provided a good sample of the sort of applause Scott would encounter when he turned to prose; and so to reflect this early popularity, a scattering of reviews of the poetry has been given in this volume. Much of the criticism is, furthermore, far from contemptible. At least on the negative side the sort of things are said that should have been said.

But although the treatment of Scott's novels is emphasized in the documents that follow, the later discussion of his verse is given more space than can be defended by citing its popularity then or now. Scott's poetry was relegated by many Victorians to the status of children's reading; and yet others, some few of their commentaries selected here, made interesting attempts to find approaches to his verse which would entitle it to adult respect and appreciation.

As for the commentaries on Scott's novels after his death, the problem is one of volume; for considering the normal posthumous erosion of an author's popularity, there was not much decline in interest in the Waverley novels throughout most of the nineteenth century, even though by 1860 newer techniques in novel writing had made much of Scott's writing appear clumsier than it seemed to his contemporaries. The terminus of 1885 has been chosen as the approximate date by which Scott ceased to be popular with the reading public at large. Some of the later documents are included as illustrative of certain trends, but on the whole they contain valid criticism in their own right.

II

Some knowledge of the publication history of Scott's works can help our understanding of his contemporary reception. His poetic career began more or less with his first major original work, *The Lay of the Last Minstrel*, a verse romance published in 1805. In spite of flaws in the story and in the versification and diction, the poem was generally well received, probably because, as Carlyle pointed out (No. 51), Scott's poetry stood out against the bleak poetic background of the time, the insipidity of William Hayley's verse, the uninspired didacticism of Erasmus Darwin's *The Loves of the Plants*, or the silliness of Della Cruscan lyrics. At least *The Lay* had a certain vigour and sharply drawn descriptions. It ran through fifteen editions by 1815, in any event, and was followed by the still more successful *Marmion* (1808) and *The Lady of the Lake* (1810). According to John Gibson Lockhart both the last-mentioned poems ran to at least 50,000 copies by 1836.[2]

But in 1814, having detected a slight decline in his poetic popularity which he himself attributed to the rise of Byron's, Scott published his first novel, *Waverley*. Much the same situation that obtained for poetry in 1805 existed for the novel in 1814. Besides Jane Austen, whose anonymous novels caused so little stir, and the more popular Maria Edgeworth, there was no other living novelist of interest; much of the fiction of the time was manufactured by the Minerva Press for circulating libraries. Consequently, fiction no longer enjoyed a high standing. Although Defoe, Richardson, Fielding, and Smollett were mentioned with respect, the genre itself had fallen in the estimation of the early nineteenth century.

Scott singlehandedly revived the reputation of the novel and showed that novel-writing could be a lucrative profession. According to Lockhart, it took five weeks to sell the first impression (1,000 copies) of *Waverley*, but by the end of the first year six editions had appeared.[3] *Old Mortality* (1816) sold 4,000 copies in the first six weeks, *Rob Roy* (1818) 10,000 copies in the first fortnight.[4] *The Fortunes of Nigel* (1822), however, makes both figures look comparatively insignificant. Archibald Constable, Scott's publisher, made him the following report on its arrival in London in May 1822:

A new novel from the author of *Waverley* puts aside—in other words, puts down for the time, every other literary performance. The Smack Ocean, by which the new work was shipped, arrived at the wharf on Sunday; the bales were got out by *one* on Monday morning, and before half-past ten o'clock 7,000 copies had been dispersed from 90 Cheapside [his London agent's address].[5]

And as for Scott's income from his publications, Lockhart claims that in 1822 the novels were bringing in between £10,000 and £15,000 per year.[6]

The speed with which Scott produced his novels and other works partly accounts for these very large sums. Between July 1814 and July 1818, six Waverley novels were published, but in 1819 and the early 1820s the novels appeared every four to six months. Indeed, *Ivanhoe* and *The Monastery* were published about two and a half months apart. The reviewer of *Quentin Durward* in the *New Monthly Magazine* (No. 34) did in fact complain, in his capacity as exhausted reviewer, of 'the announcement of "Another Novel from the Great Unknown" '.

The Waverley novels were published anonymously, the second and following ones being designated as 'by the author of *Waverley*'. Most reviewers saw through the anonymity but played along by referring to the author as, among other things, 'The Great Unknown', 'the Enchanter of the North', 'the Northern Magician', 'The Scottish Prospero', and even 'the Pet of the Public'. Some reviewers, nevertheless, occasionally retailed rumours of other authorship: Thomas Scott (Sir Walter's brother in America), Mrs. Thomas Scott, and a 'Mr. Forbes' (No. 16); and, in view of the great productivity, the collaboration of several unknown authors was seriously proposed.

The importance of the anonymity is perhaps exaggerated today, for anonymity seems to have been a literary phenomenon of the age. Wordsworth's and Coleridge's *Lyrical Ballads*, Byron's *English Bards*, *Beppo*, and *Don Juan*, and various works by Jane Austen, Thomas Moore, Samuel Rogers, Robert Southey, and Charles Lamb, together with a few verse romances by Scott himself, indicate the kind of strange attraction anonymity held for Romantic writers; and of course almost all the literary reviews were unsigned. In many cases there was an additional reason for the literary anonymity: satire, political attacks, or literary experimentation called for the cloak of mystery. In the case of the Waverley novels such motives seem largely missing; and in view of the unprecedented popularity of the works the reviewers often expressed puzzlement at the anonymity. When the veil was finally lifted in 1827, Scott claimed in his preface to *The Chronicles of the Canongate* that the anonymity began as 'the humour or caprice of the time' and was continued after the success of *Waverley* in order to avoid the dangers of immodesty incident to literary popularity.

Whatever his motives, or lack of them, the reviewers sometimes saw the anonymity as part of a wide scheme of what was called 'bookmaking'—profiteering by either raising the price or padding the contents of books. Scott had demonstrated that novel-writing could be big business and was often accused of 'bookmaking'. The mystification concerning authorship was sometimes attacked as just a further gimmick to attract attention and sustain sales. Another ploy, in the view of the *Monthly Magazine*, was used in publishing *St. Ronan's Well*:

The Scotch publishers latterly hit upon a puffing pretension, which, whatever may have been its plausibility or success, is, we fancy, by the work before us, likely to be thrown back into disuse. Thus was it: they forwarded an early copy to some favoured and friendly editor, who culled out its pretty passages, and thus beguiled the press into general commendation upon special provocatives;

while the eager readers in town were formally apprised, by daily advertisement, that the new *novel shipped from Leith* was weather-bound, while each morning ensured a variation of the needle. But the stormy winds do blow, do blow, do blow![7]

Whether a plot by Constable or not, several of the weeklies plagiarized (from the *Leeds Intelligencer*) excerpts from the novel and praised it, and then were forced to rescind their verdicts in a second review.

As we will see, Scott's poems and the novels 'by the author of *Waverley*' encountered considerable adverse criticism. And yet, as is usually the case with criticism, it seems to have had little influence on its subject. Scott's careless errors continued to the end, and even the new, complete edition which he supervised beginning in 1829 shows no major revisions, only a large number of minor stylistic changes. Scott's view of his own writing is unassuming, almost degrading: at times he saw it largely as amusement. His prefatory remarks (Nos. 32a, b) and his self-review in the *Quarterly* (No. 17) are self-defensive; in several of his poems, moreover, he had tossed back taunts to his reviewers, such as 'flow forth, flow unrestrain'd, my tale' (in the introduction to Canto III of *Marmion*) and 'little reck I of the censure sharp/May idly cavil at an idle lay' (in the epilogue to *The Lady of the Lake*).

Almost any other writer of the period would have exposed himself by such taunts and self-defences, to the charge of in fact caring a great deal about the flailings by his critics, but Scott's personality, along with his *poco-curante* view of the writing profession, provides contrary evidence. Benjamin Robert Haydon, a painter of the period, and an acquaintance of both Scott and Wordsworth, compared the two. Anyone's modesty would stand out against the background of Wordsworth's notorious egotism, but Haydon's remarks are, I believe, revealing nonetheless. Scott 'is always cool & amusing'; he 'seems to wish to seem less than he is'; his 'disposition can be traced to the effect of Success operating on a genial temperament, while Wordsworth's takes its rise from the effect of unjust ridicule wounding a deep self estimation'. 'Yet,' he continues, 'I do think Scott's success would have made Wordsworth insufferable, while Wordsworth's failures would not have rendered Scott a bit less delightful'.[8] Such a disposition is not likely to be affected much by criticism.

The contemporary reviewers of Scott's works had much to contend with. They confronted a careless, indifferent, and anonymous writer who ground out novels at an unprecedented flow for a voracious public which would not likely pay much attention to adverse critics anyway. In one sense, the reviewers were facing for the first time a modern phenomenon—the best-seller.

III

From the period of Scott's contemporary reception, roughly 1805-32, an enormous amount of data has survived. Well over 350 reviews of the novels alone exist, and mention of Scott and 'the author of *Waverley*' crops up everywhere in the correspondence and diaries of the period. To include as large and as representative a selection as possible, the letters chosen are largely those which contain criticism of the works in question; and plot synopses and quotations, which so often formed a large part of the reviews, have been omitted and described in brackets.

The reception of Scott's poetry by his reviewers was uneven, sometimes placid, sometimes stormy.[9] After the favourable reception of *The Minstrelsy of the Scottish Border*, the five major verse romances— his major poetic works—were subjected to considerable scrutiny. *The Lay of the Last Minstrel* (1805) enjoyed a generally favourable reception, while *Marmion* (1808) encountered a good deal of opposition, in spite of its popularity with the reading public. The high point of Scott's relations with his critics came with reviews of *The Lady of the Lake* (1810); the enthusiasm can be seen in the review in the *British Critic* (No. 3). The publication of *Rokeby* (1813) provoked a slight dip in Scott's reputation, and the reception of *The Lord of the Isles* (1815), published after *Waverley*, must have confirmed all Scott's fears about the demise of his poetic career. Even his friend George Ellis has not much good to say for the poem in the *Quarterly* (No. 13). A later 'dramatic sketch', *Halidon Hill* (1822), received mixed reviews; the review in the *Eclectic* (No. 33) seems to me a fair estimation of Scott's dramatic powers of dialogue and characterization in the 'sketch', seen on so much larger a scale in his novels.

The criticism of his poetry was a fitting prelude to that encountered later by his novels; in fact, as we shall see, the same criticisms were made of both. On the negative side, there was his incredible carelessness, the grammatical errors and padding. Perhaps the best exposure of this sloppiness is contained in the review in the *Literary Journal* (No. 1), where the very facile versification, the poor rhymes, and the obvious metre are also examined. The other side, a defence of Scott's versification, can be found in the *British Critic* (No. 3). Francis Jeffrey, in the *Edinburgh Review* (No. 2), made a special onslaught against the inconsistency and unnaturalness of the characterization, the insipid heroine, and the poor plot construction. The charge of 'bookmaking', moreover, is frequently on the list of Scott's offences read off with boredom or frustration after the first few publications.

At the end of Jeffrey's review there is a political note sounded in his attack on Scott's niggardly praise of Charles Fox, the deceased Whig minister. The *Edinburgh*, like almost all other reviewing periodicals of the time, had a partisan bias. That bias, however, took a form which is often misunderstood, for the two parties, Whig and Tory, were not opposed in basic principles; they shared an aristocratic view of government. Neither party, consequently, was as heated in its antagonism toward the other as were both parties toward the dangerous revolutionaries of the time—those who, whether Jacobins or Radicals, threatened to unweave the political and social fabric. Shelley, for example, received what appears to have been prejudiced treatment at times as payment for his revolutionary views. Scott, as Tory member of the two-party Establishment, had little to fear from the political prejudices of the reviewers of either party when they were rendering a purely literary assessment. It was only when partisan political issues crept into his own work that reviewers of the opposite party, like Jeffrey, would attack. And this situation did not arise all that often.

But there was also a positive side to the account of the reception of Scott's verse. There was almost always praise for particular passages, for Scott's descriptive powers, and sometimes for his display of the manners of past ages. Instances occurred, especially in the fashionable magazines (No. 10), in which this praise was mindlessly unalloyed with any of the criticisms noted above; but most often the praise and blame were mixed and the beauties said to be sufficient compensation for the flaws, a position not often taken by critics of Scott today. Coleridge's letter (No. 4) criticizing *The Lady of the Lake* is indeed modern in its almost total dismissal of the poem.

It is not accidental that contemporary criticism of Scott's verse and novels shares so many points in common. As was pointed out by J. L. Adolphus (No. 28), Scott's relatively 'unpoetical' style was easily transferred from verse to prose, and Mrs. Oliphant later in the century (No. 60) saw the same close relationship and that Scott needed the novel form to expand his sense of character.

Like the earlier verse romances, Scott's first novel, *Waverley* (1814), was a success with the public, and this success won critical endorsement from most reviewers. In its enthusiasm the *Antijacobin Review* was led to hope that *Waverley* presaged a revival of the novel, and Jeffrey in the *Edinburgh Review* (No. 9) noted that it put all other contemporary novels in the shade.[10] Even though it is not always stated, there is a sense that something new had happened; several reviewers remarked that *Waverley* would definitely not be relegated to the shelves of a circulating library.

The general points of praise and disapproval of *Waverley*, some of them already sounding like echoes from critiques of Scott's verse narratives, form the beginning of a list which was to become familiar to readers of contemporary reviews of Scott's novels. There is bountiful praise for the characterization, descriptions, the easy, flowing style, the display of past manners, and for particularly fine scenes. The adverse criticism consisted of objections to the obscurity of the Scottish dialect, the poorly constructed story, the tiresomeness of Scott's bores, the historical inaccuracies, and the very mixture itself of history and fiction. As we shall see, the last-named objection was to stimulate controversy throughout the nineteenth century. *Waverley*, furthermore, was identified by almost every reviewer as Scott's work.

Reviews of *Guy Mannering* (1815) and *The Antiquary* (1816), the following two novels, continued favourable on the whole. Although the typical adverse criticisms made of *Waverley* continued too, the praise ran only slightly abated. Several reviewers, however, thought that *Guy Mannering* was more like a common novel of the time, especially in the story. The predictions and their fulfilment, the main conventions objected to, were specifically criticized, partly for encouraging superstition, partly for being improbable. J. H. Merivale, in the *Monthly Review*, did not object to 'gross improbability' in a romance, but

. . . in a species of writing which founds its only claim to our favour on the reality of its pictures and images, the introduction of any thing that is diametrically contrary to all our ordinary principles of belief and action is as gross a violation of every rule of composition as the appendage of a fish's tail to a woman's head and shoulders, or the assemblage of any others the most discordant images on a single canvas.[11]

John Wilson Croker, reviewing *The Antiquary* in the *Quarterly* (No. 14), noted that the absence of predictions in that novel gave it an advantage over *Guy Mannering*, for he 'felt little or no interest in the fortunes of those whose fate was predestined, and whose happiness or woe depended not on their own actions, but on the prognostications of a beldam gipsy or a wild Oxonian. . . .'

The criticism of the predictions began a habit of objecting to the supernatural machinery in the novels. Likewise, the comparison of each novel with *Waverley* (and later with all the earlier novels) began in reviews of *Guy Mannering*. From this point on, even if a Waverley novel is thought not to measure up to its predecessors, it is most often said to be yet better than most, or even all, other contemporary novels. The *British Lady's Magazine* in its review of *The Antiquary* (No. 15) began still another critical tradition by remarking that the author was merely repeating his characters with different names.

The next publication, *The Tales of My Landlord* (1816), consisted of two novels, *The Black Dwarf* and *Old Mortality*. The former was attacked on almost every count; *Old Mortality* was generally well received by the critics. A second attempt to fool the public as to authorship—the *Tales* did not carry the caption 'by the author of *Waverley*'—was a total failure: they were invariably identified as being clearly in the same series. The complicated frame of the novel was generally thought clumsy and pointless, even by Scott himself in the *Quarterly* (No. 17). Most reviews continued the praise and blame given the earlier novels, but the *Critical Review* (No. 16) is especially good on the plot, characterization, and dialect of *Old Mortality*.

Scott's mixture of history and fiction had previously been discussed only in a general way. The accuracy and value of the historical aspect of the novels was applauded in reviews of the *Tales*, but an attack by Dr. Thomas M'Crie (a Scottish seceding divine) in the *Edinburgh Christian Instructor* was so severe that Scott felt it necessary to defend his delineation of the Covenanters in the *Quarterly* (No. 17).[12] The new genre of the historical novel, moreover, was discussed by several reviewers. Two of them pointed out that the mingling of fact and fiction required that historical accuracy not always be followed strictly. Jeffrey in the *Edinburgh Review* praised Scott's use of historical events to develop his characters and his making 'us present to the times in which he has placed them, less by his direct notices of the great transactions by which they were distinguished, than by his casual intimations of their effects on private persons, and by the very contrast which their temper and occupations often appear to furnish to the colour of the national story'. For, claimed Jeffrey, the conventional historian exaggerates the importance of events; most people's lives are not much affected by great events and 'all public events are important only as they ultimately concern individuals. . . .'[13] Scott himself had something to say on the subject of historical novels in the *Quarterly* (No. 17).

Rob Roy (1818), the next novel 'by the author of *Waverley*', on the whole enjoyed a favourable reception. As was to be expected, the characterization received the brunt of attention. E. T. Channing in the *North American Review* (No. 20) noted that the individual characters are never given in a lump but slowly unfold themselves. Channing, furthermore, denied that there was any repetition of characters, and several other reviewers agreed. Francis Jeffrey in the *Edinburgh*, as well as some other reviewers, objected to what he considered the improbability of Die Vernon's delineation:

A girl of eighteen, not only with more wit and learning than any man of forty, but with more sound sense, and firmness of character, than any man whatever— and with perfect frankness and elegance of manners, though bred among boors and bigots—is rather a more violent fiction, we think, than a king with marble legs, or a youth with an ivory shoulder.[14]

And yet Jeffrey found Die Vernon impressive and with enough of a mixture of truth that she soon seemed feasible and interesting. Some of the improbabilities of plot were also probed by Nassau Senior in the *Quarterly* (No. 29).

The Heart of Midlothian (1818), often cited today as the best of the Waverley novels, was not enthusiastically reviewed by Scott's contemporaries. At the time of publication, in fact, it received predominantly unfavourable reviews; only when the more influential quarterlies that reviewed it within the next few years are also considered can its overall reception be pronounced favourable. One of the major objections made, even by the favourable reviewers, was that the novel was protracted too far, that the fourth volume, coming as it did after the catastrophe, was not of much interest (Nos. 21 and 29). This objection was often accompanied by a charge of 'bookmaking'. Effie's transformation and George's death at the hand of his son were seen as gross improbabilities that did not make the last volume any more palatable.

The by now habitual praise, begun in reviews of *Waverley*, continued. The characterization of Jeanie Deans was highly esteemed, especially in view of the difficulties overcome in portraying a common, virtuous, plain heroine. And in spite of the relative unimportance of history in *The Heart of Midlothian*, the issue of historical fidelity, begun in reviews of *Old Mortality*, was revived. The *Monthly Review* discussed the difficulties of recreating the past, especially the need to reason constantly about the past from analogy with the present, and concluded that 'the author of *Waverley*' had succeeded.[15] Josiah Conder in the *Eclectic Review*, on the other hand, argued that since analogy was the only source for the historical novelist, the resultant picture is 'only a modification of the present, which comes to us under the guise and semblance of the past'. And that a genius can make us believe he has done the impossible only makes his historical novel more dangerous. It is the author's characters, Conder adds, that are the charm and merit of the Waverley novels, and yet even with characterization this author is limited to his powers of observation: he has not 'a philosophical comprehension or abstract knowledge of the internal workings of the human mind'.[16]

The reception of *The Bride of Lammermoor* and *A Legend of Montrose* (*Tales of My Landlord*, 3rd series, 1819) showed an upsurge in the critical reputation of 'the author of *Waverley*'. The unpleasantness of the tragic ending of *The Bride* was one of the worst faults many reviewers could find, whereas the tragic ending was seen by Nassau Senior in the *Quarterly* (No. 29) as one of the novel's highest recommendations. In that same review can be found an example of the comparison, usually favourable, of Scott with Shakespeare, a practice which began in reviews of this volume and which was often repeated during the remainder of the nineteenth century.

Ivanhoe (1820), the next of the Waverley novels, was a success with the critics as well as with the reading public. Only the *Eclectic* (No. 26), the *Edinburgh*, and the *Quarterly* (No. 29) showed much disapproval. Many reviewers, however, objected to what they considered too much detail in the descriptions; the *Eclectic* (No. 26) even thought the excess detail destroyed the verisimilitude, leaving only a 'pageant'. The reviewer in *Blackwood's* attempted to explain the wealth of detail by pointing out that the contemporary ignorance of the manners of an age so distant required the novelist to provide minute descriptions.[17] The descriptions themselves are parodied in a burlesque novel by William Maginn (No. 38).

The *New Edinburgh Review*, in its critique of the previous *Tales*, had suggested that Scott need not feel himself bound to Scottish subjects, and Scott did in *Ivanhoe* turn to England for his subject.[18] The *Literary*

Gazette in its review of the novel pointed out one result of the change: by choosing a period so far in the past, with a society relatively uncivilized and with so many associations with past verse romances, the novel itself turned into a romance.[19] As such, the reviewer added, it was excellent.

The term 'romance' raised new problems, for historical novels are one thing, historical romances quite another. The *New Edinburgh Review* pointed out that, in spite of the romance furniture scattered throughout the book, there was too much nature, accurate history, and realism for it to qualify strictly as a romance in the usual sense of the term.[20] And romance elements in the novel protected it from charges of historical inaccuracy in the view of the *Monthly Magazine* (No. 23). The *Monthly Review* thought an 'historical romance' a contradiction in terms, the two elements an impossible combination. 'Authenticated history, of which the leading traits are present to our remembrance, perpetually appeals against the fictions with which she is compelled to associate. . . .' 'Romance', on the other hand, 'is discouraged in her career by those whispers of incredulity, and those intimations of incongruity, which are inseparable from such an admixture: some suspicion perpetually haunts us, that the real course of events is broken up to suit the purposes of the story. . . .' 'In this conflict', the reviewer concluded,

the mind, on the one hand, refuses to acquiesce in certain and indisputable fact; while, on the other, the fiction, however ingenious may be its structure, works on us with its charm half broken and its potency nearly dissolved. In vain we would gladly give the reins of our fancy into the hands of the author, when, at every step that it takes, it stumbles on a reality that checks and intercepts it: not unlike the effect of that imperfect slumber which is interrupted by the sounds of the active world,—a confused mixture of drowsy and waking existence. It is neither perfect romance nor perfect history.[21]

The reviewer in the *Eclectic* (No. 26) agreed about the impossibility of the mixture, made (if possible) worse by the author's lack of the necessary enthusiasm for romance writing. Jeffrey in the *Edinburgh* merely pointed out the total absence of realism in characterization and background and said he preferred the early Scottish novels.[22]

After *Ivanhoe* and until Scott's last publication, that is from 1820 to 1832, his relationship with his contemporary critics was uneven. It declined sharply on the publication of *The Monastery* (1820) but returned with *The Abbot* (1820) and *Kenilworth* (1821) to something like the previous heights of *Ivanhoe*. In late 1821 and early 1822 another dip occurred with *The Pirate*; then the reviewers divided over *The Fortunes of Nigel* and *Peveril of the Peak*. His reputation again rose in 1823 with *Quentin Durward*, only to fall to its lowest level the following year with Scott's only non-historical (i.e. contemporary) novel, *St. Ronan's Well*. For the next three years, there was a slight improvement with a divided critical reception for *Redgauntlet* (1824) and *Tales of the Crusaders* (*The Talisman* and *The Betrothed*, 1825), and then a further dip with *Woodstock* (1826). Scott's last four fictional works enjoyed a generally favourable reception, but for the first time other forces may have been at work. By the publication of the first, *The Chronicles of the Canongate* (1827), Scott's authorship was public, and the additional knowledge of his financial disaster may well have won him the sympathy of his critics.

Besides the now familiar judgments pro and con—the praise of scenes and descriptions and the objections to plot construction and carelessness of style—the controversy over the mixture of history and romance continued with vigour.

First of all, however, the romance elements themselves were attacked. Several reviewers called *The Monastery* a fairy tale; and the *Literary Gazette* regretted the entry into 'absolute fairy land'.[23] The reviewer of *St. Ronan's Well* in the *Universal Review* was more sober in his attack: he had no objection to merely entertaining the public with romances as long as the author is willing to pay the price. '. . . No author will find immortality, but in the power of making his readers think, of summoning to their minds those high and passionate influences which are made to disturb and kindle the human heart. . . .'[24]

As for the historical side, inaccuracies continued to be uncovered, although sometimes fidelity of detail was said to be unimportant. Extravagant praise was not lacking, however: *Blackwoods*, in its review of *The Pirate* (possibly by J. G. Lockhart), called its author 'one of the greatest of national historians', and the *Edinburgh Magazine* thought that future historians would refer to *The Fortunes of Nigel* for the delineation of James I.[25] The most detailed attack on the historical fidelity as such occurs in the examination by the *Westminster Review* of the language used in *Woodstock* (No. 36). Accusations of Tory bias also cropped up, especially in reviews of Scott's novels of the mid '20s (see, for example, No. 34).

The mixture of history and romance brought on continual adverse criticism as well as an occasional defence, but nothing new came from the controversy. Scott himself, however, apparently thought the attacks were worth answering in his preface to *Peveril of the Peak* (No. 32b).

As for the more strictly literary criticisms, attacks on what was seen as repetition of characters and incidents became more intense. The *London Magazine* began its critique of *Woodstock*:

There is a stratagem in old-clothes dealing called *duffing*. The practitioner— as we learn from those fountains of polite knowledge, the Police Reports— raises the scanty nap of a veteran garment, gives it a gloss with some pre- paration, and passes it off as new. Sir Walter Scott has taken to *duffing* in the novel trade: he *renovates* (we believe that is the phrase) his old thread-bare stories, fresh binds them, and palming them on us as new, gives us the nap which the other sort of *duffer* endeavours to bestow on his wares. This is a kind of legerdemain utterly unworthy of a reputed wizard; but so long as the public consent to be deceived and amused by it, we cannot blame the author for practising it.[26]

Many reviews contained lists of sets of characters considered similar, one figure from the work under review, the other from a previous work. Nassau Senior in his review of *The Fortunes of Nigel* in the *Quarterly* set forth still wider similarities.

All his readers must have observed the three characters that form the prominent group of almost every novel. A virtuous passive hero, who is to marry the heroine; a fierce active hero, who is to die a violent death, generally by hanging or shooting; and a fool or bore, whose duty it is to drain to the uttermost dregs one solitary fund of humour.

The passive hero, moreover, is usually in danger from suspicious appearances in the earlier part of the novel and from the gallows in the later part.[27]

The *Literary Register*, reviewing *Peveril*, pointed out that Shakespeare, unlike the 'author of *Waverley*', never repeated his characters or incidents.[28] But in spite of this obvious dissimilarity, comparisons of the two authors nevertheless became more frequent in the 1820s, Scott often being set down as the greatest writer since Shakespeare. Several times, however, there is said to be no comparison—Shakespeare is so much the greater.

Scott's relationship with his reviewers was in general pleasant, especially contrasted to that of other writers in the period. Most reviewers did indeed harass Scott (and the 'author of *Waverley*') in hopes of his improvement, but hardly ever was a reviewer ready to damn his poems or novels, and bitterness was seldom displayed.

Scott gave the reviewers little cause to be upset in a non-literary way; he had none of Shelley's irreligion or of Hazlitt's maverick politics. And his literary experiments were confined to practice, saving him from Wordsworth's fate.

The reviewers, too, were only sanctioning a popularity that already existed with the reading public. Praise of Scott was on everyone's lips and in everyone's letters, but most of it merely described the enjoyment derived from his poems or novels as they came out. The representative selection in this regard is the letter from an anonymous shepherd (No. 27), which testifies to the sort of popularity Scott's novels had won down through a rapidly growing reading public. Sydney Smith's letters to Archibald Constable (No. 22) are valuable for their critical views as well.

Much of what is critically interesting comes from the writers of the period. Of the novelists, Maria Edgeworth was the most respected at the time *Waverley* appeared; in this light, her letter to Scott (No. 8) is much more flattering than it might otherwise appear. It is worth remembering as well, however, that letters are quite different from reviews, especially in tone. This may seem too obvious for comment, and yet it is easy to misinterpret Jane Austen's brief remarks to her sister (No. 7) as something other than casual and ironic. Thomas Love Peacock, the satirical novelist, attested to Scott's popularity and influence, both in his serious comments in an unpublished essay (No. 18) and in his caricature of Scott and his ideas in *Crotchet Castle* (No. 44). Scott himself commented on his English imitators in his journal (No. 37) and defended himself from serious attacks in a review (No. 17) and in prefaces to the novels (No. 32). Some of the most severe attacks, although not public, came from Coleridge (Nos. 4 and 24) and Wordsworth (Nos. 11 and 55).

Scott's fame spread quickly. His poems and novels were translated into a number of continental languages within ten or twenty years of their publication. French translations of the novels were often out within a year. The interest shown by the many translations is reflected also by the great admiration of contemporary continental writers. Heine (No. 39) saw Scott as the originator of the historical novel, the harmonizer, too, of democratic and aristocratic elements. Goethe (No. 40) was taken by Scott's artistic techniques; Pushkin by his objectivity and use of local colour; Balzac (No. 52d) by Scott's literary eclecticism, his fusion of the literature of ideas and of images. Sainte-Beuve, in his obituary of Scott (No. 45), stressed Scott's disinterestedness. Stendhal (No. 43), however, had serious reservations about Scott's powers of characterization and doubts about his lasting popularity.

Besides the more fragmented or incidental views of Scott, there were among contemporary assessments some precursors of the more complete, expanded criticisms of the Victorians. The first of these was John Leicester Adolphus's monograph, *Letters to Richard Heber* (No. 28). Adolphus took on the unnecessary task of proving, mainly from internal evidence, that the author of *Marmion* and the author of *Waverley* were one and the same. The first edition made quite a stir in 1821. The author of *Marmion* invited Adolphus to Abbotsford and the author of *Waverley* made mention of the monograph in his Introduction to *The Fortunes of Nigel*. William Hazlitt, the radical essayist and critic, had enormous admiration for Scott in spite of his Tory views. Hazlitt devoted a chapter of *The Spirit of the Age* (No. 35) to Scott, discussed the automatic stature assumed for romance heroes by Scott and others ('Why the Heroes of Romance are Insipid'), and disagreed that Scott was comparable to Shakespeare in invention, Scott being *only* an imitator of nature ('Sir Walter Scott, Racine, and Shakespeare'). The more subtle though rigorous criticism of some of the Victorians is present in M. D. Maurice's *Athenaeum* article (No. 42). Maurice saw Scott's novels as falling somewhere between genuinely great literature and what we today call best-sellers. The contemporary and Victorian concern about the historical novel was again articulated in a comment in 1828 by the historian Thomas Babington Macaulay (No. 41).

What I think is most impressive in the contemporary criticism of Scott is not the subtle insights into his works, although these occur. It is not even the ultimate judgment of his works, of their comparative value, although posterity has not differed much in the overall assessments. It is the great tolerance his contemporaries showed for his flaws; they were so much more willing than we are today to accept the positive values as compensation. We have perhaps lost a very valuable critical knack in our more fastidious days and, as a consequence, have foregone a good deal of enjoyment.

IV

According to James T. Hillhouse, who has made the only full-length study of Scott's reputation, the general popularity of the author of

Waverley continued for at least fifty years or so following his death.[29] There is evidence to substantiate this claim. In 1844 Francis Jeffrey reported that Robert Cadell, the publisher of the novels, claimed a sale of 60,000 volumes in the previous year alone.[30] Cadell had also written in 1848 to a prospective purchaser of the copyrights that Scott's works had already brought in 'a trifle over £76,000 and what is more surprising, as I have already said, the demand for his work continues. . . .'[31] In the early 1860s, when the copyrights began to expire, cheap editions appeared, witnessing a substantial popularity with the lower classes; a cheap edition of a biography of Scott is known to have sold 180,000 copies in 1871, a fact which indicates that that popularity had continued.[32]

In that same year, however, Leslie Stephen (No. 61) claimed that Scott's reputation was beginning to wane, and Bagehot some thirteen years earlier (No. 57) had noted the failure of the Waverley novels to satisfy the romantically inclined younger generation. And yet this last observation runs counter to a frequent remark, made by Stephen and others, that Scott's novels made fascinating reading for children, whatever other claims they might have. The conversation held by Sidney Colvin, Gladstone, and others in the 1870s (No. 64) indicates, moreover, that there was still an interest in the novels outside of public criticism, that they had not yet been totally relegated to the nursery.

From 1832 to 1885 Scott's reputation with the critics reflected his popularity with the reading public, just as had been the case with his contemporaries. Scott has never aroused much bitterness, and yet the few more famous critics, especially Carlyle (No. 51), were sometimes severe, and their attacks on Scott obscure his generally high reputation with Victorian critics as a whole.

Scott's fame and popularity spread still further after his death through continental translations. *Ivanhoe*, for example, already available in 1832 in French, Spanish, and German, was translated into Portuguese in 1838, Italian in 1840, Greek in 1847, and Polish in 1865. And yet although earlier continental critics, such as Balzac and Sainte-Beuve, were friendly enough, later critics, such as Taine (No. 58) and Brandes (No. 66), have generally been antagonistic. In the United States Scott enjoyed immense popularity both before and after his death; the only notable nineteenth-century voice raised against Scott was Twain's (No. 70).

Scott's attractive personality, his lack of vanity and pretensions, was partly responsible for his continued fame and popularity, especially after the publication of Lockhart's *Life* in 1837. Even Thomas Carlyle, in his review of that biography (No. 51), was impressed by Scott's personality, especially its healthiness. This view of Scott was shared by Bagehot and Ruskin.

In spite of his admiration, however, Carlyle wrote the severest and most influential article on Scott ever published. He claimed that although Scott was by no means a mediocre man, neither was he great. He was too worldly, even materialistic, and had little interest in the speculative life. The Waverley novels, moreover, were without a purpose or message and were therefore essentially frivolous and ephemeral. Leslie Stephen (No. 61) thought Carlyle too severe in his censure and yet nonetheless correct in principle.

Several years before Carlyle's article appeared, Harriet Martineau (No. 49), more morally engaged even than Carlyle, found Scott on the other hand a very nearly perfect model of a moral propagandist, although she did add that she thought Scott was unconsciously so. And before Carlyle's article had time to make much effect, John Henry Newman (No. 53) claimed Scott as a sort of John the Baptist preparing the way for the Catholic Revival. After Carlyle's article many Victorians gave his moral objections careful consideration, usually only to attack them at last. R. H. Hutton (No. 67) and Julia Wedgwood (No. 68), for example, flatly rejected Carlyle.

Carlyle's main objection was to Scott's supposed amoral stance: George Brandes, the Danish critic, objected to Scott's *lack* of *im*moral tendencies (No. 66). No author as inoffensive as Scott, he argued, could possibly long survive. But the final word on the issue of Scott's morals is a fitting end to a controversy which need never have arisen: in *Life on the Mississippi*, Mark Twain accused Scott and his medievalism of being largely responsible for the Southerner's chivalric fantasies and thus for the Civil War itself (No. 70).

The historical elements in Scott's novels continued to be both influential and controversial. There were many imitators of Scott's historical novels, such as G. P. R. James and Bulwer-Lytton, and historians themselves, such as Thierry and Michelet, were inspired by Scott's novels to produce more imaginative historical studies.

The controversy regarding the mixture of history and fiction, so heated among Scott's contemporaries, continued in full force in the Victorian period. At its highest level the controversy involved the question of the historical novel as a form. Bulwer-Lytton (No. 46), an historical novelist himself, praised the form and Scott's method of showing the historical times instead of great historical figures. One of the few to defend the form was Belinsky, the Russian critic, who saw Scott's genius in his blending of the historical and the private lives he dealt with (No. 54). Later in the century the form came under more vigorous attack, chiefly from H. A. Taine, the French critic (No. 58), who claimed that every 200 years or so the mainsprings of human passions changed, precluding the validity of historical novels. The anonymous writer of an earlier article (No. 56) and Leslie Stephen (No. 61) agreed with Taine's conclusions, although for differing reasons.

Scott's handling of the form generally elicited praise from those who accepted the form itself. Walter Bagehot (No. 57) liked what he called Scott's 'romantic sense', which allowed him to go from history to sentiment with ease. Richard Hutton (No. 67) especially praised Scott's passive heroes for providing insight into both sides of an historical struggle. In her review of Hutton's book, Julia Wedgwood (No. 68) praised Scott's 'broad objective painting', missing from the works of his followers. Henry James (No. 59) likewise considered that Scott's Victorian imitators differed from him—in not ignoring the crudeness of the past as Scott had done.

The more strictly literary assessments of Scott's works continued customary judgments—that the fiction was superior to the poetry, the Scottish novels to the later romances. But among such routine appraisals can be found a number of original and illuminating approaches to both the prose and poetry.

Scott's verse romances are not much esteemed today nor were they during the Victorian period. Many of the critics who bothered to discuss them took, at least, a defensive position. F. T. Palgrave, the editor of *The Golden Treasury*, considered Scott especially talented at telling a story in verse, where few before him had succeeded.[33] Richard Hutton (No. 67) praised the speed of Scott's descriptions, his strongly drawn descriptions, and his simplicity. But Hutton's most pertinent comment is that verse romances should not be read as if they were novels. In her review of Hutton's book, Julia Wedgwood (No. 68) claimed Scott's genius in verse was his ability to move the reader's feelings quickly. W. B. O. Peabody in an article published shortly after Scott's death (No. 48) warned that Scott's poetry does not satisfy the usual expectations of poetry, and like Wedgwood he saw Scott's chief merit in his conveying the excitement of action. Mrs. Oliphant, writing in 1871 (No. 60), wanted Scott to be judged as a minstrel, that is, as a poet who among other things could not afford to flag or be too deep. It is worth noting that none of these critics was without reservations and that none preferred Scott's poetry to his fiction.

The fiction itself was treated in terms both of Scott's place in the history of the English novel and of his craftsmanship. Robert Louis Stevenson (No. 65) claimed Scott had given the novel greater freedom. An anonymous critic in the *Athenaeum* (No. 62) saw that Scott avoided the psychological element in his novels—wisely in the critic's opinion; only in *Waverley* did Scott attempt any psychological experimentation, perhaps, the critic suggests, because it was the only novel Scott wrote before he read Jane Austen. Taine (No. 58) thought the Waverley novels with their realism led to the novel of manners of Jane Austen, George Eliot, and others.

Of the comments on Scott's craftsmanship a few examples will have to do. The anonymous critic in the *London Quarterly* (No. 63) found that, unlike Dickens and Thackeray, Scott never resorted to caricature, and was so talented at keeping the actions of his novels interesting that he did not even bother to explain disguises. A provocative point made in the *Athenaeum* (No. 62) was that Scott was good at delineating modest girls devoid of prudery: they do not overwhelm you; they grow on you slowly. Ruskin's excellent discussion (No. 69) of Scott's dialect involves a close reading of a text, unusual in nineteenth-century criticism. The comparisons of Scott to Shakespeare, moreover, continued through the Victorian period and often centred upon the great variety of characters created by both writers.

James T. Hillhouse, the historian of Waverley criticism, expressed surprise at the competence of the contemporary criticism of Scott.[34] I, on the other hand, am more often amazed by the fertility and rigorousness of the Victorian criticism. Not that feeble Victorian criticism does not exist: David Masson in his history of the British novel (1859) comments mindlessly, 'You do not expect me, I am sure, to criticize the Waverley novels. We all know them and we all enjoy them.'[35] But the greater part of the Victorian assessments of Scott are vigorous, pertinent, and thoughtful.

V

From about the year 1885 or so, Scott's popularity and critical reputation declined. The view of Scott as a children's-classic writer won increasing adherence after 1885. In the early years of the period there were, however, numerous editions of the Waverley novels, a fact which probably indicates Scott's confirmed status as an adult classic as well, a classic finely bound and uncut.[36]

Scott's reputation as a novelist continued fairly high with the critics for a time, but for all the interest his verse romances have aroused in this century they might as well have never been written. The amount of attention paid to the novels continued; discussion of the treatment they received from 1880 to the 1930s takes up almost one-third of Hillhouse's study of Scott's reputation.

The kind of critic and approach did, however, change somewhat in that period. For the most part Scott no longer attracted critics of the stature of Jeffrey, Hazlitt, Carlyle, Stephen, and Bagehot. There were, to be sure, essays by such well-known figures as Virginia Woolf, G. K. Chesterton, and Ford Madox Ford, but the majority of those who have written on Scott from the fin de siècle to World War II have been academics, such as Oliver Elton, W. P. Ker, and H. J. C. Grierson. Scott's fate has been in fact similar to that of Shelley, his contemporary, in that their literary stature exists almost exclusively among university scholars. But Scott, unlike Shelley, has not been attacked by major critics; he has become the ward of the literary historians almost purely by default. Few critics (as opposed to scholars) have shown much interest in him.

Although the issue of Scott's moral position died a natural death by the end of the nineteenth century, many of the traditional concerns and assessments have retained some currency, even if in a diluted form. The bulk of the interest has remained with Scott's characterization; comparison with Shakespeare for their mutual talent in creating a variety of characters has continued as well. And critical and scholarly interest has not shifted from the nineteenth-century preference for the early, Scottish novels. Benedetto Croce, moreover, has upheld the tradition of rejection of Scott by continental critics.[37]

Georg Lukacs, the Hungarian Marxist critic, however, has brought a new interest and respect to the historical novel and especially to Scott's pioneering in the form. Although there have been other studies of the historical aspects of Scott's novels since 1885, for example excellent essays by George Saintsbury (1894) and David Daiches (1951), it was Lukacs' *The Historical Novel* (first published in 1937 but not influential in English circles until translated in 1962) that has done most to revive the historical controversy.[38]

After World War II, interest in Scott has not died out, but it would be safe to say that it has stabilized while scholarly and critical books and articles on his fellow Romantic writers have been increasing at a steady pace. Among the items published on Scott, moreover, there is evidence of a revival of serious critical interest. F. R. Hart's *Scott's Novels* (1966) and chapters by E. M. W. Tillyard and Donald Davie, for example, question some of the orthodox positions on Scott and point, I believe, to the direction in which future criticism ought to head.[39] In the meantime, however, anyone who still believes in the doctrine of necessary progress would do well to compare the distinguished criticisms of Scott's contemporaries and near-contemporaries with the bulk of what has been written in this century.

NOTES

[1] 25 January 1823, 49.

[2] Lockhart, *Memoirs of the Life of Scott* (Edinburgh, 1839), III, 67 (Ch. XVI); III, 249 (Ch. XX).

[3] *Ibid.*, IV, 395 (Ch. XXXIII).

[4] *Ibid.*, V, 175 (Ch. XXXVII); V, 269 (Ch. XL).

[5] *Ibid.*, VII, 21 (Ch. LV).

[6] *Ibid.*, VII, 18-19 (Ch. LV).

[7] LVII (February 1824), 64.

[8] W. B. Pope, ed., *The Diary of Benjamin Robert Haydon* (Cambridge, Mass., 1960), II, 312.

[9] See John Hayden, *The Romantic Reviewers* 1802-24 (Chicago and London, 1969), 125-34, for a more detailed account of the critical reception of Scott's poetry and miscellaneous prose works.

[10] *Antijacobin Review*, LXVII (September 1814), 217.

[11] LXXVII 2s (May 1815), 86.

[12] Lockhart, V, 174 (Ch. XXXVII).

[13] XXVIII (March 1817), 216 & 217.

[14] XXIX (February 1818), 410.

[15] LXXXVII (December 1818), 361-62.

[16] XII 2s (November 1819), 425 & 427.

[17] VI (December 1819), 262.

[18] II (August 1819), 184.

[19] 25 December 1819, 817 & 823.

[20] III (February 1820), 164-65.

[21] XCI (January 1820), 73-74.

[22] XXXIII (January 1820), 53-54.

[23] 25 March 1820, 193.

[24] I (May 1824), 334.

[25] *Blackwood's Magazine*, X (December 1821), 713; *Edinburgh Magazine*, X 2s (May 1822), *564 (pages misnumbered).

[26] V 2s (June 1826), 173-74.

[27] XXVII (July 1822), 339-340.

[28] 25 January 1823, 49.

[29] James T. Hillhouse, *The Waverley Novels and their Critics* (Minneapolis, 1936), 225-226.

[30] Francis Jeffrey, *Contributions to the Edinburgh Review* (Phil., 1848), 523n (first footnote to his *Waverley* review).

[31] Sir Herbert J. C. Grierson, *Sir Walter Scott, Bart.* (N.Y., 1938), 304.

[32] Hillhouse, 250.

[33] F. T. Palgrave, ed., *Poetical Works of Scott* (London, 1869), xxviii.

[34] Hillhouse, ix.

[35] David Masson, *British Novelists and their Styles* (Cambridge, 1859), 193.

[36] Hillhouse, 251.

[37] B. Croce, 'Walter Scott', *The Dial*, LXXV (October 1923), 325-31.

[38] George Saintsbury, 'The Historical Novel, Pt. II. Scott and Dumas', *Macmillan's Magazine*, LXX (September 1894), 321-30; David Daiches, 'Scott's Achievement as a Novelist', in *Literary Essays* (London, 1956, first published in *Nineteenth-Century Fiction*, September 1951).

[39] E. M. W. Tillyard, *The Epic Strain in the English Novel* (Fair Lawn, N.J., 1958); Donald Davie, *The Heyday of Sir Walter Scott* (London, 1961).

THE LAY OF THE LAST MINSTREL

1805

1. Unsigned review, *Literary Journal*

March 1805, v, 271-80

The author of this poem has already distinguished himself by his regard to the remains of the minstrelsy of the Scottish border. He has now attempted to imitate what he admired; or rather to dress in such a garb as may not disgust a modern taste, the manners and customs of the Scottish borderers which are handed down to us by tradition, and by the remains of their poetry. Attempts of this sort are attended with many difficulties. Although often undertaken, they have very rarely succeeded. Oral tradition is soon corrupted. Even historical events are quickly disfigured, while every succeeding generation accommodates the narrative to its own altered ideas; and where a society is rapidly advancing towards civilization, the traces of manners, which oral tradition retains, are often too much defaced in the course of a century to give any just idea of what they really were at the period when they prevailed. What is handed down in the songs of a rude age, when the bard merely describes the scene immediately passing before his eyes, may convey a just picture as far as it goes. But to form a new piece from these scattered materials, and to fill up the outlines of manners thus presented, requires much judgment and industry, and is after all in danger of not being attended with much success. The poet feels his fancy perpetually hampered by the fear of going astray. The manners and sentiments of the age in which he lives are perpetually thrusting themselves in his way. If he carefully rejects them, and confines himself to glean the sentiments and images of the songs of the age he wishes to describe, his performance can scarcely fail to be tame, and insipid in the extreme. If he gives his fancy a freer rein, and allows himself to fill up his outlines with the ideas of his own age, the picture he presents

25

to us, not only bears no resemblance to the age he means to describe, but, unless wrought up with very great skill, seldom fails to betray such patching as forms the most whimsical appearance. It is nearly impossible in such an attempt at once to exhibit a picture that is just and pleasing. Either a mere undistinguishing outline is presented, or one of the extremes we have mentioned destroys the effect. To produce instances in support of these observations would be to enumerate nearly all those pieces which have professed to delineate the manners of a distant age. Our heroic poems and tragedies are generally of this class. Voltaire is charged with making the knights of the middle age talk like modern philosophers. The numerous imitators of Homer evidently labour under the difficulty of producing a picture of the heroic age of Greece in any degree just, and at the same time different from his. Virgil usually makes his personages view things with the eyes of a Roman of the Augustan age. Any facts he introduces with regard to their manners and customs are faithfully copied from Homer. But on these subjects he generally avoids being particular as much as possible; and hence the common observation that few of his heroes have any character at all. So captivating, however, are the strains of that poet, that while we read we cannot imagine they could be altered for the better. Another imitator of Homer, and a still more rigid one, the author of the Epigoniad, proves how very faintly the manners of a distant age can be delineated by copying the descriptions of a co-temporary poet; and how very little interesting such a representation can be made, even by great industry and some share of genius.

The difficulty of delineating manners not immediately passing under our eye, and the little success with which we have seen such attempts almost always attended, made us look with not a little distrust on the design of the performance before us, which professes to 'illustrate the customs and manners which anciently prevailed on the borders of England and Scotland'. We know, indeed, that the author possessed singular opportunities for executing this design with more than ordinary propriety. He had, in the course of his former researches, made himself acquainted with all that both ancient songs and oral tradition have preserved with regard to the customs and manners he intended to describe. He was intimately acquainted with the scene where his story is placed; and as he is himself of the race of Scottish borderers, he might be expected to delineate their ancient poets with a degree of enthusiasm. The favourable presage we drew from these circumstances has not been disappointed; and if we have met with considerable blemishes, we have also derived very considerable pleasure from the perusal of this performance.

[plot summary omitted]

Into this story, which is founded on tradition, Mr. Scott has introduced a great variety of particulars, characteristic of the manners of the ancient Scottish borderers. It is, perhaps, impossible to mark particular characters very strongly in a poem that refers to a distant age, and at the same time not to disfigure the picture by the inconsistent peculiarities of the age in which the writer himself lives. Our author has, with care, avoided the latter error. He has also given us a pretty distinct idea of the minstrel. Of the rest of the personages, the representations presented to us seem by no means so well defined. This, however, was a fault extremely difficult to be avoided. It is scarcely possible that figures seen through the mists of antiquity should not appear indistinct and disproportioned. The notes which are subjoined to the work are of much use in enabling us to comprehend the idea which the poet intends to convey to us of the different personages. We conceive that, without overburdening the poem, he might have rendered them somewhat more distinct in the text. Yet it must be owned that the ludicrous traits of the old traditions require to be softened in a poem which is supposed to be delivered by a minstrel before such dignified personages, as the heads of a feudal clan.

The machinery, adapted to the popular superstitions of the age, has, in general, a very happy effect. The wizard Michael Scott, is exactly such a wizard as we have often heard of in our childhood. We cannot say the same of the 'Spirit of the Flood', and the 'Spirit of the Fell'. The idea we are led to form of these personages from their dialogue bears some resemblance to that of Ariel and his company in the Tempest, and still more to that of Oberon and his consort in the Midsummer Night's Dream. But nothing is recalled to us of the idea we had been led by tradition to form of the *water kelpies* and the *mountain fairies*.

RIVER SPIRIT
'Sleepest thou, brother?'

MOUNTAIN SPIRIT
—— 'Brother, nay—
On my hills the moon-beams play.
From Craik-cross to Skelf hill-pen,
By every rill, in every glen,

Merry elves, their morrice pacing,
    To aerial minstrelsy,
Emerald rings on brown heath tracing,
    Trip it deft and merrily
Up, and mark their nimble feet!
Up, and list their music sweet!'

This namby-pamby dialogue has a very bad effect, and we would recommend to the author to expunge it. In the goblin-page of Lord Cranstoun we recognise completely one of those villainous imps who are perpetually busy in doing all the mischievous tricks in their power.

The story for the most part proceeds with all the connection requisite. There are, however, some incidents for which we are left by the poet to account in the best way we can. It seems strange that the lady, all skilful as she was in the occult sciences, does not make any attempt to unravel the mystery of Sir William Deloraine being found lying wounded at the door of her tower, particularly when such a very great stake as the all-powerful book of Michael Scott depended upon her discovery of this circumstance. It appears also rather odd, that she should never have suspected the manœuvres of the elfin page, especially as we are given to understand that she could have easily counteracted his spells. We understood, that in the mythology of the times described, the more powerful magician or spirit always perceived the manœuvres of their inferiors when carried on immediately within their inspection. She is also not in the least aware of the deception practised on her by Lord Cranstoun when he personates Deloraine. But what seems most unaccountable is, that no notice is taken of the doings of the elfin page, even after the heir of Buccleugh is restored to his mother, and when it was to be expected he should inform her of the manner in which he was carried off. The time allowed for the whole transactions to pass appears also unaccountably short; and the reader is perpetually expecting to hear of the spell by which the English were so soon brought in force to Branksome tower.

Were we to point out the passages of the poem which afforded us most pleasure, we should select those in which the minstrel himself makes his appearance. The introduction, and the concluding stanza of each canto, have an excellent effect, and are very pleasing. From these we shall gratify our readers by some quotations. The introduction we shall extract at length, as it affords a very good specimen of the powers of the poet.

[introduction, ll. 1-100, omitted]

The conclusion of the second canto presents a lively picture of which every one who has at any time cheered a vagrant old minstrel of our own times with a cordial cup, has seen a resemblance.

[canto II, ll. 416-34, omitted]

It is now necessary to state those circumstances in the poem which have struck us as blemishes; and this, although the most ungracious and disagreeable, is, perhaps, not the least useful part of the critic's task, at least, in respect to the author. One principal defect in the piece is the irregularity of the versification. In some ancient metrical romances, which the author in this respect professes to copy, we are willing to pardon this mark of an uncultivated taste, while the whole piece discovers the same rudeness in every particular. But indeed *The Lay of the Last Minstrel* plainly discovers in other respects a cultivation very different from that of the age to which the story refers. Nor do we account this superior polish a blemish. To write coarse doggrel because coarse doggrel was written in the age in which the scene is placed, is a strange depraved affectation of being natural, into which many inferior writers have fallen, but which Mr. Scott has had both good taste and good sense enough in general to avoid. His irregular versification, however, frequently approaches too nearly to this fault. The measure is often so abruptly altered, and without any apparent reason, that the melody is completely lost, and a very disagreeable impression left on the reader who has any ear for cadence. The verse which he sometimes uses has also no characteristic of verse, but that it is printed in one line, and rhymes to another. The following are examples of this sort.

> 'It was the Spirit of the Flood that spoke,
> And he called on the Spirit of the Fell.'

> 'When buttress and buttress alternately,
> Seem framed of ebon and ivory,
> When silver edges the imagery,
> And the scrolls that teach thee to live and die,'

> 'And the silken knots which in hurry she would make,
> Why tremble her slender fingers to tie.'

We conceive that such limping verses as these would be a blemish in any poem; nor can we see that they have the least tendency to render the description more natural. Our author hints in the advertisement prefixed to the poem that this species of verse was most suitable to the descriptions of scenery and manners he intended to introduce. We cannot see why either irregular metre or limping lines can at all improve such descriptions. The introduction is, in regard to the versification, the most regular part of the poem, nor can we see that any beauties of the succeeding cantos would have required to be retrenched by the continuation of the same measure in them. Our author, indeed, seems to have formed his taste in versification too much on the present depraved model of the German poets. How much genius has Wieland smothered under the heaps of uncouth and ill-arranged verses with which he has loaded his works!

When our author has allowed himself so very wide a latitude in the alteration of his metre, we should at least have expected him to avoid the last refuge of non-plus'd rhymesters, that of eking out his lines with unmeaning and superfluous words. Yet the following instances seem to exemplify this fault.

'In Eske, or Liddell, fords were none,
But he would ride them *one by one*—'

Did any person ever ride two fords at once?

The old eke-out *I say*, is scarcely pardonable in a poem constructed on the model of that before us, especially when no necessity calls for it as a stronger affirmation.

'Never heavier man and horse
Stemmed a midnight torrent's force;
The warrior's very plume, *I say*,
Was daggled by the dashing spray.'

The following interpolation also savours little of a lay intended for 'high dames and mighty earls':

'For, *at a word*, be it understood,
He was always for ill, and never for good.'

The ridicule of Pope has banished the eke-out *do's* and *did's*. These have, however, of late made their appearance again, under the disguise of their allies *would* and *could*. The disguise employed by our author, in the following passage, is however too thin to conceal *did* from the ridicule that pursues his poetical appearances.

'And you might hear from Branksome hill,
No sound but Teviot's gushing tide;
Save, when the changing sentinel
The challenge of his watch *could* tell.'

A degree of quaintness is allowable in a poem that describes the manners of the sixteenth century. Quaintness was the taste of that age, not only in writing, but in ordinary conversation. Our author, however, seems to carry this sometimes too far. Alliteration is a species of affectation to which our author seems much addicted, and he has unfortunately fallen sometimes upon the most grating and unmusical sounds.

> 'Where *Melros'* rose, and fair Tweed ran.'
> 'He meetly stabled his steed in stall.'

There is sometimes an affectation of imitating the sound by the sense, which recalls to us the well-known verse,

> 'Tramp, tramp, along the land,
> And plash, plash, along the sea.'

The kindred of the following verses will easily be traced:

> 'For I have seen war's lightening flashing,
> Seen the claymore with bayonet clashing,
> Seen through red blood the war-horse dashing.'

The following is also an attempt to represent by the measure the speed of Sir William Deloraine's dapple horse.

> ' "O swiftly can speed my dapple-gray steed,
> Who drinks of the Teviot clear;
> Ere break of day," the warrior 'gan say,
> "Again will I be here": '—

Perhaps a little Latin introduced into a poem may give an opinion of an author's learning; but we must own that we were tempted to laugh in the midst of a very serious subject, by the introduction of the burden of the funeral song.

> 'DIES IRÆ, DIES ILLA,
> SOLVET SÆCLUM IN FAVILLA;'—[1]

This would surely have appeared with more propriety in a note.

There is nothing more insipid, or that more effectually destroys the

---

[1]   'Day of dread, day of ire,
         When the world shall melt in fire'.
Opening lines of the Sequence from the Roman Catholic common mass for the dead.

pleasure which poetry affords, than the useless repetition of unmeaning words. Who does not feel *each* muscle of his face put out of humour by the following repetition?

> 'Each with warlike tidings fraught;
> Each from each the signal caught;
> Each after each they glanced to sight,'—

There is a species of poetry so well known in our days, that it is only necessary to mention its name. Our author has in too many instances shewn an inclination towards *namby-pamby*.

> 'Alike to him was time, or tide,
> December's snow, or July's pride;
> Alike to him was tide, or time,
> Moonless midnight, or mattin prime.'

> 'With dagger's hilt, on the wicket strong,
> *He struck full loud, and struck full long.*
> The porter hurried to the gate—
> *"Who knocks so loud, and knocks so late?"* '

> 'The unearthly voices ceast,
>   And the heavy sound was still;
> *It died on the river's breast,*
>   *It died on the side of the hill—*'

This propensity, however, sometimes has so ludicrous an effect as to relieve the insipidity of namby-pamby, although it may be questioned whether the *ridiculous* substituted in its room be less hurtful to the general effect of the poem. The dialogue of the Spirits already quoted may be ranked in this class.

> 'For mass or prayer can I rarely tarry,
> Save to patter an Ave Mary,
> When I ride on a Border foray:'—

> 'O'er ptarmigan and venison,
> The priest had spoke his benison.'

In the following passages we have something like examples of the celebrated art of sinking in poetry.

> 'Where Aill, from mountains freed,
> Down from the lakes did raving come;
> Each wave was crested with tawny foam,
>   Like *the mane of a chestnut steed.*'

> 'A hardy race, on Irthing bred,
> With kirtles white, and crosses red,
> Arrayed beneath the banner tall,
> That streamed o'er Acre's conquered wall;
> And minstrels, as they marched in order,
> Played "Noble Lord Dacre, he dwells on the Border".'

We do not blame the introduction of any of these circumstances into the poem; but certainly the suddenness of the transition has in it something of the ludicrous.

The use of antiquated language in the description of ancient manners is a folly resembling that taste for describing the manners of the common people in their own dialect. Our author has not particularly disfigured his poem by the affectation of introducing antiquated words. He has indeed his *certes* and *uneath*, and a few more of the same category. He also grates our ears by placing the accent frequently on a syllable different from that accented by the usage of the present age.

> 'Seemed dimly huge the dark *Abbaye*.'
> 'Lie buried within that proud *chapelle*.'

The word *Abbaye* is used in another place with the accent on the first syllable.

We are at a loss to interpret the following expression:

> 'From the sound of Teviot's tide,
> Chafing with the mountain's side.'

Does *with* here mean *on*, or is it altogether thrust in to make up the verse, but to mean nothing?

> 'Be it scroll, or be it book,
> Into, knight, thou must not look.'

Is *it* here left out by an error of the press? If not, it is a very whimsical ellipsis.

There are some circumstances which seem to us inconsistencies, although the poet in general is not chargeable with this fault. At a time when the monasteries were perpetually frequented by warrior devotees, we can scarcely imagine where the 'Monk of St. Mary's aisle' had hid himself, when he tells Sir William Deloraine,

> 'Now, strange to my eyes thine arms appear,
> And their iron clang sounds strange to my ear.'

33

We should scarcely have expected a specific botanical term in the mouth of an old minstrel;

> 'Like some tall rock with *lichens* grey.'

Are pity and sincerity inconsistent?

> 'He paused—the listening dames again
> Applaud the hoary Minstrel's strain;
> With many a word of kindly cheer,
> *In pity half, and half sincere,*'—

The notes, as we have already observed, are of considerable utility in explaining the allusions of the text. The author here expatiates on the subject which indeed forms the burden of the whole poem, the honours of the family of Scott. He appears to have studied the heraldry and antiquities of that name most profoundly. Perhaps those who look upon the boast of ancestry as one of the whimsical foibles of humanity, may accuse the author of too glaring vanity in sitting down in the present age to celebrate in verse the honours of his own name and family. But for our own parts we shall be always happy to see the foible exhibit itself in such a pleasing form as *The Lay of the Last Minstrel*. Not only the nature of the poem, but the superb manner in which it is printed renders it a very proper present 'for high dames and mighty earls'.

We have now endeavoured to the best of our judgment, to appreciate the principal merits and defects of this performance. In our opinion Mr. Scott, both in this and in other instances, deserves praise for the zeal with which he has laboured to throw light on the ancient manners and customs of one portion of our countrymen.

MARMION
1808

---

2. Francis Jeffrey, unsigned review, *Edinburgh Review*

April 1808, xii, 1-35

Jeffrey, editor and main literary reviewer for the *Edinburgh Review* from 1802 to 1829, was a friend of Scott. It has often been said that this critique led Scott to break with Jeffrey and his *Review* and to help found the *Quarterly*, even though Scott denied this rumour.

For Jeffrey's review of *Waverley*, see No. 9.

There is a kind of right of primogeniture among books, as well as among men; and it is difficult for an author, who has obtained great fame by a first publication, not to appear to fall off in a second—especially if his original success could be imputed, in any degree, to the novelty of his plan of composition. The public is always indulgent to untried talents; and is even apt to exaggerate a little the value of what it receives without any previous expectation. But, for this advance of kindness, it usually exacts a most usurious return in the end. When the poor author comes back, he is no longer received as a benefactor, but a debtor. In return for the credit it formerly gave him, the world now conceives that it has a just claim on him for excellence, and becomes impertinently scrupulous as to the quality of the coin in which it is to be paid.

The just amount of this claim plainly cannot be for more than the rate of excellence which he had reached in his former production; but, in estimating this rate, various errors are perpetually committed, which increase the difficulties of the task which is thus imposed on him. In the *first* place, the comparative amount of his past and present merits can only be ascertained by the uncertain standard of his reader's feelings; and these must always be less lively with regard to a second performance; which, with every other excellence of the first, must necessarily want the powerful recommendations of novelty and surprise, and, consequently, fall very far short of the effect produced by their strong cooperation. In the *second* place, it may be observed, in general, that wherever our impression of any work is favourable on the whole, its excellence is constantly exaggerated, in those vague and habitual recollections which form the basis of subsequent comparisons. We readily drop from our memory the dull and bad passages, and carry along with us the remembrance of those only which had afforded us delight. Thus, when we take the merit of any favourite poem as a standard of comparison for some later production of the same author, we never take its true average merit, which is the only fair standard, but the merit of its most striking and memorable passages, which naturally stand forward in our recollection, and pass upon our hasty retrospect as just and characteristic specimens of the whole work; and this high and exaggerated standard we rigorously apply to the first, and perhaps the least interesting parts of the second performance. Finally, it deserves to be noticed, that where a first work, containing considerable blemishes, has been favourably received, the public always expects this indulgence to be repaid by an improvement that ought not to be always expected. If a second performance appear, therefore, with the same faults, they will no longer meet with the same toleration. Murmurs will be heard about indolence, presumption, and abuse of good nature; while the critics, and those who had gently hinted at the necessity of correction, will be more out of humour than the rest at this apparent neglect of their admonitions.

For these, and for other reasons, we are inclined to suspect, that the success of the work now before us will be less brilliant than that of the author's former publication, though we are ourselves of opinion, that its intrinsic merits are nearly, if not altogether, equal; and that, if it had had the fortune to be the elder born, it would have inherited as fair a portion of renown as has fallen to the lot of its predecessor. It is a good deal longer, indeed, and somewhat more ambitious; and it is rather clearer that it has greater faults, than that it has greater beauties; though, for our own parts, we are inclined to believe in both propositions. It has more tedious and flat passages, and more ostentation of historical and antiquarian lore; but it has also greater richness and variety, both of character and incident; and if it has less sweetness and pathos in the softer passages, it has certainly more vehemence and force of colouring in the loftier and busier representations of action and emotion. The place of the prologuizing minstrel is but ill supplied, indeed, by the epistolary dissertations which are prefixed to each book of the present poem; and the ballad pieces and mere episodes which it contains, have less finish and poetical beauty; but there is more airiness and spirit in the lighter delineations; and the story, if not more skilfully conducted, is at least better complicated, and extended through a wider field of adventure. The characteristics of both, however, are evidently the same;—a broken narrative—a redundancy of minute description—bursts of unequal and energetic poetry—and a general tone of spirit and animation, unchecked by timidity or affectation, and unchastised by any great delicacy of taste, or elegance of fancy.

But though we think this last romance of Mr. Scott's about as good as the former, and allow that it affords great indications of poetical talent, we must remind our readers, that we never entertained much partiality for this sort of composition, and ventured on a former occasion to express our regret, that an author endowed with such talents should consume them in imitations of obsolete extravagance, and in the representation of manners and sentiments in which none of his readers can be supposed to take much interest, except the few who can judge of their exactness. To write a modern romance of chivalry, seems to be much such a fantasy as to build a modern abbey, or an English pagoda. For once, however, it may be excused as a pretty caprice of genius; but a second production of the same sort is entitled to less indulgence, and imposes a sort of duty to drive the author from so idle a task, by a fair exposition of the faults which are in a manner inseparable from its execution. To enable our readers to judge fairly of the present performance, we shall first present them with a brief abstract of the story; and then endeavour to point out what seems to be exceptionable, and what is praiseworthy, in the execution.

[a plot summary is omitted]

Now, upon this narrative, we are led to observe, in the first place, that it forms a very scanty and narrow foundation for a poem of such length as is now before us. There is scarcely matter enough in the main story for a ballad of ordinary dimensions; and the present work is not so properly diversified with episodes and descriptions, as made up and composed of them. No long poem, however, can maintain its interest without a connected narrative. It should be a grand historical picture, in which all the personages are concerned in one great transaction, and not a mere gallery of detached groupes and portraits. When we accompany the poet in his career of adventure, it is not enough that he points out to us, as we go along, the beauties of the landscape, and the costume of the inhabitants. The people must do something after they are described; and they must do it in concert, or in opposition to each other; while the landscape, with its castles and woods and defiles, must serve merely as the scene of their exploits, and the field of their conspiracies and contentions. There is too little connected incident in *Marmion*, and a great deal too much gratuitous description.

In the second place, we object to the whole plan and conception of the fable, as turning mainly upon incidents unsuitable for poetical narrative, and brought out in the denouement in a very obscure, laborious, and imperfect manner. The events of an epic narrative should all be of a broad, clear, and palpable description; and the difficulties and embarrassments of the characters, of a nature to be easily comprehended and entered into by readers of all descriptions. Now, the leading incidents in this poem are of a very narrow and peculiar character, and are woven together into a petty intricacy and entanglement which puzzles the reader instead of interesting him, and fatigues instead of exciting his curiosity. The unaccountable conduct of Constance, in first ruining De Wilton in order to forward Marmion's suit with Clara, and then trying to poison Clara, because Marmion's suit seemed likely to succeed with her—but, above all, the paltry device of the forged letters, and the sealed packet given up by Constance at her condemnation, and handed over by the abbess to De Wilton and Lord Angus, are incidents not only unworthy of the dignity of poetry, but really incapable of being made subservient to its legitimate purposes. They are particularly unsuitable, too, to the age and character of the personages to whom they relate; and, instead of forming the instruments of knightly vengeance and redress, remind us of the machinery of a bad German novel, or of the disclosures which might be expected on the trial of a pettifogging attorney. The obscurity and intricacy which they communicate to the whole story, must be very painfully felt by every reader who tries to comprehend it; and is prodigiously increased by the very clumsy and inartificial manner in which the denouement is ultimately brought about by the author. Three several attempts are made by three several persons to beat into the head of the reader the evidence of De Wilton's innocence, and of Marmion's guilt; first, by Constance in her dying speech and confession; secondly, by the abbess in her conference with De Wilton; and, lastly, by this injured innocent himself, on disclosing himself to Clara in the castle of Lord Angus. After all, the precise nature of the plot and the detection is very imperfectly explained, and, we will venture to say, is not fully understood by one half of those who have fairly read through every word of the quarto now before us. We would object, on the same grounds, to the whole scenery of Constance's condemnation. The subterranean chamber, with its low arches, massive walls, and silent monks with smoky torches,—its old chandelier in an iron chain,—the stern abbots and haughty prioresses, with their flowing black dresses, and book of statutes laid on an iron table, are all images borrowed from the novels of Mrs. Ratcliffe and her imitators. The public, we believe, has now supped full of this sort of horrors; or, if any effect is still to be produced by their exhibition, it may certainly be produced at too cheap a rate, to be worthy the ambition of a poet of original imagination.

In the third place, we object to the extreme and monstrous improbability of almost all the incidents which go to the composition of this fable. We know very well, that poetry does not describe what is ordinary; but the marvellous, in which it is privileged to indulge, is the marvellous of performance, and not of accident. One extraordinary rencontre or opportune coincidence may be permitted, perhaps, to bring the parties together, and wind up matters for the catastrophe; but a writer who gets through the whole business of his poem, by a series of lucky hits and incalculable chances, certainly manages matters in a very economical way for his judgment and invention, and will probably be found to have consulted his own ease, rather than the delight of his readers. Now, the whole story of *Marmion* seems to us to turn upon a tissue of such incredible accidents. In the first place, it was totally beyond all calculation, that Marmion and De Wilton should meet, by pure chance, at Norham, on the only night which either of them could spend in that fortress. In the next place, it is almost totally incredible that the former should not recognize his antient rival and antagonist, merely because he had assumed a palmer's habit, and lost a little flesh and colour in his travels. He appears unhooded, and walks and speaks before him; and, as near as we can guess, it could not be more than a year since they had entered the lists against each other. Constance, at her death, says she had lived but three years with Marmion; and, it was not till he tired of her, that he aspired to Clara, or laid plots against De Wilton. It is equally inconceivable that De Wilton should have taken upon himself the friendly office of a guide to his arch enemy, and discharged it quietly and faithfully, without seeking, or apparently thinking of any opportunity of disclosure or revenge. So far from meditating any thing of the sort, he makes two several efforts to leave him, when it appears that his services are no longer indispensable. If his accidental meeting, and continued association with Marmion, be altogether unnatural, it must appear still more extraordinary, that he should afterwards meet with the Lady Clare, his adored mistress, and the Abbess of Whitby, who had in her pocket the written proofs of his innocence, in consequence of an occurrence equally accidental. These two ladies, the only two persons in the universe whom it was of any consequence to him to meet, are captured in their voyage from Holy Isle, and brought to Edinburgh, by the luckiest accident in the world, the very day that De Wilton and Marmion make their entry into it. Nay, the king, without knowing that they are at all of his acquaintance, happens to appoint them lodgings in the same stair-case, and to make them travel under his escort! We pass the night combat at Gifford, in which Marmion knows his opponent by moonlight, though he never could guess at him in sunshine; and all the inconsistencies of his dilatory wooing of Lady Clare. Those, and all the prodigies and miracles of the story, we can excuse, as within the privilege of poetry; but, the lucky chances we have already specified, are rather too much for our patience. A poet, we think, should never let his heroes contract such great debts to fortune; especially when a little exertion of his own might make them independent of her bounty. De Wilton might have been made to seek and watch his adversary, from some moody feeling of patient revenge; and it certainly would not have been difficult to discover motives which might have induced both Clara and the Abbess to follow and relieve him, without dragging them into his presence by the clumsy hands of a cruizer from Dunbar.

In the *fourth* place, we think we have reason to complain of Mr. Scott for having made his figuring characters so entirely worthless, as to excite but little of our sympathy, and at the same time keeping his virtuous personages so completely in the back ground, that we are scarcely at all acquainted with them when the work is brought to a conclusion. Marmion is not only a villain, but a mean and sordid villain; and represented as such, without any visible motive, and at the evident expense of characteristic truth and consistency. His elopement with Constance, and his subsequent desertion of her, are knightly vices enough, we suppose; but then he would surely have been more interesting and natural, if he had deserted her for a brighter beauty, and not merely for a richer bride. This was very well for Mr. Thomas Inkle, the young merchant of London; but for the valiant, haughty and liberal Lord Marmion of Fontenaye and Lutterward, we do think it was quite unsuitable. Thus, too, it was very chivalrous and orderly perhaps, for him to hate De Wilton, and to seek to supplant him in his lady's love; but, to slip a bundle of forged letters into his bureau, was cowardly as well as malignant. Now, Marmion is not represented as a coward, nor as at all afraid of De Wilton; on the contrary, and it is certainly the most absurd part of the story, he fights him fairly and valiantly after all, and overcomes him by mere force of arms, as he might have done at the beginning, without having recourse to devices so unsuitable to his general character and habits of acting. By the way, we have great doubts whether a *convicted* traitor, like De Wilton, whose guilt was established by written evidence under his own hand, was ever allowed to enter the lists, as a knight, against his accuser. At all events, we are positive, that an accuser, who was as ready and willing to fight as Marmion, could never have condescended to forge in support of his accusation; and that the author has greatly diminished our interest in the story, as well as needlessly violated the truth of character, by loading his hero with the guilt of this most revolting and improbable proceeding. The crimes of Constance are multiplied in like manner to such a degree, as both to destroy our interest in her fate, and to violate all probability. Her elopement was enough to bring on her doom; and we should have felt more for it, if it had appeared a little more unmerited. She is utterly debased, when she becomes the instrument of Marmion's murderous perfidy, and the assassin of her unwilling rival.

De Wilton, again, is too much depressed throughout the poem. It is rather dangerous for a poet to chuse a hero who has been beaten in fair battle. The readers of romance do not like an unsuccessful warrior; but to be beaten in a judicial combat, and to have his arms reversed and tied on the gallows, is an adventure which can only be expiated by signal prowess and exemplary revenge, achieved against great odds, in full view of the reader. The unfortunate De Wilton, however, carries this stain upon him from one end of the poem to the other. He wanders up and down, a dishonoured fugitive, in the disguise of a palmer, through the five first books; and though he is knighted and mounted again in the last, yet we see nothing of his performances; nor is the author merciful enough to afford him one opportunity of redeeming his credit by an exploit of gallantry or skill. For the poor Lady Clare, she is a personage of still greater insipidity and insignificance. The author seems to have formed her upon the principle of Mr. Pope's maxim, that women have no characters at all. We find her every where, where she has no business to be; neither saying nor doing any thing of the least consequence, but whimpering and sobbing over the Matrimony in her prayer book, like a great miss from a boarding school; and all this is the more inexcusable, as she is altogether a supernumerary person in the play, who should atone for her intrusion by some brilliancy or novelty of deportment. Matters would have gone on just as well, although she had been left behind at Whitby till after the battle of Flodden; and she is daggled about in the train, first of the Abbess and then of Lord Marmion, for no purpose, that we can see, but to afford the author an opportunity for two or three pages of indifferent description.

Finally, we must object, both on critical and on national grounds, to the discrepancy between the title and the substance of the poem, and the neglect of Scotish feelings and Scotish character that is manifested throughout. Marmion is no more a tale of Flodden Field, than of Bosworth Field, or any other field in history. The story is quite independent of the national feuds of the sister kingdoms; and the battle of Flodden has no other connexion with it, than from being the conflict in which the hero loses his life. Flodden, however, is mentioned; and the preparations for Flodden, and the consequences of it, are repeatedly alluded to in the course of the composition. Yet we nowhere find any adequate expressions of those melancholy and patriotic sentiments which are still all over Scotland the accompaniment of those allusions and recollections. No picture is drawn of the national feelings before or after that fatal encounter; and the day that broke for ever the pride and the splendour of his country, is only commemorated by a Scotish poet as the period when an English warrior was beaten to the ground. There is scarcely one trait of true Scotish nationality or patriotism introduced into the whole poem; and Mr. Scott's only expression of admiration or love for the beautiful country to which he belongs, is put, if we rightly remember, into the mouth of one of his Southern favourites. Independently of this, we think that too little pains is taken to distinguish the Scotish character and manners from the English, or to give expression to the general feeling of rivalry and mutual jealousy which at that time existed between the two countries.

If there be any truth in what we have now said, it is evident that the merit of this poem cannot consist in the story. And yet it has very great merit, and various kinds of merit,—both in the picturesque representation of visible objects, in the delineation of manners and characters, and in the description of great and striking events. After having detained the reader so long with our own dull remarks, it will be refreshing to him to peruse a few specimens of Mr. Scott's more enlivening strains. The opening stanzas of the whole poem contain a good picture.

[omitted here are praise and quotations of the following passages: Canto I, stanzas I and II and ll. 460-83; Canto II, ll. 22-42 and stanza VIII, stanza XXI and ll. 471-94, 622-34; Canto III, stanza IX; Canto IV, ll. 541-56, 600-34; Canto V, ll. 186-241, 296-371, 415-20; and Canto VI, ll. 338-50, 574-89, 598-616, 750-818, 854-927, 935-61, 983-92, and 1022-59]

The powerful poetry of these passages can receive no illustration from any praises or observations of ours. It is superior, in our apprehension, to all that this author has hitherto produced; and, with a few faults of diction, equal to any thing that has *ever* been written upon similar subjects. Though we have extended our extracts to a very unusual length, in order to do justice to these fine conceptions, we have been obliged to leave out a great deal, which serves in the original to give beauty and effect to what we have actually cited. From the moment the author gets in sight of Flodden Field, indeed, to the end of the poem, there is no tame writing, and no intervention of ordinary passages. He does not once flag or grow tedious; and neither stops to describe dresses and ceremonies, nor to commemorate the harsh names of feudal barons from the Border. There is a flight of five or six hundred lines, in short, in which he never stoops his wing, nor wavers in his course; but carries the reader forward with a more rapid, sustained, and lofty movement, than any Epic bard that we can at present remember.

From the contemplation of such distinguished excellence, it is painful to be obliged to turn to the defects and deformities which occur in the same composition. But this, though a less pleasing, is a still more indispensable part of our duty; and one, from the resolute discharge of which, much more beneficial consequences may be expected. In the work which contains the fine passages we have just quoted, and many of nearly equal beauty, there is such a proportion of tedious, hasty, and injudicious composition, as makes it questionable with us, whether it is entitled to go down to posterity as a work of classical merit, or whether the author will retain, with another generation, that high reputation which his genius certainly might make coeval with the language. These are the authors, after all, whose faults it is of most consequence to point out; and criticism performs her best and boldest office,—not when she tramples down the weed, or tears up the bramble,—but when she strips the strangling ivy from the oak, or cuts out the canker from the rose. The faults of the fable we have already noticed at sufficient length. Those of the execution we shall now endeavour to enumerate with greater brevity.

And, in the *first* place, we must beg leave to protest, in the name of a very numerous class of readers, against the insufferable number, and length, and minuteness of those descriptions of antient dresses and manners, and buildings; and ceremonies, and local superstitions; with which the whole poem is overrun,—which render so many notes necessary, and are, after all, but imperfectly understood by those to whom chivalrous antiquity has not hitherto been an object of peculiar attention. We object to these, and to all such details, because they are, for the most part, without dignity or interest in themselves; because, in a modern author, they are evidently unnatural; and because they must always be strange, and, in a good degree, obscure and unintelligible to ordinary readers.

When a great personage is to be introduced, it is right, perhaps, to give the reader some notion of his external appearance; and when a memorable event is to be narrated, it is natural to help the imagination by some picturesque representation of the scenes with which it is connected. Yet, even upon such occasions, it can seldom be adviseable to present the reader with a full inventory of the hero's dress, from his shoebuckle to the plume in his cap, or to enumerate all the drawbridges, portcullisses, and diamond cut stones in the castle. Mr. Scott, however, not only draws out almost all his pictures in these full dimensions, but frequently introduces those pieces of Flemish or Chinese painting to represent persons who are of no consequence, or places and events which are of no importance to the story. It would be endless to go through the poem for examples of this excess of minute description; we shall merely glance at the First Canto as a specimen. We pass the long description of Lord Marmion himself, with his mail of Milan steel; the blue ribbons on his horse's mane; and his blue velvet housings. We pass also the two gallant squires who ride behind him. But our patience is really exhausted, when we are forced to attend to the black stockings and blue jerkins of the inferior persons in the train, and to the whole process of turning out the guard with advanced arms on entering the castle.

[Canto I, ll. 103-62, are omitted]

Sir Hugh the Heron then orders supper—

'Now broach ye a pipe of Malvoisie,
Bring pasties of the doe.'

—And after the repast is concluded, they have some mulled wine, and drink good night very ceremoniously.

'Lord Marmion drank a fair good rest,
The Captain pledged his noble guest,
The cup went round among the rest.'

In the morning, again, we are informed that they had prayers, and that knight and squire

——'broke their fast
On rich substantial repast.'
'Then came the stirrup-cup in course,' &c. &c.

And thus a whole Canto is filled up with the account of a visit and a supper, which lead to no consequences whatever, and are not attended with any circumstances which must not have occurred at every visit and supper among persons of the same rank at that period. Now, we are really at a loss to know, why the mere circumstance of a moderate antiquity should be supposed so far to ennoble those details, as to entitle them to a place in poetry, which certainly never could be claimed for a description of more modern adventures. Nobody, we believe, would be bold enough to introduce into a serious poem a description of the hussar boots and gold epaulets of a commander in chief, and much less to particularize the liveries and canes of his servants or the order and array of a grand dinner, given even to the cabinet ministers. Yet these things are, in their own nature, fully as picturesque, and as interesting, as the ribbons at the mane of Lord Marmion's horse, or his supper and breakfast at the castle of Norham. We are glad, indeed, to find these little details in *old* books, whether in prose or verse, because they are there authentic and valuable documents of the usages and modes of life of our ancestors; and we are thankful when we light upon this sort of information in an antient romance, which commonly contains matter much more tedious. Even there, however, we smile at the simplicity which could mistake such naked enumerations for poetical description; and reckon them as nearly on a level, in point of taste, with the theological disputations that are sometimes introduced in the same meritorious compositions. In a *modern* romance, however, these details being no longer authentic, are of no value in point of information; and as the author has no claim to indulgence on the ground of simplicity, the smile which his predecessors excited is in some danger of being turned into a yawn. If he wishes sincerely to follow their example, he should describe the manners of his own time, and not of theirs. They painted from observation, and not from study; and the familiarity and *naïveté* of their delineations, transcribed with a slovenly and hasty hand from what they saw daily before them, is as remote as possible from the elaborate pictures extracted by a modern imitator from black-letter books, and coloured, not from the life, but from learned theories, or at best from mouldy monkish illuminations, and mutilated fragments of painted glass.

But the times of chivalry, it may be said, were more picturesque than the present times. They are better adapted to poetry; and every thing that is associated with them has a certain hold on the imagination, and partakes of the interest of the period. We do not mean utterly to deny this; nor can we stop, at present, to assign exact limits to our assent: but this we will venture to observe, in general, that if it be true that the interest which we take in the contemplation of the chivalrous era, arises from the dangers and virtues by which it was distinguished,—from the constant hazards in which its warriors passed their days, and the mild and generous valour with which they met those hazards,—joined to the singular contrast which it presented between the ceremonious polish and gallantry of the nobles, and the brutish ignorance of the body of the people:—if these are, as we conceive they are, the sources of the charm which still operates in behalf of the days of knightly adventure, then it should follow, that nothing should interest us, by association with that age, but what serves naturally to bring before us those hazards and that valour, and gallantry, and aristocratical superiority. Any description, or any imitation of the exploits in which those qualities were signalized, will do this most effectually. Battles,—tournaments,—penances,—deliverance of damsels,—instalments of knights, &c.—and, intermixed with these, we must admit some description of arms, armorial bearings, castles, battlements, and chapels: but the least and lowest of the whole certainly is the description of servants' liveries, and of the peaceful operations of eating, drinking, and ordinary salutation. These have no sensible connexion with the qualities or peculiarities which have conferred certain poetical privileges on the manners of chivalry. They do not enter either necessarily or naturally into our conception of what is interesting in those manners; and, though protected, by their strangeness, from the ridicule which would infallibly attach to their modern equivalents, are substantially as unpoetic, and as little entitled to indulgence from impartial criticism.

We would extend this censure to a larger proportion of the work before us than we now choose to mention—certainly to all the stupid monkish legends about St. Hilda and St. Cuthbert—to the ludicrous description of Lord Gifford's habiliments of divination—and to all the various scraps and fragments of antiquarian history and baronial biography, which are scattered profusely through the whole narrative. These we conceive to be put in purely for the sake of displaying the erudition of the author; and poetry, which has no other recommendation, but that the substance of it has been gleaned from rare or obscure books, has, in our estimation, the least of all possible recommendations. Mr. Scott's great talents, and the novelty of the style in which his romances are written, have made even these defects acceptable to a considerable part of his readers. His genius, seconded by the omnipotence of fashion, has brought chivalry again into temporary favour; but he ought to know, that this is a taste too evidently unnatural to be long prevalent in the modern world. Fine ladies and gentlemen now talk, indeed, of donjons, keeps, tabards, scutcheons, tressures, caps of maintenance, portcullisses, wimples, and we know not what besides; just as they did, in the days of Dr. Darwin's popularity, of gnomes, sylphs, oxygen, gossamer, polygynia, and polyandria. That fashion, however, passed rapidly away; and if it be now evident to all the world, that Dr. Darwin obstructed the extension of his fame, and hastened the extinction of his brilliant reputation, by the pedantry and ostentatious learning of his poems, Mr. Scott should take care that a different sort of pedantry does not produce the same effects. The world will never be long pleased with what it does not readily understand; and the poetry which is destined for immortality, should treat only of feelings and events which can be conceived and entered into by readers of all descriptions.

What we have now mentioned, is the cardinal fault of the work before us; but it has other faults, of too great magnitude to be passed altogether without notice. There is a debasing lowness and vulgarity in some passages, which we think must be offensive to every reader of delicacy, and which are not, for the most part, redeemed by any vigour or picturesque effect. The venison pasties, we think, are of this description; and this commemoration of Sir Hugh Heron's troopers, who

> 'Have drunk the monks of St. Bothan's ale,
> And driven the beeves of Lauderdale;
> Harried the wives of Greenlaw's goods,
> And given them light to fet their hoods.'

The long account of Friar John, though not without merit, offends in the same sort; nor can we easily conceive, how any one could venture, in a serious poem, to speak of

> ——'the wind that blows,
> And *warms itself against his nose.*'

The speeches of squire Blount, too, are a great deal too unpolished for a noble youth aspiring to knighthood. On two occasions, to specify no more, he addresses his brother squire in these cacophonous lines—

> '*St. Anton' fire thee!* wilt thou stand
> All day with bonnet in thy hand?'
> '*Stint in thy prate,*' quoth Blount, '*thou'dst best,*
> And listen to our Lord's behest.'

Neither can we be brought to admire the simple dignity of Sir Hugh the Heron, who thus encourageth his nephew,

> ——'*By my fay,*
> Well hast thou spoke—say forth thy say.'

There are other passages in which the flatness and tediousness of the narrative is relieved by no sort of beauty, nor elegance of diction, and which form an extraordinary contrast with the more animated and finished portions of the poem. We shall not afflict our readers with more than one specimen of this falling off. We select it from the Abbess's explanation to De Wilton.

[canto V, ll. 580-602 are omitted]

In some other places, Mr. Scott's love of variety has betrayed him into strange imitations. This is evidently formed on the school of Sternhold and Hopkins.

> 'Of all the palaces so fair,
> Built for the royal dwelling,
> In Scotland, far beyond compare,
> Linlithgow is excelling.'

The following is a sort of mongrel between the same school, and the later one of Mr. Wordsworth.

> 'And Bishop Gawain, as he rose,
> Said—Wilton, grieve not for thy woes,
> Disgrace and trouble;
> For He, who honour best bestows,
> May give thee double.'

There are many other blemishes, both of taste and of diction, which we had marked for reprehension, but now think it unnecessary to specify; and which, with some of those we have mentioned, we are willing to ascribe to the haste in which much of the poem seems evidently to have been composed. Mr. Scott knows too well what is due to the public, to make any boast of the rapidity with which his works are written; but the dates and the extent of his successive publications show sufficiently how short a time could be devoted to each; and explain, though they do not apologize for, the many imperfections with which they have been suffered to appear. He who writes for immortality should not be sparing of time; and if it be true, that in every thing which has a principle of life, the period of gestation and growth bears some proportion to that of the whole future existence, the author now before us should tremble when he looks back on the miracles of his own facility.

We have dwelt longer on the beauties and defects of this poem, than we are afraid will be agreeable either to the partial or the indifferent; not only because we look upon it as a misapplication, in some degree, of very extraordinary talents, but because we cannot help considering it as the foundation of a new school, which may hereafter occasion no little annoyance both to us and to the public. Mr. Scott has hitherto filled the whole stage himself; and the very splendour of his success has probably operated, as yet, rather to deter, than to encourage, the herd of rivals and imitators: but if, by the help of the good parts of his poem, he succeeds in suborning the verdict of the public in favour of the bad parts also, and establishes an indiscriminate taste for chivalrous legends and romances in irregular rhime, he may depend upon having as many copyists as Mrs. Radcliffe or Schiller, and upon becoming the founder of a new schism in the catholic poetical church, for which, in spite of all our exertions, there will probably be no cure, but in the extravagance of the last and lowest of its followers. It is for this reason that we conceive it to be our duty to make one strong effort to bring back the great apostle of the heresy to the wholesome creed of his instructors, and to stop the insurrection before it becomes desperate and senseless, by persuading the leader to return to his duty and allegiance. We admire Mr. Scott's genius as much as any of those who may be misled by its perversion; and, like the curate and the barber in Don Quixote, lament the day when a gentleman of such endowments was corrupted by the wicked tales of knight-errantry and enchantment.

We have left ourselves no room to say any thing of the epistolary effusions which are prefixed to each of the cantos. They certainly are not among the happiest productions of Mr. Scott's muse. They want interest in the subjects, and finish in the execution. There is too much of them about the personal and private feelings and affairs of the author; and too much of the remainder about the most trite common places of politics and poetry. There is a good deal of spirit, however, and a good deal of nature intermingled. There is a fine description of St. Mary's loch, in that prefixed to the second canto; and a very pleasing representation of the author's early tastes and prejudices, in that prefixed to the third. The last, which is about Christmas, is the worst; though the first, containing a threnody on Nelson, Pitt and Fox, exhibits a more remarkable failure. We are unwilling to quarrel with a poet on the score of politics; but the manner in which he has chosen to praise the last of these great men, is more likely, we conceive, to give offence to his admirers, than the most direct censure. The only deed for which he is praised, is for having broken off the negotiation for peace; and for this act of firmness, it is added, Heaven rewarded him with a share in the honoured grave of Pitt! It is then said, that his errors should be forgotten, and that he *died* a Briton—a pretty plain insinuation, that, in the author's opinion, he did not live one; and just such an encomium as he himself pronounces over the grave of his villain hero Marmion. There was no need, surely, to pay compliments to ministers or princesses, either in the introduction or in the body of a romance of the 16th century. Yet we have a laboured lamentation over the Duke of Brunswick, in one of the epistles; and, in the heart of the poem, a triumphant allusion to the siege of Copenhagen—the last exploit, certainly, of British valour, on which we should have expected a chivalrous poet to found his patriotic gratulations. We have no business, however, on this occasion, with the political creed of the author; and we notice these allusions to objects of temporary interest, chiefly as instances of bad taste, and additional proofs that the author does not always recollect, that a poet should address himself to more than one generation.

THE LADY OF THE LAKE

1810

3. Unsigned review, *British Critic*

August 1810, xxxvi, 119-24

'To those who are truly and steadily good,' says Plutarch, 'no honour is more dear than that of conferring honour on the deserving; nor any distinction more becoming, than that of giving distinction.'[1] After the delight we have received from various compositions of Mr. Scott, we should feel degraded in our own eyes if we felt a wish to deny him the well-earned title of a poet; or even to lower and diminish his fame by captious and invidious abatements. Such attempts, however called for by the cravings of some readers, will never be made by the *British Critic*, whose editors, if they presume not to take all the praise bestowed by Plutarch, are more ambitious to deserve it, than the utmost credit that could be gained by harshness and injustice.

If we say then that the poet has consulted his own ease in the versification of this Poem, we do not mean to add that he has thereby defrauded the reader of any gratification. Many perhaps may read the Poem without perceiving that the whole narrative is given in the easiest, and generally the tamest measure that our language knows; the measure in which *improvisatori*, if England could produce them, would certainly speak or sing; the eight syllable couplet; the verse of Gay's *Fables*, Prior's *Alma*, &c. that the numbers which divide the pages, and certainly relieve the attention, are perfectly arbitrary, marking neither stanzas, nor any artificial divisions, but mere paragraphs; and that the poem might as well be printed without them, except that the reader would then feel the want of relief, which always has been felt in long poems of this construction. But, having ventured upon this style of narrative, Mr. Scott, like a man of true genius, has ennobled it; he has infused into it a vigour, which it has

[1] From 'On Listening to Lectures', in Plutarch's *Moralia*.

seldom, we might perhaps say never, been known to possess. He has enjoyed the full benefit of its freedom, and has repaid it by strength and animation. In descriptions more particularly, his touches are so lively and picturesque, that it seems as if their effect would be damped and flattened by any other mode of versification. Thus we actually see the stag setting out before the hounds.

> 'But, e'er his fleet career he took,
> The dew-drops from his flanks he shook;
> Like crested leader proud and high,
> Tossed his beamed frontlet to the sky;
> A moment gazed adown the dale,
> A moment snuffed the tainted gale,
> A moment listened to the cry,
> That thickened as the chase drew nigh:[1]
> Then, as the headmost foes appeared,
> With one brave bound the copse he cleared.'

Nor is the following picture of a calm morning, amidst mountain scenery, at all less animated.

> 'The Summer dawn's reflected hue
> To purple changed Loch-Kattrine blue;
> Mildly and soft the western breeze
> Just kissed the lake, just stirred the trees,
> And the pleas'd lake, like maiden coy,
> Trembled, but dimpled not for joy;
> The mountain shadows on her breast
> Were neither broken nor at rest;
> In bright uncertainty they lie,
> Like future joys to Fancy's eye.
> The Water-lily to the light
> Her chalice oped of silver bright;
> The doe awoke, and to the lawn,
> Begemmed with dew-drops, led her fawn;
> The grey mist left the mountain side,
> The torrent show'd its glittering pride;
> Invisible, in flecked sky,
> The lark sent down her revelry;
> The black-bird and the speckled thrush,
> Good-morrow gave from brake and bush;
> In answer cooed the cushat dove,
> Her notes of peace, and rest, and love.'

[1] The repetition of the same rhyme after only one couplet is an inadvertence easily corrected [reviewer].

But, with all this command of the versification he has chosen, the poet seems to have felt that it might want variety; for this reason apparently it is, that he has begun each canto with a stanza or two of alternate rhyme in longer measure, and throughout the whole poem has scattered lyric pieces, some of them mere ballads, the chief advantage of which, in many instances at least, is the effect of breaking the uniformity of cadence, which might otherwise hang heavy in so long a narration. Some of them, undoubtedly, but for this consideration, might as well be absent; though others have much beauty. From the whole contrivance arrives a species of tale, which if it be not easily arranged under any known class, has only the greater air of originality; and possesses eminently the qualities of fixing the attention, exciting curiosity, and repaying both, by pleasing images and splendid pictures.

The tale is in itself extremely interesting, more so perhaps than that of either of the author's former poems. But it possesses also the powerful charm of painting real manners; and displaying the character of an interesting because singular people. The clan-ship of the Highlands, the adherence of the people to their chiefs, the mode of calling them to arms, and other circumstances of their warfare, are all so peculiar and so remote from polished life, that they excite the strongest curiosity, when represented, as we have reason to suppose, with truth as well as liveliness. The following picture of the kind of ambush in which the Highland warriors could lie, among their mountains, is among the most singular and striking that poetry has ever sketched. The chief calls up five hundred warriors by a single signal, who appear, and then as suddenly are lost again.

[Canto V, stanzas IX-X are omitted]

The tale is placed in the reign of James V of Scotland, [1513-1542] a period when clanship was in its utmost vigour, and when the principal events of it, if not historically true, are yet in general consistent with probability. We say, in general, for in a few instances the author has thought fit to venture on the preternatural, a licence which we will not dispute with him; but which certainly destroys probability, and so far injures the effect. In his language Mr. S. takes the liberty of interspersing not only antiquated but Scottish terms, and some of these without interpretation. In the above extract, *bracken*[1] means fern, and had been explained; but *glinted* can only be conjectured from the

[1] So brakes in English [reviewer].

context to mean *glanced*. Nor is it a common Scottish word, since it is not noticed in the copious and excellent dictionary of Dr. Jamieson.[1]

The characters of the poem are few, but they are truly interesting, particularly the Lady of the Lake herself; and the denouement of the tale was to us unexpected, though not unlike others that have been told. But this is surely conducted with skill. Of the narrative the characteristics are general ease, and occasional vigour; and the sentiments introduced arise naturally from the incidents. The following is particularly beautiful.

> 'Some feelings are to mortals given,
> With less of earth in them than heaven;
> And if there be a human tear
> From passion's dross refined and clear;
> A tear so limpid and so meek,
> It would not stain an angel's cheek;
> 'Tis that which pious fathers shed,
> Upon a duteous daughter's head.'

In the concluding lines, after the tale is finished, Mr. S. seems to anticipate something of that caustic criticism which is but too indiscriminately bestowed by the fashion of the present day; a fashion which he, as is reported, contributed to introduce; but he supports himself by reflecting like a true poet, on the consolations he has often received from the Muse.

[Canto VI, ll. 851-59, omitted]

Far be it from us to interrupt the consolations of the poet; and though we certainly could wish that he would not always be quite so much of the Minstrel, but would rise to some higher and more regular strains of poetry, yet while he throws so much of interest and so much of genius into the compositions, which he apparently pours forth with extreme facility, we shall not wish to stand among his censurers, however small the credit may be which is attached to candid commendation.[2]

[1] Several other words of this kind are not explained. The author seems to think, and perhaps not without reason, that they have been very extensively made known by his former Poems. But he should remember that knowledge so picked up in accidental scraps is easily lost again, and that many memories are naturally short [reviewer].

[2] The notes subjoined to the poem are sufficiently illustrative both of the fictions and of the manners introduced, and are as usual written with spirit [reviewer].

4. Coleridge: a letter to Wordsworth

1810

A letter from Samuel Taylor Coleridge to William Wordsworth written in early October 1810 (extracted from E. L. Griggs, ed., *Collected Letters of Samuel Taylor Coleridge* (Oxford, 1959)).

For Coleridge's views on Scott's novels, see No. 24.

I am reading Scott's *Lady of the Lake*, having had it on my table week after week till it cried shame to me for not opening it. But truly as far as I can judge from the first 98 pages, my reluctance was not unprophetic. Merciful Apollo!—what an easy pace dost thou jog on with thy unspurred yet unpinioned Pegasus!—The movement of the Poem (which is written with exception of a multitude of Songs in regular 8 syllable Iambics) is between a sleeping Canter and a Market-woman's trot—but it is endless—I seem never to have made any way—I never remember a narrative poem in which I felt the sense of Progress so languid—. There are (speaking of the first 90 pages) two or three pleasing Images—that of the Swan, p. 25.—is the best—the following seems to me to demand something more for it's introduction than a mere description for description's sake supplies—

> With boughs that *quaked** at every breath   *!
> Gray Birch and Aspen wept beneath;
> Aloft, the ash and warrior Oak
> Cast anchor in the rifted Rock—

I wish, there were more faults of this kind—if it be a fault—yet I think, if it had been a beauty, it would not have instantly struck a perplexed feeling in my mind—as it did, & continues to do—a *doubt*—I seem to feel, that I could have used the metaphor; but not in that way, or without other images or feelings in tune with it.—That *The Lady of the Lake* is not without it's peccadillos against the 8th Commandment à la mode of Messieurs Scott & Campbell, this may suffice—

> Some feelings are to mortals *given*
> *With less* of Earth in them than *Heaven.*
> Vide Ruth, p. 110.[1]

In short, what I felt in *Marmion*, I feel still more in *The Lady of the Lake* —viz. that a man accustomed to cast words in metre and familiar with descriptive Poets & Tourists, himself a Picturesque Tourist, must be troubled with a mental Strangury, if he could not lift up his leg six times at six different Corners, and each time p— a canto.—I should imagine that even Scott's warmest admirers must acknowlege & complain of the number of prosaic lines—PROSE IN POLYSYLLABLES, surely the worst of all prose for chivalrous Poetry—not to mention the liberty taken with our Articles, & pron. relatives such as—

> And Malcolm heard his Ellen's Scream
> *As faultered thro' terrific Dream.*
> Then Roderick plunged *in sheath* his sword
> And veiled his wrath *in scornful word*
> 'Rest safe, till morning! Pity, 'twere
> Such cheek should feel the midnight air.
> Then may'st thou to James Stuart tell
> Roderick will keep the Lake & Fell
> Nor lackey, with his free-born Clan,
> [2]The pageant pomp of earthly man!—
> More would he of Clan Alpine know,
> Thou canst our Strength & Passes shew.
> Malise, what ho!'—his henchman came;
> 'Give our safe conduct to the Graeme!'
> Young Malcolm answered, calm and bold,
> [']Fear nothing for thy favourite hold.
> The Spot,[3] an Angel deigned to grace,
> Is blessed, tho' *robbers* HAUNT THE PLACE;
> Thy churlish Courtesy for those
> Reserve, who fear to be thy foes.
> As safe to me the mountain way
> At midnight, as in blaze of Day,

[1] 'Ruth', lines 124-25:
> For him, a youth to whom was given
> So much of earth—so much of heaven.

[2] *Vide* Wesley's Hymns for the Arminian Methodist Chapel [S.T.C.].

[3] Ellen: an Angel means a beautiful young Lady. I think I have met with the same thought *elsewhere*! and 'deigned to grace'—N.B. She was residing there by compulsion her father being under the wrath of '*King James*' [S.T.C.].

!!!Tho', with his boldest at his back,
Even Roderick Dhu *beset the Track*![1]
Brave Douglas—lovely Ellen—nay—
Nought here of parting will I say.
Earth does not hold a lonesome glen
So secret,[2] but we meet agen.
Chieftain! we too shall find an hour.'
He said, and left the sylvan Bower.—

On my word, I have not *selected* this Stanza—I do not say, that there
are not many better, but I do affirm, that there are some worse, and
that it is a fair specimen of the general style.—But that you may not
rely on my Judgment I will transcribe the next Stanza likewise, the
36th—

Old Allan[3] followed to the Strand
(Such was the Douglas's Command)
And anxious told, how, on the morn,
The stern Sir Roderick *deep had sworn*,
The fiery Cross should circle o'er
Dale, Glen, & Valley, Down, & Moor.
Much were the Peril to the Graeme
From those, who to the signal came;
Far up the Lake 'twere *safest land*,
Himself would row him to the Strand.
He gave his Counsel to the wind,
While Malcom did, unheeding, bind,
Round Dirk & Pouch and broad-sword roll'd,
His ample Plaid in tightened *fold*,
And stripped his Limbs *to such array*
As best might suit the watery way.

37
Then spoke abrupt: 'Farewell to thee,
Pattern of old Fidelity!'
The Minstrel's hand he kindly prest,—
'O! could I *point a place* of rest!

[1] What a thumping Braggadocio this youthful Lover is! [S.T.C.].
[2] S. has been called the Caledonian Comet; but Comets move in ellipses—
and this is doubtless a most eccentric Ellipse, which would frighten Priscian
[S.T.C.].
[3] A miserable copy of Bracy the Bard—Allan too has a *prophetic Dream*; and
what is it? The very ancient Story to be met with in all books of second Sight,
that a Gentleman travelling found a dinner prepared for him at a place where he
had never been before (as related in Humphrey Clinker, *et passim*)! [S.T.C.].

> My Sovereign holds in ward my land,
> My Uncle leads my vassal band;
> To tame his foes, his friends to aid,
> Poor Malcolm has but heart & blade.[']

Poor Malcolm! a hearty Blade, that I will say for him!—

The Poem commences with the poorest Paraphrase-Parody of *The Hart Leap Well*—.

I will add but one extract more, as an instance of the Poet's ear for lyric harmony—Observe, this a poem of the dark Ages, & admire with me the felicity of aiding the imagination in it's flight into the Ages past, & oblivion of the present by—God save the King! & other savory Descants.

> Boat Song. (Canto 2, *19*.p. 69)
>
> Hail to the Chief who in triumph advances,
> Honour'd & blest be the evergreen Pine!
> Long may the Tree in his banner that glances,
> Flourish, the Shelter and grace of our line!
> Heaven send it happy dew,
> Earth lend it sap anew,
> Gayly to bourgeon and *broadly to grow*,
> While every highland Glen
> Sends our shouts back agen,
> 'Roderigh Vich Alpine dhu, ho! ieroe!'

Now, that will tell! that last Gaelic Line is 'a damn'd hard Hit'—as Renyolds [*sic*] said of a passage in King Lear—I suppose, there is some untranslatable Beauty in the Gaelic words, which has preserved this one line in each stanza unenglished—even as the old Popish Translators left the Latin Words & Phrases of the Vulgate sticking, like raisins in a pudding, in the English Text.—

In short, my dear William!—it is time to write a Recipe for Poems of this sort—I amused myself a day or two ago on reading a Romance in Mrs. Radcliff's style with making out a scheme, which was to serve for all romances a priori—only varying the proportions—A Baron or Baroness ignorant of their Birth, and in some dependent situation—Castle—on a Rock—a Sepulchre—at some distance from the Rock—Deserted Rooms—Underground Passages—Pictures—A ghost, so believed—or—a written record—blood on it!—A wonderful Cut throat—&c &c &c—Now I say, it is time to make out the component parts of the Scottish Minstrelsy—The first Business must be, a vast

c*

string of patronymics, and names of Mountains, Rivers, &c—the most commonplace imagery the Bard gars look almaist as well as new, by the introduction of Benvoirlich, Uam Var,

> on copse-wood gray
> That *waved & wept* on *Loch Achray*,
> And mingled with the pine trees *blue*
> On the bold Cliffs of Benvenue—

> How should the Poet e'er give o'er,
> With his eye fix'd on Cambus-More—
> Need reins be tighten'd in Despair,
> When rose Benledi's ridge *in air*
> Tho' not one image grace the Heath,
> It gain such charm from flooded Teith—
> Besides, you need not travel far,
> To reach the Lake of Vennachar—
> Or *ponder refuge* from your Toil
> By far Lochard or Aberfoil!—

Secondly, all the nomenclature of Gothic Architecture, of Heraldry, of Arms, of Hunting, & Falconry—these possess the same power of reviving the caput mortuum & rust of old imagery—besides, they will stand by themselves, Stout Substantives, if only they are strung together, and some attention is paid to the sound of the words—for no one attempts to understand the meaning, which indeed would snap the charm—3—some pathetic moralizing on old times, or any thing else, for the head & tail pieces—with a *Bard* (that is absolutely necessary) and Songs of course—For the rest, whatever suits Mrs. Radcliff, i.e. in the Fable, and the Dramatis Personae, will do for the Poem— with this advantage, that however thread-bare in the Romance Shelves of the circulating Library it is to be taken as quite new as soon as told in rhyme—it need not be half as interesting—& the Ghost may be a Ghost, or may be explained—or both may take place in the same poem—Item—the Poet not only may but must mix all dialects *of all ages*—and all styles from Dr. Robertson's to the Babes in the wood—

I have read only two Cantos out of six—it is not that it would be any act of self-denial to send you the Poem, neither is it for the pain, which, I own, I should feel, and shrink *at* but not *from*, of asking Southey to permit me to send it—that I do not send you the Poem today—but because I think, you would not wish me to ask Southey, who perhaps would refuse, and certainly would grant it with reluctance

& fear—& because I take for granted, that you will have a copy sent
you shortly—
    I send the Brazil which has entertained & instructed me. The
Kehama is expected.
    May God bless you!—I am curious to see the Babe; but long more
anxiously to see little Catherine—

S. T. COLERIDGE—

ROKEBY

1813

---

5. Unsigned review, *British Review*

May 1813, iv, 126-33

Amongst the fashionable arrivals which we are accustomed to read of in our daily newspapers, we feel ourselves now fully prepared for an annual visitor from Edinburgh, in the shape and under the title of Mr. Walter Scott's muse. Accustomed to present herself so frequently to the eyes of an admiring public, like other young ladies she has long ago acquired (to use her own language)

'the ease
That marks security to please.'

But we must take the liberty of observing (for Reviewers ought to be plain-spoken men) that she seems to us, according to a very natural course in the progress of every habit which is not on the side of excellence, to be approaching the brink of a slippery descent which threatens to precipitate the fair adventurer from the point of careless and haughty security into a fatal forgetfulness of her dependence on the rules of propriety, and the laws of correct taste.

Let it be remembered, too, (to carry the parallel a step further) that while the young lady is in progress towards the attainment of this confident ease, the beholder is also recovering from the first impression, and gaining that ease on *his* part, which is necessary to enable him coolly to criticize the charms which first took his judgment captive:— that if the propensity to admire is lessened by frequency and familiarity, the disposition to censure is augmented by defiance, and stimulated by neglect; while, perhaps, something too like disgust is the effect of a monotonous repetition of the same dress, the same airs, and the same fascinations.

Our allegory has been of little service, unless it has enabled our readers to anticipate our general opinion of *Rokeby*. We will endeavour to give a hasty sketch of the story; and it will be a very hasty and meagre sketch, because we do not deem it sufficiently complimentary to Mr. Scott to suppose our readers to have suffered the long interval of time which has elapsed since the publication of the poem to have passed without their perusal of it. If they have perused it and have not understood the story, which we venture to say was very possible without any imputation on their understandings, we are sure they will not be induced to read it again after having the story related to them in prose.

If some of our readers have not read the poem, we despair of enabling them to follow the course of the narration by any previous preparation short of a complete paraphrase of each canto, which, to be plain and honest, we could not bring ourselves to do, even if the demands of other articles allowed us sufficient room. A very slight sketch, however, we will give for the sake of rendering intelligible the few remarks upon the execution of the poem, which we shall feel it our duty to offer.

[a plot summary, including scattered quotations, omitted. The scene with Oswald and Bertram is praised highly. Scott's descriptions of rapid action are said to hurry the reader on, 'giving him hardly time to breathe, much less to examine']

We have thus endeavoured to give a condensed narrative of this poem. The task, we must confess, has not been of the pleasantest kind, but it may have spared us the necessity of taking any particular pains to point out its deficiencies. It is in itself very intricate, and puts the reader to a necessity, when his mind should be engaged by the poetry, of turning the leaves backwards and forwards, in the dry pursuit of the connecting incidents, and in tracing an outline of facts amidst a crowd of descriptions, and transactions.

We have no hesitation in stating it as our opinion, that a complicated tale is unfit for poetical effect, and that where the imagination is to be exalted, and the feelings excited, the mind ought not to be put upon any strong spontaneous effort. The happiest posture in which the mind of the reader can be for the purposes of the poet, is that docile resignation of feeling, which submits to be moved and directed whichever way the poet turns his magic sceptre, whether to scenes of beauty, grandeur, and delight, or to the gloomy sojourn of terror and despair. But when we are involved in the entanglements of an intricate plot, we feel either in a state of actual embarrassment, or in the perpetual peril of losing ourselves, from which the effort to escape agitates and fatigues the mind, and creates a sort of friction that retards the wheels of imagination.

To this difficulty in following the grand outline of the story, the poet has greatly added by the disproportionate and sometimes oppressive attention bestowed upon events holding only a secondary consideration in the action of the piece. This is a fault, however, to which genius is always liable, and we doubt whether it was ever more excusable than in the productions of our author, whose detached pieces have so much separate excellence. Still, however, this want of uniform care, and particularly an inattention to those incidents which form, as it were, the hinges of the story, give to the whole narrative an appearance of obscurity, abruptness, and negligence. An observation which we think may be fairly extended to all the productions of this poet.

Still, however, with this injurious consequence fully before us, we cannot help thinking that much of Mr. Scott's characteristic beauty has arisen from that indulgence of his own genius, which has carried to the different parts of his poems so partial a distribution of his favour. To observe that proportion and harmony between the several parts which are necessary to keep them in a just correspondence with each other, and to harmonize them into a whole, is not one of the excellences of Mr. Scott. His genius seems rather to riot in the breach of these rules, and to recreate its playful vigour in a capricious selection of its favourite themes. Thus, in many instances, a transaction of the highest interest is very slightly or faintly recorded, while an incident of subordinate or collateral importance rises to view in the brightest tints of poetical lustre.

One of the peculiar perfections of this author's poetical style is that bold negligence, and vigorous ease, by which it is often characterized. He regularly succeeds best where he appears most secure of success, and the spontaneous force which marks his happiest passages, has reminded us very often of the muse of Dryden.

The passage in *The Lady of the Lake*, which describes the ancient harper's reverie, serves so well to illustrate what we mean that we shall borrow it for that purpose.

> 'Yet ere his onward way he took
> The stranger cast a lingering look,
> Where easily his eye might reach,

The Harper on the islet beach,
Reclined against a blighted tree
As wasted, grey, and worn as he.
To minstrel meditation given,
His reverend brow was raised to heaven,
As from the rising sun to claim
A sparkle of inspiring flame;
His hand, reclined upon the wire,
Seemed watching the awakening fire;
So still he sate, as those who wait
Till judgment speak the doom of fate;
So still, as if no breeze might dare
To lift one lock of hoary hair;
So still, as life itself were fled,
In the last sound his harp had sped.'

We will offer another illustration from the poem before us; most, indeed, of the happiest passages from any of Mr. Scott's productions will second the remark we have above made.

[Canto III, Stanza V is omitted]

In the above passages, as, indeed, in by far the greater part of those which we should select for their beauty, it is observable that there is a sprinkling of ordinary, dull, and common-place sentiment; and, perhaps, we should scarcely exaggerate were we to say that the staple of Mr. Scott's poetry does not consist of new sentiments, new images, or new expressions. His excellence lies in a fascinating mode of working up the common and stock materials of poetry into new fabrics, and dazzling the eye by the profusion, the splendour, and the gaiety of the assortment. The wild traditions, the fierce enthusiasm, the warlike habits, the inspiring songs, the savage scenery, and sequestered solitudes, of the people, and the regions of the north of Scotland, afforded to the genius of Mr. Scott a fund of stories, adventures, characters, and localities, almost new to the poetry of this country, and which when wrought into combination with images, sentiments, and expressions, of the most popular and general cast, imparted to them an air of novelty, and freshness, which gave them back their original influence on the heart and the fancy. To this felicitous and almost accidental union of the new and the common, the surprising and the natural, Mr. Scott seems to have been principally indebted for the almost unprecedented success of his poetical effusions. That he has brought to these grand rudiments the vivifying powers of a true poetical mind, can scarcely be denied. To call this mass together, to organize it into active existence, and to endow it with intelligence, grace, and beauty, requires the creative force of genius; and after what Mr. Scott has accomplished he may laugh at those critics who deny him the credit of original genius.

Yet there are gradations and denominations of genius; and we are by no means disposed to place Mr. Scott in the highest rank. We have said as much, indeed, when we ascribed his success in great part to accident, and we are the more induced to maintain this opinion, by observing with how much tenacity he clings to the same system of manners, the same imagery, and the same scenes, in all his poems. In his last poem, which is now before us, this adherence to his first plan has betrayed him into something of anachronism in the habits, usages, and manners, in which he has dressed up his story. He has made Yorkshire, in the middle of the seventeenth century, exhibit the same moral, social, and physical appearance as the north of Scotland in the beginning of the same century, or as England in the reign of Henry the Eighth. Except the poem of Don Roderick, in which the poet most assuredly achieved nothing worthy of himself, or his former reputation, the muse of Mr. Scott has hitherto shown herself able to repeat only her first inspirations, and the Lay of the *last* Minstrel has, in truth, proved only the *first* of a series of songs, pretty much of the same burthen.

Neither can we let the poet escape us without another remark on the disparaging side, with which we will close our article. We cannot help complaining of his too frequent repetitions of the same images in the same poems. His perpetual recurrence to bowers and towers is perfectly fatiguing; wherever we see the one, we may be sure the other is not far behind. Take away any one of his favourite phrases and a gaping wound would appear in each of his poems. Of all the poets he appears to have the largest interest in the moon; and we cannot help giving him a friendly hint, that if he draws so often upon his funds there, his drafts may come at length to be refused in this planet. We shall rejoice if these observations shall have the good fortune to induce Mr. Scott, if only for the bare purpose of shewing how incapable we are of appreciating him, to introduce his muse to us in a different costume, speaking a different language, and displaying new graces and fascinations.

WAVERLEY

1814

---

6. Unsigned review, *British Critic*

August 1814, ns ii, 189-211

There is a certain gratification felt in introducing two distinguished
personages to each other, although it may be ascertained, from various
circumstances, that they must necessarily have been soon acquainted,
without the formality of the said introduction. Such a gratification
will be our's in the present instance: we request permission, therefore,
to introduce '*Waverley, or 'Tis Sixty Years since*,' a publication which has
already excited considerable interest in the sister kingdom, to the
literary world on this side of the Tweed. It is with the more satisfaction
that we undertake this duty, as it is an office which but seldom falls
to the share of the conductors of a critical journal to execute. So rapid
is the circulation of those works, to which the public attention has
been by anticipation directed, that it is our province rather to confirm
or correct a judgment already formed, than to direct it to a new and
undiscovered object. Where however an opportunity occurs of
performing our duty in this latter respect, we undertake it with
pleasure, because commendation is generally its end; and it is with
peculiar pleasure that we undertake it in the present instance, because
we are assured that in such commendation the public will coincide.
We have now the start both of general curiosity and general opinion;
lest therefore we should lose the vantage ground, we shall proceed
in the execution of our duty, and present to the public a work, in
which, before many weeks are passed, they will feel a very lively
interest.

A very short time has elapsed, since this publication made its
appearance in Edinburgh, and though it came into the world in the
modest garb of anonymous obscurity, the northern literati are

unanimous, as we understand, in ascribing part of it at least to the pen of W. Scott. As that gentleman has too much good sense to play the coquet with the world, we understand that he perseveres in a formal denial of the charge; though from all we can learn, the *not guilty* which he pleads to the indictment, proceeds almost as faintly from his mouth, as from the tongue of a notorious offender at the bar of the Old Bailey. Of the circumstances which form the external evidence in proof of this charge, we must of course be supposed essentially ignorant, as we in the south can have no opportunity of entering into the secret history of the literary world in the north; nor if we had, should we attempt to enter into its detail, as to the generality of our readers it could afford neither amusement nor interest. In the internal evidence alone we can feel a concern, and, such as it is, we shall present it to our readers, that they may be enabled to form their opinions upon the same ground with ourselves. We shall only add, that upon this evidence principally the tale in question has been ascribed to our favourite poet, as before it was actually presented to the public in Edinburgh, no expectation had been formed of the appearance of such a work.

The time which the author has chosen for the historical part of his tale, is a period to which no Briton can look back without the strongest emotions, and the most anxious interest. It is the year 1745, the last fatal year when the blood of our countrymen was spilt on its own shores, when Briton met Briton on his native land. It has pleased Providence, in his mercy to this favoured country, for a space of now nearly seventy years, to secure it not only from the invasions of foreign foes but to preserve it from the still more fearful and deadly scenes of civil commotion. By the restoration of peace to the whole European world a mighty machine of national strength is suddenly diverted from those external objects to which it has been so long and so powerfully directed; it is our earnest hope, as it is our most confident trust, that its gigantic force may not, by an unnatural revulsion, be turned inwardly upon itself, and that the same energies which blessed us with victory, and crowned us with glory in our operations abroad, may not inflame us with the ardour of contention, nor curse us with the spirit of discord at home.—May the peace, which our exertions in the cause of all that is great and good have purchased and secured to the world around us, descend 'twice blessed' upon our native land. If the history of those bloody days, which is embodied in this tale, shall by an early and awful warning inspire the nation with a jealous vigilance against the very first symptoms of their recurrence, we shall consider that not even the light pages of fiction have trifled in vain.

[plot summary and quotations omitted. The reviewer praises the humour of the introduction, the delineation of Fergus MacIvor, and the descriptions of the clan feast, the Battle of Preston, and the last parting of Waverley and Fergus]

We have thus given a short sketch of the story, which is in itself too interesting for an abridgement, and too replete with varied incident to bear the rapidity of a dry detail. If, however, from our imperfect outline, we shall have induced the reader to enjoy the full colouring in the original, we shall not have failed in our desire of discovering to his mind a source of valuable and legitimate amusement.

We are unwilling to consider this publication in the light of a common novel, whose fate it is to be devoured with rapidity for the day, and to be afterwards forgotten for ever; but as a vehicle of curious accurate information upon a subject which must at all times demand our attention—the history and manners of a very, very large and renowned portion of the inhabitants of these islands; of a race who, within these few years, have vanished from the face of their native land, but have left their names and their actions behind them as monuments of spirited independence, and of intrepid loyalty to that unfortunate family, who now with their brave defenders are for ever gone. We would recommend this tale, as faithfully embodying the lives, the manners, and the opinions of this departed race, and as affording those features of ancient days, which no man probably, besides its author, has had the means to collect, the desire to preserve, or the power to pourtray. This tale should be ranked in the same class with the Arabian Nights' entertainments, in which the story, however it may for a moment engage the attention, is but of little consequence, in proportion to the faithful picture which they present of the manners and customs of the east.

Although there are characters sufficient to awaken the attention, and to diversify the scenes, yet they are not in sufficient number to perplex the memory, or to confuse the incidents. Their spirit is well kept up till the very last, and they relieve one another with so much art, that the reader will not find himself wearied even with the pedantic jargon of the old baron of Bradwardine.

Upon the character of Davy Gellatly we must observe, that although this sort of personage is but little known in England, yet in Scotland it is by no means uncommon. In almost every small town there is a sort of public idiot, bearing the proportion, as we conceive, of about two of knave to three of fool, who is considered so necessary an appendage to the dignity of the place, that when he grows old, there is generally a young one in training as his successor. Davy appears to have been formed by the author, in some measure, upon the model of Shakespeare's fools, and we think that the similarity between himself and the fool in King Lear is peculiarly striking. We shall also call the attention of our readers to a circumstance in which they have doubtless anticipated us, the strong similarity between some turns in the character of Davy and those of Blanche of Devon: particularly the warning given by both in wild and incoherent song. There is a melancholy tale also attached to both their histories which strongly marks their resemblance. Not indeed that we would prove the one to be a copy of the other, this would be too much for our purpose: the peculiar traits of similarity are just strong enough to mark them the offspring of the same hand, and the creatures of the same poetic mind.

Fergus Mac Ivor is a character drawn by a master's pencil, from his first introduction in the wilds of the Highlands to the final scene before his execution, all the various features which the author conceived are fully expressed. Even in his last moments, while we shudder at his wild and intriguing ambition, we admire his original and powerful genius, we honour his generous and intrepid fidelity. If feminine softness, joined to the most romantic patriotism, can delight our readers, of Flora they will feel themselves the devoted admirers. Of Rose Bradwardine we read more than we see; the sweetness of her character, and the silent warmth of her affection for our hero, render her worthy of him.

Of Waverley himself we shall say but little, as his character is far too common to need a comment; we can only say that his wanderings are not gratuitous, nor is he wavering and indecisive only because the author chooses to make him so. Every feature in his character is formed by education, and it is to this first source that we are constantly referred for a just and sufficient cause of all the wandering passions as they arise in his mind.

The secondary personages are drawn with much spirit and fidelity, and with a very striking knowledge of the peculiarities of the Scotch temper and disposition. The incidents are (to use a very vile phrase) all founded on fact, and the historical parts are related with much accuracy. The time which has elapsed since the year 1745 has allowed the author the liberty of introducing feigned characters as actors in those real scenes, without wearying the patience or disgusting the credulity of the reader. Here our author has a powerful advantage over our celebrated novellist of modern days, Miss Edgeworth: that Fergus Mac Ivor should have been a partizan of the Stuart race, that he should have fought at Culloden, and have been executed at Carlisle, we can, as far as the purposes of the tale are concerned, readily and sufficiently believe; but that Lord Oldborough should have been a minister of the King's in 1808, is a height of absurdity to which no vigour of imagination or power of fancy can possibly reach. The character of Donald Bean, for instance, upon whose agency so much of the tale depends, was by no means uncommon upon the Highland borders. There are those still living who well remember the ravages inflicted by the clan of the Macgregors, and their chief, Rob Roy, who inhabited the caves which are concealed amidst the inaccessible passes and insurmountable steeps of the northern side of Ben Lomond.

The livelier scenes which are displayed in the course of the tale are of the most amusing species, because they flow so naturally from the personages before us, that the characters, not the author, appear to speak. A strong vein of very original humour marks the whole; in most instances it is indeed of a local and particular nature, but in many cases it assumes a more general appearance. A scene between Sir Everard's Jacobite chaplain and his bookseller is drawn in a style which shews the author to have read and relished Swift in no ordinary degree.[1]

[a quotation from chapter 6 'Here he produced' to 'packed in his saddle-bags' is omitted]

Of the more serious portions of the history we can speak with unqualified approbation; the very few pathetic scenes which occur are short, dignified, and affecting. The love scenes are sufficiently contracted to produce that very uncommon sensation in the mind, a wish that they were longer. The sentiments are uniformly good, and such as cannot fail to make a strong impression upon the mind of a thinking reader. We were much pleased with the following remarks upon a mode of education which is daily gaining ground, and threatens, by

---

[1] We are happy to hear that a splendid edition of the works of Swift have been just published, with a preface and notes by Walter Scott: we trust that we shall soon present an account of them to our readers [reviewer].

its extension to more advanced periods of youth, to render the minds of the rising generation pert, superficial, and effeminate.

[a quotation from chapter 3 'But the character' to 'his character, happiness, and utility' is omitted]

Let those who are engaged in forming the minds of the youth of this country not disdain to receive a hint even from the trifling pages of a novel, and let those who are placed under their care, as they value both themselves and their best hopes, learn from the character of Waverley early to distrust that inordinate self-confidence, and that over-bearing petulance, which teaches them to despise that order, that labour, and that discipline of the mind, which can alone secure to them the full completion of their ambitious views. The most fatal enemies to the bright prospects of future distinction are the ramblings of superficial enquiry, and the pride of conceited indolence.

The religious opinions expressed in the course of the tale are few, but of those few we fully approve. The loyalty and strength of the political sentiments clearly prove their author to be a man of a sound and vigorous mind, whose talents have not been lowered, nor whose spirit debased by the flimsy theories and the mawkish speculations of modern metaphysical politics. The humourous and happy adaptation of legal terms shew no moderate acquaintance with the arcana of the law, and a perpetual allusion to the English and the Latin classics no common share of scholarship and of taste.

That there are faults in the work we cannot deny, and some glaring errors, which we could heartily wish in a second edition were altered or erased, as they have a tendency to lessen the permanent value of the work, and to place it in the scale of a more common production. The pieces of intelligence which are represented as appearing in the newspapers, savour much more of modern manners, than 'sixty years since;' such as the supersession of Waverley in the form of a paragraph.

'We understand that this same Richard Waverley, who hath done all this, is not the only example of the *Wavering Honour of* W-v-r-l-y H-n-r. See the *Gazette* of this day.'

Now this is a pun which would disgrace even the *Morning Post* of the present day, and sixty years since we believe the paradise of fools was not blessed with so congenial an archivist. We object, upon the same grounds, to the relation of the death of R. Waverley, and of the exhibition of old Bradwardine's absurdity in pulling off the boot of the Prince. 'Something too much of this;' even were the anecdote in character, we think that the indication of the Baron's intention to perform it would have been sufficient. There is here and there a tendency to caricature and broad farce, which we are persuaded that the good taste of the author himself will discover, and his good sense will correct. Of the poetry which is interspersed we can speak in the highest terms. The following is a poem on the oak tree which grew over the tomb of the gallant Wogan, a name which will stand for ever honoured in the memory of every loyalist and patriot:—

['To an Oak Tree' is omitted]

If the testimony of this witness be not sufficient to work conviction in the reader's mind as to the name of the author, he will find still fuller testimony in other poems, which we have not room to extract. Whoever may be the author of the prose, we strongly suspect that the poetry at least was written by W. Scott; if our conjecture is unfounded, we congratulate the world on the appearance of a new poet, whose genius bears so striking a resemblance to their old favourite. Respecting the prose, we own that our suspicions are very strong of Walter Scott, as in very few besides himself are united that strength of feeling, that richness of anecdote, that store of historical knowledge, that accuracy of legal information, and above all, those high constitutional principles which dignify and adorn the mind of that original and native poet.

Much, however, as we respect the attachment of the author to the peculiarities of his country, we could wish that in a second edition he would sacrifice some few of them to our foolish prejudices in the south, and restore to the following lines, as to the old Baron of Bradwardine, their forfeited quantity:—

> '*Moritur*, et dulces moriens reminiscitur Argos.'
> '*fungarque* inani
> Munere.'[1]

Leaving, however, these trifling inaccuracies, we can earnestly recommend these volumes to our readers, as containing a treasure of anecdote and information upon these subjects, which few but the author of the present tale could so accurately present or so successfully embody.

We ought to have before observed, that to justify the second name,

---

[1] 'He dies and, dying, remembers sweet Argos' and 'I will perform an empty service'. The reviewer is here criticizing the metrics of the lines, both of which were presumably written by Scott.

''Tis sixty years since', the author informs us that this tale was written in the year 1805; of this we have no reason to doubt; the first sketches were probably drawn at that period, although, from the use of certain cant words of the present year, such as *tact, bivouacking, the Cossacks,* &c. we are of opinion that the finishing stroke has been but very lately applied.

7. Jane Austen: a comment

1814

A brief extract from a letter to Anna Austen dated 28 September 1814 (taken from R. W. Chapman, ed., *Jane Austen's Letters,* 2nd ed. (London, 1952)).

Walter Scott has no business to write novels, especially good ones.—It is not fair.—He has Fame and Profit enough as a Poet, and should not be taking the bread out of other people's mouths.—I do not like him, & do not mean to like *Waverley* if I can help it—but fear I must.

8. Maria Edgeworth: a letter

1814

A letter from Maria Edgeworth, the novelist, to 'the author of *Waverley*', 23 October 1814.

Upon receiving a presentation copy 'from the author', she sent this letter to James Ballantyne, Scott's literary agent. It carried the motto, '*Aut Scotus, aut Diabolus*', either Scott or the Devil.

We have this moment finished *Waverley*. It was read aloud to this large family, and I wish the author could have witnessed the impression it made—the strong hold it seized of the feelings both of young and old—the admiration raised by the beautiful descriptions of nature—by the new and bold delineations of character—the perfect manner in which every character is sustained in every change of situation from first to last, without effort, without the affectation of making the persons speak in character—the ingenuity with which each person introduced in the drama is made useful and necessary to the end—the admirable art with which the story is constructed and with which the author keeps his own secrets till the proper moment when they should be revealed, whilst in the mean time, with the skill of Shakespeare, the mind is prepared by unseen degrees for all the changes of feeling and fortune, so that nothing, however extraordinary, shocks us as improbable; and the interest is kept up to the last moment. We were so possessed with the belief that the whole story and every character in it was real, that we could not endure the occasional addresses from the author to the reader. They are like Fielding; but for that reason we cannot bear them, we cannot bear that an author of such high powers, of such original genius, should for a moment stoop to imitation. This is the only thing we dislike, these are the only passages we wish omitted in the whole work; and let the unqualified manner in which I say this, and the very vehemence of my expression of this disapprobation, be a sure pledge to the author of the sincerity of all the admiration I feel for his genius.

I have not yet said half we felt in reading the work. The characters are not only finely drawn as separate figures, but they are grouped with great skill, and contrasted so artfully, and yet so naturally, as to produce the happiest dramatic effect, and at the same time to relieve the feelings and attention in the most agreeable manner. The novelty of the Highland world which is discovered to our view excites curiosity and interest powerfully; but though it is all new to us it does not embarrass or perplex, or strain the attention. We never are harassed by doubts of the probability of any of these modes of life; though we did not know them, we are quite certain they did exist exactly as they are represented. We are sensible that there is a peculiar merit in the work which is in a measure lost upon us, the *dialects* of the Highlanders and the Lowlanders, etc. But there is another and a higher merit with which we are as much struck and as much delighted as any true born Scotchman could be; the various gradations of Scotch feudal character, from the high-born chieftain and the military baron, to the noble-minded lieutenant Evan Dhu, the robber Bean Lean, and the savage Callum Beg. The *Pre*— the Chevalier is beautifully drawn—

'A prince: aye, every inch a prince!'

His polished manners, his exquisite address, politeness and generosity, interest the reader irresistibly, and he pleases the more from the contrast between him and those who surround him. I think he is my favorite character; the Baron Bradwardine is my father's. He thinks it required more genius to invent, and more ability uniformly to sustain this character than any one of the masterly characters with which the book abounds. There is indeed uncommon art in the manner in which his dignity is preserved by his courage and magnanimity, in spite of all his pedantry and his *ridicules*, and his bear and bootjack, and all the raillery of MacIvor. MacIvor's unexpected 'bear and bootjack' made us laugh heartily.

But to return to the dear good baron; though I acknowledge that I am not as good a judge as my father and brothers are of his recondite learning and his law Latin, yet I feel the humor, and was touched to the quick by the strokes of generosity, gentleness, and pathos in this old man, who is, by the bye, all in good time worked up into a very dignified father-in-law for the hero. His exclamation of 'Oh! my son! my son!' and the yielding of the fictitious character of the baron to the natural feelings of the father is beautiful. (Evan Dhu's fear that his father-in-law should die quietly in his bed, made us laugh almost as much as the bear and bootjack.)

Jinker, in the battle, pleading the cause of the mare he had sold to Balmawhapple, and which had thrown him for want of the proper bit, is truly comic; my father says that this and some other passages respecting horsemanship could not have been written by any one who was not master both of the great and little horse.

I tell you without order the great and little strokes of humor and pathos just as I recollect, or am reminded of them at this moment by my companions. The fact is that we have had the volumes only during the time we could read them, and as fast as we could read, lent to us as a great favor by one who was happy enough to have secured a copy before the first and second editions were sold in Dublin. When we applied, not a copy could be had; we expect one in the course of next week, but we resolved to write to the author without waiting for a second perusal. Judging by our own feeling as authors, we guess that he would rather know our genuine first thoughts, than wait for cool second thoughts, or have a regular eulogium or criticism put in the most lucid manner, and given in the finest sentences that ever were rounded.

Is it possible that I have got thus far without having named Flora or Vich Ian Vohr—the *last Vich Ian Vohr!* Yet our minds were full of them the moment before I began this letter; and could you have seen the tears forced from us by their fate, you would have been satisfied that the pathos went to our hearts. Ian Vohr from the first moment he appears, till the last, is an admirably drawn and finely sustained character—new, perfectly new to the English reader—often entertaining—always heroic—sometimes sublime. The gray spirit, the Bodach Glas, thrills *us* with horror. *Us!* What effect must it have upon those under the influence of the superstitions of the Highlands? This circumstance is admirably introduced; this superstition is a weakness quite consistent with the strength of the character, perfectly natural after the disappointment of all his hopes, in the dejection of his mind, and the exhaustion of his bodily strength.

Flora we could wish was never called *Miss MacIvor,* because in this country there are tribes of vulgar Miss *Macs,* and this association is unfavorable to the sublime and beautiful of *your* Flora—she is a true heroine. Her first appearance seized upon the mind and enchanted us so completely, that we were certain she was to be your heroine, and the wife of your hero—but with what inimitable art you gradually convince the reader that she was not, as she said of herself, *capable of making Waverley happy*; leaving her in full possession of our admiration, you first make us pity, then love, and at last give our undivided affection to Rose Bradwardine—sweet Scotch Rose! The last scene between Flora and Waverley is highly pathetic—my brother wishes that *bridal garment* were *shroud*; because when the heart is touched we seldom use metaphor, or quaint alliteration; bride-favor, bridal garment.

There is one thing more we could wish changed or omitted in Flora's character. I have not the volume, and therefore cannot refer to the page; but I recollect in the first visit to Flora, when she is to sing certain verses, there is a walk, in which the description of the place is beautiful, but *too long*, and we did not like the preparation for *a scene*—the appearance of Flora and her harp was too like a common heroine, she should be far above all stage effect or novelist's trick.

These are, without reserve, the only faults we found or *can* find in this work of genius. We should scarcely have thought them worth mentioning, except to give you proof positive that we are not flatterers. Believe me, I have not, nor can I convey to you the full idea of the pleasure, the delight we have had in reading *Waverley*, nor of the feeling of sorrow with which we came to the end of the history of persons whose real presence had so filled our minds—we felt that we must return to the *flat realities* of life, that our stimulus was gone, and we were little disposed to read the 'Postscript, which should have been a Preface'.

'Well, let us hear it,' said my father, and Mrs. Edgeworth read on.

Oh! my dear sir, how much pleasure would my father, my mother, my whole family, as well as myself have lost, if we had not read to the last page! And the pleasure came upon us so unexpectedly—we had been so completely absorbed that every thought of ourselves, of our own authorship, was far, far away.

Thank you for the honor you have done us, and for the pleasure you have given us, great in proportion to the opinion we had formed of the work we had just perused—and believe me, every opinion I have in this letter expressed was formed before any individual in the family had peeped to the end of the book, or knew how much we owed you.

Your obliged and grateful

MARIA EDGEWORTH.

9. Francis Jeffrey, *Edinburgh Review*

November 1814, xxiv, 208-43

For Jeffrey's review of *Marmion*, see No. 2.

It is wonderful what genius and adherence to nature will do, in spite of all disadvantages. Here is a thing obviously very hastily, and, in many places, very unskilfully written—composed, one half of it, in a dialect unintelligible to four-fifths of the reading population of the country—relating to a period too recent to be romantic, and too far gone by to be familiar—and published, moreover, in a quarter of the island where materials and talents for novel-writing have been supposed to be equally wanting; and yet, by the mere force and truth and vivacity of its colouring, already casting the whole tribe of ordinary novels into the shade, and taking its place rather with the most popular of our modern poems, than with the rubbish of provincial romances.

The secret of this success, we take it, is merely that the author is a person of genius; and that he has, notwithstanding, had virtue enough to be true to nature throughout, and to content himself, even in the marvellous parts of his story, with copying from actual existences, rather than from the phantasms of his own imagination. The charm which this communicates to all works that deal in the representation of human actions and characters, is more readily felt than understood, and operates with unfailing efficacy even upon those who have no acquaintance with the originals from which the picture has been borrowed. It requires no ordinary talent, indeed, to choose such realities as may outshine the bright imaginations of the inventive, and so to combine them as to produce the most advantageous effect; but when this is once accomplished, the result is sure to be something more firm, impressive, and engaging, than can ever be produced by mere fiction. There is a consistency in nature and truth, the want of which may always be detected in the happiest combinations of fancy; and the consciousness of their support gives a confidence and assurance to the artist, which encourages him occasionally to risk a strength of colouring, and a boldness of drawing, upon which he would scarcely have ventured in a sketch that was purely ideal. The reader, too, who by these or still finer indications, speedily comes to perceive that he is engaged with scenes and characters that are copied from existing originals, naturally lends a more eager attention to the story in which they are unfolded, and regards with a keener interest what he no longer considers as a bewildering series of dreams and exaggerations—but an instructive exposition of human actions and energies, and of all the singular modifications which our plastic nature receives from the circumstances with which it is surrounded.

The object of the work before us, was evidently to present a faithful and animated picture of the manners and state of society that prevailed in this northern part of the island, in the earlier part of last century; and the author has judiciously fixed upon the era of the Rebellion in 1745, not only as enriching his pages with the interest inseparably attached to the narration of such occurrences, but as affording a fair opportunity for bringing out all the contrasted principles and habits which distinguished the different classes of persons who then divided the country, and formed among them the basis of almost all that was peculiar in the national character. That unfortunate contention brought conspicuously to light, and for the last time, the fading image of feudal chivalry in the mountains, and vulgar fanaticism in the plains; and startled the more polished parts of the land with the wild but brilliant picture of the devoted valour, incorruptible fidelity, patriarchal brotherhood, and savage habits, of the Celtic Clans on the one hand,—and the dark, untractable, and domineering bigotry of the Covenanters on the other. Both forms of society had indeed been prevalent in the other parts of the country,—but had there been so long superseded by more peaceable habits, and milder manners, that their vestiges were almost effaced, and their very memory nearly forgotten. The feudal principalities had been extinguished in the South for near three hundred years,—and the dominion of the Puritans from the time of the Restoration. When the glens of the central Highlands, therefore, were opened up to the gaze of the English, it seemed as if they were carried back to the days of the Heptarchy;—when they saw the array of the West-country Whigs, they might imagine themselves transported to the age of Cromwell. The effect, indeed, is almost as startling at the present moment; and one great source of the interest which the volumes before us undoubtedly possess, is to be sought in the surprise that is excited by discovering, that in our own country, and almost in our own age, manners and characters existed, and were conspicuous, which we had been accustomed to consider as belonging to remote antiquity, or extravagant romance.

The way in which they are here represented must satisfy every reader, we think, by an inward *tact* and conviction, that the delineation has been made from actual experience and observation;—experience and observation employed perhaps only on a few surviving relics and specimens of what was familiar a little earlier—but generalized from instances sufficiently numerous and complete, to warrant all that may have been added to the portrait:—And indeed the records and vestiges of the more extraordinary parts of the representation are still sufficiently abundant, to satisfy all who have the means of consulting them, as to the perfect accuracy of the picture. The great traits of Clannish dependence, pride, and fidelity, may still be detected in many districts of the Highlands, though they do not now adhere to the chieftains when they mingle in general society; and the existing contentions of Burghers and Antiburghers, and Cameronians, though shrunk into comparative insignificance, and left indeed without protection to the ridicule of the profane, may still be referred to, as complete verifications of all that is here stated about Gifted Gilfillan, or Ebenezer Cruickshank. The traits of Scottish national character in the lower ranks, can still less be regarded as antiquated or traditional; nor is there any thing in the whole compass of the work which gives us a stronger impression of the nice observation and graphical talents of the author, than the extraordinary fidelity and felicity with which all the inferior agents in the story are represented. No one who has not lived extensively among the lower orders of all descriptions, and made himself familiar with their various tempers and dialects, can perceive the full merit of those rapid and characteristic sketches; but it requires only a general knowledge of human nature, to feel that they must be faithful copies from known originals; and to be aware of the extra-ordinary facility and flexibility of hand which has touched, for instance, with such discriminating shades, the various gradations of the Celtic character, from the savage imperturbability of Dugald Mahony, who stalks grimly about with his battle-axe on his shoulder, without speaking a word to any body,—to the lively unprincipled activity of Callum Beg,—the coarse unreflecting hardihood and heroism of Evan Maccombich,—and the pride, gallantry, elegance and ambition of Fergus himself. In the lower class of the Lowland characters, again, the vulgarity of Mrs. Flockhart and of Lieutenant Jinker is perfectly distinct and original;—as well as the puritanism of Gilfillan and Cruickshank—the atrocity of Mrs. Mucklewrath—and the slow solemnity of Alexander Saunderson. The Baron of Bradwardine, and Baillie Macwheeble, are caricatures no doubt, after the fashion of the caricatures in the novels of Smollet,—or pictures, at the best, of individuals who must always have been unique and extraordinary: but almost all the other personages in the history are fair representatives of classes that are still existing, or may be remembered at least to have existed, by many whose recollections do not extend quite so far back as to the year 1745. We are speaking, however, of the book, as if our readers were already familiar with its contents—and its great popularity perhaps entitles us to do so: But it will be safer, and more decorous, at all events, to preface the extracts we propose to make from it, with a short account of the story.

It is not very skilfully adjusted—though narrated with so much ease and rapidity as to be on the whole very interesting.

[plot summary omitted. The description of the house and household of Tully-Veolan is praised, but the Baron is said to have more peculiarities 'than can be decently accumulated in one character']

Such is the outline of the story;—although it is broken and diversified with so many subordinate incidents, that what we have now given, will afford but a very inadequate idea even of the narrative part of this performance. Though that narrative is always lively and easy, however, we think the great charm of the work consists in the characters and descriptions—of which we must now present our readers with a few specimens. We may begin with the hero's first approach to the mansion of Tully-Veolan; in which those who have visited the more unfrequented parts of our country, will easily recognize many features with which they must be familiar.

[the following quotations are omitted: chapter 8 'It was about noon' to 'had conjured up' (with some omissions); chapter 10 'At his first address' to 'in the year 1713', and 'They were all' to 'persons eminent in the law'; chapter 11 'At length' to 'a greyhound called Whistler,' and 'Edward rushed forward' to 'Centaurs and Lapithae'; chapter 16 'While they' to 'suck the marrow' and 'It was towards evening' to 'with great rapidity' (with some omissions); chapter 17 'The party preserved' to 'proudly denominated' (with some omissions); chapter 18 'When Edward' to 'her solitary journey' and 'An air of openness' to 'the close of evening' (with some omissions); chapter 20 'The hall in which the feast was prepared' to 'their usual channel' (with some omissions); chapter 35 'They soon recognized' to ' "to your custody" ' (with some omissions)]

Most of the extracts we have now made are somewhat of a ludicrous character; but the author's powers are by no means limited to representations of this description—nor are we aware of many things, either in poetry or prose, more striking and impressive than the closing scene of the gallant Fergus and his faithful attendant. They were made prisoners, as has been already mentioned, in the night skirmish at Clifton, and arraigned at Carlisle when the law came to glean what had escaped the merciless sword of the victor. Waverley arrived just as the fatal verdict had been given in.

[the following quotations are omitted: chapter 68 'He pressed into the court' to 'a dead silence ensued', and 'The messenger brought back' to ' "my dear, dear Fergus" '; chapter 69 'After a sleepless night' to 'describe his sensations' (with some omissions); chapter 65 ' "I must go back" ' to ' "for an old soldier" '; chapter 71 ' "Since, you have lawfully" ' to ' "to its value" ', and 'The dinner was excellent' to 'more happily fulfilled'. The final parting of Waverley and Fergus is highly praised, and the account of the Baron's situation in hiding from the soldiers is said to contain 'a happy mixture of the ludicrous and the interesting']

Though in these extracts we have greatly exceeded the limits we usually impose on ourselves with regard to performances of this description—and trespassed indeed considerably on space which we had reserved for more weighty matters, we have, after all, afforded but an imperfect specimen of the variety which this work contains.— The gay scenes of the Adventurer's court—the breaking up of his army from Edinburgh—the battle of Preston—and the whole process of his disastrous advance and retreat from the English provinces, are given with the greatest brilliancy and effect—as well as the scenes of internal disorder and rising disunion that prevail in his scanty army— the quarrel with Fergus—and the mystical visions by which that devoted chieftain foresees his disastrous fate. The lower scenes again with Mrs. Flockhart, Mrs. Nosebag, Callum-Beg, and the Cumberland peasants, though to some fastidious readers they may appear coarse and disgusting, are painted with a force and a truth to nature, which equally bespeak the powers of the artist, and are incomparably superior to any thing of the sort which has been offered to the publick for the last sixty years. There are also various copies of verses scattered through the work, which indicate poetical talents of no ordinary description—though bearing, perhaps still more distinctly than the prose, the traces of considerable carelessness and haste.

The worst part of the book by far is that portion of the first volume which contains the history of the hero's residence in England—and next to it is the laborious, tardy, and obscure explanation of some puzzling occurrences in the story, which the reader would, in general, be much better pleased to be permitted to forget—and which are neither well explained after all, nor at all worth explaining. The passages in which the author speaks in his own person, and assumes the smart and flippant style of modern makers of paragraphs, are also considerably below mediocrity—and form a strange and humiliating contrast with the force and freedom of his manner when engaged in those dramatic or picturesque representations to which his genius so decidedly inclines.

There has been much speculation, at least in this quarter of the island, about the author of this singular performance—and certainly it is not easy to conjecture why it is still anonymous.—Judging by internal evidence, to which alone we pretend to have access, we should not scruple to ascribe it to the highest of those authors to whom it has been assigned by the sagacious conjectures of the public;—and this at least we will venture to say, that if it be indeed the work of an author hitherto unknown, Mr. Scott would do well to look to his laurels, and to rouse himself for a sturdier competition than any he has yet had to encounter.

THE FIELD OF WATERLOO
1815

---

10. Unsigned review, *La Belle Assembleé*

Supplement for 1815, ns xii, 340–42

La Belle Assembleé was a fashionable lady's magazine.

The story of this interesting Poem is too well known, and too deeply felt, for us to attempt to give any outline of what is engraven in letters of adamant on the heart of every Briton; neither shall we offer any criticism on a work above all praise, both for its own peculiar merit, and the benevolent purpose for which it was written. If the hasty productions of Mr. Scott are thus replete with poetic excellence and interest, we may venture to affirm he need never bestow much time or labour in the charming productions which issue from his pen.

After bestowing this tribute of praise which we find ourselves incapable of withholding from a work appropriately dedicated to the Duchess of Wellington, the consort of England's immortal Hero, we proceed to lay before our readers such extracts from Mr. Scott's Poem, which we find most descriptive and beautiful.

[various passages of the poem are quoted]

GUY MANNERING

1815

---

11. Wordsworth on Scott's first novels

Extract from a letter from William Wordsworth to R. P. Gillies, dated 25 April 1815 (from Ernest De Selincourt, ed., *The Letters of William and Dorothy Wordsworth: The Middle Years* (Oxford, 1937)).

For Wordsworth's later comments on Scott, see No. 55.

You mentioned *Guy Mannering* in your last. I have read it. I cannot say that I was disappointed, for there is very considerable talent displayed in the performance, and much of that sort of knowledge with which the author's mind is so richly stored. But the adventures I think not well chosen, or invented, and they are still worse put together; and the characters, with the exception of Meg Merrilies, excite little interest. In the management of this lady the author has shown very considerable ability, but with that want of taste which is universal among modern novels of the Radcliffe school; which, as far as they are concerned, this is. I allude to the laborious manner in which everything is placed before your eyes for the production of picturesque effect. The reader, in good narration, feels that pictures rise up before his sight, and pass away from it unostentatiously, succeeding each other. But when they are fixed upon an easel for the express purpose of being admired, the judicious are apt to take offence, and even to turn sulky at the exhibitor's officiousness. But these novels are likely to be much overrated on their first appearance, and will afterwards be as much undervalued. *Waverley* heightened my opinion of Scott's talents very considerably, and if *Mannering* has not added much, it has not taken much away. Infinitely the best part of *Waverley* is the pictures of Highland manners at Mac Ivor's castle, and the delineation of his character, which are done with great spirit. The Scotch baron, and

86

all the circumstances in which he is exhibited, are too peculiar and *outré*. Such caricatures require a higher condiment of humour to give them a relish than the author of *Waverley* possesses. But too much of this gossip.

12. Unsigned review, *Augustan Review*

July 1815, i, 228-33

We think the writer of this work is intitled, as well for this as for his former production, to take an elevated station among the Novelists of the present age. His claim, indeed, is not founded on the portion of delight he affords—on the strong interest he excites; or on that unbroken charm with which some authors encircle us, and transport us from the painful realities of this world into regions of a purer mould. The spell which he employs is perpetually broken by the *variety of talent* which he displays. At one moment he enraptures us with associations quite romantic, or almost suspends our breath with images of horror: and next moment he elaborates with prodigious skill, pictures of disgusting coarseness and vulgarity. This incongruous combination destroys the interest we feel in the story, while it forces us to acknowledge the talents of the writer. It is like an attempt to combine in the same picture, the humor of Hogarth—with the wild and savage energy of Salvator Rosa.

The chief merit of the present romance consists in its novel situations —its enchanting descriptions of natural scenery—and the strength and power of the terrific objects which it exhibits. The last is, upon the whole, the most striking of its qualities, and is wielded the most evidently with the hand of a master. There is a wild uncertainty about his mysterious incidents, and a darkness of coloring in the delineation of his barbarous characters, which sometimes remind us of Caleb Williams, though without nearly approaching the excellence of that wonderful production. Mr. Godwin's triumph is great in the *quality*, this writer in the *quantity* of his fearful instruments. The latter can 'on horror's head horrors accumulate;' but the former has shaken deeper strings of the soul, and has maintained an elevation and a magnificence in his machinery which we altogether miss in *Guy Mannering*. The affrightments of the work before us have all the power, but not the dignity of imagination—the strength without the majesty—the fearfulness and rapidity of lightning without the grandeur which its aerial course exhibits. But it is time to present the reader with an outline of the fable, and with a sketch of the principal characters.

[plot summary omitted]

Such is the brief outline of the story of the work before us; which is in no respect commendable, except as it affords scope for the display of the author's genius. Its improbabilities are glaring; and its moral might, in the time of Lord Hale, have subjected the printer to an indictment for supporting astrology and witchcraft. It is conducted too with very little skill; for at the very beginning of the second volume, the reader knows very nearly as much as he is acquainted with at the conclusion of the last. Not that we ever desire to be startled at the ending, by some strange event contrary to all the expectations excited—which generally occurs when the author has changed his design, or very imperfectly conceived it. We have no objection to approach the catastrophe, as we do in the novels of Richardson—by regular gradations, like the avenue to a venerable building which we discern from afar, and the towers of which we distinguish one by one, till the whole edifice appears in the full majesty of its proportions: but, we do not like to see the whole machinery at once, and to be carried to the end by the mere genius of the writer, even where, as in the work before us, it alone is capable of delighting us.

Most of the persons introduced are, we fear, also rather insipid. Guy Mannering is a mere *chorus* to unite the parts of the narrative. The young ladies 'have no character at all'. Bertram and Hazlewood are only handsome young men in love with the young ladies. Mr. Pleydell is a humorous old barrister fond of good eating, and Glossin a knavish attorney. On the other hand Dominie Sampson, the awkward instructor of Miss Bertram, is admirably delineated—his amiable simplicity of heart would almost assimilate him to Parson Adams; were he not as taciturn as that worthy Clergyman was loquacious. Dirk Haiteraick, too, is a very striking though disgusting portrait of hard-featured villainy combined with invincible selfishness. Meg Merrilies is, however, the great agent—the genius of the author shines forth in every line she utters and every scene in which she appears. There is a wild sublimity about her, a magnanimity in her revenge, a devotedness in her attachment to the family who have injured her tribe, and a heroism in her death, which form an object at once original and exalted. The speech she makes to the old Laird of Ellangowan immediately after the expulsion of the gypsies from their dwellings, is filled with wild pathos, while the image of the heart-struck sybil is highly picturesque:

[a quotation from chapter 8, 'She was standing' to 'overtake the caravan' is omitted]

We had intended to transcribe a part of the terrible scene where Bertram is concealed among the banditti, as well as the descriptions of his faint recollections, and strange emotions on revisiting the castle of his fathers. But we have exceeded our limits, and we console ourselves with the belief that our readers will peruse the novel for themselves, which we advise them to do. Upon the whole we regard it as superior to *Waverley*, both in its description and the force of its characters. The enthusiasm is wilder and more moving, because it is the fire of imagination not of faction, with which the loftiest personage is endowed. The genius of poetry must be more uniformly lofty than that of politics—when the greatness of the latter is displayed in rebellion. As to the name of the author, we are not particularly anxious to ascertain it: we only say that, if *Guy Mannering* be the production of Mr. Scott, it is of a higher order than any metrical romance to which he has given the sanction of his distinguished name.

THE LORD OF THE ISLES
1815

---

13. George Ellis, *Quarterly Review*

Dated July 1815, issued between 2 November and
6 December 1815, xiii, 287-309

George Ellis, a politician and writer of the period, was a friend
of Scott, and Scott was a contributor to the *Quarterly*.

If poets were to take precedency of each other according to the
number of their admirers, we are inclined to think that the author
before us, and one or two of his contemporaries, might fairly enter
into competition with some of the greatest names which the annals
of our literature can boast. The writings of Homer, and Virgil, and
Milton, have not perhaps so many genuine admirers as is commonly
supposed; because the merit which they possess is of a quality so far
above the standard to which the state of the general reader is adapted,
that it can be duly appreciated, we imagine, only by minds of some
considerable cultivation. Magni est viri, says Quintilian, speaking of
Homer, virtutes ejus non æmulatione (quod fieri non potest) sed
intellectu sequi.[1] The works of our modern bards, however, are
obviously calculated for a much larger description of readers; the
characters and sentiments which they contain, the species of interest
which they inspire, are, for the most part, level to all capacities; while
their faults and deficiencies are such that none but persons of refined
and practised taste are in any sensible degree affected by them. Whether
this be a sort of merit which indicates great and uncommon talents,
may perhaps admit a doubt; but at all events it is a very useful one to
the public at large. The productions of Mr. Scott, possibly, bear no

---

[1] 'It requires a powerful mind, I will not say to imitate, for that is impossible,
but even to appreciate his excellence.' Quintillian's *Institutio Oratoria*, X, i, 50,
trans. H. E. Butler.

more proportion to the *Iliad* or the *Paradise Lost,* than the excellent Tales of Miss Edgeworth to the *Histories* of Tacitus or Clarendon; but this is a separate question. Such men as Homer and Milton are of rare occurrence; in the mean time we are in the enjoyment of a description of poetry, which is adapted to the genius of a greater number of writers, and is capable of affording amusement to a greater variety of readers than any which antiquity possessed.

But although it is clear, that some conveniences have resulted from thus lowering the qualification formerly required even from the readers of good poetry; it has also been attended with some disadvantages. Authors will not, any more than other men, bestow upon their wares a greater degree of polish and perfection, than their customers generally require; and since all that the purchasers of poetry seem now to insist upon is an interesting story, spirited narrative, and good and picturesque descriptions of visible objects, it cannot be expected that poets should feel very anxious to furnish them with any thing besides. There is certainly no great amusement to be extracted from the *nine years labour* of revising the language and composition of a long poem; and as no commensurate increase of fame, or at least of popularity, would probably ensue from it, a poet who, like the author before us, seems to write merely with a view to please himself and his contemporaries, has no adequate inducement for devoting himself to so irksome an occupation. But if it be, in this point of view, possible for a poet to bestow upon his writings a superfluous degree of care and correction, it may also be possible, we should suppose, to bestow too little. Whether this be the case in the poem before us, is a point upon which Mr. Scott can possibly form a much more competent judgment than ourselves; we can only say, that without possessing greater beauties than its predecessors, it has certain violations of propriety both in the language and in the composition of the story, of which the former efforts of his muse afford neither so many nor such striking examples.

We have ever shewn ourselves much more disposed to praise the many excellencies of Mr. Scott's poetry than to censure its faults. We have not now any quarrel with Mr. Scott on account of the measure which he has chosen; still less on account of his subjects; we believe that they are both of them not only pleasing in themselves, but well adapted to each other and to the bent of his peculiar genius. On the contrary, it is because we admire his genius and are partial to the subjects which he delights in; that we so much regret he should leave room for any difference of opinion respecting them, merely from not bestowing upon his publications that common degree of labour and meditation, which, we cannot help saying, it is scarcely decorous to withhold.

It seems idle to offer any general remarks upon this subject; let the essence of poetry be defined as it may, still it is plain that whatever tends to give grace and delicacy to the pleasure which it imparts, cannot be without importance. Those qualities which result from taste and judgment constitute perhaps rather the ornaments than the elements of poetry specifically considered; they are, however, such as in different proportions necessarily enter into the composition of every poem, and unless they be to a certain degree attended to, it is impossible to prevent other feelings than those of pleasure from predominating in the mind. We are far from meaning to say that such is the case in the composition before us; in this, as in all Mr. Scott's productions, pleasure is unquestionably the prevailing feeling which is excited; yet we cannot but think that this feeling is more frequently counteracted by others of an opposite description in the poem which we are now considering, than even the licence of popular taste can reasonably be expected to sanction.

We do not found this opinion upon a consideration of the faults which we may have observed in this or that passage, or even in any single department of the poem; but we speak from the general impression which a perusal of it has left upon our minds. It would not of course be possible to convey this to the minds of our readers by any extracts; and as the faults to which we allude differ from those which we have had occasion to point out in Mr. Scott's former productions, not in kind but in degree, particular examples, in the present instance, must be altogether unnecessary; and as to any general remarks which we may have to offer, they will probably be better understood, when we shall have put our readers in possession of the story upon which the poem is founded.

After some introductory lines rather pleasing than appropriate, the poem is opened by a party of minstrels assembled 'from mainland and from isle', in the castle of Artornish, for the purpose of celebrating the bridal-day of the chief to whom it belongs, and who is the hero of the tale, with the sister of a neighbouring chieftain.

[plot summary and quotations omitted. The description of the landing at the castle is praised]

The scene between Edith and her nurse is spirited, and contains many very pleasing lines. The description of Lord Ronald's fleet, and of the bark endeavouring to make her way against the wind, more particularly of the last, is executed with extraordinary beauty and fidelity. So is the picture of Ronald himself during the feast.

[plot summary and quotations omitted. The song of the minstrel is said not to contain 'any great merit']

Such is the story of the second canto. It exhibits fewer of Mr. Scott's characteristical beauties than of his characteristical faults. The scene itself is not of a very edifying description, nor is the want of agreeableness in the subject compensated by any detached merit in the details. Of the language and versification in many parts, it is hardly possible to speak favourably. The same must be said of the speeches which the different characters address to each other. The rude vehemence which they display seems to consist much more in the loudness and gesticulation with which the speakers express themselves, than in the force and energy of their sentiments, which, for the most part, are such as the barbarous chiefs to whom they are attributed might, without any great premeditation, either as to the thought or language, have actually uttered. To find language and sentiments proportioned to characters of such extraordinary dimensions as the agents in the poems of Homer and Milton, is indeed an admirable effort of genius; but to make such as we meet with in the epic poetry of the present day, persons often below the middle size and never very much above it, merely speak in *character*, is not likely to occasion either much difficulty to the poet or much pleasure to the reader. As an example, we might adduce the speech of 'stout Dunvegan's knight', which is not the less wanting in taste because it is natural and characteristic.

[plot summary and quotations omitted. The opening of Canto III is praised, but the scene of Ronald, Torquil, and Bruce is criticized as too merely conversational. The description of Scavigh Bay is said to be 'admirably touched']

This canto is full of beauties: the first part of it, containing the conference of the chiefs in Bruce's chamber, might perhaps have been abridged, because the discussion of a mere matter of business is unsuited for poetry; but the remainder of the canto is unobjectionable; the scenery in which it is laid excites the imagination; and the cave scene affords many opportunities for the poet, of which Mr. Scott has very successfully availed himself. The description, which we have extracted, of Allan's watch is particularly pleasing; indeed, the manner in which he is made to fall asleep, mingling the scenes of which he was thinking, with the scene around him, and then mingling with his dreams the captive's sudden scream, is, we think, among the most happy passages of the whole poem.—

[plot summary and quotations omitted. The opening of Canto IV receives praise, as well as Allan's funeral and voyage to the Isle of Arran]

The above is an outline of the fourth canto, which cannot be very greatly praised. It contains, indeed, many pleasing passages, but the merit which they possess is too much detached from the general interest of the poem. The only business is Bruce's arrival at the isle of Arran: the voyage is certainly described with spirit, but the remainder of the canto is rather tedious, and might, without any considerable inconvenience, have been left a good deal to the reader's imagination. Mr. Scott ought to reserve, as much as possible, the interlocutory parts of his narrative, for occasions which admit of high and animated sentiment, or the display of powerful emotion, because this is almost the only poetical beauty of which speeches are susceptible. But to fill up three-fourths of a canto with a lover's asking a brother in a quiet and friendly manner for permission to address his sister in marriage, and a brother's asking his sister whether she has any objections, is, we think, somewhat injudicious.

[plot summary of, and quotations from, Canto V are omitted]

This Canto is not distinguished by many passages of extraordinary merit; as it is, however, full of business, and comparatively free from those long rhyming dialogues which are so frequent in the poem, it is upon the whole spirited and pleasing. The scene in which Ronald is described sheltering Edith under his plaid, for the love which he bears to Isabel, is, we think, more poetically conceived than any other in the whole poem—and contains some touches of great pathos, and beauty.

Having thus put Bruce in possession of his paternal hall, the poem pauses for about eight years! during which interval the poet desires us to believe that many things have taken place, and among others, that the mute page having resumed the attire of her sex, has taken up her abode with Isabel, now a nun, in the convent of St. Bride. In this retreat, days and months and years had passed away in calm seclusion, when news is brought to the convent, that Bruce had recovered the whole of Scotland from the hands of the English, with the exception of Stirling castle, the governor of which had entered into a stipulation for surrendering the fortress committed to his charge, unless, by a day fixed upon, the English should raise the siege. On the morning after the news arrived, Isabel takes an opportunity of informing Edith, that they must part. By the death and flight of her kindred, it seems that Edith was now heiress to all the lands of the house of Lorn; and Bruce, being naturally desirous of preventing so powerful a fief from devolving upon any person of equivocal fidelity, proposed renewing the long suspended treaty of marriage between the houses of Lorn and Clan-Colla. In this politic wish, the king was still farther confirmed, by having observed, that since the hopes of Ronald had been closed on the side of Isabel, he had gradually become sensible of the merits of Edith, and penitent for the cruelty, or at least for the imprudence of his former conduct towards her. Under these circumstances Bruce had dispatched a messenger, acquainting Isabel with the prosperous state of his affairs, and requesting her to send Edith to him under the protection of a knight whom he had directed to take charge of her. The 'Maid of Lorn' of course makes many coy excuses; (as well she might, for the transaction was not remarkable for its delicacy;) they are all, however, overruled by the kind persuasion of Isabel, and Edith finally sets out, equipped in male attire, in order that she may have an opportunity of being an eye-witness of Ronald's remorse. She arrives at the camp of Bruce on the eve of the battle of Bannock-burn, which is described with considerable spirit. The event it is unnecessary to relate: as soon as the battle is terminated, Bruce issues orders for the celebration of the nuptials; whether they were ever solemnized it is impossible to say; as *critics* we should certainly have forbidden the banns; because, although it is conceivable that the mere lapse of time might not have eradicated the passion of Edith, yet how such a circumstance alone, without even the assistance of an interview, could have created one in the bosom of Ronald, is altogether inconceivable. He must have proposed to marry her, merely from compassion, or for the sake of her money and lands, and upon either supposition, it would have comported with the delicacy of Edith to refuse his proffered hand.

Such is an outline of the story upon which the poem before us is founded; and in whatever point of view it be regarded, whether with reference to the incidents it contains, or the agents by whom it is carried on, we think that one less calculated to keep alive the interest and curiosity of the reader could not easily have been contrived. Of the characters, we cannot say much; they are not conceived with any great degree of originality, nor delineated with any particular spirit. Neither are we disposed to criticize with minuteness the incidents of the story; but we conceive that the whole poem, considering it as a narrative poem, is projected upon wrong principles.

The story is obviously composed of two independent plots, connected with each other merely by the accidental circumstances of time and place. The liberation of Scotland by Bruce has not naturally any more connection with the loves of Ronald and the Maid of Lorn, than with those of Dido and Æneas; nor are we able to conceive any possible motive which should have induced Mr. Scott to weave them as he has done into the same narrative, except the desire of combining the advantages of an heroical, with what we may call, for want of an appropriate word, an *ethical* subject; an attempt which we feel assured he never would have made had he duly weighed the very different principles upon which these dissimilar sorts of poetry are founded. This is a subject upon which we cannot now expatiate; we may however observe, that to engraft a domestic episode upon an heroical subject, is a very different thing from engrafting an heroical episode upon a domestic subject. When the leading object of the poet is to interest his reader in some great historical catastrophe, as this can only be brought about by the agency of individuals, of course it is impossible to suppose, but that in the progress of a long poem, frequent occasions must arise in which the reader will be called upon to sympathize with their particular disasters. Such occasions however are only incidental; they should grow out of the poem, and in this case, when they do occur, the feelings which they will excite, merely pass through the mind, without heating the imagination, or greatly disturbing the curiosity with which it still looks forward to the general catastrophe. But when the interest of a poem is principally founded upon the fortunes of individuals—as all novels and romances, whether in prose or verse, ought to be—nothing can be more contrary, we conceive, either to prudence or propriety, than to attach those fortunes to the fate of states and empires: because, when the imagination is filled with great events, we are always apt to calculate things in the gross, and, as common experience shews, to estimate the value of particular interests, not by themselves, but with reference to the importance which they possess, as items in the great account. Thus, had Mr. Scott introduced the loves of Ronald and the Maid of Lorn as an episode of an epic poem upon the subject of the battle of Bannockburn, its want of connection with the main action might have been excused in favour of its intrinsic merit; but by a great singularity of judgment, he has introduced the battle of Bannockburn as an episode in the loves of Ronald and the Maid of Lorn. To say nothing of the obvious preposterousness of such a design, abstractedly considered, the effect of it has, we think, decidedly been to destroy that interest which either of them might separately have created; or if any interest remain respecting the fate of the ill-requited Edith, it is because at no moment of the poem do we feel the slightest degree of it, respecting the enterprize of Bruce.

We have now put our readers in possession both of the story upon which the poem is built, and of our opinions as to its merits. The many beautiful passages which we have extracted from it, combined with the brief remarks subjoined to each canto, will sufficiently shew, that although the 'Lord of the Isles' is not likely to add very much to the reputation of Mr. Scott, yet this must be imputed rather to the greatness of his previous reputation than to the absolute inferiority of the poem itself. Unfortunately, its merits are merely incidental, while its defects are mixed up with the very elements of the poem. But it is not in the power of Mr. Scott to write with tameness; be the subject what it will, (and he could not easily have chosen one more impracticable,) he impresses upon whatever scenes he describes so much movement and activity—he infuses into his narrative such a flow of life, and, if we may so express ourselves, of animal spirits, that without satisfying the judgment, or moving the feelings, or elevating the mind, or even very greatly interesting the curiosity, he is still able to seize upon, and, as it were, exhilarate the imagination of his readers, in a manner which is often truly unaccountable. This quality Mr. Scott possesses in an admirable degree; and supposing that he had no other object in view than to convince the world of the great poetical powers with which he is gifted, the poem before us would be quite sufficient for his purpose. But this is of very inferior importance to the public; what they want is a good poem, and, as experience has shewn, this can only be constructed upon a solid foundation of taste and judgment and meditation.

THE ANTIQUARY
1816

---

14. John Wilson Croker, *Quarterly Review*

Dated April 1816, issued August 1816, xv, 125-39

Croker, First Secretary to the Admiralty and a scholar of some repute, was also a frequent contributor to the *Quarterly*. He is best known for the review of *Endymion* that was supposed to have sent Keats to an early grave.

Having already delivered our opinion on the general character of *Waverley* and *Guy Mannering*, we have little or, indeed, nothing to add on that subject with regard to the present novel, which professes to be a third brother of the same family. We doubt whether the voice of the public has ratified the preference which we so decidedly gave to *Waverley* over *Guy Mannering*; but a second perusal of both has convinced us that our judgment was not incorrect; and we are satisfied that the time is not far distant, if it be not already arrived, when the best claim of *Guy Mannering* on the attention of its readers will be the line of the title-page, in which it is described as the work of the author of *Waverley*.

The Antiquary is a work of precisely the same style; it unites to a considerable degree the merits of *Waverley* with the faults of *The Astrologer*; and we have no hesitation in placing it, with the crowd of modern novels, below the former, and, with very few modern novels, above the latter.

The author tells us in his preface, that 'the present work completes a series of fictitious narratives intended to illustrate the manners of Scotland at three different periods. *Waverley* embraced the age of our fathers, *Guy Mannering* that of our own youth, and *The Antiquary* refers to the last ten years of the eighteenth century' (p. v.). This may, in an occult sense, be true; but if it means, as it at first view imports to state, that the three novels have been written with this original intention, and that they were meant, in their first conception, to exhibit three different stages of society, we presume to doubt a little the literal authenticity of the statement.

In the first place we hardly think that so skilful an observer of manners could have imagined that in sixty years such changes could take place in national language, manners, habits, and character, as to warrant, *a priori*, the design of three distinct pictures. In the second place we find the author himself confessing that he has, '*especially* in his two last works, sought his principal personages in that class of society who are the last to feel the polish which assimilates to each other the manners of different nations' (p. vi); or, in other words, which change most slowly; and of course it follows that so far from endeavouring to illustrate the manners of three different periods, he has endeavoured to describe three different periods of which the manners were very much the same. And, finally, we appeal to our southern readers, at least, whether they can distinguish between the Astrologer and the Antiquary, and whether, with equal probability and appearance of truth, Jonathan Oldbuck, and his associates, might not have preceded in chronological order Guy Mannering and his dramatis personæ. We admit that, provided the author succeeds in amusing us, it is, in ordinary cases, of little consequence on what theory he may choose to proceed, or to say that he proceeds; but when he affects, as in the present instance, to write a work in some degree historical of men, and professedly historical of manners, it becomes our duty, as contemporaries, as well as reviewers, to withhold our testimony from what we consider a misrepresentation. We believe that the manners of Guy Mannering are as much the existing manners of the day as those of the Antiquary; and we are satisfied that the able and ingenious author, after having written these three very amusing romances, has indulged himself in a fanciful classification of them, and, waiving his higher claims, prefers the humbler one of writing on a *system*, which he never thought of, and in which, if he had designed it, we should have no hesitation in saying that he has, by his own confession, failed.

That, however, in which he has not failed is the higher duty of the novelist—character, interest, eloquence; something that hurries rather than leads you on; traits of feeling that melt, and strokes of humour that enliven the heart; all these he, in an eminent degree possesses; with them he combines so curious and accurate a delineation of human nature, that, through the Scottish garb, and the Scottish dialect, we distinguish the characteristic follies, foibles, and virtues, which belong to our own acquaintance, and to all mankind.

This is the peculiar merit of the author of these works, and no slight merit it is, for the want of it constitutes, as we have said on another occasion, the chief fault of some of our most eminent novelists, and the possession of it, the chief merit of the greatest poet that ever lived—of Shakspeare. His Romans, his Frenchmen, his Englishmen, are all *men*; the features of the national character are varied and amusing, but the great charm of his exhibitions of human life is, that, modified a little by their age and their country, his characters are all human beings, to whose pains and whose pleasures our own hearts are responsive, and to whose reasons and motives of action our own minds assent.

Our readers will recollect that our dissatisfaction with some parts of *Guy Mannering* was excited by the gratuitous introduction of supernatural agency, and that we said quodcunque ostendis mihi sic, incredulus odi.[1] Even Shakspeare, who has been called the mighty magician, was never guilty of this mistake. His magic was employed in fairy land, as in *The Tempest*, and his ghosts and goblins in dark ages, as in *Macbeth* and *Hamlet*. When he introduces a witch in *Henry VI* it is because, historically, his representation was true; when he exhibits the perturbed dreams of a murderer in *Richard III* it was because his representation was morally probable; but he never thought of making these fancies actual agents in an historical scene. There are no ghosts in *Henry VIII* and no witches in *The Merry Wives of Windsor*, (except the merry ladies;) and when, in one of his comedies, he chooses to wander out of nature, he modestly calls his drama a *Dream*, and mixes up fairies, witchery, mythology, and common life in a brilliant extravaganza which affects no historical nor even possible truth, and which pretends to represent neither actual nor possible nature. Not so *Guy Mannering*,—it brings down witchery and supernatural agency into our own times, not to be laughed at by the better informed, or credited by the vulgar; but as an active, effective, and real part of his machinery. It treats the supernatural agency not as a superstition, but as a truth; and the result is brought about, not by the imaginations of men deluded by a fiction, but by the actual operation of a miracle contrary to the opinion and belief of all the parties concerned.

From this blame the present work is not wholly free; there are two

[1] 'Whatever you show me thus, I reject and hate.'—Horace, *Ars Poetica*, 188.

or three marvellous dreams and apparitions, upon which, we suspect, the author intended to ground some important parts of his denouement; but his taste luckily took fright, the apparitions do not contribute to the catastrophe, and they now appear in the work as marks rather of the author's own predilection to such machines, than as any assistance to him in the way of machinery.

This, then, is a manifest advantage which the present work has over *Guy Mannering*; and we own, that while we felt little or no interest in the fortunes of those whose fate was predestined, and whose happiness or woe depended not on their own actions, but on the prognostications of a beldam gipsy or a wild Oxonian, we are very differently affected for those who, like the characters in *Waverley* and *The Antiquary*, work out their own destinies, and must stand or fall (to use a common phrase) by their own virtue or folly, courage or weakness.

Some strong defects it must be admitted this work has; the story of the novel is not very novel, nor yet very probable.

[a short plot summary is omitted]

It will be seen from the summary, that though the antiquary gives his name to the work, he can hardly be called its hero; and, indeed, though the peculiarity of his character induces the author to produce him very frequently and forwardly in the scene, he has not any great share in the plot, and is evidently recommended to the high station which he occupies by his humour rather than his use. This character is, indeed, drawn with great truth and spirit; we should have praised its originality too, if we did not remember, with equal pleasure and affection, our admirable friend the Baron of Bradwardine, of whom Mr. Oldbuck sometimes reminds us, and never without at once gaining and losing a little by the recollection—gaining by his resemblance to that delightful portrait, and losing by a manifest inferiority to his striking original. In another character also, we have to observe a similar instance of self imitation—Edie Ochiltree, a kind of licensed beggar, is but a male Meg Merrilies; his character is, however, admirably drawn, and, in this case, we must confess, that we prefer the copy to the original. Edie is nothing supernatural, and therefore not so *striking* a personage as Meg; but there is great skill and great effect, as well as great simplicity and truth, in this portrait, and his contribution to the progress of the story is easy and probable, and, on that account, to us, more interesting, than the incantations and prophecies of the witch of the ashen wand.

We shall extract a description of Edie, not as the most amusing specimen we could produce, but because it is a living portrait of a singular class of the Scottish poor.

[a quotation from chapter 4 'He had the exterior appearance' to 'vulgarly, blue-gowns' is omitted]

Scanty as our limits are, we think that we should scarcely do justice to the author, if we did not make room for the following extract. It greatly exceeds the length in which we commonly indulge; but for this, its uncommon merits will find a ready excuse in the minds of our readers. It is a description of the danger to which Sir Arthur and Miss Wardour are exposed, when caught, by the rising of the tide in a stormy evening, on sands surrounded by inaccessible precipices, the base of which the tide at its full rising would overflow. The scenery is undoubtedly delineated by an imagination at once fervid and poetical, and it is marked by such traits of character and truth, that every craig, and breaker, and precipice are brought distinctly before us.

[a quotation from chapter 7 'When the knight and his daughter' to 'beyond the reach of the billows' (passage since slightly revised) is omitted]

This will give the readers a notion of the dialect in which great part of the work is written, and we shall now select a couple of scenes as descriptive of its peculiar taste, and attention to nature:—the first shall be one of a lighter cast, which we quote, not because it is the best of the kind, but that it happens to be the first which we have been able to discover of a manageable length.

[a quotation from chapter 11 'Upon the links' to 'be prepared for dinner' is omitted]

Our other quotation shall be the funeral of this *'fish-wife's'* son, who within a few days after the foregoing conversation, afforded a melancholy illustration of his mother's forcible expression, that it was not fish but men's lives that the Antiquary was buying.—He had been drowned, and the body, washed ashore, was now to be buried after the fashion of the country. 'It is a scene,' says the author, 'which our Wilkie *alone* would have painted with that exquisite feeling of nature that characterizes his enchanting productions'; but the author is too modest, and too unjust to his own art. Wilkie, with all his enchanting qualities, could not, the pencil cannot, paint this scene with such touching strokes of nature as we find in the dramatic narration of our author. It is too long to be extracted *in extenso*, but, at the risk of diminishing its effect, we shall venture to put together some detached sentences.

[a quotation from chapter 31 'The body was laid' to 'dispersed the mourners' (with some omissions) is omitted]

This, it will be confessed, is fine moral painting, the father unable to look *at* or yet *away* from his son's coffin, is a touch of nature not inferior to Madame de Sévigné's famous description of Madame de Longueville's inquiry after her son;—the 'Grecian painter's veil' is not so natural and touching as the poor fish-woman's apron; the divided sensations of the children and the involuntary motion of the poor old woman's hands, from which the implements of spinning had been removed, are admirable; and the 'creak of the screws' produces an effect on us almost equal to the sound of Clarissa's coffin on the narrow stairs.

We hope we have now said enough to induce our readers to think this novel well worth reading, and we shall only add, that it is impossible to read it without feeling the highest respect for the talents, both gay and pathetic, of the author, for the bold impartiality of his national delineations, and for the taste and discrimination with which he has rescued, from the overwhelming march of time and change of manners, these historical representations of a state of society, which even now is curious, but which in no long period will become 'a tale of other times'; and be examined not merely by the listless reader of novels but by the moralist and the antiquary.

It may be useful to apprise our readers (a circumstance which we unfortunately did not discover till we had got to the end of the third volume), that there is there to be found a glossary, which is indeed almost indispensable to the understanding of nine-tenths of the work. Those ingenious persons, therefore, who begin to read novels by the latter end, have had, in this instance, a singular advantage over those who, like us, have laboured regularly on through the dark dialect of Anglified Erse.

If, as we expect, new editions of *Waverley*, *Guy Mannering*, and *The Antiquary*, should be required by the public, we suggest that the glossary should be placed conspicuously at the beginning of the first volume of the series.

15. Unsigned review, *British Lady's Magazine*

August 1816, iv, 103-105

The merited attention which *Waverley* and *Guy Mannering* have excited, as spirited sketches of local character and manners, naturally led us to an eager perusal of *The Antiquary*. It has somewhat disappointed us, but only in a way which a little previous consideration might have prepared us to expect. Most novelists, if that term is not degrading to accurate delineators of common life, decline after a second or third production of consequence, because there is infinitely less variety in human nature than is generally supposed; and, when an author's first and most lively impressions have been conveyed, he follows with his more remote and less natural combinations. The *Persiles and Sigismunda* of Cervantes, the *Amelia* of Fielding, the *Sir Lancelot Greaves* of Smollet, the *Patronage* of Miss Edgeworth, the *Wanderer* of Madame D'Arblay, and, lastly, *The Antiquary* of the present author, are all proofs of this fact; and many more might be adduced if it were necessary. If such be the case generally, it must be still more in course when peculiarity of language, and local ideas and habits, form the chief materials for the canvas. The three works, *Waverley*, *Guy Mannering*, and *The Antiquary*, considering their length, have followed each other very rapidly; the last in particular, which the author (possibly with a perception of the truth we have been maintaining) announces to be his last in this line of composition.

In its construction as a story, which we do not think so absolutely a consequence of a too frequent appearance as a failure in characteristic delineation, *The Antiquary* even falls below its brethren: but, as the author frankly acknowledges this defect in all his labours, there is no more to be said. It happens, however, unfortunately, that he ceases to be strong in the place of his strength, and that his characters are little more than repetitions. Thus, the Antiquary is the Pleydel of *Guy Mannering*, whose Meg Merrilies is split into two personages, called Edie Ochiltree and Elspeth; Sir Arthur Wardour is Sir Robert Hazlewood, and so on.—But, with all this, is the book without merit? —by no means: the author of *Guy Mannering* may fall below himself, but cannot be dull. In fact, Oldbuck is too much a wit for an antiquary, as his pleasantry upon his nephew sufficiently evinces. The repetition of Ossian, and the seal adventure of the latter, abound in genuine satire and irresistible humour; the passage, however, is too long for quotation: as a specimen of the author's best serious manner, we therefore give the following sketch of a female *Struldbrugg*, which seems a kind of filling-up of the outline of Swift. The scene is in the cabin of a poor fisherman, whose eldest son has been drowned in his vocation; the subject, his funeral.

[a quotation from chapter 31 'In the inside' to 'with her withered and pallid hand', is omitted]

In taking leave of *The Antiquary*, however, we cannot help remonstrating with the author on the outrageous history of the Glenallans, in a work which professes to take the last ten years as its time of action. To say nothing of the illiberality of appropriating dark and horrible doings to Catholic families, we cannot recognize the propriety of murdering infants with golden bodkins, &c., as at all in nature during the last ten years; and fairly attribute the absurdity in an author so able and quick-witted as the one before us, to the prevalence of the mania alluded to in the first article of our present Magazine—namely, a perverted train of associations, which has mastered the common sense of the town, to the disorder of the finest brains in it. May it disappear with the existing weather, to which, in the dark, the cloudy, and the unnatural, it bears no slight resemblance; although (as there is no answering for tastes) some people may deem both one and the other agreeable. If so, we humbly enter our caveat and conclude.

16. Unsigned review, *Critical Review*

December 1816, 5th Series, iv, 614-25

These two novels comprised *Tales of My Landlord*, first series.

It is impossible to read the first sheet of this production without a conviction that it is by the author of *Waverley*, *Guy Mannering*, and *The Antiquary*, though the title-page gives us no such information. It is not difficult to conjecture why it should have been omitted when we recollect the concluding sentence of the preface to *The Antiquary*, in which the writer took leave of the public 'as one not likely soon to trouble it again'. Eight months, however, are scarcely elapsed before he once more introduces himself to our notice in four volumes of the *Tales of my Landlord*.

Besides the reason above given, several others may have induced Mr. Forbes (or whoever the writer in reality be) to persevere in his anonymous system of authorship; in the first place, the volumes on our table are by no means equal to his other productions; and although an indication on the title-page would greatly have assisted the sale, and enhanced the price of the copyright, he may have been unwilling to risk his nameless fame in this new experiment; or, in the next place, he may have been desirous of ascertaining whether the popularity his novels have hitherto acquired, ought in any large proportion to be attributed to the often-repeated, and as often-refuted report, that Mr. Walter Scott, at least, had 'a main finger in their composition'. It is, however, not very material to settle these questions, nor to indulge in further fruitless conjecture as to the author's motives for persevering in a provoking concealment (as most of his female readers term it), which appears to answer no purpose but that of exciting curiosity by withholding its gratification, as appetite is created by the refusal of sustenance.

The tales before us are two in number, and are called *The Black Dwarf*, and *Old Mortality*: the scenes of both lie in Scotland, and the design of the author is declared to be, to pourtray the manners of his countrymen; and they are to be followed by others of the same character at a future period. They are both compounded of fiction and history, the latter being ingeniously made to assist the former in the developement of the characters, and the production of the events. There is, however, a defect in their arrangement, for *The Black Dwarf* refers to the state of Scotland in the reign of Queen Anne, while *Old Mortality* speaks of its condition during the struggles by the Presbyterians in favour of 'the solemn league and covenant', in the latter end of the reign of Charles II. For this reason, we wish that the order had been reversed—that as far as any difference exists, not only the historical transactions, but the manners and habits of the people, might have been displayed chronologically. In another respect also, this change might have been advantageous; for although the first story, according to the present arrangement, bears the more tempting title, it is much inferior to that which follows in most of the respects in which this author's novels are excellent.

The general title of *Tales of my Landlord* is derived from the circumstance, that they are supposed to have been collected from the relations of different persons at the Wallace Inn at Gandercleugh: this is rather a clumsy expedient, for they are the tales of any body but the landlord, and *Old Mortality* does not profess to have its origin even in that source. It is a little surprising that an individual who has shewn so much skill in interweaving facts with fiction, and heightening the one by the other, should have so completely failed in his endeavours to give an appropriate introduction to these entertaining relations. Mr. Peter Pattieson is supposed to have been the writer and compiler of the tales, who, dying young, left them to the care of Mr. Jedediah Cleishbotham, the schoolmaster, to whom he had been usher and assistant. The clumsiness of this contrivance, and the aukward manner in which it is executed, have nothing, however, to do with the merits of the novels themselves.

In speaking of these separate productions, we shall take them in the order of time and of comparative merit and importance, beginning therefore with *Old Mortality*, which occupies the three last of the four volumes. It is not to be supposed, that in the limits to which we are compelled to restrict ourselves, we can enter even into a brief detail of the story, which is somewhat complicated, and the less necessary, because the historical matters introduced and contributing to the unwinding of the plot, are generally known to all readers but those who would read this story as a mere novel for the amusement the fable will afford.

Old Mortality is a sort of nick-name given by the people of Scotland to an antiquated Presbyterian, who having engaged and suffered in the struggles of 1679, preserved his unshaken zeal for his party, and in his declining years, journied from burial-ground to burial-ground with his hammer and chissel, renewing the decaying names on the tombstones of those who had fought and fallen in the cause he reverenced: from the details he supplied, Peter Pattieson is supposed to have framed the novel which bears his title.

There is considerable bustle and business in the story, not merely from the numerous conflicts in which the covenanters are engaged with their enemies, in which the hero and some of the principal characters are concerned, but from the great number of personages introduced; they are not less than sixteen or eighteen in number, to nearly all of whom parts of importance are assigned; and in the space of the whole three volumes, the author has not room completely to develope any of their characters: some are killed off earlier and some later, according to convenience; so that at the end they are reduced to three or four individuals, who, according to custom, are dismissed as happy as love, matrimony, and money can make them. The man who forms the principal feature, and who first excites and afterwards heads the Covenanters in the battles of London Hill and Bothwell Bridge, is John Balfour, of Burley, who assassinated Dr. Sharpe, Archbishop of St. Andrew's, and whose temper and dispositions are described, and kept up with great consistency throughout. He is a Highlander, or 'one of the hill-folk', of uncommonly sturdy proportions, and of a mind corresponding with his make—undaunted, fierce, and zealous to the last degree in the holy cause he had espoused. He has fled from the murder he has committed, and is sheltered as a distressed traveller merely by Henry Morton, the hero of the tale, a young man of benevolence, courage, and of handsome proportions, who is in love with Miss Edith Bellenger, the grand-daughter of Lady Margaret Bellenger, and niece to Major Bellenger, who are both well supported characters, though the idea of the latter is evidently derived from My Uncle Toby. The rival of Morton is Lord Evandale, who, though unsuccessful with the lady, is, we apprehend, too successful with the reader, for he attracts even more interest than Morton, and he is not disposed of until the novel is nearly concluded.

Henry Morton unites himself to the Covenanters, and becomes one of their leaders, his associates besides Balfour being the fanatical preachers, who put themselves at the head of the rebels to vindicate the cause against the Prelatists, upon whom they denounce, and often execute, the most bloody vengeance. To these persons are assigned various ridiculous names, such as Poundtext, Kettledrummle, &c. which are employed, we understand, as a sort of shorthand to save the trouble of entering into the detail of their conduct and objects; in various parts, however, we have a little too much of their incoherent scrutinizing.

On the other side, at the head of the Royalists, is Colonel Grahame, of Claverhouse, afterwards created for his services Viscount Dundee, who subsequently commanded the Highlanders in their resistance to the revolution, and the expulsion of the Stuarts. At the period embraced by this story, he is the enterprising, courageous, and skilful antagonist of Balfour and his zeal-blinded friends, and is supported principally by Lord Evandale, Ensign Grahame, Bothwell, Inglis, and others, who all contribute their share to the advancement of the plot. It is an excellence of modern novelists, almost peculiar to the author before us, that instead of occupying a great number of pages in dull and trite description of the various persons who constitute the machinery of the work, detailing first their personal advantages in the usual style of disgusting hyperbole, and afterwards their intellectual endowments and accomplishments in a strain equally extravagant and absurd, he leaves the reader to form his own notions by hints as the story proceeds, or by the actions in which the parties are severally engaged. For this reason we can seldom extract any particular passages which at one view will afford a portrait of any one of the characters: there is, however, one little exception to this remark in the person of the heroine, Edith Bellenger, who is thus spoken of: the author first mentions her grandmother, Lady Margaret.

[a quotation from chapter 2 'Near to the enormous' to 'the figure of her palfry' is omitted]

We shall now, without further preface, extract some parts of these volumes, noticing so much of the story as is necessary to render them intelligible, and to enable the reader to appreciate their merit: some passages may stand by themselves as separate pictures, which require little or no illustration from surrounding objects. Such is the case with the following humorous account of an old penurious Scotch Laird's table and family party dinner about the year 1680.

[a quotation from chapter 8 'The Laird of Milnwood' to 'this very cormorant' is omitted]

Henry Morton, the hero, joined the Calvinistical covenanters, and one defect, and no inconsiderable defect of this story is, that he is made, almost without motive, to desert the side on which his love, his relatives, and his interest all lay: this inconsistency might have been remedied, had the author described him with a little more enthusiasm than he appears to have possessed, more justifiable hatred of the tyranny and cruelty of the royal party, and warmer admiration of the principles, however perverted, of the cause which he espoused. This, however, is not done, and the only inducement he appears to have had, consists in revenge for ill treatment he received from a party of life-guards. After he had declared his intention to Balfour of Burley, the latter introduces him to the council of the Covenanters: the manner in which business was conducted at these assemblies, may be judged of from the subsequent extract.

[a quotation from chapter 22 ' "We will not" ' to 'by his pouring forth' is omitted]

The insurgents, as most of our readers will recollect, after taking Glasgow, were defeated with great slaughter at Bothwell-bridge; a great number of prisoners are made, and among them, Morton and Macbriar, a young firm misguided zealot, who had vehemently and unceasingly preached up the doctrine of cutting the throats of the prelates for the glory of God. The latter is brought before the privy-council, and the torture of *the boots* is inflicted upon him, which he bears with unshrinking firmness, proclaiming his principles to his latest gasp. In his description of this punishment, the author seems to be a little misinformed as to the mode in which this torture was inflicted; an accurate account of it will be found in Douce's *Illustration of Shakespeare*. Morton, at the instance of Col. Grahame, of Claver-house, and Lord Evandale, is banished, instead of suffering death like the other prisoners.

Much of the interest of the tale depends upon the mutual obligations of the hero and Lord Evandale; who, though rivals in love, and fighting on contrary sides, behave with the most disinterested generosity towards each other. This part of the story is well invented and well supported. Henry Morton returns to his native country with the Prince of Orange, and discovers the retreat of Balfour, who had taken refuge in the fastnesses of the Highlands and who afterwards breaks from his retreat to prosecute revenge against Lord Evandale, who had been a successful opponent of the Covenanters: he is shot by Balfour, who is pursued by some troopers to a river, into which he plunges on horseback: the description of his death is very powerful, and well suited to the character and temper of the man.

[a quotation from chapter 44 'A hasty call to surrender' to 'a ruder epitaph' is omitted]

Morton and Edith Bellenger, are, of course, afterwards happily united.

The other story, called *The Black Dwarf*, only occupies one volume, and neither in point of interest nor execution, is to be compared with *Old Mortality*. The individual, who gives a name to the piece, is a deformed misanthrope; who having been betrayed in a love affair by his bosom friend, retires in disgust to a wild waste, called Mucklestane Muir, where he builds himself a hut, and from the singularity of his person, dress, and deportment, is taken by the ignorant country-people for a supernatural being, who holds converse with the devil and familiar spirits, and has unlimited power over the fortunes and fates of all who live in his neighbourhood. Indeed, there are several parts of his conduct that bear a very ambiguous appearance, until they are afterwards explained.

Near to the place where the Dwarf has settled his habitation, resides a Mr. Vere, in a sort of feudal castle, whose beautiful daughter is in love with a young man named Earnscliff, who has a rival in the person of Sir Frederick Langley. Mr. Vere is, in truth, the friend who had injured the Black Dwarf, whose real name is Sir Edward Mauley; and, by his interposition, a midnight match between Sir E. Langley and Miss Vere is prevented. The discovery is made in the chapel; and Vere, who had been concerned in some treasonable plots, flies to France, while young Earnscliff and Miss Vere are married with his consent, and with the approbation of the Black Dwarf, who, retiring into undiscovered seclusion, bestows upon them the bulk of a very large fortune. This story possesses considerable capabilities; but the fault is, as in the former, the multiplication of characters, by which are rendered imperfect: the following specimen is taken from that part of the story, in which the Dwarf intercepts the ceremony where Vere is endeavouring to compel his daughter to marry Sir P. Langley.

[a quotation from chapter 17 'The clergyman opened his prayer-book' to 'with a gesture of mute despair' is omitted]

We do not think the state in which these volumes are written, by any means so good as that of *Guy Mannering*, or even *The Antiquary*: the author becomes a little careless as he gains confidence by approbation; and, for merely English readers, too much of the Scotch dialect is introduced into the speeches. It is sometimes employed, however, with admirable effect; according to the character of the individual who speaks, it seems to add characteristic ferocity to the ruffian, or simplicity to the innocence of youth, and tenderness to the effusions of love. On other occasions it not a little heightens the comic effect of rustic humour.

While exhibiting the manners, the author has endeavoured also to employ something of the language of the times: he describes, but he has now and then gone too far back into antiquity, and has brought forward words that had even then been long obsolete. The error was, however, on the right side, and it would be advantageous, if, instead of the prevailing fashion of importing French terms, we resorted more to the wells of undefiled English, afforded by our elder writers.

17. Walter Scott: an unsigned review, *Quarterly Review*

Dated January 1817, issued April 1817, xvi, 430-80

The review was actually written in collaboration, mostly by Scott but partly by his friend, William Erskine, and contains editorial emendation by William Gifford, editor of the *Quarterly*.

For speculation on authorship of the various parts of the review, see Martin Lightfoot, 'Scott's Self-Reviewal: Manuscript and Other Evidence', *Nineteenth-Century Fiction* (Sept. 1968), xxiii, 150-60.

These Tales belong obviously to a class of novels which we have already had occasion repeatedly to notice, and which have attracted the attention of the public in no common degree,—we mean *Waverley*, *Guy Mannering*, and *The Antiquary*, and we have little hesitation to pronounce them either entirely, or in a great measure, the work of the same author. Why he should industriously endeavour to elude observation by taking leave of us in one character, and then suddenly popping out upon us in another, we cannot pretend to guess without knowing more of his personal reasons for preserving so strict an incognito than has hitherto reached us. We can, however, conceive many reasons for a writer observing this sort of mystery; not to mention that it has certainly had its effect in keeping up the interest which his works have excited.

We do not know if the imagination of our author will sink in the opinion of the public when deprived of that degree of invention which we have been hitherto disposed to ascribe to him; but we are certain that it ought to increase the value of his portraits, that human beings have actually sate for them. These coincidences between fiction and reality are perhaps the very circumstances to which the success of these novels is in a great measure to be attributed: for, without depreciating the merit of the artist, every spectator at once recognizes in those scenes and faces which are copied from nature an air of distinct reality, which is not attached to fancy-pieces however happily conceived and elaborately executed. By what sort of free-masonry, if we may use the term, the mind arrives at this conviction, we do not pretend to guess, but every one must have felt that he instinctively and almost insensibly recognizes in painting, poetry, or other works of imagination, that which is copied from existing nature, and that he forthwith clings to it with that kindred interest which thinks nothing which is human indifferent to humanity. Before therefore we proceed to analyse the work immediately before us, we beg leave briefly to notice a few circumstances connected with its predecessors.

Our author has told us it was his object to present a succession of scenes and characters connected with Scotland in its past and present state, and we must own that his stories are so slightly con-structed as to remind us of the showman's thread with which he draws up his pictures and presents them successively to the eye of the spectator. He seems seriously to have proceeded on Mr. Bays's maxim—'What the deuce is a plot good for, but to bring in fine things?'—Probability and perspicuity of narrative are sacrificed with the utmost indifference to the desire of producing effect; and provided the author can but contrive to 'surprize and elevate', he appears to think that he has done his duty to the public. Against this slovenly indifference we have already remonstrated, and we again enter our protest. It is in justice to the author himself that we do so, because, whatever merit individual scenes and passages may possess, (and none have been more ready than ourselves to offer our applause,) it is clear that their effect would be greatly enhanced by being disposed in a clear and continued narrative. We are the more earnest in this matter, because it seems that the author errs chiefly from carelessness. There may be something of system in it however: for we have remarked, that with an attention which amounts even to affectation, he has avoided the common language of narrative, and thrown his story, as much as possible, into a dramatic shape. In many cases this has added greatly to the effect, by keeping both the actors and action continually before the reader, and placing him, in some measure, in the situation of the audience at a theatre, who are compelled to gather the meaning of the scene from what the dramatis personæ say to each other, and not from any explanation addressed immediately to themselves. But though the author gain this advantage, and thereby compel the reader to think of the personages of the novel and not of the writer, yet the practice, especially pushed to the extent we have noticed, is a principal cause of the flimsiness and incoherent texture of which his greatest admirers are compelled to complain. Few can wish his success more sincerely than we do, and yet without more attention on his own part, we have great doubts of its continuance.

In addition to the loose and incoherent style of the narration, another leading fault in these novels is the total want of interest which the reader attaches to the character of the hero. Waverley, Brown, or Bertram in *Guy Mannering*, and Lovel in *The Antiquary*, are all brethren of a family; very amiable and very insipid sort of young men. We think we can perceive that this error is also in some degree occasioned by the dramatic principle upon which the author frames his plots. His chief characters are never actors, but always acted upon by the spur of circumstances, and have their fates uniformly determined by the agency of the subordinate persons. This arises from the author having usually represented them as foreigners to whom every thing in Scotland is strange,—a circumstance which serves as his apology for entering into many minute details which are reflectively, as it were, addressed to the reader through the medium of the hero. While he is going into explanations and details which, addressed directly to the reader, might appear tiresome and unnecessary, he gives interest to them by exhibiting the effect which they produce upon the principal person of his drama, and at the same time obtains a patient hearing for what might otherwise be passed over without attention. But if he gains this advantage, it is by sacrificing the character of the hero. No one can be interesting to the reader who is not himself a prime agent in the scene. This is understood even by the worthy citizen and his wife, who are introduced as prolocutors in Fletcher's *Knight of the Burning Pestle*. When they are asked what the principal person of the drama shall do?—the answer is prompt and ready—'Marry, let him come forth and kill a giant.' There is a good deal of tact in the request. Every hero in poetry, in fictitious narrative, ought to come forth and do or say something or other which no other person could have done or said; make some sacrifice, surmount some difficulty, and become interesting to us otherwise than by his mere appearance on the scene, the passive tool of the other characters.

The insipidity of this author's heroes may be also in part referred to the readiness with which he twists and turns his story to produce some immediate and perhaps temporary effect. This could hardly be done without representing the principal character either as inconsistent or flexible in his principles. The ease with which Waverley adopts and afterwards forsakes the Jacobite party in 1745 is a good example of what we mean. Had he been painted as a steady character, his conduct would have been improbable. The author was aware of this; and yet, unwilling to relinquish an opportunity of introducing the interior of the Chevalier's military court, the circumstances of the battle of Preston-pans, and so forth, he hesitates not to sacrifice poor Waverley, and to represent him as a reed blown about at the pleasure of every breeze: a less careless writer would probably have taken some pains to gain the end proposed in a more artful and ingenious manner. But our author was hasty, and has paid the penalty of his haste.

We have hinted that we are disposed to question the originality of these novels in point of invention, and that in doing so, we do not consider ourselves as derogating from the merit of the author, to whom, on the contrary, we give the praise due to one who has collected and brought out with accuracy and effect, incidents and manners which might otherwise have slept in oblivion. We proceed to our proofs.[1]

[a long passage suggesting historical precedents for incidents in *Waverley* is omitted]

The traditions and manners of the Scotch were so blended with superstitious practices and fears, that the author of these novels seems to have deemed it incumbent on him, to transfer many more such incidents to his novels, than seem either probable or natural to an English reader. It may be some apology that his story would have lost the national cast, which it was chiefly his object to preserve, had this been otherwise. There are few families of antiquity in Scotland, which do not possess some strange legends, told only under promise of secrecy, and with an air of mystery; in developing which, the influence of the powers of darkness is referred to. The truth probably is, that the agency of witches and demons was often made to account for the sudden disappearance of individuals and similar incidents, too apt to arise out of the evil dispositions of humanity, in a land where

[1] It will be readily conceived that the curious MSS. and other information of which we have availed ourselves were not accessible to us in this country: but we have been assiduous in our inquiries; and are happy enough to possess a correspondent whose researches on the spot have been indefatigable, and whose kind, and ready communications have anticipated all our wishes [reviewer].

revenge was long held honourable—where private feuds and civil broils disturbed the inhabitants for ages—and where justice was but weakly and irregularly executed. Mr. Law, a conscientious but credulous clergyman of the Kirk of Scotland, who lived in the seventeenth century, has left behind him a very curious manuscript, in which, with the political events of that distracted period, he has intermingled the various portents and marvellous occurrences which, in common with his age, he ascribed to supernatural agency. The following extract will serve to illustrate the taste of this period for the supernatural. When we read such things recorded by men of sense and education, (and Mr. Law was deficient in neither,) we cannot help remembering the times of paganism, when every scene, incident, and action, had its appropriate and presiding deity. It is indeed curious to consider what must have been the sensations of a person, who lived under this peculiar species of hallucination, believing himself beset on all hands by invisible agents; one who was unable to account for the restiveness of a nobleman's carriage horses otherwise than by the immediate effect of witchcraft: and supposed that the *sage femme* of the highest reputation was most likely to devote the infants to the infernal spirits, upon their very entrance into life.

[passages on superstitions, on the past conviviality of Scottish lawyers, and on the past situation of Scottish idiots are omitted]

It has been generally supposed that in the case of these as of other successful novels, the most prominent and peculiar characters were sketched from real life. It was only after the death of Smollet, that two barbers and a shoemaker contended about the character of Strap, which each asserted was modelled from his own: but even in the lifetime of the present author, there is scarcely a dale in the pastoral districts of the southern counties but arrogates to itself the possession of the original Dandie Dinmont. As for Baillie Mac Wheeble, a person of the highest eminence in the law perfectly well remembers having received fees from him. We ourselves think we recognize the prototype of Meg Merrilies, on whose wild fidelity so much of the interest of *Guy Mannering* hinges, in the Jean Gordon of the following extract:

[an excerpt on Jean Gordon from the *Edinburgh Monthly Magazine* is omitted]

Although these strong resemblances occur so frequently, and with such peculiar force, as almost to impress us with the conviction that the author sketched from nature, and not from fancy alone; yet we hesitate to draw any positive conclusion, sensible that a character dashed off as the representative of a certain class of men will bear, if executed with fidelity to the general outlines, not only that resemblance which he ought to possess as 'knight of the shire', but also a special affinity to some particular individual. It is scarcely possible it should be otherwise. When Emery appears on the stage as a Yorkshire peasant, with the habit, manner, and dialect peculiar to the character, and which he assumes with so much truth and fidelity, those unacquainted with the province or its inhabitants see merely the abstract idea, the beau ideal of a Yorkshireman. But to those who are intimate with both, the action and manner of the comedian almost necessarily recal the idea of some individual native (altogether unknown probably to the performer) to whom his exterior and manners bear a casual resemblance. We are therefore on the whole inclined to believe, that the incidents are frequently copied from *actual* occurrences, but that the characters are either entirely fictitious, or if any traits have been borrowed from real life, as in the anecdote which we have quoted respecting Invernahyle, they have been carefully disguised and blended with such as are purely imaginary. We now proceed to a more particular examination of the volumes before us.

They are entitled *Tales of my Landlord*: why so entitled, excepting to introduce a quotation from Don Quixote, it is difficult to conceive: for Tales of my Landlord they are *not*, nor is it indeed easy to say whose tales they ought to be called. There is a proem, as it is termed, supposed to be written by Jedediah Cleishbotham, the schoolmaster and parish clerk of the village of Gandercleugh, in which we are given to understand that these Tales were compiled by his deceased usher, Mr. Peter Pattieson, from the narratives or conversations of such travellers as frequented the Wallace Inn, in that village. Of this proem we shall only say that it is written in the quaint style of that prefixed by Gay to his Pastorals, being, as Johnson terms it, 'such imitation as he could obtain of obsolete language, and by consequence in a style that was never written nor spoken in any age or place.'

The first of the Tales thus ushered in is entitled *The Black Dwarf*. It contains some striking scenes, but it is even more than usually deficient in the requisites of a luminous and interesting narrative, as will appear from the following abridgment.

[plot summary and a quotation from chapter 3 of *The Black Dwarf* 'The height of the object' to ' "for the last time" ' are omitted]

The domestic scene is painted with the knowledge of the language and manners of that class of society, which give interest to the picture of Dandie Dinmont and his family, in *Guy Mannering*. But we do not think it equal to the more simple sketch contained in the earlier novel. This must frequently be the case, when an author, in repeated efforts, brings before us characters of the same *genus*. He is, as it were, compelled to dwell upon the specific differences and distinctions instead of the general characteristics, or, in other words, rather to shew wherein Hobbie Elliot differs from Dandie Dinmont than to describe the former as he really was.

The mysterious dwarf, with speed almost supernatural, builds himself a house of stones and turf, incloses it with a rude wall, within which he cultivates a patch of garden ground, and all this he accomplishes by the assistance of chance passengers who occasionally stopped to aid him in a task which seemed so unfitted for a being of his distorted shape. Against this whole tale we were tempted to state the objection of utter improbability. We are given however to understand that such an individual, so misused by nature in his birth, did actually, within these twenty years, appear in a lone valley in the moors of Tweedale, and so build a mansion without any assistance but that of passengers as aforesaid, and said house so constructed did so inhabit. The singular circumstances of his hideous appearance, of the apparent ease with which he constructed his place of abode, of the total ignorance of all the vicinity respecting his birth or history, excited, in the minds of the common people, a superstitious terror not inferior to that which the romance describes the appearance of the Black Dwarf to have spread through Liddesdale. The real recluse possessed intelligence and information beyond his apparent condition, which the neighbours, in their simplicity, were sometimes disposed to think preternatural. He once resided (and perhaps still lives) in the vale formed by the Manor-water which falls into the Tweed near Peebles, a glen long honoured by the residence of the late venerable Professor Ferguson.

[plot summary is omitted]

This list of personages is not numerous, yet the tale is far from corresponding in simplicity. On the contrary, it abounds with plots, elopements, ravishments, and rescues, and all the violent events which are so common in romance, and of such rare occurrence in real life.

Willie of Westburnflat, the robber aforesaid, opens the campaign by burning the house of our honest friend Hobbie Elliot. The gathering of the borderers for redress and vengeance, their pursuit of the freebooter, and the siege of his tower, are all told with the spirit which shews a mind accustomed to the contemplation of such scenes. The robber, for his ransom, offers to deliver up his fair prisoner, who proves to be, not Grace Armstrong, but Miss Vere, whom her father, finding his plans on her freedom of choice likely to be deranged by the interference of the steward Ratcliffe, who seems to possess a mysterious authority over the conduct of his patron, had procured to be carried off by this freebooter, in order to place her the more absolutely at his paternal disposal. She is restored to the Castle of Ellieslaw by her lover Earnscliff, who (of course) had been foremost in her rescue. This ought not to be slurred over, being one of the few attempts which the poor gentleman makes to *kill a giant*, or otherwise to distinguish himself during the volume. In the meanwhile, the influence of the Black Dwarf with the robber obtains the freedom of Grace Armstrong, and the Solitary contrives also to throw in the way of her betrothed husband a purse of gold, sufficient to reimburse all his losses.

[plot summary is omitted]

Such is the brief abstract of a tale of which the narrative is unusually artificial. Neither hero nor heroine excites interest of any sort, being just that sort of *pattern* people whom nobody cares a farthing about. The explanation of the dwarf's real circumstances and character, too long delayed from an obvious wish to protract the mystery, is at length huddled up so hastily that, for our parts, we cannot say we are able to comprehend more of the motives of this principal personage than that he was a mad man, and acted like one—an easy and summary mode of settling all difficulties. As for the hurry and military bustle of the conclusion, it is only worthy of the farce of the *Miller and his Men*, or any other modern melo-drama, ending with a front crouded with soldiers and scene-shifters, and a back scene in a state of conflagration.

We have dealt with this tale very much according to the clown's argument in favour of Master Froth—'Look upon his face, I will be sworn on a book that his face is the worst part about him, and if his face be the worst part about him, how could Master Froth do the constable's wife any harm?' Even so we will take our oaths that the narrative is the worst part of *The Black Dwarf*, and that if the reader can tolerate it upon the sketch we have given him, he will find the work itself contains passages both of natural pathos and fantastic terror, not unworthy of the author of the scene of Stanie's burial, in *The Antiquary*, or the wild tone assumed in the character of Meg Merrilies.

The story which occupies the next three volumes is of much deeper interest, both as a tale and from its connexion with historical facts and personages. It is entitled *Old Mortality*, but should have been called the Tale of Old Mortality, for the personage so named is only quoted as the authority for the incidents. The story is thus given in the introduction:

[a quotation from chapter 1 ' "According to the belief" ' to ' "appellation of Old Mortality" ' is omitted]

We believe we can add a local habitation and a name to the accounts given of this remarkable old man. His name was Robert Patterson, and in the earlier part of his life he lived in the parish of Closeburn, in Dumfriesshire, where he was distinguished for depth of piety and devotional feeling. Whether domestic affliction, or some other cause, induced him to adopt the wandering course of life described in the tale which bears his name, we have not been informed: but he continued it for many years, and about fifteen years since closed his weary pilgrimage in the manner described in the introduction, 'being found on the highway, near Lockerby, in Dumfriesshire, exhausted and just expiring. The old pony, the companion of his wanderings, was found standing by the side of his master.' This remarkable personage is mentioned in a note upon Swift's Memoirs of Captain John Creighton, in Mr. Scott's edition of that author.

[plot summary and quotations from chapter 3 'No sooner had the horses' to 'which he was muffled', and chapter 4 'His comrade' to 'were left alone' are omitted]

We may here briefly notice that Francis Stewart, the grandson and representative of the last Earl of Bothwell, who was himself a grandson of James V of Scotland, was so much reduced in circumstances, as actually to ride a private in the Life-guards at this period, as we learn from the Memoirs of Creighton, who was his comrade. Nothing else is known of him, and the character assigned to him in the novel is purely imaginary.

Balfour and Morton having left the village together, the former in the course of their journey discovers himself to Morton as an ancient comrade of his father, and on hearing the kettle-drums and trumpets of a body of horse approaching, prevails upon him to give him refuge in his uncle's house of Milnwood. And here, like Don Quixote, when he censured the anachronisms of Mr. Peter's puppet-show, we beg to inform our novelist that cavalry never march to the sound of music by night, any more than the Moors of Jansuena used bells.

It must be remarked that by the cruel and arbitrary laws of the time, Morton, in affording to the comrade of his father a protection which he could not in humanity refuse him, incurred the heavy penalty attached to receiving or sheltering intercommuned persons. There was, by the severity of government, a ban put upon the refractory calvinists, equal to the *aquæ et ignis interdictio*[1] of the civil law, and whoever transgressed it by relieving the unhappy fugitive, involved himself in his crime and punishment. Another circumstance added to the hazard which Morton thus incurred. The ploughman of Lady Margaret Bellenden, Cuddie Headrigg by name, had been, with his mother, expelled from the castle of Tillietudlem, on account of his refusing to bear arms at the weapon-showing, and thereby occasioning the substitution of Goose-Gibbie, to the disgrace, as we have already seen, of Lady Margaret's troop. The old woman is described as a zealous extra-presbyterian; the son as an old-fashioned Scotch boor, sly and shrewd in his own concerns, dull and indifferent to all other matters; reverencing his mother, and loving his mistress, a pert serving damsel in the castle, better than was uniformly expressed by his language. The submission of this honest countryman, upon a martial summons, to petticoat influence, was not peculiar to his rank of life. We learn from Fountainhall, that when thirty-five heritors of the kingdom of Fife were summoned to appear before the council for neglecting to join the King's host, in 1680, with their horses and arms, some of their apologies were similar to those which Cuddie might have preferred for himself. 'Balcanquhal of that ilk alleged that his horses were robbed, but shunned to take the declaration for fear of disquiet from his wife.'—'And Young of Kirkton stated his lady's dangerous sickness, and bitter curses if he should leave her; and the appearance of abortion on his offering to go from her.' Now as there was a private understanding between Morton and the fair Edith Bellenden, the former is induced, at the request of the young lady, to use his interest with his uncle and his uncle's favourite housekeeper to

[1] 'Interdiction of fire and water'—formula of banishment.

122

receive the two exiles as menials into the house of Milnwood. The family there are seated at dinner when they are disturbed by one of those tyrannical domiciliary visits which the soldiers were authorized and encouraged to commit. The scene may very well be extracted as a specimen of the author's colouring and outline.

[quotations from chapter 8 'While the servants' to 'Scotland had said it', and ' "Well," said Bothwell' to ' "armed fanatics?" ', and 'Old Milnwood cast' to ' "lad awa' to captivity" ' and plot summary are omitted]

The scene which we have transcribed seems to have been sketched with considerable attention to the manners. But it is not quite original, and probably the reader will discover the germ of it in the following dialogue, which Daniel Defoe has introduced into his History of the Church of Scotland. It will be remembered that Defoe visited Scotland on a political mission, about the time of the Union, and it is evident that the anecdotes concerning this unhappy period, then fresh in the memory of many, must have been peculiarly interesting to a man of his liveliness of imagination, who excelled all others in dramatizing a story, and presenting it as if in actual speech and action before the reader.

[an excerpt from Defoe's *History of the Church of Scotland* is omitted]

This story seems to intimate, that the inhumanity of the soldiers did not in all instances keep pace with the severity of their instructions. Indeed even the curates sometimes were said to connive at the recusancy of their parishioners, and held it as a sufficient compliance with the orders of the council, that their parishioners should keep the church, if they occasionally walked in at one door, and out at the other, though without remaining during divine service. To return to our tale.

[plot summary and quotations from chapter 12 'Grahame of Claver-house was in the prime' to 'of their lustre', and chapter 13 ' "Be it so then" ' to ' " this morning's work" ', and chapter 16 ' "You are the murdering villain" ' to 'they were spoken' are omitted. The description of Claverhouse and the fight between Bothwell and Balfour are praised. The last quotation concerns the Battle of Loudon-hill]

This is a lively, but exaggerated account of a remarkable skirmish, the only one in which Claverhouse was ever worsted. The relation betwixt him and the Cornet Grahame who was slain is quite imaginary. The accounts given by Creighton, and by Guild, (author of a Latin poem, called Bellum Bothuellianum,) state that the body of this officer was brutally mangled after death, by the conquerors, from a belief that it was that of his commander Claverhouse. A curious detail of the action which we should be tempted to transcribe had we space, from the manuscript of James Russell, one of the murderers of Archbishop Sharpe, and who was himself present, ascribes the mangling of the corpse of Cornet Grahame, to some indiscreet language which he was reported to have held on the morning of the fight. Both parties, no doubt, made a point of believing their own side of the story, which is always a matter of conscience in such cases.

Morton, set at liberty by the victorious Covenanters, is induced to join their cause and accept of a command in their levy; as well by the arguments of Burley and a deep sense of the injustice with which the insurgents have been treated by government, as by natural indignation at the unworthy and cruel treatment which he had himself experienced. But, although he adopts this decisive step, yet it is without participating the narrow minded fanaticism and bitter rancour with which most of the persecuted party regarded the prelatists, and not without an express stipulation, that, as he joined a cause supported by men in open war, so he expected it was to be carried on, according to the laws of civilized nations. If we look to the history of these times, we shall find reason to believe, that the Covenanters had not learned mercy in the school of persecution. It was perhaps not to be expected, from a people proscribed and persecuted, having their spirits embittered by the most severe personal sufferings. But that the temper of the victors of Drumclog was cruel and sanguinary, is too evident from the report of their historian, Mr. Howie, of Lochgoin; a character scarcely less interesting or peculiar, than Old Mortality, and who, not many years since, collected, with great assiduity, both from manuscripts and traditions, all that could be recovered concerning the champions of the Covenant. In his History of the rising at Bothwell-bridge and the preceding skirmish of Drumclog, he records the opinions of Mr. Robert Hamilton, who commanded the Whigs upon the latter occasion, concerning the propriety and legality of giving quarter to a vanquished enemy.

'Mr. Hamilton discovered a great deal of bravery and valour, both in the conflict with and pursuit of the enemy; but when he and some others were pursuing the enemy, others flew too greedily upon the spoil, small as it was, instead of pursuing the victory; and some, without Mr. Hamilton's knowledge, and directly contrary to his express command, *gave five of these bloody enemies quarters, and then let them go; this greatly grieved Mr. Hamilton, when he saw some of Babel's brats spared, after the Lord had delivered them to their hands, that they might dash them against the stones. Psal. 137—9.*—In his own account of this he reckons the sparing of these enemies and the letting them go, to be among their first stepping aside; for which he feared that the Lord would not honour them to do much more for him; and he says, that he was neither for taking favours from, nor giving favours to, the Lord's enemies.'—*Battle of Bothwell Bridge*, p. 9.

The author therefore has acted in strict conformity with historical truth (whether with propriety we shall hereafter inquire) in representing the covenanters or rather the ultra-covenanters, for those who gained the skirmish fell chiefly under this description, as a fierce and sanguinary set of men, whose zeal and impatience under persecution had destroyed the moral feeling and principle which ought to attend and qualify all acts of retaliation. The large body of Presbyterians, both clergy and people, were far from joining in these extravagances, and when they took up arms to unite themselves to the insurgents, were received with great jealousy and suspicion by the high-flyers of whom we have spoken. The clergy who had been contented to exercise their ministry by the favour of the government, under what was called the Indulgence, were stigmatized by their opponents as Erastians and will-worshippers, while they, with more appearance of reason, recriminated upon their adversaries that they meant, under pretence of establishing the liberty and independence of the kirk, altogether to disown allegiance to the government. The author of Old Mortality has drawn a lively sketch of their distracted councils and growing divisions, and has introduced several characters of their clergy, on each of whom religious enthusiasm is represented as producing an effect in proportion to its quality, and the capacity upon which it is wrought. It is sincere but formal in the indulged Presbyterian clergyman Poundtext, who is honest, well-meaning, and faithful, but somewhat timorous and attached to his own ease and comfort. The zeal of Kettledrummle is more boisterous, and he is bold, clamorous, and intractable. In a youth called Mac Briar, of a more elevated and warm imagination, enthusiasm is wild, exalted, eloquent, and impressive; and in Habbakuk Mucklewrath it soars into absolute madness.

We have been at some pains to ascertain that there were such dissensions as are alluded to in the novels, and we think it is but fair to quote the words of those who lived at the period. James Russell has left distinct testimony on this subject.

[excerpts from various historical sources to validate Scott's presentation of the Covenanters are omitted, along with some plot summary. The siege of Tillietudlem is said to be 'perhaps' too detailed. The proposed execution of Lord Evandale by the Covenanters is last mentioned]

This incident is not in any respect strained. From the principles expressed in former quotations, it seems that the Cameronian part of the insurgents had resolved to refuse quarter to their prisoners. It appears, from the joint testimony of Creighton and Guild, countenanced by a passage in Blacader's Manuscript Memoirs, that they set up in the centre of their camp at Hamilton, a gallows of unusual size and extraordinary construction, furnished with hooks and halters for executing many criminals at once; and it was avowed that this machine was constructed for the service of the malignants: nor was this an empty threat, for they actually did put to death, in cold blood, one Watson, a butcher in Glasgow, whose crime was that of bearing arms for the government. This execution gave great displeasure to that portion of their own friends whom they were pleased to call Erastians, as appears from Russell's Memoirs, already quoted.

The deliverance of Lord Evandale occasions an open breach betwixt Morton, the hero of the novel, and his father's friend Burley, who considered himself as specially injured in the transaction. While these dissensions are rending asunder the insurgent army, the Duke of Monmouth, at the head of that of Charles II, advances towards them, like the kite in the fable, hovering over the pugnacious frog and mouse, and ready to pounce on both. Morton goes as an envoy to the Duke, who seems inclined to hear him with indulgence, but is prevented by the stern influence of Claverhouse and General Dalzell. In this last point, the author has cruelly falsified history, for he has represented Dalzell as present at the battle of Bothwell Bridge; whereas that 'old and bloody man', as Wodrow calls him, was *not* at the said battle, but at Edinburgh, and only joined the army a day or two afterwards. He also exhibits the said Dalzell as wearing *boots*, which it appears from the authority of Creighton the old general never wore. We know little the author can say for himself to excuse these sophistications, and, therefore, may charitably suggest that he was writing a romance, and not a history. But he has done strict justice to the facts of history in representing Monmouth as anxious to prevent bloodshed, both before and after the engagement, and as overpowered by the fiercer spirits around him when willing to offer favourable terms to the insurgents.

Morton, after having, as is incumbent on him as the hero of the tale, done prodigious things to turn the scale of fortune, is at last compelled to betake himself to flight, accompanied by the faithful Cuddie, the companion of his distress.

[plot summary is omitted. The reprieve of Morton from the death penalty is last mentioned]

But he witnesses the dreadful examination by torture imposed upon one of his late companions. The scene is described in language which seems almost borrowed from the records of those horrible proceedings, and, with many other incidents, true in fact, though mingled with a fictitious narrative, ought to make every Scotchman thank God that he has been born a century and a half later than such atrocities were perpetrated under the sanction of law. The accused person sustains the torture with that firmness which most of the sufferers manifested, few of whom, excepting Donald Cargil the preacher, who is said by Fountainhall to have behaved very timorously, lost their fortitude even under these dreadful inflictions. Cuddie Headrigg, whose zeal was by no means torture-proof, after as many evasions as were likely from his rank and country, for Scotch country-people are celebrated for giving indirect answers to plain questions, is at length brought to confess his error, drink the king's health, recant his whiggish principles, and accept a free pardon. The scene of his examination is characteristic, but we have not room for its insertion.

Morton receives a second communication from his old friend Burley, stating that he possessed unbounded influence over the fortune of Edith Bellenden, to whom he knew Morton's attachment, and would exercise it in his favour in case of his perseverance in the Presbyterian cause. The reason given for this unexpected change of conduct is Burley's having witnessed Morton's gallant behaviour at Bothwell Bridge. But we consider the motive as inadequate, and the incident as improbable. Morton being on ship-board when he receives the letter, has no opportunity to take any step in consequence of it.

[plot summary is omitted]

Balfour is slain after a most desperate resistance well and strikingly described. The intrusive heir male is killed in the fray—which opens to Lady Margaret an easy access to her rightful inheritance; and Miss Edith, who must now have obtained the ripe age of *thirty* years, bestows her hand on Morton.

We have given these details partly in compliance with the established rules which our office prescribes, and partly in the hope that the authorities we have been enabled to bring together might give additional light and interest to the story. From the unprecedented popularity of the work, we cannot flatter ourselves that our summary has made any one of our readers acquainted with events with which he was not previously familiar. The causes of that popularity we may be permitted shortly to allude to; we cannot even hope to exhaust them, and it is the less necessary that we should attempt it, since we cannot suggest a consideration which a perusal of the work has not anticipated in the minds of all our readers.

One great source of the universal admiration which this family of Novels has attracted, is their peculiar plan, and the distinguished excellence with which it has been executed. The objections that have frequently been stated against what are called Historical Romances, have been suggested, we think, rather from observing the universal failure of that species of composition, than from any inherent and constitutional defect in the species of composition itself. If the manners of different ages are injudiciously blended together,—if unpowdered crops and slim and fairy shapes are commingled in the dance with volumed wigs and far-extending hoops,—if in the portraiture of real character the truth of history be violated, the eyes of the spectator are necessarily averted from a picture which excites in every well regulated and intelligent mind the hatred of incredulity. We have neither time nor inclination to enforce our remark by giving illustrations of it. But if those unpardonable sins against good taste can be avoided, and the features of an age gone by can be recalled in a spirit of delineation at once faithful and striking, the very opposite is the legitimate conclusion: the composition itself is in every point of view dignified and improved; and the author, leaving the light and frivolous associates with whom a careless observer would be disposed to ally him, takes his seat on the bench of the historians of his time and country. In this proud assembly, and in no mean place of it, we are disposed to rank the author of these works; for we again express our conviction—and we desire to be understood to use the term as distinguished from *knowledge*—that they are all the offspring of the same parent. At once a master of the great events and minuter incidents of history, and of the manners of the times he celebrates, as distinguished from those which now prevail,—the intimate thus of the living and of the dead, his judgment enables him to separate those traits which are characteristic from those that are generic; and his imagination, not less accurate and discriminating than vigorous and vivid, presents to the mind of the reader the manners of the times, and introduces to his familiar acquaintance the individuals of his drama as they thought and spoke and acted. We are not quite sure that any thing is to be found in the manner and character of the Black Dwarf which would enable us, without the aid of the author's information, and the facts he relates, to give it to the beginning of the last century; and, as we have already remarked, his free-booting robber lives, perhaps, too late in time. But his delineation is perfect. With palpable and inexcusable defects in the *denouement*, there are scenes of deep and overwhelming interest; and every one, we think, must be delighted with the portrait of the Grandmother of Hobbie Elliott, a representation soothing and consoling in itself, and heightened in its effect by the contrast produced from the lighter manners of the younger members of the family, and the honest but somewhat blunt and boisterous bearing of the shepherd himself.

The second tale however, as we have remarked, is more adapted to the talents of the author, and his success has been proportionably triumphant. We have trespassed too unmercifully on the time of our gentle readers to indulge our inclination in endeavouring to form an estimate of that melancholy but, nevertheless, most attractive period in our history, when by the united efforts of a corrupt and unprincipled government, of extravagant fanaticism, want of education, perversion of religion, and the influence of ill-instructed teachers, whose hearts and understandings were estranged and debased by the illapses of the wildest enthusiasm, the liberty of the people was all but extinguished, and the bonds of society nearly dissolved. Revolting as all this is to the Patriot, it affords fertile materials to the Poet. As to the *beauty* of the delineation presented to the reader in this tale, there is, we believe, but one opinion: and we are persuaded that the more carefully and dispassionately it is contemplated, the more perfect will it appear in the still more valuable qualities of fidelity and truth. We have given part of the evidence on which we say this, and we will again recur to the subject. The opinions and language of the *honest party* are detailed with the accuracy of a witness; and he who could open to our view the state of the Scottish peasantry, perishing in the field or on the scaffold, and driven to utter and just desperation, in attempting to defend their first and most sacred rights; who could place before our eyes the leaders of these enormities, from the notorious Duke of Lauderdale downwards to the fellow mind that executed his behest, precisely as they lived and looked,—such a chronicler cannot justly be charged with attempting to extenuate or throw into the shade the corruptions of a government that soon afterwards fell a victim to its own follies and crimes.

Independently of the delineation of the manners and characters of the times to which the story refers, it is impossible to avoid noticing, as a separate excellence, the faithful representation of general nature. Looking not merely to the litter of novels that peep out for a single day from the mud where they were spawned, but to many of more ambitious pretensions—it is quite evident that in framing them, the authors have first addressed themselves to the involutions and developement of the story, as the principal object of their attention; and that in entangling and unravelling the plot, in combining the incidents which compose it, and even in depicting the characters, they sought for assistance chiefly in the writings of their predecessors. Baldness, and uniformity, and inanity are the inevitable results of this slovenly and unintellectual proceeding. The volume which this author has studied is the great book of Nature. He has gone abroad into the world in quest of what the world will certainly and abundantly supply, but what a man of great discrimination alone will find, and a man of the very highest genius will alone depict after he has discovered it. The characters of Shakspeare are not more exclusively human, not more perfectly men and women as they live and move, than those of this mysterious author. It is from this circumstance that, as we have already observed, many of his personages are supposed to be sketched from real life. He must have mixed much and variously in the society of his native country; his studies must have familiarized him to systems of manners now forgotten; and thus the persons of his drama, though in truth the creatures of his own imagination, convey the impression of individuals who we are persuaded must exist, or are evoked from their graves in all their original freshness, entire in their lineaments, and perfect in all the minute peculiarities of dress and demeanour. The work now more immediately under our consideration is accordingly equally remarkable for the truth and the endless variety of its characters. The stately and pompous dignity of Lady Margaret

Bellenden, absorbed in the consciousness of her rank;—the bustling importance and unaffected kindliness of Mrs. Alison Wilson, varying in their form, but preserving their substance, with her variations of fortune;—the true Caledonian prudence of Neil Blane;—we cannot stay to examine, nor point out with what exquisite skill their characteristic features are brought to the reader's eye, not by description or enumeration, but by compelling him, as in real life, to observe their effect when forced into contact with the peculiarities of others. The more prominent personages it would be superfluous to notice. We must be pardoned, however, for offering one slight tribute of respect to the interesting old woman by whom Morton is directed to Burley's last retreat: she is portrayed as a patient, kind, gentle, and generous being, even in the lowest state of oppression, poverty and blindness; her religious enthusiasm, unlike that of her sect, is impressed with the pure stamp of the Gospel, combining meekness with piety, and love to her neighbour with obedience and love of the Deity. And the author's knowledge of human nature is well illustrated in the last glimpse he gives us of our early acquaintance, Jenny Dennison. When Morton returns from the continent, the giddy *fille de chambre* of Tillietudlem has become the wife of Cuddie Headrigg, and the mother of a large family. Every one must have observed that coquetry, whether in high or low life, is always founded on intense selfishness, which, as age advances, gradually displays itself in its true colours, and vanity gives way to avarice; and with perfect truth of representation, the lively, thoughtless girl has settled into a prudent housewife, whose whole cares are centered in herself, and in her husband and children, because they are *her* husband and children. Nor in this rapid and imperfect sketch can we altogether pass over the peculiar excellence of the *dialogue*. We do not allude merely to its dramatic merit, nor to the lively and easy tone of natural conversation by which it is uniformly distinguished: we would notice the singular skill and felicity with which, in conveying the genuine sentiments of the Scottish peasant in the genuine language of his native land, the author has avoided that appearance of grossness and vulgarity by which the success of every similar attempt has hitherto been defeated. The full value of this praise we, on this part of the island, cannot, perhaps, be expected to feel, though we are not wholly insensible to it. The Scottish peasant speaks the language of his native country, his *national* language, not the *patois* of an individual district; and in listening to it we not only do not experience even the slightest feeling of disgust or aversion, but our bosoms are responsive to every sentiment of sublimity, or awe, or terror which the author may be disposed to excite. Of the truth of all this, Meg Merrilies is a sufficiently decisive instance. The terrible graces of this mysterious personage, an outcast and profligate of the lowest class, are complete in their effect, though conveyed by the *medium* of language that has hitherto been connected with associations that must have altogether neutralized them. We could, with much satisfaction to ourselves, and much we fear to the annoyance of our patient readers, dilate on this part of the subject, and illustrate our views by quotations from some of the scenes that peculiarly struck ourselves; but we have trespassed much on their indulgence, and there is one not unimportant view we have still to open to them. This chiefly relates to the historical portraits with which the author has presented us. We propose to examine these somewhat in detail, and we trust the information we have collected from sources not often resorted to, may be an apology for the length of the Article.

Most of the group are drawn in harsh colours, and yet the truth of the resemblances, when illustrated by historical documents, will scarcely be disputed, except by those staunch partizans whose religious or political creed is the sole gauge for estimating the good or bad qualities of the characters of past ages. To such men an extensive knowledge of history is only the means of further perversion of its truth. The portraits of their favourites (as Queen Elizabeth is said to have required of her own) must be drawn without shadow, and the objects of their political antipathy be blackened, horned, hoofed, and clawed ere they will acknowledge the likeness of either. But if we are to idolize the memory of deceased men of worth and piety of our own persuasion, as if they had not been fallible mortals, it is in vain that we are converted from paganism, which transformed deceased heroes into deities; and if we damn utterly the characters and motives of those who stood in opposition to their opinions, we have gained little by leaving the Church of Rome, in whose creed heresy includes every other possible guilt.

The most prominent portrait, historically considered, is that of John Grahame, of Claverhouse, afterwards Viscount of Dundee; and its accurate resemblance can hardly be disputed, though those who only look at his cruelty towards the Presbyterians will consider his courage, talents, high spirit, and loyal devotion to an unfortunate master, as ill associated with such evil attributes. They who study his life will have some reason to think that a mistaken opinion of the absolute obedience due by an officer to his superiors, joined to unscrupulous ambition, was the ruling principle of many of his worst actions. Yet he was not uniformly so ruthless as he is painted in the Tales. In some cases he interceded for the life of those whom he was ordered to put to death; and particularly, he pleaded hard with Sir James Johnstone, of Westerhall, for the life of one Hyslop, shot on Eskdale moor. It appears also, from his correspondence with Lord Lithgow, that he was attentive to his prisoners, as he apologizes for not bringing one of them, who laboured under a disease rendering it painful for him to be on horseback. From the following anecdote it would seem that his activity against the Whigs did not always correspond with the wishes of those in power:

'The Thesr. Queensberry having taken some disgust at Claverhouse, *for not being so active against the Whigs as he ought*, (they having killed two men, and made one Mr. Shaw, a minister, swear never to preach under bishops,) orders his brother, Colonel Douglas, to take two hundred men of his regiment and attack the rebels. But having one day with a party of his men met with as many of the rebels in a house, they killed two of his men and Captain Urquhart Meldrum's brother, and was near being shot himself, had not a Whig's carabine misgiven, (the more pity, considering what a vile traitor the Colonel after proved to King James VII.), that Douglas therefore shot the said Whig, January, 1685.'—*Fountainhall's MS Diary.*

Something is also to be given to the exaggeration of political and polemical hatred. For example, John Brown of Muirkirk is, in Wodrow's history, said to have been shot by Claverhouse with his own hand. But in the *Life of Peden*, which gives a minute and interesting account of this execution, the particulars whereof the author had from the unfortunate widow, we are expressly told that Brown was shot by a file of soldiers, Claverhouse looking on and commanding. Enough will, however, remain, after every possible deduction, to stigmatize Claverhouse during this earlier part of his military career, as a fierce and savage officer; the ready executioner of the worst commands of his superiors, forgetting that no officer is morally justifiable in the execution of cruelty and oppression, however the commands of his superiors may be his warrant in an earthly court of justice: for the alternative of surrendering his commission being at all times in his power, he who voluntarily continues in a service where such things are exacted at his hand, cannot be judged otherwise than as one who prefers professional advancement and private interest to good faith, justice, and honour. But there are circumstances in

Grahame's subsequent conduct which have gilded over cruelties that, we shall presently shew, belonged as much to the age as to the man, and they have been glossed over, if not extenuated, by the closing scenes of his life.

During the general desertion of James II, Claverhouse, then Viscount of Dundee, remained inalienably firm to his benefactor. In his personal expenses he had been a rigid economist, but he was profuse of his fortune when it could aid the cause of his misguided prince. When James had disbanded his army, and was about to take the last and desperate step of leaving Britain, Claverhouse withstood it. He maintained, that the army, though disembodied, was not so dispersed but that they could be again assembled; and he offered to collect them under the king's standard, and to give battle to the Dutch.[1] Disappointed in this enterprize by the pusillanimity of the king, he did not desert his sinking cause. He fought his cause in the convention of estates in Scotland; and finally retreating to the Highlands, raised the clans in his defence. No name is yet so loved and venerated among the Highlanders as that of Dundee, and the influence which he had been able to acquire over the minds of this keen-spirited and aboriginal race is of itself sufficient to prove his talents. Sir John Dalrymple has idly represented him as studying their ancient poetry, and heating his enthusiasm with their ancient traditions. The truth is, that Dundee did not even understand their language, and never learned above a few words of it. His ascendancy over them was acquired by his superior talents and the art which he possessed of managing minds inferior to his own. He fell in the moment of a most decided victory, gained over troops superior to his own in number, in equipment, in military skill, in every thing but the valour and activity of the soldiers and the military talents of the general. Few men have left to posterity a character so strikingly varied. It is not shaded—it is not even chequered—it is on the one side purely heroic, on the other, cruel, savage and sanguinary. The old story of the gold and silver shield is but a type of the character of Claverhouse; and partizans on either side may assail or defend his character with as good faith as the knights in the fable. The minstrels have not been silent on the occasion, and the censure of the amiable Grahame may be well contrasted with the classical epitaph of Pitcairn.

Claverhouse is the only cavalier of importance upon whom our author has dwelt, though he has touched slightly on Sir John Dalzell

[1] See MacPherson's State Papers [reviewer].

and the Duke of Lauderdale. Among the Covenanters, the character of Balfour is most prominent. This man (for he actually existed) was a gentleman by birth, and brother-in-law to Hackstorne of Rathillet, an enthusiast of another and more unmixed mould. In point of religious observances he did not act up to the strictness of his sect, but he atoned for such negligence by his military enterprize and unsparing cruelty. This we learn from Howie, whose work we have already quoted; and at the same time we become acquainted with what the honest man considered as the criterion of a soldier of the Covenant.

'He joined with the more faithful part of our late sufferers, and although he was by some reckoned none of the most religious, yet he was always zealous and honest-hearted, courageous in every enterprize, and a brave soldier, *seldom any escaping that came in his hands.'—Scottish Worthies*, p. 563.

From another passage we gain something of his personal appearance, which seems to have been as unattractive as his proceedings were ruthless.

'At that meeting at Loudon Hill, dispersed May 5th, 1681, it is said that he disarmed one of Duke Hamilton's men with his own hand, taking a pair of fine pistols belonging to the duke from his saddle, telling him to tell his master, he would keep them till meeting. Afterwards, when the Duke asked his man, What he was like? he told him he was a little man, squint eyed, and of a very fierce aspect; the Duke said, he knew who it was, and withal prayed that he might never see his face, for if he should, he was sure he would not live long.'— *Ibidem.*

Burley appears to have been wounded in the battle of Bothwell Bridge, for he was heard to execrate the hand which had fired the shot. He fled to Holland, where his company was shunned by such of the Scottish fugitives as had their religious zeal qualified by moral considerations, and he was refused the communion by the Scottish congregation. He is said to have accompanied Argyle in his unfortunate attempt, along with one Fleming, also an assassin of the Archbishop. And finally, he joined the expedition of the Prince of Orange, but died before the disembarkation; an event to which Mr. Howie fondly ascribes the limitation of the revenge which would otherwise have been taken on the persecutors of the Lord's people and cause in Scotland.

'It is said he (Balfour) obtained liberty from the prince for that purpose, but died at sea before their arrival in Scotland. Whereby that design was never accomplished, and so the land was never purged by the blood of them who had shed innocent blood, according to the law of the Lord, Gen. ix. 6. *Whoso sheddeth man's blood, by man shall his blood be shed.'—Scottish Worthies, ibidem.*

It will hardly be alleged that our author has greatly misrepresented this singular character. On the contrary, he appears to have imputed to Burley, as the prime motive of his actions, a deep though regulated spirit of enthusiasm, which, from Howie's account, he seems not to have in reality possessed, and so far has rendered him more interesting and terrible, than if he had been painted as the thorough-going, bloody-minded ruffian, with little religion and less mercy, in which character he figures among the Scottish Worthies.

Admitting, however, that these portraits are sketched with spirit and effect, two questions arise of much more importance than any thing affecting the merits of the novels—namely, whether it is safe or prudent to imitate, in a fictitious narrative, and often with a view to a ludicrous effect, the scriptural style of the zealots of the seventeenth century; and secondly, whether the recusant presbyterians, collectively considered, do not carry too reverential and sacred a character to be treated by an unknown author with such insolent familiarity.

On the first subject, we frankly own we have great hesitation. It is scarcely possible to ascribe scriptural expressions to hypocritical or extravagant characters without some risk of mischief, because it will be apt to create an habitual association between the expression and the ludicrous manner in which it is used, unfavourable to the reverence due to the sacred text. And it is no defence to state that this is an error inherent in the plan of the novel. Bourdaloue, a great authority, extends this restriction still farther, and denounces all attempts to unmask hypocrisy by raillery, because in doing so the satirist is necessarily compelled to expose to ridicule the religious vizard of which he has divested him. Yet even against such authority it may be stated, that ridicule is the friend both of religion and virtue, when directed against those who assume their garb, whether from hypocrisy or fanaticism. The satire of Butler, not always decorous in these particulars, was yet eminently useful in stripping off their borrowed gravity and exposing to public ridicule the affected fanaticism of the times in which he lived. It may also be remembered, that in the days of Queen Anne a number of the Camisars or Huguenots of Dauphiné arrived as refugees in England, and became distinguished by the name of the French prophets. The fate of these enthusiasts in their own country had been somewhat similar to that of the Covenanters. Like them, they used to assemble in the mountains and desolate places, to the amount of many hundreds, in arms, and like them they were hunted and persecuted by the military. Like them, they were enthusiasts, though their enthusiasm assumed a character more decidedly absurd. The fugitive Camisars who came to London had convulsion-fits, prophesied, made converts, and attracted the public attention by an offer to raise the dead. The English minister, instead of fine and imprisonment and other inflictions which might have placed them in the rank and estimation of martyrs, and confirmed in their faith their numerous disciples, encouraged a dramatic author to bring out a farce on the subject which, though neither very witty nor very delicate, had the good effect of laughing the French prophets out of their audience and putting a stop to an inundation of nonsense which could not have failed to disgrace the age in which it appeared. The Camisars subsided into their ordinary vocation of psalmodic whiners, and no more was heard of their sect or their miracles. It would be well if all folly of the kind could be so easily quelled: for enthusiastic nonsense, whether of this day or of those which have passed away, has no more title to shelter itself under the veil of religion than a common pirate to be protected by the reverence due to an honoured and friendly flag.

Still, however, we must allow that there is great delicacy and hesitation to be used in employing the weapon of ridicule on any point connected with religion. Some passages occur in the work before us for which the writer's sole apology must be the uncontroulable disposition to indulge the peculiarity of his vein of humour—a temptation which even the saturnine John Knox was unable to resist either in narrating the martyrdom of his friend Wisheart or the assassination of his enemy Beatson, and in the impossibility of resisting which his learned and accurate biographer has rested his apology for this mixture of jest and earnest.

'There are writers,' he says, (rebutting the charge of Hume against Knox,) 'who can treat the most sacred subjects with a levity bordering on profanity. Must we at once pronounce them profane, and is nothing to be set down to the score of natural temper inclining them to wit and humour? The pleasantry which Knox has mingled with his narrative of his (Cardinal Beatson's) death and burial is unseasonable and unbecoming. But it is to be imputed not to any pleasure which he took in describing a bloody scene, but to the strong propensity which he had to indulge his vein of humour. Those who have read his history with attention must have perceived that he is not able to check this even on very serious occasions.'—*Macrie's Life of Knox*, p. 147.

Indeed Dr. Macrie himself has given us a striking instance of the indulgence which the Presbyterian clergy, even of the strictest persuasion, permit to the *vis comica*. After describing a polemical work as 'ingeniously constructed and occasionally enlivened with strokes of humour', he transfers, to embellish his own pages (for we can discover no purpose of edification which the tale serves,) a ludicrous parody made by an ignorant parish-priest on certain words of a Psalm, too sacred to be here quoted. Our own innocent pleasantry cannot, in this instance, be quite reconciled with that of the learned biographer of John Knox, but we can easily conceive that his authority may be regarded in Scotland as decisive of the extent to which a humourist may venture in exercising his wit upon scriptural expressions without incurring censure even from her most rigid divines.

It may however be a very different point how far the author is entitled to be acquitted upon the second point of indictment. To use too much freedom with things sacred is a course much more easily glossed over than that of exposing to ridicule the persons of any particular sect. Every one knows the reply of the great Prince of Condé to Louis XIV, when this monarch expressed his surprize at the clamour excited by Molière's Tartuffe, while a blasphemous farce called *Scaramouche Hermite* was performed without giving any scandal: 'C'est parceque Scaramouche ne jouoit que le ciel et la religion, dont les dévots se soucioient beaucoup moins que d'eux-mêmes.'[1] We believe, therefore, the best service we can do our author in the present case is to shew that the odious part of his satire applies only to that fierce and unreasonable set of extra-presbyterians, whose zeal, equally absurd and cruel, afforded pretexts for the severities inflicted on nonconformists without exception, and gave the greatest scandal and offence to the wise, sober, enlightened, and truly pious among the Presbyterians.

The principal difference betwixt the Cameronians and the rational presbyterians has been already touched upon. It may be summed in a very few words.

After the restoration of Charles II, episcopacy was restored in Scotland, upon the unanimous petition of the Scottish parliament. Had this been accompanied with a free toleration of the presbyterians, whose consciences preferred a different mode of church-government, we do not conceive there would have been any wrong done to that

---

[1] 'It's because *Scaramouche* only ridicules heaven and religion, about which the pious are much less concerned than about themselves.'

ancient kingdom. But instead of this, the most violent means of enforcing conformity were resorted to without scruple, and the ejected presbyterian clergy were persecuted by penal statutes and prohibited from the exercise of their ministry. These rigours only made the people more anxiously seek out and adhere to the silenced preachers. Driven from the churches, they held conventicles in houses. Expelled from cities and the mansions of men, they met on the hills and deserts like the French huguenots. Assailed with arms, they repelled force by force. The severity of the rulers, instigated by the episcopal clergy, increased with the obstinacy of the recusants, until the latter, in 1666, assumed arms for the purpose of asserting their right to worship God in their own way. They were defeated at Pentland; and in 1669 a gleam of common sense and justice seems to have beamed upon the Scottish councils of Charles. They granted what was called an *indulgence* (afterwards repeatedly renewed) to the presbyterian clergy, assigned them small stipends, and permitted them to preach in such deserted churches as should be assigned to them by the Scottish Privy Council. This 'indulgence', though clogged with harsh conditions and frequently renewed or capriciously recalled, was still an acceptable boon to the wiser and better part of the presbyterian clergy, who considered it as an opening to the exercise of their ministry under the lawful authority, which they continued to acknowledge. But fiercer and more intractable principles were evinced by the younger ministers of that persuasion. They considered the submitting to exercise their ministry under the controul of any visible authority as absolute erastianism, a desertion of the great invisible and divine Head of the church, and a line of conduct which could only be defended, says one of their tracts, by nullifidians, time-servers, infidels, or the Archbishop of Canterbury. They held up to ridicule and abhorrence such of their brethren as considered mere toleration as a boon worth accepting. Every thing, according to these fervent divines, which fell short of re-establishing presbytery as the sole and predominating religion, all that did not imply a full restoration of the Solemn League and Covenant, was an imperfect and unsound composition between God and mammon, episcopacy and prelacy. The following extracts from a printed sermon by one of them, on the subject of 'soul-confirmation', will at once exemplify the contempt and scorn with which these high-flyers regarded their more sober-minded brethren, and serve as a specimen of the homely eloquence with which they excited their followers. The reader will probably be of opinion that it is worthy of Kettledrummle himself, and will serve to clear Mr. Jedediah Cleishbotham of the charge of exaggeration.

'There is many folk that has a face to the religion that is in fashion, and there is many folk, they have ay a face to the old company, they have a face for godly folk, and they have a face for persecutors of godly folk, and they will be daddies bairns and minnies bairns both; they will be *prelates* bairns and they will be *malignants* bairns and they will be the people of God's bairns. And what think ye of that bastard temper? Poor Peter had a trial of this soupleness, but God made Paul an instrument to take him by the neck and shake it from him: And O that God would take us by the neck and shake our soupleness from us.

'Therefore you that keeps only your old job-trot, and does not mend your pace, you will not wone at *soul-confirmation*, there is a whine (i.e. *a few*) old job-trot, and does not mend your pace, you will not wone at *soul-confirmation*, there is a whine old job-trot ministers among us, a whine old job-trot professors, they have their own pace, and faster they will not go; O therefore they could never wine to *soul-confirmation* in the mettere of God. And our old job-trot ministers is turned *curates*, and our old job-trot professors is joined with them, and now this way God has turned them inside out, and has made it manifest and when their heart is hanging upon this braw, I will not give a grey groat for them and their profession both.

'The devil has the ministers and professors of Scotland, now in a sive, and O as he sifts, and O as he riddles, and O as he rattles, and O the chaff he gets; And I fear there be more chaff nor there be good corn, and that will be found among us or all be done: but the *soul-confirmed* man leaves ever the devil at two more, and he has ay the matter gadged, and leaves ay the devil in the lee side,—Sirs O work in the day of the cross.'

The more moderate presbyterian ministers saw with pain and resentment the lower part of their congregation, who had least to lose by taking desperate courses, withdrawn from their flocks, by their more zealous pretenders to purity of doctrine, while they themselves were held up to ridicule, old jog-trot professors and chaff-winnowed out and flung away by Satan. They charged the Cameronian preachers with leading the deluded multitude to slaughter at Bothwell, by prophesying a certainty of victory, and dissuading them from accepting the amnesty offered by Monmouth. 'All could not avail', says Mr. Law, himself a presbyterian minister, 'with M'Cargill, Kidd, Douglas, and other witless men amongst them, to hearken to any proposals of peace. Among others that Douglas, sitting on his horse, and preaching to the confused multitude, told them that they would come to terms with them, and like a drone was always droning on these terms with them: "they would give us a half Christ, but we will have a whole Christ," and such like impertinent speeches as these, good enough to feed those that are served with wind and not with the sincere milk of the word of God.' Law also censures these irritated and extravagant enthusiasts, not only for intending to overthrow the government, but as binding themselves to kill all that would not accede to their opinion, and he gives several instances of such cruelty being exercised by them, not only upon straggling soldiers whom they shot by the way or surprized in their quarters, but upon those who, having once joined them, had fallen away from their principles. Being asked why they committed these cruelties in cold blood, they answered, 'they were obliged to do it by their sacred bond.' Upon these occasions they practised great cruelties, mangling the bodies of their victims that each man might have his share of the guilt. In these cases the Cameronians imagined themselves the direct and inspired executioners of the vengeance of heaven. Nor did they lack the usual incentives of enthusiasm. Peden and others among them set up a claim to the gift of prophecy, though they seldom foretold any thing to the purpose. They detected witches, had bodily encounters with the enemy of mankind in his own shape, or could discover him as, lurking in the disguise of a raven, he inspired the rhetoric of a Quaker's meeting. In some cases, celestial guardians kept guard over their field-meetings. At a conventicle held on the Lomond-hills, the Rev. Mr. Blacader was credibly assured, under the hands of four honest men, that at the time the meeting was disturbed by the soldiers, some women who had remained at home, 'clearly perceived as the form of a tall man, majestic-like, stand in the air in stately posture with the one leg, as it were, advanced before the other, standing above the people all the time of the soldiers shooting.' Unluckily this great vision of the Guarded Mount did not conclude as might have been expected. The divine sentinel left his post too soon, and the troopers fell upon the rear of the audience, plundered and stripped many, and made eighteen prisoners.

But we have no delight to dwell either upon the atrocities or absurdities of a people whose ignorance and fanaticism were rendered frantic by persecution. It is enough for our present purpose to observe that the present Church of Scotland, which comprizes so much sound doctrine and learning, and has produced so many distinguished characters, is the legitimate representative of the indulged clergy of the days of Charles II settled however upon a comprehensive basis. That after the revolution, it should have succeeded episcopacy as the national religion, was natural and regular, because it possessed all the sense, learning, and moderation fit for such a change, and because among its followers were to be found the only men of property and influence who acknowledged presbytery. But the Cameronians continued long as a separate sect, though their preachers were bigoted and ignorant, and their hearers were gleaned out of the lower ranks of the peasantry. Their principle, so far as it was intelligible, asserted that paramount species of presbyterian church-government which was established in the year 1648, and they continued to regard the established church as erastian and time-serving, because they prudently remained silent upon certain abstract and delicate topics, where there might be some collision between the absolute liberty asserted by the church and the civil government of the state. The Cameronians, on the contrary, disowned all kings and government whatsoever, which should not take the Solemn League and Covenant; and long retained hopes of re-establishing that great national engagement, a bait which was held out to them by all those who wished to disturb the government during the reign of William and Anne, as is evident from the Memoirs of Ker of Kersland, and the Negotiations of Colonel Hooke with the jacobites and disaffected of the year.

A party so wild in their principles, so vague and inconsistent in their views, could not subsist long under a free and unlimited toleration. They continued to hold their preachings on the hills, but they lost much of their zeal when they were no longer liable to be disturbed by dragoons, sheriffs, and lieutenants of Militia.—The old fable of the Traveller's Cloak was in time verified, and the fierce sanguinary zealots of the days of Claverhouse sank into such quiet and peaceable enthusiasts as Howie of Lochgoin, or Old Mortality himself. It is, therefore, upon a race of sectaries who have long ceased to exist, that Mr. Jedediah Cleishbotham has charged all that is odious, and almost all that is ridiculous, in his fictitious narrative; and we can no more suppose any moderate presbyterian involved in the satire, than we should imagine that the character of Hampden stood committed by a little raillery on the person of Ludovic Claxton, the Muggletonian. If, however, there remain any of those sectaries who, confining the beams of the Gospel to the Goshen of their own obscure synagogue, and with James Mitchell, the intended assassin, giving their sweeping testimony against prelacy and popery, The Whole Duty of Man and bordles, promiscuous dancing and the Common Prayer-book, and all the other enormities and backslidings of the time, may perhaps be offended at this idle tale, we are afraid they will receive their answer in the tone of the revellers to Malvolio, who, it will be remembered, was something a kind of Puritan: 'Doest thou think because thou art virtuous, there shall be no more cakes and ale?—Aye, by Saint Anne, and ginger will be hot in the mouth too.'

We intended here to conclude this long article, when a strong report reached us of certain transatlantic confessions, which, if genuine, (though of this we know nothing,) assign a different author to these volumes, than the party suspected by our Scottish correspondents. Yet a critic may be excused seizing upon the nearest suspicious person, on the principle happily expressed by Claverhouse, in a letter to the Earl of Linlithgow. He had been, it seems, in search of a gifted weaver, who used to hold forth at conventicles: 'I sent to seek the webster, (weaver) they brought in his *brother* for him: though he maybe cannot preach like his brother, I doubt not but he is as well principled as he, wherefore I thought it would be no great fault to give him the trouble to go jail with the rest.'

18. Thomas Love Peacock in a serious mood

1818

Extracts from an article, 'An Essay on Fashionable Literature', by Peacock, written in 1818 but never published (taken from A. B. Young, 'T. L. Peacock's "Essay on Fashionable Literature"', *Notes and Queries*, II 2nd series (2 July 1910), 4-5, II 2nd series (23 July 1910), 62-63).

For a more humorous approach by Peacock, see No. 44.

Immediately before the first passage, Peacock has been discussing the instability of fashionable popularity.

Mr. Walter Scott seems an exception to this. Having long occupied the poetical throne, he seems indeed to have been deposed by Lord Byron, but he has risen with redoubled might as a novelist, and has thus continued from the publication of *The Lay of the Last Minstrel* the most popular writer of his time—perhaps the most universally successful in his own day of any writer that ever lived. He has the rare talent of pleasing all ranks and classes of men, from the peer to the peasant, and all orders and degrees of mind, from the philosopher to the man-milliner 'of whom nine make a taylor'. On the arrival of *Rob Roy*, as formerly on that of *Marmion*, the scholar lays aside his Plato, the statesman suspends his calculations, the young lady deserts her hoop, the critic smiles as he trims his lamp, thanking God for his good fortune, and the weary artisan resigns his sleep for the refreshment of the magic page. . . .

. . . Cervantes—Rabelais—Swift—Voltaire—Fielding—have led fancy against opinion with a success that no other names can parallel. Works of mere amusement that treat nothing may have an accidental and transient success, but cannot, of course, have influence in their own times, and will certainly not pass to posterity. Mr. Scott's success has been attributed, in a great measure, to his keeping clear of opinion.

But he is far from being a writer who teaches nothing. On the contrary, he communicates fresh and valuable information. He is the historian of a peculiar and minute class of our own countrymen who, within a few years, have completely passed away. He offers materials to the philosopher in depicting, with the truth of life, the features of human nature in a peculiar state of society before comparatively little known.

ROB ROY

1818

---

19. Unsigned review, *European Magazine*

February 1818, lxxiii, 137-39

Although we opened these volumes with strong anticipations of pleasure, we did not calculate upon reading it twice; first, because we could not help it; and secondly because, having satisfied the childish impatience excited by the fable, we wished to examine at our leisure the dramatis personæ. The result of our comparisons is highly favourable to *Rob Roy*; for although Meg Merrilies and Edie Ochiltree are still unrivalled as single portraits, there will be found in the present Work a richer variety of figures than have been exhibited on the same canvass within the last half century. The scene is laid in the early part of the reign of George the First, a few months previous to the insurrection of the Highlanders in 1715. By this felicitous choice of his subject, the author has ample scope for those picturesque descriptions so congenial to his talents; and, quitting altogether the level line of ordinary life, he is at liberty to introduce a series of eccentric personages, who in any other situation would almost appear to outstep the modesty of nature. These personages are, with scarcely one exception, invested with the attraction of strongly marked individuality: from the formal arithmetical Owen to the jovial Justice; from the conceited shrewd Andrew Fairservice to the bold unconquerable MacGregor; from the comfortable, self-complacent, thrifty, yet kind-hearted Baillie, Nicol Jervie, to the vindictive Helen, or the high-spirited romantic Diana Vernon; all are sketched by the hand of a master at once exact and bold, possessing a vigorous imagination, an observant eye, and an almost unlimited invention. If there be one character less discriminated, it is that of the hero Francis Osbaldistone, but the deficiency is disguised by his telling his own story; a task which he performs with such admirable address, that it is impossible to lose sight of him for a single

146

moment. This interesting narrative might, however, be comprised in a brief argument. Francis Osbaldistone, a young man of a poetical taste, offends his father, a wealthy merchant, by refusing to become his partner, and, as a consequence of his delinquency, is exiled to the seat of his ancestors in Northumberland, and associated with a family of Jacobites and Papists; till, from the treachery of one of them, he is induced to visit Scotland, where, as might be expected, he meets with many strange adventures. There are many striking scenes in this work which are worthy of graphic illustration. The introduction of the hero to Sir Hildebrand and his rustic sons—the evening colloquy with sly Andrew Fairservice—the meeting between Campbell and Morris at Justice Inglewood's—the exquisite description of the cathedral at Glasgow—the scene in the subterraneous aisle—the rencontre on the Brigg—the recognition of MacGregor and Jervie in the prison—the battle of the inn at Aberfoil—and, neither last nor least, the sudden apparition of Helen Campbell to the military invaders of the Glen.

[a quotation from chapter 30 'We approached' to 'hung suspended by the loins' is omitted]

20. E. T. Channing, *North American Review*

July 1818, vii, 149–84

Edward Tyrrell Channing was editor of the *North American Review* at the time of the review and was later a professor at Harvard.

It is not possible that the fame or attraction of these writings should be increased, by fixing them upon any living author,—there is no living author, who would not add to his celebrity by owning them. If the writer, however, chooses to hide himself and 'feed unenvied' upon his glory, it is his own affair—we wish for his name, merely that we may refer to him more conveniently.

Some of his tales are admirable histories of Scotland, all of them lie chiefly there, and most of the characters are natives. His own country is the home and school of his genius—it is familiar to him, and thus, as the scene of his stories, it gives them an air of easy reality. He found it a new and unexhausted country in fiction, at least for his purposes; on all sides there was a boundless variety and striking distinctness in the face of the earth, the modes of life and the character of man, and just such a union of the chivalrous and wild with the later habits of a busier and more worldly race, as would enable him to be at once a poet and a practical, philosophical observer.

We have here his fifth tale, founded upon Scottish character, manners, antiquities and scenery. Like the others, it is supported in some measure by fact, and all are faithful sketches of society and nature at different periods. They have the truth, without the formality and limitations of history, for men here are grouped and at work, very much as they are in life; society never stands still and is never lost sight of, that battles may be fought or great men display themselves,— the anvil is ringing, as well that the poor traveller's beast may not go unshod, as that the soldier may be equipped, who is to fight for a realm.—It was said anciently of the Greek tragedies, that they were wholly 'of kings and princes, of rich or ambitious personages;—you never see a poor man have a part, unless it be as a chorus, or to fill up the scenes, to dance or to be derided.' There is a livelier and juster diversity in the views of things presented here. We are not kept forever upon the high grounds of life, and oppressed with the solemn air and motion, the perpetual stateliness of leading characters. There are cottages and workshops on the slopes and in the vallies, and beings in sight there, who are the secret strength and life of society,—the unobtrusive, poor and labouring have a place here, as important as that which they fill in the real world. And besides this natural mixture and diversity of classes, each individual is suffered to lay open his whole mind; there is no attempt to give an artificial unity and condensation to the character, by placing him under one set of influences only, and thus forcing him to exhibit the workings of a single feeling, and all for the sake of producing a violent effect on us. He is here allowed to be affected naturally by every thing he encounters in the common course of things; and the principle, that gives the character its form in one place, may change it a little with the change of circumstances.

The author seems to be at home every where, and know every thing. His knowledge, however, has not the air of learning, amassed to be told; it is something gathered incidentally, whilst he was studying men in their pursuits, customs and amusements,—something fallen in with rather than sought. The commonest things, the lowest characters belong to the action,—it rarely stands still for the sake of description. You are in the midst of life, gaining knowledge as well as entertainment, by a process akin to actual experience and observation. Every man is in his proper situation, and suitable discourse is put into his mouth,—we have the peculiarities of his gait, the expression of his face, the tone of his voice, every thing, in short, which is significant of character, or that adds to its reality;—and these are not given once for all in a formal description, but they come out in connexion with his feelings, situation or employment, and vary with them. He is allowed to unfold himself, to practise upon others, to utter fine thoughts or foolish ones, and betray all his infirmities and motives and every influence that presses on him, without the dread that he is destined for a book and therefore upon his good behaviour. The author is extremely generous to his characters. He is never afraid of them, or anxious to give you a full preparatory account of them, to excite your interest, or save you from mistakes. If a man has any individuality, he is sure to have fair play; and it is more than probable that you will at first be told, merely how he is regarded by people about him; and if you receive a wrong impression, you may correct it as you go along, just as you are set right in the living world. The profusion and huddle of characters and interests make no disturbance and jostling, which are not sufficiently balanced. It is but setting powers against each other, so as to keep up a perpetual agitation.

If we come to his descriptions of nature, we find there a presence, a visibility, that sets us in the midst of things. He unfolds the region about him freely and easily, as creation is revealed in the sunshine,— by a full and yet noiseless disclosure;—nothing is displaced; the forms and relations of objects are undisturbed, and the light, in which they rest, gives perfect harmony. The facility and vividness of his descriptions shew that his heart is open to beauty and truth, and that he conveys the simple impression he has received. He is abroad for his own exhilaration, and the healthful exercise of his mind in minute, distinguishing observation; and in all his pictures, there is a cordial exposure of beauty, reality, perfect life, as if the communication of his enjoyment made a part of it.

He does not always depend for the effect of his painting, upon the enumeration of particulars or a broad, complete presentment of things; but a great deal upon your interest in the action and characters that are introduced. He knows that the mind once kindled, will throw light all around it. You feel an interest in the place by your interest in what is passing there—you perceive a union between the action and the scene, so that a hint, a word is enough to open the whole upon you— you are made happy by finishing the picture yourself, and in the process, you are visited by old recollections and associations, till the prospect grows as familiar as home. His most scattered and irregular description, coming in here and there in the midst of a wild and hurried narrative,—such as Waverley's night adventure on the heath, after his rescue,—has kept its hold on the memory, while others, more compact and finished, but less essential to the action, have faded. It may be well, some time after reading these works, when the excitement is gone, but the impression is unworn, to turn back to passages which interested us the most, and chiefly for description, and see how much their effect was owing to the excited state of the mind, to the watchful notice it took and the wide use it made of the smallest hints. We almost wonder on a second, cooler reading, that the effect should have been so powerful, and the scene so full and distinct.—And if we may judge from our own feelings, as distinct views are received from his light and rapid touches, some little intimations which make the mind busy in its own way, as from his more laboured pictures, which he sometimes draws as if for the mere pleasure they give him, and in looking at which we are obliged to follow him step by step, and observe the parts till we sometimes almost fail of a whole. He shews every where the greatest delicacy of feeling and observation, in the selection of some little picturesque circumstance, to suggest and illuminate every thing else, to provoke our imaginations to independent action and perception, and thus give a vivid reality to things. And we all know that trifles enter as largely into our poetical as our every-day happiness,—the imagination and affections attach themselves to the smallest things, and are carried by them into endless and ever-varying creations.

We may also remark his peculiar way of bringing us acquainted gradually with some new region, where we are to stay awhile. He conducts us, from time to time, as events may require, from one apartment to another or to new views of the same building, or to some unnoticed opening into the hills, or creek or cavern that lay hid in the windings of the shore. We feel the changes of season, and of day and night in their effect upon the prospect. The weary heath and moors sink us into 'endless reverie', and our spirits are brisk as we come upon the heights. We carry from description like this, feelings that spring from beholding the world, rather than reading of it.

The author notices and preserves with perfect facility, all the connexions between the small and vast, the ludicrous and awful, the melancholy and thoughtless, which nature herself has ordained. And when he makes use of contrast,—and he certainly makes a most powerful one,—it is never or rarely brought in violently, but in the same easy way with the diversities and irregularities, that enter into and enliven the established order of the world. Sometimes,—when we are absorbed by a picturesque or dramatic scene, and our curiosity and anxiety are so balanced that we can hardly turn over the leaf,—we meet with characters of a very different complexion from all which has wrought upon us so powerfully; and they will be sure to enter at once into affairs in their own way, even at the risk of disturbing our rapture;—but we never imagine that they were brought there to produce the effect of forced contrast, of violent transition,—they are in their places and talk and act as they should, sustaining relations to everything about them, and obeying influences which perhaps they never think of. This natural contrast is observed every where in some shape or other, giving at one time a refreshing, at others an oppressive distinctness to objects, or presenting them in various lights and connexions, always deepening the interest which it threatens to thwart or divert. We need not admonish any reader, that Edie's gamesomeness in the storm and Elspeth's pledge at the funeral, enter, more than words can well express, into the incommunicable feelings which both those scenes leave in the heart. No one, who remembers the maniac Balfour in his fearful retreat, has forgotten the little light-footed guide that conducted Henry Morton thither 'in the grey of the morning'.

And tenderness too is brought in, in the same vivid way, softening the harsher features of characters and actions, shedding all around the most assuasive influence, and yet possessing dignity and power in the midst of hard-wrung tears and sad remembrances. It is as the morning mist that hangs thinly on the cliff, or as the hush, the pause in the tempest. When Meg is conducting Bertram and Dinmont to the cavern on the sea-shore, at the moment when the scattered interests of the story are all thronging together, and she feels that the uses of life are nearly ended with her, an air of decay, of decline,—without the least of imbecility,—seems to pass over the grandeur and stern irregularity of her mind. 'She moved up the brook, until she came to the ruined hamlet, where, pausing with a look of peculiar and softened interest before one of the gables which was still standing, she said in a tone less abrupt, though as solemn as before, "Do you see that blackened and broken end of a sheeling?—there my kettle boiled for forty years—there I bore twelve buirdly sons and daughters—where are they now?—where are the leaves that were on that auld ash-tree at Martinmas?—the west wind has made it bare, and I'm stripped too. Do you see that saugh tree?—it's but a blackened rotten stump now—I've sate under it mony a bonny summer afternoon when it hung its gay garlands ower the poppling water. I've sate there, and," elevating her voice, "I've held you on my knee, Henry Bertram, and sung ye sangs of the old barons and their bloody wars. It will ne'er be green again, and Meg Merrillies will never sing blithe sangs mair." '

We may call these works novels, or what we please,—they are after all nothing but views of the real world, given by a man who observes it widely, justly and feelingly, and passes by nothing however low, and shrinks from nothing however terrible, which God has placed here as a part of his system. The earth is large enough for the safe expansion and action of all minds however opposite, and he delights to contemplate the workings, and see the same principles struggling or playing freely in the various conditions of life, differently combined indeed and receiving different shades and modifications, according to the diversity of influences which help to make the character, and yet all betraying the universal alliance of man. With all the strangeness of his personages, the violence of the life he describes, and the local air of his sketches, his genius is still spread out over the earth,—'one touch of nature makes the whole world kin,'—hardly a feeling or motive is given, but we all own it, or a course of action detailed, but it has authority apart from its historical truth. It is the truth more than the marvellous, that affects us in his most fearful sketches of an erring mind, self-persuaded of its supernatural power, and acquiring, from this very conviction, an energy and over-awing influence which help it in some degree to fulfil the destinies it unrols. It is the same truth that touches us, when he presents the mysterious creations of 'the sleeping fancy', and especially the whimsical forms that crowd upon the mind just as it dawns from sleep, and the senses are faintly affected by outward objects. In the same spirit is the description of the almost visionary returns of memory, 'the dreams of early and shadowy recollections', which broke upon young Bertram, as he was walking unconsciously among the scenes of his infancy. The author is always teaching us a large philosophy in the midst of visible scenes and living beings.

The imagination is never straitened by the perpetual reality of things, nor does it lose itself in endless and vain illusions,—its excitement and adventures here are spontaneous and begin in truth, and have warmth, support and reach, yielding us always an untreacherous satisfaction, and the most wholesome practical influences. The earth is no longer a mere clod, of uneven surface, fertile mould and varied colour,—it acquires a new and moral interest by its power of carrying us to something higher, and leading us to connect all that we behold here with our own minds and with God.—The romantic and poetical, both in the human character and the world which helps to form it, are naturally blended,—no man will be made an idle visionary by the union between life and poetry in these works, for it is just such a union as is established by nature, and admirably fitted to open the whole mind and harmonize the character of such a being as man, with powers so various, but all given for his happiness and perfection, and naturally tending thither, and yet in danger of subjection to the lowest and most narrowing influences of this mixed world.

It was not to be expected that a writer should observe so minutely and justly, without investing objects with something of his own,— the imagination cannot be so busy, and the heart unmoved. But he does not visit the world with a diseased heart, and discolour its beauties, and turn them to false uses. 'His mind apprehends objects and occurrences in their reality, and yet communicates to them a tincture of its own colouring and tone.' And this is the way with all men who have sympathy with creation. He who observes and paints truly, must make his feelings, his delight a part of the picture, and there will be an exquisite accordance between what flows from himself and what he borrows from nature. And the reader of a kindred mind will trust more warmly in the truth of descriptions, which, besides presenting colour, situation and form, express distinctly his own secret though undefined feelings, in the prospect of like beauties, and thus interpret, as it were, his own heart.

With his love of the picturesque and romantic, the author unites a singular intimacy with men in the practical, common pursuits. There are very few economists or observers, who can talk more sagaciously of mere business and calculation, or send a young man into life with safer rules of conduct, or determine more accurately the influence of occupation, accident and every outward circumstance upon character and happiness. So far from disdaining our regular society, he is sometimes in the midst of us, perfectly familiar with citizens and affairs, and the tradeful stir and habits of the town. Only give him strong character, and the free expression of it,—and he will be sure to observe and make something of it, whether it be found in the city or mountains. But he feels, and with reason, that in populous settle-ments, every thing is under cultivation, and tending too much to assimilation and consequent lassitude. He is weary and impatient there, —he cannot tolerate the shifting, arbitrary fashions of artificial life, the formalities and observances, which shew the condition of society more than the elements of character, what is accidental rather than what is essential, the present and fleeting, not the universal and ever-lasting in man. When he talks of mere ladies and gentlemen, and makes them witty, or puts them in love, it is hard to say which is most to be pitied,—he or they. The amiable and generous feelings are seldom and but poorly delineated in the merely domestic, industrious and cultivated,—they are reserved for beings formed upon a larger scale and of rougher and harder materials; and in them these qualities are certainly exhibited to greater advantage, partly from their relation to the rest of the character, and partly from their possessing an originality and distinctness, and expressing themselves with a fervour and reckless vehemence, which are not quite so observable in more educated virtue.

He does not carry us into the wilderness of life, merely because it is new and attractive,—he there finds man in harmony with the land-scape, and at home, in the presence of objects that were about him in infancy, which have grown into his soul, and are now secretly incorporated with all he feels of pride and sorrow and happiness. 'The heather that I have trod upon when living, must bloom ower me when I am dead—my heart would sink, and my arm would shrink and wither like fern in the frost, were I to lose sight of my native hills; nor has the world a scene that would console me for the loss of the rocks and cairns, wild as they are, that you see around us.' In such a region, we are put upon a fresh study of real, though it may be daring and impetuous character; if we are moved violently, we are yet purified and invigorated, and rescued from utter slavery to the habits and tone of subdued society.

We hope no one will find fault with the author's vagabond charac-ters, for their presumption in exhibiting sentiments and actions wholly incompatible with their condition. We should be sorry to think that the humour, poetry, sagacity, high feeling and roguish propensities of the Beggar, were not the fair result of his way of life acting upon a neglected but gifted mind. The school of the world, we must remember, is free and generous, and has little system. It will indeed be sure to mould the character in some way or other,—but a man, who is wholly bare to its influences, will generally be formed by those which best suit his genius and natural tendencies; he will find enough on every side to expand and invigorate his whole mind, and the result, however unfit for a useful life, may be magnificent beyond all that teaching could effect.

The author has his faults,—he must needs illustrate in himself the mixture of imperfection which he observes in every thing about him. But we can say of him, and it will hold true of every man of genius, that his failures are not to be found where his mind is most kindled. So long as he is given up to his subject, he is sustained and unerring; but he fails, the very moment he begins to talk or trifle *confidentially* with the reader, or to display superfluously in himself the humour or drollery, which comes so admirably from his characters,—the very moment he forsakes invention and precipitates the story, by adopting the common artifices of relieving a hero, or lifting instead of attending him into new situations. But his failures often give us breathing time after excitement, and when he is ready, he falls into the natural course of things as easily as he deserted it.

Objections are made to the similarity that runs through all his works. Different persons resort perpetually to the same attitudes and motions, to shew their feelings to advantage, or to make their follies or infirmities more ludicrous. Majestic forms are placed again and again in the same commanding situations. Helen Campbell on the summit of the rock has no doubt brought to many a mind the Gipsey on the high bank that overhung the road, and the Gipsey perhaps has recalled the warriors on the turrets in the opening of *Marmion*. The situation is fine and never to be forgotten, especially in connexion with such beings,—and yet men, trees, steeples and chimnies may be seen almost every day, with the same advantage of light, effect of elevation and distinctness of outline.

But readers, who can perceive prominent resemblances, may not so readily detect minute discriminations, or probably we should not have heard quite so much about the sameness of his characters. He is not only rebuked for his attachment to gypsies, beggars, smugglers, &c. as Shakespeare will soon be for his clowns, constables, witches and grave-diggers,—(for the vulgar and vicious are to be outlaws in fiction, however privileged in life,) but, what is worse, his low characters are thrown together as copies of each other, and his offence of borrowing from himself is set down in the same easy way, in which Miss Burney has been reproved for her everlasting Mr. Dubster, Mrs. Mittin, and other small teasing creatures, which, because she had done well with them once, she thought proper to introduce forever after. It may be that Meg, Elspeth, Edie and Mause are one and the same person, with only a slight change in circumstances, and so of Callum Beg, Dougal and others. Our friend Dandie Dinmont, the shrewd, resolute, free hearted Borderer, may be of the same family with Cuddie Headrigg, that inimitable compound of good-nature, timidity, selfish cunning and utter worldliness;—and the kindred will probably be extended now to Mr. Andrew Fairservice. And we know not what objection there is to following the same character into different situations, allowing that it is variously and brightly developed. But we have not perceived this offensive sameness in the characters,—

some of those, which have been thus strangely huddled together, are so broadly and essentially different, that it was mortifying to see the comparison made; and the rest appear to be as distinct and individual, as we should expect of men in similar pursuits and condition in life, where there is no attempt to give them exaggerated and even violent peculiarities, for the sake of effect. The great question is, are you willing to have such persons introduced?—and if so, will you consent to observe nice shades of character in the vulgar and wicked, and can you relish romantic feeling and a highly poetical language in men and women who are little better, after all, than rogues? If you are not disposed to do and enjoy this, you are merely narrowing your field of observation, and with it your pleasures, and no doubt your own minds too.—One word more of the supposed sameness in the author's low characters,—they all have a strong *nationality*, very different from our own, and with which we are but little acquainted. It may be then, that the traits which belong to all impress us so strongly, that we pay less attention to individual differences than we should do in our own country, where, as the *nationality* is shared by all and observed by none, the study of character is confined to individual peculiarities.

In *Rob Roy*, we are not so much struck with the want of freshness, as with the imperfect execution, if not conception. In the other tales, there are great defects in the story, but there is little or no anxiety to interest you in it,—the present scene is enough, the characters have sufficiently strong motives for what they do; and so long as your attention is engrossed, and those in whom you are most interested are suitably disposed of, it is of very little importance that the events are sometimes clumsily woven together, and still less, whether the hero and his mistress are married at the end of the book or not. In fact, we would rather hear no more of them, than be called to witness the great stir at the close, merely to make people happy, whom we thought very little of in the course of the story. In the present work, however, there is a great attempt to make an interesting fable. Characters are brought forward, and sketched finely, and undertake a great deal and do little or nothing. The reader's curiosity is perpetually awakened by doubtful intimations, and he is extremely busy and ingenious to look into the mysteries of character and the bearings of plots, and after all he finds that very little was intended or at least accomplished, but an unfair excitement and baffling of his acuteness and eagerness. The story is in mist throughout, lest it should be seen through too soon and too easily; and devices the most awkward are

resorted to, to keep it in motion, when it threatens to come suddenly
to a close. There is everywhere a want of object, of something about
which these restless agents may revolve, and which may give meaning
and consequence to the preparations which are going on. There is no
commanding spirit here, whose presence is felt the moment he appears,
not because his purposes are seen through, but from some nameless
influence, which touches us as if we were by, and saw everything, and
had something to do or suffer with the rest. In parts, there is a great
hurry and sudden shifting of scenes, arising from impatience, not from
the bustle or thickening interest of the story. In other places, there is a
dead pause for the hero to talk needlessly of himself, or to make
explanations, and stand in the way of other people and of animated
conversation. And even his explanations are lame,—he evidently
wants information of what is going on at a distance, so that matters,
which ought to be important, are left in obscurity. We do not carry
from this tale the distinct remembrance of everything, which is left
by the others. And yet *Rob Roy*, though it have faults enough to put
any other man in peril, has beauties with them that might make any
other man immortal.

In the opening, we are made acquainted with the hero's father, a
London merchant, who does very little for the story but set it a-going;
the author however is prodigal of his genius, and has given a sketch
of this man which has great truth and spirit. The hero is nothing, unless
you will take him for a satire personified upon the whole class. And
we may say this of his brethren in the other tales. They are the only
persons that the author labours to make something of, as if in pity for
their incapacity, and they are the only indifferent beings that he has
any concern with. You would never think of Frank Osbaldistone,
were he not kindly telling the story, or sometimes teasing you by his
insignificant interference with actions and characters that are wholly
beyond him. But his father, who lives in a counting-house, and goes
once to Holland upon a matter of no importance to any one but the
Company, is never forgotten. Most writers would have fastened him
upon us as an excellent moral lesson, and told us of his good habits
and hours, and of his stern integrity,—in short, made him a very
Thorowgood. Our author does as well, not by making us own that
indeed the man led an honest life, but by exciting a deep respect for the
principles and views of the merchant, and leading us to conclude the
inevitable virtue and consistency of his actions, without enumerating
them. He carries us into the man's mind by every thing which is related

of his conduct or appearance, till we think a great deal more about his character than his particular pursuits, and are satisfied what would be his behaviour, if, instead of merchandise, he had turned to any other profession, or been cast in a different situation.

Frank was a little too romantic for trade, and his father sufficiently self-willed not to humour his boy. Owen, the head clerk,—a character made up of simplicity, affectionateness and the ledger,—does all he can to effect a reconciliation, but in vain; and accordingly our hero is sent to Northumberland to cure his folly, by fair experience of the life, which country gentlemen lead. We feel the author very sensibly in the course of Frank's journey, but we pass over Mr. Morris with his portmanteau, and the Landlord's sunday dinner to his guests, as we probably shall many other scenes as admirable in their way, merely because it is too late in the day to give them at full. We wish, however, that Rob Roy had sustained throughout, all the interest which he excites as plain Mr. Campbell, the Scotch dealer in cattle. His character is more poetical in the highlands, but less peculiar, though we would not intimate that there is in it the slightest incongruity.

Frank was now on his first visit to Osbaldistone Hall in Northumberland, the abode of his ancestors, and in the possession of his uncle, Sir Hildebrand. As he approached, he heard the sounds of the chase, and began to revolve the sad time he should have in a family of mere sportsmen.

[plot summary is omitted, as well as the following quotations: chapter 5 'A vision' to 'unexpected appearance', and 'I observed them both look' to 'poor kinswoman', and ' "But here we are" ' to 'piercing hazel eyes', and 'I called' to 'my six cousins and my uncle']

There are characters however to redeem the Northumbrian family, and which owe some of their effect to the strange group and the fine old castle, in which they are introduced. Die Vernon is not only very unlike, and very far beyond the cultivated females of the other stories, but our favourite among all the romantic heroines we have yet encountered. She is just such a civilized woman as the author might be expected to sketch successfully.—Her form and disposition begin to open upon us, the moment she appears, and the imagination is never fairly rid of the beautiful vision,—old Owen Feltham would have said of her, 'she hangs upon all the retirements of a man like a perpetual enchantment.' Her beauty is not 'inventoried', as Olivia would have it, but comes out, as does her character, by degrees and always in connexion with something she feels or utters,—her mind appears to have formed her countenance and figure, as if to give itself a full, visible expression. We almost hear the tones of her voice; and when she pours out her indignation, enthusiasm or devotedness, we see the attitude and action, perfectly natural, unconfined, unthought of—it is 'beauty in the act of expanding into grandeur'. A perpetual grace, lightness and over-frankness of feeling and manner, are united with the delicacy and dignity of an innocent and exalted spirit. There is nothing conventional about her; she has known little of polished life or feminine sympathy. 'I would fain,—she says,—have the freedom of wild heath and open air with the other commoners of nature'—and she seems indeed to have grown up with the wild plants around her, and to have been formed by the free, kind, adorning touches of nature. But beneath her intrepidity and independence, there is a soothing tenderness, a quiet not enfeebling sadness, which soften and ripen the whole character, and give it an air the most exquisitely feminine.

Her cousin Rashleigh, Sir Hildebrand's youngest son, is not so original a being as Diana, nor quite so original as the author would have him, though unlike every thing at the Hall. He is of a hideous mind and person, but with nothing vulgar in the deformity of either. Once seen, he is fatally fastened upon the memory forever. He seems to fight against his personal defects in spite as much as ambition, while every mischievous and ferocious principle within him is nourished and kept in sound health and action, but all controlled by art and caution. He inspires at once dread and disgust, and these are not lessened, we suspect, by the rich tones of his voice, and the gentle but full flow of his conversation.

The strange darkness which hangs over the purposes of Rashleigh and the situation of Diana, is favourable to the effect of that part of the work in which they are chiefly concerned. For all that the reader knows, there may something come of this fine opening—and when we learn at the close, that Rashleigh has only been working some indistinct mischief at a distance, and that Diana, in the good old-fashioned way, has renounced every thing we cared for, for the sake of a lover, our only consolation is to go back to the time, when she was 'the heath-bell of Cheviot and the blossom of the border'. Her character was formed then in her utterly unprotected state,—professing a persecuted faith, doomed to a convent, or to be the wife of one of her scorned cousins, her father under sentence of death living in disguise beneath the same roof, and the secret known only to Rashleigh. And what were the relations between this man and herself?

[a quotation from chapter 13 ' "Let me know" ' to ' "this accomplished villain" ' is omitted]

With this extract we take leave of Die Vernon. We regard that part of the book, which belongs to her, as a precious fragment, and unlike all that has come from the same hand. Every event is plainly designed for her and has but slender intimacy with any thing hereafter. There is nothing disturbing in the narrative—and very little variety of interest, but always a beautiful transparency and flow in the style, and great spirit in the conversation. The most bustling scene is at Justice Inglewood's, where the author brings together, in his peculiar way, a variety of characters, that he may set them against each other and observe the contrasts, and the influence which men unconsciously exert in bringing each other out.

[plot summary and a quotation from chapter 6 'I hae been flitting' to 'her ain private supper' are omitted. The political machinations are said to be 'a dim, clumsy affair' and Andrew Fairservice is described as 'very diverting and vexatious']

Frank applied to him for a guide to Glasgow, whereupon Andrew, who knew as well as any one how to 'cuitle up the daft young English Squire', offered his own services, and after a journey, distinguished chiefly from the beginning by Mr. Fairservice's knavery, the travellers reach Glasgow on Sunday. They follow the crowd to the cathedral, which, with the grave yard, and the congregation in the sepulchral church, is described with singular distinctness and simplicity. The whole scene is perfectly new to us, and the effect throughout is to inspire a still religious awe, and to recal a thousand early remembrances of Sabbath-days, and unfilled graves. A voice in the crowd whispers Frank to be on the bridge at midnight, and we are soon brought to one of the finest night scenes in a city that we can recollect. There is no vulgar terror here, nothing overdone for effect,—the growing stillness and desertion of the streets, the dim melancholy grandeur of the river and arches are enough of themselves to inspire deep and sad thought. The meeting of Frank and the stranger, their walk through the city to the prison, the chilling allusions of the outlaw to the risk he now encounters for his young companion, are all in the same spirit. And the half-savage joy, idolatry and alarm of Dougal the turnkey, when he recognizes in the stranger and at such a place, his own proscribed leader, serve but to heighten the effect of this perfectly simple and awful scene.—Frank finds Owen in the jail, where he had been cast on his arrival, by some ungrateful Scotch correspondents, who had claims against the House, but no mercy for its present embarrassments. Explanations and sympathy follow of course, and are soon interrupted, to our great satisfaction and the alarm of the intruders, by the arrival and bustling entrance of Baillie Nicol Jarvie, another correspondent of quite an opposite character. And once for all, we must say of Mr. Jarvie, that he is our chief delight among the men. He is an easy, knowing man, of a very ancient school, we should think, not perfectly original, and yet not the less agreeable for that. His prejudices, old proverbs, magisterial airs and commercial habits mix in so naturally with his vanity, benevolence, and blunt good nature, that they all appear to have been born with him. He is sagacious and often discreet, and has a very suitable love of life and comfort; but with these he has a great share of natural intrepidity and self-esteem, and he is excessively fond of hearing himself talk, let the hazard be what it may. 'I trow I hae a Scotch tongue in my head—if they speak, I'se answer.' And it is delightful to hear him talk. Every thing is entertaining when he is by, and the author has dealt liberally with him, as he does with all his favourites.

[plot summary is omitted, as well as the following quotations: chapter 23 'The first whom he approached' to ' "disposed to be seen" ', and ' "I tell you Robin" ' to ' "Sunday or Saturday" '; chapter 26 ' "The times came hard" ' to ' "became a broken man" ']

We shall now follow the Baillie, Frank and Andrew Fairservice to the Highlands. If the author is ever more successful in one kind of description than another, we suspect it is when he describes heaths, and low, swampy regions, that are desolate and yet tame.

[plot summary is omitted, as well as the following quotations: chapter 27 'The road which we travelled' to 'peasweep and whaup'; chapter 28 'The interior presented' to 'their scabbards'; chapter 30 'I shall never forget' to ' "what we'll land in" '. The reviewer praises the scene at the Inn of Aberfoil and the march to the ambush that followed]

Dougal carried the party to a pass where a fatal contest with some of Rob's followers was inevitable, and in the confusion of the battle he crept into a thicket and Frank after him, leaving the Baillie and Andrew to provide for themselves. We have pitied the honest Baillie all along, for being plunged into such irregular and perilous life; and we confess, we could scarcely laugh, when we saw him dangling in mid air from a thorn branch, which caught him in his flight as he was stepping from one rock to another. It was much more diverting to see Andrew on the top of a cliff, fully possessed that he was in the midst of danger, and capering and writhing to avoid the balls, which he conceived to be whistling around him.

Helen Campbell, Rob's wife, was at the head of the Highland party—an injured, fierce, iron-hearted woman, presented in majestic attitudes, and rarely speaking but in wrath, indignation or anguish. Her character is overdone and, we should think, fails of the effect intended. She has very little to do, but the author has connected with her one of his most awful scenes.

[plot summary and a quotation from chapter 31 'The wife of MacGregor' to 'the sum of human existence' are omitted]

After the blood has curdled at this, it is quite restoring to hear from Mad. de Stael, that 'the love of life appears to man the most ridiculous and the most vulgar of feelings; and the laughter, which seizes upon mortal beings, when contemplating the object of one of their fellow-mortals, suffering under the apprehension of death, must be confessed to be a noble attribute of the human understanding.'

We have next a fruitless negotiation between Frank, on the part of Helen, and the commander of the enemy, for Rob's freedom. Accordingly, Rob takes his escape upon himself, though he was to hang next morning and was surrounded by guards. He effects his object as the party is crossing the Forth at sunset; and the attempts to retake or destroy him, by the horsemen in the river, or along the steep banks, the shouts, straggling pistol shots, splash of water, the wildness of the country and the gathering darkness altogether are enough to put one out of breath.

Then follows the interview between the travellers and Rob at the inn and afterwards at his 'puir dwelling', and then the final parting. The poetry of Rob's character is here given with great warmth and eloquence, and it is the more affecting from its harmony with the picturesque scene that surrounds him, and from the contrast between the ever-changing lights, in which his heart is laid open, and the

Rob Roy

undisturbed, funereal gloom that hangs over Helen Campbell. But we can extract no more.

We never intended to tell the whole story, or how all were made happy in the end, who deserved to be,—and we are the more willing to stop here, as the remaining fifty pages,—if we except 'the rescue' and Rashleigh's death at the very close,—are a sad falling off from all that the author ever wrote.—If we were asked, which of the tales we liked most, we should say, *The Antiquary*; and which least,— *Rob Roy*. But this is a very shallow sort of criticism, and a very unfair way to treat the present work. It has blemishes enough as a whole; but how many parts are there,—perfectly new ones too,—which could come from no other mind on earth! The descriptions of Scottish scenery appear to us as fine as any in the other stories; and we have rarely felt that we were looking upon old prospects. We have here many new and very minute views of Highland manners and usages, and much eloquent expression of the wild, free character and feelings of the mountaineers. It may not be easy to find in the other tales more graphic descriptions of buildings, especially their interior, than are given here. We do not allude merely to the Hall and the cathedral; the author is perhaps even more successful in the Highland hovel, and in the contrast between its smoke and filth, its wretched furniture and vulgar brawls, and the fresh, tranquil, pastoral beauties which surround it. He always delights in the picturesque effect of such scenes. But we must not go over the ground again. On the whole, there is matter here for a better book, and proofs on all hands that the author is not exhausted, that he has not yet forsaken invention and become an artisan.

THE HEART OF MIDLOTHIAN
1818

21. Unsigned review, *British Review*

November 1818, xii, 396-406

This book came under the heading *Tales of My Landlord*, second series.

In concluding our review of *Rob Roy*, in the Number for February, we predicted that, as the author had kept one of his masks in reserve, we should soon see more Tales of my Landlord. We however spoke at random, and had certainly no expectation that, in so short a time, four new volumes from the same hand, and almost of the same materials, could again be conjured upon our table. But this ingenious and hitherto successful author, we are now sorry to say, seems to set no value on literary reputation but as it contributes to the sale of his books. The opinion of the world comes authenticated to him through the medium of bank-bills; and, judging from the unpardonable haste and carelessness with which his latter productions have been sent forth from the press, we may safely infer that, author as he is, a name upon the Stock Exchange is dearer to him than the highest niche in the temple of fame. On all occasions we experience more satisfaction in speaking well of a book than in condemning it; but on all occasions we must pass an honest judgment on the books under review. It is not maintained, indeed, that there is any great falling off in point of genius, or even in the technical skill of constructing a story: on the contrary, the powers of the author seem neither decayed nor exhausted, and his greatest admirers have all along admitted that he was never very successful in putting together the materials of a narrative. Our disapprobation, therefore, has a much juster object than if it were directed against weakness or inanity. We are angry at him for holding the public so very cheap as to invite their attention to a work which he seems not to have taken the trouble to revise before he sent it to the press, nor even to correct whilst it was passing through the hands of the printer. Repetition, tautology, with clumsiness of every species and degree, meet our eyes in almost every page; and we have, moreover, some reason to be dissatisfied with him for attacking so unmercifully our patience and our purses, by protracting so doggedly and heavily an exhausted subject, merely, as it should seem, to comply with the mercenary condition of extending the tale to four volumes. Nor will the morality of the piece endure examination; although it must be owned that every thing which is bad in this respect, has so little of the touch of truth and life in it that its impression is likely to be as weak in effect as in tendency it is vicious. But of these particulars we shall be able to speak with more effect when we have given a *precis* of the words and deeds which constitute *The Heart of Mid-Lothian*; and, as most of our readers are in all likelihood already acquainted with its details, we shall discharge this part of our office with due regard to brevity.

[plot summary omitted]

Now for a short sketch of the dramatis personæ.—With the young man, who is exhibited to us in this narrative as a smuggler, rioter, and seducer, there is an unwarrantable degree of liberty taken in regard to fiction; and as the whole character is made up in direct opposition to well-known facts, we feel the incongruity and violence so much the more strongly. George Robertson, the smuggler and robber, was in reality a stable-keeper in Edinburgh, as may be seen in the *Criminal Trials*, published for the express purpose of illustrating this very tale; but instead of this humble calling and unpromising destiny, he figures out upon us towards the close of his career as Sir George Staunton, of Wilmingham. It is not easy to define poetical licence, and it is perhaps not very generous to restrict it; but, we are satisfied that, if the author had been aware that his publisher meant to print a volume of *facts* to illustrate his four volumes of *fiction*, he would have adhered more closely to historical truth. David Deans, the father of the two girls, Jeanie and Effie, is a fine specimen, without either caricature or inconsistency, of the old Cameronian covenanter; of which class of puritanical religionists and disaffected subjects we have one or two members in every tale or novel which has passed through the hands of the extraordinary writer to whom they are usually ascribed. But David Deans is no copy from a feigned original. We have indeed all the bigotry and much of the canting and misapplication of Scripture-language which were shown forth in the Kettledrummles, Macbriars, and Mucklewraths of *Old Mortality*; but we have more of human nature in its every-day phrases and expressions combined with the dark and unyielding stoicism of the mountain preacher. We see in him a father, and a father, too, in the most trying of all circumstances, the witness of his child's guilt, infamy, and condemnation. The war between his feelings as a parent, and that high-strained sense of religious obligation, which identifies all human feelings with weakness or positive sin, is finely pourtrayed in the character of Douce Davie; and, indeed, the great and almost sole merit of the romance now before us arises from the successful exhibition of this old peasant's principles, whilst in contact with less pure society; and of the rare goodness of his eldest daughter's heart, in the varied circumstances in which she is called upon to manifest her heroic generosity, and most invincible resolution. Jeanie and her father are finished pictures; the rest are sketches. The hand of a master is perceptible in every one of them, no doubt, but they are merely *rubbed in*; and as usual in all large collections, we have several daubs which can only serve as foils to set off the *chef-d'œuvres*. We have, for example, an old saddler who has lost his reason from attending courts of justice, and who is ever and anon spouting bad law and worse Latin to the annoyance of all around him:—next, the wife of this cracked tradesman, a notable woman in her way, and profuse of practical morality, and cutting jibes upon her husband—then the two lairds of Dumbiedikes, abominable caricatures both; and lastly, Mr. Reuben Butler, the lover; and in due season, the husband of Jeanie Deans, a decent common-place character, who seems to have very little business in the piece, and whose room could have been as well filled by any body else. He is of use, however, upon the following occasion.

[plot summary is omitted as well as the following quotations: chapter 35 'Argyle was alone' to ' "frae southerners and strangers?" ' (with some omissions); chapter 37 ' "What is your particular interest" ' to ' "at the tail of ae tow" ' (with some omissions). The interview of Jeanie Deans with the Duke is said to have been done 'uncommonly well' and that some pains are bestowed on the passage]

The result has been already mentioned:—Euphemia Deans obtained a pardon and was set at liberty; and moreover before she was well out of prison she was carried off by her former paramour Geordie

Robertson, alias Sir George Staunton, conducted to Italy, taught all sorts of fashionable accomplishments, whence she returns, after the lapse of a few years, to sparkle a distinguished belle in the highest rank and most polished society of England. We leave it to the author to reconcile such an issue either with common probability or with the moral object which he professes to have in view. Effie Deans, the daughter of a poor, rude, vulgar milkman, herself an illiterate, giddy girl, trained to the society of smugglers, thieves, and Gypseys, imprisoned, tried, and condemned, for the murder of her bastard infant, comes forward in a brief space thereafter, to claim the admiration of the reader, as a lady of the most elegant manners and refined accomplishments, 'the blazing star, the universal toast of the winter, and really the most beautiful creature that was seen at court upon the birth-day.' And, what is more, she is in habits of intimacy with the Duke of Argyle, who had saved her from the gallows: she is honoured with his company in her box at the theatre, where he tells her all the story of Jeanie's heroism, as connected with her jaunt to London, and thereby makes Lady Staunton betray her consciousness, by falling into a swoon; and yet she is not recognized. Nay, the author, in order to expose his indiscretion still further, and to show still further his contempt of all semblance of probability, assures us that the Duke discovered a very strong likeness between her Ladyship and her more humble sister, now the wife of the Rev. R. Butler, and yet his Grace is never led to suspect that the former might be the runaway Effie, thus strangely metamorphosed. But we wrong Argyle's discernment, perhaps, as the change in the damsel's character can hardly be said to be in nature; for the maxim that woman is a thing '*varium et mutabile semper*',[1] applies to any other point rather than to change of habits and disposition for the better, particularly when under the tuition of a rake. The author is at some pains, indeed, to convince us that Sir George Staunton and his Lady, though rich, gay, and admired, are not happy, thereby endeavouring, of course, to save his reputation for sound and teachable morality; and he even proceeds so far as to tell us, in a formal address, that the lesson conveyed by his tale is very useful and very obvious; but we have uniformly observed that, when the writer of a novel, or apologue, manifests any anxiety about the *moral* of it, and takes more than ordinary trouble to point it out, the said moral is very deficient either with regard to its precise meaning or its immediate tendency:

[1] 'Ever fickle and changing', Virgil, *Aeneid*, IV, 569.

'This tale,' says he, 'will not be told in vain, if it shall be found to illustrate the great truth, that guilt, though it may attain temporal splendour, can never confer real happiness; that the evil consequences of our crimes long survive their commission, and like the ghosts of the murdered, for ever haunt the steps of the malefactor; and that the paths of virtue, though seldom those of worldly greatness, are always those of pleasantness and peace.'

As an instrument of vengeance upon the heads of his guilty parents, the youth, for whose supposed death when an infant, Euphemia Deans had been sentenced as a murderer, is brought upon the stage in the character of a smuggler, or freebooter, on the Highland border, and has the part assigned to him of shooting his father, in a random fire of musketry. This event, so unnatural and unexpected, is another atonement made to the stinted morality of the tale—a kind of constrained *amende honorable* to the claims of virtue—all meant, it is presumed, to prove that vice brings misery, and that early profligacy terminates in a horrible death, as an effect results from a cause. But, exclaims the reader, what is the connexion between Geordie Robertson's libertinism and Sir George Staunton's tragical end, further than that he begat a son, which added one to the number of a thousand million of human beings, and thereby added one more to the sum total of those who handle guns and pistols! It is a poor device for so great an author; and if he had not been compelled by his mercantile engagement to spin out the thread of his story, with or without materials, so as to make out a *fourth* volume, and by that means to secure the *fourth* thousand pounds,[1] he would have scorned to introduce any part of the trash, of which he has composed the latter part of his work.

Far are we from entertaining any wish to run down this performance, or to depreciate the undisputed and excellent talents of its author; on which account, we feel no disposition to go out of our way in search of faults, or to lend an ear to every surmise which would deprive him of the merit of originality in incident or description. We pay no regard, for example, to the circumstance which we have heard dwelt upon by gossipping critics, that the long journey to London on foot to procure a pardon, in this case, was evidently suggested by the story of Elizabeth in the *Exiles of Siberia*, who walked from Tobolsk to St. Petersburgh to implore the clemency of the Emperor in behalf of her father. We have even been told that there is to be found, somewhere in the annals of Edinburgh, a fact corresponding in its main circum-

---

[1] Four thousand pounds is the sum said to have been the purchase-money of the copy-right [reviewer].

stances to the exploit which was performed by the virtuous and affectionate Jeanie Deans: but all this goes for nothing. If pure and absolute originality is to be held as an essential requisite in authorship, we shall not find that Virgil, Chaucer, Shakspeare, and even Milton himself, are entitled to much praise. Subjects and materials for novels, tales, and plays, lie scattered around like the potter's earth or the marble in the rock; but it requires the head of genius to mould them into those beautiful forms of art, which so frequently rival the products of nature. To apply these remarks to the volumes before us, we may observe that there could not be a greater proof of talent than that, with such materials as he has chosen to work upon, the author should have succeeded in creating so much interest, and in so deeply touching the feelings of his readers. Two girls, of low extraction and vulgar manners, and an old man of a repulsive and morose disposition, are all that we have for heroines and a hero; and yet such is the power of the writer, and such is his knowledge of human nature, whether acting or suffering, that, we will venture to assert, his description of the prison scene, before and after trial—the trial itself—the parting of Jeanie from her father and lover, and several other passages in the second and third volumes, take a firmer hold of the sympathies of humanity, and call forth more profound sorrow, love, and admiration from the heart, than has yet been awakened by all the frothy sentimentality and desperado enterprize of the modern school. So much the greater pity is it, therefore, and so much the more justly is our indignation excited, that a person of such brilliant genius should bargain away its dignity: that, in order to have the sum contracted for a few months sooner, he should hurry on the performance with so little regard to his own reputation as to leave it stained with blunders, which would disgrace any boy who has well learned his grammar; and that, to have the sum a little larger, he should have crammed into his work all the common places, low jokes, and second-hand incidents, which seem to have been thrown aside by him as unworthy of a place in any of his former books.

We have nothing to do with booksellers' bargains further than as the ware which they bring into the market may appear to have suffered from the terms of the negotiation; for as cupidity is no breach of a human law, we willingly leave it to that severe retribution which sooner or later overtakes it in the contempt and avoidance of good-hearted men. In the present case, we believe the punishment has trodden hard upon the heels of the transgression; and, if we have been rightly informed, both author and publisher have had reason to repent of their ill-timed avarice. No second edition of the new series has as yet been called for; and we have even heard that the first sells slowly in the shops, at a considerable reduction from the regular price.

But we will not part with the author in anger. We hold ourselves greatly indebted to him for much amusement and for some instruction; and in return we should be inclined to proffer him a piece of counsel as to all his future undertakings of this delicate nature. Let him have regard to his literary character on the one hand, and to public feeling on the other, and he may hope that, in the long run, he will make more money, if that is so much his object, than he possibly can by sending masses of manuscript to the press before the ink has dried upon it, and thereby irretrievably disgusting those who are most inclined to become his patrons. He has shown that he can write; and the public are fairly entitled to insist that he shall write, as well as he can, as often as he invites them to peruse his works. There is no harm in 'making hay whilst the sun shines'; but it is incumbent upon him, truly and honestly to *make* his hay, and not send forth musty, raw, unpalatable stuff, as the fruits of his hasty labour. If he has, indeed, succeeded in erecting a 'second story with attics to his domicile at Ganderclough'; and the good Dominie is said to have achieved great things; and if he continues to fix his eyes upon the 'Pendicle of seven acres, three roods, and four perches, called the Carlines croft'; and report says, that such an acquisition would count as nothing when compared with the acres and roods which already own him as their lord (laird); let him be reminded of the words of Solomon, still a wiser teacher than Jedediah Cleishbotham; 'He that maketh haste to be rich falleth into grievous snares.'

Since we sent these few paragraphs to the press, we have been informed that there is a third Series of *Tales of my Landlord* going forward at Edinburgh. *The Arabian Nights*, so long admired for never-ending incident and seducing narrative, are now likely to be surpassed, at least in number, although they were in reality, what they are in name, a Thousand and One.

22. Sydney Smith on the novels

1819-23

Letters from Sydney Smith, Anglican minister, wit, and *Edinburgh* reviewer, to Archibald Constable, Scott's publisher, thanking him for complimentary copies (from N. C. Smith, ed., *The Letters of Sydney Smith* (Oxford, 1953), 328, 342, 350-1, 373, 384-5, 389, 394, 404-5).

Scott had written at the end of *The Bride of Lammermoor* that he was 'retiring from the field'.

The Bride of Lammermoor

York, June 28th, 1819

Dear Sir,

I am truly obliged by your kindness in sending me the last novel of Walter Scott. It would be profanation to call him Mr. Walter Scott. I should as soon say Mr. Shakespeare or Mr. Fielding. Sir William and Lady Ashton are excellent, and highly dramatic. Drumthwacket is very well done; parts of Caleb are excellent. Some of the dialogues between Bucklaw and Craigengelt are as good as can be, and both these characters very well imagined. *As the author has left off writing*, I shall not again be disturbed so much in my ordinary occupations. When I get hold of one of these novels, turnips, sermons, and justice-business are all forgotten.

Your sincere well-wisher

SYDNEY SMITH

Ivanhoe

Foston, Dec. 25th, 1819

Dear Sir,

I waited to thank you until I had read the novel. There is *no doubt* of its success. There is nothing very powerful and striking in it; but it is uniformly agreeable, lively and interesting, and the least dull, and

172

most easily read of any novels I remember. Pray make the author go
on; I am sure he has five or six more such novels in him, therefore
five or six holidays for the whole kingdom

Truly yours

SYDNEY SMITH

The Monastery

Foston, March 25th, 1820

Dear Sir,

I am much obliged by your present of *The Monastery*, which I have
read, and which I must frankly confess I admire less than any of the
others—much less. Such I think you will find the judgment of the
public to be. The idea of painting ancient manners in a fictitious story
and in well-known scenery is admirable, and the writer has admirable
talents for it; but nothing is done without pains, and I doubt whether
pains have been taken in *The Monastery*,—if they have, they have failed.
It is quite childish to introduce supernatural agency; as much of the
terrors and follies of superstition as you please, but no actual ghosts
and hobgoblins. I recommend one novel every year, and more pains.
So much money is worth getting; so much deserved fame is worth
keeping, so much amusement we ought all to strive to continue for
the public good. You will excuse my candour,—you know I am your
wellwisher. I was the first to praise *Ivanhoe*, as I shall be to praise the
next, if I can do so conscientiously

Yours sincerely

SYDNEY SMITH

Kenilworth

Foston, Jan. 26th, 1821

Dear Sir,

Very good indeed; there cannot and will not be two opinions upon
it. The dialogues are a little too long. Pray let us have no more
Dominie Sampsons—good, but stale. These are trifling faults, but the
author has completely recovered himself, and the novel is excellent.

Yours very truly

SYDNEY SMITH

Flibbertigibbet is very good and very new.

The Pirate

Foston, Dec. 21st, 1821

Dear Sir,

I am much obliged by your kindness in sending me *The Pirate*. You know how much I admire the genius of the author, but even that has its limits, and is exhaustible. I am afraid this novel will depend upon the former reputation of the author, and will add nothing to it. It may sell, and another may *half* sell, but that is all, unless he comes out with something vigorous, and redeems himself. I do not blame him for writing himself out, if he knows he is doing so, and has done his *best*, and his *all*. I am for the mixture of history and fiction. If the native land of Scotland will supply no more scenes and characters, for he is always best in Scotland, though he was very good in England the [time] he was there; but pray (wherever the scene is laid) no more *Meg Merrilies* and *Dominie Sampson*—very good the first and second times, but now quite worn out, and always recurring. All human themes have an end (except Taxation); but I shall heartily regret my annual amusement if I am to lose it.

I am very sorry to hear you are unwell; it is because you are so rich. If you were poor and had much to fret you, you would be better; but do not be alarmed, you have yet twenty or thirty years good. When you go off at that distant period, I think you should leave me a handsome legacy in books, as the first person who gave you a start in life.

Your sincere well-wisher

SYDNEY SMITH

The Fortunes of Nigel

Foston, June 21st, 1822

Dear Sir,

Many thanks for *Nigel*; a far better novel than *The Pirate*, though not of the highest order of Scott's novels. It is the first novel in which there is no Meg Merrilies. There is, however, a Dominie Sampson in the horologer. The first volume is admirable. Nothing can be better than the apprentices, the shop of old Heriot, the state of the city. James is quite excellent wherever he appears. I do not dislike Alsatia. The miser's daughter is very good; so is the murder. The story execrable; the gentlemanlike, light, witty conversation always (as in all his novels) very bad. Horrors or humour are his forte. He must avoid running into length—great part of the second volume very long and tiresome; but upon the whole the novel will do—keeps up the reputation of the author; and does not impair the very noble and honourable estate which he has in his brains.

I hope you are better, that you are leaving it to your deputies to increase your wealth, and making it your care and the care of your doctors to amend your health.

Your sincere well-wisher
SYDNEY SMITH

Peveril of the Peak

Foston, Jan. 21st, 1823

Dear Sir,

A good novel, but not so good as either of the two last, and not good enough for such a writer. The next must be better or it will be the last. There is I see Flibbertigibbet over again. Bridgenorth is not new, Charles is the best done. My opinion is worth but little, but I am always sincere. There is one comfort, however, in reading Scott's novels, that his worst are better than what are called the successful productions of other persons. Many thanks for your kindness, and recollections of me.

Yours very truly
SYDNEY SMITH

St. Ronan's Well

Foston, Dec. 28th, 1823

Dear Sir,

Many thanks for St. Ronan, by far the best that has appeared for some time,—I mean the best of Sir Walter's, and therefore, of course, better than all others. Every now and then there is some mistaken and over-charged humour—but much excellent delineation of character,—the story very well told, and the whole very interesting. Lady Binks, the old landlady, and Touchwood are all very good. Mrs. Blower particularly so. So are MacTurk and Lady Penelope. I wish he would give his people better names: Sir Bingo Binks is quite ridiculous. I was very glad to find Dryasdust and Meg Merrilies excluded; one was never good, and the other too often good. The curtain should have dropped on finding Clara's glove. Some of the serious scenes with Clara and her brother are very fine,—the Knife scene masterly. In her light and gay moments Clara is very vulgar; but Sir Walter always fails in well bred men and women,—and yet, who has seen more of both? and who in the ordinary intercourse of Society is better bred? Upon the whole, I call this a very successful exhibition. I hope you are rich, healthy, and thinner.

Yours truly

SYDNEY SMITH

IVANHOE

1820

---

23. Unsigned notice, *Monthly Magazine*

February 1820, xlix, 71

The champion novelist of the day has again exhibited himself on a new arena,—in *Ivanhoe*, or the *Jew of York*,—equipped in the trappings of the feudal times, and in the chivalric character of an accomplished young Saxon of the woods. Though not perfectly historical in giving such a pompous picture of chivalric society at so early a period, (as it rather resembles Francis I, than Richard), yet, as it serves to represent characters of untamed life, judiciously mingled with those of 'high thoughts seated in a heart of courtesy', the union of two different periods of society may be admissible in *a romance*. With this, and the single exception of the want of a real story, we do not recollect perusing any work of Walter Scott's that has afforded us more pleasure than the present. The exquisite description, and dramatic power of character, are sufficient to redeem greater faults than are perceptible in the novels of this original author.

24. Coleridge on the novels

1820s

Extracts (*a*) from a letter of Samuel Taylor Coleridge to Thomas
Allsop, 8 April 1820, and (*b*) January 1821, and from (*c*) marginalia written by Coleridge between 1823 and his death in 1834.
The letters are taken from Thomas Allsop, *Letters, Conversations
and Recollections of S. T. Coleridge*, 3rd ed. (London, 1864),
25-29, 79, and the marginalia from T. M. Raysor, ed., *Coleridge's
Miscellaneous Criticism* (London, 1936), 328, 329, 331, 335.

(*a*) . . . I occasioned you to misconceive me respecting Sir Walter
Scott. My purpose was to bring proofs of the energetic or inenergetic
state of the minds of men, induced by the excess and unintermitted
action of stimulating events and circumstances,—revolutions, battles,
newspapers, mobs, sedition and treason trials, public harangues,
meetings, dinners; the necessity in every individual of ever increasing
activity and anxiety in the improvement of his estate, trade, &c., in
proportion to the decrease of the actual value of money, to the
multiplication of competitors, and to the almost compulsory expedience of expense, and prominence, even as the means of obtaining or
retaining competence; the consequent craving after amusement as
proper *relaxation*, as *rest* freed from the tedium of vacancy; and,
again, after such knowledge and such acquirements as are *ready coin*,
that will pass *at once*, unweighed and unassayed; to the unexampled
facilities afforded for this end by reviews, magazines, &c., &c. The
theatres, to which few go to see *a play*, but to see Master Betty or
Mr. Kean, or some one individual in some *one* part: and the single
fact that our neighbour, Mathews, has taken more, night after night,
than both the regular theatres conjointly, and when the best comedies
or whole plays have been acted at each house, and those by excellent
comedians, would have yielded a striking instance, and illustration of
my position. But I chose an example in literature, as more in point
for the subject of my particular remarks, and because every man of

genius, who is born for his age, and capable of acting *immediately* and widely on that age, must of necessity *reflect* the age in the first instance, though as far as he is a man of genius, he will doubtless be himself reflected by it reciprocally. Now I selected Scott for the very reason, that I do hold him for a man of *very extraordinary* powers; and when I say that I have read the far greater part of his novels twice, and several three times over, with undiminished pleasure and interest; and that, in my reprobation of *The Bride of Lammermoor* (with the exception, however, of the almost Shakspearian old witch-wives at the funeral) and of the *Ivanhoe*, I mean to imply the grounds of my admiration of the others, and the permanent nature of the interest which they excite. In a word, I am far from thinking that *Old Mortality* or *Guy Mannering* would have been less admired in the age of Sterne, Fielding, and Richardson, than they are in the present times; but only that Sterne, &c., would not have had the same *immediate* popularity in the present day as in their own less stimulated and, therefore, less languid reading world.

Of Sir Walter Scott's poems I cannot speak so highly, still less of the Poetry in his Poems; though even in these the power of presenting the most numerous figures, and figures with the most complex movements, and under rapid succession, in *true picturesque unity*, attests true and peculiar genius. You cannot imagine with how much pain I used, many years ago, to hear ——'s contemptuous assertions respecting Scott; and if I mistake not, I have yet the fragments of the rough draft of a letter written by me so long ago as my first lectures at the London Philosophical Society, Fetter Lane, and on the backs of the unused admission tickets.

One more remark. My criticism was *confined* to the one point of the higher degree of intellectual activity implied in the reading and admiration of Fielding, Richardson, and Sterne;—in moral, or, if that be too high and inwardly a word, in *mannerly* manliness of taste the present age and its *best* writers have the decided advantage, and I sincerely trust that Walter Scott's readers would be as little disposed to relish the stupid lechery of the courtship of Widow Wadman, as Scott himself would be capable of presenting it. And, that though I cannot pretend to have found in any of these novels a character that even approaches in genius, in truth of conception, or boldness and freshness of execution, to Parson Adams, Blifil, Strap, Lieutenant Bowling, Mr. Shandy, Uncle Toby and Trim, and Lovelace; and though Scott's *female* characters will not, even the very best, bear a comparison with Miss Byron, Clementina, Emily, in *Sir Charles Grandison*; nor the comic ones with Tabitha Bramble, or with Betty (in Mrs. Bennet's *Beggar Girl*); and though, by the use of the Scotch dialect, by Ossianic mock-highland motley-heroic, and by extracts from the printed sermons, memoirs, &c., of the fanatic preachers, there is a good deal of *false effect* and stage trick: still the number of characters *so good* produced by one man, and in so rapid a succession, must ever remain an illustrious phenomenon in literature, after all the subtractions for those borrowed from English and German sources, or compounded by blending two or three of the old drama into one—*ex. gr.*, the Caleb in *The Bride of Lammermoor*.

Scott's great merit, and, at the same time, his *felicity*, and the true solution of the long-sustained *interest* novel after novel excited, lie in the nature of the subject; not merely, or even chiefly, because the struggle between the Stuarts and the Presbyterians and sectaries, is still in lively memory, and the passions of the adherency to the former, if not the adherency itself, extant in our own fathers' or grandfathers' times; nor yet (though this is of great weight) because the language, manners, &c., introduced are sufficiently different from our own for *poignancy*, and yet sufficiently near and similar for sympathy; nor yet because, for the same reason, the author, speaking, reflecting, and descanting in his own person, remains still (to adopt a painter's phrase) in sufficient *keeping* with his subject matter, while his characters can both talk and feel interesting to *us* as men, without recourse to *antiquarian* interest, and nevertheless without moral anachronism (in all which points the *Ivanhoe* is so wofully the contrary, for what Englishman cares for Saxon or Norman, both brutal invaders, more than for Chinese and Cochin-Chinese?)—yet great as all these causes are, the essential wisdom and happiness of the subject consists in this,—that the contest between the loyalists and their opponents can never be *obsolete*, for it is the contest between the two great moving principles of social humanity; religious adherence to the past and the ancient, the desire and the admiration of permanence, on the one hand; and the passion for increase of knowledge, for truth, as the offspring of reason—in short, the mighty instincts of *progression* and *free agency*, on the other. In all subjects of deep and lasting interest, you will detect a struggle between two opposites, two polar forces, both of which are alike necessary to our human well-being, and necessary each to the continued existence of the other. Well, therefore, may we contemplate with intense feelings those whirlwinds which are for free agents the appointed means, and the only possible condition of that equilibrium in which our moral Being subsists; while the disturbance of the same constitutes our sense of life. Thus in the ancient Tragedy, the lofty struggle between irresistible fate and unconquerable free will, which finds its equilibrium in the Providence and the future retribution of Christianity. If, instead of a contest between Saxons and Normans, or the Fantees and Ashantees,—a mere contest of indifferents! of minim surges in a boiling fish-kettle,—Walter Scott had taken the struggle between the men of arts and the men of arms in the time of Becket, and made us feel how much to claim our well-wishing there was in the cause and character of the priestly and papal party, no less than in those of Henry and his knights, he would have opened a new mine, instead of translating into Leadenhall Street Minerva Library sentences, a cento of the most common incidents of the stately self-congruous romances of D'Urfé, Scudéri, &c. N.B. I have not read *The Monastery*, but I suspect that the thought or element of the faery work is from the German. I perceive from that passage in the *Old Mortality*, where Morton is discovered by old Alice in consequence of calling his dog Elphin, that Walter Scott has been reading *Tieck's Phantasies* (a collection of faery or witch tales), from which both the incident and name is borrowed.

(*b*) Walter Scott's poems and novels (except only the two wretched abortions, *Ivanhoe* and *The Bride of Ravensmuir*, or whatever its name may be) supply both instance and solution of the *present* conditions and components of popularity, viz. to amuse without requiring any effort of thought, and without exciting any deep emotion. The age seems *sore* from excess of stimulation, just as, a day or two after a thorough debauch and long sustained drinking match, a man feels all over like a bruise. Even to admire otherwise than *on the whole*, and where 'I admire' is but a synonym for 'I remember I *liked* it very much *when I was reading it*', is too much an effort, would be too disquieting an emotion. Compare *Waverley*, *Guy Mannering*, and Co., with works that had an *immediate run* in the last generation, *Tristram Shandy*, *Roderick Random*, *Sir Charles Grandison*, *Clarissa Harlowe*, and *Tom Jones* (all which became popular as soon as published, and therefore instances fairly in point), and you will be convinced that the difference of taste is real, and not any fancy or croaking of my own.

A Legend of Montrose

(c) If Sir Walter Scott could on any fair ground be compared with Shakespeare, I should select the character of Dalgetty as best supporting the claim. Brave, enterprising, intrepid, brisk to act, stubborn in endurance: these qualities, virtues in a soldier, grounded on wrong principles, but yet *principles*. Wrong [?] indeed, but clear, intelligible, and of precalculable influence and in all circumstances coercive; and unbent by accident. I exceedingly admire Captain Dalgetty. S. T. C.

Ivanhoe

[End of *Ivanhoe*.] I do not myself know how to account for it, but so the fact is, that tho' I have read, and again and again turned to, sundry chapters of *Ivanhoe* with an untired interest, I have never read the whole —the pain or the perplexity or whatever it was always outweighed the curiosity. Perhaps the foreseen hopelessness of Rebecca—the comparatively feeble interest excited by Rowena, the from the beginning foreknown bride of Ivanhoe—perhaps the unmixed atrocity of the Norman nobles, and our utter indifference to the feuds of Norman and Saxon (*N.B.* what a contrast to our interest in the Cavaliers and Jacobites and the Puritans, Commonwealthmen, and Covenanters from Charles I to the Revolution)—these may, or may not have been the causes, but *Ivanhoe* I never have been able to summon fortitude to read thro'. Doubtless, the want of any one predominant interest aggravated by the want of any one continuous thread of events is a grievous defect in a novel. Therefore the charm of Scott's *Guy Mannering*, which I am far from admiring the most but yet read with the greatest delight—spite of the *falsetto* of Meg Merrilies, and the absurdity of the tale. But it contains an amiable character, tho' a very commonplace and easily manufactured compound, Dandy Dinmont— and in all Walter Scott's novels I know of no other. Cuddy in *Old Mortality* is the nearest to it, and certainly much more of a *character* than Dinmont. But Cuddy's consenting not to see and recognize his old master at his selfish wife's instance, is quite inconsistent with what is meant by a *good heart*. No wife could have influenced *Strap* to such an act. I have no doubt, however, that this very absence of *heart* is one and not the least operative of the causes of Scott's unprecedented favour with the higher classes.

The Abbot

[Ch. III. Sir Halbert chafes over his humble origin.]

Sir Walter Scott should never have meddled with the supernatural, for he cannot blend it with the natural. Imagine the supposed experiences of Halbert in *The Monastery*—and you feel how impossible these in themselves justly delineated natural feelings become. The *supernaturalist's* must be a transitory character, never *carried* on. He must exist only in and for the supernatural tale.

[*Ibid.* Sir Halbert unceremoniously reverses his wife's order that the dog should be kept chained up.]

And yet Sir Walter would describe Sir Halbert as an amiable character, a kind husband. But the truth probably is, that the whole of this *Abbot* was written because a novel for £2,000 or £3,000 was engaged for. S. T. C.

[*Ibid.* Sir Halbert prefers the dog Wolf to his wife's page.]

Surely a very cruel and unamiable speech for the peasant's son to the Lady of Avenel.

[Ch. XXVII. Roland makes love to the supposed Catherine Seyton, who is really her twin brother dressed as a woman.]

Shakespeare has left us one *farce*—the classical model of that *genus* of the drama which begins by taking some improbability for granted and then works a comic interest out of it. But even in the *Comedy of Errors* Shakespeare would not have made a *male* after close examination and excited doubt indistinguishable from a female. The improbability of this scene is so monstrous, and Roland's stupidity so inconceivable, that even its actual occurrence would not have justified its introduction in such a work.

Peveril of the Peak

[Fly-leaves.] The absence of the higher beauties and excellencies of style, character, and plot has done more for Sir Walter Scott's European, yea, plusquam-European popularity, than ever the abundance of them effected for any former writer. His age is an age of *anxiety* from the crown to the hovel, from the cradle to the coffin; all is an anxious straining to maintain life, or *appearances*—to *rise*, as the only condition of not falling.—Interest? A few girls may crave purity, and weep over *Clarissa Harlowe,* and the old novelists! For the public at large, every man (for every man is now a reader) has too much of it in his own needs and embarrassments. He reads, as he smokes, takes snuff, swings [?] a chair, goes to a concert, or a pantomime, to be *amused,* and forget himself.—When the desire is to be *a* musas how can it be gratified *apud* musas?[1]

The great felicity of Sir Walter Scott is that his own intellect supplies the place of all intellect and all character in his heroes and heroines, and *representing* the intellect of his readers, supersedes all motive for its exertion, by never appearing alien, whether as above or below. S. T. C.

[1] That is, when one desires to be *amused or distracted* how can one be gratified *by* the muses.

THE MONASTERY

1820

25. Unsigned review, *Ladies' Monthly Museum*

May 1820, 3rd Series, xi, 273-80

When the work of a long acknowledged favourite is put into our hands, we cannot help preparing ourselves for a treat. The remembrance of former excellence dwells on our fancy, and with something like an eager impatience we turn over its pages. Whether this prepossession be justifiable, or whether it be right to look for undiminished merit from any author, however qualified his abilities may be, we will not determine; we know it is natural, and we feel, that in the event of its being wrong, we are sufficiently punished in the double disappointment which attends the failure of our expectations. Such is our situation at the present moment: never, that we remember, were we more disappointed than in the novel now before us, a production so infinitely inferior to every other that we have seen from the same celebrated author, that it is, in our opinion, unworthy of him. In vain we look for those great powers of genius in the masterly delineation of character, the glowing description of scenery, the faithful and exquisite touches of nature, or the wild, but poetic fancy, that formerly so much delighted us. Father Eustace, Halbert Glendenning, and Henry Warden, are undoubtedly pourtrayed in a manner which few but the author of *Waverley* could have done, and many other parts are extremely well written; but these are but gleams of excellencies, and bear no proportion to the general defects. The incidents are improbable and extravagant; the plot, if any it have, we have been unable to discover; and we do not think it altogether unexceptionable in a moral point of view. We are old-fashioned people, and may have old-fashioned notions, but we can never approve of the manner in which a volume, that we have ever considered too sacred to be lightly mentioned, is introduced, and we are not more at a loss to conceive the necessity, than to reconcile ourselves to the propriety of it. The devils, it is true, believe and tremble; but there is something repugnant to our feelings in making a fairy, or phantom, whichever the Maid of Avenal may be designated, the guardian of the Bible, and we think it neither complimentary to the holy book itself, nor tending to preserve its sanctity in the eyes of the reader. No part, however, of this Maid of Avenal meets with our approbation; on the contrary, whatever concerns her is such an infringement on common sense, and is, in some respects, so ridiculous, that we should be inclined to suppose, that in the spirit of our first James, who boasted what a king would do in the plenitude of his power, this celebrated writer has endeavoured to shew what an author might do in the plenitude of his, and ascertain what degree of absurdity would be tolerated by an indulgent public. The character of Sir Piercie Shafton, the great admirer of Euphuism, is well sustained; but he is a very disagreeable personage; and the story of the silver bodkin is absurd in the extreme. Except in the case of Rebecca, we have always preferred this author's old ladies to his young ones, and we are not now more inclined to change our opinion: the heroine is very uninteresting, and Missie Happer, the Miller's daughter, not much better. Our readers, however, must not suppose that they will not derive any pleasure from the perusal of these volumes; on the contrary; they must remember that it is very possible for an author of celebrity to write unworthy of himself, and yet infinitely superior to any one else, in the same line; and the same work which, when weighed in the scale of his own merits, sinks infinitely below the balance, will, when compared with others, rise equally above the general standard. The following beautiful extracts alone, would make ample atonement for many blemishes; and the fine scene, between the Sub-Prior and Henry Warden, deserves and receives our warmest commendation. The first is supposed to be spoken by Father Eustace, and the latter is part of a dialogue between Halbert Glendinning and his old domestic Martin.

[quotations from chapter 8 ' "There," said he' to ' "which she is assailed" '; chapter 17 ' "Halbert," said the old man' to ' "and by example" '; chapter 2 'Amongst the troops' to ' "these boys" '; and chapter 10 ' "I would ask" ' to ' "my mercy" ', and ' "with our reverend" ' to ' "to heaven" ' are omitted]

The character of the Sub-Prior is a very fine one. If there be moments in which his religious zeal approaches to intolerance, he amply redeems this only fault in his otherwise perfect character, by his native goodness of heart and strength of understanding. The incident of his revealing his adventure with the White Spirit, and thereby subjecting himself, merely from conscientious motives, to the censure of those weak minds he had, till then, governed, is well conceived; and the above scene with the ruffian Christie of the Clinthill, places his character in a really resplendent point of view: it is one of the most beautiful examples of the pure spirit of Christian charity which we ever remember to have met with. Father Eustace, in fact, rises upon us throughout the whole work; the heroic firmness with which he braves what he conceives certain death, in the discharge of his duty, and his refusal to purchase his own safety, and that of his monastery, by surrendering Sir Piercie Shafton to the Protestant forces, are pourtrayed in the author's best manner.

The versatility of this author's powers is one of his principal excellencies; in the foregoing extracts, we have given our readers a beautiful specimen of the elegance, and even sublimity, of his style; and the following, which we have taken from the introductory epistle, supposed to be written by Captain Clutterbuck to the author of *Waverley*, giving him an account of the manner in which he received the MSS. on which the romance is founded, so strongly marks the spirit and humour which distinguish it, and forms so good a contrast to the former, that we cannot forbear subjoining it.

[a quotation from the Introductory Epistle, 'I never could conceive' to ' "an inch of clean linen" ' is omitted]

The incidents on which this romance is founded are supposed to have taken place in the reign of Elizabeth, at a time when the power of the Romish Church was tottering on the eve of destruction, and the picture of the different parties of the day is finely pourtrayed. The scene is laid in Scotland, and almost entirely confined to the monastery and tower of Glendearg; but we have already so much encroached upon our limits, that we must now refer our readers to the volumes themselves for further information.—We understand that this undefatigable author has another work in the press; and we look forward to its publication with considerable interest, in the hope that it will repay us for our present disappointment.

IVANHOE

1820

26. Unsigned review, *Eclectic Review*

June 1820, 2nd Series, xiii, 526-40

There are several good reasons for our not saying much about the present production of the Author of *Waverley*. In the first place, it belongs to a class of works which has but doubtful claims upon our notice; in the next place we have recently delivered our sentiments pretty much at large upon some preceding publications of the same Author; and we shall only add, though we have twenty reasons quite as strong in reserve, that most of our readers have before this time made up their own opinion about the merits of *Ivanhoe*, and will therefore care less about ours. It is almost impossible to keep pace with the pen of this prolific Writer. Before the novel in question could have completed the circulation of the reading societies, or half the subscribers to the libraries could have been satisfied, a new series of volumes is in the hands of the public, and more are understood to be behind. We might regret this rapidity of composition in a writer of so much talent, were there not reason to believe, that he is one who can execute with spirit only his first warm conceptions, and that the attempt to elaborate would, with him, be as unsuccessful as it would be irksome. He has probably taken greater pains, if not in writing, yet, in order to write the present work, than in the case of any of the preceding tales: accordingly, it contains more information of a certain kind, is in parts more highly wrought, and is richer in antiquarian details, than perhaps any other; but it has less of verisimilitude, and makes a much more evanescent, if not a less vivid impression upon the reader's fancy.

The Author was himself aware that he was making an experiment very different from any of his previous attempts, when he undertook to carry his readers six hundred years back, instead of sixty, and 'to obtain an interest for the traditions and manners of old England, similar to that which has been excited in behalf of those of our poorer and less celebrated neighbours'. In the Dedicatory Epistle to the Rev. Dr. Dryasdust, he anticipates and replies to the objections which *à priori* lie against such an attempt, founded on the remote distance of the state of society in which the scene is laid, the total dissimilarity of the circumstances and manners of that era, to any thing which comes within the range of an Englishman's experience, and the scantiness of the materials for memoirs of the domestic life of our Saxon and Norman ancestors. English is a term scarcely applicable, indeed, to the times of Richard I. At that period, the very language of the country was undergoing a transition correspondent to the change which was being wrought upon the people, by the blending down of the conquerors and the conquered into one nation; and while Norman French was the only language 'of honour, of chivalry, and of justice', which continued to be the case to the time of Edward the Third, it is not without a contradiction in terms that we can speak of old English manners, as having under such circumstances come into existence. Whether we term them English, or French, or Anglo-Norman, they were still, however, the manners of our ancestors, and as such, a legitimate matter of curiosity. The only question is, whether they admit of being brought before us with a graphic force of description, that shall transport us in imagination back to the times to which the tale refers, and deceive us into the belief that in the pictures of the Novelist, we have represented to us the realities of history.

From one obvious means of aiding to produce such an illusion, the Writer is of necessity debarred by the circumstance, that the language he is compelled to employ, is not the language of the times in which his *dramatis personæ* are supposed to have lived: at the same time there is, in the present instance, just a sufficient mixture of foreign and antiquated phraseology, to fix the reader's attention upon the circumstance, and to give the medium employed, the awkwardness of translation. The extent of this disadvantage can be judged of only by calling to mind how much of the spirit and effect of the dialogue in the preceding tales of the Author of *Waverley*, arise from the recognized peculiarities of provincial idiom, and the comic force of quaint or familiar turns of expression. We could point out more than one of the ideal actors, who is indebted to this circumstance for nearly the whole of his dramatic individuality and importance. The character of the

Jester in *Ivanhoe*, is one of the most interesting in the Tale; strange to say, however, it is an interest of an heroic kind, arising from the touching display of his fidelity to his master, and his other very singular good qualities. His appropriate excellence as a professed humourist, is very tolerably vindicated by the occasional sallies of his wit; yet, in spite of his best efforts, he is, take him altogether, an exceedingly less amusing and less comic personage than either Captain Dugald Dalgetty, or Dousterswivel, or Dominie Sampson. In a pure romance, the modern flavour of the language put into the mouths of the ladies and gentlemen of remote times, is not felt to be a discrepancy; but the present work has for its design, in common with all the inimitable productions of its Author, to present to us, with antiquarian fidelity, the manners and customs of the age. Every part, therefore, must be in more than dramatic consistency; every thing bordering upon palpable anachronism, must be carefully avoided; and although the language 'must not be exclusively obsolete and unintelligible', yet 'no word or turn of phraseology betraying an origin directly modern', is, if possible, to be admitted into the composition. All that the romance-writer is concerned to make us believe, is, that the events he details, took place in the order and under the circumstances described, and that the parties whose names are given, had an existence, and did and said in substance the things ascribed to their agency. But the Author of *Ivanhoe*, not content with this, aims to produce the conviction in his readers, that the personages of the tale performed their part in a specific manner, and used certain specific modes of speech; that the events recorded not merely took place, but took place under such and such minutely defined peculiarities of scene and circumstance. The consequence is, that the moment the antiquary is at fault, the pseudo-historian is detected in his forgeries; every incongruity in the narrative, operates as an impeachment of his testimony; the costume which the actors have borrowed from ancient times, is perceived to be the only thing which claims affinity with reality; and while we admire the ingenuity and inventive fertility of the Writer, no other impression is left on the mind, than that of a pageant or a masquerade.

It is a fatal disadvantage in all historical romances, that they attempt to combine two opposite kinds of interest; that arising from general views of society connected with moral and political considerations, and implying a certain degree of abstraction, which is the proper interest of history, and that resulting from an engrossing sympathy with the feelings and fortunes of individuals, which is the appropriate charm of fictitious narrative. It is true that sometimes the historian, by deviating into the province of the biographer, succeeds in bespeaking a very strong feeling of interest on behalf of some favourite hero; but neither the design nor the excellence of history consists in producing any such effect upon the feelings through the medium of the imagination. The effect, however, is still in sufficient harmony with that of the general narrative, the mind being in either case occupied with realities. In the state of feeling requisite to the full enjoyment of a work of fiction, the realities of history can, on the contrary, please only as they are disguised by circumstances which give them the power of acting upon the imagination. The sole purpose which they are adapted to serve, is, to lend an appearance of verity to the supposititious details which are built upon them; for which purpose it is requisite that they should occupy the mere back-ground, so as never to become the object of distinct attention. But in that anomalous sort of production which is perpetually hovering between history and romance without possessing the genuine character of either, the illusion is never complete: the grand facts of history are perpetually forcing themselves upon the recollection in all their unromantic truth and moral importance, while a competitor interest to which the imagination is quite disposed to yield, is ever soliciting the feelings, and awakening emotions of an opposite nature. We think that if the readers of such works were at sufficient leisure to attend to the operation of their own minds under the excitation of perusal, they would find that they never entered into the full spirit of the fiction, except when they fairly lost sight of the history.

The historical plays of Shakspeare may seem to require our notice as a grand exception to this remark. The fact is, that they please, not as romance, but as history: the illusion is complete, but it is produced by different means from those employed by the Novelist; and the high tragic interest which is for the most part excited by the graver scenes of the great Dramatist, bears a much nearer relation to what the same scenes in real life would produce, than is the case with any other species of fiction. Add to this, that the charm of the language, and the beauty and elevation of the sentiment, qualities substantially real, have no small share in the effect produced upon the imagination.

A comparison has been more than indirectly suggested between Shakspeare and the Author of *Waverley*. No better illustration could have been furnished than that with which the Novelist has himself supplied us in *Ivanhoe*, for the purpose of pointing out the extent of the difference. Shakspeare is *all true*; he is always true to nature, and where he differs from the truth of history, it is only by strong and repeated efforts that the mind can disengage itself from the thraldom of his authority. In the delineation of the Scottish and Gaelic national characters, the Author of the Novels is equally faithful, and, within a certain range, the power of observation supplies to him the place of that mighty creative genius which made Shakspeare free of the universe. Nothing since Hamlet and Falstaff took their place among the real existences of history, has ever approached so near to those splendid creations of fancy, in individuality and verisimilitude, as some of the familiar personages in these tales. But we must not confound the description of talent, any more than the degree of talent, which has originated the latter, with the comprehensive genius of the great Expositor of Nature.

Ivanhoe is perhaps one of the cleverest of all our Author's productions; but in those respects in which it was an experiment, it is, in our opinion, a failure. It professes to be a romance; but the talents of the Author are not adapted to romance-writing. He is, if we mistake not, destitute of the requisite enthusiasm. The writer of a romance must at least seem to be in earnest, and by this means he may succeed in engaging the reader's attention to his narrative, how improbable soever it may be, and how foreign soever the events to his experience. A sort of reflected belief is awakened by the recital of wonders which are known to have exerted on the minds of others the effect of reality, provided there is nothing in the air and manner of the reciter to counteract it. Our Author refers to the goblin tale written by Horace Walpole, 'which has thrilled many a bosom', and it furnishes an instance in point. *The Castle of Otranto* is so admirable an imitation of the old romances, that it passes with the reader, not simply as a *record* of the times to which it relates, but as a *production* of those times; and hence it is that the enchanted casque, which, viewed as a modern fiction, would be too palpably false to awaken any sensation of terror, is an incident perfectly proper and highly impressive. In like manner, *The Lay of the Last Minstrel* derives from the character of the imaginary bard, a charm which none of the subsequent poems of the same Author possess. The authenticity of tales of gramarye and witchcraft, is quite equal to that of the more plausible fictions about damsels and warriors; and as to the various degrees of credibility which respectively attach to them, that circumstance can make no difference, when there is, in either case, absolutely no ground of belief, but the reader is called upon to place himself in the situation of those persons by whom they were alike received with implicit credulity.

If there be any justice in these remarks, it will be sufficient to say, that Ivanhoe has no pretensions to the character of an ancient legend: it has none of the musty odour of antiquity about it. The diction of the narrative is unaffectedly modern; and it is only in the dialogue that any attempt is made to give an antique cast to the phraseology. Instead of the grave and somewhat dignified style in which it behooved the celebrator of ancient deeds of chivalry to describe such high achievements, a vein of facetiousness runs through the composition, which is not always in unison with good taste; and the Author throughout the narrative, takes especial care to keep himself distinct from the subjects of the fiction, ever and anon pretending to translate from the language of the original, or inserting parenthetical notes and reflections, such as might be looked for in a genuine and veritable history. The effect of this, is positively bad; and the alternate description and dialogue present a species of patchwork, which has neither beauty, nor apparent necessity, nor correctness to recommend it. There are many parts of the Tale which are strikingly picturesque and dramatic, and the characters of some of the personages are very finely discriminated; all this we readily admit; but what we complain of, and what we think most readers on a cool perusal will perceive to be matter of just complaint, is, that the Author has not given us either genuine romance or genuine history; he has furnished us with neither a memoir nor a legend of the times,—certainly with nothing that can convey any idea of the living manners of our ancestors, beyond what may easily be picked out of the History of England, except as to a few points of costume; nor yet with a work of pure entrancing fiction; but with that mongrel sort of production, an historical novel,—as inferior in point of interest (we do not say in point of merit) to *The Castle of Otranto*, or *The Mysteries of Udolpho*, as it is to *The Chronicle of the Cid*, or the inimitable Froissart.

In conformity to equitable custom, we shall now proceed, without further prologue, to select a few extracts from the work before us, which we shall leave to speak for themselves. The tournament is, unquestionably, one of the very best things in the Tale, but its length will preclude our giving the whole of the scene.

[a quotation from chapter 7 'The scene was singularly' to 'prepared to guess'; and chapter 8 'At length the barriers' to 'they had forfeited' is omitted]

The siege of the castle of Torquilstone by the Black Knight and his strange ally, Locksley, at the head of a band of heroic outlaws, is another of those admirably painted scenes which exhibit the master hand. Wilfrid of Ivanhoe, wounded and a prisoner, is stretched upon a bed of pain. His attendant is a lovely Jewess, the magnanimous heroine of the tale, upon the delineation of whose character, the Author has bestowed his very best efforts.

[a quotation from chapter 29 ' "And I must lie here" ' to ' "triumph over hundreds" ' is omitted]

The death-scene of Front de Bœuf is not half so thrilling as that of old Dumbiedikes, nor does the Saxon maniac, Ulrica, horrible even to disgusting as is the whole conception, equal in sublimity the character of old Elspeth in *The Antiquary*. The fact is, that the historic truth of terrible realities like those to which we are at present alluding, forms no apology for the introduction of them into Romance. Our last specimen must be, the trial of Rebecca on the charge of witchcraft.

[a quotation from chapter 37 'At this period' to 'the whole assembly' (with some omissions) is omitted]

27. A shepherd's tribute

1820

Extract from an anonymous letter to Scott dated 24 June 1820 (from Wilfred Partington, ed., *The Private Letter-Books of Sir Walter Scott* (London, 1930), 321-24).

The letter, endorsed by Scott as being written by a shepherd, begins, 'I am an obscure, solitary individual, and have almost all my life, which is now better than fifty years, lived in the wildest districts in the south of Scotland'. Early in the letter he informs Scott of a similar village, called Glendayrg, to one mentioned in *The Monastery* and discusses the existence of elves.

I cannot help telling you that I am astonished, perfectly astonished, how ye have acquired the Scottish dialect and phraseology so exactly. Certainly neither your education nor studies could discover ought of that antiquated language: yet when ye chuse to adopt it ye have it as truly as if ye knew no other, but had lived in the most sequestered nook of the Forest all your life. Of all your writings that I have seen, I like the *Legend of Montrose* and *The Monastery* best. Edie Ochiltree in *The Antiquary* is very good: whenever he speaks it is always what one in his situation and of his trade would say; and when the adept broke the pick in digging for the treasure; and Edie exclaim'd against the folk of Fairport for selling such useless things, it is really extraordinary. But I think I never saw nor read nothing truer to nature than when the Duke of Argyle gave a look to his sore arm that was swinging in a napkin by his side when the marshal airs that were heard among the hills announced that a party of horse was coming to the field: this is up to nature—and up to nature in its most intricate and nicest parts. I have for the last three or four days been tending my sheep on a high hill named Penvallah: there is no human being near, and I have been most agreeably entertained with *The Monastery*. I can scarcely select one passage more beautiful than another, yet when ye

195

say that Halbert alighted from the heart of the oak with as little injury as the falcon stooping for his meal, it is truly excellent. On a tranquil summer's evening I have sometimes witnessed the aptness of this comparison: the eagle, that noble bird, wheels her spiral course to such a height that she appears like a small dot on the clear sky; sometimes the eye loses her altogether: anon, she appears like a speck of vapour wandering over the blue void; after taking a number of circles at that extraordinary elevation she descends by the same winding course she arose, but only in larger circles, keeping her wings as steady and expanded all the while as ever ye saw the arms of a mock-man that had been set up to fray the crows from a field of new sown barley. When she comes near her favourite cliff she stretches out her legs to meet its ragged point, yet alights as safe and easy as if she had descended to the ground and meadow from only a few yards elevation. So fell Halbert from his oak, and so stoops the eagle from her airy flight.

I should now, Sir, give some reasons for sending you an anonymous letter. Indeed, I have none that can fully justify my conduct: I only saw there was a resemblance between old Simon's Glendayrg and the one in Etterick head, and I thought it would not be unentertaining to let you know in what that resemblance consisted. My fancy has been strongly excited by reading these books, especially *The Monastery*, and I could not help freely telling you my thoughts on some passages. You will find bad grammar in almost every sentence, but I know ye will have the goodness to dispense with this. I cannot rectify it myself. That ye may long enjoy the honors conferred upon you by your Sovereign is the ardent and genuine wish of your Humble servt. &c.

[unsigned.]

28. J. L. Adolphus on the works
and their authorship

1821

Extracts from the anonymous *Letters to Richard Heber, Esq. M.P.*, 2nd ed. (1822).

The author was John Leicester Adolphus, a lawyer and minor author. The monograph, originally published in 1821, is a long, detailed comparison of the Waverley novels with the poems and other signed works by Scott with the conclusion that all were written by the same hand.

One of the first inquiries that suggest themselves in such investigations as the present is, how far the authors resemble each other in their style of composition. You must have observed, however, that in the novels, as well as in the prose works of the author of *Marmion*, the style seldom presses itself on our consideration: some glorious and some discreditable exceptions will immediately occur to you; but, generally speaking, it is the spirit, not the structure, of the sentence that obtains our attention, and if the language becomes elevated and enriched, the thought also rises in proportion, and maintains its ascendency. In this respect the novels before us differ strikingly from the work of Mr. Hope, already alluded to, where the elegance and aptness of the style add sensibly, nay, perhaps too obviously, to the effect of every passage, and equally assert their claim to praise in the gayest, the saddest, and the tenderest scenes.

You will remark also, that those parts of the novels in which fine thoughts and fine composition have been most successfully united, are evidently from the peculiar nature of their subjects, and from their highly imaginative or passionate character, unfit to be placed in comparison with any passage of a sober literary essay, or historical memoir, though proceeding from the same pen. I might transcribe the parting harangue of Meg Merrilies to Godfrey Bertram, the young fisherman's funeral in the *Antiquary*, the death of Mucklewrath the preacher, Jeanie Deans's supplication to Queen Caroline, the dissolution of the Chapter at Templestowe by Cœur-de-Lion, or Elizabeth's torchlight procession to Kenilworth, all specimens of admirable composition; but would it not be absurd to inquire what these extracts have in common with any page selected from the Life of Swift or Dryden, from the Essay on Border Manners and History, or even from Paul's Letters?

If, however, we view the style of the novels at its ordinary level, we shall, I think, find it bear as great resemblance to that of the other prose works as can exist between two modes of writing, when both are unmarked by any strong characteristic feature. Neither the author of *Waverley*, nor the editor of Dryden, is to be recognized by a frequent or ambitious use of antithesis, inversion, re-iteration, or climax; by sententious brevity, or sounding circumlocution; by studied points or efforts to surprise; or, in short, by any of those artifices which, often repeated, form obvious peculiarities in style. The prose of these writers is, on the contrary, remarkable (if it can in any respect be deemed so) for plainness, and for the rare occurrence of ornaments produced by an artful collocation of words. Nothing seems attempted or desired, except to compose at as little expense of labour as possible consistently with the ease of the reader. Their style is therefore fluent, often diffuse, but generally perspicuous: if it is sometimes weakened by a super abundance, it is seldom darkened by a penury of words. We may remark as a characteristic circumstance, that they constantly express thoughts in the regular form of simile, which other writers would condense into metaphor. Their usual phraseology is of that learned and somewhat formal description, very generally adopted for the ordinary purposes of literature, and which, with reference to the business of authorship, may be called technical; a kind of language differing from that in which we converse, or correspond on familiar subjects, as printed characters from a free hand-writing. Yet the tone and spirit in which they deliver themselves are remarkably free from all appearance of pedantry and authoritative stiffness; there is, on the contrary, a winning air of candour in their address, which deserves to be numbered among their chief excellencies. They urge opinions and impart knowledge in the frank, unassuming, and courteous manner of a friend communicating with a friend. The use of irony or sarcasm appears repugnant to their natural openness and good humour; and accordingly they seldom employ these weapons unless it be for the prosecution of fictitious conflicts between imaginary personages. But there is a kind of serious banter, a style hovering between affected gravity and satirical slyness, in which both writers take an unusual delight: it is a vein which may be traced through almost all their compositions, even, I think, to the poems, but which most frequently discloses itself in the telling of a story.—One or two brief instances will bring a multitude to your remembrance.

But if the comparison be restricted to those points in which a near resemblance may be reasonably expected, an examination of the dialogue will, I think, go far in confirming our assurance of the novelist's identity with the poet.

Their address in combining narrative with conversation, so that each supports and animates the other, has been too long admired and cele-brated to need illustration by particular examples. I cannot, however, forbear mentioning two splendid instances; the death of Marmion, and the distress of Sir Arthur and Miss Wardour on Knockwinnock Sands.

Not less remarkable are the nicety of perception and felicity of execution with which they adapt language to the sex, age, character, and condition of the speaker. A few examples will show how similarly (if not equally in degree) the same talent is developed by these authors in both modes of composition: how each (as the author of *Marmion* says of Swift) 'seems, like the Persian dervise, to' possess 'the faculty of transfusing his own soul into the body of any one whom he' may select;—'of seeing with his eyes, employing every organ of his sense, and even becoming master of the powers of his judgment.'

In the reply of young Buccleuch to the English archer, observe the admirable combination of childish simplicity with native haughtiness and courage:

[ll. 234-61 of Canto III of *The Lay of the Last Minstrel* were quoted]

The scene I have quoted has perhaps reminded you of that in which old Stawarth Bolton places his red cross in the bonnet of little Halbert Glendinning, and the boy indignantly 'skims it into the brook'. 'I will not go with you,' said Halbert boldly, 'for you are a false-hearted southern; and the southerns killed my father: and I will war on you to the death, when I can draw my father's sword.'[1]

---

[1] 'And if I live to be a man,
My father's death revenged shall be.'
Lay of the Last Minstrel, Canto I. St. 9 [Adolphus].

'God-a-mercy, my little levin-bolt,' said Stawarth, 'the goodly custom of deadly feud will never go down in thy day, I presume.' *The Monastery*, vol. i. ch. 2.

To infuse into conversation a spirit truly and unaffectedly feminine appears to me one of the most difficult tasks that can be undertaken by a writer of our sex: yet this is in many instances happily achieved by the author of *Marmion*, although the somewhat antiquated turn of his style is unfavourable to such an attempt. I think his greatest felicity in this respect lies in occasional snatches of speech interwoven with animated description; as when, in Holy-rood palace, Lady Heron

> 'rises with a smile
> Upon the harp to play.'

> ★　★　★　★　★

> '—And first she pitch'd her voice to sing,
> Then glanced her dark eye on the king,
> And then around the silent ring;
> And laugh'd and blush'd, and oft did say
> Her pretty oath, by Yea, and Nay,
> She could not, would not, durst not play!'
> *Marmion*, Canto V. St. 11.

But of all the dramatic scenes in which this writer has depicted female manners and character, there is none perhaps so purely natural and irresistibly pathetic as the first interview of Jeanie Deans with her imprisoned sister in the presence of Ratcliffe: a piece of writing which alone might entitle its author to sit down at the feet of Shakspeare. I cannot forego the pleasure of adorning this unworthy page with an extract, though it is almost profanation to dismember so beautiful a scene.

[a quotation from chapter 20 'O, if ye had spoken' to 'and was silent' from *Heart of Midlothian* is omitted]

The colloquial felicity of these writers is shewn not only in their skilful adaptation of discourse to the natural varieties of age, sex, and disposition, but in the wonderful address and versatility with which they suit it to all acquired habits and peculiarities, whether national or professional, the effect of accident or result of education. If we look into the poems, the gentle Fitz-Eustace and the 'sworn horse-courser' Harry Blount, the rough English soldier John of Brent, and his pert but courtly captain, are marked and obvious instances; and the manners and circumstances of every personage in *The Lay of the Last Minstrel* are as vividly pictured in his language as in the description by which the poet introduces him.

If further illustration were required, I might transcribe at random from the discourse of MacIvor's clansmen in *Waverley*, Serjeant Bothwell (or indeed any other character) in *Old Mortality*, Mr. Owen or the Baillie in *Rob Roy*, Abbot Boniface in *The Monastery* and *Abbot*, and Sir Dugald Dalgetty in *A Legend of Montrose*. The wanton exuberance of the novelist's dramatic talent is singularly evinced in this last story, by his introducing, without any absolute necessity, a professional conference between two second-sighted prophets: a short dialogue, but extremely forcible and poetical. The colloquies of Ailsie Gourlay and her fellow-aspirants in witchcraft may be mentioned as similar prodigalities of eccentric and luxuriant imagination.

The excellencies I have thus inadequately praised are sometimes accompanied by kindred faults; and these also are common to both writers. The author of *Waverley* is perhaps unrivalled in the learned ease and happy address with which he handles the phraseology of remote times; there is scarcely a chapter in *Kenilworth* which does not exhibit this talent in matchless perfection. But he sometimes, either from precipitation, or disgust at his task, or simple negligence, allows his dialogue to languish in a bald verbosity, and sink into that weak and affected strain, which, although sufficiently formal and antiquated, can never, by the greatest stretch of indulgence, be accepted as the similitude of real conversation in any age or class of society. The same occasional error had been imputed to the author of *Marmion*, before *Waverley* saw the light.

To make their characters discourse by the book is a fault which many novelists commit through barrenness of fancy, or ignorance of the world. It cannot be imputed to either of these causes that the authors of *Waverley* and *Marmion* sometimes impart a tinge of their own archæological erudition to the sallies of playful gallantry and of homely humour. Thus in *The Lady of the Lake*, Fitz-James and Ellen grow absolutely pedantic in their continued allusions to the old romances. Fitz-Eustace in *Marmion* touches on the same extreme, but the nature of his character allows, or indeed requires it. Roland Græme and Catherine Seyton, in *The Abbot*, carry the humour farther, and with less excuse.

The following passage very palpably betrays its bookish origin. When Ellen Douglas and Allanbane the harper arrive at Stirling, escorted by a soldier, his comrade asks—

[ll. 126-31 of Canto VI of *The Lady of the Lake* were quoted]

It may be answered, that although the glee-maiden, ape, and harper of an ancient juggler's troop are known to us only by the aid of antiquarian research, they were common and familiar enough in the time of James the Fifth, to be a subject of popular raillery. But the qualities of all dialogue must be estimated by the effect it produces on the reader or hearer. Now it is true that, within a certain limit, allusions proper to the age or place in which the scene is laid tend powerfully to strengthen the dramatic effect, and assist us in imagining that we listen to a real conversation, or at least hear it reported by a witness bearing all the passages freshly in his memory. But when, in the midst of a flowing and easy colloquy, we encounter some pointed reference, and that not inevitably suggested by the occasion, to an object or custom with which even well-educated persons are not universally familiar, a momentary pause ensues, while we recur in mind to the learned sources whence the author derived his information; meanwhile our fancy drops from its flight; the illusion of the scene forsakes us; and, after the charm is dissolved, we care but little for being convinced that we ought still to have remained under its dominion. When Arruntius, in Jonson's tragedy of Sejanus, satirically tells the courtiers to 'run a lictor's pace', and bids one get 'Liburnian porters' to bear his 'obsequious fatness', I suppose every reader's imagination is transported instantly from the streets of Rome to a college library; yet lictors and their paces, and Liburnian porters, were as well known to the fellow-citizens of Sejanus as glee-maidens and jugglers to the garrison of Stirling.

Another practice which I think materially injures the *vraisemblance* of a scene, is to represent persons celebrated in history, as indulging in idle and sportive allusions to their own and each other's most famous adventures and sayings. This is so much the error of a novice, and therefore so surprising in the authors of *Waverley* and *Marmion*, that, however rare in its occurrence, it cannot pass wholly unnoticed.

When the meteor which had lured Bruce and his followers from Arran to the coast of Carrick, sank down and left them in darkness,

[ll. 350-7 of Canto V of *Lord of the Isles* were quoted]

The Duke of Argyle's prattle with his children, in the presence of Jeanie Deans, about Sheriff-muir and the Bob of Dumblane, is still more inartificial, and, indeed, falls so much below the author's usual style, that I have no inclination to extract the passage.

I know not whether it is owing to any perverseness of our nature, that a fictitious conversation, presenting these broad references to the recorded history of the speakers, awakens incredulity, and arms us against illusion. It certainly is not impossible that a statesman or warrior should at a given time be heard familiarly discoursing on his own most celebrated exploit or memorable saying; neither is it absolutely incredible that a portrait-painter should surprise a member of parliament musing over a favourite bill, or an officer unrolling the plan of a boasted position or manœuvre; yet the limner obtains small credit for his ingenuity in choosing such situations, and the novelist and poet, in my opinion, achieve as little for the honour of their art by their direct and palpable appeals to our commonest historical recollections. Experience, I think, tells us, that most persons, during the active season of life at least, are sparing of allusions to great and momentous incidents in their own past career, partly from natural reserve, and partly, it may be, because such events, at the time of their occurrence, so entirely fill the thoughts, and exhaust every sensation they are capable of producing, that they do not afterwards, on common occasions, recur to the mind with that freshness which prompts the tongue to utterance. Whether this observation be well or ill founded, it is at least certain, that when the celebrated characters introduced in a fictitious tale seem over-forward in reminding us of their own deeds and sayings, the propriety of the scene is almost as much violated as if they announced themselves like Holofernes's nine worthies:

> 'My scutcheon plain declares, that I am Alisander.'
> *Love's Labour Lost*, Act V. Sc. 2.

Or,

> 'I Pompey am, Pompey surnamed the Great,
> That oft in field, with targe and shield, did make my foe to sweat.'
> *Ibid.*

Little, I believe, can be added to this catalogue of faults, which has been thus prolonged, not because the enumeration gave me any pleasure, but that corresponding blemishes are usually thought to afford stronger presumption of affinity than similar perfections.

It may be worth while, however, in concluding, to notice one insignificant exception to what has been said of the versatility exhibited by our authors in their dramatic pictures of character: I mean the marked failure of both in scenes of bold and unmitigated vulgarity. These are but seldom attempted, and it is evident they are not written *con amore*; they appear sordidly coarse, and want that free spirit of joyous insolence which alone, on such occasions, can compel us to overlook the vileness of the subject. John of Brent and his comrades, in the *Lady of the Lake*, are at least as saucy and irreverent as Burns's Merry Beggars; but the soldiers, with all their licence, are coldly and formally debauched; while the joviality of Posie-Nansie's is so animated and glowing, that the whole spirit of the revel rushes upon us, and vagrancy appears almost sublime in the lines—

'Here's to budgets, bags, and wallets!
Here's to all the wandering train!
Here's our ragged brats and callets!
One and all cry out, Amen!

A fig for those by law protected,
Liberty's a glorious feast!
Courts for cowards were erected,
Churches built to please the priest!'

Inglis the trooper, in *Old Mortality*, Frank Levitt the thief, in *The Heart of Mid-Lothian*, and noble Captain Craigengelt, in *The Bride of Lammermoor*, are at times even repulsively coarse; but their coarseness is of that kind which neither illustrates the character nor invigorates the language; it is at once overcharged and ineffective, plainly indicating that the writer, unsuccessful in seizing the spirit of genuine *black-guardism*, has made an aggravated display of its outward signs, to conceal or atone for the essential deficiency. In portraying that unconscious vulgarity which results from selfishness, conceit, and bad education, the author of *Waverley* exhibits all his accustomed felicity, as in the character of Mrs. Nosebag, and occasionally in that of Sir Dugald Dalgetty; but he has not yet caught, with his usual nice apprehension, the reckless and ribald audacity of the 'lewd rabble', and those who adopt their manners; and his essays of this kind, having all the rudeness of reality, without affording the pleasure which is produced by judicious imitation, remind us of the economical humorist in Miss Burney's *Cecilia*, who appears at a masquerade with the borrowed suit of a real chimney-sweeper.

In the general remarks which I offered on the style of these two writers, I mentioned, as one of its distinguishing features, a tendency to diffuseness. This, however, is by no means a prevailing characteristic of their dialogue, which, in all its happiest parts, is peculiarly terse and compact, and becomes, according to the occasion, sententious or epigrammatic, without any diminution of ease, or sacrifice of propriety. Hence it is, that when the stories of these authors have been compressed for the stage (as the Constrictor serpent compresses a lordly stag), it has commonly been found expedient to retain the original dialogue, not only of the novels, but occasionally even of the poems, as more effective than any which could be substituted, and better calculated for developing the fable with animation, propriety, and distinctness.

I cannot support these observations better than by referring to that scene in *Marmion* where the hero is received by King James in the banqueting room at Holy-rood.

It is observable throughout the novels and poems, that wherever the interest rises to a very high pitch, there the dialogue, if that form of composition be employed, becomes in a peculiar degree condensed and pointed. Let me call to your mind, as instances, the scene of Fergus M'Ivor's condemnation; that in which Edgar Ravenswood arrives at the Lord Keeper's to claim a final interview with Miss Ashton; and the altercation between Malcolm Græme and the chief of Clan-Alpine. Indeed, all the quarrels in these romances appear to me, as Sir Lucius O'Trigger would say, the prettiest quarrels in the world: every kind of heroic or gentlemanlike dissension is managed with admirable skill and spirit; and sometimes conducted through the requisite stages of Retort, Quip, Reply, Reproof, and Countercheck, with a lofty-minded discretion which would hardly have mis-become the days of Saviolo and Caranza.

Yet, with all their address in carrying on that kind of dispute which tends to martial defiance, both writers are, I think, unfortunate in their endeavours to imitate the conflict of acrimonious but polished raillery, as it is waged by well-bred malice on peaceable occasions. The mutual taunts of Marmion and Sir Hugh the Heron, when the knight asks his guest, of the page that used to attend him,

> 'Say, hast thou given that lovely youth
> To serve in lady's bower?
> Or was the gentle page, in sooth,
> A gentle paramour?'

and the baron, remarking in his turn the absence of Heron's flighty consort, ironically inquires—

> '—has that dame, so fair and sage,
> Gone on some pious pilgrimage?'

are somewhat rude, even for Norham castle. In the *Abbot*, the war of sarcasm between Mary Stuart and the Lady of Lochleven usually ends in bringing down both disputants to the common level of incensed females; a circumstance perhaps strictly natural, but pertaining to that kind of nature which, as we fly from it in real life, we are not greatly pleased to encounter in fiction; certainly not where the fable is of an elevated and romantic cast.

In attempting to draw the poetical character of the author of *Marmion*, I have dwelt particularly on his judgment in selecting, enthusiasm in feeling, and energy in painting. From the union of these qualities arises that particular excellence in which, rivalled only by the author of *Waverley*, he far surpasses all other contemporary poets and descriptive writers, and is little inferior, if inferior, to the greatest of any age. I mean that realizing power which brings the imagined scene so forcibly to our minds, that we almost seem to behold it with our eyes. If there is any single perfection which, beyond all the rest, distinguishes either the author of *Marmion*, or the novelist, considered as a poet, it is the freshness, the living truth, the ἐνάργεια of his narrative and description. Both seem to transport themselves at pleasure, by a strong effort of fancy, into the midst of the objects they propose to represent; and hence the composition of their stories, in every important part, is either picturesque or dramatic, or partakes of both qualities; and the circumstances are so well chosen and aptly combined, and the incidents follow one another so naturally, that we cannot but suppose the entire scene to have existed at once, or the whole action to have passed uninterruptedly, in the author's imagination, and to have been transferred thence to his paper, like a minute of actual observations, or an abstract of real occurrences.

The picturesque mode of narrative, which impresses an event or situation on the fancy by a vivid representation of all the outward circumstances as they unitedly offer themselves to the sense, is brilliantly exemplified in this passage of *Kenilworth*:

[a quotation from chapter 10 'The door was unlocked' to 'to Richard Varney' of *Kenilworth* is omitted]

The liveliness and air of truth which these writers have given to their narrative and descriptive passages, is attained sometimes by the felicitous combination of several particulars at once natural and striking; sometimes by the opportune suggestion of a single circumstance so manifestly proper to the occasion, that, having it before us, we cannot conceive the action to have happened without it, yet so far unexpected, that it appears unlikely to have entered the imagination of a person contriving a fictitious story, or to have engaged any man's notice except in connexion with real facts.

The following descriptions owe their vivacity and truth of effect to the cause first mentioned:

'It was with such feelings that I eyed the approach of the new coach lately established on our road, and known by the name of the Somerset.—The distant tremulous sound of its wheels was heard just as I gained the summit of the gentle ascent, called the Goslin-brae, from which you command an extensive view down the valley of the river Gander.'—'I must own I have had great pleasure in watching the approach of the carriage, where the openings of the road permit it to be seen. The gay glancing of the equipage, its diminished and toy-like appearance at a distance, contrasted with the rapidity of its motion, its appearance and disappearance at intervals, and the progressively increasing sounds that announce its nearer approach, have all to the idle and listless spectator, who has nothing more important to attend so, something of awakening interest.'—'On the present occasion, however, fate had decreed that I should not enjoy the consummation of the amusement, by seeing the coach rattle past me as I sat on the turf, and hearing the hoarse grating voice of the guard, as he skimmed forth for my grasp the expected packet, without the carriage checking its course for an instant. I had seen the vehicle thunder down the hill that leads to the bridge with more than its usual impetuosity, glittering all the while by flashes from a cloudy tabernacle of the dust which it had raised, and leaving a train behind it on the road resembling a wreath of summer mist. But it did not appear on the top of the nearer bank within the usual space of three minutes.'—*Heart of Mid Lothian*, introductory chapter.

In pointing out the faculty which these authors exert, of comprehending at once, in the mind's eye, both the general effect of a scene, and the mutual bearing of its several parts, I should have added, but for interrupting the course of observation, that they possess, in subserviency to this talent, the power of embracing with the same masterly and accurate *coup d'œil*, all the external appearances that characterize individual persons. Their scrupulous particularity in the description of physiognomy, demeanour, form, and even dress, often imparts to their stories the air of real memoirs. Where, indeed, the fable treats of personages who have actually existed, such minuteness is not surprising, because we then conclude that the details are borrowed from some picture, or sculptured monument, or written record; but it is a distinguishing mark of strong and original fancy to bestow on a fictitious character, not merely the general cast of countenance and figure which we are accustomed to associate with certain qualities and habits, and the outline of a suitable costume, but also such peculiarities, both of aspect and of external ornament, as oblige us to imagine that we see the copy of an individual, not the abstract of a class.

Any writer, attentive to minute points of tradition, might have represented John Balfour, or the Marquis of Argyle with an oblique cast of vision; but the scar on Bois-Guilbert's stern brow, which had communicated 'a sinister expression', and a slight appearance of distortion, to one of his eyes, is the stroke by which an accomplished artist gives his fancy-piece the air of a portrait.

As the beauty of these tales is often enhanced by their admirable dramatic effect, so too they occasionally lose in elegance and simplicity by an over-ambitious seeking after what are technically called coups-de-théâtre. There are some, I will not say many passages of both writers, in which either the transactions themselves are so remote from common nature, or the coincidences of time, place, situation of parties, and other accidents, are contrived with such apparent study, and so much previous sacrifice of probability, that the scene when fully developed appears not properly dramatic, but melodramatic.

In *Ivanhoe*, when the castle of Front-de-bœuf is wrapped in flames, and its besiegers stand waiting its downfall, behold! the Saxon Ulrica, by whose hand the conflagration was kindled, appears on a turret, 'in the guise of one of the ancient furies, yelling forth a war-song,' her hair dishevelled, and insanity in her eyes. Brandishing her distaff, she stands (like Fawdoun's Ghost), among the crashing towers, till, having finished several stanzas of her barbarous hymn, she at last sinks among the fiery ruins. The whole incident is described with much spirit, and may not be inconsistent with manners and customs at some time prevalent in our country: it would, no doubt, have made the fortune of a common romance; but in such a work as *Ivanhoe*, it appears, I think, too glaring and meretricious an ornament, and too much in the taste of the Miller and his Men. The same melo-dramatic turn is observable in that striking passage of *The Lady of the Lake*, where a

Saxon soldier is employed, during the battle at Loch Katrine, to bring off a boat from the island on which Sir Roderick's clansmen have placed their wives and families:

[ll. 561-73 of Canto VI of *The Lady of the Lake* were quoted]

An incident of the same class, and remarkable both for its fantastic effect, and for the improbable means and abrupt manner of its accomplishment, is the interruption of Miss Vere's marriage, by the Black Dwarf issuing from behind a monument in the family chapel, and proclaiming himself the rightful lord of Ellieslaw, his pretensions being supported by a party who had opportunely assembled in arms for another purpose, at the moment when their aid was wanted in this adventure; and the plot having been still further assisted by the castle doors standing all open, and the servants being all intoxicated. Another scene of the same character occurs in *Rokeby*, where Philip Mortham, supposed to have been assassinated at Marston-Moor, starts up from behind the tomb of his wife exactly in time to parry the stab which Risingham aims at Wilfrid.

To vary narrative by the introduction of detached lyrical pieces, is a practice resorted to with characteristic frequency by the poet, and occasionally, though more sparingly, adopted by the novelist. In this, too, both, at times, become a little theatrical. The scene contrived for *Waverley* by Miss Mac-Ivor, at the cascade, where, after terrifying the Southron by a display of her activity in walking 'over four-inched bridges', she seats herself on a mossy fragment of rock, at a convenient distance from the waterfall, and touching her harp, pours forth a long but spirited Jacobite invocation, is got up with too evident an attention to stage effect; and the performance of Ellen Douglas before Fitz-James, under circumstances not very dissimilar, has something of the same fault.

We now and then find entire songs deliberately executed in situations which are usually (except in operas,) considered the most uninviting to vocal exhibition. Thus, in *The Lady of the Lake*, a bridegroom summoned away in the midst of the nuptial ceremony, to forward Sir Roderick's fiery cross, breaks out in 'voluntary song', and completes three long stanzas of the impromptu, while 'glancing o'er bank and brae', with the speed of 'fire from flint'. And I have already mentioned the passage of *Ivanhoe*, where the Saxon virago chants fifty lines of martial poetry from the top of a burning castle in which she is about to perish.

It has been frequently noticed as a fault in the stories of both these authors, that the hero (by which name, according to romantic etiquette, we are to understand the personage who marries the heroine,) is not sufficiently important, and fails to maintain his legitimate pre-eminence above the other characters. This deficiency is, I think, attributable, in different instances, to different causes, and not uniformly to the same, as critics seem to have assumed, who lay the whole blame on the general faultlessness or inactivity of these nominal heroes.

One circumstance very common in the novels and poems, and highly disadvantageous to the principal personage, is, that during a great part of the story, he is made the blind or involuntary instrument of another's purposes, the attendant on another's will, and the sport of events over which he exercises no controul. Such, for example, is Waverley; a hero, who, from beginning to end of his history, is scarcely ever left upon his own hands, but appears almost always in the situation of pupil, guest, patient, protégé, or prisoner; engaged in a quarrel from which he is unconsciously extricated; half duped and half seduced into rebellion; ineffectually repenting; snatched away by accident from his sinking party; by accident preserved from justice; and restored by the exertions of his friends to safety, fortune, and happiness. Such a hero is De Wilton, who is introduced as the vanquished rival of Marmion, becomes by mere chance the Baron's attendant and guide, and obtains in his execution of that office the means and opportunity of achieving the few acts we find recorded of him. Malcolm Græme, in *The Lady of the Lake*, is a royal ward, without command of vassals or lands; makes a truant expedition (for a generous purpose, indeed,) to Loch Katrine, where he hears the proposal of Roderick Dhu for the hand of Ellen discussed and rejected without his interference, draws on a momentary quarrel with the chieftain by a somewhat unseasonable act of gallantry, incurs the rebuke of Douglas, and, returning homewards, is consigned to prison, from which he is released at the end of the story by his mistress's interest with the Monarch. Henry Bertram might justly claim to be the hero of *Guy Mannering*, if perils, labours, and courageous achievements, could of themselves confer such a dignity; but it is difficult to consider him in that light, because we see him the mere king of a chess-board, advanced, withdrawn, exposed and protected, at the pleasure of those who play the game over his head. The character of Francis Osbaldistone is not too insipidly immaculate to engage sympathy or awaken curiosity; but it wants that commanding interest which should surround the first personage of a novel; and the reason is, that in almost every part of the story we find him played upon as a dupe, disposed of as a captive, tutored as a novice, and unwittingly exciting indignation as a Marplot. Omitting other instances of the same kind, I will produce one character for the purpose of contrast. The Master of Ravenswood performs fewer feats of knight-errantry than any of the worthies I have mentioned, except, perhaps, Malcolm Græme: to shoot a bull; to cross swords with Bucklaw; to stare down and buffet Craigengelt; and (a more desperate venture than any) to brave the acrimony of Lady Ashton, forms, I think, the sum of his achievements. Yet no individual in any of the novels or poems more completely maintains his pre-eminence as the hero; for the whole action depends upon, and centres in him: his ruling influence is always felt, whether he be absent or present; and of all the passions, whether hatred, love, admiration, hope, or fear, which vary and animate the successive scenes, he is the grand, ultimate, and paramount object.

It is also the misfortune of many heroes in these works to be constantly thrown into shade by some more prominent character. This is particularly the case with De Wilton and Græme; with Redmond O'Neale in *Rokeby*, who shrinks to a mere idle stripling beside the dignified Mortham and the awful barbarian Risingham; with Ronald of the Isles, who, throughout the tale which takes its name from him, is evidently a subordinate agent to the real hero, Robert Bruce; with Waverley, with Henry Bertram, with Francis Osbaldistone, who plays a second-part alternately to Diana Vernon, to Baillie Jarvie, to Rob Roy, and even to Rashleigh; with Ivanhoe, whose best gifts dwindle to insignificance before the prowess and magnanimity of Richard, and the sense and fortitude of Rebecca: but such is not the predicament of Ravenswood, who preserves the same majestic ascendency over all the various characters, of whatever quality, humour, or disposition, with whom he is placed in contact.

Another circumstance which has wrought irreparable disadvantage to some heroes of great promise, is their being suffered to remain so long inactive, as entirely to forfeit their importance, and almost to run the risk of being forgotten by slow or negligent readers. Wilfrid of *Ivanhoe*, and Lovel in *The Antiquary*, are placed in this situation; and Malcolm Græme continues in retirement till we hardly wish for his return.

But there is an error, if possible, still more fatal, which both the novelist and the poet have incautiously committed in more than one instance. It is in vain that the hero is kept almost perpetually in view, that he seeks desperate adventures, and defies danger and hardship; in vain that he moves conspicuous, nay, pre-eminent, in most scenes, and, in many, engrosses our whole anxiety—if, upon some one important occasion, when the great interests of the story are at stake, and our concern in the action is wound up to its highest pitch, he is permitted to be absent, or, still worse, to stand by as an idle spectator. Heroic importance, like political influence, or female ascendency, must be guarded with incessant care, for a moment's rivalry may sometimes be fatal.

In all the works of the novelist, there is no character of the same class more vigorously drawn, or variously illustrated, than that of Henry Morton: his qualities are such as at once compel our sympathy and command our respect, and many principal events of the story receive their whole impulse and direction from his will. But, during those spirited and intensely agitating scenes with the insurgents at Loudonhill, which have never been surpassed by the present or perhaps by any other fabulous writer, Henry Morton is quietly seated on a hill, awaiting the event, and only contrives at the close of the engagement to incur some danger by interposing in behalf of Lord Evandale. When the resolution is taken to defend Lady Margaret's castle, the moment, perhaps, at which the interest of the story arrives at its highest point, Henry Morton is hearing sermons in the fanatical camp. When his fellow-rebels appear before the council, and the enthusiast Macbriar is enduring torture with a martyr's constancy, Henry Morton is standing aloof, with his pardon in his hand, though not an unconcerned, yet a passive spectator. When the gallant Evandale falls a victim to his own high spirit and the baseness of his enemies, Henry Morton, though hastening to his rescue, comes too late to succour, or to assist personally in avenging him. Thus, at several of the most important conjunctures, our whole interest and sympathy are demanded for Claverhouse, for Bothwell, for Cornet Grahame, for Lord Evandale, and for the Covenanters; while for Morton we have only the observation of Henri IV to the brave Crillon, 'Tu n'y étois pas.'[1]

Malcolm Græme is the 'brave Crillon' of *The Lady of the Lake*; Roderick Dhu is vanquished; Malcolm is not there; a battle is fought

[1] 'You were not there.'

at Loch Katrine; he is not there; Douglas mixes in the royal sports, offends the king, and is borne off a prisoner; Malcolm is not there; the fair Ellen makes her way through the soldiery at Stirling Castle, and presses for access to the monarch; Malcom is not there. The protracted and total inactivity of a hero himself is not so fatal to his credit as the exploits performed by others without his participation. De Wilton is the Crillon of Flodden Field. In the magnificent and energetic description of that battle, our enthusiasm is excited for Surrey, Stanley, Tunstall, Dacre; we hang in suspense on the fates of Marmion, plunge eagerly into the fight with Blount and Fitz-Eustace, and look with sympathy and admiration on the deserted Clare. But when the damsel naturally asks, 'Is Wilton there?' the poet does not care to give an answer; and it matters little that after the battle is over, the slain buried, and the funeral oration spoken, we are charged, on pain of being set down as 'dull elves', to believe, that 'Turk Gregory never did such deeds in arms', as this same De Wilton.

The character of Ivanhoe, again, suffers more in my opinion, by his quiescence during the siege of Torquilstone, than it gains by his gallant bearing at Ashby, or his truly chivalrous self-devotion in the lists at Templestowe; and Waverley sinks into absolute insignificance, by sustaining only the part of a common spectator in the highly tragic scene of Mac-Ivor's and Evan Dhu's condemnation.

There is, I think, in the minds of most readers, a natural and not ungenerous prejudice against him who, by whatever means, escapes from the disaster in which his party or friends are involved, and is seen enjoying security, or even pursuing his way to happiness, while they encounter their fate. Our affections and sympathies obstinately adhere to the falling, more especially if they fall bravely and becomingly; we are disposed, at the same time, to entertain something like contempt for the inglorious safety of those who survive the ruin; and to cry out, like the indignant father of the last remaining Horatius, 'Qu'il mourût!'[1] The contrast of Henry Morton pardoned by the government and pursuing his fortune in Holland, with Macbriar tortured and put to death, with Burley, a wanderer in the desert hills, and with so many other associates of their rebellion slain, persecuted, and proscribed, is almost fatal to the romantic interest of his character: and I do not know that I have ever cordially forgiven Waverley for not being hanged with Fergus Mac-Ivor; though the chieftain, it must be owned, had by far the stronger vocation to that destiny.

[1] Corneille. Horace, acte, iii. sc. 6 [Adolphus].

It would perhaps be too much to pronounce in general, that the dignity of a hero is compromised by his cherishing an unrequited passion. In subordinate personages, as Wilfrid in *Rokeby*, Lord Evandale in *Old Mortality*, and Edward Glendinning in *The Monastery*, disappointment of this kind has an effect by no means ungraceful, nor is it any serious disparagement, even to the principal character, to be once denied, if ultimately successful, like Lovel in *The Antiquary*. But I think the hero appears in no very flattering light, when, after neglecting a lady who was willing to be won, for the sake of some haughtier beauty, he finds his suit rejected, not in favour of any earlier lover, but from mere disinclination, and at length, despairing of success, returns for consolation to the once slighted but still compassionate fair one,—

'Flava excutitur Chloë,
Rejectæque patet janua Lydiæ.'[1]

This proceeding, however frequent it may be in actual life, is not, I believe, very common in romance; and we may therefore observe, as a remarkable coincidence, that the whole story, exactly as I have given it, occurs once at least in the poems, and again in the novels. The Lord of the Isles, beloved by Edith, to whom he has long been contracted, takes advantage of a somewhat unhandsome pretext to throw off his engagement, and prefers his suit to Isabel, the sister of Bruce; but when this lady has declined his addresses, and retired into a convent, he begins to perceive the merit of her affronted rival; then

——'dwells he on' her 'juster claims,
And oft his breach of faith he blames,'

and at length he decently resigns himself to her disposal on the field of Bannockburn. The situation of Waverley with Miss Bradwardine and Flora Mac-Ivor is precisely the same, except that in this case there is no violated contract. The rejection here is accompanied with some appearance of contempt for the gallant's character; and in both instances the inflexible damsel is so sincerely indifferent, that she exerts considerable industry in promoting the revolt of her admirer.

In *Harold the Dauntless*, a story not otherwise resembling either of those last mentioned, the patient Eivir makes prize of the hero's rugged heart, after he has failed in his courtship to the outlaw's daughter.

---

[1] 'Fair-haired Chloe is put aside and the door thrown open to rejected Lydia.' Horace, *Odes*, III, ix; trans. C. E. Bennett.

29. Nassau Senior surveys the novels, *Quarterly Review*

1821

Unsigned review of *Rob Roy*, *Heart of Midlothian*, *Bride of Lammermoor*, *Legend of Montrose*, *Ivanhoe*, *The Monastery*, *The Abbot*, and *Kenilworth*, *Quarterly Review* (October 1821), xxvi, 109-48 (issued December 1821).

The reviewer was Nassau Senior, a lawyer and the first professor of Political Economy at Oxford.

The reader may expect an apology for our having delayed noticing the works that compose the long list prefixed to this article. We are disposed to apologize for noticing them at all. And, certainly, most of the motives which direct us in the selection of writers to be reviewed, are in this case wanting. We cannot propose to draw the public attention to works, which are bought, and borrowed, and stolen, and begged for, a hundred times more than our dry and perishable pages. We have little expectation that the great author, who tosses his works to us with such careless profusion, will take the trouble of examining our strictures—and still less that he will be guided by them. Our praise or blame cannot well be heard among the voices of a whole nation. It is by these motives, or rather by this absence of motive, that our silence has been principally occasioned. But it cannot be persisted in. One of our duties is, to give a literary history of the times we live in—to tell those who follow us what were the subjects and the writers which chiefly engaged the attention of our contemporaries.—And it would be a strange omission if we were to pass over the works, which, from their number, their merit, their originality, and their diffusion, have more influence than is exercised by any others within the whole scope of our literature.

Our deliberation has been quickened by feeling that this really is no case for further delay. We have suffered three years to elapse since we reviewed the first series of the *Tales of my Landlord*—and in that interval a line of three-and-twenty new volumes has covered our table. A sight which, as we sit with it before us, might alarm even German diligence. It is in some measure a compensation, that we consequently address readers who are masters of their subject, and may engage in criticism without previous exposition. Our present situation has all the advantages over our ordinary one, which the comedian in Athenæus attributes to tragedy over his own art.

> '——In every sense
> This tragedy's a blessed kind of writing:
> For first, before your Prologue opes his mouth,
> The audience know the tale, and catch your drift
> From a mere hint. Mention but Oedipus—
> They knew the rest by rote, "his sire was Laius;
> His mother, Queen Jocasta; such and such
> His sons and daughters; such his former deeds,
>   And such (anon) his fate." Or name Alcmæon,
> "The madman, is it not, that slew his mother?"
> Echoes each urchin.—
>   ——Now we poor Comedians
> Get no such lucky lifts—our toiling brains
> Must coin new names, new circumstances past,
> New present incidents, new introductions,
> And new catastrophes; and if we blunder
> In this same dull explanatory task,
> We get hiss'd off; while your high tragic dons
> May boggle by prerogative forsooth.'

But to business. First, in order of time, comes *Rob Roy*. We never rejoiced more in the circumstances which exempt us from endeavouring to relate our author's plots: for though we have this instant closed the last volume, and though one of the objects of our re-perusal was to make out the story, we are by no means sure that we have succeeded. Nothing but the novel's being in the first person, so that the author appears bound only to relate the events which his hero saw and heard, without detailing the steps by which they are brought about, could have enabled him to make it hang together, even with the small portion of plausibility which it now possesses. He must have been sorely puzzled, if he had been forced, in his own person, to account for the influence which constrained Rashleigh to produce Campbell, in order to extricate his hero at Justice Inglewood's, or for the success of such an extraordinary proceeding. It is equally difficult to account for the interposition of Rashleigh's political friends, to oblige him to give up the assets, which he had taken in order to forward (though in a most unintelligible way) their views as well as his own—and for the effect of that interference, at a time when he had determined to quit their party. Indeed, the whole business of the assets—what they were— the objects for which they were taken—the manner in which they are recovered, is one mass of confusion and improbability. The author himself, as he goes on, finds himself so thoroughly involved in the meshes of his plot, that seeing no legitimate extrication, he clears himself at last by the most absolute, we had almost said the most tyrannical, exercise of the empire which authors must be acknowledged to have over their personages and events, which we recollect, even in the annals of that despotic class of sovereigns. C'est un vrai coup d'état[1]—and one which we should have expected rather from an Asiatic writer, than from a novelist 'in this free country'. He had resolved that his hero should, after the custom of heroes, enjoy the family estate and marry the heroine. But the estate is in the hands of an uncle, with six healthy sons; the heroine is pledged either to marry one of them or to take the veil. *Opposuit Natura alpesque nivemque*[2]. First comes the estate. An ordinary novelist would have felt that his hero could not have it; or, if he had set his heart upon giving it him, would have made out some story of an old entail, or a forged will, or have tried to find some other expedient, by which, with a resemblance to the common course of events, he might obtain it. It would not have been easy to do it well, and we cannot find out any plan by which it could have been done tolerably. One plan only, we can confidently say, he would *not* have adopted. He would not have killed all the six sons by different violent deaths, and the father of a broken heart for their loss, within the space of six months. If the sudden death of one person is a most inartificial mode of bringing about

---

[1] 'It is truly a coup d'état (or successful use of force).'
[2] 'Nature throws in his way Alps and snow'. Juvenal, *Satires*, X, 152. Trans. G. G. Ramsey.

a catastrophe, what shall we say of this literary execution of a whole family?

But the marriage was as difficult a business as the succession. Diana was opposed to the hero in religion and in principles; she was under the absolute influence of her father, and he is determined, at their last appearance, Vol. III, p. 316, and p. 345, with her apparent acquiescence, to 'dedicate her to God'. It appears, from a hint in p. 345, that our author had thoughts of recurring to his old method, and killing Sir Frederick Vernon before his daughter should be irrevocably vowed to the cloister, and then making her change her mind and marry. Whether the clumsiness of these expedients disgusted him when he came to put them into execution, or whether, when in sight of land, he was too anxious to scramble ashore to wait for the ordinary means, we are not informed—but, in fact, he has left the difficulty as he found it. He tells us indeed that Diana Vernon became Mrs. Francis Osbaldistone—and he tells Will Tresham that *he* knows how it took place, but he does *not* tell the reader. We recollect, when we were beginners in chess, our indignation at the abrupt ends of some of Philidor's games, in which, the pieces and pawns appearing to our ignorant eyes pretty well balanced, we were told, 'The white King wins in seven moves'. When we played out the game, sometimes the white king won in four moves, sometimes in twenty, sometimes he was check-mated in six moves, and sometimes he gave a stale mate in five. But what were the seven moves thus obscurely indicated, we could not for our lives find out. How Mr. Osbaldistone 'sped in his wooing' is still more mysterious.

The characters are, as usual, admirable. The best, perhaps, of the men is the Baillie. Nothing can promise less originality or interest than the portrait of a conceited, petulant, purse-proud tradesman; full of his own and his father's local dignity and importance, and of mercantile and presbyterian formalities, and totally without tact or discretion, who does nothing in the story but give bail, take a journey, and marry his maid. But the courage, the generosity, and the frank naïveté and warm-heartedness, which are united to these unpromising ingredients, and above all, perhaps, the 'Hieland blude of him that warms at thae daft tales o' venturesome deeds and escapes—tho' they are all sinfu' vanities', and makes him affirm before the council that Rob Roy 'set apart what he had dune again the law o' the country, and the hership o' the Lennox' (i.e. the laying waste and plundering a whole country), 'and the misfortune o' some folk losing life by him, was an honester man than stude on any o' their shanks', make him both original and interesting in the highest degree. Rashleigh is among the best portraits of that difficult subject, a well-drawn villain, that we recollect. The reader feels that his hypocrisy might have deceived— that of the common fictitious rascal would only disgust. Rob Roy himself well answers our preconceptions of his character. The man who, without rank or fortune, could for thirty or forty years set all law at defiance, who, though peculiarly obnoxious to the government, not merely as breaking its laws and plundering its subjects, but as a rebel and a traitor, and at deadly feud with the great men on whose property he lived, could resist all their power, and elude all their stratagems, without being ever overwhelmed by superior force, or betrayed by the treachery of his own companions—taken, as many of them must have been, from among the least trust-worthy of men— must have been a man of extraordinary talents and, mixed with his great vices, of extraordinary virtues. He must have had the first in order to play his own part well, the second in order to retain in devoted fidelity his associates.

And he must have been a man of extraordinary courage. Some of our readers may perhaps be surprized at hearing that the last has been doubted; and, certainly, on the occasions which are the most usual tests of courage, he behaved ill. He fought two duels, and in both of them yielded almost immediately, in no very honourable manner. And, at Sheriff Muir, on the only occasion in which, with the temporary command of the clan, he had an opportunity of showing at once his spirit and his devotion,

> 'He never advanced
> From the place he was stanced
> Till nae mair was to do there at a' man.'

But the fact is, that no two things can be more different than the courage of an outlaw and that of a soldier. The first is founded on familiarity with danger,—it is the virtue of rude times, and can be obtained only by repeated exposure to peril. The second is founded on the point of honour—it can exist only in a most artificial state of society, and is so far from requiring repeated exposure, that it is often most perfectly exhibited by men who were never in danger before in their lives. The first arises from the contempt which is the proverbial result of familiarity. A man who has been often in danger has learnt to distinguish its real, from its apparent, symptoms—to fear the lightning, not the thunder. He has learnt to balance the hazards of different modes of escape—to wait the opportunity for putting in practice that which appears most promising, and to snatch that opportunity when, on the whole, it appears probable that a better will not offer. All this supposes great calmness and presence of mind—but is compatible with a thorough detestation of all unnecessary risk. It not only is compatible with such a detestation, but its natural tendency, if uncounteracted by other causes, must be to produce it. The constant association, in such a man's mind, with danger has been, that it is a thing to be as much as possible avoided. His constant meditation has been, how shall I attain my object with the least hazard, and, having attained it, how shall I best provide for my safety? Such habits fit him admirably for avoiding danger—and for encountering it when it cannot be avoided; but very ill for thrusting himself into it when it can—or for continuing in it when any mode of escape is open. No man can show more calmness in danger, than a North American Indian, or try more frightful modes of escape, if they are the best that offer,—or fight more desperately if he is absolutely forced to fight. But he will not fight *unless* he is forced. He will rather endure any fatigue, cold, sleeplessness, and famine, to surprize his deadliest enemy, than meet him on fair, or nearly fair, terms.

Military courage is founded on the glory attached to the endurance of danger, and to the infamy attached to undue fear. And, as no natural bounds can be assigned to qualities, which are themselves unnatural, the necessary endurance was first raised to insensibility, and, at last, to delight, in danger. In that most artificial period which followed both the English and the French civil wars, when the minds of men, deprived of the violent sources of excitement to which they had been accustomed, ran into every sort of affectation and absurdity, a gentleman seems to have been bound to hold any opportunity of encountering danger a source of unalloyed enjoyment. Any ulterior purpose, however frivolous, was not to be required. A man who was so fortunate as to receive, or to have a fair opportunity of giving, a challenge, had the patronage of inviting three or four friends to partake in the amusement; and while the principals, who might be supposed to have some object in it, were fighting, the seconds, instead of minding their duty as umpires, fought too, to show how much they enjoyed a chance of being wounded or killed. The story is well known of the man who offered to Lord Stair such an opportunity, provided he would exercise this patronage in his favour; and who refused to interfere further when he found he could derive no advantage from the transaction, as his lordship's list was full for his next three affairs. The story is probably coloured, but it shows what were the feelings, at least the cant, of the times in which it could be circulated. A man so trained would have shone on those occasions, on which we have described Rob Roy as failing—but it may be questioned whether he would have heard, with the same presence of mind, the Baillie's step on the Tolbooth's stairs; and whether, if strapped, like him, to Evan Bigg, he would have had sufficient boldness to plan his escape, sufficient composure to execute it, or sufficient patience to delay it to the most favourable instant.

But what of 'Die Vernon, the heath-bell of Cheviot, the blossom of the Border'? To say the truth we had rather say nothing, for we fear we may not be impartial judges. We are now old and grey-headed, and, even when young, we do not recollect that we ever were in love; a passion, of which Bacon remarks that great and worthy persons are unsusceptible. But if we could suspect ourselves of admitting a feeling so inconsistent with our age and situation, we should believe ourselves in love with Die Vernon. We have what has always been considered as the first and most fatal symptom—'We like her faults as much as if they were our own.' We acknowledge that her debut is coarse and unnatural—that her telling Osbaldistone, in the first five minutes of their acquaintance, that she thinks him handsome, is shocking—that her selecting their first meeting at dinner, when all eyes and ears would naturally be open upon the stranger, to abuse the whole family seriatim, by name, is absolutely impossible. And yet we dwell upon all these passages with pleasure. But certainly the damage was not done on the first day. The next we were very much amused. We were delighted with her during her ride to Justice Inglewood's, and still more during her return—laughed most heartily at her meeting with Jobson, sympathized with her three subjects of pity, envied Osbaldistone his situation as her confidant and counsellor 'tho' he was to know nothing of her affairs'; admired her collection of treasures, and were pleased even with her blue-ism, so different was it from any to which we had been accustomed. By this time we probably were in some danger, but we are not sure whether she completed our conquest in the masterly scene, in which she drew from Osbaldistone the account of Rashleigh's falsehoods, or in that, perhaps still finer, in which, after her unsuccessful defence of the mysterious glove, she baffled her cousin's curiosity, and defied his jealousy, without diminishing one shade of his esteem or his love. We have heard the character called unnatural throughout. She ought, perhaps, to be somewhat older, twenty-two would have been better than eighteen; but grant the author what he has always a right to claim for his heroine, if he is bold enough to think he can support them, great talents and excellence of disposition, and add, what certainly is possible, an education perfectly unfemale, under the superintendance of two men of talent and learning, and add the pride of high birth, and the enthusiasm of an adherent to a persecuted religion and an exiled king—exclude her from the ordinary wishes and schemes of young girls by predestining her to a hateful object or a cloister, and give her, instead of their ordinary amusements and employments, political intrigues, Greek and Latin, and field-sports, and you have the rough outlines of the portrait, to which our author has given such relief and colouring.

But we must hasten to *The Heart of Mid-Lothian*, with the exception perhaps of *Waverley*, the most perfect of the whole set. And we are not sure that even *Waverley* may not owe the superiority in our eyes, which, on reconsideration, we still feel that it possesses, to the circumstances under which we first read it. We shall never forget the disappointment and listlessness with which, in the middle of a watering-place long vacation, we tumbled a new, untalked of, anonymous novel out of the box, which came to us from our faithless librarian, filled with substitutes for every thing we had ordered. Any where else we might have returned it uncut; but a watering-place makes a man acquainted with strange companions for his reading, as well as his talking, hours. So we opened it, at hazard, in the second volume, and instantly found ourselves, with as much surprise as Waverley himself, and with about the same effect, in the centre of the Chevalier's court. Little did we suspect, while we wondered who this literary giant might be, that seven years after, we should be reviewing so many more of his volumes in one article, and that the mystery would be, except by internal evidence, as dark as ever.

But, abstracting from *Waverley* the advantage of its primogeniture, the two novels, different as they appear, have many points in common; they are unequalled in the happiness of their subjects. The story of Prince Charles is a piece of the wildest romance, in the midst of the dullest flats of history, as if the cave of Staffa could rise in the middle of the Zuyder Zee. *The Heart of Mid-Lothian* is as fortunately chosen. The escape of Robertson, the murder of Porteous, and the pardon of Effie, though the principal facts of the last are true, and even the minutest details of the two former, are as marvellous in their way as the enterprise of Prince Charles; and the characters in both novels derive the same advantage from our imperfect knowledge of the class from which they are taken. All our author's readers must have observed how much better he paints beggars, gipsies, smugglers, and peasants, the favourites of kings and queens, and kings and queens themselves, the very lowest and the very highest ranks of society, than that rank to which he must himself belong. How superior is Effie Deans to Lady Staunton, and Daddie Ratton to Sir George? How much bolder, and how much more accurate, appears to us the pencil that struck out Dandie Dinmont than that which drew, though with far more elaboration, Mr. Pleydell? How much more do his Mary of Scotland and Elizabeth of England appear to resemble queens, than his Julia Mannering does, a young lady? How comes he to copy more correctly what he knows imperfectly, than what he knows well?

Our first answer is, 'We doot the fact.' We suspect that his gentlemen and ladies are, in truth, more faithful portraits than his princes, his beggars, or his rustics; but that the familiarity of his readers with the originals makes their examination of his faithfulness too severe. They are more struck by the deficiencies than by the merits; by what varies from their own standard, than by what coincides with it. No jockey was ever satisfied with the horses even of Phidias. But when the author paints a peasant, a cowfeeder, or a queen, he takes from a class with which the reader is so little acquainted, that, if the figure be but spirited and consistent, and contain nothing obviously incompatible with its supposed situation, we are willing, indeed we are forced, to take its resemblance upon trust. And perhaps the author's consciousness of the reliance of his reader is even more valuable to him than that reliance itself. It leaves him at liberty to dress his characters, not in the most appropriate, but the most picturesque, habiliments. If he draws from his own sphere of life, it is from a finished model, where every detail is prescribed to him. If from any other, it is from a sketch of which only one or two leading features are marked, and his imagination may supply, as he likes best, the remainder. He has the same advantage which Dryden translating Chaucer had over Dryden translating Virgil. He is saved too from the danger of losing *general* resemblance in too close a copy of the individuals with whom he is intimate; and from that of introducing something of effort, something of overcolouring and caricature, into his figures, in his endeavours to render striking, the representations of a well-known class. A painter may be tempted to put horses and cows into some studied attitude, or to group them too artificially, who would not think of any thing more than an unaffected resemblance of an hippopotamus.

Our general admiration of the story of *The Heart of Mid-Lothian* does not, of course, extend to the management of all the details. The beginning, or rather the beginnings, for there are half a dozen of them, are singularly careless. The author, in his premature anxiety to get in medias res, introduces us at the point where the different interests converge; and then, instead of floating down the united stream of events, we are forced separately to ascend each of its tributary branches, like Humboldt examining the bifurcations of the Oroonoko, until we forget, in exploring their sources, the manner in which they bear on one another. We regret too, that he should have violated the simplicity of his narrative by that novel-like incident, the testimonial from Butler's grandfather through which, in some degree, Jeannie obtains the assistance of Argyle. Its introduction is, if we may be allowed to revert to a distinction which we endeavored to establish in a former article, vol. xxiv, p. 355, both improbable and unnatural. Improbable, because, that Jeannie should, the instant she wanted a great protector, have found her obscure lover possessed of the strongest claims on the man best fitted for the purpose, was, to a degree almost beyond the powers of numeration, against the chances of real life. Unnatural, because it was absolutely impossible that a family, holding a document which gave them unlimited access to the patronage of the most powerful nobleman in Scotland, should have suffered it to remain unemployed, like Aladdin's rusty lamp, while they struggled through three generations in poverty and disappointment. If our author thinks even *this* more natural, than that Argyle should have been induced, by Jeannie's representations, to examine into her sister's case, by his doubts as to her guilt to interfere in her favour, and by his sympathy with Jeannie's heroism to bestow his benefits on her and her family, we must say that he thinks much worse, than we do, of the characters he has drawn.

We are not sure too, that it might not have been politic in the author to suppress almost all his fourth volume. We are very glad that he did not, for it is all very amusing. Knockdunder is excellent; and so is the transformation of Gentle Geordie and Effie into Sir George and Lady Staunton, particularly the latter; and we revisited with pleasure, in Sir George's company, the Tolbooth door and

Saddletree's shop. A new and most entertaining light is likewise thrown upon the character of David Deans; his feelings on Dumbie-dike's marriage, his reconciliation of his speculative principles with existing circumstances, and his discussion with Butler as to his acceptance of the Duke's preferment, are delightful. But all this has the effect of a farce after a tragedy. Where the ludicrous is interwoven with the pathetic or the terrible, it heightens the effect, both by contrast and by the appearance which it gives of authenticity. Saddle-tree's absurdities have certainly a good effect in the trial scene; but a whole train of light amusing narrative, in which the very persons, whose previous history has harrowed the reader's mind with pity and terror, or swelled it with admiration, have nothing to do but to show foibles and enjoy prosperity, lowers sadly their poetical dignity, little perhaps as they themselves would have been aware of it.

Among the exquisite scenes, on which the opinion that we have just ventured to express is founded, perhaps the most perfect is the meeting of the sisters before the trial. We will own, that on our first perusal, we trembled for the author when we found that he really meant to exhibit it. We felt that such a meeting must create emotions almost beyond the power of words; and yet that a single expression exaggerated, or constrained, or artificial, would poison the whole. The trial has not perhaps the same merit from its difficulty, but is as striking in its execution. Effie is a perfect specimen of the fit subject for fictitious misfortune. Not so good as to make her calamities absolutely revolting; not so bad as to make them appear appropriate punishments. Her crime is precisely the $\alpha\mu\alpha\rho\tau\iota\alpha$ $\mu\epsilon\gamma\alpha\lambda\eta$ of Aristotle.[1] Had it been deeper, her sufferings would, of course, have excited less pity; had it been none at all, they would have raised, instead of pity, horror and indignation. As it is, our exquisite pity for *her*, and our pity, mingled with admiration, for her father, produce an intensity of interest, which extends itself, not only to the important incidents, but to the minute formalities, of the trial, which is even heightened, as we observed before, by the foolery of Saddletree, and the bad taste of her advocate, and is not destroyed even by our constant anticipation of the event. We wait with almost as much anxiety during Jeannie's silence after Fairbrother's question, 'And what was the answer she made,' and while the yet unpublished verdict is sealed and recorded, as if we did not well know what must, in each case, be the result.

We cannot bestow the same unqualified praise on another celebrated

[1] The great tragic flaw. See Aristotle's *Poetics*, section XIII.

scene, Jeannie's interview with Queen Caroline. Jeannie's pleading appears to us much too rhetorical for the person and for the occasion; and the queen's answer, supposing her to have been overpowered by Jeannie's entreaties, 'This is eloquence', is still worse. Had it *been* eloquence it must necessarily have been unperceived by the queen. If there is any art of which *celare artem*[1] is the basis, it is this. The instant it peeps out, it defeats its own object, by diverting our attention from the subject to the speaker, and that, with a suspicion of his sophistry equal to our admiration of his ingenuity. A man who, in answer to an earnest address to the feelings of his hearer, is told, 'you have spoken eloquently', feels that he has failed. Effie, when she entreats Sharpitlaw to allow her to see her sister, *is* eloquent, and his answer accordingly betrays perfect unconsciousness that she has been so, 'You shall see your sister,' he began, 'if you'll tell me', then interrupting himself, he added in a more hurried tone, 'no, you shall see your sister whether you tell me or no.'

The duke himself is, perhaps, a little too fine spoken in his opening conversation with the queen, but his character is in general happily finished. The vanity, which covered his great qualities with a varnish, that has perhaps contributed to the permanence of his reputation, is very gracefully insinuated. Douce Davie Deans is magnanimous in his affliction, and amusing in his prosperity. We have but one fault to find with him, the laugh which is constantly raised by his religious peculiarities. It may be said, that the weight of his religion, like that of armour of proof, if it sometimes repels the impulses of nature, when they are right, always secures him from them when they are wrong; that, if it loads him with unnecessary scruples, it arms him with heroic self-devotion and constancy; and if it sometimes makes him absurd, leaves him often venerable, and always respectable, in his absurdity. But it is precisely to this union of good and evil consequences, that, *as a subject of general representation*, we object. When religion, or what resembles it, is represented as rendering sanguinary and merciless such a fanatic as Burley, every reader can perceive that his belief does not create his bad passions, but only decides their course. Pride, violence, and malignity, are essential parts of his character; and if he had been an Atheist instead of a Cameronian, they would have only changed their objects. But the religion of David Deans is the basis of his whole character; his faults and follies seem, no less than his virtues, to spring from it. And we can conceive a reader, without much power of

[1] The concealment of art.

discrimination, so strongly associating them together, as to believe the one as necessary a consequence of it as the other; and to congratulate himself that *he* is a man of the world, above all silly scruples. We refer, as an illustration of our remark, to his conversation with Saddletree and Butler, on the choice of a counsel for Effie, at the end of the first volume.

To get rid of the little we have remaining of blame, we must add, that we do not think George Robertson quite worthy of his author. He is somewhat too melo-dramatic. Men, whatever may be their remorse, do not profusely apply to themselves the terms villain, murderer and devil; or calmly affirm themselves predestined to evil here and hereafter. They have always a reserve as to the goodness of their hearts, especially where they are ready, as Robertson is described to be, to sacrifice their lives to save that of another. Saddletree is less annoying than our author's fool generally is, because there is less of him. He is not, like Fair Service, locomotive, so that when we escape from Edinburgh and its neighbourhood, we leave him. His wife is happily contrasted to him. We thoroughly enter into her dislike of her husband's gossips, and her indignation to 'see sae mony o'them set up yonder in their red gowns and black gowns, and a' to take the life o' a bit senseless lassie.' What to say of Madge Wildfire we scarcely know. The outline is bold and the colouring vivid; and it is more like what we suppose madness to be than any other representation of it that we recollect. But whether it is really like, those only can tell who have had the misfortune to see more of the insane than has fallen to our lot. Her introduction, to warn Robertson by her songs that an enemy is at hand, rather too much resembles the incident in *The Lady of the Lake*, where Fitz James is warned of the ambush by the song of the maniac Blanch. The novel, however, tells the story with more plausibility.

We must not close our remarks without taking a more formal leave of Jeannie. She is a perfect model of sober heroism; of the union of good sense with strong affections, firm principles and perfect dis-interestedness; and of the calm superiority to misfortune, danger and difficulty, which such an union must create. A hero so characterized gen-erally spoils the interest of a novel, both because the reader knows him to be protected, among all his dangers, by the strong arm of poetical justice, and because his conduct, upon every occasion, is anticipated. The first of these inconveniences is skilfully obviated, by making another person the object of the dangers on which the interest of the story depends, and using Jeannie only as the means of averting them; the second, by placing her in humble life, and then exposing her to situations in which no good sense could supply the want of experience. As it is, she is a splendid exception to the insipidity of perfect characters, and excites and retains the reader's deepest interest, without possessing the advantage of a single fault.

We are almost inclined to renounce the supremacy of *Waverley*, and of *The Heart of Mid-Lothian*, when we come to *The Bride of Lammermoor*. It is a tragedy of the highest order, and unites excellence of plot to our author's usual merits of character and description. It may be objected, that poor Lucy Ashton's misfortunes are too much the sufferings of innocence to be the fit subjects of tragical sympathy. Her forming the engagement with Ravenswood cannot, as it is described, be considered even as an error. She adheres to it, through every persecution of violence and art, while her reason remains unimpaired; and her final breach of it is scarcely an act of the will. Perhaps the answer is, that a voluntary breach of engagement is a fault, to which so much disapprobation is attached, that some degree of disapprobation—that degree which affords a pretext for the misfortunes of tragedy—is attached to one that is involuntary. No combination of circumstances will perfectly wipe off the stain of a breach of chastity, and constancy is the chastity of the affection, and is as necessary to the security of unmarried love, as that of the person is to married love. Both are, therefore, fenced with the same jealousy; and a woman who has been surprised, or seduced, or impelled into a violation of either, though under circumstances that may acquit her in foro conscientiæ, is guilty foro imaginationis. To this arbitrary tribunal the poet resorts; here Miss Ashton will be tried, and though her case is a very hard one, we fear the verdict will be against her.

Although there is no deficiency of faults in Ravenswood, it is perhaps a blemish, that his faults are so remotely connected with his misfortunes. They set in motion, it is true, the train of causes on which his misery and his death ultimately depend. If he had not been violent and revengeful, the lord keeper would not have feared him; if the lord keeper had not feared him, he would not have endeavoured to soften him by effecting an intimacy with Lucy Ashton. Without that intimacy there would have been no engagement; without the engagement he would not have received the challenge, or been lost on his way to meet it. But it is not to the remote and accidental, but to the immediate and appropriate, effects that the reader looks. Now all the immediate effects of Ravenswood's spirit of pride and vengeance are advantages; it frightens a powerful enemy into a friend, gives him the affections of a charming girl, and appears to have great influence in obtaining a valuable patron. His misfortunes spring from the enmity of Bucklaw and Lady Ashton; both arising from causes out of his own controul, and as likely to have arisen if he had been the meekest of mankind. If this *is* a fault, it is an unlucky one, as it might have been so easily avoided. His own temper might have been made to afford far more obvious, and more probable, causes of offence, than a gaucherie of Caleb's, or the hereditary dislike of Lady Ashton. As a character he is excellent, admirably drawn, and admirably grouped and contrasted with those around him. Indeed we recollect no work of our author's in which contrast is more skilfully used. Ravenswood is opposed to Lucy, and Sir William to his lady; and those characters, which at first appear the same, are beautifully distinguished from each other. Sir William and Lucy are flexible and timid; Ravenswood and Lady Ashton firm and decisive. But the flexibility of Sir William, arising from fear of personal consequences, and fickleness of purpose, differs as much from that of his daughter, which springs from affectionateness of disposition, anxiety not to give pain, and preference of others to herself, as the firmness of Lady Ashton does from that of Ravenswood. Lady Ashton's firmness is nurtured in affluence and power, strengthened by the subservience of him who fills the station of her superior, and confirmed by the direction of all her purposes to family aggrandizement. Ravenswood's is grounded, in a great measure, on the want of those advantages, the possession of which contributes to that of Lady Ashton; on an habitual feeling that he is defrauded of his just rank in society, and habitual exertions to force those who cross him to acknowledge it. He treats them as inferiors, whom accident and injustice have made his equals, and follows his own impulses without deference for their opinions or their feelings. But, as one impulse succeeds another, his course, though vehement and intrepid, is not always consistent. Lady Ashton's is governed by calculation, and is therefore unvarying.

The engagement between the lovers is beautifully managed, and with the more merit, as it is a scene in which ordinary novelists so often fail. They generally seem to select it as an opportunity for fine writing—for long flowery 'declarations in form', to use their own expression, on the part of the hero, and pretty disclaimers on that of the lady. Now in fact, where such a scene is merely the eclaircissement of a previous mutual affection, (and those are the cases of which we are speaking,) nothing can be shorter, less impassioned, or less 'in form' than the really important parts of it. The veil between them has become so slight that the least touch tears it down. Short half-hints of attachment on *his* part, and of acquiescence on hers, are enough to explain their mutual feelings, and both parties are anxious, as quickly as possible, to consider the explanation as made. There may, or may not, be protestations and vehemence in the conversation that follows; we only wish to exclude them from those very few words which, with the reply or silence by which they are followed, actually form the declaration and acceptance; and we will admit, too, a great distinction between the case we have supposed and one of indifference on the man's side. Where an Irish captain woos a city widow, or a boarding-school heiress, he may make all his approaches in form, and when he thinks he can venture to batter in breach, may open with vows and protestations,

> And all the 'great' artillery of love;

but the conduct of a lover will differ as much from that of a fortune-hunter as his feelings.

The three hags are a bold, we had almost said a not unequal, rivalry of the Weird Sisters. Their professional praise of Ravenswood is whimsically horrible.

[a quotation from chapter 23 of *The Bride of Lammermoor* ' "He is a frank man" ' to 'replied the sage' is omitted]

We wish Ailsie Gourlay's prediction had been omitted. Like the apparition of Alice Gray, and the prophecy that the last Lord of Ravenswood would stable his steed in the Kelpie's flow, it is a useless improbability. If the latter had been made a mere vague presage of evil, it might have produced equal effect, in deepening the gloom which always overshadows the hero's destiny, without requiring us to mix a belief of actual supernatural agency with the actions and habits of the world as we see it. Or if Ravenswood had been a knight of romance, in habitual intercourse with giants and dæmons, we might as easily have supposed him to encounter a ghost as a dragon. But in a novel, in which the main instrument is a suit in the Scotch courts carried by appeal into the House of Lords, where the only knight is a lawyer, the principal incident a change in the ministry, and the most affecting scene, the signing of marriage settlements, we cannot believe that an infant's fortune was truly spaed before the sark gaed over its head, that a circumstantial prophecy was accurately fulfilled, or that an old woman made mouths at a young man after she was dead.—Ghosts have no business to appear to mortgagers or mortgagees.

But Caleb is a more serious blemish. Of all our author's fools and bores, and we acknowledge we dislike the whole race of them, from Monk Barns down to the Euphuist, he is the most pertinacious, the most intrusive, and, from the nature of his one monotonous note, the least pardonable in his intrusion. His silly buffoonery is always marring, with gross absurdities and degrading associations, some scene of tenderness or dignity. Our author's eminent success in the difficult and almost untrodden path of tragi-comedy (few writers before him, excepting Shakspeare, having ever ventured to bring the ludicrous into close contrast with the pathetic) has probably tended, as is often the case, to tempt him into carrying the expedient to an excess. Such contrasts occur in nature; and when represented as they occur in nature, have an interesting and agreeable effect, in a great measure, as we hinted before, from the vivid resemblance to reality thus produced. But they will not admit of being violently and ambitiously introduced. It is the old mistake of the first landscape gardeners, who, in their rage to imitate nature, used to plant dead trees, and build ant-hills, close to a house: if it be intolerable to have every circumstance of horror or pathos artificially crowded together, with a studied exclusion of every lighter character and event, still less tolerable is it to have an equally artificial effort after the contrasts of tragi-comedy; to have the broadest and most extravagant caricature continually dragged into studied opposition to the tragic characters and incidents.

We must not quit *The Bride of Lammermoor* without remarking its deviation from the usual management of a narrative. The fatal nature of the catastrophe is vaguely indicated in the very beginning; at every rest in the story it is more and more pointedly designated; and long before the conclusion we are aware of the place and means of its accomplishment. We are first told of the malignant fiend under whose influence the tissue of incidents is to be woven. We are told that a dreadful punishment awaits Sir William's selfish calculations on the supposed attachment of Ravenswood and Lucy. Before the lovers have thrice met we are told what were his remarks after the catastrophe of their love; and, however he might disregard, in real life, the ominous fatality of the mermaiden's well, the raven that is killed as the lovers quit it, the thunderstorm that marks their interview at

Wolf's Craig, or even the prophecies of Ailsie Gourlay and True Thomas, every reader feels that, in fiction, these are tokens true as holy writ; and yet our interest in the story is strengthened, instead of being destroyed, by our fore-knowledge of the conclusion. How is this managed? How is that which generally deadens the reader's interest made, in this instance, its auxiliary?

We believe that *The Bride of Lammermoor* owes to the nature of its catastrophe its exemption from the usual necessity of reserve—it is the privilege of tragedy. We will assume that every fiction must contain Aristotle's μεταβασις,[1] dangers terminating in happiness, or happiness converted into misery. In the former case the impending evils, the probability of which formed the danger, do not actually take place; in the latter, during the apparent safety of the characters, evils are brooding which ultimately destroy it. They are disturbed, in the one case, by causeless fears, and, in the other, lulled in fatal security; and if the reader is aware of this, he in both cases sympathizes, not with their actual feelings, but with what would be their feelings if they knew their situation. In the first case, if they knew their own safety they would laugh at the danger; and accordingly there is nothing more ludicrous than a man, who thinks himself in danger, when he is not. If the seconds have resolved to charge the pistols merely with powder, we defy their principals, however cool may be their courage, with whatever calmness they may make preparations for a fatal result, to excite any emotions but ridicule. Sancho, clinging in darkness to a ledge of rock with firm ground, where he supposes an unfathomable abyss, six inches below him, has every reason to think himself in the most frightful danger; but we know that he is safe, and we laugh. If we are to sympathize with the courage, we must sympathize with the fear of the hero; to do that, we must, like him, be ignorant of the event. But though a man who is safe, when he thinks himself in danger, is only an object of amusement, a man who is in danger, when he thinks himself safe, may be an object of the deepest interest;—we feel as he would feel if he knew his situation—we appear even to feel more deeply, when we contrast it with his enjoyment and his gaiety.

> Regardless of the sweeping whirlwind's sway,
> That, hushed in grim repose, expects his evening prey.

There is no picture more affecting, than that of high hopes and

Change of fortune. See Aristotle's *Poetics*, section XIII.

brilliant expectations, when the reader, alone, hears the wheels of an avenging fortune 'groan heavily along the distant road'. It is a consequence of this distinction that Tragedy is allowed to take her plots from known events, while Comedy must invent them herself. We use the word comedy, somewhat improperly, to designate the class of fictions which end happily; for danger, which the spectator knows to be unfounded, makes an admirable subject for comedy in its narrow sense of ludicrous fiction, on the very same ground that it is an improper subject of serious fiction. How utterly would the Judgment-scene in *The Merchant of Venice* have been ruined if it had been preceded by the conference between Bellario and Portia, and the reader had been warned of the flaw by which Antonio is to be saved! and how carefully has Shakspeare provided, by the interference of Portia, and her reiterated advice and entreaty to the Jew to accept the money, (which are in fact unnatural, as she was provided with a better remedy,) to convince the spectator that the issue will be fatal! If we could put ourselves in the situation of those for whom Shakspeare wrote; if we could take a draught of Lethe, and then read it as for the first time; or if it could have been concealed from us till our taste was ripe, how much would the scene, beautiful as it is, be improved! But our interest in *Lear* or *Othello* is not diminished by a tenth perusal. It is probable that they would lose by that ignorance of the events by which *The Merchant of Venice* would be improved. A fiction which ends happily may give as much pleasure on a first perusal, as one which ends unfortunately; but a great part of its power is exhausted by that first perusal. We have been admitted behind the scenes, and though we may admire the skill with which the giant is compounded, we know that his bones are made of wicker, and his muscles of straw. But the evils of tragedy are 'no sham', and the knowledge that they are impending, renders affecting even the tranquil scenes by which they are preceded—we feel them to be the calm before the tempest,

The torrent's smoothness ere it dash below.

The Legend of Montrose will not detain us so long as its predecessors. It is, we think, inferior to them all. The plot, if it can be called one, is a fragment of the history of Montrose, without middle or end; to which two or three well-known stories of no great merit, such as that of the Chieftain who cheated his English friends of a fairly won bet, the amputated head which the Macgregors placed at the table once its own, with bread between its jaws, and the assassination of Lord

Kilpont by Stuart of Ardvoirlich, are, with new names and dates, inartificially stuck on. A love-story, of slight materials, is interwoven to give it some consistency, and there are in this, as in every other of our author's novels, some splendid purpurei panni.[1] It differs from them all in one respect, that the Bore, Dugald Dalgetty, is perhaps the best drawn character. There is a great deal too much of him, as is always the case, but he has more variety in his note than they usually possess. The whole-length portrait of a mere mercenary, whom constant exposure to the violence of his enemies, and the selfishness of his friends, had covered with a callous integument, equally proof against fear, generosity, and delicacy, would have been tiresome, but for the ludicrous tinge of a pedantry, partly scholastic, partly military, and partly national;—and the wild figures among whom he is placed, show off well his regulated vices and his mechanical virtues. His merit is increased by his originality: in ordinary novels high personal courage, and a strict adherence to whatever may have been laid down as the point of honour, are almost entirely confined either to the characters that are intended to be amiable, or to those that, however unamiable, possess a certain lofty and Satanic ferocity—to those whom we intended to love or to fear—to the Æneas or the Mezentius. In Dugald Dalgetty, we find cool intrepidity, arising from long familiarity with danger, and habitual adherence to his own point of honour, combined (as is often the case in real life, and so seldom, as we have said, in fiction) with a calculating and sordid disposition—qualities that, instead of love or fear, excite contempt. The escape from Inverara, with all its improbabilities, is among the splendid patches we have alluded to. Another is the battle of Inverlochy, with the gradual approach of Montrose's army that precedes, and the contest over the body of the Knight of Ardenvohr, that concludes it. Allen M'Aulay and Mac Eagh would have been fine characters in a poem—we are not sure whether their features are not exaggerated in what purports to be a representation of real events. One cannot believe Mac Eagh's parting injunction to Kenneth to have been delivered—but it is a beautiful piece of Ossianic declamation. His vengeance on Allan M'Aulay is perhaps too artificial and too sentimental for the contriver—particularly as two of his enemies were to gain by it, much more than M'Aulay was to lose. Menteith is in perfectly good taste, but too unambitious a character to give scope for much praise or blame: and history has shed a light over the disastrous heroism of Montrose, as

[1] Purple passages.

disastrous to his country as it was glorious to himself, which debarred our author from individualizing him by a nice selection and compensation of qualities. The opportunities, however, which he had, he has used successfully; and mixed well, with his general panegyric, the alloy of personal motives, which may be supposed to have produced the memorable invasion of Argyleshire.

Next comes the splendid masque, *Ivanhoe*. Of all our author's works, this is formed of the most peculiar materials. Kings, crusaders, knights, and outlaws, Cœur de Lion, and the Templars, and Robin Hood, and Friar Tuck, and the Forest of Sherwood, the names, and the times, and the scenes, which are entwined with our earliest and dearest recollections, but which we never hoped again to meet with in serious narrative, become as familiar in our mouths as household terms. Names coupled with such associations would be interesting, however trivial the actions in which they were engaged—and they are used as profusely as they are collected. We have the public and private life of our Saxon and of our Norman ancestors, the domestic meal, the formal banquet, the tournament in both its forms, the storm of a baronial castle, the solemn trial, and the judicial combat. These are among the scenes immediately before us, and, as we pass through them, views perpetually open on each side of our path, that show the contemporary state of Europe and Asia, with glimpses of Palestine, and Saladin, and the Crusaders in the distance.

We recollect that, on our first perusal, we thought *Ivanhoe*, though not the best, the most brilliant and most amusing of this whole family of novels. We are not sure that it has stood a second so well. Its principal deficiency is one which besets ordinary novelists, but from which our author is in general eminently free—want of individuality in the principal characters. Ivanhoe, Rowena, Front de Bœuf, Locksley, the Templar, and even the grace of the whole story, Rebecca, are each marked with one, or at most two, predominating qualities, without the counterbalancing merits and defects, which, by reciprocally modifying each other, distinguish every man, in real life, from his neighbour. Ivanhoe and Rowena are the traditionary hero and heroine of romance. He, brave, and strong, and generous; she, beautiful and amiable; and both of them constant—very well qualified for their employment at the end of the story, to marry and live happily together, but a little insipid during its progress. Front de Bœuf is the traditional giant—very big and very fierce—and his active and passive duties are those always assigned to the giant—the first consisting in seizing travellers on the road, and imprisoning them in his castle, to the danger of the honour of the ladies, the life of the knights, and the property of all others; and the second, in being beaten at tournaments and killed by the knight-errant, to whom the author at length issues his commission of general castle-delivery. Brian de Bois Guilbert belongs to that hacknied class, the men of fixed resolve and indomitable will—fine ingredients in a character, which is marked by other peculiarities, but too uniform and inartificial, and, in fictitious life, too trite, to serve, as they do here, for its basis. To say the truth, we have been lately so bored by the continual recurrence of the Impiger, iracundus, inexorabilis, acer,[1] who allows no law, but that of arms, that if we had found a novel, which we were trying as an experiment, begin with a description of a person, in whom 'the projection of the veins of the forehead, and the readiness with which the upper lip and its thick black mustachios quivered upon the slightest emotion, plainly indicated that the tempest might be again, and easily awakened'— whose 'keen, piercing, dark eyes told in every glance a history of difficulties subdued, and dangers shared, and seemed to challenge opposition to his wishes, for the pleasure of sweeping it from his road by a determined exertion of courage, and of will'—we fear we should have been apt to push the inquiry no farther. As Bois Guilbert is almost all in shadow, Rebecca is all in light. Brought up among examples of nothing but extortion and cruelty on one side, and cowardice, meanness, and avarice on the other, in the situation most certain to break the courage, and sour the temper, and narrow the heart, she emerges—perfect. From an education combining every disadvantage, she rises, such as no advantages could have made her. But in Rebecca the beauty of the execution more than redeems the improbability of the conception. We only regret that her love for Ivanhoe, which is so exquisitely described, is not better accounted for. When we recollect that she knew, when she first saw him, that their difference of race raised between them an impassable barrier; and that, in their first conversation, she discovered where his affections were fixed, it is scarcely possible that love, so totally without hope, could have arisen in a well disciplined mind, even with the assistance of similarity of character and frequent intercourse. And even these are, in this case, wanting. They are described as opposed in all their feelings, and habits, and prejudices, and associations—and it is in only their second interview that her passion has reached such a height, that, in

[1] 'Impatient, passionate, ruthless, fierce.' Horace, *Ars Poetica*, 121.

despair at its hopelessness, she murmurs a welcome to the random shaft which should put an end to her life.

But perhaps the greatest failure, if that term can be applied where so little is attempted, is Locksley. He has precisely that set of qualities, honour, disinterestedness, generosity, and justice, which always mark the outlaw of a novel, at least of a bad novel, and never the outlaw of real life—and he has no others. We have the more right to complain, when we compare this vulgarly featured daub, which is affixed to such a name as Robin Hood, with the living portraits of Donald Bean, and Julian Avenel, and the Children of the Mist, and Rob Roy, which show how the painter can treat such a subject if he chooses. It is true that he was hampered by the historical features of Robin Hood; but our very complaint is, that *circa vilem patulumque moratur orbem*,[1] without venturing to add a shade, or a colour, which shall make the picture more individual, or less improbable.

But our censure must end here. In the rest of the characters we recognize the author of *Waverley*. Nothing can be more bold than the conception, or more vigorous than the representation, of Richard and Friar Tuck. It is difficult to choose between subjects of such excellence— but of the two, we think the Friar is our favourite. Scarcely any other author could have ventured to engraft the outlaw on the priest, or could have prevented the union from being unnatural or hateful. But the humour, which is thrown over it, solders together its heterogeneous parts, and makes the compound as amusing as it is original. As for Richard, we will confess that, long before *Ivanhoe* was written, he had been a subject of our meditation. We have often endeavoured to picture to our minds the appearance and the manners of the man, whom history appears to have amused herself with dressing in the colours of fable. Our author has done for us, what we never could do satisfactorily for ourselves. We acknowledge his Richard with the same conviction of his identity, and the same wonder that we could ever have supposed him any thing different, with which we recognize, in a long separated friend, the features and address which we had in vain tried to imagine in his absence. Prince John, and Cedric, and Athelstan, and De Bracy, and Prior Aymer, and Gurth, are all good, though of coarser materials —and even Higg the son of Snell, and Hubert the forester, and Father Dennett, though their outlines are indicated only by a few negligent strokes, stand out from the canvass with all the prominence of real

---

[1] 'He lingers along the easy and open path'—adapted from Horace, *Ars Poetica*, 132.

existence. But we find that it is at the scenes in which Richard, or the Friar, is engaged, that our volumes open of themselves—and a well thumbed passage is that in which, at their first meeting, the ascetic reserve, which the hermit seems to have adopted rather as a vehicle for his humour than as a cloak, relaxes before the bold frankness and irresistible smile of the Knight. Another is, the resurrection of the Friar from the dungeons of Front de Bœuf, with his 'captive to his bow and his halbert'—his account of his controversy with the Jew— and his memorable exchange of buffets with Richard, taken of course from the similar contest between Richard and Ardour, so amusingly related by Mr. Ellis. This, however, is hardly imitation—a real incident in Richard's life probably forms the basis, of which the old chronicler and the modern novelist have given us variations. But we have little doubt that the mode in which Rebecca repels the Templar, is borrowed from the celebrated scene in which Clarissa (vol. vi, letter 13) awes Lovelace by a similar menace of suicide. As they are scenes in which these great writers appear both to have put forth their strength, we would extract them, if our limits, already almost exceeded, permitted us, and as they do not, we recommend our readers to compare them: the cautious, minute, and reiterated strokes of Richardson afford a striking contrast to the bold semi-poetical rapidity of his modern rival.

We have little to say as to the story, but that it is totally deficient in unity of action, and consists, in fact, of a series of events, which occurred, at about the same time, to a set of persons who happened to be collected at the lists of Ashby. The associations, however, which are connected with the actors and the times, and the vividness of the narration prevent the interest from flagging—or rather renew it with each adventure—and the want of one concentrated interest may only make the different scenes more amusing, by allowing the reader leisure to pause and look round him as he passes. Perhaps the scene that bears this examination worst, is the tournament. Our first objection to it is, that it is managed in what we should almost call a childish way, with a profuseness of success, first on the side of the challengers, and then on that of the hero, so glaringly improbable, as to destroy the reality produced by the general minuteness of description. We almost tremble at our rashness when we presume to add a doubt of the antiquarian accuracy of some of the details. We had always supposed the forfeiture of arms and horse to be a punishment reserved for unknightly conduct, and not the necessary result of the slightest preponderance of success on either side, in each encounter. Front de

Bœuf is described as incurring this forfeiture, because he loses a
stirrup; Malvoison, because he is unhelmed—and Grant Mesnil
because his horse swerves; on these terms no challenger could have
expected to retain his horse and arms during a day. We object, indeed,
generally to our author's representation of a tournament as a personal
contest, in which one knight was to be declared conqueror, and the
other conquered. Our ancestors seem to have considered it as a knightly
game, in which the antagonists might mutually show their address,
and which did not imply victory or defeat in either. We equally
doubt the correctness of our author's distinction (vol. i, p. 169)
between the effects of a blow on the helmet, and one on the shield—
or rather we admit the distinction, but believe that the superiority
attributed by him to the former, in fact belonged to the latter. As a
general illustration of our remarks, we refer to the most detailed
account, which is extant, of such a scene, in Froissart's description of
the great tournament held by three French knights at St. Inglevere,
lib. x. cap. 11, particularly to the courses run by Sir J. Rosseau, Sir P.
Sherborne, and Sir Herchance.

But the most striking scene in the whole work, is the storming of
Front de Bœuf's castle. Every reader must have felt the peculiar
vividness with which the first assault is painted. Much as we have
exceeded our usual limits, we will make a short extract from it.

[a quotation from chapter 29 of *Ivanhoe* 'It was not, however, by
clamor' to 'than upon battle' is omitted]

It may be worth while to examine the means by which this vividness
has been obtained, and by which the reader feels himself more present
at that part of this scene, which is described by Rebecca, than at that
which is described by the author in his own person. Had he really
been present at that part which is described by the author, he would
have seen and heard certain sensible objects, from which he might
have inferred, with more or less propriety, that certain events were
taking place. Had he been among the assailants, he might have inferred,
from the number of men whom he saw bleeding and falling, the loss
that his companions were suffering. Had he been on the ramparts, he
might have drawn the same inference as to the defenders. From the
effect produced on their armour by the arrows, and the mode in which
they exposed themselves, he might have judged whether their armour
were, or were not, of proof, and whether they did or did not, trust
to it. By accurate observation, of the points struck by the arrows, he

might have inferred whether they had, or had not, each an individual aim. And, if accustomed to such scenes, he might have judged whether the defence were more or less obstinate, or the attack more or less furious, than was usual. But, unless the reader's experience has been such as to associate in his mind these appearances and inferences, he must feel that, had he been present, these appearances would not have suggested to him these inferences, and, being absent, the inferences do not suggest to him what must have been the appearances. He cannot, therefore, fancy himself to have been present at the event. He cannot even fancy the author to have been present *at the whole*, for no one person could have seen enough to make, with certainty, all these inferences. He must suppose him to have been informed by many other persons of the inferences drawn by them, from what they saw and heard, and from these accounts to have himself inferred the whole event. It is thus that a narrative is usually formed. And such a narrative may often enable us to judge perfectly of the *consequences* of an event, and leave us perfectly in the dark as to the actual *appearances* of which it really consisted. We, who are now writing, will confess that nothing can be more vague than our ideas of a battle or a siege. When we hear of an assault, or a charge, an advance, or a rout, we have an indistinct conception of blood, and fire, and smoke, red coats, and blue coats, and gun, drum, trumpet, blunderbuss, and thunder;—but it is a conception, of which the parts are very inconsistent with one another, and all of them, we have no doubt, with the reality. Yet, when we have a full narration of a victory or a storm, we often think we can estimate both the causes and the consequences of these events, far better than a common soldier, though he may have been present at all that *one* person could witness, and may have a clear conception of the *things*, of which we blindly use the *names*. Yet so far are we from fancying ourselves present at the scene, that, as in the novel, we cannot even fancy the relator to have been. When he tells of events, which took place at different places at the same time, we know that he must be repeating the inferences drawn by different persons from what they saw in different situations. Such a narrative affords the greatest body of information, in the most concise form, to the intellect, but can suggest no new image to the imagination. It is, as we have said, the common and historical one. We lose in the extent, but gain in the apparent authenticity, of our information, when the narrator gives us only the inferences which might have been drawn by one witness. We may then suppose him to have been that witness, and are more disposed to believe his inferences correct, than if he had made them at second hand, and also to sympathize with his feelings when a witness. This authenticity and power of creating sympathy are, as we observed in a late Number (vol. xxiv., p. 361) the advantages of novels in the first person: the narrow sources of information to which they are confined, is their defect. We approach a step nearer still to being actually present, when the narrator gives us, not his inferences, but the sensible objects themselves. This, only, can be called a description; but, to make it worth having, the objects must be interesting, or we should not listen—they must be new, or we should anticipate them— and they must be intelligible, or we could draw no conclusions from them. The remaining merit is, that the spectator should have been affected by them as we should have been ourselves. It is this which makes a traveller so much better a describer than a native—which would make us listen rather to a passenger's account of a shipwreck than to that of a sailor. The native and the sailor are much more familiar with the objects they describe—and therefore describe them more correctly, but with that familiarity we do not sympathize. We wish for first impressions, because we wish to feel as we should have felt if we had been present.

Rebecca's description unites all these merits in a higher degree than any that we remember. The objects are interesting and perfectly new. The previous detail, and Ivanhoe's explanation, make them intelligible, and enable us to infer the progress of events; and her wonder, her horror, and her intense anxiety, are exactly the feelings which we should expect to feel ourselves, if exposed, for the first time, to such a scene, as inactive spectators. We think that, in her place, we should have seen the same sights, heard the same sounds, drawn the same inferences, and felt the same emotions. And our perfect sympathy produces its usual effect, of making us fancy ourselves, as we read, in her situation. Before we quit this scene, we must observe that it contains an heraldic error, remarkable in itself, when we consider the antiquarian knowledge of our author, and still more from its coincidence with a similar mistake in his great rival, Sir Walter Scott. The Black Knight bears what Rebecca calls 'a bar and padlock painted blue', or, as Ivanhoe corrects her, 'a fetterlock and shackle bolt azure' on a black shield; that is, azure upon sable. This, we believe, as colour upon colour, to be false heraldry. Now on the shield of Sir Walter's Marmion, a falcon

'Soared sable in an azure field.'

The same fault reversed. It is a curious addition to the coincidences of these two great writers, that, with all their minute learning on chivalrous points, they should both have been guilty of the same oversight.

The peculiarity, as well as the merit, of *Ivanhoe*, has seduced us beyond our usual limits. We are in less danger of exceeding them with *The Monastery*. Without disputing the general verdict, which places this below the rest of our author's works, we shall endeavour to ascertain the grounds on which it may be supposed to be founded. We believe the principal deficiency lies in, what is usually our author's principal excellence, the female characters. In general, his men add to the boldness and animation of the scene, but his women support almost all its interest. Perhaps this must always be the case where both are equally well drawn. We sympathize more readily with simple, than with compound, feelings; and therefore less easily with those characters, the different ingredients of which, have, by mutual subservience, been moulded into one uniform mass, than with those in which they stand unmixed and contrasted. Courage restrained by caution, and liberality, by prudence, loyalty, with a view only to the ultimate utility of power, and love, never forgetting itself in its object, are the attributes of men. Their purposes are formed on a general balance of compensating motives, and pursued only while their means appear not totally inadequate. The greater susceptibility, which is always the charm, and sometimes the misfortune, of women, deprives them of the same accurate view of the proportion of different objects. The one upon which they are intent, whether it be a lover, a parent, a husband, a child, a king, a preacher, a ball, or a bonnet, swallows up the rest. Hence the enthusiasm of their loyalty, the devotedness of their affection, the abandonment of self, and the general vehemence of emotion, which, in fiction as well as in reality, operate contagiously on our feelings. But our author has, in *The Monastery*, neglected the power of representing the female character, which he possesses so eminently, and, in general, uses so liberally. The heroine is milk and water, or any thing still more insipid: Dame Glendenning and Tibbie are the common furniture of a farm-house; and Mysie Happer and poor Catherine, though beautiful, are mere sketches.

This deficiency might have been supplied by the skilful complication and disentanglement of a well constructed plot. But all that resembles a plot is the union of Halbert Glendinning with his demure, pale-faced love—and that is effected by mere accident, his introduction to Murray, and Murray's unforeseen march to Kennaquair. We cannot help suspecting that our author began to tell his story with very vague plans for its progress. We can conceive him to have sketched the characters of Halbert, Edward, Mary, Boniface, Eustace, Warden, and Shafton—to have resolved to marry Halbert and Mary, make Edward a monk, say a good deal about *The Monastery*, and bring in, and get rid of, the Euphuist as he could; and then to have set to work, trusting that the White Lady would help him whenever he stuck fast. His trust was certainly well founded, for he could not doubt the willingness or the power of a being who was to act with no assignable objects, and to be restrained by no assignable limits. With such machinery, constructing stories is as easy as lying. We could invent them so for eight years together: dinners and suppers, and sleeping hours, excepted. But he must know that such props to the author are stumbling-blocks to the reader. We tolerate a supernatural agent only when

> Actoris partes, officiumque virile
> Sustinet——[1]

when its purposes and means are referable to some standard. Without such a standard, we can neither enter into the conduct of a being that appears to have no motives, nor estimate the skill of an author who has not let us know what he intends to represent.

A natural consequence, of writing without a well digested plan, is disproportion of parts. Too long a beginning is a common fault of our author's, but we know no instance of it so glaring as the work before us. Until the morning when Halbert leaves his companions at their lessons, and runs up the glen to invoke the white lady, the real story can scarcely be said to begin. Edward, Mary, and Halbert, till then, are children, and a whole volume has been employed in introducing to us the trite characters of Espeth, and Tibbie, and Martin, and of the fierce borderer, the good-natured luxurious abbot, and the pious sub-prior; and in relating the absolutely trifling legerdemain which transports to and fro the black book. We could almost venture to assert that the first nine chapters might be compressed without injury into nine pages. And even when the narrative is at last set flowing from the capacious cistern of the first volume, it breaks, almost immediately, like a stream in a flat country, into three or four independent channels. We have the stories of Mysie, and Sir Piercy Shaftone, of Halbert, of Henry Warden, and of the inhabitants of the

---

[1] 'He maintains the role of an actor and the function of a man.'

convent, and the tower of Glendinning, all diverging in different directions, and only connected by terminating in Murray's march. The only individual for whom we feel much interest, is poor Mysie, for she is almost the only one who acts on natural motives. Halbert is a fine high-spirited youth, but when we are told that his character is altered by his being conversant with high matters, and called to a destiny beyond that of other men, and by his communications with a supernatural being, and find that his fate is to be swayed by the capricious exertions of her indefinite power; the one ceases to be intelligible, and the other to be interesting. Henry Warden's perils are too soon over, and Eustace's begin too late, and the motives of both are too artificial, to be the subjects of much sympathy. Espeth, Tibbie, and Mary cannot be interesting, for they do nothing and suffer nothing, and the only scene in which Edward is so, is that, in which he resolves to assume the cowl. As for Sir Piercy, he is as incomprehensible as the white lady. We might let his Euphuism pass, for it would be rash to set any bounds to the possible influence of affectation, but from the manner in which the story of his birth is mentioned by Stawarth Bolton, it could not have been a matter of deep mystery; and if it had, his conduct, when the bodkin is presented to him, is the most absurd piece of exaggeration even in our author's pages, subject as they are to that fault. And the conclusion is as hurried as the commencement is drawled out. The troops of Murray and Foster are let down e machina[1] on the stage, to kill Julian, Kate, and Christie, betray Shafton's genealogy, change Abbot Boniface into Abbot Eustace, and, *de more*,[2] marry the two pair of lovers.

And yet no reader can doubt the genuineness of *The Monastery*. 'Many men, many women, and many children' might have avoided its faults—but we know no man or woman, besides 'the Author of *Waverley*', who could have painted the scene which follows the entrance of Halbert and Henry Warden into the Castle of Avenel, the meeting between Warden and Eustace, or Halbert's ride to the scene where the battle was fought. To *one* other name alone could we ascribe the poetry, so wild, so varied, and so powerful, that flows from the White Lady; and *he* is a champion who seems to have retired from the literary lists, and is suspected to see, without bitter regret, his proudly-earned honours matched, perhaps eclipsed, by those of his masked successor.

[1] That is, unnaturally, as an expedient.
[2] According to custom.

But the great merit of *The Monastery* is, that it is a foundation for *The Abbot*. This not only relieves, in a great measure, the reader from the slow detail, or the perplexing retracings and eclaircissements, which detain or interrupt him in a narrative that is purely fictitious, but is an improvement on some of the peculiar advantages of one that is historical. In the latter, the hard and meagre outline of his previous knowledge seldom contains more than the names and mutual relations of the principal personages, and what they had previously *done*, with very little of what they had previously *felt*. But where one fiction is founded on another we are introduced, not merely to persons who are notorious to us, but to old acquaintances and friends. The Knight of Avenel, the Abbot Ambrosius, and the Gardener Blinkhoolie, are the Halbert, and Edward, and Boniface, into whose early associations and secret feelings we had been admitted. We meet them, as we meet, in real life, with those whom we have known in long-past times, and in different situations, and are interested in tracing, sometimes the resemblance, and sometimes the contrast, between what has past and what is present; in observing the effect of new circumstances in modifying or confirming their old feelings, or in eliciting others which before lay unperceived. We view with interest the fiery freedom of Halbert's youth ripened into the steady and stern composure of the approved soldier and skilful politician; and when, as Knight of Avenel, he sighs for birth and name, we recognize the feelings, that drove him from the obscure security of a church vassal, to seek with his sword the means of ranking with those proud men that despised his clownish poverty. And when Ambrose acknowledges that, bent as he is by affliction, he has not forgotten the effect of beauty on the heart of youth—that even in the watches of the night, broken by the thoughts of an imprisoned Queen, a distracted kingdom, a church laid waste and ruinous, come other thoughts than these suggest, and feelings that belong to an earlier and happier course of life; a single allusion sends us back through the whole intervening time, and we see him again in the deep window recess of Glendearg, and Mary's looks of simple yet earnest anxiety watching for his assistance in their childish studies. The allusion would have been pretty, but how inferior, if Ambrose had been a new character, and we had been forced to account for it by some vague theory as to his former history.

The Abbot has, however, far greater advantages over its predecessor than those, great as they are, that arise from their relative situation. We escape from the dull tower of Glendearg, with its narrow valley and homely inmates, to Edinburgh, and Holy Rood House, and Lochleven Castle, and the field of Langside, and to high dames and mighty earls, and exchange the obscure squabbling of the hamlet and the convent, for events where the passions of individuals decided the fate of kingdoms, and, above all, we exchange unintelligible fairy-ism for human actors and human feelings.

It is true there is a sorceress on the stage, but one endued with powers far greater 'for evil or for good' than the White Lady.

History has never described, or fiction invented, a character more truly tragic than Queen Mary. The most fruitful imagination could not have adorned her with more accomplishments, or exposed her to greater extremes of fortune, or alternated them with greater rapidity. And the mystery which, after all the exertions of her friends and enemies, still rests on her conduct, and which our author has most skilfully left as dark as he found it, prevents our being either shocked or unmoved by her final calamities. The former would have been the case, if her innocence could have been established. We could not have borne to see such a being plunged, by a false accusation, from such happiness into such misery. The latter would have followed, if she could have been proved to be guilty. Her sufferings, bitter as they were, were less unmixed than those of Bothwell. He too endured a long imprisonment, but it was in a desolate climate, without the alleviations which even Elizabeth allowed to her rival, without the hope of escape, or the sympathy of devoted attendants: such was his misery, that his reason sunk under it. And though his sufferings were greater than those of his accomplice, if such she were, his crime was less. He had not to break the same restraints of intimate connection and of sex. But nobody could read a tragedy of which his misfortunes formed the substance; because we are sure of his guilt, they would excite no interest. While we continue to doubt her's, Mary's will be intensely affecting.

And yet no poet has, with success, taken her for a heroine. The last and most distinguished of those who have made the attempt, Alfieri, who might have been expected, from his peculiar situation, to write con amore, has only failed the most conspicuously. By selecting the murder of Darnley for his subject, he has, at once, given up almost all the advantages that her history afforded. His Maria Stuarda is merely an affectionate, sweet-tempered wife, who loses a sulky husband. She incurs neither guilt nor danger; and the story, after languishing through five declamatory uneventful acts, breaks off, at the first incident, which gives the reader hopes that something is to happen, and leaves him to guess what that something must have been, not from the situation of the characters, with which it is totally irreconcileable, but from an obscure prophetic denunciation. But Mary has at length fallen into the hands of an author that deserves her. He had not only to paint the queen, the beauty, and the accomplished women, to embody all our ideas of the majestic, the pleasing, and the brilliant, but to shade his picture with the weaknesses that were necessary to its probability, without diminishing its fascination; to allude constantly to past events, without implying the innocence or guilt of the principal character, and to make us lament the failure of schemes, under which, if they had succeeded, we should probably ourselves be this instant suffering. Never was there a more difficult attempt, or a more splendid execution.

For a purpose, of which we shall speak hereafter, he has given her a companion from that class of characters, which it seems his delight to draw, and we are sure it is ours, to read; in which the arch buoyancy and lightheartedness of youth are united to the arduous designs and firm resolves of maturer age; and where all that is lovely, and playful, and fragile in woman, is mixed with the deep cares, and adventurous enterprise of man. Not even in Flora Mac Ivor, or Diana Vernon, is this union more bewitching than in Catherine Seyton.

Our author, to be sure, was put upon his mettle. The hero was to betray his trust, to desert the religion of which he began to feel the truth, and to engage in schemes, the success of which endangered the ruin of his country, and was certain to effect that of the protectors of his infancy. Strong temptations were necessary, and strong temptations are applied; we feel that an older and more thinking mind than Roland's would not have resisted them. We admit the probability and the interest of the narrative, and yet we wish it could have been altered. The picture of stern duty opposed to violent temptation is only safe, either where, as in the case of Jeannie Deans, duty prevails, or where its failure, as in that of Lucy Ashton, is followed by misfortunes, which are to be the subjects of our sympathy. The rule of poetical justice has obtained such currency, that whatever the author rewards he is supposed to approve. Our author appears to have felt this objection, and to have endeavoured to obviate it by expedients, which strike us as aggravations. He makes Roland rejoice that Morton's interruption enabled him to part from the Regent, without plighting his troth to fulfil his orders, and feel himself at liberty, without any breach of honour, to contribute to the Queen's escape, as soon as he has intimated to Dryfesdale that he refuses trust. But, when he proceeded on his office, after a full explanation from the person who entrusted him with it, of the duties to which it was attached, it is mere jesuitism to say, that he was not bound by its conditions, because he had given to them only a tacit consent; or that he could be released from them, after having acquired, by a long apparent acquiescence, the means of defeating them, by any declaration even to his principal, much less to a subordinate agent. We do not deny, that his situation was one of extreme difficulty, that to have refused Murray's trust would have been immediate ruin, and that every motive which can soften, and subdue, and delude, the firmest principle and the clearest perception, was accumulated to induce him to betray it. In real life, all would forgive, some would even admire, his conduct; but a writer of fiction has no right to dress, what is fundamentally wrong, in a covering that can attract sympathy or admiration. *He* is not exposed to the same difficulties as his heroes, and has no right to make their reward *depend* on that part of their conduct which does not deserve unmixed approbation. Still less has he a right to sanction a parley between duty and passion, and to countenance the sophistry that attacks the understanding through the heart. To him, still more forcibly than to Hiero, may Pindar's caution be applied.

$$\ddot{a}\text{-}$$
$$\text{-}\psi\epsilon\upsilon\delta\epsilon\hat{\iota}\ \pi\rho\grave{o}\varsigma\ \ddot{a}\kappa\mu o\nu\iota\ \chi\acute{a}\lambda\text{-}$$
$$\text{-}\kappa\epsilon\upsilon\epsilon\ \gamma\lambda\hat{\omega}\sigma\sigma\alpha\nu.$$
$$E\check{\iota}\ \tau\iota\ \kappa\alpha\grave{\iota}\ \phi\lambda\alpha\hat{\upsilon}\rho o\upsilon\ \pi\alpha\rho\alpha\iota\theta\upsilon\varsigma\text{-}$$
$$\text{-}\sigma\epsilon\iota,\ \mu\acute{\epsilon}\gamma\alpha\ \tau o\iota\ \phi\acute{\epsilon}\rho\epsilon\tau\alpha\iota$$
$$\pi\grave{\alpha}\rho\ \sigma\acute{\epsilon}\theta\epsilon\nu.\ \ \Pi O\Lambda\Lambda\Omega N\ TAMI'A\Sigma$$
$$E\Sigma\Sigma I.^1$$

But this blemish, the importance of which we must not dissemble, is the only material fault we have to find with the story. It is, in general, beautifully conceived, and beautifully executed. The author has selected the only part of Mary's life which, from the magnitude of the events, their connection with each other, and the short time within which they occurred, affords fit materials for poetical narrative. We have a beginning which excites curiosity, a middle which keeps it up,

---

[1] 'If any word, be it ever so light, falleth by chance, it is borne along as a word of weight, when it falleth from thee. Thou art the faithful steward of an ample store. Thou hast many trusty witnesses to thy deeds of either kind.' Pindar, *Pythian Odes*, I, 85; trans. Sir John Sandys.

and an end by which it is satisfied. And the loves of Catherine and Roland are most skilfully interwoven with the fate of their mistress. Never was a double plot better connected. From our first entrance into the Castle of Loch Leven, to the last signal of adieu waved by Mary in the Firth of Galloway, our interest is concentrated on the three principal characters, interrupted by no episodes, and broken by few improbabilities.

We are criticizing an author too enterprizing to be deterred by any difficulties of execution. We have no doubt, therefore, that in suppressing the visit paid by the Regent to Mary, during her imprisonment, he decided wisely; but we must own we were watching for it as we read, and felt disappointed when we found it was to be omitted. We know that it was, in fact, deeply affecting to Mary; and when we recollect the relation, in which he stood to the principal persons in the castle, the circumstances under which he met the sister, to whom he owed so much, whom he once served so faithfully, and appears to have once loved so truly, now deposed for his advantage, and imprisoned by his authority, the mixed feelings of pride and shame with which he must have been received by Lady Lochleven, the outward deference that must have covered the fear and dislike of George Douglas, the unrestrained hatred of Catherine Seyton, and the awe of Roland Græme, we cannot conceive a finer picture, than would have been the result of such a subject, in the hands of such a master. Perhaps he did not like to injure his fine sketch of Murray's character, by the unnecessary cruelty of that visit; perhaps he feared that he must degrade that of Roland, by forcing from him promises of a fidelity that he was to abandon. Whatever were his motives for the suppression, we cannot well doubt, as we said before, they were sufficient; but we regret that his management of the plot made it necessary.

Where all is so excellent it is difficult to select particular points. We are not sure whether we prefer the busy scenes of Holy Rood House, the interview in which Roland yields himself up to Catherine, as she signs the cross over his forehead, the scene in which Mary anticipates one blithesome day at their blithesome bridal, or the morning that she awakes at West Niddie. Perhaps they are all inferior to the battle, painted in the favourite manner of our author, and of Sir Walter Scott, from the point of view occupied by the ladies and the squires who protect them. But there is no end of enumerating beauties, and we have not time or inclination to search for blemishes.

In *Kenilworth* our author is again upon tragic ground; a ground which, either from the advantages we have ascribed to tragedy, in its independence of any concealment of the catastrophe, and wider admission of historical subjects, or from the peculiar bent of his talents, he always appears to us, on a reperusal, to tread most successfully. But though *Kenilworth* must rank high among his works, we think it inferior, as a whole, to his other tragedies, *The Bride of Lammermoor*, the historical part of *Waverley*, and *The Abbot*, both in materials and in execution. Amy Robsart and Elizabeth occupy nearly the same space upon the canvass as Catherine Seyton and Mary. But almost all the points of interest, which are divided between Amy and Elizabeth, historical recollections, beauty, talents, attractive virtues and unhappy errors, exalted rank and deep misfortune, are accumulated in Mary; and we want altogether that union of the lofty and the elegant, of enthusiasm and playfulness, which enchanted us in Catherine. Amy is a beautiful specimen of that class which long ago furnished Desdemona; the basis of whose character is conjugal love, whose charm consists in its purity and its devotedness, whose fault springs from its undue prevalence over filial duty, and whose sufferings are occasioned by the perverted passions of him, to whom it is addressed. Elizabeth owes almost all her interest, to our early associations, and to her marvellous combination of the male and female dispositions, in those points in which they seem most incompatible. The representation of such a character loses much of its interest in history, and would be intolerable in pure fiction. In the former, its peculiarities are softened down by the distance, and Elizabeth appears a fine, but not an uncommon object, a great, unamiable sovereign; and the same peculiarities, shown in the microscopic exaggeration of fiction, would, if judged only by the rules of fiction, offend as unnatural; but supported by the authority of history, they would be most striking. A portrait might be drawn of Elizabeth, uniting the magnanimous courage, the persevering, but governable, anger, the power of weighing distant against immediate advantages, and the brilliant against the useful, and of subjecting all surrounding minds, which dignify men, and men only of the most manly character, with the most craving vanity, the most irritable jealousy, the meanest duplicity, and the most capricious and unrelenting spite, that ever degraded the silliest and most hateful of her sex.

Our author has not, we think, made the most of his opportunities. He has complied with the laws of poetical consistency, without recollecting that, in this instance, the notoriety of Elizabeth's history warranted their violation. Instead of pushing to the utmost the opposing qualities that formed her character, he has softened even the incidents that he has directly borrowed. When Leicester knelt before her at Kenilworth, 'ere she raised him, she passed her hand over his head, so near as *almost* to touch his long curled and perfumed hair, and with a movement of fondness that seemed to intimate, she would, *if she dared*, have made the motion a slight caress.' Listen to Sir James Melvil's account of the real occurrence. 'I was required to stay till he was made Earl of Leicester, which was done at Westminster, the Queen herself helping to put on his ceremonial, he sitting upon his knees [kneeling] before her with great gravity; but she could not refrain from putting her hands into his neck, *smilingly tickling him*, the French ambassador and I standing by. Then she turned, asking at me how I liked him?' Again, when she discovers Leicester's conduct, in which every cause of personal irritation is most skilfully accumulated, she punishes him only by a quarter of an hour's restraint under the custody of the earl marshal. When, at a later period, and under circumstances of much less aggravation, she detected his marriage with Lady Essex, she actually imprisoned him. Our author has not ventured on the full vehemence of her affection or her rage. But, after all, his picture of the lion-hearted Queen, though it might perhaps have been improved by the admission of stronger contrasts, is so vivid, and so magnificent, that we can hardly wish it other than it is.

We are not sure that we have suggested any improvement in Elizabeth. We have none to offer in Leicester. His struggles under the contest between love, ambition, and vanity, the subservience of his spirits and his feelings to the associations of time and place; Amy's power when present, and weakness when absent; his half formed resolution to abandon for her the court, and its flight at the thought, not of what he would lose, but of what his rivals would gain; his devotion to Elizabeth, only equalled by his fear, are the best picture extant

'Of the old courtier of the queen and the queen's old courtier'—

of the man who, without hereditary rank or fortune, the son and the grandson of attainted and forfeited traitors, without talents in affairs or in war, a dangerous counsellor and an unfortunate commander, stained by the imputation of almost every crime, and the commission of many, unfaithful to his mistress in love, and hurtful in business, managed to deceive, and practically to retain in subjection, for thirty years, the most jealous woman, the most imperious sovereign, and the most acute discerner, to whose scrutiny his vices and deficiencies could have been exposed; for whose sake she endured, during her whole life, the slander, to which she was most sensible, and reposed the land-defence of her kingdom, at the time when the Armada threatened its greatest danger, in hands notoriously incompetent.

Varney belongs to the class, so rare, if it really exist, of unmixed villains, in whom, with vigorous intellectual powers, the moral sense is totally deficient, and who accordingly select their objects with perfect selfishness, and pursue them with unrelenting earnestness, softened by no compunction, and awed by no fear, but that of failure. Our author apologizes for his introduction, by assuring us, from time to time, that there *are* such men. We are willing to surrender our previous opinion to the authority of one so intimately acquainted with human nature: but the necessity of this apology ought, perhaps, to have led him to doubt the propriety of introducing the character that required it. If the mixture of human feeling, which we think would have been found in the real Varney, could have been infused into the fictitious one, without defeating the plan of the novel, it certainly would have improved it, by rendering more natural one of the principal characters. We are reminded by Tressilian of the Wilfred of *Rokeby*. They are both executions of the difficult task of giving dignity to an unsuccessful lover. They are both men of deep thought and retired habits; both nourish an early, long, and unfortunate attachment. In both it sinks so deep into the mind, that it becomes their dream by night, and their vision by day; mixes itself with every source of interest and enjoyment, and when blighted and withered by final disappointment, it seems, in both, as if the springs of the heart were dried up along with it. But as Tressilian is to support more of the plot than Wilfred, he has a firmer bodily and mental temperament; and his mind, instead of having mere sorrows to brood over, is steeled by injuries to avenge. They are fine variations of what appears to be one conception.

Blount and Raleigh are very good, particularly Blount at his knighthood; but when we arrive at the end of the journey, at the beginning of which they were so specially introduced to us, and during the course of which they have occupied so much of our time, and find that they have no influence whatever on the catastrophe, we are inclined to ask what procured us the honour of their company? Our author sometimes reminds us of the magician, that accompanied Benvenuto Cellini to the Coliseum, and whose misfortune it was, that his powers of evoking spirits were greater than his means of employing or removing them. No man has more influence in the vasty deep. They come when he does call them; but for any thing they have to do, it often seems that they might as well have been left there.

The fault of Raleigh and Blount is, that they are supernumeraries. Wayland Smith is not that; but if another agent could have been found to conduct the countess to Kenilworth, we cannot but wish that the whole episode of 'Wayland the cunning smith', (though the clink of his ghostly hammer still frightens the children of Uffington and Compton,) and of the semi-miraculous cure of Sussex, could have been omitted. They are an unnecessary waste of time and violation of probability. But a legendary hint affects our author, like a sound which reaches the ear in imperfect sleep. He instantly builds on it a super-structure of persons and events, as disproportioned to its origin, as if the mouse had brought forth the mountain.

The last volume and the opening of the first are, we think, superior to the rest. The author seems to have found some difficulty in filling the interval between Amy's parting with Leicester at Cumnor, and her journey to Kenilworth. For this purpose we have the episodes of Wayland Smith, and Sussex, and Raleigh, the pleasing anachronism of Shakspeare, the bear-bait taken from the contemporary cockney description of such a scene reprinted by Andrews:[1] Wayland's intro-duction to Amy, in the disguise of a pedlar, borrowed from the common stock of Novel-ism—and the scene in which Janet detects the person, copied almost faithfully from Artaserse. But as the action proceeds, as the early events begin, in their consequences, to bear more and more upon each other, and the clashing interests to muster their forces on each side, our author's genius seems roused as the demands on him increase. Like Sir Walter's Minstrel, when at last 'he caught the measure wild', he is *cursu concitus heros*.[2] Nothing can be finer than the evening which Amy passes in Mervyn's tower—more striking than the conclusion of her interview with Leicester, or more affect-ing than its beginning. The paleness that indicates Varney's purpose to Foster, and is told only by the dialogue, is a splendid imitation of Buckingham's question to Dorset, in Richard the Third:

'Look I so pale, Lord Dorset, as the rest?'

[1] Orson Penner's supplication (for the outlines of the story are true) was in fact successful. The biped performers were restrained from acting on certain days in the week, lest they should interfere with the quadrupeds [N. W. Senior].

[2] 'The hero roused on the run'. Virgil's *Aenead, XII*, 902.

At every page the catastrophe seems impending, yet none of the events which defer it appear forced. And so skilful is the preparation of the mine, which is to overturn Leicester's confidence in his wife, that though all the circumstances, by which his jealousy is to be fired, have taken place under our eyes, we are unconscious of her danger, till Varney's rapid recapitulation lights the train.

> 'Then come at once the lightning and the thunder,
> And distant echoes tell that all is rent asunder.'[1]

It is a fault perhaps of the conclusion, that it is too uniformly tragical. In *Waverley* and *The Abbot*, the happiness of Rose and Waverley, and of Catherine and Roland, is entwined, like the ivy of a ruined window, with the calamities of their unfortunate associates, and relieves us from one unvaried spectacle of misery. And even in *The Bride of Lammermoor*, our author relents from what appears to have been his earlier intention, restores Bucklaw to health, and pensions Craigengelt, and suffers the whole weight of the catastrophe to fall only on his hero and heroine. But in *Kenilworth*, the marriage of Wayland Smith and Janet (an event which scarcely excites any interest) is the only instance of mercy. The immediate circumstances of Amy's death, as she rushes to meet, what she supposes to be, her husband's signal, almost pass the limit that divides pity from horror. It is what Foster calls it, 'a seething of the kid in the mother's milk'. All our author's reiterations of Varney's devilishness, do not render it credible. Tressilian, Sir Hugh Robsart, Varney, Foster, Demetrius, Lambourne, almost every agent in the story, perish prematurely or violently. Elizabeth is reserved for the sorrows of disappointed love and betrayed confidence, and Leicester for misery, such as even our author has not ventured to describe.

We doubt, also, the propriety of utterly confounding all biographical truth, in a life so well known as Leicester's. We do not object to the alteration of events that are neither notorious nor important, nor to supplying the details of what is imperfectly known. The reader of *The Abbot* may know, if he choose to inquire, that Murray was not in Scotland at the time when Mary is represented to have signed the relinquishment of her power. And he has no reason to suppose that Sir Halbert Glendinning, or Catherine Seyton, or Roland Græme ever existed. But, as to Murray, if we discover the variation of the story told

---

[1] We wish we could persuade our author to let us have this 'old play'.—We suspect that he has the only copy—and if the rest resembles his quotations, it will be worth all our new ones [N. W. Senior].

in *The Abbot* from that of other histories, we treat it merely as one of the discrepancies frequently found in the details of different historians. It does not diminish our belief in the fidelity of the general outline: and as to the imaginary figures, with which our author has adorned his canvass, if we have no reason to suppose that they have, we have none to suppose that they have not, existed. They are neither supported nor contradicted by our previous opinions; if they fit in well, we admit them with confidence, as supplementary details. But all who started with an acquaintance with Leicester's history, or have been led by our author to examine it, and we think this division embraces all his readers, must feel that neither his detail nor his outline bears any resemblance to the truth. Leicester's union with Amy appears to have been a marriage *de convenance*, publicly celebrated, when both parties were very young, and long before Elizabeth's accession, and from which he was freed, after having publicly supported it for several years, by her violent and mysterious death, as soon as the situation of England and Scotland opened to him a double hope of royal alliance. Many years after occurred the celebrated visit to Kenilworth,—and at a still later period, his marriage with Lady Essex, the discovery of which occasioned the burst of fury in Elizabeth, to which we have alluded. Such a perversion of known facts not only deprives the story of the credibility, which an historical fiction derives from our conviction that the outline is true, but even of the temporary belief that we give to a well constructed tale. Even our author's ordinary legal accuracy fails him. Leicester's treason could not, as he supposes (vol. iii, 213), have enriched his widow; it would have forfeited her dower. Nor is his topography more correct. We think he never was at Cumnor—we are sure he never rode from thence to Woodstock—or found a bog near Wayland Smith's stone.

We have dwelt so long on the novels in detail, that our readers will gladly be spared any general remarks. Our parting exhortation to the 'Great Unknown' must be, if he would gratify the impatience of his contemporary readers, to write as much and as quickly as possible: if he would transmit his name to posterity, in such a manner as to do full justice to his extraordinary powers, to bestow a little more time and leisure in giving them their scope; in concentrating those excellencies which he has shown to be within his reach, and in avoiding those blemishes, which he cannot but have taste to perceive.

THE PIRATE

1821

30. Unsigned review, *Examiner*

30 December 1821, 826-27

The review is signed 'Q.', a probable indication that it was written
by Albany Fonblanque, later editor of the *Examiner* (see John
Hayden, *The Romantic Reviewers* (Chicago and London, 1969),
68). *The Pirate* carries an official publication date of 1822, but
was actually published in December 1821.

Sir Walter Scott—for we presume it will now be considered affected
to say the 'great unknown'—has in the present instance resorted to the
ultima Thule to prove his mastery over peculiar localities and manners,
the scene of the present volumes being the Shetland and Orkney
Islands exclusively. In an Advertisement which serves as an introduction, we are led to understand that the tale before us was suggested by
the fate of a pirate of the name of *Gow*, who was captured on the coast
of the Orkneys in 1723, and executed. Some daring peculiarities in his
deportment, but especially his success in obtaining the affections of a
young lady of family and property before his honourable occupation
was discovered, have furnished the outline of *The Pirate*; but with no
great resemblance either in character or catastrophe. Compared with the
original, or even with the recent efforts of the same author, we have
reason to believe it will be found almost as barren as the scene of its
incident; but it is only comparatively, and in reference to his own
productions, that we venture to say so, for there is much of the same
happy power of informed and accurate description—of filling up the
meagre outline supplied by faint traditions—and of giving spirit,
interest and nature to sketches of inevitable ignorance and prejudice.
There is also a similar, but possibly not quite so happy an intermixture
of the romantic and imaginative in character and transaction; although

256

in both, it must be admitted that there is no small repetition and loan from previously exhausted conceptions. In short, there is not a personage in the story with whom we have not before been made acquainted by the author himself; a fact which is by no means concealed by the novelty of the site. But in truth this novelty is a very bounded one, and naturally limits the author to a certain stock of associations, as the following sketch of the story will make manifest:—

[a portion of the plot summary is omitted]

The sole remaining interest, independent of occasional humour and miscellaneous character, is supplied by another variation—a fifth or sixth we believe,—from the unrivalled Meg Merrilies; a mixture of pretension and insanity in the person of a mysterious female who is skilled in the runic rhyme, and believes herself endowed with supernatural powers, and in consequence makes every one else believe the same. An old secret this, and the foundation of much of that delusion in the world, which is half artful and half the result of self-deception. We cannot recollect the exact words, but is it not Swift who says, that 'when once the imagination gets astride of the senses, and reason goes to buffets with fancy, a man first deceives himself and then other people; the disease possessing the nature of an epidemic.' So it is with the Enchantress of Shetland, who is made to do too much to be merely a mad woman, and too little to be any thing else. Upon the fact of this mysterious personage being really the mother of the pirate, and thinking herself so of the youth who saves him, a great portion of the interest is founded. The catastrophe is poor—the pirate is finally apprehended, but pardoned, and dies heroically in the service of his country. The heroine retains an interest in him, but follows her high notions and her duty; and the younger sister and the gallant and active son of the recluse, marry in the usual common way and carry on the business of life. We need state no more in the way of outline, for no more is necessary.

In the management of the story of this production we possibly perceive more want of keeping than usual even in the works of an author whose tissue of incident has uniformly been inferior to his conception of character. In point of fact, we are very slightly interested for any of the parties. The simplicity of the heroine is too *ignorant*—the pirate is neither virtuous nor vicious enough to be any thing at all; and the latter part of his conduct has no sympathy with the beginning. The recluse is a nonentity; his son a mere good natured young man; and the witch a slovenly impression from a fine but worn out conception. The younger sister has merit; and simply because she possesses characteristics which the author cannot help discovering to be valuable, although somewhat against the grain. For instance, she is slightly sceptical on the subject of mysterious pretension; and has an involuntary disposition to be satirical upon solemn fantasticality; and to see things as they are,— an amazing unsentimental qualification. With all this she is amiable and natural, which we fear is much beyond what the author has made her sister, although intended to be a great deal more.

But if *The Pirate* falls short in general character, it is by no means destitute of that happy exhibition of habits and manners, the capability of supplying which in point of fact, is the highest qualification of its author. We are made actors in local customs, and spectators of local incident and enterprise, with the usual easy and spontaneous felicity. The attack of a stranded whale is described to the life; and the *morale* of the Shetlanders in regard to wrecks, might pass for nature even in Cornwall. Still, owing to the scantiness of the principal canvass, some patchwork has been joined to it, which whatever it may afford in the way of variety, materially detracts from the *nature* of the grouping. Such, for instance, is the introduction of a rhimer who has attended Will's Coffee House, and borrowed importance from having listened to Dryden, as also a very artificial agricultural improver, who in 1723 was struck with much of the speculation and enthusiasm, which were scarce commodities until several years later. For the disposition to amuse himself with a portion of this agricultural *mania* no fault can be found with Sir Walter Scott; but his satire fails, because it is indiscriminate. In the spirit of too much of the incidental sentiment of this gifted writer, one might be led to regard all improvement as useless and dangerous innovation; and to sanctify ignorance and prejudice as estimable *per se*. Notions and habits are too often exalted by Sir Walter Scott into principles. A ridicule of mere theory as opposed to practice is fair enough; but is a bad plough, like a vicious mode of government, to be retained simply because it is ancient. We have no sort of objection to a little raillery upon the theoretical agriculturist; he is fair game if marked with discrimination; but we must not allow of the occasional weakness of this or of any other character, to form a covert defence for all sorts of ancient absurdity. Sir Walter Scott by a dexterous introduction of transient flashes of humour and candour, has a pleasant mode of qualifying this illiberality; yet, not so much so, but it is easy enough to

perceive that one of the axioms in his philosophy is,—right or wrong,—
to keep mankind as much as possible eternally in the same state.

We must not be prevented by respect for acknowledged genius from
repeating, that the catastrophe of *The Pirate* is extremely lame and
inconsistent; nor is it mending the matter, to add, that we are so
uninterested for the characters generally, as to care little for their disposal. The sudden sobering of the mind of the half artful and half insane
Norna, by the discovery that her imaginary magical endowments had
nearly rendered her the destroyer of her son, as she had before been of
her father, is well conceived; but the remainder is managed in the
commonest manner of the commonest novel of Messrs. Newman.
Upon the whole, with quite enough to mark the author and ascertain
his powers, we are unequivocally of opinion that *The Pirate* will rank
decidedly behind every one of its predecessors.

There is one grand moral defect in this novel, which as it is in a more
or less degree common to the whole series, and has never to our
knowledge been attended to by others, we shall take the liberty to
notice—We mean the countenance afforded to much dark and absurd
superstition, by an unaccountable fulfilment of its omens and predictions, and by clothing what must necessarily be either madness or
imposture, with loftier attributes than certainly belong to them. This
may pass in direct romance; but when the story treats of times so
recent as 1723, we cannot so well away with it; and feel more positively
the impropriety of regularly establishing the fatality of the dreams of
old women, and giving weight to barbarous notions and practices by
supporting them with a show of necessary sequence and completion.
Thus in *The Pirate*, the crazed Norna seems to calm a tempest; and
passes out of a company no one can tell how. The Shetlanders have,
or *had* a superstition growing out of their profitable occupation of
plundering wrecks. It was peculiarly amiable, for it implied that people
are uniformly in danger of some mortal injury from those they save
from drowning, and in consequence, struggling mariners were usually
left to perish; which at once prevented the dreaded injury and every
claim to a property in the bill of lading. A gallant youth of the Isles
saves the pirate, and the honest Shetlanders prophesy the result; the
pirate in his turn saves the young man, and the prophecies are repeated,
and what is worse the author takes care to fulfil them, without rendering
the prevalence of the notion in any respect the cause. This is decidedly
bad; and more mischievous than even eternally exalting the state of the
rude and the barbarous, and sneering at every attempt to exalt them

into creatures which shall not be the mere slaves of habit and impulse. In a word, the feudal dependance of the middle ages, is evidently the *beau-ideal* of Sir Walter Scott; and in order to sanctify and exalt the ties which bind the vassal to the lord, he takes under his especial protection, not only the social and hospitable virtues which really belonged to it, but its superstition, its ignorance, its habits, and its prejudices, which are softened into pictorial beauty, and tinted *couleur de rose*. All this is bearable within bounds; but becomes irksome as part of a system, the object of which is a studied repression of every progress, which by exalting the many, can in the slightest degree affect the power or the profit of the few.

To conclude, we repeat that we regard *The Pirate* as much below the preceding Works by the same pen; but we by no means intend to convey any censure beyond that fact. The Author is one who can scarcely write what will not be eagerly read; but respect neither for genius or authority ought to bribe us in the unbiassed exercise or expression of our judgment; in the spirit of which conviction we have written, and leave the rest to our readers.   Q.

THE FORTUNES OF NIGEL

1822

31. From an unsigned review, *General Weekly Register*

2 June 1822, 345-52; 9 June 1822, 377-83

This extract, taken from the beginning of the review, is prefaced as usual with the title of the book under review: '*The Fortunes of Nigel*; by the Author of *Waverley, Kenilworth, &c*'.

Well may the author of *Waverley* terminate his ambiguous designation with an *&c*.: so prolific a writer, who chuses to be known only by the titles of his works, would, without that useful contraction, be compelled to convert his title page into a catalogue. We know of no people, but that of the unfortunate republic of authors, who like the Jews and the Gypsies, are scattered among all the other nations of the earth, and like them are distinguished by a striking similitude of habits and features, who amplify their *cognomina* from the names of their progeny rather than from those of their progenitors. This custom seems to be rapidly increasing among the voluminous writers of the present day, and we have recently seen a title page so abundant in these *filiisnymies*, that the name of the worthy bookseller was obliged to be thrust into the corner, in the smallest type. It is not, indeed, every author that could venture upon that abbreviation of his claim to the notice of the public which is understood in an *&c*.; but surely the writer now under review might have confined himself to his earliest appellation, without even the honourable *&c*. itself, and certainly without the partial selection of *Kenilworth* from among his multitudinous offspring. On the score of merit we see no ground whatever for this selection, except perhaps that in some points it has more resemblance to the present work, than any other of this writer's productions; yet these points are not the most valuable in either of the novels, they are those in which it is admitted that the author has least succeeded; namely, in pourtraying ancient English manners from documents obtained by antiquarian researches, while in his delineations of Scottish manners we meet with more vitality, because he has in depicting them had opportunities of drawing from various living vestiges of the times he describes. It is remarkable also, that in his best and earliest novels he never ventured to carry us much further into antiquity than the commencement of the last century; a period of singular events, strong characters, and great changes in his native country; where the impressions and recollections of the public occurrences which influence the particular and personal interests of the agents of his tales, were deep and indelible in the minds of many persons, and were the immediate causes of many of the existing circumstances of that portion of the kingdom. As he led us into the higher ages of our history, he had to depend more on books than on existing feelings and on living traditions. The perusal of *Waverley*, and even *Old Mortality*, resembled the attention paid to a man who repeats to us what he had heard of the events of his father's youth from the lips of his father himself. When we came to *Ivanhoe*, *The Monastery* and *The Abbot*, we seemed to be called to a lecture upon an ancient cemetery, where the bones and ashes of priests, chieftains and buffoons were indeed discoverable, and, by means of the mutilated inscriptions, partially distinguishable, but which not all the galvanism of genius could make again to move as they moved, or to feel as they felt. We saw the personages of these romances, as a person, intimately acquainted with theatrical performers, sees a tragedy; they were every-day companions assuming ancient dresses and extravagant attitudes: and all the forgotten superstitions and hearsay eccentricities with which they were accompanied, could no more preserve the intended illusion, than could the violence of the scenic storm prevent the well-known artist in the pit from exclaiming 'that's my own thunder'. We do not mean to undervalue those productions which rest upon the higher antiquity. They are curious and instructive; but it cannot be expected that they should affect and interest so deeply as those of more modern date, which differ indeed from our own habits and manners, but are not so completely separated from them as to render our knowledge the constant and cold companion of our feelings.

32. Scott: plot construction and the historical novel

1822

Extracts from (a) Scott's Introductory Epistle to *The Fortunes of Nigel* (1822) and (b) Scott's Prefatory Letter to *Peveril of the Peak* (1822).

Both selections are in the form of a dialogue between a vision of the unknown author of *Waverley* and one of two imaginary correspondents, Captain Clutterbuck and the Reverend Doctor Dryasdust.

(a) *Captain.* This may justify a certain degree of rapidity in publication, but not that which is proverbially said to be no speed. You should take time at least to arrange your story.

Author. That is a sore point with me, my son. Believe me, I have not been fool enough to neglect ordinary precautions. I have repeatedly laid down my future work to scale, divided it into volumes and chapters, and endeavoured to construct a story which I meant should evolve itself gradually and strikingly, maintain suspense, and stimulate curiosity; and which, finally, should terminate in a striking catastrophe. But I think there is a demon who seats himself on the feather of my pen when I begin to write, and leads it astray from the purpose. Characters expand under my hand; incidents are multiplied; the story lingers, while the materials increase; my regular mansion turns out a Gothic anomaly, and the work is closed long before I have attained the point I proposed.

Captain. Resolution and determined forbearance might remedy that evil.

Author. Alas! my dear sir, you do not know the force of paternal affection. When I light on such a character as Bailie Jarvie, or Dalgetty, my imagination brightens, and my conception becomes clearer at every step which I take in his company, although it leads me many a weary mile away from the regular road, and forces me to leap hedge and ditch to get back into the route again. If I resist the temptation, as you advise me, my thoughts become prosy, flat, and dull; I write painfully to myself, and under a consciousness of flagging which makes me flag still more; the sunshine with which fancy had invested the incidents, departs from them, and leaves every thing dull and gloomy. I am no more the same author I was in my better mood, than the dog in a wheel, condemned to go round and round for hours, is like the same dog merrily chasing his own tail, and gambolling in all the frolic of unrestrained freedom. In short, sir, on such occasions, I think I am bewitched.

(b) *Dryasdust*. Craving, then, your paternal forgiveness for my presumption, I only sighed at the possibility of your venturing yourself amongst a body of critics, to whom, in the capacity of skilful anti-quaries, the investigation of truth is an especial duty, and who may therefore visit with the more severe censure those aberrations, which it is so often your pleasure to make from the path of true history.

Author. I understand you. You mean to say these learned persons will have but little toleration for a romance, or a fictitious narrative, founded upon history?

Dryasdust. Why, sir, I do rather apprehend, that their respect for the foundation will be such, that they may be apt to quarrel with the inconsistent nature of the superstructure; just as every classical traveller pours forth expressions of sorrow and indignation, when, in travelling through Greece, he chances to see a Turkish kiosk rising on the ruins of an ancient temple.

Author. But since we cannot rebuild the temple, a kiosk may be a pretty thing, may it not? Not quite correct in architecture, strictly and classically criticised; but presenting something uncommon to the eye, and something fantastic to the imagination, on which the spectator gazes with pleasure of the same description which arises from the perusal of an Eastern tale.

Dryasdust. I am unable to dispute with you in metaphor, sir; but I must say, in discharge of my conscience, that you stand much censured for adulterating the pure sources of historical knowledge. You approach them, men say, like the drunken yeoman, who, once upon a time, polluted the crystal spring which supplied the thirst of his family, with a score of sugar loaves and a hogshead of rum; and thereby converted a simple and wholesome beverage into a stupifying, brutifying, and intoxicating fluid; sweeter, indeed, to the taste, than the natural lymph, but, for that very reason, more seductively dangerous.

Author. I allow your metaphor, Doctor; but yet, though good punch cannot supply the want of spring-water, it is, when modestly used, no *malum in se*[1]; and I should have thought it a shabby thing of the parson of the parish, had he helped to drink out the well on Saturday night, and preached against the honest hospitable yeoman on Sunday morning. I should have answered him, that the very flavour of the liquor should have put him at once upon his guard; and that, if he had taken a drop over much, he ought to blame his own imprudence more than the hospitality of his entertainer.

Dryasdust. I profess I do not exactly see how this applies.

Author. No; you are one of those numerous disputants, who will never follow their metaphor a step farther than it goes their own way. I will explain. A poor fellow, like myself, weary with ransacking his own barren and bounded imagination, looks out for some general subject in the huge and boundless field of history, which holds forth examples of every kind—lights on some personage, or some combination of circumstances, or some striking trait of manners, which he thinks may be advantageously used as the basis of a fictitious narrative—bedizens it with such colouring as his skill suggests—ornaments it with such romantic circumstances as may heighten the general effect—invests it with such shades of character, as will best contrast with each other—and thinks, perhaps, he has done some service to the public, if he can present to them a lively fictitious picture, for which the original anecdote or circumstance which he made free to press into his service, only furnished a slight sketch. Now I cannot perceive any harm in this. The stores of history are accessible to every one; and are no more exhausted or impoverished by the hints thus borrowed from them, than the fountain is drained by the water which we subtract for domestic purposes. And in reply to the sober charge of falsehood, against a narrative announced positively to be fictitious, one can only answer, by Prior's exclamation,

'Odzooks, must one swear to the truth of a song?'

Dryasdust. Nay; but I fear me that you are here eluding the charge. Men do not seriously accuse you of misrepresenting history; although

[1] Evil in itself.

I assure you I have seen some grave treatises, in which it was thought necessary to contradict your assertions.

Author. That certainly was to point a discharge of artillery against a wreath of morning mist.

Dryasdust. But besides, and especially, it is said that you are in danger of causing history to be neglected—readers being contented with such frothy and superficial knowledge as they acquire from your works, to the effect of inducing them to neglect the severer and more accurate sources of information.

Author. I deny the consequence. On the contrary, I rather hope that I have turned the attention of the public on various points, which have received elucidation from writers of more learning and research, in consequence of my novels having attached some interest to them. I might give instances, but I hate vanity—I hate vanity. The history of the divining rod is well known—it is a slight valueless twig in itself, but indicates, by its motion, where veins of precious metal are concealed below the earth, which afterwards enrich the adventurers by whom they are laboriously and carefully wrought. I claim no more merit for my historical hints; but this is something.

Dryasdust. We severer antiquaries, sir, may grant that this is true; to wit, that your works may occasionally have put men of solid judgment upon researches which they would not perhaps have otherwise thought of undertaking. But this will leave you still accountable for misleading the young, the indolent, and the giddy, by thrusting into their hands, works, which, while they have so much the appearance of conveying information, as may prove perhaps a salve to their consciences for employing their leisure in the perusal, yet leave their giddy brains contended with the crude, uncertain, and often false statements, which your novels abound with.

Author. It would be very unbecoming in me, reverend sir, to accuse a gentleman of your cloth of cant; but, pray, is there not something like it in the pathos with which you enforce these dangers? I aver, on the contrary, that by introducing the busy and the youthful to 'truths severe in fairy fiction dressed',[1] I am doing a real service to the more

[1] The Doctor has denied the author's title to shelter himself under this quotation; but the author continues to think himself entitled to all the shelter, which, threadbare as it is, it may yet be able to afford him. The *truth severe* applies not to the narrative itself, but to the moral it conveys, in which the author has not been thought deficient. The 'fairy fictions' is the conduct of the story which the tale is invented to elucidate [Scott].

ingenious and the more apt among them; for the love of knowledge wants but a beginning—the least spark will give fire when the train is properly prepared; and having been interested in fictitious adventures, ascribed to an historical period and characters, the reader begins next to be anxious to learn what the facts really were, and how far the novelist has justly represented them.

But even where the mind of the more careless reader remains satisfied with the light perusal he has afforded to a tale of fiction, he will still lay down the book with a degree of knowledge, not perhaps of the most accurate kind, but such as he might not otherwise have acquired. Nor is this limited to minds of a low and incurious description; but, on the contrary, comprehends many persons otherwise of high talents, who, nevertheless, either from lack of time, or of perseverance, are willing to sit down contented with the slight information which is acquired in such a manner. The great Duke of Marlborough, for example, having quoted, in conversation, some fact of English history rather inaccurately, was requested to name his authority. 'Shakspeare's Historical Plays', answered the conqueror of Blenheim; 'the only English history I ever read in my life.' And a hasty recollection will convince any of us how much better we are acquainted with those parts of English history which that immortal bard has dramatized, than with any other portion of British story.

Dryasdust. And you, worthy sir, are ambitious to render a similar service to posterity?

Author. May the saints forefend I should be guilty of such unfounded vanity! I only show what has been done when there were giants in the land. We pigmies of the present day, may at least, however, do something; and it is well to keep a pattern before our eyes, though that pattern be inimitable.

Dryasdust. Well, sir, with me you must have your own course; and for reasons well known to you, it is impossible for me to reply to you in argument. But I doubt if all you have said will reconcile the public to the anachronisms of your present volumes. Here you have a Countess of Derby fetched out of her cold grave, and saddled with a set of adventures dated twenty years after her death, besides being given up as a Catholic, when she was in fact a zealous Huguenot.

Author. She may sue me for damages, as in the case Dido *versus* Virgil.

Dryasdust. A worse fault is, that your manners are even more incorrect than usual. Your Puritan is faintly traced, in comparison to your Cameronian.

Author. I agree to the charge; but although I still consider hypocrisy and enthusiasm as fit food for ridicule and satire, yet I am sensible of the difficulty of holding fanaticism up to laughter or abhorrence, without using colouring which may give offence to the sincerely worthy and religious. Many things are lawful which we are taught are not convenient; and there are many tones of feeling which are too respectable to be insulted, though we do not altogether sympathize with them.

Dryasdust. Not to mention, my worthy sir, that perhaps you may think the subject exhausted.

Author. The devil take the men of this generation for putting the worst construction on their neighbour's conduct!

HALIDON HILL

1822

---

33. Unsigned review, *Eclectic Review*

1822

An extract from a joint review of Scott's little-known drama *Halidon Hill* and Allan Cunningham's *Sir Marmaduke Maxwell*, *Eclectic Review* (September 1822), 2nd series xviii, 259-79.

The reviewer has just quoted Scott's prefatory remark that *Halidon Hill* was not designed for the stage.

Certainly this drama is not calculated for the stage, for it is free from both ribaldry and rant; and when did ever play succeed on an English stage without these? We cannot conceive of a greater degradation of a genuine poet, than writing for the stage. Shakspeare was degraded, and his works have been infinitely deteriorated by his writing with this view; but he wrote for bread. Sir Walter Scott shews his good taste in disclaiming any such intention; and we question whether even his great name, aided by all the scene-painter's art, and dress-maker's skill, with real armour from Marriott's, and genuine old English cross-bows, would procure it a week's run. But, drama or no drama, in the technical sense, it is a poem, and a beautiful one, worthy of the Author of *Marmion*. Nothing can be more simple in its construction. It is divided into two acts. The scene throughout is the same—different parts of the field of action, Halidon Hill. The whole interest arises from the characters of Sir Alan Swinton and young Adam Gordon, between whose houses there has existed a deadly feud, which had swept off the four sons of the aged Knight, and left the Gordon fatherless. Swinton and Gordon, who is unacquainted with the person of his father's murderer, meet for the first time on the eve of the battle; when the young chief is with difficulty restrained from drawing his sword on the enemy of his house, on discovering his name. But his vindictive feelings gradually give way before those of the patriot; and won to the admiration of Swinton's noble character, he proffers his forgiveness, and kneels to him for knighthood. They perish together in the onset, being basely deserted by the main body of the Scottish army under the Regent Douglas, from motives of pique and jealousy. The bickerings of the Scottish chiefs, and a brief scene or two in which King Edward is introduced, fill up the interstices. It is a touching tale, and abounds with passages of genuine pathos; yet, strange to say, there is scarcely a word about love, and though there is mischief enough, there is not a woman in the story. The poem opens well.

[Act I, scene 1: lines 37-48 and 115-69; Act I, scene 2: lines 216-29; Act II, scene 2: lines 29-55; Act II, scene 3: lines 19-64 are omitted. The conflict in Adam Gordon is said to be 'finely imagined', but some casual conversation of the King and the Abbot is criticized as gross]

This is a 'sketch', but it is from the hand of a master; and there is a chasteness and simplicity in the poetry, such as are displayed in our ancient ballads, which might have suffered from elaboration. The marks of rapidity and carelessness are obvious. Simon de Vipont is christened Adam in the dramatis personæ. The first line of the poem is disfigured by a jingle of words almost as bad as a pun—'No farther, Father;'—and 'Baron's banner' offend the ear in the next line but two. But we cannot open a work of the Author's, without detecting similar instances of utter disinclination to the irksome and humiliating process of revision. There is, perhaps, some pride in this indolence: he presumes on his opulence in going slovenly. But we can easily conceive that much of the spirit of the composition arises from its being struck off while the mind is yet warm with its own conceptions. Shakspeare, doubtless, wrote rapidly. The great difference between him and our Author, is, that he thought more deeply, and drew more from the profound and astonishing stores of his own mind—a mind not more observant than contemplative, and possessed of a native grandeur which found in the sublimest regions of thought its element. But, to compare Sir Walter with his peers, what living poet could have written *Halidon Hill*? Not the Author of *Sardanapalus* with all his pomp of diction and all his splendour of declamation. Long before his Lordship had tried his hand at dramas and mysteries, we ventured the opinion that he had not that creative faculty which can give to airy nothings a personality abstract and distinct, as it were, from himself. All his characters are the children of his feelings, and we may trace them by their family likeness to himself. The Giaour, Conrad, Manfred, Harold, Mazeppa, the Doge, Cain, Satan,—compare their portraits:—amid all these transformations, it is *Matthews still*. He has not been able to go out of himself in a single instance. He can describe most exquisitely, declaim most eloquently; he can throw himself into any attitude, any imaginable situation. But, till he produces something wholly different in kind from what he has yet done, we still say, with deference to the Edinburgh Reviewers, that he has not the dramatic faculty,—the power of imbodying distinct conceptions of individual character,—the spell by which the mighty masters of the art conjure up phantoms who take their place in the ranks of historic realities, seeming to think and speak from themselves, as if they had a being independent of the charm which raised them. When we hear Lear, or Richard, or Wolsey speak in Shakspeare, who thinks of the poet—who doubts that they did so talk and act? And so, in this poem of Scott's, the Swinton and the Gordon—they are living, tangible men, with voices and characters of their own, and they go to swell the ideal population of the mind. This is the test of the poet, epic or dramatic, who aspires to the palm of invention, who would become the historian, the biographer of persons and things which never were till he gave them being; and it is this wonderful talent which raises the Author of *Waverley* to the eminence he occupies, as either the first poet of his age or something greater.

QUENTIN DURWARD

1823

34. Unsigned review, *New Monthly Magazine*

July 1823, viii, 82-7

> 'What! will the line stretch out to the crack of doom?
> Another yet! a seventh!'   MACBETH.

Notwithstanding the amusement which the 'Novels by the author of *Waverley*' afford in the perusal, the astounding rapidity with which they succeed to each other gives—the *reviewer* at least, something more to do than is absolutely pleasant. The *New Monthly Magazine* is not more regular in its periodic appearances than these works; yet the necessity of reading whatever bears the signature, or rather the enigma, of their author, is absolute; and this necessity, we must confess, has more than once given birth within us to a movement of impatience and waspishness on the announcement of 'Another Novel from the great Unknown', something analogous to that betrayed by Macbeth, in the passage which serves as our motto at the head of the page. Latterly also, to make matters worse, these announcements have so enchained themselves one within the other, that it has been impossible to engage them single-handed, or to encounter the perusal of one production without the appalling consciousness that its younger brother is 'in the press', ready to pounce upon us the moment that the work in hand shall have done its business with the public. Thus the labour of the reader is brought to resemble that of the Danaides; and the 'never-ending, still beginning' task occasions a flutter of the nerves, which requires all the charm of this author's dialogue and description to dissipate and appease.

Determined to 'strike whilst the iron is hot',—or, to use a proverb more congenial to July weather, 'to make hay while the sun shines', and resolved, like good Queen Elizabeth, with her prayer-loving subjects, to give his readers '*enough of it*', the author of *Waverley* does not neglect the harvest of his popularity: and the expedition with which he conducts his movements, seems to indicate that, like some popular engravers, he must employ many assistants, to whose labours, after due touching up and polishing, he puts his own all-powerful signature —a letter of recommendation to the whole reading public of Great Britain, Germany, and France.

Every thing about these works, in truth, is singular. The dexterity, with which the friends of the 'great poet of the north' contrive to keep the public unsatisfied respecting his share in their production,—the number of extrinsic causes, (dramatizing, illustrating by engravings, music, and subsidiary publications, &c. &c.) that are brought to bear in support of their popularity,—the intrinsic interest they possess,— and the nature and management of the means which are made to produce this interest, no less than the rapidity of their succession,—all combine to render their appearance one of the most striking phænomena in the literature of the present age, and a marked sign of the times in which we live.

Those who are unacquainted with *the business* of novel-writing, imagine that nothing more is necessary than to sit down before a ream of paper, and pour forth the products of a teeming brain, with about the same degree of effort that it requires to assure some 'Dear Cousin' in the country that 'all at home are well', and that we are, 'with best love to enquiring friends', the said dear Cousin's 'very affectionate and obedient servant'.—The reverse of all this is, however, the case. The quantity of reading in history, geography, chronology, antiquities, and even in arts and sciences, necessary to give consistency, probability, and colouring to a work of imagination, requires, with the most industrious, the labour of months, before a pen is put to paper for the immediate purpose of composition.[1]

For the 'getting up', as the stage-manager would call it, of *Quentin Durward*, for instance, besides a diligent search through the historians, through Commines, Brantome, Jean de Troyes, and the rest of the memoir-writers, an immense quantity of Scottish lore must have been collected in order to trick out the Scotch guard in all the verisimilitudes of names, families, manners, and domestic anecdote. The trifling scene of the false herald alone, could not be detailed without a more intimate acquaintance with the pseudo-science of blazonry than usually falls to

[1] It has been the custom of our popular novelist to commence by drawing up a map of the scene of action, in the same way that a general would trace a geographical sketch of his intended campaign [reviewer].

the lot of any man, save a German Baron, or a thorough-paced and inveterate antiquarian.

Those who profess the faith, or the heresy, that Sir Walter Scott is the author of these works, relate that he 'writes' them during his hours of attendance in the courts: but, besides the ingenuity he must practise to hide his operations from the notice of the public, by which he is at those times surrounded, he must possess the more wonderful property of knowing by intuition facts, of which others obtain the knowledge by the most intense application. Sir Walter Scott is not only represented as a man of official occupation, as a politician actively participating in the wrangling polemics of the Edinburgh parties, but as a very convivial and social member of a remarkably social community, as a bustling farmer, and a constant improver of his favourite demesne at Abbotsford. That, amidst all these associations, he should be the sole 'Author of *Waverley*' and of its successors, seems next to a physical impossibility. The mere mechanical task of putting together the materials of a three-volume novel, after they have been collected,— supposing the book to be written *currente calamo*,[1] without reconsideration or recopying,—would occupy months of exclusive and laborious application; and this is a necessity which no genius can avert, a labour no talent can abbreviate. In this respect, some little advantage of habit apart, Sir W. Scott and the writers of the Leadenhall press are on a perfect equality. If this gentleman, therefore, is the 'Brazen mask' of the literary pantomime of hide and seek, it amounts almost to demonstration that he is powerfully assisted by a knot of subaltern drudges; and that he does little more than select the story, dispose the plan, write particular scenes, and give that sort of finish to the whole, which preserves to the book the unity of its colouring.[2] It has indeed been asserted respecting *The Pirate*,—we know not with what truth,—that it is the exclusive production of a certain member of Sir Walter Scott's family; and that it received only the revision and the adoption of the 'Author of *Waverley*'.

Some probability perhaps is added to this hypothetical notion by a marked difference observable at the first glance over the different novels in the single particular of character. In the earlier, and more appropriately called 'Scotch Novels', there is often displayed an intense

[1] 'With swift pen'.
[2] The Editor of the *New Monthly Magazine* sanctions the publication of this theory for the amusement of his readers, but begs not to be made responsible for believing it [reviewer].

degree of moral interest, in which the majority of the later productions are comparatively deficient. The death of the heroic Jacobites in *Waverley*, the strongly conceived, and finely shaded contrasts of the Serjeant and Burley, the whole description of the fanatic march, and the scene of torturing the preacher in *Old Mortality*, possess an unspeakable grasp on our sympathy; for they abound with traits of humanity, in its striking and important modifications. Rob Roy is a master's sketch of a fine, bold, generous disposition, worked upon and demoralized by the force of events; and even the Baillie's eccentricities are set off with such touches of nature and feeling as often remind us—what more *can* we say?—of Shakspeare himself. Of this excellence a smaller degree exists in the more recent productions; in which the characters differ from each other, chiefly in the shades of that weakness, or of that wickedness, which are common to them all.

In Quentin Durward, partly perhaps from the selection of the age and scene, the defect of character is singularly discoverable. Throughout all the novels, indeed, the author has shewn a stronger disposition to pourtray external nature, than to study and develope the workings of internal moral feeling and truth. Even when he enters deepest into pathos and intellectual character, his effort is always connected with a view rather to please us with the picturesque, than to sublimate our ethical principles. But in his later productions, he seems to sacrifice more than ever to picturesque effect, and he even exercises his ingenuity in giving relief to the most degraded characters which history exhibits, and in shedding the lights of an innocent and humorous peculiarity over the deepest and darkest shades of vice and crime. That the author of these novels, whoever he may be, is a devoted tory, will be no matter of new information to any of his readers; and on the ground of simple and abstracted opinion, it would be illiberal to quarrel with him. That he should even have glossed over the political offences of a Charles and a James, in order to paint those heroes of legitimacy under the traits of an amiable and gossiping privacy, may not be thought to exceed that measure of misrepresentation which the temper of our times, heated by incessant conflict and mutual injustice, appears to tolerate; but when he selects as a fit object for pencilling and adornment the infamous Louis XI, and when he dwells with a minute and complacement satisfaction on Tristrem l'Hermite, and the two canting and jesting buffoons, his subaltern executioners, we cannot help objecting to a taste and moral tact, apparently at variance with the mind which conceived and delineated a Jenny Deans.

With all the fascination which the author's vividness of genius throws over the characters of this story, there is still something in them all that is repulsive to a mind of moral and contemplative sensibility. Quentin himself, though he has energy and decision, is an adventurer and a mercenary, who offers his courage and his sinews to the furtherance of the most atrocious and perfidious tyranny that the barbarism of modern Europe has produced, with an indifference which, however natural in the feudal aristocrat of the Scotland of those days, ought to disqualify him for the attachment of a heart of civilized times. The band of Scottish archers, which he sought to join from so vast a distance, in addition to the characteristics of cruelty and licentiousness common to all mercenaries, was marked for avoidance by its recent treachery in quitting the service of Charles VII and joining the party of his rebellious and unnatural son, for a round sum of money. This circumstance should have made a deep impression on the mind of an ingenuous boy of gentle culture, whose love for his own parents must have been exalted by their bloody and unrevenged death; and the little coquetting squeamishness introduced to palliate the hero's conduct, serves only to place his moral obtuseness in a stronger light. Even Charles the Bold, whose chivalrous and unsuspecting frankness might have afforded some bright lights to the picture, is by a felicitous exercise of the author's colouring, shaded down below the tone of his ferocious rival, whose gloomy criminality shews like philosophy, as it is set off by the mere animal impulses which are made to actuate the conduct of the Duke of Burgundy.

Much of this moral defect, it is true, may perhaps follow unconsciously from the author's obstinate determination to defend indefensible points of history, to diminish the keen sensibility of the public to political truth, and to generate that indifference to public interests which is favourable to the propagation of the Tory creed. The romantic and picturesque points of feudality brought forward on the canvass may serve to beget a distaste for the colder and sterner aspects of a civilized and philosophical æra; and state criminals, portrayed with dramatic effect, and ornamented with the mock jewelry of candle-light virtues, may be made to engender a pernicious tolerance for political offenders; but, to produce this effect, the reader must be hurried forward, as over a quaking marsh, which affords no permanent footing for his steps; events must be presented with something of the vagueness of a dream; visions must succeed to visions, with a rapidity that leaves no pause for reflection; the imagination must alone be kept alert, and judgment be drugged into a diseased and unnatural slumber. Still, however, the later publications of the Author of *Waverley* are more surcharged with this defect, which we feel ourselves thus called upon to censure, than is necessary for the object that seems in a great degree to influence his writings; and a shade of probability arises, that the excess may be the work of coarser and clumsier spirits, which, in imitating their original and following the plan he has chalked out for them, have caricatured his system, and introduced faults which the master's hand has been unable to correct.

But, whatever inference may be drawn from the author's increased appetite for painting mankind under their worst aspects, it is a circumstance that becomes more striking at each succeeding publication. The system of decorating despotism is persevered in with unbated vigour, and each new novel is a special pleading in favour of passive obedience. We are not without apprehension that these observations may appear to some persons to be harsh and excessive. But let it be recollected against what evil we protest—against the misfortune of the greatest genius of the age conveying false impressions to the public of the great political concerns of man—of his blunting the sympathies of youth with the cause of human civilization, and begetting a precocious indifference to public interests. The licentiousness of the old novels was open to view; but the mischief of which we complain is more dangerous because it is more concealed. A certain public functionary is said to have written a History of England for children, in which the Revolution is purposely omitted. This act of bad faith is comparatively trifling to that of distorting facts, misrepresenting characters, and accustoming the mind to the contemplation of political vice unaccompanied by censure, or rather dressed out in the garb of amiability and goodness.

This is no imaginary offence. Its reality was well illustrated the other day in a member of our own family. A young female, of considerable liveliness, and talent beyond her years, who had just finished the perusal of *Quentin Durward*, being asked which of the characters she liked best, replied without hesitation, 'Louis XI; he is such a pleasant gentleman.' That this was a legitimate deduction in a child from the pages she had been reading, will not be disputed; and what can be more deplorable than the total confusion of right and wrong thus produced? Nor is it enough to say these works are not intended for youth; for youth will read them; and not only so, but even those of riper years will find it difficult to resist their influence, unless their moral principles are the result of a stronger character, and a deeper thought, than are often to be found among the general mass of novel-reading mankind.

We have dwelt on these generalities at some length, because we consider them important; and because the popularity of our author exempts us from the necessity of analytical criticism. *Quentin Durward* every body has read, or every body will read; and it is as useless to anticipate the pleasure of perusal by a bald abstract, as it is superfluous to fatigue our readers by an idle repetition. For the encouragement of those who have not yet commenced the perusal, we may say that it is altogether superior to its immediate predecessors, the scenes are more connected, the events more naturally conducted, the *denouement* better. The author has broken new ground, and seems invigorated by the freshness of his subject. For the rest, this novel possesses all the merits and defects of its brethren. It is formed on the same *cadre*, has the same tendencies, the same sort of adventure, the same vigour of picture-writing. One circumstance is peculiar;—the palpable, and perhaps careless, departure from the truth of history. The transactions which occasioned the imprisonment of Louis at Peronne[1] were many years antecedent to the murder of the Bishop of Liege, by William de la Mache.[2] In the insurrection which caused Louis's arrest, W. de la Mache's name is not mentioned; and his introduction as an agent in the story, seems only for the purpose of an additional gibe at popular revolutions. Again, when he did murder the Bishop, it was his son and not himself he named as the successor. The bearer of Charles the Bold's defiance to Louis in the castle of Plessis was the 'Sire de Chimay, and not the Sire de Cordés, an historical personage'. (See Anquetil.) Inbercourt, who is represented as first hearing of the siege of Tongres from Durward, was present at it himself, and was taken prisoner with the Bishop. Cardinal Baluc's confinement in his own iron cage, at Loches, was posterior to the King's captivity in Peronne. The false herald sent to England by Louis, and alluded to in the conference, is also an anachronism. These deviations from historic truth are material blemishes in the story. The author of an historic novel may omit facts, or add to them inventions which are in keeping with what is known. But he is not at liberty to distort the truth by a transfer of events and personages, by which, under the disguise of amusement, he gives false impressions, unsettles men's notions, and renders in a great degree nugatory, one of the most laborious and useful of human studies.

[1] 1468 [reviewer].   [2] 1482 [reviewer].

35. Hazlitt: Scott and the spirit of the age, *New Monthly Magazine*

1825

A chapter from William Hazlitt's *The Spirit of the Age* (taken here from the first edition). The chapter was originally published in the *New Monthly Magazine*, No. IV in a series entitled 'The Spirits of the Age'. April 1824, X, 297-304.

Sir Walter Scott is undoubtedly the most popular writer of the age—the 'lord of the ascendant' for the time being. He is just half what the human intellect is capable of being: if you take the universe, and divide it into two parts, he knows all that it *has been*; all that it *is to be* is nothing to him. His is a mind brooding over antiquity—scorning 'the present ignorant time'. He is 'laudator temporis acti'—a '*prophesier* of things past'. The old world is to him a crowded map; the new one a dull, hateful blank. He dotes on all well-authenticated superstitions; he shudders at the shadow of innovation. His retentiveness of memory, his accumulated weight of interested prejudice or romantic association have overlaid his other faculties. The cells of his memory are vast, various, full even to bursting with life and motion; his speculative understanding is empty, flaccid, poor, and dead. His mind receives and treasures up every thing brought to it by tradition or custom—it does not project itself beyond this into the world unknown, but mechanically shrinks back as from the edge of a prejudice.[1] The land of pure reason is to his apprehension like *Van Dieman's Land*;—barren, miserable, distant, a place of exile, the dreary abode of savages, convicts, and adventurers. Sir Walter would make a bad hand of a description of the *Millennium*, unless he could lay the scene in Scotland five hundred years ago, and then he would want facts and worm-eaten parchments to support his drooping style. Our historical novelist firmly thinks that

[1] In both the P. P. Howe edition and the Waller and Glover edition of Hazlitt's *Works*, 'prejudice' was replaced with 'precipice'.

nothing *is* but what *has been*—that the moral world stands still, as the material one was supposed to do of old—and that we can never get beyond the point where we actually are without utter destruction, though every thing changes and will change from what it was three hundred years ago to what it is now,—from what it is now to all that the bigoted admirer of the good old times most dreads and hates!

It is long since we read, and long since we thought of our author's poetry. It would probably have gone out of date with the immediate occasion, even if he himself had not contrived to banish it from our recollection. It is not to be denied that it had great merit, both of an obvious and intrinsic kind. It abounded in vivid descriptions, in spirited action, in smooth and flowing versification. But it wanted *character*. It was poetry 'of no mark or likelihood'. It slid out of the mind as soon as read, like a river; and would have been forgotten, but that the public curiosity was fed with ever-new supplies from the same teeming liquid source. It is not every man that can write six quarto volumes in verse, that are caught up with avidity, even by fastidious judges. But what a difference between *their* popularity and that of the Scotch Novels! It is true, the public read and admired *The Lay of the Last Minstrel, Marmion,* and so on, and each individual was contented to read and admire because the public did so: but with regard to the prose-works of the same (supposed) author, it is quite *another-guess* sort of thing. Here every one stands forward to applaud on his own ground, would be thought to go before the public opinion, is eager to extol his favourite characters louder, to understand them better than every body else, and has his own scale of comparative excellence for each work, supported by nothing but his own enthusiastic and fearless convictions. It must be amusing to the Author of *Waverley* to hear his readers and admirers (and are not these the same thing?[1]) quarrelling which of his novels is the best, opposing character to character, quoting passage against passage, striving to surpass each other in the extravagance of their encomiums, and yet unable to settle the precedence, or to do the author's writings justice—so various, so equal, so transcendant are their merits! His volumes of poetry were received as fashionable and well-dressed

[1] No! For we met with a young lady who kept a circulating library and a milliner's-shop, in a watering-place in the country, who, when we inquired for the *Scotch Novels,* spoke indifferently about them, said they were 'so dry she could hardly get through them', and recommended us to read *Agnes.* We never thought of it before; but we would venture to lay a wager that there are many other young ladies in the same situation, and who think 'Old Mortality' 'dry' [Hazlitt].

acquaintances: we are ready to tear the others in pieces as old friends. There was something meretricious in Sir Walter's ballad-rhymes; and like those who keep opera *figurantes*, we were willing to have our admiration shared, and our taste confirmed by the town: but the Novels are like the betrothed of our hearts, bone of our bone, and flesh of our flesh, and we are jealous that any one should be as much delighted or as thoroughly acquainted with their beauties as ourselves. For which of his poetical heroines would the reader break a lance so soon as for Jeanie Deans? What *Lady of the Lake* can compare with the beautiful Rebecca? We believe the late Mr. John Scott went to his death-bed (though a painful and premature one) with some degree of satisfaction, inasmuch as he had penned the most elaborate panegyric on the *Scotch Novels* that had as yet appeared!—The *Epics* are not poems, so much as metrical romances. There is a glittering veil of verse thrown over the features of nature and of old romance. The deep incisions into character are 'skinned and filmed over'—the details are lost or shaped into flimsy and insipid decorum; and the truth of feeling and of circumstance is translated into a tinkling sound, a tinsel *common-place.* It must be owned, there is a power in true poetry that lifts the mind from the ground of reality to a higher sphere, that penetrates the inert, scattered, incoherent materials presented to it, and by a force and inspiration of its own, melts and moulds them into sublimity and beauty. But Sir Walter (we contend, under correction) has not this creative impulse, this plastic power, this capacity of reacting on his first impressions. He is a learned, a literal, a *matter-of-fact* expounder of truth or fable:[1] he does not soar above and look down upon his subject, imparting his own lofty views and feelings to his descriptions of nature —he relies upon it, is raised by it, is one with it, or he is nothing. A poet is essentially a *maker*; that is, he must atone for what he loses in individuality and local resemblance by the energies and resources of his own mind. The writer of whom we speak is deficient in these last. He has either not the faculty or not the will to impregnate his subject by an effort of pure invention. The execution also is much upon a par with the more ephemeral effusions of the press. It is light, agreeable, effeminate, diffuse. Sir Walter's Muse is a *Modern Antique*. The smooth, glossy texture of his verse contrasts happily with the quaint, uncouth, rugged materials of which it is composed; and takes away any appearance of heaviness or harshness from the body of local traditions and obsolete costume. We see grim knights and iron armour; but then they

---

[1] Just as Cobbett is a *matter-of-fact reasoner* [Hazlitt].

are woven in silk with a careless, delicate hand, and have the softness of flowers. The poet's figures might be compared to old tapestries copied on the finest velvet:—they are not like Raphael's *Cartoons*, but they are very like Mr. Westall's drawings, which accompany, and are intended to illustrate them. This facility and grace of execution is the more remarkable, as a story goes that not long before the appearance of *The Lay of the Last Minstrel* Sir Walter (then Mr.) Scott, having, in the company of a friend, to cross the Firth of Forth in a ferry-boat, they proposed to beguile the time by writing a number of verses on a given subject, and that at the end of an hour's hard study, they found they had produced only six lines between them. 'It is plain', said the unconscious author to his fellow-labourer, 'that you and I need never think of getting our living by writing poetry!' In a year or so after this, he set to work, and poured out quarto upon quarto, as if they had been drops of water. As to the rest, and compared with true and great poets, our Scottish Minstrel is but 'a metre ballad-monger'. We would rather have written one song of Burns, or a single passage in Lord Byron's *Heaven and Earth*, or one of Wordsworth's 'fancies and good-nights', than all his epics. What is he to Spenser, over whose immortal, ever-amiable verse beauty hovers and trembles, and who has shed the purple light of Fancy, from his ambrosial wings, over all nature? What is there of the might of Milton, whose head is canopied in the blue serene, and who takes us to sit with him there? What is there (in his ambling rhymes) of the deep pathos of Chaucer? Or of the o'er-informing power of Shakespeare, whose eye, watching alike the minutest traces of characters and the strongest movements of passion, 'glances from heaven to earth, from earth to heaven', and with the lambent flame of genius, playing round each object, lights up the universe in a robe of its own radiance? Sir Walter has no voluntary power of combination; all his associations (as we said before) are those of habit or of tradition. He is a mere narrative and descriptive poet, garrulous of the old time. The definition of his poetry is a pleasing superficiality.

Not so of his NOVELS AND ROMANCES. There we turn over a new leaf—another and the same—the same in matter, but in form, in power how different! The author of *Waverley* has got rid of the tagging of rhymes, the eking out of syllables, the supplying of epithets, the colours of style, the grouping of his characters, and the regular march of events, and comes to the point at once, and strikes at the heart of his subject, without dismay and without disguise. His poetry was a lady's waiting-maid, dressed out in cast-off finery: his prose is a beautiful, rustic nymph, that, like Dorothea in *Don Quixote*, when she is surprised with dishevelled tresses bathing her naked feet in the brook, looks round her, abashed at the admiration her charms have excited! The grand secret of the author's success in these latter productions is that he has completely got rid of the trammels of authorship; and torn off at one rent (as Lord Peter got rid of so many yards of lace in the *Tale of a Tub*) all the ornaments of fine writing and worn-out sentimentality. All is fresh, as from the hand of nature: by going a century or two back and laying the scene in a remote and uncultivated district, all becomes new and startling in the present advanced period.— Highland manners, characters, scenery, superstitions, Northern dialect and costume, the wars, the religion, and politics of the sixteenth and seventeenth centuries, give a charming and wholesome relief to the fastidious refinement and 'over-laboured lassitude' of modern readers, like the effect of plunging a nervous valetudinarian into a cold-bath. The *Scotch Novels*, for this reason, are not so much admired in Scotland as in England. The contrast, the transition is less striking. From the top of the Calton-Hill, the inhabitants of 'Auld Reekie' can descry, or fancy they descry the peaks of Ben Lomond and the waving outline of Rob Roy's country: we who live at the southern extremity of the island can only catch a glimpse of the billowy scene in the descriptions of the Author of *Waverley*. The mountain air is most bracing to our languid nerves, and it is brought us in ship-loads from the neighbourhood of Abbot's-Ford. There is another circumstance to be taken into the account. In Edinburgh there is a little opposition and something of the spirit of cabal between the partisans of works proceeding from Mr. Constable's and Mr. Blackwood's shops. Mr. Constable gives the highest prices; but being the Whig bookseller, it is grudged that he should do so. An attempt is therefore made to transfer a certain share of popularity to the second-rate Scotch novels, 'the embryo fry, the little airy of *ricketty* children', issuing through Mr. Blackwood's shop-door. This operates a diversion, which does not affect us here. The Author of *Waverley* wears the palm of legendary lore alone. Sir Walter may, indeed, surfeit us: his imitators make us sick! It may be asked, it has been asked, 'Have we no materials for romance in England? Must we look to Scotland for a supply of whatever is original and striking in this kind?' And we answer—'Yes!' Every foot of soil is with us worked up: nearly every movement of the social machine is calculable. We have no room left for violent catastrophes; for grotesque quaintnesses; for wizard spells. The last skirts of ignorance and barbarism are seen hovering (in Sir Walter's pages) over the Border. We have, it is true, gipsies in this country as well as at the Cairn of Derncleugh: but they live under clipped hedges, and repose in camp-beds, and do not perch on crags, like eagles, or take shelter, like sea-mews, in basaltic subterranean caverns. We have heaths with rude heaps of stones upon them: but no existing superstition converts them into the Geese of Micklestane-Moor, or sees a Black Dwarf groping among them. We have sects in religion: but the only thing sublime or ridiculous in that way is Mr. Irving, the Caledonian preacher, who 'comes like a satyr staring from the woods, and yet speaks like an orator!' We had a Parson Adams not quite a hundred years ago—a Sir Roger de Coverley rather more than a hundred! Even Sir Walter is ordinarily obliged to pitch his angle (strong as the hook is) a hundred miles to the North of the 'Modern Athens' or a century back. His last work,[1] indeed, is mystical, is romantic in nothing but the title-page. Instead of 'a holy-water sprinkle dipped in dew', he has given us a fashionable watering-place—and we see what he has made of it. He must not come down from his fastnesses in traditional barbarism and native rusticity: the level, the littleness, the frippery of modern civilization will undo him as it has undone us!

Sir Walter has found out (oh, rare discovery) that facts are better than fiction; that there is no romance like the romance of real life; and that if we can but arrive at what men feel, do, and say in striking and singular situations, the result will be 'more lively, audible, and full of vent', than the fine-spun cobwebs of the brain. With reverence be it spoken, he is like the man who having to imitate the squeaking of a pig upon the stage, brought the animal under his coat with him. Our author has conjured up the actual people he has to deal with, or as much as he could get of them, in 'their habits as they lived'. He has ransacked old chronicles, and poured the contents upon his page; he has squeezed out musty records; he has consulted wayfaring pilgrims, bed-rid sibyls; he has invoked the spirits of the air; he has conversed with the living and the dead and let them tell their story their own way; and by borrowing of others, has enriched his own genius with everlasting variety, truth, and freedom. He has taken his materials from the original, authentic sources, in large concrete masses, and not tampered with or too much frittered them away. He is only the amanuensis of truth and history. It is impossible to say how fine his writings in con-

---

[1] *St. Ronan's Well* [Hazlitt].

sequence are, unless we could describe how fine nature is. All that portion of the history of his country that he has touched upon (wide as the scope is), the manners, the personages, the events, the scenery, lives over again in his volumes. Nothing is wanting—the illusion is complete. There is a hurtling in the air, a trampling of feet upon the ground, as these perfect representations of human character or fanciful belief come thronging back upon our imaginations. We will merely recall a few of the subjects of his pencil to the reader's recollection; for nothing we could add, by way of note or commendation, could make the impression more vivid.

There is (first and foremost, because the earliest of our acquaintance) the Baron of Bradwardine, stately, kind-hearted, whimsical, pedantic; and Flora MacIvor (whom even *we* forgive for her Jacobitism), the fierce Vich Ian Vohr, and Evan Dhu, constant in death, and Davie Gellatly roasting his eggs or turning his rhymes with restless volubility, and the two stag-hounds that met Waverley, as fine as ever Titian painted, or Paul Veronese:—then there is old Balfour of Burley, brandishing his sword and his Bible with fire-eyed fury, trying a fall with the insolent, gigantic Bothwell at the 'Change-house, and vanquishing him at the noble battle of Loudonhill; there is Bothwell himself, drawn to the life, proud, cruel, selfish, profligate, but with the love-letters of the gentle Alice (written thirty years before), and his verses to her memory, found in his pocket after his death: in the same volume of *Old Mortality* is that lone figure, like a figure in Scripture, of the woman sitting on the stone at the turning to the mountain, to warn Burley that there is a lion in his path; and the fawning Claverhouse, beautiful as a panther, smooth-looking, blood-spotted; and the fanatics, Macbriar and Mucklewrath, crazed with zeal and sufferings; and the inflexible Morton, and the faithful Edith, who refused to 'give her hand to another while her heart was with her lover in the deep and dead sea'. And in *The Heart of Mid-Lothian* we have Effie Deans (that sweet, faded flower) and Jeanie, her more than sister, and old David Deans, the patriarch of St. Leonard's Crags, and Butler, and Dumbie-dikes, eloquent in his silence, and Mr. Bartoline Saddle-tree and his prudent helpmate, and Porteous swinging in the wind, and Madge Wildfire, full of finery and madness, and her ghastly mother.—Again, there is Meg Merrilies, standing on her rock, stretched on her bier with 'her head to the east', and Dirk Hatterick (equal to Shakespear's Master Barnardine), and Glossin, the soul of an attorney, and Dandy Dinmont, with his terrier-pack and his pony Dumple, and the fiery

Colonel Mannering, and the modish old counsellor Pleydell, and Dominie Sampson,[1] and Rob Roy (like the eagle in his eyry), and Baillie Nicol Jarvie, and the inimitable Major Galbraith, and Rashleigh Osbaldistone, and Die Vernon, the best of secret-keepers; and in *The Antiquary*, the ingenious and abstruse Mr. Jonathan Oldbuck, and the old beadsman Edie Ochiltree, and that preternatural figure of old Edith Elspeith, a living shadow, in whom the lamp of life had been long extinguished, had it not been fed by remorse and 'thick-coming' recollections; and that striking picture of the effects of feudal tyranny and fiendish pride, the unhappy Earl of Glenallan; and the Black Dwarf, and his friend Habbie of the Heughfoot (the cheerful hunter), and his cousin Grace Armstrong, fresh and laughing like the morning; and the *Children of the Mist*, and the baying of the blood-hound that tracks their steps at a distance (the hollow echoes are in our ears now), and Amy and her hapless love, and the villain Varney, and the deep voice of George of Douglas—and the immoveable Balafre, and Master Oliver the Barber in *Quentin Durward*—and the quaint humour of *The Fortunes of Nigel*, and the comic spirit of *Peveril of the Peak*—and the fine old English romance of *Ivanhoe*. What a list of names! What a host of associations! What a thing is human life! What a power is that of genius! What a world of thought and feeling is thus rescued from oblivion! How many hours of heartfelt satisfaction has our author given to the gay and thoughtless! How many sad hearts has he soothed in pain and solitude! It is no wonder that the public repay with lengthened applause and gratitude the pleasure they receive. He writes as fast as they can read, and he does not write himself down. He is always in the public eye, and we do not tire of him. His worst is better than any other person's best. His *backgrounds* (and his later works are little else but back-grounds capitally made out) are more attractive than the principal figures and most complicated actions of other writers. His works (taken together) are almost like a new edition of human nature. This is indeed to be an author!

The political bearing of the *Scotch Novels* has been a considerable recommendation to them. They are a relief to the mind, rarefied as it has been with modern philosophy, and heated with ultra-radicalism. At a time also, when we bid fair to revive the principles of the Stuarts, it is interesting to bring us acquainted with their persons and misfortunes. The candour of Sir Walter's historic pen levels our bristling

[1] Perhaps the finest scene in all these novels, is that where the Dominie meets his pupil, Miss Lucy, the morning after her brother's arrival [Hazlitt].

prejudices on this score, and sees fair play between Roundheads and Cavaliers, between Protestant and Papist. He is a writer reconciling all the diversities of human nature to the reader. He does not enter into the distinctions of hostile sects or parties, but treats of the strength or the infirmity of the human mind, of the virtues or vices of the human breast, as they are to be found blended in the whole race of mankind. Nothing can shew more handsomely or be more gallantly executed. There was a talk at one time that our author was about to take Guy Faux for the subject of one of his novels, in order to put a more liberal and humane construction on the Gunpowder Plot than our 'No Popery' prejudices have hitherto permitted. Sir Walter is a professed *clarifier* of the age from the vulgar and still lurking old-English antipathy to Popery and Slavery. Through some odd process of *servile* logic, it should seem, that in restoring the claims of the Stuarts by the courtesy of romance, the House of Brunswick are more firmly seated in point of fact, and the Bourbons, by collateral reasoning, become legitimate! In any other point of view, we cannot possibly conceive how Sir Walter imagines 'he has done something to revive the declining spirit of loyalty' by these novels. His loyalty is founded on *would-be* treason: he props the actual throne by the shadow of rebellion. Does he really think of making us enamoured of the 'good old times' by the faithful and harrowing portraits he has drawn of them? Would he carry us back to the early stages of barbarism, of clanship, of the feudal system as 'a consummation devoutly to be wished'? Is he infatuated enough, or does he so dote and drivel over his own slothful and self-willed prejudices, as to believe that he will make a single convert to the beauty of Legitimacy, that is, of lawless power and savage bigotry, when he himself is obliged to apologise for the horrors he describes, and even render his descriptions credible to the modern reader by referring to the authentic history of these delectable times?[1]

[1] And here we cannot but think it necessary to offer some better proof than the incidents of an idle tale, to vindicate the melancholy representation of manners which has been just laid before the reader. It is grievous to think that those valiant Barons, to whose stand against the crown the liberties of England were indebted for their existence, should themselves have been such dreadful oppressors, and capable of excesses, contrary not only to the laws of England, but to those of nature and humanity. But alas! we have only to extract from the industrious Henry one of those numerous passages which he has collected from contemporary historians, to prove that fiction itself can hardly reach the dark reality of the horrors of the period.

'The description given by the author of the Saxon Chronicle of the cruelties

He is indeed so besotted as to the moral of his own story, that he has even the blindness to go out of his way to have a fling at *flints* and *dungs* (the contemptible ingredients, as he would have us believe, of a modern rabble) at the very time when he is describing a mob of the twelfth century—a mob (one should think) after the writer's own heart, without one particle of modern philosophy or revolutionary politics in their composition, who were to a man, to a hair, just what priests, and kings, and nobles *let* them be, and who were collected to witness (a spectacle proper to the times) the burning of the lovely Rebecca at the stake for a sorceress, because she was a Jewess, beautiful and innocent, and the consequent victim of insane bigotry and un-bridled profligacy. And it is at this moment (when the heart is kindled and bursting with indignation at the revolting abuses of self-constituted power) that Sir Walter *stops the press* to have a sneer at the people, and to put a spoke (as he thinks) in the wheel of upstart innovation! This is what he 'calls backing his friends'—it is thus he administers charms and philtres to our love of Legitimacy, makes us conceive a horror of all reform, civil, political, or religious, and would fain put down the *Spirit of the Age.* The author of *Waverley* might just as well get up and make a speech at a dinner at Edinburgh, abusing Mr. Mac-Adam for his improvements in the roads, on the ground that they were nearly *impassable* in many places 'sixty years since;' or object to Mr. Peel's *Police-Bill,* by insisting that Hounslow-Heath was formerly a scene of greater interest and terror to highwaymen and travellers, and cut a greater figure in the Newgate-Calendar than it does at present.—Oh! Wickliff, Luther, Hampden, Sidney, Somers, mistaken Whigs, and thoughtless Reformers in religion and politics, and all ye, whether poets or philosophers, heroes or sages, inventors of arts or sciences, patriots, benefactors of the human race, enlighteners and civilisers of

---

exercised in the reign of King Stephen by the great barons and lords of castles, who were all Normans, affords a strong proof of the excesses of which they were capable when their passions were inflamed. "They grievously oppressed the poor people by building castles; and when they were built, they filled them with wicked men or rather devils, who seized both men and women who they imagined had any money, threw them into prison, and put them to more cruel tortures than the martyrs ever endured. They suffocated some in mud, and suspended others by the feet, or the head, or the thumbs, kindling fires below them. They squeezed the heads of some with knotted cords till they pierced their brains, while they threw others into dungeons swarming with serpents, snakes, and toads." But it would be cruel to put the reader to the pain of perusing the remainder of the description.'—*Henry's Hist.*, edit. 1805, vol. vii. p. 346 [Hazlitt].

the world, who have (so far) reduced opinion to reason, and power to law, who are the cause that we no longer burn witches and heretics at slow fires, that the thumb-screws are no longer applied by ghastly, smiling judges, to extort confession of imputed crimes from sufferers for conscience sake; that men are no longer strung up like acorns on trees without judge or jury, or hunted like wild beasts through thickets and glens, who have abated the cruelty of priests, the pride of nobles, the divinity of kings in former times; to whom we owe it, that we no longer wear round our necks the collar of Gurth the swineherd, and of Wamba the jester; that the castles of great lords are no longer the dens of banditti, from whence they issue with fire and sword, to lay waste the land; that we no longer expire in loathsome dungeons without knowing the cause, or have our right hands struck off for raising them in self-defence against wanton insult; that we can sleep without fear of being burnt in our beds, or travel without making our wills; that no Amy Robsarts are thrown down trap-doors by Richard Varneys with impunity; that no Red Reiver of Westburn-Flat sets fire to peaceful cottages; that no Claverhouse signs cold-blooded death-warrants in sport; that we have no Tristan the Hermit, or Petit-Andrè, crawling near us, like spiders, and making our flesh creep, and our hearts sicken within us at every moment of our lives—ye who have produced this change in the face of nature and society, return to earth once more, and beg pardon of Sir Walter and his patrons, who sigh at not being able to undo all that you have done! Leaving this question, there are two other remarks which we wished to make on the Novels. The one was, to express our admiration at[1] the good-nature of the mottos, in which the author has taken occasion to remember and quote almost every living author (whether illustrious or obscure) but himself—an indirect argument in favour of the general opinion as to the source from which they spring—and the other was, to hint our astonishment at the innumerable and incessant instances of bad and slovenly English in them, more, we believe, than in any other works now printed. We should think the writer could not possibly read the manuscript after he has once written it, or overlook the press.

[a long attack on Scott's politics is omitted]

[1] In both the P. P. Howe edition and the Waller and Glover edition of Hazlitt's *Works*, 'at' was replaced with 'of'.

WOODSTOCK

1826

36. From an unsigned review, *Westminster Review*

April 1826, v, 399-457

George L. Nesbitt in his study of the *Westminster* (*Benthamite Reviewing* (N.Y., 1934), 105) suggests that this review is politically biassed, but no proof is given for the assertion.

As *Woodstock* may stand for the representative of its class, or at least for the defects of that class, a more minute examination of some passages will perhaps tend to illustrate the character of these English historical romances.

In a species of composition that professes to give the image of the times it treats of, the language is an important consideration. It is curious to remark how uniformly the speakers in these romances express themselves after the same manner, however various their degrees of rank, and remote from each other the periods of their existence. Gurth the swineherd and Wamba the jester, Saxons of Richard 1st's reign, might, if centuries could have been annihilated, have communed freely and sociably with Joceline Joliffe, the park-keeper, and sir Henry Lee, the ranger of Woodstock, under Charles 1st.

To characterize generally the language of the dialogue—it is copious and even redundant; with an affectation of quaintness; metaphorical and figurative; occasionally witty but oftener poetical; and larded with familiar phrases and household words to make it colloquial. The author having undertaken to deal with the characters of past ages, it was incumbent upon him to accommodate them with a language that should savour more or less of antiquity. And hence his violent endeavour after quaintness, the most palpable effect of which is, to render the dialogue unnatural and stiff. As he is deeply read in the old comedy, his language is not merely tinged with its peculiarities, but studiously enriched with its quaint and curious phrases. Yet the latter, whether more or less thickly sown, make but a beggarly show, and being patched upon a ground-work of decidedly modern construction, give to the dialogue an air of pedantry rather than of age. It will be found that its pretensions to antiquity are for the most part supported by little else than a plentiful use of 'thou' and 'thee', and such expletives as 'truly', 'entirely well', 'ay marry', 'go to', 'why look you', 'albeit', 'therewithal', 'an it please you', 'I wot not', 'by the mass', and so forth; together with many forms of expression which an assiduous perusal of the old dramatists has left in a tenacious memory.

The following are a few of the archaisms, with which the author has garnished his pages:

'Marry,' says the park-keeper of Woodstock, speaking of his master, 'it might be that he has *lacked* silver of late to pay groom and lackey.'

'A *potential* reason for the diminution of a household', said the soldier.

'Right, sir, even so, replied the keeper, but in my *poor* judgment', &c. 'Art thou not an *inconsequential* weather-brained fellow, remonstrates Everard to Wildrake, to set forth, as thou wert about to do, without any thing to *bear thy charges?*' '*Fair kinsman, it pleases me* that you are come to Woodstock', is the ironical salutation of the knight to his nephew, the roundhead colonel. 'Worthy colonel, you are *simply* the most welcome man that has come to Woodstock since the days of old king Harry', is the more cordial greeting of the presbyterian divine. 'Well, *will you shog*—will you on—will you take sasine and livery?' is the rough invitation of Joliffe, the park-keeper, to Tomkins, the Steward. 'I will *pink* his plaited armour for him', is the magnanimous resolve of cavaliero Wildrake. 'When did *I take spleen at a man* for standing his ground against me?' angrily demands the old knight of his attendant; 'Roundhead as he is, man, I like him the better of that, not the worse. I hunger and thirst to have another turn with him. I have thought on his passado ever since, and I believe, were it to try again, *I know a feat would control it.*'

'Here is the gentleman whose *warrant I must walk by*', is the simple mode in which a servant and a countryman is made to say, 'Here is the gentleman whose orders I must obey'. One man is said to be 'unsusceptible of his duty;' another, 'coughs and cries hem', a third is eternally for 'crushing an honest cup', and flinging on his 'castor;' the belly of a fourth, it is reported, 'rings cupboard;' 'it skills not talking now', observes a fifth, and so on.

The author whose phrases the dialogue most frequently echoes is Shakspeare. Many of the idioms, which in the preceding romances contributed to give the language its peculiar tone, were traceable to Shakspeare; but there is in the present work an infusion so unusually great, as to make one imagine that the writer must have come to his work fresh from a more than ordinarily close perusal of that poet. This is not evinced so much by the quotations which are thickly strewed up and down, as by the unconscious adoption of Shakspearian forms of speech by almost every character in the story. Not only does the old knight (whose love of Shakspeare is exceeded only by his loyalty) speak of one man's 'foining well—very sufficient well', and of 'fattening the region kites with the offal' of another, and of 'quoiting' a third down stairs, but even Pearson, Cromwell's aide de camp, 'trusts to see his lordship quoit them all [the parliament] down stairs;' and Charles, who affectedly ridicules Shakspeare for his 'wilderness of scenes, which the English call a play', uses the language of Shakspeare equally with the rest. 'Dear Alice,' said the king, 'I like your Everard much. I would to God he were *of our determination;*' whilst his companion, colonel Albert Lee, exclaims, 'God forbid we should be under the necessity of trusting any one who ever wore the parliament colours in a matter of such *dear concernment.*'—And Joceline Joliffe, in the same strain, speaks of their being '*heinously impoverished* down yonder at the cottage'. Then cavaliero Wildrake, in a manner meant to be insinuating, implores somebody or other to hear his story out, and 'just sip a glass of *this* very *recommendable strong waters.*—' 'He would have battered the Presbyterian spirit out of him *with a wanion*', swears the hearty old knight, speaking of the 'worthy and learned' Dr. Rochecliffe. 'However I am glad the young man is no sneaker; for were a man of the devil's opinion in religion and of old Noll's in politics, he were better open on it *full cry*, than deceive you by *hunting counter*, or *running a false scent*. Come—wipe thine eyes'—(addressing his daughter) '*the fray is over, and not like to be stirred again* soon, I trust.' Here the author's favourite reading and what is understood to have been his favourite pursuit, combine to furnish figures of speech. Let this one more citation suffice; 'Unbaptised dog,' shouts the old knight in a rage, 'speak civil of the martyr in my presence, or I will do a deed, misbecoming of me, on that caitiff corpse of thine.'—Marry, this is king Cambyses' vein with a vengeance.

There is another peculiarity of the dialogue, which is derived from the author's habits of poetical composition. Every man, woman, and child, that has aught to say, speaks by figure, and is ready with an illustration. 'Oliver's sword' metaphorically used for his authority, is said by the military preacher to be 'as pretty a bit of steel as ever dangled from a corslet, or rung against a steel saddle;' words more appropriate in the mouth of the bard of the Borders than in that of a Cromwellian saint, even though clad in 'buff and bandeliers'. Cromwell too, the most homely of speakers, has his metaphor; 'Sayst thou me?' said the general [to the impudent cavalier,] 'I profess thou art a bold companion, that can bandy words so wantonly; thou ringest somewhat too loud to be good metal, methinks;' and again when urged to punish the cavalier for an attempt upon his life, 'eagles stoop not at mallards or *wild drakes* either;' punning upon the name. Even the apparition that confounds the intellects of the grave colonel Everard, at Woodstock, addresses him through the medium of a metaphor more befitting the mouth of Adam Woodcock, the falconer of Avenel, than a commissioner from the other world: 'Thou art of a falcon breed,' it said, 'and noble in thy disposition, though unreclaimed and ill-nurtured, thou hauntest with kites and carrion crows.' The old knight is particularly ingenious. In answer to colonel Everard's assurance that he will be permitted to reside at the lodge on sufferance, he rejoins, 'Yes, I understand you. I am to be treated like the royal coin, marked with the ensign of the rump to make it pass current, although I am too old to have the royal insignia grinded off from me?'

The free use of images is not confined to rank and education; the author is profuse of his gifts; and Joceline Joliffe, no less than his master, speaks the language of poetry. 'A young maiden will laugh as a tender flower will blow—ay, and a lad will like her the better for it; just as the same blithe spring that makes the young birds whistle bids the blithe fawns skip.'—'The very deer there will butt a sick or wounded buck from the herd; hurt a dog and the whole kennel will fall on him and worry him; fishes devour their own kind when they are wounded with a spear; cut a crow's wing or break his leg the others will buffet him to death'—the purport of all which is, that when misfortunes assail us our friends are apt to forsake us. Now 'handy dandy, which is the master, which is the man?' The first sentiment smacks of youth, the second of age; but there is nothing in the diction by which to distinguish the speakers. 'We must trail bats now, Joceline,' says the old knight, intimating his acquiescence in what he could not alter, 'our time of shouldering them is passed. It skills not striving against the hill—the devil rules the roost, &c.' 'Our evil days are come with a vengeance,' sighs forth the man, 'we are fairly at bay, and fairly hunted down.' The brandisher of the quarter-staff, judge him by his speech, is a more refined person than the master of the rapier, and both are more polite than the learned divine, who remarks 'that it is best sitting near the fire when the chimney smokes'.

A wonderful aptitude at illustration is another prevailing characteristic. In the conversation of ordinary persons a speaker who ventures to commit himself in a similitude, seldom comes roundly and creditably off. But the personages of a Waverley romance are, as if by charter, universally exempt from all liability to hesitation. 'Yaw-ha,' responds cavaliero Wildrake to a proposition of colonel Everard's, after a solemn draught of something mightier than the mightiest juice of the barley-corn, 'my brain cannot compass it now; it whirls round like a toast in a bowl of muscadine.'—'I would rather drink like a hermit all my life,' is the rash asseveration of the old knight, 'than seem to pledge such scoundrels as these in their leavings, like a miserable drawer, who drains off the ends of bottles after the guests have paid their reckoning and gone off.'—'But to share my confidence,' Cromwell is made to say to the cavalier, 'is like keeping a watch over a powder-magazine; the least and most insignificant spark blows thee to ashes.'—'I will uphold thee as safe as pure gold in a miser's chest,' says one.—'They are as welcome to me as salt to sore eyes,' says another.—'They are like to frighten them thence, as a cat scares doves from a pigeon-house', says a third.—'What do you here, sitting like two crows in a mist?' inquires a fourth.—'Cupid must have bolted out of the window,' says the author himself, 'like a wild duck from a culverin.'—'On my soul,' says Pearson to his general, 'I have watched as closely as a cat a mouse-hole—made my rounds as often as a turnspit.' Even Phoebe Whitehorn has her illustration, 'the crust of a certain venison pasty', she affirms, 'is as thick as the walls of Rosamond's tower'. The only person that fails is the park-keeper, who being, in his own conceit, honester than he can find words to express, is at a loss for a subject of comparison.—'Whereas, I being as honest a fellow'—he begins, 'As ever stole venison', subjoins Tomkins the steward, befriending him at his utmost need.

Another peculiarity common to the speakers is a propensity to alliteration, a habit contracted from the study of old metrical ballads, such as the 'Battle of Flodden Field', in which almost every line is thus made sonorous. Phoebe Whitehorn, for instance, is prayed by her admirer in one breath, to trip it down to his lodge 'as fast as a fawn', and in another, to hie her down to the same place 'like a lapwing'. Then she is bid to 'wrap her cloak round her comely body', and to provide herself with 'a basket and a brace of trenchers and towels'. Phoebe retorts upon her admirer, 'Your lodge, indeed! you are very bold for a poor kill-buck that never frightened any thing before, save a *dun* deer;'—a rebuke to which the swain replies only by borrowing of her another similitude, and bidding her to get 'down to the hut like a deer'. The old knight in one place talks of having been left on the field of Edgehill 'bleeding like a bullock', and in another, to intimate his preference of direct opposition to subterfuge and evasion, remarks, 'he ever loved the buck best that stood boldest at bay.' 'My business,' says Joliffe, to signify that he was simply a park-keeper, 'is with bolts and bucks;' and he observes, in commendation of the good old times, that if 'there was a bout at single-stick, or a belly-full of boxing, it was all for love and kindness.' And the saintly soldier responds in a similar strain; that it is not likely the forester should find pleasant savour in wholesome food, if his 'ear is so much tickled with tabor tunes and morris tripping'.

The poet is constantly betrayed also by the use of redundant words, which in verse are required for the gratification of the ear, but which are heavy incumbrances in a prose dialogue. 'Now,' says the park-keeper, bewailing the forlorn estate of the may-pole, which, like the merry folk who once danced round it, was suffering in these severe times, 'it is warped, and withered, and twisted like a wasted briar tree.' 'Destruction hovers over you,' is the warning of colonel Everard to the obstinate old knight, 'ready to close her pinions to stoop, and her talons to clutch.'—'Is there not moisture on thy brow, Mark Everard? —Is there not trouble in thine eye?—Is there not a failure in thy frame?—And who ever saw such things in noble and stout Markham Everard, whose brow was only moist after having worn the helmet for a summer's day—whose hand only shook when it had wielded for hours the weighty falchion?'—And Alice Lee in a burst of indignation at hearing something to the disadvantage of her lover, declares that 'for Markham Everard, he would not for *broad* England, *had she the treasures of Peru in her bosom, and a paradise on her surface,* do a deed that would disgrace his name.'

Whilst the dialogue, on the one hand, is converted almost into poetry, it exhibits, on the other, an abundance of colloquial affectation. This consists in the use of a periphrastic mode of speech, which so far from being idiomatic is often mere verbiage. For example, when one of the hearty free-spoken characters has occasion to mention a door as being between himself and another, he quaintly calls it 'two inches of oak plant;' and little Spitfire, the messenger, who is charged with the symbolical feather to be delivered to mistress Alice Lee, declares he cannot do his devoir, with a 'three inch-board between them'. Phoebe is desired by the park-keeper to 'tell softly and hastily' what there is in the pantry; and Cavaliero having mounted upon a buttress to take a view of the interior of an apartment, drops himself 'sweetly' on the grass, and runs 'trippingly' off on being discovered. The long heavy sword of the republican soldier, is invariably, a 'ton', or a 'hundred-weight of rusty iron', in the language of the younger cavalier. The old knight swears that if a certain door is not opened to him instantly, 'he will play the locksmith with his foot;' and speaks of the soldier with whom he had crossed swords and who had made his weapon fly out of his hand, as having sent his 'rapier a hawking through the air'. It would be something strange to hear a pick-pocket thank heaven for having taught him by experience to 'carry hooks at his finger ends;' yet such is the phrase of the park-keeper. Colonel Everard, to intimidate the parliamentary commissioners, who seemed disposed to resist the order obtained from Cromwell for the evacuation of Woodstock, observes, that they ought to know 'in what characters this army of England and their general write their authority. I fear me', he adds, 'the annotation on this precept of the general will be expressed by a march of a troop of horse from Oxford to see it executed.' And sir Henry Lee, sighing at the thought that whether the restoration took place or not, he at least should not live to see it, expresses himself in terms surely very affected for a plain old man;—'If there be such a white page in the heavenly book, it will not be turned until long after my day.'—'So my tough old knight and you were at drawn bilbo, by way of afternoon service, sir preacher', is the salutation of the park-keeper to the Independent; 'Well for you I came not up till the blades were done jingling, or I had rung even-song upon your pate.' Of this part of the subject we take leave in the words of the motto to one of the chapters of the present work, in which the author has very aptly characterized the style of his own dialogue.

'My tongue pads slowly under this new language,
And starts and stumbles at these uncouth phrases.

They may be great in worth and weight, but hang
Upon the native glibness of my language
Like Saul's plate-armour on the shepherd boy,
Encumbering and not arming him.'

This subject has been dwelt upon at greater length both because the dialogue forms the chief part of a Waverley romance, and because the marks which characterize the present work are equally discernible in its predecessors. These peculiarities are neither those of the age nor of the persons treated of, but originate entirely with the author, and are derived from his own habits and pursuits. A style which combines the features of ages widely remote from each other, and which, along with the smoothness and facility of modern dialogue, affects the quaintness of antiquity, cannot be characteristic of any particular period. And since it has now been employed in a variety of works, comprehending nearly as many centuries as there are romances, should it even be found to suit the time of some one it cannot be appropriate to those of the remainder. Neither is it fitted for a nice display of character, since it invariably savours too strongly of the author, and is used indiscriminately by all the speakers. If it be accommodated to one class of men it must be equally unfit for the rest; if it be the language of the high-born and accomplished, it cannot become the mouths of the low and the rustic. And, though phrases peculiar to certain conditions of life are ambitiously affected, yet, with even these indications, it would be often difficult to decide from the evidence of the language, whether a particular speech came from the mouth of the master or the man, the knight or the serf, the king or the beggar. Neither is it much diversified by difference of education, for, though the soldier obtrudes upon you the remembrance of his profession by an assiduous use of military tropes and figures; and the presbyterian is easily distinguished from the cavalier because the one fetches his illustrations from scripture, and the other from the tavern; yet the genius and prevailing tone of their language is the same, revealing every where one mind, one speaker. It is, in short, a language *sui generis*; and, if it indicates any character at all, indicates none but its author's. The brazen head may now represent a Mercury and now a Mars, but it is one and the same voice that speaks through the mouthpiece.

There is, however, a species of diversity in the language, which is the most curious feature of the dialogue. The cavalier knight, an old man of the old school, speaks quaintly and curiously; but the knight's son and daughter use nearly the language of the present day, whilst the king is a gallant of the nineteenth century, and makes love in terms certainly never heard by the Cethegi. Colonel Everard being, after the manner of his sect, more sedate than is usual with men of his age, is endowed with only a limited portion of quaintness, and his language forms nearly the comparative degree between these two extremes. As speech is the principal medium by which character is expressed, it is impossible that the latter should be rightly represented when the medium itself is thus arbitrarily chosen.

It was long ago remarked by Dick Tinto, that his friend Peter Pattieson's heroes 'pattered' too much—made too free use of the 'gob-box'. This fault, if it *then* amounted to a fault, has arrived at a much higher degree of flagrancy. The present work is almost all dialogue, the consequence of which is, that the latter seldom manifests any dramatic spirit. It is in fact made to do double duty; and not only has to express the thoughts and sensations of the speaker; but, in the absence of narra-tive, is used by the author as a medium by which to convey an idea of the accompanying circumstances and the surrounding objects. What it gains in the picturesque it more than loses in dramatic force and propriety. Then the author keeps no measures, but without remorse pours from the mouths of blunt cavaliers and serving-men his own accumulation of bright fancies and ingenious thoughts. It is to be wished the author had reserved these ornaments to enrich the narrative portions of his romance; where if the thoughts had been over-ingenious, or the allusions far-fetched and ill brought in, they would have marred only themselves, and done no further mischief. When the author, for instance, speaking in his own person says, that the limbs of colonel Desborough resembled 'the disputatious representatives of a federative congress rather than the well-ordered union of the orders of the state in a firm and well-compacted monarchy', we only despise the cant, and laugh at a freak of fancy that could introduce so monstrous a similitude on so small an occasion. But when the king is made to rally colonel Everard, and to tell him that his 'round execration (the presbyterian colonel having just muttered an oath) bolted like a cork from a bottle of cyder, and now allows his wrath to come foaming after it in the honest unbaptized language of common ruffians;'—the propriety of character and language is sacrificed to a worthless and vulgar image; and the idea of the king is violently expelled by that of the hackneyed writer. To this use and abuse of the dialogue—this wanton indulgence of the author's fancy, and revelling in the *copia verborum* with which long study has enriched him—may be attributed, in a great measure, the failure of the present work, both in the production of dramatic effect, and in the delineation of character. To subject the dramatis personæ to the perils of a perpetual dialogue is to encounter a needless and an almost certain hazard of destroying their consistency. It may suit well enough with gossiping cavaliers and presbyterian divines to be eternally prating; but there are times at least, among persons of a particular stamp, when any conversation at all, would be the grossest violation of propriety. But to convert the dialogue into a vehicle for a display of ingenious writing, and to make all the characters alike, young and old, high and low, use the same elaborate imagery and the same artificial language, is to obliterate at once all marks of individuality.

37. Scott on his imitators

1826

Extracts from Scott's journal, 17 and 18 October 1826 (from J. G. Tait and W. M. Parker, eds., *The Journal of Sir Walter Scott* (Edinburgh, 1939-47)).

Sir John Chiverton was an historical novel by William Harrison Ainsworth.

Read over *Sir John Chiverton* and *Brambletye House*—novels in what I may surely claim as the stile

'Which I was born to introduce—
Refined it first, and showd its use.'

They are both clever books; one in imitation of the days of chivalry; the other (by Horace Smith, one of the authors of the *Rejected Addresses*) dated in the time of the Civil Wars, and introducing historical characters. I read both with great interest during the journey.

I am something like Captain Bobadil who trained up a hundred gentlemen to fight very nearly, if not altogether, as well as myself. And so far I am convinced of this, that I believe were I to publish *Canongate Chronicles* without my name (*nomme de guerre*, I mean) the event would be a corollary to the fable of the peasant who made the real pig squeak against the imitator, while the sapient audience hissed the poor grunter as if inferior to the biped in his own language. The peasant could, indeed, confute the long-eared multitude by showing piggy; but were I to fail as a knight with a white and maiden shield, and then vindicate my claim to attention by putting 'By the Author of *Waverley*' in the title, my good friend *Publicum* would defend itself by stating I had tilted so ill, that my course had not the least resemblance to my former doings, when indisputably I bore away the garland. Therefore I am as firmly and resolutely determined that I will tilt under my own cognizance. The hazard, indeed, remains of being beaten. But there is a prejudice (not an undue one neither) in favour of the original patentee; and Joe Manton's name has borne out many a sorry gun-barrel. More of this to-morrow.

October 18.—I take up again my remarks on imitations. I am sure I mean the gentlemen no wrong by calling them so, and heartily wish they had followd a better model; but it serves to show me *veluti in speculo* my own errors, or, if you will, those of the *style*.[1] One advantage, I think, I still have over all of them. They may do their fooling with better grace; but I, like Sir Andrew Aguecheek, do it more natural. They have to read old books and consult antiquarian collections to get their information; I write because I have long since read such works, and possess, thanks to a strong memory, the information which they have to seek for. This leads to a dragging-in historical details by head and shoulders, so that the interest of the main piece is lost in minute descriptions of events which do not affect its progress. Perhaps I have sind in this way myself—indeed, I am but too conscious of having considered the plot only as what Bayes calls the means of bringing in fine things; so that in respect to the descriptions, it re-sembled the string of the showman's box, which he pulls to show in succession Kings, Queens, the Battle of Waterloo, Bonaparte at Saint Helena, Newmarket Races, and White-headed Bob floored by Jemmy from town. All this I may have done, but I have repented of it; and in my better efforts, while I conducted my story through the agency of

[1] '*Just as in a mirror* my own errors, or, if you will, those of the *genre*.'

historical personages and by connecting it with historical incidents, I have endeavoured to weave them pretty closely together, and in future I will study this more. Must not let the background eclipse the principal figures—the frame overpower the picture.

Another thing in my favour is, that my contemporaries steal too openly. Mr. Smith has inserted in *Brambletye House* whole pages from Defoe's *Fire and Plague of London*.

> 'Steal! foh! a fico for the phrase—
> Convey, the wise it call!'

When *I convey* an incident or so, I am [at] as much pains to avoid detection as if the offence could be indicted in literal fact at the Old Bailey.

But leaving this, hard pressd as I am by these imitators, who must put the thing out of fashion at last, I consider, like a fox at his last shifts, whether there be a way to dodge them, some new device to throw them off, and have a mile or two of free ground, while I have legs and wind left to use it. There is one way to give novelty: to depend for success on the interest of a well-contrived story. But woe's me! that requires thought, consideration—the writing out a regular plan or plot—above all the adhering to [one]—which I never can do, for the ideas rise as I write, and bear such a disproportioned extent to that which each occupied at the first concoction, that (cocksnowns!) I shall never be able to take the trouble; and yet to make the world stare, and gain a new march ahead of them all!!! Well, something we still will do.

> 'Liberty 's in every blow;
> Let us do or die!'

38. William Maginn: burlesque as criticism

1827

An extract from William Maginn's novel burlesquing Scott and his imitators, *Whitehall; or, The Days of George IV* (1827).

William Maginn was a journalist and miscellaneous writer; he was a frequent contributor to *Blackwood's Magazine* and established *Fraser's Magazine*. According to the preface, the novel was published 400 years in the future in Yankeedoodoolia. The title page contains the motto, 'God save the King!—*Old Song*'. The following passage is a take-off of Scott's detailed descriptions.

He was a tall man, standing six feet four inches, with a countenance indicative of determination, if not of ferocity. A circular mark, in which the blue colour had begun to yield to the yellow, round his left eye, testified that he had not long before been engaged in personal rencontre; while the pustulary excrescences that disfigured his aquiline nose, shewed that he was not less accustomed to the combats of Bacchus than those of Mars. He wore a fur tiara, of enormous dimensions and a conical figure. A pewter plate, indented with the royal arms of England—gules sable, on a lion passant, guarded by a unicorn wavy, on a fess double of or argent, with a crest sinople of the third quarter proper, and inscribed with the names of several victories, won or claimed by the household troops of England, proved him to be a member of the Horse Guards. A red doublet, with a blue cuff, cape, and lappelles, was buttoned with mother-of-pearl buttons reaching from his waist to his chin, where they were met by a black leather stock, garnished and fastened by a brass clasp, on which was inscribed, *Dieu et mon Droit*, the well known war-cry of the English nation. White kerseymere trousers, buttoned at the knee, and a pair of D. D. boots— as they were called, from the circumstance of their having been invented by a Duke of Darlington—completed his dress. His arms were a ponderous cut-and-thrust sword, with a handle imitating a lion's head, sheathed in an iron scabbard, that clanked as he moved along. Over his shoulder was slung a carbine, or short gun, which military law required to be always primed, loaded, and cocked. A pair of horse-pistols were stuck in his leathern belt, and in his hand he bore a large spontoon, or pike. Such was the dress of the[1] Hanoverian Horse Guards of England at that period; and such, even in secondary occasions, their formidable armour; for the absence of the hauberk, (or morion) and of the ponderous target of bull's-hide and ormolu, showed that the gigantic Hussar was not at present upon actual duty.

[1] See Cobbett, vol. 317, p. 1248; *ibid*, p. 716 (note), &c., &c. Consult also Sir Francis Burdett's *Ode to Earl Canning*, stanza 37.

> Nor pass, dear friend, the dark array,
> Beneath their mercenary sway
>   The blood of England flows,
> Base instruments of despot's ire,
> That trample in insanguined mire
>   Britannia's virgin rose.
> Their hands the iron fetters forge,
> By whose fell means the tyrant George
>   Keeps freemen's spirit dumb;
> What time from whiskered Gottingen
> (Immortal thanks to Canning's pen!)
>   To London town they come—&c., &c. [Maginn].

39. Heinrich Heine on Scott

1828, 1837

Extracts from (*a*) Heinrich Heine's review of Scott's *The Life of Napoleon* in *Politische Annalen* (1828), xxvi, 173–81 (translation by C. G. Leland), and from (*b*) Heine's introduction to his edition of *Don Quixote* (1837) (translation by Mr. Fleishman).

(*a*) Strange! the dead Emperor is, even in his grave, the bane of the Britons, and through him Britannia's greatest poet has lost his laurels!

He *was* Britannia's greatest poet, let people say and imagine what they will. It is true that the critics of his romances carped and cavilled at his greatness, and reproached him that he assumed too much breadth in execution, that he went too much into details, that his great characters were only formed by the combination of a mass of minor traits, that he required an endless array of accessories to bring out his bold effects; but, to tell the truth, he resembled in all this a millionaire, who keeps his whole property in the form of small specie, and who must drive up three or four waggons full of sacks of pence and farthings when he has a large sum to pay. Should any one complain of the ill-manners of such a style of liquidation, with its attendant troubles of heavy lifting and hauling and endless counting, he can reply with perfect truth that, no matter *how* he gives the money, he still gives it, and that he is in reality just as well able to pay and quite as rich as another who owns nothing but bullion in bars; yes, that he even has an advantage greater than that of mere facility of transport, since in the vegetable market gold bars are useless, while every huckster woman will grab with both hands at pence and farthings when they are offered her.

(*b*) We do not find in Cervantes this one-sided tendency to portray the vulgar only; he intermingles the ideal and the common; one serves as light or as shade to the other, and the aristocratic element is as prominent in it as the popular. But this noble, chivalrous, aristocratic element disappears entirely from the novels of the English, who were the first to imitate Cervantes, and to this day always keep him in view as a model. These English novelists since Richardson's reign are prosaic natures; to the prudish spirit of their time even pithy descriptions of the life of the common people are repugnant, and we see on yonder side of the channel those *bourgeois* novels arise, wherein the petty, humdrum life of the middle classes is depicted. The public were surfeited with this deplorable class of literature until recently, when appeared the great Scot, who effected a revolution, or rather a restoration, in novel-writing. As Cervantes introduced the democratic element into romance, at a time when one-sided knight-errantry ruled supreme, so Walter Scott restored the aristocratic element to romance when it had wholly disappeared, and only a prosaic *bourgeoisie* was found to be there. By an opposite course Walter Scott again restored to romance that beautiful symmetry which we admire in Cervantes's *Don Quixote*.

I believe that the merits of England's second great poet have never in this respect been recognised. His Tory proclivities, his partiality for the past, were wholesome for literature, and for those masterpieces of his genius that everywhere found favour and imitators, and which drove into the darkest corners of the circulating libraries those ashen-grey, ghostly remains of the *bourgeoisie* romances. It is an error not to recognise Walter Scott as the founder of the so-called Historical Romance, and to endeavour to trace the latter to German initiative. This error arises from the failure to perceive that the characteristic feature of the Historical Romance consists just in the harmony between the aristocratic and democratic elements, and that Walter Scott, through the re-introduction of the aristocratic element, most beautifully restored that harmony which had been overthrown during the absolutism of the democratic element, whereas our German romanticists eliminated the democratic element entirely from their novels, and returned again to the ruts of those crazy romances of knight-errantry that flourished before Cervantes.

40. Goethe on Scott

1828, 1831

Excerpts from *Conversations of Goethe with Eckermann and Sonet*, trans. John Oxenford (London, 1901).

(*a*) 3 October 1828

'But,' continued Goethe, with animation, 'Walter Scott's *Fair Maid of Perth* is excellent, is it not? There is finish! there is a hand! What a firm foundation for the whole, and in particulars not a touch which does not lead to the catastrophe! Then, what details of dialogue and description, both of which are excellent.

'His scenes and situations are like pictures by Teniers; in the arrangement they show the summit of art, the individual figures have a speaking truth, and the execution is extended with artistical love to the minutest details, so that not a stroke is lost. How far have you read?'

'I have come,' said I, 'to the passage where Henry Smith carries the pretty minstrel girl home through the streets, and round about lanes; and where, to his great vexation, Proudfoot and Dwining met him.'

'Ah,' said Goethe, 'that is excellent; that the obstinate, honest blacksmith should be brought at last to take with him not only the suspicious maiden, but even the little dog, is one of the finest things to be found in any novel. It shows a knowledge of human nature, to which the deepest mysteries are revealed.'

'It was also,' said I, 'an admirable notion to make the heroine's father glover, who, by his trade in skins, must have been long in communication with the Highlanders.'

'Yes,' said Goethe, 'that is a touch of the highest order. From this circumstance spring the relations and situations most favourable for the whole book, and these by this means also obtain a real basis, so that they have an air of the most convincing truth. You find everywhere in Walter Scott a remarkable security and thoroughness in his delineation, which proceeds from his comprehensive knowledge of the real world, obtained by life-long studies and observations, and a daily discussion of the most important relations. Then come his great talent and his comprehensive nature. You remember the English critic, who compares the poets to the voices of male singers, of which some can command only a few fine tones, while others have the whole compass, from the highest to the lowest, completely in their power. Walter Scott is one of this last sort. In the *Fair Maid of Perth* you will not find a single weak passage to make you feel as if his knowledge and talent were insufficient. He is equal to his subject in every direction in which it takes him; the king, the royal brother, the prince, the head of the clergy, the nobles, the magistracy, the citizens and mechanics, the Highlanders, are all drawn with the same sure hand, and hit off with equal truth.'

(b) 9 October 1828

'But,' continued Goethe, after a pause, 'we will not give ourselves up to melancholy thoughts. How do you get on with your *Fair Maid of Perth*? How far have you read? Tell me all about it.'

'I read slowly,' said I. 'However, I am now as far as the scene where Proudfoot, when in Henry Smith's armour he imitates his walk and whistle, is slain, and on the following morning is found in the streets of Perth by the citizens, who, taking him for Smith, raise a great alarm through the city.'

'Ay,' said Goethe, 'that scene is remarkable; it is one of the best.'

'I have been particularly struck,' said I, 'with Walter Scott's great talent for disentangling confused situations, so that the whole separates itself into masses and quiet pictures, which leave on our minds an impression as if, like omniscient beings, we had looked down and seen events which were occurring at the same time in various places.'

'Generally,' said Goethe, 'he shows great understanding of art; for which reason we, and those like us, who always particularly look to see how things are done, find a double interest and the greatest profit in his works.

'I will not anticipate, but you will find in the third volume an admirable contrivance. You have already seen how the prince in council makes the wise proposal to let the rebel Highlanders destroy one another in combat, and how Palm Sunday is appointed for the day when the hostile clans are to come down to Perth, and to fight for life or death, thirty against thirty. You will see with admiration how Scott manages to make one man fail on one side on the decisive day, and with what art he contrives to bring his hero Smith from a distance into the vacant place among the combatants. This is admirably done; and you will be delighted when you come to it.

'But, when you have finished the *Fair Maid of Perth*, you must at once read *Waverley*, which is indeed from quite a different point of view, but which may, without hesitation, be set beside the best works that have ever been written in this world. We see that it is the same man who wrote the *Fair Maid of Perth*, but that he has yet to gain the favour of the public, and therefore collects his forces so that he may not give a touch that is short of excellence. The *Fair Maid of Perth*, on the other hand, is from a freer pen; the author is now sure of his public, and he proceeds more at liberty. After reading *Waverley*, you will understand why Walter Scott still designates himself the author of that work; for there he showed what he could do, and he has never since written anything to surpass, or even equal, that first published novel.'

(c) 9 March 1831

Goethe continued to speak of Sir Walter Scott with the highest acknowledgement.

'We read far too many poor things,' said he; 'thus losing time, and gaining nothing. We should only read what we admire, as I did in my youth, and as I now experience with Sir Walter Scott. I have just begun *Rob Roy*, and will read his best novels in succession. All is great—material, import, characters, execution; and then what infinite diligence in the preparatory studies! what truth of detail in the execution! We see, too, what English history is; and what a thing it is when such an inheritance falls to the lot of a clever poet.'

41. Macaulay: Scott as historical novelist

1828

An extract from a review of Henry Neale's *The Romance of History: England* by Thomas Babington Macaulay, *Edinburgh Review* (May 1828), xlvii, 331-67.

Macaulay is describing the ideal historian.

If a man, such as we are supposing, should write the history of England, he would assuredly not omit the battles, the sieges, the negotiations, the seditions, the ministerial changes. But with these he would intersperse the details which are the charm of historical romances. At Lincoln Cathedral there is a beautiful painted window, which was made by an apprentice out of the pieces of glass which had been rejected by his master. It is so far superior to every other in the church, that, according to the tradition, the vanquished artist killed himself from mortification. Sir Walter Scott, in the same manner, has used those fragments of truth which historians have scornfully thrown behind them in a manner which may well excite their envy. He has constructed out of their gleanings works which, even considered as histories, are scarcely less valuable than their's. But a truly great historian would reclaim those materials which the novelist has appropriated. The history of the government, and the history of the people, would be exhibited in that mode in which alone they can be exhibited justly, in inseparable conjunction and intermixture. We should not then have to look for the wars and votes of the Puritans in Clarendon, and for their phraseology in *Old Mortality*; for one half of King James in Hume and for the other half in *The Fortunes of Nigel*.

42. An early voice of dissent

1828

An extract from an unsigned article in a series of 'Sketches of Contemporary Authors' in the *Athenaeum*, 11 March 1828, 217-19.

The author was Frederick Denison Maurice, an Anglican divine and miscellaneous writer of the period. In the section previous to the selection below, Maurice praises Scott's powers of observation and description of external nature; in the passage that follows the selection Scott's *Life of Napoleon* is criticized severely.

Yet there is, in all his writings, the evidence of this main defect; he knows what is, but not how or why it is so. He has seen the outward, but he has not connected it with that which is within. He has looked at the conduct, and listened to the speech, of men; but he has not understood from what kind of central source their deeds and words are drawn. He seems to have no fondness for referring things to their origin; and instead of considering men's actions as worth observation, only in so much as they illustrate the essential character of the being from which they spring, he has treated them as if they had in themselves a definite and positive value, modified, in the hands of the poet and the novelist, by nothing but the necessity of exciting interest and giving pleasure. It is not that he has no systematic theory of human nature, for if he had, he would, to an absolute certainty, be in error. But he does not appear to believe that there is any human nature at all, or that man is aught more than a means to certain external results, the which when he has described, he has done his task and fulfilled his ministry. There is incomparably more freedom and truth in his picture of our species, than in the books of any of the systematic speculators, Locke, for instance, or Helvetius; because he has seen the inexhaustible varieties of our doings, and has exhibited them fairly and sincerely, while such writers as those to whom we allude, have assumed some one small base, and attempted to rear upon it a fabric which, restricted and low as it is, is yet infinitely too wide and lofty for the narrowness of the foundation. But *his* idea of man is meagre and wretched, compared to that of the philosophers who have contemplated the mind, instead of measuring the footsteps; who have not sought to number the hairs upon our heads, but have dealt, as it were, with the very elements of our creation. This defect shows itself very strongly in every part of his works, where he attempts to cope alone with the thoughts of any of his personages. In his dialogues, he in some degree gets over the difficulty, by repartees, passion, and mimicry of the language of the time; but, in soliloquies, how barren and incomplete appears to be his psychology! and compare these, or even the best parts of the conversations, with a scene of Shakspeare, and the difference may at once be perceived between writers, the one of whom knows nothing but phenomena, while the other, with to the full as much of individual observation, was also imbued with the largest abundance that any man ever had of universal truth. There is scarce a page of Shakspeare that does not present us with the deepest and finest moral meditations, and with a living image of those thoughts which occupy men's minds, when they reflect upon their own nature, and attempt to overleap the bounds of the present and the actual. There is rarely any thing in Scott that pretends to this, the highest of all merit; we doubt if there are a dozen attempts at reflection in his voluminous works; and the standard of good which he exhibits, in so far as it differs from the merest worldliness, is only raised above it by something more than usual of a certain shrewd good-humour.

Exactly similar observations hold good with regard to his treatment of things inanimate. He sees, neither in the world, nor in human works, any thing more than so much positive existence, more beautiful or more uninteresting, larger or smaller, as the case may be, but always something to be looked at solely for itself. And herein he would be perfectly right, if men had no faculty except that which has beauty for its object. There is doubtless a pleasure and a good in the contemplation of those things which are in conformity with the original idea of the beautiful in our minds; but there is also a nobler good in viewing all things around us, not merely by this one faculty, but as manifestations of still higher principles, and in connection with moral and religious truth. Even as ends in themselves, almost all the objects around us have their beauty; but it is as forms and symptoms of superior and invisible powers, that it is most truly useful to regard them. Nor is it necessary to put forward broadly the intention of a writer on this point; but, if he has the feeling and the law within himself, their influence will be seen in every line he writes; just as in speaking of a picture, we need not explain the construction of the eye, or the science of optics, though it will be obvious that we could not have thought one word about the matter without possessing the faculty of sight. It is from the want of this habit of mind, that Sir Walter Scott's descriptions of scenery are in general so completely separate parts of his works; they stand out from the rest of the narrative, instead of being introduced casually, indicated by an occasional expression, or shown as the drapery of the thoughts.

Besides his mode of dealing with the results of his observations of men and nature, we mentioned, as connected with it, his way of regarding history; and this is certainly no less striking than the points we have just been treating of. If the narrative of past events exhibits them to us as naked facts, it does nothing; if it presents them with their immediate causes and consequences in the minds of the actors, it does much, and what few histories have done; if it displays them justly as exponents of principles, and results of the great scheme for the education of mankind, it does all that it can do. The knowledge of an occurrence is of no value whatsoever in itself. The most spirited description of it, which merely lets us know the dresses of the chief personages, how this man looked, and what that man ate, and tells us whether a sovereign died on a bed or a battlefield, gives us knowledge of nothing worth knowing. The points which deserve to be examined, are those which make manifest the feelings of the persons concerned, the spirit of the times, the great designs that were at work, and were spreading to embrace ages in their circuit, the peculiarities and progress of national character; in short, what the mind of the world was, and what means were operating to improve it. The events themselves are of interest only as exhibiting human motives, either in the individual or the mass, and thereby opening to us some new recesses of the soul, containing perhaps powers of which we were previously unconscious, like titles to wealth, or symbols of empire, discovered in some dark and long-forgotten chamber. Yet, in reading history, it is not upon such matters as these that Sir Walter Scott has turned his attention, but to the mere external changes and salient occurrences, to triumphs or tournaments, battles or hunting matches, to whatever can be converted into a picture, or emblazoned in a show. He has not read the annals of the earth as they ought to be studied; but he would probably not be nearly so popular a writer if he had. As it is, he has filled his mind with all that is most stirring and gorgeous in the chronicles of Europe, superstitions the more impressive because forgotten, brilliant assemblages of kings, and barons, hard-fought battles, and weary pilgrimages, characters the most desperately predominating, and events the most terrible or fantastic. Of these he has made a long phantasmagoria, the most exciting and beautiful spectacle of our day; and who can wonder or complain, if he, who delights mankind with so glorious a pageant, is held by almost general consent to be the greatest of modern authors.

The tendency, which we have now dwelt upon at some length, to look at humanity and nature in their outward manifestations, instead of seizing them in their inward being, has decided in what class Sir Walter Scott must be placed with reference to the moral influence he exercises. He would commonly be called one of the most moral of writers; for he always speaks of religion with respect, and never depraves his writings by indecency. But ethics and religion would be the least important of studies, and the human mind the simplest object in the creation, if nothing more than this were needful to constitute a moral writer. However, it is not so. He, and he alone, is a moral author, whose works have the effect of flinging men back upon themselves; of forcing them to look within for the higher principles of their existence; of teaching them that the only happiness, and the only virtue, are to be found by submitting themselves uniformly to the dictates of duty, and by aiming and struggling always towards a better state of being than that which ourselves, or those around us, have hitherto attained. Sir Walter Scott has observed men's conduct instead of his own mind. He has presented to us a fair average of that conduct: but he knows nothing of the hidden powers which, if strenuously and generally called forth, will leave his books a transcript of the world, as erroneous as they are now accurate and honest. He has, therefore, no influence whatever in making men aim at improvement. He shows us what is, and that, Heaven knows, is discouraging enough; but he does not show us what we have the means of being, or he would teach us a lesson of hope, comfort, and invigoration.

> 'It is our will
> Which thus enchains us to permitted ill.
> We might be otherwise; we might be all
> We dream of—happy, high, majestical.
> Where is the love, beauty, and truth we seek,
> But in our minds? And if we were not weak,
> Should we be less in deed than in desire?

* * * * *

313

Those who try may find
How strong the chains are which our spirit bind,
Brittle, perchance, as straw. We are assured
Much may be conquered, much may be endured,
Of what degrades and crushes us. We know
That we have power over ourselves to do
And suffer—*what*, we know not till we try;
But something nobler than to live and die;
So taught the kings of old philosophy.

*   *   *   *   *

And those who suffer with their suffering kind,
Yet feel this faith religion.'

Though, therefore, it would be an insane malignity to call him indi-vidually an immoral writer, as he has always recognized the distinction between right and wrong, and never knowingly inculcated evil; yet it would be folly to pretend that he produces much moral effect upon the world, as his works do scarcely any thing towards making men wiser or better.

The most obvious ground, on which to fix his claim of a strong and beneficial influence over men, is the general and good-humoured benevolence apparent in his writings. In an age of so much affected misanthropy and real selfishness, this is, doubtless, a high merit, and it is one which, in the works of Sir Walter Scott, does not carry with it the slightest symptom of pretence, or even of exaggeration. We feel, at once, that we are in presence of a man of free and open heart, disposed to laugh at every man's jest, treat every man's foibles with gentleness, and spread over the path of life as much as possible of manly generosity. It would be difficult not to feel, after reading his books, that peevishness and envy are bad and foolish propensities, that earth yields better fruits than scorn and hatred, and, above all, that there is nothing impressive in diseased melancholy—nothing sublime in assumed misery. His mind is evidently of the very healthiest and most genial sort that society will admit, without avenging itself, by calumny and oppression, for a superiority which reproaches its own viciousness. But it should be borne in recollection, that, excellent in themselves as are such qualities, and unalloyed, as they probably are, in Sir Walter Scott, a very considerable share of them is perfectly compatible with that kind of feeling which confines itself entirely within the boundaries of our personal connections; and, though it would give up the most delicate morsel to another at the same dinner-table, would not sacrifice a farthing to do good to a kingdom or a continent. A similar character to that displayed in the writings of Sir Walter Scott, is the result, in many cases, of mere temperament and circumstance; though we perfectly believe that it exists, in his own breast, in its purest and most meritorious *avatar*. The benevolence that spends itself upon whatever may be brought by chance within its view, is an infinitely more agreeable quality than mere selfishness, but one that is very little likely to do any more good to mankind. We see it constantly around us, exerting itself towards every particular object it happens to stumble on; and yet perfectly indifferent and cold to the greater general designs, which would do good an hundred times as extensive, and a thousand times as certain.

We are not sure that Sir Walter Scott's political opinions are to be explained in this way, for we well know the vast allowances that must be made for early prejudice, confirmed by subsequent connections, habits, and interests. But we confess that it does seem to us a melancholy and painful contrast, when we think of the many warm and honest sympathies expressed and embodied in the writings of this author, and then compare them with the narrow and degraded cast of his political feelings. We think of the statue with the feet of clay; of the king in the Arabian tales, the half of whose body had been changed to insensible stone; of the woman in Milton, so fair above, yet terminating in such monstrous foulness; of all, in short, that is strangely and fearfully discordant: for nothing in fable or vision can be more so than the politics and the romance of the writer in question. He, above all other men, would be likely to fall into such an error as this; because, from his attachment to the forms of one state of society, and his indifference to the spirit of all, he could hardly avoid imagining that those forms were valuable for themselves, and applicable to our own times as well as to the thirteenth century, and to London as well as to Lochaber. The crown and the coronet still seem to him the emblems of law as opposed to anarchy, though the only countries in Europe where anarchy exists, are those where the government is peculiarly despotic, as in Southern Italy, Spain, Turkey, and Ireland. He still thinks of feudalism and hereditary nobility, as the causes no less than the glories of the most brilliant of modern ages, though the remains of the system are even now the greatest curses to England, and the very name of hereditary wisdom has become a mockery and a hissing. To his eyes a splendour appears to have vanished from the world, since mankind have omitted that custom now confined, (except among soldiers,) to kings and courtiers, the wearing arms in peace, which, much more than two thousand years ago, was cited, by the best of historians, as the most evident relic of the rudest barbarism.[1] We fear, however, that even Sir Walter Scott himself would apostatise from the ninth to the nineteenth century, if a party of English borderers were making a forage, and threatening to burn Abbotsford. It is true, that no people ever existed, not living under some form of government which has, of course, grown out of their character, and adapted itself, in a considerable degree, to their peculiar circumstances. We are irrevocably connected with the past,—the prolongation of an antiquity which reaches back from us into the dim shades of an almost immeasurable remoteness. Every nation has within itself the germs and types of those institutions which are the most likely to produce its happiness, and which can alone be in conformity with its hereditary spirit. But these institutions must needs be altered, to fit them to the varying occasions and silent revolutions of society. It is thus that Solon reformed the government of Athens, when he saw that it was necessary, from the increasing power of the inferior classes, to give it a more democratic character; it is thus that the Licinian rogations admitted to a larger share of authority a commonalty which had become too numerous and too strong to be safely contemned; and thus it is, that, in spite of the opposition even of such men as Sir Walter Scott, the wardens, who guard the cob-webbed doors of the English constitution, will be compelled to turn the rusty hinges, and draw back the rotten bolts, and to admit to the political sanctuary an equal representation of the people.

We have spoken of the mode in which he looks at men, at nature, and at history; and attempted to show how one great defect accompanies him in each. We have said something of his claims to be considered as a moral writer; and something of his political opinions and feelings; but connected more or less with all these subjects, there is another on which we have not hitherto touched, the necessary influence, namely, of the whole class of composition for which Sir Walter Scott is distinguished: and in speaking of the great bulk of his writings, as forming a class, we include both verse and prose, for the character of his rhymed and of his unmetrical romances is essentially the same. The great classes into which fiction may be divided are made up of those that please chiefly by the exhibition of the human mind, and those that please chiefly by the display of incident and situation. The former are

[1] Thucydides, b. i., c. 5, 6 [F. D. Maurice].

the domain of the mightier teachers of mankind; the kingdom of Homer, of Cervantes, of Shakspeare, of Milton, and of Schiller,—a realm allied, indeed, to this world, and open to the access of men, but pure from our infirmities, and far raised above the stir of our evil passions,—a sphere with which the earth is connected, and moves in accordance, but which, like to the sun itself, only shines upon the world to be its illumination and its law. Here is the true and serene empire of man's glory and greatness; and from this sanctuary issue the eternal oracles of consolation, which tell us to how free and sublime a destiny the human soul may lift itself. But the other class of writers, who find their resources in every thing that can create an interest, however transitory and vulgar, who describe scenes merely for the purpose of describing them, and heap together circumstances that shall have a value in themselves, quite independently of the characters of those whom they act upon;—it is the doom of such men to compound melo-dramas, and the prize of their high calling to produce excitement without thought; and to relieve from listlessness, without rousing to exertion. To neither of those does Sir Walter Scott exclusively belong. That he is not one of the latter order of authors, witness much of *Old Mortality*, of *The Antiquary*, of *The Bride of Lammermoor*, and *The Heart of Mid-Lothian*, and yet, unhappily, the larger proportion of his works would seem to separate him entirely from the former; and, on the whole, he has ministered immensely to the diseased craving for mere amusement, so strikingly characteristic of an age in which men read as a relaxation from the nobler and more serious employments of shooting wild-fowl or adding together figures. Literature has become the property of the crowd, before the crowd have been made fit auditors of truth; literature has, consequently, been divorced from truth, and degraded to their level. But, alas! that men of genius, instead of doing something to reform their age, should submit themselves to the meanest eddies of that current which they might have turned from its wanderings, to flow between banks of fragrance and beauty, and sparkle over sands of gold! Therefore, when it shall fill its appointed channel, it will leave their reputations but decaying wrecks upon the barren sands it will have deserted; and float forward, in the prouder triumph, the argosies from which it may now have shrunk away.

43. Stendhal on Scott, *Le National*

1830

An article by Stendhal (Henri Beyle), the French novelist; it was
entitled 'Walter Scott and La Princesse de Clèves' and appeared
in *Le National*, 19 February 1830. The translator is Geoffrey
Strickland.

La Princesse de Clèves was a novel by Mme. de Lafayette.

These two names indicate the two extremes in the novel. Should the
novelist describe the dress worn by the various characters, the landscape around them and their physiognomy, or would he do better to
depict the passions and sentiments which agitate their souls? My
reflections will not be welcome. An immense body of men of letters
finds it in its own interest to praise Sir Walter Scott to the skies,
together with his method of composition. The doublet and leather
collar of a medieval serf are easier to describe than the movements of
the human heart. One can either imagine or describe inaccurately
medieval costume (we have only a half-knowledge of the customs and
the dress worn in Cardinal Richelieu's ante-chamber); whereas we
throw the book down in disgust if the author fails to describe the
human heart, and ascribes, say, to an illustrious companion-in-arms of
the son of Henri IV the ignoble sentiments of a lackey. Everyone
recalls Voltaire's famous story. One day he was giving a lesson in tragic
diction to a young actress, who recited a lively passage with the utmost
coldness. 'But, my dear young lady', cried Voltaire. 'You ought to be
acting as though the devil were in you. What would you do if a cruel
tyrant had just separated you from your lover?' 'I should take another',
was her reply.

I do not wish to suggest that all the makers of historical novels think
as reasonably as this prudent young pupil of Voltaire's; but even the
most susceptible among them will not suspect me of calumny if I say
that it is infinitely easier to describe in picturesque detail a character's

dress than to say what he feels and to make him speak. Let us not forget another advantage which is offered by the school of Sir Walter Scott: the description of the costume and posture of a character, however minor he may be, takes at least two pages. The movements of the heart, which, to begin with, are so difficult to discern and so difficult to describe with precision and without either timidity or exaggeration, would scarcely furnish a few lines. Open at random ten pages from one of the volumes of *La Princesse de Clèves*; then compare them with ten pages from *Ivanhoe* or *Quentin Durward*; it will be found that the latter display a *historical merit*.

They teach those who know little or nothing about history a number of minor details concerning the past. Their historical merit has already given great pleasure. I do not wish to deny this, only it is the historical merit which will grow old the soonest. The century will move towards a more true and natural form of expression; and the mannered approximations of Sir Walter Scott will one day seem as distasteful as they at first seemed charming. Perhaps it would be wise if I were to develop these rapid hints and say something more of the future destiny of the fashionable novel.

See what a crowd of men and women have found it in their interest to maintain that Sir Walter Scott is a great man. Despite their numbers, I have no intention of borrowing the mask of hypocrisy which the nineteenth century finds so fashionable. I shall pronounce with all frankness my conviction that, in ten years time, the reputation of the Scottish novelist will have declined by half. Richardson's fame in France was equal to Scott's. Diderot used to say, 'In exile or prison I would ask for only three books: Homer, the Bible, and *Clarissa Harlowe*.' Like Sir Walter Scott, Richardson had a more distinguished reputation in Paris than in England.

Every work of art is a charming lie; anyone who has written knows this well. There is nothing more ridiculous than the advice commonly given to the writer in society: 'Imitate nature.' Confound it, I know that the writer should imitate nature, but to what extent? That is the whole question. Two men of equal genius, Racine and Shakespeare, have depicted, one of them Iphigenia at the moment when her father is about to sacrifice her in Aulis, the other the young Imogen at the moment when a husband she adores is about to have her stabbed somewhere in the mountain country near Milford Haven.

These great poets have both imitated nature; but one wished to amuse country gentlemen who still had the rough stern frankness which was the fruit of the long Wars of the Roses. The other sought the applause of the polite courtiers who, imitating the genteel forms established by Lauzun and the Marquis de Vardes, wished to win favour in the eyes of the king and the general approval of the ladies. 'Imitate nature' is therefore meaningless advice. To what extent must one imitate nature if one is to give pleasure to the reader? This is the main question.

I think that I should insist on one childish detail. If all that had been said at Aulis when Iphigenia was about to be murdered had been taken down on paper and preserved, we would possess five or six volumes, even if we confined ourselves to what was said by the principal characters of Racine's play. It was first necessary to reduce these six volumes to eighty pages. Furthermore, most of what was said by Agamemnon and Calchas would be unintelligible today and, even if we did understand it, would fill us with horror.

Art, then, is nothing more than a charming lie; only Sir Walter Scott has been too much of a liar. He would give greater pleasure to those higher natures who ultimately decide the fate of all literature, if, in his portrayal of the passions, he had admitted a greater number of natural traits. His characters, when they are moved by passion, seem ashamed of themselves, altogether like Mlle Mars when she is playing the part of a stupid, frivolous woman. When she comes on to the stage, this great actress glances meaningfully at the audience with a look that seems to say: 'Now don't go away thinking that I am nothing but a silly goose myself. I've got my wits about me just as much as you have. I merely want you to tell me one thing: in order to give you pleasure and deserve your applause, this being my greatest desire, I have chosen to impersonate this sort of woman. Have I succeeded or not?'

One would say of a painter who displayed this fault, which is to be found in both Scott and Mlle Mars, that his colours lacked freshness and were unnatural.

I will go even further. The more elevated the sentiments which Walter Scott's characters have to express, the less they are bold or confident. I am forced to confess this and it is this which I find most painful in what I have to say about the author and his work. One sees here all the experience and wiliness of an old judge. This is the man who, having been admitted to the table of George IV, when the latter was visiting Edinburgh, enthusiastically asked for the glass in which the King had just drunk the health of his people. Sir Walter Scott was given the precious goblet and placed it in his overcoat pocket. On returning home, however, forgetting this honour for an instant, he threw down his coat and broke the glass, an accident which threw him into despair. Would the elderly Corneille or the excellent Ducis have understood such feelings? In a hundred and forty-six years time, Scott will be less esteemed than Corneille still is a hundred and forty-six years after his death.

44. Peacock: Mr. Chainmail and the enchanter

1831

Excerpts from Thomas Love Peacock's *Crotchet Castle* (1831)— taken here from the first edition. For more serious remarks by Peacock, see No. 18.

Of the personages represented in the dialogue, Lady Clarinda and the Rev. Dr. Folliott are 'straight' characters, the latter being even a sort of touchstone to Peacock's own views; Mr. MacQuedy and Mr. Trillo are caricatures, the first of a Scotch political economist, the second perhaps of the poet Thomas Moore. The split between Sir Walter Scott the poet and the anonymous author of *Waverley* allowed Scott to be represented by both Mr. Chainmail and the enchanter.

LADY CLARINDA

Next to Mr. Skionar, sits Mr. Chainmail, a good-looking young gentleman, as you see, with very antiquated tastes. He is fond of old poetry, and is something of a poet himself. He is deep in monkish literature, and holds that the best state of society was that of the twelfth century, when nothing was going forward but fighting, feasting, and praying, which he says are the three great purposes for which man was made. He laments bitterly over the inventions of gunpowder, steam, and gas, which he says have ruined the world. He lives within two or three miles, and has a large hall, adorned with rusty pikes, shields, helmets, swords, and tattered banners, and furnished with yew-tree chairs, and two long old worm-eaten oak tables, where he dines with all his household, after the fashion of his favorite age.

At Godstow, they gathered hazel on the grave of Rosamond; and, proceeding on their voyage, fell into a discussion on legendary histories.

LADY CLARINDA

History is but a tiresome thing in itself: it becomes more agreeable the more romance is mixed up with it. The great enchanter has made me learn many things which I should never have dreamed of studying, if they had not come to me in the form of amusement.

THE REV. DR. FOLLIOTT

What enchanter is that? There are two enchanters: he of the north, and he of the south.

MR. TRILLO

Rossini?

THE REV. DR. FOLLIOTT

Aye, there is another enchanter. But I mean the great enchanter of Covent Garden: he who, for more than a quarter of a century, has produced two pantomimes a year, to the delight of children of all ages; including myself at all ages. That is the enchanter for me. I am for the pantomimes. All the northern enchanter's romances put together, would not furnish materials for half the southern enchanter's pantomimes.

LADY CLARINDA

Surely you do not class literature with pantomime?

THE REV. DR. FOLLIOTT

In these cases, I do. They are both one, with a slight difference. The one is the literature of pantomime, the other is the pantomime of literature. There is the same variety of character, the same diversity of story, the same copiousness of incident, the same research into costume, the same display of heraldry, falconry, minstrelsy, scenery, monkery, witchery, devilry, robbery, poachery, piracy, fishery, gipsy-astrology, demonology, architecture, fortification, castrametation, navigation; the same running base of love and battle. The main difference is, that the one set of amusing fictions is told in music and action; the other in all the worst dialects of the English language. As to any sentence worth remembering, any moral or political truth, any thing having a tendency, however remote, to make men wiser or better, to make them think, to make them ever think of thinking; they are both precisely alike: *nuspiam: nequaquam: nullibi: nullimodis.*[1]

LADY CLARINDA

Very amusing, however.

THE REV. DR. FOLLIOTT

Very amusing, very amusing.

MR. CHAINMAIL

My quarrel with the northern enchanter is, that he has grossly misrepresented the twelfth century.

THE REV. DR. FOLLIOTT

He has misrepresented every thing, or he would not have been very amusing. Sober truth is but dull matter to the reading rabble. The angler, who puts not on his hook the bait that best pleases the fish, may sit all day on the bank without catching a gudgeon.[2]

MR. MAC QUEDY

But how do you mean that he has misrepresented the twelfth century? By exhibiting some of its knights and ladies in the colors of refinement and virtue, seeing that they were all no better than ruffians, and something else that shall be nameless?

MR. CHAINMAIL

By no means. By depicting them as much worse than they were, not, as you suppose, much better. No one would infer from his

---

[1] 'Nobody, by no means, nowhere, in no way.'

[2] Petronius Arbiter, *Satyricon*, section 3 [Peacock].

pictures, that theirs was a much better state of society than this which we live in.

MR. MAC QUEDY

No, nor was it. It was a period of brutality, ignorance, fanaticism, and tyranny; when the land was covered with castles, and every castle contained a gang of banditti, headed by a titled robber, who levied contributions with fire and sword; plundering, torturing, ravishing, burying his captives in loathsome dungeons, and broiling them on gridirons, to force from them the surrender of every particle of treasure which he suspected them of possessing; and fighting every now and then with the neighbouring lords, his conterminal bandits, for the right of marauding on the boundaries. This was the twelfth century, as depicted by all contemporary historians and poets.

MR. CHAINMAIL

No, sir. Weigh the evidence of specific facts; you will find more good than evil. Who was England's greatest hero; the mirror of chivalry, the pattern of honor, the fountain of generosity, the model to all succeeding ages of military glory? Richard the First. There is a king of the twelfth century. What was the first step of liberty? Magna Charta. That was the best thing ever done by lords. There are lords of the twelfth century. You must remember, too, that these lords were petty princes, and made war on each other as legitimately as the heads of larger communities did or do. For their system of revenue, it was, to be sure, more rough and summary than that which has succeeded it, but it was certainly less searching and less productive. And as to the people, I content myself with these great points: that every man was armed, every man was a good archer, every man could and would fight effectively, with sword or pike, or even with oaken cudgel; no man would live quietly without beef and ale; if he had them not, he fought till he either got them, or was put out of condition to want them. They were not, and could not be, subjected to that powerful pressure of all the other classes of society, combined by gunpowder, steam, and *fiscality*, which has brought them to that dismal degradation in which we see them now. And there are the people of the twelfth century.

MR. MAC QUEDY

As to your king, the enchanter has done him ample justice, even in your own view. As to your lords and their ladies, he has drawn them too favorably, given them too many of the false colors of chivalry, thrown too attractive a light on their abominable doings. As to the people, he keeps them so much in the background, that he can hardly be said to have represented them at all, much less misrepresented them, which indeed he could scarcely do, seeing that, by your own showing, they were all thieves, ready to knock down any man for what they could not come by honestly.

MR. CHAINMAIL

No, sir. They could come honestly by beef and ale, while they were left to their simple industry. When oppression interfered with them in that, then they stood on the defensive, and fought for what they were not permitted to come by quietly.

MR. MAC QUEDY

If A., being aggrieved by B., knocks down C., do you call that standing on the defensive?

MR. CHAINMAIL

That depends on who or what C. is.

THE REV. DR. FOLLIOTT

Gentlemen, you will never settle this controversy, till you have first settled what is good for man in this world; the great question, *de finibus*, which has puzzled all philosophers. If the enchanter has represented the twelfth century too brightly for one, and too darkly for the other of you, I should say, as an impartial man, he has represented it fairly. My quarrel with him is, that his works contain nothing worth quoting; and a book that furnishes no quotations, is *me judice*, no book,—it is a plaything. There is no question about the amusement,— amusement of multitudes; but if he who amuses us most, is to be our enchanter κατ' ἐξοχὴν,[1] then my enchanter is the enchanter of Covent Garden.

[1] Par excellence.

45. Sainte-Beuve: a French obituary, *Le Globe*

1832

An obituary notice from *Le Globe*, 27 September 1832, by Charles Augustan Sainte-Beuve, the French literary critic. This translation is by Elizabeth Lee.

The long hopeless agony which for several months beset one of the most glorious and brilliant lives of the age has at length ended: Walter Scott died last Friday, at his estate of Abbotsford. It is not a grief for England only; it is a sorrow for France and the whole civilised world, for whom Walter Scott, more than any other writer of the time, was, as it were, a generous wizard and a kindly benefactor. Doubtless the vigorous and fertile genius to which we owe so much noble enjoyment, so many hours of pure emotion, so many marvellous creations which have become a portion of ourselves and of our memories, doubtless the splendid genius had begun to grow sensibly weaker. We dared no longer expect of it masterpieces to be compared with the old ones; we even feared to see it regard complacently a feeble posterity, as happens with great men in their decline, as Corneille in his old age could not quite avoid. It is permissible to believe that, in dying, Walter Scott has not taken with him any great unfinished idea; his genius had expanded at ease and with abundance; he had said enough for his glory and our delight. Although he was only sixty-two years old he died full of works, and had satisfied the world. But it is always a profound grief, an irreparable loss, to see one of the lives that have instructed and charmed us, extinguished.

[a passage concerning the recent death of great literary figures and expressing hope for the new generation is omitted]

Walter Scott, if he lacked the political character suited to the new requirements, and was on that point the slave of the prejudices of his education, and perhaps also of his poetical predilections, had the good fortune to combat very seldom in word or deed the legitimate development in which nations are engaged. France addressed several reproaches to him on account of the strange opinions with which he filled *Paul's Letters to his Kinsfolk* and *The History of Napoleon Bonaparte*; but it was on his part thoughtlessness and habitual prejudice rather than ill-will and system. Author, poet, story-teller above all, he obeyed, in the course of a long and laborious career, an easy, fertile inspiration, independent of pressing questions, a stranger to the struggles of the time, loving past ages, whose ruins he frequented and whose spirits he invoked, searching out every tradition to revive and rejuvenate it. He was, in his novels, one of the natures we are forced to call impartial and disinterested, because they can reflect life as it is in itself, describe man in all the varieties of passion or circumstances, while they apparently mingle in the paintings and faithful representations nothing of their own impressions or personality. Those kinds of natures which have the gift of forgetting themselves and of transforming themselves into an infinitude of personages, whom they make live, speak, and act in countless pathetic or diverting ways, are often capable of ardent passion on their own account, although they never express it directly. It is difficult to believe, for instance, that Shakespeare and Molière, the two highest types of that order of mind, did not feel the affairs of life with a deep and sometimes unhappy passion. It was not thus with Scott, though he was of the same family; he possessed neither their power of combination, their philosophical reach, nor their genius of style. Of a kindly, facile, pleasantly cheerful disposition, of a mind eager for culture and various sorts of knowledge, accommodating himself to prevailing manners and accredited opinions, of a somewhat dispassionate soul in so far as it appears habitually fortunate and favoured by circumstances, he developed on a brilliant and animated plane, attaining without effort those of his creations which will remain the most immortal, complacently looking on, so to speak, at their birth, and nowhere stamping them with the indescribable excess of sharp, personal imprint which always betrays an author's secrets. If he described himself in any character of his novels, it was in persons such as Morton in *Old Mortality*, that is to say in a pale, undecided, honest, and good type.

[a passage concerning Scott's life is omitted. Scott's poems are said to be 'full of charm and freshness']

Waverley appeared in 1814, and was the first of the series of masterpieces which have been the delight and joy of Europe for the last fifteen years. Several critical, antiquarian, and editorial works were written in the short intervals of the enchanting productions that succeeded each other every six months. After *The Fair Maid of Perth*, which deserved its title, a rapid decline, and symptoms of exhaustion were observed. Walter Scott's last years were saddened by losses and money difficulties, due to the failure of his publishers. Universal sympathy, a redoubling of respect and veneration, the homage of his sovereign and the British nation in that last voyage undertaken at the expense of the State, helped to compensate him, and he died as he had lived, happy, kindly, peaceable, and even in his extremest sufferings not out of love with life. Posterity will doubtless admire his works less than we do, but he will always remain a great creator, a grand man, an immortal painter of humanity!

46. Bulwer-Lytton on historical romance, *Fraser's Magazine*

1832

From an unsigned review of *Tales of My Landlord*, 4th Series (*Count Robert of Paris* and *Castle Dangerous*), *Fraser's Magazine*, February 1832, v, 6-19.

Edward George Bulwer-Lytton was himself the author of historical novels.

Sir Walter Scott had not all those aids of which his successors and imitators may take advantage. The historical romance was as much a distinct species of prose narrative fiction as the historical play was of dramatic poetry. He, however, had sufficient tact to detect at once the way in which it should be conducted, and continued to work upon the same principle, notwithstanding the warnings and oppositions of critics not submissive to the authority of contemporary genius, nor finding their canon of rules in the nature of the productions themselves, but reasoning from analogy, if not deciding on the grounds of hereditary prejudices. Mr. Allan Cunningham, in his *Paul Jones*, adopted the opposite course; and, in imitation of Miss Jane Porter's *Scottish Chiefs*, made the historical personages the principal actors of his romance, and thereby subjected himself to all the disadvantages of the historical fable. We suspect, however, that this sort of fable may have been improperly named. Miss Porter herself denominated it the 'Biographical Romance;' and this is, in fact, the character of this sort of works: they bear a resemblance to the *Achilleid* of Statius rather than to the *Iliad* and *Odyssey* of Homer. Homer's great epic does not seek to describe all the events of the hero's life, or all the circumstances of the Trojan war, but is content with an episode in its history, and finds it possible to introduce, within the limits afforded by the development of a single fact, descriptions of all the varieties of battle, and all the historical persons that he was acquainted with. The contrary practice, whether in prose or verse, leads to numberless inconveniences,—it destroys the simplicity of construction, and makes a work, however brief, unwieldy and unrememberable. It is also observable, that all the persons of the ancient poem strike the reader, on the perusal, to have been real, and not imaginary. The prose epic condescends to introduce fictitious characters and action. Of this, more hereafter.

With respect to the historical drama, the case has been somewhat different. The Italian tales, which supplied materials even for the inexhaustible imagination of Shakespeare, gave birth to that peculiar turn of comic interest with which the most numerous and noble race of our dramatic poets have enlivened the solemn scenes of gorgeous tragedy, and, in consequence, increased greatly their effect by contrast. It is to this that we owe the introduction of Falstaff and his company, male and female, and a fund of character drawn from familiar life. Other poets have taken advantage of the privilege to introduce fictitious characters of a serious cast; and when they are of so beautiful a kind as Schiller's Thekla, in *Wallenstein*, we have no very strong desire to quarrel with them for the license, which is rather of romantic than dramatic propriety. But to make ideal characters the principal agents of such dramas, would be as improper as it is comparatively unprecedented.

The drama is a concise poem, and has only room sufficient to develop a few historical characters and events; and the introduction of much legendary or fictitious action would occupy the station that might be filled with more propriety by the former. The novel, on the other hand, is a diffuse form of composition; and there is danger, not imaginary, but sufficiently exemplified in all historical novels constructed on the old principle, that, from the extent of ground to be covered, the writer will be inclined to ascribe incidents and relations to the historical hero inconsistent with all our previous associations, and destroy that degree of nascent belief which is indispensable to the enjoyment of fictitious composition. Besides which, it will be found to militate against the best interests of this kind of writing, and deprive it of those advantages which it has, in some measure, over history and even poetry itself. It has been well observed, that in history there is too little individuality, and in poetry there is too much effort, to permit the poet and historian to portray the living manners as they rise. Poetry and history have more elevated claims,—they deal with large masses—with prominent outlines, and permanent forms; it is reserved for prose fiction, and other popular media of instruction or amusement, to catch the evanescent shades—the lighter detail—and the temporary traits. The historical romance is not so denominated, because it develops an historical event, or introduces characters whose names are enrolled in the annals of antiquity, but because it professes to delineate the distinctive peculiarities and costumes of the times to which it is understood to relate. The historical event is referred to for the purpose of giving consistency and probability to the plot, and the persons are introduced as the landmarks of the age whereof the manners are representative. Opportunity is thus afforded to instruct as well as to amuse, and to make an effort of a higher kind than is necessary to the description of the other characters, in the careful elaboration of a vigorous sketch or full-length portrait of the Colossus who then 'bestrode our little world'. If, however, he had all the stage to himself, this opportunity would be effectually precluded. The greater portion of it he must have, if the plot relate principally to his fortunes and characters, and the *dénouement* would, moreover, have the disadvantage of being foreseen from the beginning; so that no curiosity could be possibly excited for the result.

The course adopted by our modern novelist suspends the interest in a twofold way. The inferior appetite of curiosity is quickened for the upshot of the fictitious narrative, while a higher expectation is kept athirst respecting the mode in which the prose poet will accomplish the more arduous part of his labour—the ultimate dramatic development of the history,—which, as it can derive nothing from the satisfaction of that lower feeling, must depend for its effect upon excellence of execution, and upon that alone. This is an advantage derived to the historical novel from the practice and on the authority of a master, the loss of which it is not extremely well calculated to sustain: it is an advantage which enables it to take its stand as a distinct class of literary production, and removes all objection against it—an objection not felt on account of any inherent defect in the thing itself, but from the constant failure of all previous attempts, which now, we think we are enabled to say, with some confidence, arose from the principles of its construction not being properly understood. These, indeed, could not be understood until they were illustrated, as they have been, by the practical evolution of them in the efforts of a writer of indisputable power. The critic must wait until the experiment is successfully made by the force of productive genius; then, compelled inward upon the laws by which he judges, he decides according to the conformity of the production with the invariable rules of his understanding. But it is absolutely requisite that he should have the materials given upon which he is to arbitrate, before the applicable principles can be ascertained or developed. Even then, he is inclined to decide hastily in the face of precedent; and it is not until the reality of individual genius has been acknowledged generally, that he feels himself justified in recognising its claims and yielding to its authority.

47. Scott's intellectual qualities, *Monthly Repository*

1832

Excerpts from an unsigned article entitled 'On the Intellectual Character of Sir Walter Scott', which appeared in the *Monthly Repository* (November 1832), 2nd Series lxxi, 721-8.

The distinguishing quality of Scott's mind, and the source of his literary power, was the faculty which has been termed *conception*, that faculty by which the various component parts of a transaction, a character, or a scene, are combined into a whole, which is distinctly and vividly presented to the mind. Phrenologists, we suppose, would say that he had the organ of constructiveness, it was rather that of re-constructiveness. Had he when a boy been turned into a disarranged armoury, we should have expected to have speedily seen him picking out the corslet here and the greaves there, and fitting the different pieces together, until the perfect form of the antique warrior stood before us, the trophy of his peculiar skill. His forte was description; and in this, whether it be of objects material or mental, he has, probably, never been surpassed. His delineations are never either on the one hand the creations of his own phantasy, or, on the other, a mere catalogue of uncombined particulars. Our notion of his intellectual rank is, that he occupied a midway station between the man of memory who merely reproduces what he found *as* he found it; and the man of poetical imagination, or of creative power. It is true that imagination must derive its materials from actual existence; but the combination is original: the parts may be, but the whole is not, a re-production. It is no disparagement of Scott to say, that to this 'highest heaven of invention' he never ascended. Many a character which Shakspeare drew *was* an original: every character which Scott drew *had* an original. But if he could not create like Shakspeare, he was only second to Shakspeare for presenting the vivid portraiture of what nature had

332

created. The temples which he restored from materials that, in other hands, would have been only isolated, scattered, and shapeless fragments, shewed not unworthy their original architect. He was an admirable renovator. It was beyond him to mould the form of a Pandora, but he had power to re-animate the mummy of a Cheops.

The limitation of Scott's power, and his occasional failures, are, as well as his success, to be traced to the peculiar mental character which we have endeavoured to indicate. The process which he pursued was, as we have shewn, one of practical observation and logical induction, rather than of poetical creation. Hence he never succeeded in the supernatural. His materials failed him. His creatures were all of the earth, earthy. He could scarcely rise enough above the actual world even to depict effectively an unwavering faith in starry, or spiritual influences. Mannering does not believe in his own calculations, and Norna has doubts of her own conjurations. His best believers are Meg Merrilies and M'Aulay, and even their faith he has neutralised by throwing into the scale a grain or two of insanity. The White Lady is but a lady in white; and he seldom got safely beyond the letter of his legend; he wanted documents. His country was very rich, and he coined and circulated the wealth, in superstitious records, but there were none of these which could help him to penetrate, as Shakspeare did, into the innermost workings of the thoughts of a spirit of the air, or a soul in purgatory. Hence, too, there is little in his writings of that elevated, generous, unworldly character, which has so often constituted the power and charm of romance. He could not enter thoroughly into such a character. He was no enthusiast. And his characters always become unsubstantial and deficient in vitality, in proportion as they recede from the times in which authentic and abundant information could be obtained. He failed, also, in all his dramatic attempts. The drama requires imagination in addition to conception. Its rapid developments, its selection of contrasted situations, its bounding over long intervals of the process to fix at once and exclusively on the more striking and startling points; these were beyond the sphere of his peculiar faculty. The narrow space of five acts did not afford him room enough. His novels are better than his poems, for the same reason that his poems are better than his dramas. As he arrived at his idea of a character by the combination of a multitude of particulars, fitting them together, and building them up into an harmonious entirety, so he required, for the conveyance of his idea to the reader's mind, full space for the converse process, scope for unfolding and exhibiting it by particulars as minute and multitudinous as those from which it was concocted. His most congenial model for the drama would have been the German who produced a comedy in four volumes octavo. The preparatory writing in his novels is often rather lengthy. Had he written without regard to booksellers, his narratives would have been interminable. There seems no good reason (except the shop) why his people should not have carried on their sayings and doings in the same amusing way, through thirty volumes instead of three. Hence though his characters are often very dramatic, his mode of developing and disposing of them is usually most undramatic. He plays with them, and 'exquisite fooling' it is, till the required quantity of letter-press is completed, and then he huddles up the catastrophe, and sends them about their business in a hurry. The school breaks up; go home, boys, and be good; and then he briefly tells us that they were, or shall be, very happy all their lives ever after.

Scott is said to have been so delighted with 'the Pleasures of Hope', that, the manuscript having been left with him late one night, he was able, after twice reading it, to repeat the whole poem next morning, with only a few trifling omissions. We should have thought that the Pleasures of Memory (not Rogers's) had been more to his taste. His genius was no Janus. The future did not divide its regards with the past: it looked only backward. He was eminently the man of the past. In a literary sense, he thought little of the world to come; his heart was in the bygone world. Reform was a trouble to his mind; he dwelt in the fading shadows of feudality, and was appalled at the growing glare of democracy; he knew not the people; and *as* the people he loved them not. The king's evil of aristocracy was hereditary in his moral constitution, and the disease was incurable; in fact, he died of it: the spirit of aristocracy was his murderer; it made him undervalue those laurels which, had he rightly prized them, would have saved his brows from the flash which scathed him. He more gloried in being the laird of Abbotsford than the author of *Waverley*. His passion for becoming the connecting link of a broken feudal chain was his ruin. The purchase and improvement of his 'policy' outran even the unprecedented profits of his publications. He became involved in the unfortunate speculations of Constable's house, and the tenacity with which he clung to the retention of Abbotsford, and the preservation of its entail, impelled him to the gigantic attempt of writing down a debt of one hundred thousand pounds. One-half of this mountain he did heave off, and then sunk, crushed beneath the remaining portion. The laird destroyed the novelist. A popular journal has suggested a national subscription in order to free Abbotsford from the claims of the creditors, and entail it on the heirs of the baronetcy. This would be like honouring the memory of Achilles by raising the *effigies* of his vulnerable heel as a monument. Let the nation endow his family, if there be occasion, and amply too; and let Abbotsford be purchased, but rather to be preserved as the author's monument, than by being made an aristocratical *appanage* cherish the folly which hastened the extinction of so much mental energy and moral worth. That has already cost us enough, for it cost us Scott. It will be long ere aristocracy will balance that account. But for his healthy habits, his regularity of application, his cheerfulness of disposition, his good heart and conscience, it would have inflicted the loss upon us long before. The kingdom which he ruled in the regions of literature dissolves with his death. 'The age of chivalry is gone.' The age of improvement is come, and futurity will now be the poet's inspiration. 'Let bygones be bygones'; they have been nobly chronicled, and peace to the manes of the *ultimus Romanorum*; 'We ne'er shall look upon his like again'; that is too much to hope for. Let his toryism 'lie with him in his grave, but not remembered in his epitaph'; it did not mar his kindheartedness; it did not disfigure, or but very faintly, his beautiful sketches. If he did not rightly estimate what a people is, collectively, he well appreciated what they had been individually; he did them justice, and rendered them affection,

> 'For this single cause
> That we have, all of us, ONE HUMAN HEART.'

In theory he was no disciple of Bentham; no advocate of the 'greatest happiness principle'; but practically, and considering only the immediate result, who is there of our times, either among the living or the dead, that has generated a greater amount of human enjoyment?

48. W. B. O. Peabody defends Scott's poetry

1833

An extract from an unsigned review of Allan Cunningham's *Some Account of the Life and Works of Sir Walter Scott, North American Review* (April 1833), xxxvi, 289-315.

The reviewer was William Bourn Oliver Peabody, a Unitarian minister and miscellaneous writer.

It has been fashionable enough to say, that the poetry of Scott is not destined to be read hereafter; some infer this from its unusual popularity, as if nothing could be seen aright, except at the distance of a century. Even Sir James Mackintosh, no common judge, believed that it could not last, because none but the most elaborate poetry had yet defied the test of time. This is, after all, only saying, that it does not square with our notions of what poetry ought to be. Some believe, that the poet trespasses upon the province of another, when he deserts nature to find a subject in the world of art; others imagine, that the heart is his only true dominion; and there are very few, who do not set up a poetical definition of their own, like the image in the plain of Dura, and measure the desert of all by the zeal with which they do it homage. But this is partial judgment; it takes one quality for all, unlike the Oriental tale, which represents the foot that kicked a vessel of water to a thirsty animal, as conveyed to Paradise to enjoy its reward, while the remainder of the man found no such recompense. It is possible, after all, that the waters of Israel may be found of no less healing virtue than the rivers of Damascus;—that the very qualities which in our opinion lead to death, may be the very ones which shall make the works of genius live. The poetry of Scott falls within none of these definitions. His versification, perfect as much of it may be, betrays in many instances very little of the care of preparation; there is nothing so aristocratic in his love of nature, as to make him look with indifference on art; nothing so fervent in his contemplation of the heart, as to make him insensible to human action. Action is indeed the living soul, which quickens and informs the whole; the heart of his reader beats high as it is borne along with the rush and sweep of its movement; and it is vain to say, that there is nothing of poetry in what so excites us; we might as well deny, that there was music in the harpstring of the ancient bard. The truth is, that it was a development of the same qualities, which were afterwards manifested in his romances with such commanding power, in a form, less fitted to reveal them in their full perfection. Fortunate indeed it was, if that can be attributed to fortune, which is an accident befalling genius only, that he afterwards assumed another form, better calculated for the exhibition of character in all its shifting alternations of light and shade, its infinite varieties of stern feeling, of high resolve, of playful humor, of every thing, in short, from the loftiest to the lowest. The ancients understood this, when they placed the region of song upon the mountain's brow, open to communion with the grand and beautiful, the sunlight and the storm, and lifted above the crowd, that hurry onward in the paths of life around its base. Shakespeare understood it no less, and uniformly throws aside the restraint of verse, when he has to deal with the familiar and the common. The romance, as Scott afterwards presented it, was the discovery of his maturity; it was poetry still; but he had laid aside conventional restraint, and gone forth with the active bound of the mountaineer, when his foot is on his native hills. Any one will feel the force of this remark, who considers how perfectly impossible it would have been to present such a personage as Captain Dalgetty in verse; while Ellen Douglas is as delightful a vision as his pencil ever drew. It was thus that the form of verse became a limitation of his power. Still, though we do not incline to place the metrical romances among the highest efforts of talent, not even of his own, we believe that there are redeeming virtues in them, which will not suffer them to be forgotten. What can be richer or more glowing than his descriptions? They are not like the images reflected dimly in the dark chamber, when the sun is shut in by clouds; they stand out in full distinctness and reality, like the outline of the mountains on the evening skies of autumn. What was ever more beautiful or truer, than his picture of the scenery of Loch Katrine in *The Lady of the Lake*, a poem by which the pilgrim traces out his path, as if directed by a golden bough? This is the first of his poems, in which his descriptive power is revealed in a perfection, which not even he could afterwards excel; though probably no traveller will visit Melrose or Flodden, made so celebrated by his earlier ones, hereafter, without recollecting their departed minstrel, or gaze upon a lake or mountain of Scotland, without bidding his gentle spirit rest. It is a great prerogative of genius, thus to write its name upon every hill and valley of its native land, so that all coming generations shall read it there. Then his sentiments are always just, and flow naturally, without enthusiasm, as if they merely shadowed forth the prevailing temper of his soul. But the real, in-wrought, undying charm is that of which we have already spoken;—the life and spirit of the action, rolling onward in a deep and flashing tide; and this, in spite of all definitions, will hardly fail to be regarded as an evidence of the existence and power of the art divine.

Certain it is, that no conqueror ever gained a victory more decisive and complete, than that which was accomplished by the author of *The Lay of the Last Minstrel*; and yet it is far from being the best of the class to which it belongs. Its characters are dim and shadowy, and betray very little of that perfect mastery of the heart, which was after-wards so strikingly displayed. His heroes of border chivalry are no more distinguished by any peculiar qualities, than Gyas and Cloanthus; the Lady of Buccleugh is of a higher mood; but it is vain to attempt to feel much interest in the others. There are many defects in the con-struction of the story, which seems to have been formed without any regular plan, the writer having evidently drifted with the tide; and the superstitions, however characteristic and true, are sometimes startling and repulsive. All this is probably owing to the manner in which the tale was written. Scott was requested to write a ballad upon the legend of Gilpin Horner, which was expanded in its progress into this poem; and it was thus prepared under all the disadvantages of an involuntary, if not of a reluctant task. But all this and more would be atoned for by the bursts of genuine poetry, which are perpetually breaking forth; yet we remember it rather as a succession of beautiful fragments, than a well compacted and perfect whole. In *Marmion*, which appeared three years after, there were the same defects and beauties, each in less degree, but other excellencies were added, which the Lay had not revealed. The action of the Lay was spiritless, while that of *Marmion* was full of life; the construction of the story was not perfect, and the versification, though in many places rich and beautiful, was in many others rude and careless; but it led right onward to the glorious battle scene, one of the finest passages of narrative poetry in the language; of which it is hard to believe that, in its present form, it required the labor only of a single afternoon. Thus the various excellencies of Scott were gradually exhibiting themselves, like stars above the horizon: in the first instance, we find true sentiment, and passages of uncommon beauty; then comes the animated and varied action; and the fullness of his descriptive power is reserved for *The Lady of the Lake*, the most popular of all his metrical romances, and the best deserving of its reputation. Its characters are beautifully drawn, and the story proceeds with undiminished interest to its close; nothing in poetry surpasses the magic beauty of its scenery; it shows, on the whole, more inventive skill as well as varied power, than any of his former works. But it is needless to enter into an inquiry respecting the merit of poems, which have been read with admiration wherever the English language is known. *Rokeby* and *The Lord of the Isles* were the only remarkable ones which followed; these were distinguished by other traits than any which preceded them; they exhibited far more variety and precision in their views of character, and greater hurry in the preparation.

49. Harriet Martineau: Scott as moral hero, *Tait's Edinburgh Magazine*

1833

Extract from an article by Harriet Martineau, *Tait's Edinburgh Magazine* (January 1833), ii, 445-60.

Harriet Martineau was a writer and popularizer with a heavy moral bent; here she sees Scott as leading the way in the field of moral propaganda. The first paragraph is a recapitulation of the previous section of the article.

These, then, are the moral services,—many and great,—which Scott has rendered, positively and negatively, consciously and unconsciously, to society. He has softened national prejudices; he has encouraged innocent tastes in every region of the world; he has imparted to certain influential classes the conviction that human nature works alike in all; he has exposed priestcraft and fanaticism; he has effectively satirized eccentricities, unamiablenesses, and follies; he has irresistibly recommended benignity in the survey of life, and indicated the glory of a higher kind of benevolence; and finally, he has advocated the rights of woman with a force all the greater for his being unaware of the import and tendency of what he was saying.—The one other achievement which we attribute to him, is also not the less magnificent for being overlooked by himself.

By achieving so much within narrow bounds, he has taught how more may be achieved in a wider space. He has taught us the power of fiction as an agent of morals and philosophy; 'and it shall go hard with us but we will better the instruction'. Every agent of these master spirits is wanted in an age like this; and he who has placed a new one at their service, is a benefactor of society. Scott might have written, as he declared he wrote, for the passing of his time, the improvement of his fortunes, and the amusement of his readers: he might have believed, as he declared he believed, that little moral utility arises out of works of fiction: we are not bound to estimate his works as lightly as he did, or to agree in his opinions of their influences. We rather learn from him how much may be impressed by exemplification which would be rejected in the form of reasoning, and how there may be more extensive *embodiments* of truth in fiction than the world was before thoroughly aware of. It matters not that the truth he exemplified was taken up at random, like that of all his predecessors in the walks of fiction. Others may systematize, having learned from him how extensively they may embody. There is a boundless field open before them; no less than the whole region of moral science, politics, political economy, social rights and duties. All these, and more, are as fit for the process of exemplification as the varieties of life and character illustrated by Scott. And not only has he left the great mass of material unwrought, but, with all his richness of variety, has made but scanty use of the best instruments of illustration. The grandest manifestations of passion remain to be displayed; the finest elements of the poetry of human emotion are yet uncombined; the most various dramatic exhibition of events and characters is yet unwrought; for there has yet been no recorder of the poor; at least, none but those who write as mere observers; who describe, but do not dramatize humble life. The widest interests being thus still untouched, the richest materials unemployed, what may not prove the ultimate obligations of society to him who did so much, and pointed the way towards doing infinitely more; and whose vast achievements are, above all, valuable as indications of what remains to be achieved? That this, his strongest claim to gratitude, has not yet been fully recognised, is evident from the fact, that though he has had many imitators, there have been yet none to take suggestion from him; to employ his method of procedure upon new doctrine and other materials. There have been many found to construct fiction within his range of morals, character, incident, and scenery; but none to carry the process out of his range. We have yet to wait for the philosophical romance, for the novels which shall relate to other classes than the aristocracy; we have yet to look for this legitimate offspring of the productions of Scott, though wearied with the intrusions of their spurious brethren.

The progression of the age requires something better than this imitation;—requires that the above-mentioned suggestion should be used. If an author of equal genius with Scott were to arise to-morrow, he would not meet with an equal reception; not only because novelty

is worn off, but because the serious temper of the times requires a new
direction of the genius of the age. Under the pressure of difficulty, in
the prospect of extensive change, armed with expectation, or filled with
determination as the general mind now is, it has not leisure or disposition to receive even its amusements unmixed with what is solid and
has a bearing upon its engrossing interests.

50. J. G. Lockhart on Scott

1837

Extracts from John Gibson Lockhart, *Memoirs of the Life of Sir
Walter Scott, Bart.*, first published in 1837. (These selections are
taken from the 1839 ed. (Edinburgh, London), v, 176-7 (ch. 37),
vi, 255-7 (ch. 50), vii, 117-18 (ch. 57).)

Lockhart was Scott's son-in-law and editor of the *Quarterly
Review* for many years (1825-53).

Old Mortality

Old Mortality . . . is remarkable as the *novelist's* first attempt to repeople
the past by the power of imagination working on materials furnished
by books. In *Waverley* he revived the fervid dreams of his boyhood,
and drew, not from printed records, but from the artless oral narratives
of his *Invernahyles*. In *Guy Mannering* and *The Antiquary* he embodied
characters and manners familiar to his own wandering youth. But
whenever his letters mention *Old Mortality* in its progress, they
represent him as strong in the confidence that the industry with which
he had pored over a library of forgotten tracts would enable him to
identify himself with the time in which they had birth, as completely
as if he had listened with his own ears to the dismal sermons of Peden,

ridden with Claverhouse and Dalzell in the rout of Bothwell, and been an advocate at the bar of the Privy-Council, when Lauderdale catechized and tortured the assassins of Archbishop Sharpe. To reproduce a departed age with such minute and lifelike accuracy as this tale exhibits, demanded a far more energetic sympathy of imagination than had been called for in any effort of his serious verse. It is indeed most curiously instructive for any student of art to compare the Roundheads of *Rokeby* with the Bluebonnets of *Old Mortality*. For the rest—the story is framed with a deeper skill than any of the preceding novels; the canvas is a broader one; the characters are contrasted and projected with a power and felicity which neither he nor any other master ever surpassed; and, notwithstanding all that has been urged against him as a disparager of the Covenanters, it is to me very doubtful whether the inspiration of romantic chivalry ever prompted him to nobler emotions than he has lavished on the re-animation of their stern and solemn enthusiasm. This work has always appeared to me the *Marmion* of his novels.

The Monastery

It was considered as a failure—the first of the series on which any such sentence was pronounced;—nor have I much to allege in favour of the White Lady of Avenel, generally criticised as the primary blot, or of Sir Percy Shafton, who was loudly, though not quite so generally, condemned. In either case, considered separately, he seems to have erred from dwelling (in the German taste) on materials that might have done very well for a rapid sketch. The phantom with whom we have leisure to become familiar, is sure to fail—even the witch of Endor is contented with a momentary appearance and five syllables of the shade she evokes. And we may say the same of any grotesque absurdity in human manners. Scott might have considered with advantage how lightly and briefly Shakspeare introduces *his* Euphuism—though actually the prevalent humour of the hour when he was writing. But perhaps these errors might have attracted little notice had the novelist been successful in finding some reconciling medium capable of giving consistence and harmony to his naturally incongruous materials.

The beautiful natural scenery, and the sterling Scotch characters and manners introduced in *The Monastery*, are, however, sufficient to redeem even these mistakes; and, indeed, I am inclined to believe that it will ultimately occupy a securer place than some romances enjoying hitherto a far higher reputation, in which he makes no use of *Scottish* materials.

Peveril of the Peak

Its reception was somewhat colder than that of its three immediate predecessors. The post-haste rapidity of the Novelist's execution was put to a severe trial, from his adoption of so wide a canvass as was presented by a period of twenty busy years, and filled by so very large and multifarious an assemblage of persons, not a few of them, as it were, struggling for prominence. Fenella was an unfortunate conception; what is good in it is not original, and the rest extravagantly absurd and incredible. Even worse was that condescension to the practice of vulgar romancers, in his treatment of the trial scenes—scenes usually the very citadels of his strength—which outraged every feeling of probability with those who had studied the terrible tragedies of the Popish Plot, in the authentic records of, perhaps, the most disgraceful epoch in our history. The story is clumsy and perplexed; the catastrophe (another signal exception to his rules) foreseen from the beginning, and yet most inartificially brought about. All this is true; and yet might not criticisms of the same sort be applied to half the masterpieces of Shakspeare? And did any dramatist—to say nothing of any other novelist—ever produce, in spite of all the surrounding bewilderment of the fable, characters more powerfully conceived, or, on the whole, more happily portrayed, than those (I name but a few) of Christian, Bridgenorth, Buckingham, and Chiffinch—sketches more vivid than those of Young Derby, Colonel Blood, and the keeper of Newgate?

51. Carlyle: the amoral Scott,
London and Westminster Review

1838

Unsigned review by Thomas Carlyle of the first six volumes of Lockhart's *Life of Sir Walter Scott, Baronet* (quoted here from Carlyle's *Miscellaneous Essays*, III (London, 1888, 167-223). This review first appeared in the *London and Westminster Review* (January 1838), xxviii, 293-345, and became a reference point for many later critics.

An introductory section, which has here been omitted, deals first with hero worship and then with Lockhart's *Life*.

Into the question whether Scott was a great man or not, we do not propose to enter deeply. It is, as too usual, a question about words. There can be no doubt but many men have been named and printed *great* who were vastly smaller than he: as little doubt moreover that of the specially *good*, a very large portion, according to any genuine standard of man's worth, were worthless in comparison to him. He for whom Scott is great may most innocently name him so; may with advantage admire his great qualities, and ought with sincere heart to emulate them. At the same time, it is good that there be a certain degree of precision in our epithets. It is good to understand, for one thing, that no popularity, and open-mouthed wonder of all the world, continued even for a long series of years, can make a man great. Such popularity is a remarkable fortune; indicates a great adaptation of the man to his element of circumstances; but may or may not indicate anything great in the man. To our imagination, as above hinted, there is a certain apotheosis in it; but in the reality no apotheosis at all. Popularity is as a blaze of illumination, or alas, of conflagration, kindled round a man; *showing* what is in him; not putting the smallest item more into him; often abstracting much from him; conflagrating the poor man himself into ashes and *caput mortuum*! And then, by the nature of it, such popularity is transient; your 'series of years', quite unexpectedly, sometimes almost all on a sudden, terminates! For the stupidity of men, especially of men congregated in masses round any object, is extreme. What illuminations and conflagrations have kindled themselves, as if new heavenly suns had risen, which proved only to be tar-barrels and terrestrial locks of straw! Profane Princesses cried out, 'One God, one Farinelli!'—and whither now have they and Farinelli danced?

In Literature too there have been seen popularities greater even than Scott's, and nothing perennial in the interior of them. Lope de Vega, whom all the world swore by, and made a proverb of; who could make an acceptable five-act tragedy in almost as many hours; the greatest of all popularities past or present, and perhaps one of the greatest men that ever ranked among popularities: Lope himself, so radiant, far-shining, has not proved to be a sun or star of the firmament; but is as good as lost and gone out; or plays at best in the eyes of some few as a vague aurora-borealis, and brilliant ineffectuality. The great man of Spain sat obscure at the time, all dark and poor, a maimed soldier; writing his *Don Quixote* in prison. And Lope's fate withal was sad, his popularity perhaps a curse to him; for in this man there was something ethereal too, a divine particle traceable in few other popular men; and such far-shining diffusion of himself, though all the world swore by it, would do nothing for the true life of him even while he lived: he had to creep into a convent, into a monk's cowl, and learn, with infinite sorrow, that his blessedness had lain elsewhere; that when a man's life feels itself to be sick and an error, no voting of bystanders can make it well and a truth again.

Or coming down to our own times, was not August Kotzebue popular? Kotzebue, not so many years since, saw himself, if rumour and hand-clapping could be credited, the greatest man going; saw visibly his Thoughts, dressed-out in plush and pasteboard, permeating and perambulating civilised Europe; the most iron visages weeping with him, in all theatres from Cadiz to Kamtchatka; his own 'astonishing genius' meanwhile producing two tragedies or so per month: he, on the whole, blazed high enough: he too has gone out into Night and *Orcus*, and already is not. We will omit this of popularity altogether; and account it as making simply nothing towards Scott's greatness or non-greatness, as an accident, not a quality.

Shorn of this falsifying *nimbus*, and reduced to his own natural dimensions, there remains the reality, Walter Scott, and what we can find in him: to be accounted great, or not great, according to the dialects of men. Friends to precision of epithet will probably deny his title to the name 'great'. It seems to us there goes other stuff to the making of great men than can be detected here. One knows not what idea worthy of the name of great, what purpose, instinct or tendency, that could be called great, Scott ever was inspired with. His life was worldly; his ambitions were worldly. There is nothing spiritual in him; all is economical, material, of the earth earthy. A love of picturesque, of beautiful, vigorous and graceful things; a genuine love, yet not more genuine than has dwelt in hundreds of men named minor poets: this is the highest quality to be discerned in him.

His power of representing these things, too, his poetic power, like his moral power, was a genius *in extenso*, as we may say, not *in intenso*. In action, in speculation, *broad* as he was, he rose nowhere high; productive without measure as to quantity, in quality he for the most part transcended but a little way the region of commonplace. It has been said, 'no man has written as many volumes with so few sentences that can be quoted'. Winged words were not his vocation; nothing urged him that way: the great Mystery of Existence was not great to him; did not drive him into rocky solitudes to wrestle with it for an answer, to be answered or to perish. He had nothing of the martyr; into no 'dark region to slay monsters for us', did he, either led or driven, venture down: his conquests were for his own behoof mainly, conquests over common market-labour, and reckonable in good metallic coin of the realm. The thing he had faith in, except power, power of what sort soever, and even of the rudest sort, would be difficult to point out. One sees not that he believed in anything; nay he did not even disbelieve; but quietly acquiesced, and made himself at home in a world of conventionalities; the false, the semi-false and the true were alike true in this, that they were there, and had power in their hands more or less. It was well to feel so; and yet not well! We find it written, 'Woe to them that are at ease in Zion'; but surely it is a double woe to them that are at ease in Babel, in Domdaniel. On the other hand, he wrote many volumes, amusing many thousands of men. Shall we call this great? It seems to us there dwells and struggles another sort of spirit in the inward parts of great men!

Brother Ringletub, the missionary, inquired of Ram-Dass, a Hindoo man-god, who had set up for godhood lately, What he meant to do, then, with the sins of mankind? To which Ram-Dass at once answered, He had *fire enough in his belly* to burn-up all the sins in the world. Ram-Dass was right so far, and had a spice of sense in him; for surely it is the test of every divine man this same, and without it he is not divine or great,—that he *have* fire in him to burn-up somewhat of the sins of the world, of the miseries and errors of the world: why else is he there? Far be it from us to say that a great man must needs, with benevolence prepense, become a 'friend of humanity'; nay that such professional self-conscious friends of humanity are not the fatalest kind of persons to be met with in our day. All greatness is unconscious, or it is little and nought. And yet a great man without *such* fire in him, burning dim or developed, as a divine behest in his heart of hearts, never resting till it be fulfilled, were a solecism in Nature. A great man is ever, as the Transcendentalists speak, possessed with an *idea*.

Napoleon himself, not the superfinest of great men, and ballasted sufficiently with prudences and egoisms, had nevertheless, as is clear enough, an idea to start with: the idea that 'Democracy was the Cause of Man, the right and infinite Cause. Accordingly, he made himself the armed Soldier of Democracy'; and did vindicate it in a rather great manner. Nay, to the very last, he had a kind of idea; that, namely, of '*La carrière ouverte aux talens*, The tools to him that can handle them;' really one of the best ideas yet promulgated on that matter, or rather the one true central idea, towards which all the others, if they tend anywhither, must tend. Unhappily it was in the military province only that Napoleon could realise this idea of his, being forced to fight for himself the while: before he got it tried to any extent in the civil province of things, his head by much victory grew light (no head can stand more than its quantity); and he lost head, as they say, and became a selfish ambitionist and quack, and was hurled out; leaving his idea to be realised, in the civil province of things, by others! Thus was Napoleon; thus are all great men: children of the idea; or, in Ram-Dass's phraseology, furnished with fire to burn-up the miseries of men. Conscious or unconscious, latent or unfolded, there is small vestige of any such fire being extant in the inner-man of Scott.

Yet on the other hand, the surliest critic must allow that Scott was a genuine man, which itself is a great matter. No affectation, fantasticality or distortion dwelt in him; no shadow of cant. Nay withal, was he not a right brave and strong man, according to his kind? What a load of toil, what a measure of felicity, he quietly bore along with him; with what quiet strength he both worked on this earth, and enjoyed in it;

invincible to evil fortune and to good! A most composed invincible man; in difficulty and distress knowing no discouragement, Samson-like carrying off on his strong Samson-shoulders the gates that would imprison him; in danger and menace laughing at the whisper of fear. And then, with such a sunny current of true humour and humanity, a free joyful sympathy with so many things; what of fire he had all lying so beautifully *latent*, as radical latent heat, as fruitful internal warmth of life; a most robust, healthy man! The truth is, our best definition of Scott were perhaps even this, that he was, if no great man, then something much pleasanter to be, a robust, thoroughly healthy and withal very prosperous and victorious man. An eminently well-conditioned man, healthy in body, healthy in soul; we will call him one of the *healthiest* of men.

Neither is this a small matter: health is a great matter, both to the possessor of it and to others. On the whole, that humorist in the Moral Essay was not so far out, who determined on honouring health only; and so instead of humbling himself to the highborn, to the rich and well-dressed, insisted on doffing hat to the healthy: coroneted carriages with pale faces in them passed by as failures, miserable and lamentable; trucks with ruddy-cheeked strength dragging at them were greeted as successful and venerable. For does not health mean harmony, the synonym of all that is true, justly-ordered, good; is it not, in some sense, the net-total, as shown by experiment, of whatever worth is in us? The healthy man is the most meritorious product of Nature so far as he goes. A healthy body is good; but a soul in right health,—it is the thing beyond all others to be prayed for; the blessedest thing this earth receives of Heaven. Without artificial medicament of philosophy, or tight-lacing of creeds (always very questionable), the healthy soul discerns what is good, and adheres to it, and retains it; discerns what is bad, and spontaneously casts it off. An instinct from Nature herself, like that which guides the wild animals of the forest to their food, shows him what he shall do, what he shall abstain from. The false and foreign will not adhere to him; cant and all fantastic diseased incrustations are impossible;—as Walker the *Original*, in such eminence of health was *he* for his part, *could* not, by much abstinence from soap-and-water, attain to a dirty face! This thing thou canst work with and profit by, this thing is substantial and worthy; that other thing thou canst not work with, it is trivial and inapt: so speaks unerringly the inward monition of the man's whole nature. No need of logic to prove the most argumentative absurdity absurd; as Goethe says of himself, 'all this ran down from me like water from a man in wax-cloth dress'. Blessed is the healthy nature; it is the coherent, sweetly coöperative, not incoherent, self-distracting, self-destructive one! In the harmonious adjustment and play of all the faculties, the just balance of oneself gives a just feeling towards all men and all things. Glad lights from within radiates outwards, and enlightens and embellishes.

Now all this can be predicated of Walter Scott, and of no British literary man that we remember in these days, to any such extent,— if it be not perhaps of one, the most opposite imaginable to Scott, but his equal in this quality and what holds of it: William Cobbett! Nay there are other similarities, widely different as they two look; nor be the comparison disparaging to Scott: for Cobbett also, as the pattern John Bull of his century, strong as the rhinoceros, and with singular humanities and genialities shining through his thick skin, is a most brave phenomenon. So bounteous was Nature to us; in the sickliest of recorded ages, when British Literature lay all puking and sprawling in Werterism, Byronism, and other Sentimentalism tearful or spasmodic (fruit of internal *wind*), Nature was kind enough to send us two healthy Men, of whom she might still say, not without pride, 'These also were made in England; such limbs do I still make there!' It is one of the cheerfulest sights, let the question of its greatness be settled as you will. A healthy nature may or may not be great; but there is no great nature that is not healthy.

Or, on the whole, might we not say, Scott, in the new vesture of the nineteenth century, was intrinsically very much the old fighting Borderer of prior centuries; the kind of man Nature did of old make in that birthland of his? In the saddle, with the foray-spear, he would have acquitted himself as he did at the desk with his pen. One fancies how, in stout *Beardie* of Harden's time, he could have played Beardie's part; and *been* the stalwart buff-belted *terrae filius* he in this late time could only delight to draw. The same stout self-help was in him; the same oak and triple brass round his heart. He too could have fought at Redswire, cracking crowns with the fiercest, if that had been the task; could have harried cattle in Tynedale, repaying injury with compound interest; a right sufficient captain of men. A man without qualms or fantasticalities; a hard-headed, sound-hearted man, of joyous robust temper, looking to the main chance, and fighting direct thitherward; *valde stalwartus homo!*[1]—How much in that case had slumbered in him, and passed away without sign! But indeed who knows how much

[1] 'A very stalwart man.'

slumbers in many men? Perhaps our greatest poets are the *mute* Miltons; the vocals are those whom by happy accident we lay hold of, one here, one there, as it chances, and *make* vocal. It is even a question, whether, had not want, discomfort and distress-warrants been busy at Stratford-on-Avon, Shakspeare himself had not lived killing calves or combing wool! Had the Edial Boarding-school turned out well, we had never heard of Samuel Johnson; Samuel Johnson had been a fat schoolmaster and dogmatic gerundgrinder, and never known that he was more. Nature is rich: those two eggs thou art eating carelessly to breakfast, could they not have been hatched into a pair of fowls, and have covered the whole world with poultry?

But it was not harrying of cattle in Tynedale, or cracking of crowns at Redswire, that this stout Border-chief was appointed to perform. Far other work. To be the song-singer and pleasant tale-teller to Britain and Europe, in the beginning of the artificial nineteenth century; here, and not there, lay his business. Beardie of Harden would have found it very amazing. How he shapes himself to this new element; how he helps himself along in it, makes it too do for him, lives sound and victorious in it, and leads over the marches such a spoil as all the cattle-droves the Hardens ever took were poor in comparison to; this is the history of the life and achievements of *our* Sir Walter Scott, Baronet;—whereat we are now to glance for a little! It is a thing remarkable; a thing substantial; of joyful, victorious sort; not unworthy to be glanced at. Withal, however, a glance here and there will suffice. Our limits are narrow; the thing, were it never so victorious, is not of the sublime sort, nor extremely edifying; there is nothing in it to censure vehemently, nor love vehemently; there is more to wonder at than admire; and the whole secret is not an abstruse one.

Till towards the age of thirty, Scott's life has nothing in it decisively pointing towards Literature, or indeed towards distinction of any kind; he is wedded, settled, and has gone through all his preliminary steps, without symptom of renown as yet. It is the life of every other Edinburgh youth of his station and time. Fortunate we must name it, in many ways. Parents in easy or wealthy circumstances, yet un-encumbered with the cares and perversions of aristocracy; nothing eminent in place, in faculty or culture, yet nothing deficient; all around is methodic regulation, prudence, prosperity, kind-heartedness; an element of warmth and light, of affection, industry and burgherly comfort, heightened into elegance; in which the young heart can wholesomely grow. A vigorous health seems to have been given by

Nature; yet, as if Nature had said withal, 'Let it be a health to express itself by mind, not by body,' a lameness is added in childhood; the brave little boy, instead of romping and bickering, must learn to think; or at lowest, what is a great matter, to sit still. No rackets and trundling-hoops for this young Walter; but ballads, history-books and a world of legendary stuff, which his mother and those near him are copiously able to furnish. Disease, which is but superficial, and issues in outward lameness, does not cloud the young existence; rather forwards it towards the expansion it is fitted for. The miserable disease had been one of the internal nobler parts, marring the general organisation; under which no Walter Scott could have been forwarded, or with all his other endowments could have been producible or possible. 'Nature gives healthy children much; how much! Wise education is a wise unfolding of this; often it unfolds itself better of its own accord.'

Add one other circumstance: the place where; namely, Presbyterian Scotland. The influences of this are felt incessantly, they stream-in at every pore. 'There is a country accent,' says La Rochefoucault, 'not in speech only, but in thought, conduct, character and manner of existing, which never forsakes a man.' Scott, we believe, was all his days an Episcopalian Dissenter in Scotland; but that makes little to the matter. Nobody who knows Scotland and Scott can doubt but Presbyterianism too had a vast share in the forming of him. A country where the entire people is, or even once has been, laid hold of, filled to the heart with an infinite religious idea, has 'made a step from which it cannot retrograde'. Thought, conscience, the sense that man is denizen of a Universe, creature of an Eternity, has penetrated to the remotest cottage, to the simplest heart. Beautiful and awful, the feeling of a Heavenly Behest, of Duty god-commanded, over-canopies all life. There is an inspiration in such a people: one may say in a more special sense, 'the inspiration of the Almighty giveth them understanding.' Honour to all the brave and true; everlasting honour to brave old Knox, one of the truest of the true! That, in the moment while he and his cause, amid civil broils, in convulsion and confusion, were still but struggling for life, he sent the schoolmaster forth to all corners, and said, 'Let the people be taught:' this is but one, and indeed an inevitable and comparatively inconsiderable item in his great message to men. His message, in its true compass, was, 'Let men know that they are men; created by God, responsible to God; who work in any meanest moment of time what will last through eternity.' It is verily a great message. Not ploughing and hammering machines, not patent-digesters (never so ornamental) to digest the produce of these: no, in no wise; born slaves neither of their fellow-men, nor of their own appetites; but men! This great message Knox did deliver, with a man's voice and strength; and found a people to believe him.

Of such an achievement, we say, were it to be made once only, the results are immense. Thought, in such a country, may change its form, but cannot go out; the country has attained *majority*; thought, and a certain spiritual manhood, ready for all work that man can do, endures there. It may take many forms: the form of hard-fisted money-getting industry, as in the vulgar Scotchman, in the vulgar New Englander; but as compact developed force and alertness of faculty, it is still there; it may utter itself one day as the colossal Scepticism of a Hume (beneficent this too though painful, wrestling Titan-like through doubt and inquiry towards new belief); and again, some better day, it may utter itself as the inspired Melody of a Burns: in a word, it is there, and continues to manifest itself, in the Voice and the Work of a Nation of hardy endeavouring considering men, with whatever that may bear in it, or unfold from it. The Scotch national character originates in many circumstances; first of all, in the Saxon stuff there was to work on; but next, and beyond all else except that, in the Presbyterian Gospel of John Knox. It seems a good national character; and on some sides not so good. Let Scott thank John Knox, for he owed him much, little as he dreamed of debt in that quarter! No Scotchman of his time was more entirely Scotch than Walter Scott: the good and the not so good, which all Scotchmen inherit, ran through every fibre of him.

[a strictly biographical passage has been omitted]

The Minstrelsy of the Scottish Border proved to be a well from which flowed one of the broadest rivers. Metrical Romances (which in due time pass into Prose Romances); the old life of men resuscitated for us: it is a mighty word! Not as dead tradition, but as a palpable presence, the past stood before us. There they were, the rugged old fighting men; in their doughty simplicity and strength, with their heartiness, their healthiness, their stout self-help, in their iron basnets, leather jerkins, jackboots, in their quaintness of manner and costume; there as they looked and lived: it was like a new-discovered continent in Literature; for the new century, a bright El Dorado,—or else some fat beatific land of Cockaigne, and Paradise of Donothings. To the opening nineteenth century, in its languor and paralysis, nothing could have been welcomer. Most unexpected, most refreshing and exhilarating; behold our new El Dorado; our fat beatific Lubberland, where one can enjoy and do nothing! It was the time for such a new Literature; and this Walter Scott was the man for it. The *Lays*, the *Marmions*, the *Ladys* and *Lords* of Lake and Isles, followed in quick succession, with ever-widening profit and praise. How many thousands of guineas were paid-down for each new Lay; how many thousands of copies (fifty and more sometimes) were printed off, then and subsequently; what complimenting, reviewing, renown and apotheosis there was: all is recorded in these Seven Volumes, which will be valuable in literary statistics. It is a history, brilliant, remarkable; the outlines of which are known to all. The reader shall recall it, or conceive it. No blaze in his fancy is likely to mount higher than the reality did.

At this middle period of his life, therefore, Scott, enriched with copyrights, with new official incomes and promotions, rich in money, rich in repute, presents himself as a man in the full career of success. 'Health, wealth, and wit to guide them' (as his vernacular Proverb says), all these three are his. The field is open for him, and victory there; his own faculty, his own self, unshackled, victoriously unfolds itself,—the highest blessedness that can befall a man. Wide circle of friends, personal loving admirers; warmth of domestic joys, vouchsafed to all that can true-heartedly nestle down among them; light of radiance and renown given only to a few: who would not call Scott happy? But the happiest circumstance of all is, as we said above, that Scott had in himself a right healthy soul, rendering him little dependent on outward circumstances. Things showed themselves to him not in distortion or borrowed light or gloom, but as they were. Endeavour lay in him and endurance, in due measure; and clear vision of what was to be endeavoured after. Were one to preach a Sermon on Health, as really were worth doing, Scott ought to be the text. Theories are demonstrably true in the way of logic; and then in the way of practice they prove true or else not true: but here is the grand experiment, Do they turnout well? What boots it that a man's creed is the wisest, that his system of principles is the superfinest, if, when set to work, the life of him does nothing but jar, and fret itself into *holes*? They are untrue in that, were it in nothing else, these principles of his; openly convicted of untruth;— fit only, shall we say, to be rejected as counterfeits, and flung to the dogs? We say not that; but we do say, that ill-health, of body or of mind, is *defeat*, is battle (in a good or in a bad cause) with bad success; that health alone is victory. Let all men, if they can manage it, contrive to be healthy! He who in what cause soever sinks into pain and disease, let him take thought of it; let him know well that it is not good *he* has arrived at yet, but surely evil,—may, or may not be, on the way towards good.

Scott's healthiness showed itself decisively in all things, and nowhere more decisively than in this: the way in which he took his fame; the estimate he from the first formed of fame. Money will buy money's worth; but the thing men call fame, what is it? A gaudy emblazonry, not good for much,—except, indeed, as it too may turn to money. To Scott it was a profitable pleasing superfluity, no necessary of life. Not necessary, now or ever! Seemingly without much effort, but taught by Nature, and the instinct which instructs the sound heart what is good for it and what is not, he felt that he could always do without this same emblazonry of reputation; that he ought to put no trust in it; but be ready at any time to see it pass away from him, and to hold on his way as before. It is incalculable, as we conjecture, what evil he escaped in this manner; what perversions, irritations, mean agonies without a name, he lived wholly apart from, knew nothing of. Happily before fame arrived, he had reached the mature age at which all this was easier to him. What a strange Nemesis lurks in the felicities of men! In thy mouth it shall be sweet as honey, in thy belly it shall be bitter as gall! Some weakly-organized individual, we will say at the age of five-and-twenty, whose main or whole talent rests on some prurient susceptivity, and nothing under it but shallowness and vacuum, is clutched hold of by the general imagination, is whirled aloft to the giddy height; and taught to believe the divine-seeming message that he is a great man: such individual seems the luckiest of men: and, alas, is he not the unluckiest? Swallow not the Circe-draught, O weakly-organized individual; it is fell poison; it will dry up the fountains of thy whole existence, and all will grow withered and parched; thou shalt be wretched under the sun!

Is there, for example, a sadder book than that *Life of Byron* by Moore? To omit mere prurient susceptivities that rest on vacuum, look at poor Byron, who really had much substance in him. Sitting there in his self-exile, with a proud heart striving to persuade itself that it despises the entire created Universe; and far off, in foggy Babylon, let any pitifulest whipster draw pen on him, your proud Byron writhes in torture,—as if the pitiful whipster were a magician, or his pen a galvanic wire struck into the Byron's spinal marrow! Lamentable, despicable,—one had rather be a kitten and cry mew! O son of Adam, great or little, according as thou art lovable, those thou livest with will love thee. Those thou livest *not* with, is it of moment that they have the alphabetic letters of thy name engraved on their memory, with some signpost likeness of thee (as like as I to Hercules) appended to them? It is not of moment; in sober truth, not of any moment at all! And yet, behold, there is no soul now whom thou canst love freely,—from *one* soul only art thou always sure of reverence enough; in presence of no soul is it rightly well with thee! How is thy world become desert; and thou, for the sake of a little babblement of tongues, art poor, bankrupt, insolvent not in purse, but in heart and mind! 'The Golden Calf of self-love,' says Jean Paul, 'has grown into a burning Phalaris' Bull, to consume its owner and worshipper.' Ambition, the desire of shining and out-shining, was the beginning of Sin in this world. The man of letters who founds upon his fame, does he not thereby alone declare himself a follower of Lucifer (named *Satan*, the Enemy), and member of the Satanic school?——

It was in this poetic period that Scott formed his connexion with the Ballantynes; and embarked, though under cover, largely in trade. To those who regard him in the heroic light, and will have *Vates* to signify Prophet as well as Poet, this portion of his biography seems somewhat incongruous. Viewed as it stood in the reality, as he was and as it was, the enterprise, since it proved so unfortunate, may be called lamentable, but cannot be called unnatural. The practical Scott, look-ing towards practical issues in all things, could not but find hard cash one of the most practical. If by any means cash could be honestly produced, were it by writing poems, were it by printing them, why not? Great things might be done ultimately; great difficulties were at once got rid of,—manifold higglings of booksellers, and contradictions of sinners hereby fell away. A printing and bookselling speculation was not so alien for a maker of books. Voltaire, who indeed got no copy-rights, made much money by the war-commissariat, in his time; we believe, by the victualling branch of it. St. George himself, they say, was a dealer in bacon in Cappadocia. A thrifty man will help himself towards his object by such steps as lead to it. Station in society, solid power over the good things of this world, was Scott's avowed object; towards which the precept of precepts is that of Iago, *Put money in thy purse.*

Here, indeed, it is to be remarked, that perhaps no literary man of any generation has less value than Scott for the immaterial part of his mission in any sense: not only for the fantasy called fame, with the fantastic miseries attendant thereon; but also for the spiritual purport of his work, whether it tended hitherward or thitherward, or had any tendency whatever; and indeed for all purports and results of his working, except such, we may say, as offered themselves to the eye, and could, in one sense or the other, be handled, looked at and buttoned into the breeches-pocket. Somewhat too little of a fantast, this *Vates* of ours! But so it was: in this nineteenth century, our highest literary man, who immeasurably beyond all others commanded the world's ear, had, as it were, no message whatever to deliver to the world; wished not the world to elevate itself, to amend itself, to do this or to do that, except simply pay him for the books he kept writing. Very remarkable; fittest, perhaps, for an age fallen languid, destitute of faith and terrified at scepticism? Or, perhaps, for quite another sort of age, an age all in peaceable triumphant motion? Be this as it may, surely since Shakspeare's time there has been no great speaker so unconscious of an aim in speaking as Walter Scott. Equally unconscious these two utterances: equally the sincere complete products of the minds they came from: and now if they were equally *deep*? Or, if the one was living fire, and the other was futile phosphorescence and mere resinous firework? It will depend on the relative worth of the minds; for both were equally spontaneous, both equally expressed themselves unencumbered by an ulterior aim. Beyond drawing audiences to the Globe Theatre, Shakspeare contemplated no result in those plays of his. Yet they have had results! Utter with free heart what thy own *dæmon* gives thee: if fire from heaven, it shall be well; if resinous firework, it shall be—as well as it could be, or better than otherwise!

The candid judge will, in general, require that a speaker, in so extremely serious a Universe as this of ours, have something to speak about. In the heart of the speaker there ought to be some kind of gospel-tidings, burning till it be uttered; otherwise it were better for him that he altogether held his peace. A gospel somewhat more decisive than this of Scott's,—except to an age altogether languid, without either scepticism or faith! These things the candid judge will demand of literary men; yet withal will recognise the great worth there is in Scott's honesty if in nothing more, in his being the thing he was with such entire good faith. Here is a something, not a nothing. If no skyborn messenger, heaven looking through his eyes; then neither is it a chimera with his systems, crotchets, cants, fanaticisms, and 'last infirmity of noble minds,'—full of misery, unrest and ill-will; but a substantial, peaceable, terrestrial man. Far as the Earth is under the Heaven does Scott stand below the former sort of character; but high as the cheerful flowery Earth is above waste Tartarus does he stand above the latter. Let him live in his own fashion, and do honour to him in that.

It were late in the day to write criticisms on those Metrical Romances: at the same time, we may remark, the great popularity they had seems natural enough. In the first place, there was the indisputable impress of worth, of genuine human force, in them. This, which lies in some degree, or is thought to lie, at the bottom of all popularity, did to an unusual degree disclose itself in these rhymed romances of Scott's. Pictures were actually painted and presented; human emotions conceived and sympathised with. Considering what wretched Della-Cruscan and other vamping-up of old worn-out tatters was the staple article then, it may be granted that Scott's excellence was superior and supreme. When a Hayley was the main singer, a Scott might well be hailed with warm welcome. Consider whether *The Loves of the Plants*, and even *The Loves of the Triangles*, could be worth the loves and hates of men and women! Scott was as preferable to what he displaced, as the substance is to wearisomely repeated shadow of a substance.

But, in the second place, we may say that the *kind* of worth which Scott manifested was fitted especially for the then temper of men. We have called it an age fallen into spiritual languor, destitute of belief, yet terrified at Scepticism; reduced to live a stinted half-life, under strange new circumstances. Now vigorous whole-life, this was what of all things these delineations offered. The reader was carried back to rough strong times, wherein those maladies of ours had not yet arisen. Brawny fighters, all cased in buff and iron, their hearts too sheathed in oak and triple brass, caprioled their huge war-horses, shook their death-doing spears; and went forth in the most determined manner, nothing doubting. The reader sighed, yet not without a reflex solacement: 'O, that I too had lived in those times, had never known these logic-cobwebs, this doubt, this sickliness; and been and felt myself alive among men alive!' Add lastly, that in this new-found poetic world there was no call for effort on the reader's part; what excellence they had, exhibited itself at a glance. It was for the reader not the El Dorado only, but a beatific land of Cockaigne and Paradise of Donothings! The reader, what the vast majority of readers so long to do, was allowed to lie down at his ease, and be ministered to. What the Turkish bathkeeper is said to aim at with his frictions, and shampooings, and fomentings, more or less effectually, that the patient in total idleness may have the delights of activity,—was here to a con-

siderable extent realized. The languid imagination fell back into its
rest; an artist was there who could supply it with high-painted scenes,
with sequences of stirring action, and whisper to it, Be at ease, and let
thy tepid element be comfortable to thee. 'The rude man,' says a
critic, 'requires only to see something going on. The man of more
refinement must be made to feel. The man of complete refinement
must be made to reflect.'

We named *The Minstrelsy of the Scottish Border* the fountain from
which flowed this great river of Metrical Romances; but according
to some they can be traced to a still higher, obscurer spring; to Goethe's
Götz von Berlichingen with the Iron Hand; of which, as we have seen,
Scott in his earlier days executed a translation. Dated a good many years
ago, the following words in a criticism on Goethe are found written;
which probably are still new to most readers of this Review:

'The works just mentioned, *Götz* and *Werter*, though noble specimens of
youthful talent, are still not so much distinguished by their intrinsic merits as
by their splendid fortune. It would be difficult to name two books which have
exercised a deeper influence on the subsequent literature of Europe than these
two performances of a young author; his first-fruits, the produce of his twenty-
fourth year. *Werter* appeared to seize the hearts of men in all quarters of the
world, and to utter for them the word which they had long been waiting to hear.
As usually happens too, this same word, once uttered, was soon abundantly
repeated; spoken in all dialects, and chanted through all notes of the gamut, till
the sound of it had grown a weariness rather than a pleasure. Sceptical sentimentality, view-hunting, love, friendship, suicide and desperation, became the
staple of literary ware; and though the epidemic, after a long course of years,
subsided in Germany, it reappeared with various modifications in other
countries, and everywhere abundant traces of its good and bad effects are still
to be discerned. The fortune of *Berlichingen with the Iron Hand*, though less
sudden, was by no means less exalted. In his own country, *Götz*, though he
now stands solitary and childless, became the parent of an innumerable progeny
of chivalry plays, feudal delineations, and poetico-antiquarian performances;
which, though long ago deceased, made noise enough in their day and generation: and with ourselves his influence has been perhaps still more remarkable.
Sir Walter Scott's first literary enterprise was a translation of *Götz von Berlichingen*: and, if genius could be communicated like instruction, we might call this
work of Goethe's the prime cause of *Marmion* and *The Lady of the Lake*, with
all that has followed from the same creative hand. Truly, a grain of seed that
has lighted in the right soil! For if not firmer and fairer, it has grown to be taller
and broader than any other tree; and all the nations of the earth are still yearly
gathering of its fruit.'

How far *Götz von Berlichingen* actually affected Scott's literary destination, and whether without it the rhymed romances, and then the prose romances of the Author of *Waverley*, would not have followed as they did, must remain a very obscure question; obscure, and not important. Of the fact, however, there is no doubt, that these two tendencies, which may be named *Götzism* and *Werterism*, of the former of which Scott was representative with us, have made, and are still in some quarters making the tour of all Europe. In Germany too there was this affectionate half-regretful looking-back into the Past; Germany had its buff-belted watch-tower period in literature, and had even got done with it before Scott began. Then as to *Werterism*, had not we English our Byron and his genus? No form of Werterism in any other country had half the potency; as our Scott carried Chivalry Literature to the ends of the world, so did our Byron Werterism. France, busy with its Revolution and Napoleon, had little leisure at the moment for Götzism or Werterism; but it has had them both since, in a shape of its own: witness the whole 'Literature of Desperation' in our own days; the beggarliest form of Werterism yet seen, probably its expiring final form: witness also, at the other extremity of the scale, a noble-gifted Chateaubriand, Götz and Werter both in one.—Curious: how all Europe is but like a set of parishes of the same county; participant of the self-same influences, ever since the Crusades, and earlier;—and these glorious wars of ours are but like parish-brawls, which begin in mutual ignorance, intoxication and boastful speech; which end in broken windows, damage, waste and bloody noses; and which one hopes the general good sense is now in the way towards putting down, in some measure!

But leaving this to be as it can, what it concerned us here to remark, was that British Werterism, in the shape of those Byron Poems, so potent and poignant, produced on the languid appetite of men a mighty effect. This too was a 'class of feelings deeply important to modern minds; feelings which arise from *passion incapable of being converted into action*, which belong to an age as indolent, cultivated and unbelieving as our own!' The 'languid age without either faith or scepticism' turned towards Byronism with an interest altogether peculiar: here, if no cure for its miserable paralysis and languor, was at least an indignant statement of the misery; an indignant Ernulphus' curse read over it,—which all men felt to be something. Half-regretful lookings into the Past gave place, in many quarters, to Ernulphus' cursings of the Present. Scott was among the first to perceive that the day of Metrical Chivalry

Romances was declining. He had held the sovereignty for some half-score of years, a comparatively long lease of it; and now the time seemed come for dethronement, for abdication: an unpleasant business; which however he held himself ready, as a brave man will, to transact with composure and in silence. After all, Poetry was not his staff of life; Poetry had already yielded him much money; *this* at least it would not take back from him. Busy always with editing, with compiling, with multiplex official commercial business, and solid interests, he beheld the coming change with unmoved eye.

Resignation he was prepared to exhibit in this matter;—and now behold there proved to be no need of resignation. Let the Metrical Romance become a Prose one; shake off its rhyme-fetters, and try a wider sweep! In the spring of 1814 appeared *Waverley*; an event memorable in the annals of British Literature; in the annals of British Bookselling thrice and four times memorable. Byron sang, but Scott narrated; and when the song had sung itself out through all variations onwards to the *Don Juan* one, Scott was still found narrating, and carrying the whole world along with him. All bygone popularity of chivalry-lays was swallowed up in a far greater. What 'series' followed out of *Waverley*, and how and with what result, is known to all men; was witnessed and watched with a kind of rapt astonishment by all. Hardly any literary reputation ever rose so high in our Island; no reputation at all ever spread so wide. Walter Scott became Sir Walter Scott, Baronet, of Abbotsford; on whom Fortune seemed to pour her whole cornucopia of wealth, honour and worldly good; the favourite of Princes and of Peasants, and all intermediate men. His 'Waverley series', swift-following one on the other apparently without end, was the universal reading; looked for like an annual harvest, by all ranks, in all European countries.

A curious circumstance superadded itself, that the author though known was unknown. From the first most people suspected, and soon after the first, few intelligent persons much doubted, that the Author of *Waverley* was Walter Scott. Yet a certain mystery was still kept up; rather piquant to the public; doubtless very pleasant to the author, who saw it all; who probably had not to listen, as other hapless individuals often had, to this or the other long-drawn 'clear proof at last', that the author was not Walter Scott, but a certain astonishing Mr. So-and-so; —one of the standing miseries of human life in that time. But for the privileged Author it was like a king travelling incognito. All men know that he is a high king, chivalrous Gustaf or Kaiser Joseph; but he mingles in their meetings without cumber of etiquette or lonesome ceremony, as Chevalier du Nord, or Count of Lorraine: he has none of the weariness of royalty, and yet all the praise, and the satisfaction of hearing it with his own ears. In a word, the Waverley Novels circulated and reigned triumphant; to the general imagination the 'Author of *Waverley*' was like some living mythological personage, and ranked among the chief wonders of the world.

How a man lived and demeaned himself in such unwonted circumstances, is worth seeing. We would gladly quote from Scott's correspondence of this period; but that does not much illustrate the matter. His letters, as above stated, are never without interest, yet also seldom or never very interesting. They are full of cheerfulness, of wit and ingenuity; but they do not treat of aught intimate; without impeaching their sincerity, what is called sincerity, one may say they do not, in any case whatever, proceed from the innermost parts of the mind. Conventional forms, due consideration of your own and your correspondent's pretensions and vanities, are at no moment left out of view. The epistolary stream runs on, lucid, free, glad-flowing; but always, as it were, *parallel* to the real substance of the matter, never coincident with it. One feels it hollowish under foot. Letters they are of a most humane man of the world, even exemplary in that kind; but with the man of the world always visible in them;—as indeed it was little in Scott's way to speak, perhaps even with himself, in any other fashion. We select rather some glimpses of him from Mr. Lockhart's record. The first is of dining with Royalty or Prince-Regentship itself; an almost official matter:

[a strictly biographical passage has been omitted]

Surely all this is very beautiful; like a picture of Boccaccio's: the ideal of a country life in our time. Why could it not last? Income was not wanting: Scott's official permanent income was amply adequate to meet the expense of all that was valuable in it; nay, of all that was not harassing, senseless and despicable. Scott had some 2,000*l.* a-year without writing books at all. Why should he manufacture and not create, to make more money; and rear mass on mass for a dwelling to himself, till the pile toppled, sank crashing, and buried him in its ruins, when he had a safe pleasant dwelling ready of its own accord? Alas, Scott, with all his health, was *infected*; sick of the fearfulest malady, that of Ambition! To such length had the King's baronetcy, the world's

favour and 'sixteen parties a-day', brought it with him. So the inane
racket must be kept up, and rise ever higher. So masons labour,
ditchers delve; and there is endless, altogether deplorable correspondence about marble-slabs for tables, wainscoting of rooms, curtains and
the trimmings of curtains, orange-coloured or fawn-coloured: Walter
Scott, one of the gifted of the world, whom his admirers call the most
gifted, must kill himself that he may be a country gentleman, the
founder of a race of Scottish lairds.

It is one of the strangest, most tragical histories ever enacted under
this sun. So poor a passion can lead so strong a man into such mad
extremes. Surely, were not man a fool always, one might say there
was something eminently distracted in this, *end* as it would, of a Walter
Scott writing daily with the ardour of a steam-engine, that he might
make 15,000*l.* a-year, and buy upholstery with it. To cover the walls
of a stone house in Selkirkshire with nicknacks, ancient armour and
genealogical shields, what can we name it but a being bit with delirium
of a kind? That tract after tract of moorland in the shire of Selkirk
should be joined together on parchment and by ring-fence, and named
after one's name,—why, it is a shabby small-type edition of your vulgar
Napoleons, Alexanders, and conquering heroes, not counted venerable
by any teacher of men!—

> 'The whole world was not half so wide
> To Alexander when he cried
> Because he had but one to subdue,
> As was a narrow paltry tub to
> Diogenes; who ne'er was said,
> For aught that ever I could read,
> To whine, put finger i' the eye and sob,
> Because he had ne'er another tub.'

Not he! And if, 'looked at from the Moon, which itself is far from
Infinitude', Napoleon's dominions were as small as mine, *what*, by any
chance of possibility, could Abbotsford landed-property ever have
become? As the Arabs say, there is a black speck, were it no bigger than
a bean's eye, in every soul; which, once set it a-working, will overcloud
the whole man into darkness and quasi-madness, and hurry him bale-
fully into Night!

With respect to the literary character of these Waverley Novels, so
extraordinary in their commercial character, there remains, after so
much reviewing, good and bad, little that it were profitable at present
to say. The great fact about them is, that they were faster written and

better paid for than any other books in the world. It must be granted, moreover, that they have a worth far surpassing what is usual in such cases; nay, that if Literature had no task but that of harmlessly amusing indolent languid men, here was the very perfection of Literature; that a man, here more emphatically than ever elsewhere, might fling himself back, exclaiming, 'Be mine to lie on this sofa, and read everlasting Novels of Walter Scott!' The composition, slight as it often is, usually hangs together in some measure, and *is* a composition. There is a free flow of narrative, of incident and sentiment; an easy master-like coherence throughout, as if it were the free dash of a master's hand, 'round as the O of Giotto'.[1] It is the perfection of extemporaneous writing. Farthermore, surely he were a blind critic who did not recognise here a certain genial sunshiny freshness and picturesqueness; paintings both of scenery and figures, very graceful, brilliant, occasionally full of grace and glowing brightness blended in the softest composure; in fact, a deep sincere love of the beautiful in Nature and Man, and the readiest faculty of expressing this by imagination and by word. No fresher paintings of Nature can be found than Scott's; hardly anywhere a wider sympathy with man. From Davie Deans up to Richard Coeur-de-Lion; from Meg Merrilies to Die Vernon and Queen Elizabeth! It is the utterance of a man of open soul; of a brave, large, free-seeing man, who has a true brotherhood with all men. In joyous picturesqueness and fellow-feeling, freedom of eye and heart; or to say it in a word, in general *healthiness* of mind, these Novels prove Scott to have been amongst the foremost writers.

Neither in the higher and highest excellence, of drawing character,

---

[1] '... He proceeded to Florence' (the messenger of the Pope) 'and repaired one morning to the workshop where Giotto was occupied with his labours. He declared the purpose of the Pope, and the manner in which that pontiff desired to avail himself of his assistance, and finally, requested to have a drawing, that he might send it to his holiness. Giotto, who was very courteous, took a sheet of paper, and a pencil dipped in a red colour; then, resting his elbow on his side, to form a sort of compass, with one turn of the hand he drew a circle, so perfect and exact that it was a marvel to behold. This done, he turned, smiling to the courtier, saying, "Here is your drawing".... From which the Pope, and such of his courtiers as were well versed in the subject, perceived how far Giotto surpassed all the other painters of his time. This incident becoming known, gave rise to the proverb, still used in relation to people of dull wits—"*Tu sei più tondo che l'O di Giotto*"—the significance of which consists in the double meaning of the word "tondo", which is used in the Tuscan for slowness of intellect and heaviness of comprehension, as well as for an exact circle.' [Quoted by Carlyle (in Italian) from Vasari's *Life of Giotto*. Trans. here by Mrs. Jonathan Foster.]

is he at any time altogether deficient; though at no time can we call him, in the best sense, successful. His Baillie Jarvies, Dinmonts, Dalgettys (for their name is legion), do look and talk like what they give themselves out for; they are, if not *created* and made poetically alive, yet deceptively *enacted* as a good player might do them. What more is wanted, then? For the reader lying on a sofa, nothing more; yet for another sort of reader, much. It were a long chapter to unfold the difference in drawing a character between a Scott, and a Shakspeare, a Goethe. Yet it is a difference literally immense; they are of different species; the value of the one is not to be counted in the coin of the other. We might say in a short word, which means a long matter, that your Shakspeare fashions his characters from the heart outwards; your Scott fashions them from the skin inwards, never getting near the heart of them! The one set become living men and women; the other amount to little more than mechanical cases, deceptively painted automatons. Compare Fenella with Goethe's Mignon, which, it was once said, Scott had 'done Goethe the honour' to borrow. He has borrowed what he could of Mignon. The small stature, the climbing talent, the trickiness, the *mechanical case*, as we say, he has borrowed; but the soul of Mignon is left behind. Fenella is an unfavourable specimen for Scott; but it illustrates in the aggravated state, what is traceable in all the characters he drew.

To the same purport indeed we are to say that these famed books are altogether addressed to the every-day mind; that for any other mind there is next to no nourishment in them. Opinions, emotions, principles, doubts, beliefs, beyond what the intelligent country gentleman can carry along with him, are not to be found. It is orderly, customary, it is prudent, decent; nothing more. One would say, it lay not in Scott to give much more; getting out of the ordinary range, and attempting the heroic, which is but seldom the case, he falls almost at once into the rose-pink sentimental,—descries the Minerva Press from afar, and hastily quits that course; for none better than he knew it to lead nowhither. On the whole, contrasting *Waverley*, which was carefully written, with most of its followers, which were written extempore, one may regret the extempore method. Something very perfect in its kind might have come from Scott; nor was it a low kind: nay, who knows how high, with studious self-concentration, he might have gone; what wealth Nature had implanted in him, which his circumstances, most unkind while seeming to be kindest, had never impelled him to unfold?

But after all, in the loudest blaring and trumpeting of popularity, it is ever to be held in mind, as a truth remaining true forever, that Literature *has* other aims than that of harmlessly amusing indolent languid men: or if Literature have them not, then Literature is a very poor affair; and something else must have them, and must accomplish them, with thanks or without thanks; the thankful or thankless world were not long a world otherwise! Under this head there is little to be sought or found in the Waverley Novels. Not profitable for doctrine, for reproof, for edification, for building up or elevating, in any shape! The sick heart will find no healing here, the darkly-struggling heart no guidance: the Heroic that is in all men no divine awakening voice. We say, therefore, that they do not found themselves on deep interests, but on comparatively trivial ones; not on the perennial, perhaps not even on the lasting. In fact, much of the interest of these Novels results from what may be called contrasts of costume. The phraseology, fashion of arms, of dress and life, belonging to one age, is brought suddenly with singular vividness before the eyes of another. A great effect this; yet by the very nature of it, an altogether temporary one. Consider, brethren, shall not we too one day be antiques, and grow to have as quaint a costume as the rest? The stuffed Dandy, only give him *time*, will become one of the wonderfulest mummies. In antiquarian museums, only two centuries hence, the steeple-hat will hang on the next peg to Franks and Company's patent, antiquarians deciding which is uglier: and the Stulz swallow-tail, one may hope, will seem as incredible as any garment that ever made ridiculous the respectable back of man. Not by slashed breeches, steeple-hats, buff-belts, or antiquated speech, can romance-heroes continue to interest us; but simply and solely, in the long-run, by being men. Buff-belts and all manner of jerkins and costumes are transitory; man alone is perennial. He that has gone deeper into this than other men, will be remembered longer than they; he that has not, not. Tried under this category, Scott, with his clear practical insight, joyous temper, and other sound faculties, is not to be accounted little,—among the ordinary circulating-library heroes he might well pass for a demi-god. Not little; yet neither is he great; there were greater, more than one or two, in his own age: among the great of all ages, one sees no likelihood of a place for him.

What, then, is the result of these Waverley Romances? Are they to amuse one generation only? One or more! As many generations as they can; but not all generations: ah no, when our swallow-tail has become fantastic as trunk-hose, they will cease to amuse!—Meanwhile, as we can discern, their results have been several-fold. First of all, and certainly not least of all, have they not perhaps had this result: that a considerable portion of mankind has hereby been sated with mere amusement, and set on seeking something better? Amusement in the way of reading can go no farther, can do nothing better, by the power of man; and men ask, Is this what it can do? Scott, we reckon, carried several things to their ultimatum and crisis, so that change became inevitable: a great service, though an indirect one.

Secondly, however, we may say, these Historical Novels have taught all men this truth, which looks like a truism, and yet was as good as unknown to writers of history and others, till so taught: that the bygone ages of the world were actually filled by living men not by protocols, state-papers, controversies and abstractions of men. Not abstractions were they, not diagrams and theorems; but men, in buff or other coats and breeches, with colour in their cheeks, with passions in their stomach, and the idioms, features and vitalities of very men. It is a little word this; inclusive of great meaning! History will henceforth have to take thought of it. Her faint hearsays of 'philosophy teaching by experience' will have to exchange themselves everywhere for direct inspection and embodiment: this, and this only, will be counted experience; and till once experience have got in, philosophy will reconcile herself to wait at the door. It is a great service, fertile in consequences, this that Scott has done; a great truth laid open by him;— correspondent indeed to the substantial nature of the man; to his solidity and veracity even of imagination, which, with all his lively discursiveness, was the characteristic of him.

A word here as to the extempore style of writing, which is getting much celebrated in these days. Scott seems to have been a high proficient in it. His rapidity was extreme; and the matter produced was excellent, considering that: the circumstances under which some of his Novels, when he could not himself write, were dictated, are justly considered wonderful. It is a valuable faculty this of ready-writing; nay farther, for Scott's purpose it was clearly the only good mode. By much labour he could not have added one guinea to his copyright; nor could the reader on the sofa have lain a whit more at ease. It was in all ways necessary that these works should be produced rapidly; and, round or not, be thrown off like Giotto's O. But indeed, in all things, writing or other, which a man engages in, there is the indispensablest beauty in knowing *how to get done*. A man frets himself to no purpose; he has not the sleight of the trade; he is not a craftsman, but an unfortunate borer and bungler, if he know not when to have done. Perfection is unattainable: no carpenter ever made a mathematically accurate right-angle in the world; yet all carpenters know when it is right enough, and do not botch it, and lose their wages, by making it too right. Too much painstaking speaks disease in one's mind, as well as too little. The adroit sound-minded man will endeavour to spend on each business approximately what of pains it deserves; and with a conscience void of remorse will dismiss it then. All this in favour of easy-writing shall be granted, and, if need were, enforced and inculcated.

And yet, on the other hand, it shall not less but more strenuously be inculcated, that in the way of writing, no great thing was ever, or will ever be done with ease, but with difficulty! Let ready-writers with any faculty in them lay this to heart. Is it with ease, or not with ease, that a man shall *do his best*, in any shape; above all, in this shape justly named of 'soul's travail', working in the deep places of thought, embodying the True out of the Obscure and Possible, environed on all sides with the uncreated False? Not so, now or at any time. The experience of all men belies it; the nature of things contradicts it. Virgil and Tacitus, were they ready-writers? The whole *Prophecies of Isaiah* are not equal in extent to this cobweb of a Review Article. Shakspeare, we may fancy, wrote with rapidity; but not till he had thought with intensity: long and sore had this man thought, as the seeing eye may discern well, and had dwelt and wrestled amid dark pains and throes,—though his great soul is silent about all that. It was for him to write rapidly at fit intervals, being ready to do it. And herein truly lies the secret of the matter: such swiftness of mere writing, after due energy of preparation, is doubtless the right method; the hot furnace having long worked and simmered, let the pure gold flow out at one gush. It was Shakspeare's plan; no easy-writer he, or he had never been a Shakspeare. Neither was Milton one of the mob of gentlemen that write with ease; he did not attain Shakspeare's faculty, one perceives, of even writing fast *after* long preparation, but struggled while he wrote. Goethe also tells us he 'had nothing sent him in his sleep;' no page of his but he knew well how it came there. It is reckoned to be the best prose, accordingly, that has been written by any modern. Schiller, as an unfortunate and unhealthy man, '*könnte nie fertig werden*, never could get done;' the noble genius of him struggled not wisely but too well, and wore his life itself heroically out. Or did Petrarch write easily? Dante sees himself 'growing lean' over his *Divine Comedy*; in stern

solitary death-wrestle with it, to prevail over it, and do it, if his uttermost faculty may: hence, too, it is done and prevailed over, and the
fiery life of it endures forevermore among men.

No: creation, one would think, cannot be easy; your Jove has severe
pains, and fire-flames, in the head out of which an armed Pallas is
struggling! As for manufacture, that is a different matter, and may
become easy or not easy, according as it is taken up. Yet of manufacture too, the general truth is that, given the manufacturer, it will be
worthy in direct proportion to the pains bestowed upon it; and worthless always, or nearly so, with no pains. Cease, therefore, O ready-
writer, to brag openly of thy rapidity and facility; to thee (if thou be
in the manufacturing line) it is a benefit, an increase of wages; but to
me it is sheer loss, worsening of my pennyworth: why wilt thou brag
of it to me? Write easily, by steam if thou canst contrive it, and canst
sell it; but hide it like virtue! 'Easy writing,' said Sheridan, 'is sometimes d—d hard reading.' Sometimes; and always it is sure to be rather
useless reading, which indeed (to a creature of few years and much
work) may be reckoned the hardest of all.

Scott's productive facility amazed everybody; and set Captain Hall,
for one, upon a very strange method of accounting for it without
miracle;—for which see his Journal, above quoted from. The Captain,
on counting line for line, found that he himself had written in that
Journal of his almost as much as Scott, at odd hours in a given number
of days; 'and as for the invention,' says he, 'it is known that this costs
Scott nothing, but comes to him of its own accord.' Convenient
indeed!—But for us too Scott's rapidity is great, is a proof and consequence of the solid health of the man, bodily and spiritual; great,
but unmiraculous; not greater than that of many others besides Captain
Hall. Admire it, yet with measure. For observe always, there are two
conditions in work: let me fix the quality, and *you* shall fix the quantity!
Any man may get through work rapidly who easily satisfies himself
about it. Print the *talk* of any man, there will be a thick octavo volume
daily; make his writing three times as good as his talk, there will be
the third part of a volume daily, which still is good work. To write
with never such rapidity in a passable manner, is indicative not of a
man's genius, but of his habits; it will prove his soundness of nervous
system, his practicality of mind, and in fine, that he has the knack of his
trade. In the most flattering view, rapidity will betoken health of mind:
much also, perhaps most of all, will depend on health of body. Doubt
it not, a faculty of easy-writing is attainable by man! The human

THE AMORAL SCOTT *London and Westminster Review* 1838

genius, once fairly set in this direction, will carry it far. William
Cobbett, one of the healthiest of men, was a greater improviser even
than Walter Scott: his writing, considered as to quality and quantity, of
Rural Rides, Registers, Grammars, Sermons, Peter Porcupines,
Histories of Reformation, ever-fresh denouncements of Potatoes and
Paper-money, seems to us still more wonderful. Pierre Bayle wrote
enormous folios, one sees not on what motive-principle: he flowed-on
forever, a mighty tide of ditch-water; and even died flowing, with the
pen in his hand. But indeed the most unaccountable ready-writer of
all is, probably, the common Editor of a Daily Newspaper. Consider
his leading articles; what they treat of, how passably they are done.
Straw that has been thrashed a hundred times without wheat; ephemeral sound of a sound; such portent of the hour as all men have seen a
hundred items turn out inane: how a man, with merely human faculty,
buckles himself nightly with new vigour and interest to this thrashed
straw, nightly thrashes it anew, nightly gets-up new thunder about it;
and so goes on thrashing and thundering for a considerable series of
years; this is a fact remaining still to be accounted for, in human
physiology. The vitality of man is great.

Or shall we say, Scott, among the many things he carried towards
their ultimatum and crisis, carried this of ready-writing too, that so all
men might better see what was in it? It is a valuable consummation.
Not without results;—results, at some of which Scott as a Tory
politician would have greatly shuddered. For if once Printing have
grown to be as Talk, then DEMOCRACY (if we look into the roots of
things) is not a bugbear and probability, but a certainty, and event as
good as come! 'Inevitable seems it me.' But leaving this, sure enough
the triumph of ready-writing appears to be even now; everywhere the
ready-writer is found bragging strangely of his readiness. In a late
translated *Don Carlos*, one of the most indifferent translations ever done
with any sign of ability, a hitherto unknown individual is found
assuring his reader, 'The reader will possibly think it an excuse, when
I assure him that the whole piece was completed within the space of ten
weeks, that is to say, between the sixth of January and the eighteenth
of March of this year (inclusive of a fortnight's interruption from over-
exertion); that I often translated twenty pages a-day, and that the
fifth act was the work of five days.'[1] O hitherto unknown individual,
what is it to me what time it was the work of, whether five days

[1] *Don Carlos*, a Dramatic Poem, from the German of Schiller. Mannheim and
London, 1837 [Carlyle].

or five decades of years? The only question is, How well hast thou done it?

So, however, it stands: the genius of Extempore irresistibly lording it, advancing on us like ocean-tides, like Noah's deluges—of ditch-water! The prospect seems one of the lamentablest. To have all Literature swum away from us in watery Extempore, and a spiritual time of Noah supervene? That surely is an awful reflection; worthy of dyspeptic Matthew Bramble in a London fog! Be of comfort, O splenetic Matthew; it is not Literature they are swimming away; it is only Book-publishing and Book-selling. Was there not a Literature *before* Printing or Faust of Mentz, and yet men wrote extempore? Nay, before Writing or Cadmus of Thebes, and yet men spoke extempore? Literature is the Thought of thinking Souls; this, by the blessing of God, can in no generation be swum away, but remains with us to the end.

Scott's career, of writing impromptu novels to buy farms with, was not of a kind to terminate voluntarily, but to accelerate itself more and more; and one sees not to what wise goal it could, in any case, have led him. Bookseller Constable's bankruptcy was not the ruin of Scott; his ruin was, that ambition, and even false ambition, had laid hold of him; that his way of life was not wise. Whither could it lead? Where could it stop? New farms there remained ever to be bought, while new novels could pay for them. More and more success but gave more and more appetite, more and more audacity. The impromptu writing must have waxed ever thinner; declined faster and faster into the questionable category, into the condemnable, into the generally condemned. Already there existed, in secret, everywhere a considerable opposition party; witnesses of the Waverley miracles, but unable to believe in them, forced silently to protest against them. Such opposition party was in the sure case to grow; and even, with the impromptu process ever going on, ever waxing thinner, to draw the world over to it. Silent protest must at length have come to words; harsh truths, backed by harsher facts of a world-popularity over-wrought and worn-out, behoved to have been spoken;—such as can be spoken now without reluctance, when they can pain the brave man's heart no more. Who knows? Perhaps it was better ordered to be all *otherwise*. Otherwise, at any rate, it was. One day the Constable mountain, which seemed to stand strong like the other rock mountains, gave suddenly, as the icebergs do, a loud-sounding crack; suddenly, with huge clangor, shivered itself into ice-dust; and sank, carrying much along with it. In one day Scott's high-heaped money-wages became fairy-money and nonentity; in one day the rich man and lord of land saw himself penniless, landless, a bankrupt among creditors.

It was a hard trial. He met it proudly, bravely,—like a brave proud man of the world. Perhaps there had been a prouder way still: to have owned honestly that he *was* unsuccessful, then, all bankrupt, broken, in the world's goods and repute; and to have turned elsewhither for some refuge. Refuge did lie elsewhere; but it was not Scott's course, or fashion of mind, to seek it there. To say, Hitherto I have been all in the wrong, and this my fame and pride, now broken, was an empty delusion and spell of accursed witchcraft! It was difficult for flesh and blood! He said, I will retrieve myself, and make my point good yet, or die for it. Silently, like a proud strong man, he girt himself to the Hercules' task, of removing rubbish-mountains, since that was it; of paying large ransoms by what he could still write and sell. In his declining years, too; misfortune is doubly and trebly unfortunate that befalls us then. Scott fell to his Hercules' task like a very man, and went on with it unweariedly; with a noble cheerfulness, while his life-strings were cracking, he grappled with it, and wrestled with it, years long, in death-grips, strength to strength;—and *it* proved the stronger; and his life and heart did crack and break: the cordage of a most strong heart! Over these last writings of Scott, his *Napoleons, Demonologies, Scotch Histories*, and the rest, criticism, finding still much to wonder at, much to commend, will utter no word of blame; this one word only, Woe is me! The noble war-horse that once laughed at the shaking of the spear, how is he doomed to toil himself dead, dragging ignoble wheels! Scott's descent was like that of a spent projectile; rapid, straight down;—perhaps mercifully so. It is a tragedy, as all life is; one proof more that Fortune stands on a restless *globe*; that Ambition, literary, warlike, politic, pecuniary, never yet profited any man.

Our last extract shall be from Volume Sixth; a very tragical one. Tragical, yet still beautiful; waste Ruin's havoc borrowing a kind of sacredness from a yet sterner visitation, that of Death! Scott has withdrawn into a solitary lodging-house in Edinburgh, to do daily the day's work there; and had to leave his wife at Abbotsford in the last stage of disease. He went away silently; looked silently at the sleeping face he scarcely hoped ever to see again. We quote from a Diary he had begun to keep in those months, on hint from Byron's *Ravenna Journal*: copious sections of it render this Sixth Volume more interesting than any of the former ones:

[passages from Scott's journal have been omitted]

This is beautiful as well as tragical. Other scenes, in that Seventh Volume, must come, which will have no beauty, but be tragical only. It is better that we are to end here.

And so the curtain falls; and the strong Walter Scott is with us no more. A possession from him does remain; widely scattered; yet attainable; not inconsiderable. It can be said of him, When he departed, he took a Man's life along with him. No sounder piece of British manhood was put together in that eighteenth century of Time. Alas, his fine Scotch face, with its shaggy honesty, sagacity and goodness, when we saw it latterly on the Edinburgh streets, was all worn with care, the joy all fled from it;—ploughed deep with labour and sorrow. We shall never forget it; we shall never see it again. Adieu, Sir Walter, pride of all Scotchmen, take our proud and sad farewell.

52. Balzac on Scott

1838, 1840

Extracts from (a) a letter to Mme. Hanska, dated 20-22 January 1838 (in *Lettres à l'etrangère*, Paris, 1899, pp. 453-4); (b) the preface to the 1st ed. of *La Femme Superieure*, 1838; (c) a review of James Fenimore Cooper's *The Pathfinder* in the *Revue Parisienne*, 25 July 1840, pp. 73-5, 76-8; (d) a review of Stendhal's *La Chartreuse de Parme* in the *Revue Parisienne*, 25 September 1840, 274. Translations are by Katherine P. Wormeley.

(a) It is twelve years since I have been saying of Walter Scott what you have now written to me. Beside him, Lord Byron is nothing, or almost nothing. But you are mistaken as to the plot of *Kenilworth*. To the minds of all makers of romance, and to mine, the plot of that work is the grandest, most complete, most extraordinary of all; the book is a masterpiece from this point of view, just as *St. Ronan's Well* is a masterpiece for detail and patience of finish, as the *Chronicles of the Canongate* are for sentiment, as *Ivanhoe* (the first volume, be it understood) is for history, *The Antiquary* for poesy, and *The Heart of Mid-Lothian* for profound interest. All these works have their own especial merit, but genius shines throughout them all. Scott will still be growing greater when Byron is forgotten: I speak of Byron translated; for the poet in the original must last, if only for his form and his powerful inspiration. Byron's brain had never any other imprint than that of his own personality; whereas the whole world has posed before the creative genius of Scott and has there, so to speak, beheld itself.

(*b*) ['BUREAUCRACY', 'NUCINGEN AND CO.', 'ESTHER'.] 1838.
These are three fragments which will, later, be found in their place in the *Études de Mœurs*. Here the author owns with a good grace one of the thousand little miseries of his literary life, which is, beyond question, the only point he can have in common with one of the noblest geniuses of modern times, Walter Scott, on whose authority he now bases his own defence. If this anomaly of publication is open to criticism, the illustrious Scotchman would be without excuse, whereas the poor French author presents himself with a touching accompaniment of attenuating circumstances before the areopagus so amusingly personified by the ingenious Scotchman in his prefaces as Captain Clutterbuck, Doctor Dryasdust, and other charming myths, to whom he renders his accounts, hidden beneath pseudonyms—other figures not less charming. Before the disaster which poisoned his latter days Sir Walter Scott lived as a feudal lord in his castle of Abbotsford, surrounded by a magnificence worthy of his literary royalty, and endowed with a civil list of three hundred thousand francs. He wrote, at his ease and as he pleased, one work in six months without other obligations than those he was under to fame. In such a situation a writer is expected to publish only completed works. The French author has, alas! an uncivil list and many obligations to meet; consequently, the differences that exist between him and that great genius in the spiritual order are not less extensive in the physical order.

Walter Scott might have avoided this assumed defect, which he defined himself when replying to critics eager to convert his brilliant qualities into vices,—eternal manœuvre of literary calumny. This vice consisted in not following his original plans, constructed with the depth that characterizes the Scotch nature, the structure of which became broken under the developments which he gave to the characters of certain personages. In working from the glowing sketch which all literary painters design upon the canvas of their brain, he saw emerging larger, as in a stereopticon, a figure so attractive, existences so magnificent, a character so new, that instead of leaving them in minor places he let them expand and develop grandly in his work. That fickle goddess Fancy invited him so persuasively with a touch of her rosy fingers, and a smile so fascinating, she made herself so coquettish in Fenella, so profound in the Laird o' Dumbiedikes, so varied in the neighbourhood of Saint Ronan's Well that he—child as naïve as the man was great—let himself go and followed her into all the dark corners it pleased her to illuminate. This great genius, the dupe of his own poesy, explored and ferreted with the goddess; he turned over all the stones in the road beneath which lay the souls of licentiates; he let himself be led to the sea-shore to see a marsh; he listened to the delightful chatter of that fairy and reproduced it in leafy arabesques profoundly pondered, long prepared, his glory to the eyes of connoisseurs, though wearisome to superficial minds, in which each detail is so essential that the personages, the events, would be incomprehensible if a single one of them were omitted.

See how he dashes the jesting personages of his preface on the critics! Like splendid hunting-dogs they rush at their quarry and, with a single snap of the jaws, bite the said aristarchs to the bone. These ingenious prefaces, without gall yet *malicieux*, ironical with good nature, in which reason shines, resplendent as Molière could make it, these prefaces are masterpieces to studious minds which have preserved the taste for atticism. Sir Walter Scott, a rich man, a Scotchman with ample leisure, having a whole horizon blue before him, might, if he had thought proper, have ripened his plans and composed his work in a manner to insert with regularity all the beautiful precious stones he had found on his way. But he thought that all did well *as he produced them*; and he was right.

(c) That which renders Cooper inferior to Walter Scott is his profound and radical impotence for the comic, and his perpetual intention to divert you, in which he never succeeds. I feel, in reading Cooper, a singular sensation, as if while listening to beautiful music there was near me some horrible village fiddler scraping his violin and harrowing me by playing the same air. To produce what he thinks to be comic he puts into the mouth of one of his personages a silly joke, invented *a priori*, some notion, a mental vice, a deformity of mind, which is shown in the first chapters and reappears, page after page, to the last. This joke and this personage form the village fiddler I speak of. To this system we owe David in *The Mohicans*, the English sailor and Lieutenant Muir in *The Pathfinder*; in short, all the so-called comic figures in Cooper's works.

The originator of this malady was Walter Scott. The visit of King Charles, of which Lady Bellenden speaks seven or eight times in *The Puritans*, and other like features of which Walter Scott, as a man of genius, was chary, have been the ruin of Cooper. The great Scotchman never abused this means, which is petty, and reveals an aridity, a barrenness of mind. Genius consists in making gush from a situation the words by which a character reveals itself, and not in bedizening a personage with a speech adapted to the occasion. It is perfectly permissible to pose a man as gay, or gloomy, or ironical; but his gaiety, his gloom, his irony must be manifested by traits of character. After painting your personage, make him talk; but to make him always say the same thing is impotent. It is in the invention of circumstances and in that of characteristic traits that the genius of the modern *trouvère* reveals itself. If you do not feel within you the power of creating thus, remain *yourself*; seek, work out the resources that are really within you. In *Redgauntlet* there is an old smuggler who repeatedly remarks: 'And therefore, consequently,' but Walter Scott has made that expression a source of inextinguishable humour which never wearies us.

The difference that exists between Walter Scott and Cooper is derived essentially from the nature of the subjects towards which their genius led them. From Cooper's scenes nothing philosophical or impressive to the intellect issues when, the work once read, the soul looks back to take in a sense of the whole. Yet both are great historians; both have cold hearts; neither will admit passion, that divine emanation, superior to the virtue that man has constructed for the preservation of society; they have suppressed it, they have offered it as a holocaust to the bluestockings of their country; but the one initiates you into great human evolutions, the other into the mighty heart of Nature herself. One has brought literature to grasp the earth and ocean, the other makes it grapple body to body with humanity. Read Cooper, and this will strike you, especially in *The Pathfinder*. You will not find a portrait which makes you think, which brings you back into yourself by some subtle or ingenious reflection, which explains to you facts, persons, or actions.

He seems, on the contrary, to wish to plunge you into solitude and leave you to dream there. Whereas Scott gives you, wherever you are, a brilliant company of human beings. Cooper's work isolates; Scott weds you to his drama as he paints with broad strokes the features of his country at all epochs. The grandeur of Cooper is a reflection of the Nature he depicts; that of Walter Scott is more peculiarly his own. The Scotchman procreates his work; the American is the son of his. Walter Scott has a hundred aspects; Cooper is a painter of sea and landscape, admirably aided by two academies—the Savage and the Sailor. His noble creation of Leather-Stocking is a work apart. Not understanding English I cannot judge of the style of these two great geniuses, happily for us so different, but I should suppose the Scotchman to be superior to the American in the expression of his thought and in the mechanism of his style. . . .

To sum up once more: one is the historian of Nature, the other of humanity; one attains to the glorious ideal by imagery, the other by action, though without neglecting poesy, the high-priestess of art: the high tide in *The Antiquary*, the first landscape in *Ivanhoe* testify to a talent for painting equal to Cooper's.

(*d*) . . . Certain rounded and completed beings, certain *bifron* intellects, embracing all, want lyric and action, drama and ode, believing that perfection requires a sense of the total. This school, which must be named that of *literary eclecticism*, demands a representation of the world as it is: images and ideas; the idea in the image, or the image in the idea, movement, and revery. Walter Scott satisfied completely these eclectic natures.

53. Cardinal Newman: Scott prepared the way, *British Critic*

1839

An excerpt from an unsigned review, 'The State of Religious Parties', *British Critic* (April 1839), xxv, 395-426.

The writer was John Henry Cardinal Newman; or at least he claims total authorship in a note appended to a reprint of the article in his *Collected Works* (London, 1874-1921), iii, 308.

According to Newman in his *Apologia pro Vita Sua* this article 'contains the last words which I ever spoke as an Anglican to Anglicans. It may now be read as my parting address and valediction, made to my friends.' In the passage immediately preceding the excerpt below, Newman has enumerated several causes for the progress of the tractarian movement.

But besides these, and similar causes of the moment, there has been for some years, from whatever cause, a growing tendency towards the character of mind and feeling of which Catholic doctrines are the just expression. This manifested itself long before men entered into the truth intellectually, or knew what they ought to believe, and what not; and what the practical duties were to which a matured knowledge would lead them. During the first quarter of this century a great poet was raised in the North, who, whatever were his defects, has contributed by his works, in prose and verse, to prepare men for some closer and more practical approximation to Catholic truth. The general need of something deeper and more attractive than what had offered itself elsewhere, may be considered to have led to his popularity; and by means of his popularity he re-acted on his readers, stimulating their mental thirst, feeding their hopes, setting before them visions, which, when once seen, are not easily forgotten, and silently indoctrinating them with nobler ideas, which might afterwards be appealed to as first principles. Doubtless there are things in the poems and romances alluded to of which a correct judgment is forced to disapprove; and which must be ever a matter of regret; but contrasted with the popular writers of the last century, with its novelists, and some of its most admired poets, as Pope, they stand almost as oracles of Truth confronting the ministers of error and sin.

54. Belinsky: a Russian contemporary looks at Scott

1844

An extract from an article by Vissarion Belinsky, the Russian Romantic literary critic and philosopher. The article is ostensibly a review of a text-book by S. Smaragdov, *A Guide to the Study of Modern History*, and first appeared in *Otechestvenniye Zapiski* (1844). The selection is here taken from *V. G. Belinsky, Selected Philosophical Works* (Moscow, 1956).

Among the men who have contributed most to the cultivation of a true view on history an honourable place belongs to the man who has written one very bad history and a multitude of excellent novels: we have in mind Walter Scott. The ignorant have proclaimed his novels to be the illegitimate product of the liaison of history with fiction. Evidently, the idea of history and fiction did not dovetail in their narrow conception. Thus, there are people who cannot for the life of them see any sense in opera as a production of art because the actors do not speak, but sing, and that does not happen in real life. Thus, there are people who consider verse as nonsense, rightly claiming that no one speaks in verse. There are different kinds of people and different kinds of narrowmindedness! The people who are seduced by the blending of history with romance regard history as a military and diplomatic chronicle, from which point of view they are, of course, right. They do not understand that the history of customs and morals, which change with every new generation, is more interesting than the history of wars and treaties, and that the renovation of morals through the renovation of generations is one of the principal means by which Providence leads mankind to perfection. They do not understand that the historic and private lives of people are mingled together and fused like holidays with workdays. Walter Scott, as a man of genius, fathomed this with his instinct. Being familiar with the chronicles, he was able not only to read their lines, but between the lines. His novels are filled with a moving crowd, are alive with passions and seething interests great and small, base and lofty, and everywhere we feel the pathos of the epoch which the author has grasped with amazing skill. To read his novel is like living the age he describes, becoming for a moment a contemporary of the characters he portrays, thinking for a moment their thoughts and feeling their emotions. He was able, as a man of genius, to throw a retrospective glance at the sanguinary intestine disturbances of ancient England and turbulences of the new England which assumed the form of conservatism and opposition, and disclosed their meaning in history, and he himself explained the origin of the French revolution to be a result of *thirteen centuries* of strife between the Frank and Gallic elements.

55. Wordsworth's later views

1844

Extracts from reminiscences of Wordsworth by (a) Mrs. Davy and (b) Lady Richardson (from A. B. Grosart, ed., *The Prose Works of William Wordsworth* (London, 1876), iii, 442-3, 445). The first selection (a) is taken from a conversation dated 11 July 1844; the second (b) 12 July 1844.

For Wordsworth's earlier opinion of Scott, see No. 11.

(a) Mr. Wordsworth, in his best manner, with earnest thoughts given out in noble diction, gave his reasons for thinking that as a poet Scott would not live. 'I don't like,' he said, 'to say all this, or to take to pieces some of the best reputed passages of Scott's verse, especially in presence of my wife, because she thinks me too fastidious; but as a poet Scott *cannot* live, for he has never in verse written anything addressed to the immortal part of man. In making amusing stories in verse, he will be superseded by some newer versifier; what he writes in the way of natural description is merely rhyming nonsense.' As a prose writer, Mr. Wordsworth admitted that Scott had touched a higher vein, because there he had really dealt with feeling and passion. As historical novels, professing to give the manners of a past time, he did not attach much value to those works of Scott's so called, because that he held to be an attempt in which success was impossible. This led to some remarks on historical writing, from which it appeared that Mr. Wordsworth has small value for anything but contemporary history.

(b) He discoursed at great length on Scott's works. His poetry he considered of that kind which will always be in demand, and that the supply will always meet it, suited to the age. He does not consider that it in any way goes below the surface of things; it does not reach to any intellectual or spiritual emotion; it is altogether superficial, and he felt it himself to be so. His descriptions are not true to Nature; they are addressed to the ear, not to the mind. He was a master of bodily movements in his battle-scenes; but very little productive power was exerted in popular creations.

56. A question of history, *Fraser's Magazine*

1847

An unsigned article entitled 'Walter Scott—Has History Gained by His Writings?' published in *Fraser's Magazine* (September 1847), xxxvi, 345-51.

The 'Mr. James' mentioned in the opening paragraph and elsewhere is G. P. R. James, an historical novelist.

We have been informed by our elders, that the present generation, brought up under the shadow of a Bulwer and a Disraeli, a Mr. James and a Mrs. Trollope, is quite incapable of appreciating the particular kind of success which the early novels of Scott obtained. Every one of us has, probably, a distinct idea of what a novel is;—a book, which while in the embryotic state of preliminary puff and advertisement is of neither good nor evil name, but which must be finally brought up for sentence before every man who belongs to a book club, or subscribes to a circulating library. But thirty years ago, neither had the machinery which diffuses Mr. Colburn's publications over the face of the country come into existence, nor was this *primâ facie* character of theirs, or rather this absence of character, at all acknowledged. In fact, every novel came into the world with a brand upon it. The trail of the 'Minerva Press' was over all. In writings intended more especially for the lower and middle classes, the good old cottage tracts, which used to enforce order and morality with edifying stories of rustic worthies and their miraculous success in life, we remember to have seen the respectable and decorous effusions of Mrs. Barbara Redgauntlet, and such small deer, denounced in language which one would, now-a-days, think strong if applied to Paul de Kock or Pigault le Brun; while essayists, the forcible-feebles of higher pretension, over whose dreary pages many of our readers have doubtless yawned in the countless editions and imitations of the *Elegant Extracts*, sneered magnificently at fiction, as unworthy to occupy the time which a man of intellect must spend in reading, much more in writing it. A few might still cling to a belief in Fielding and Smollett, and the world did actually make clear exceptions in favour of Miss Edgeworth and Mackenzie; but, in glancing at the contemporary criticisms on these last writers, one can hardly help being amused by the evident anxiety shewn to separate them from the class to which they belonged, and the undaunted chivalry with which the critic insisted on saving his author's fair fame, at the expense of a total abandonment for the nonce of the common meaning of the most common words. In short, to the largest part of the reading public, including, perhaps, the worthiest portion of it, it must be confessed that the novel, like the pole-cat, was known only by name and a reputation for bad odour.

This state of things was completely changed in less than two years by the irresistible popularity of Scott. Alike intelligible to all, and appreciable by all, he became at once as much the darling of the milliner's apprentice as of the *bas bleu*,[1] and the overflowing stream of refreshment found a thousand channels, conducting it to regions where nothing so exhilarating, so fertilizing, had been known or felt before. But men's prepossessions, though easily enough overruled by a sense of new gratification, do yet, in some degree, demand to be explained and accounted for. There were not wanting persons—among them men of the most various bents, dandy *littérateurs* like Rose; cool, clear-sighted analysts like Jeffrey—who set themselves energetically to speculate on the strange vicissitude in taste through which that department of literature, which was of late shunned by all, had now become the resort and delight both of the undiscerning public and of their critical selves. We must remember that but slender count was taken of Scott's peculiar merits—that few would admit his strength to lie in the liberality with which he had drawn on the common and patent

[1] Bluestocking.

stock of every-day life. No break in the continuity of fiction was discerned; the novel was the novel still; and accordingly the change from disgust to admiration looked very much like an impeachment of former tastes and preferences.

The device lighted upon to reconcile the contradiction was characteristic of the day—characteristic of that school of criticism, which, professing the keenest relish for the new-born literature it had undertaken to review, persisted meanwhile in the constant endeavour to explain its excellence by a reference to recognized standards, *generally* but slightly applicable,—*frequently* governed by conditions of thought and feeling entirely different. The process seems to have been something like this. There is apparent on the face of the Waverley Novels a certain connexion with and dependence on History; that is, in many instances the characters introduced are the representatives of men who in their day existed—of what are called historical personages; and the dramatic action and business of the plot frequently profess to proceed in periods, whose chronicles it is the province of History to examine, explain, and develope. This gave rise to the presumption, that it was the deliberate design of Scott to create a literature which should be strictly ancillary to History, and, though filling a subordinate office, should promote the same philosophy and contribute to the same ends. Accordingly, the term 'Historical Novels' was invented,—an appellation which Scott himself, who certainly was not ignorant of the real character of history, never (such is our impression), in one instance, countenanced. Now, History was a good thing: for had it not been so said by them of old? and a Waverley Novel was a good thing, in virtue of one of those facts on which it is impossible to reason. It followed, therefore, that Scott's merits were exactly measured by the degree in which the inherent value of History overbalanced the intrinsic worthlessness of the novel. We are here inventing no imaginary paradox. In proof of what we have stated, we might refer our readers to the *Critical, Monthly,* and *Quarterly Reviews,*—in short, to almost all the constituents of contemporary criticism. There is now open before us an article in the *Quarterly,* the writer of which—supposed to have been Lord Dudley—cites in proof of this identical position, not without much jubilant exultation, an edition of *Philippe de Comines,* which appeared soon after the publication of *Quentin Durward.*

We believe it may be shewn to demonstration, that in these views, frequently urged on a public completely enslaved to the periodical critics, originated this belief in Scott's services to History. We need scarcely add, that the same theory, advanced by abler, or at least more unprejudiced, men, and supported by better arguments, has, in our own day, obtained so widely as to have almost passed into a literary canon. It is, for instance, a leading tenet of Macaulay, who, in several passages, has contrasted the meagreness of History, as long as it was entombed in chronicles, with its vivacious energy after Scott had breathed into the dead bones the breath of life. At the same time it is necessary to remark, that this question of Scott's furtherance of History is quite distinct from that of his influence on it. The first we are heretical enough to doubt, but we think that no one can reasonably hesitate as to the last. For good or for evil, it was an important day for History when Walter Scott first decided on translating from the German, *Götz with the Iron Hand*, the prolific origin of a world-famous progeny. It is true that, properly speaking, there is not at present in England anything like systematic History written; at the same time, the ground, which in an age more earnest and less accustomed to loose habits of thinking would be filled by the historian, is now occupied by a swarm of essayists, article-writers, and inditers of Historic Fancies,—which last term shall at present only tempt us to remark, that it indicates great confusion of idea in the era which countenances its adoption. The whole of this scattered literature presents, more or less, the characteristic peculiarity of Scott's influence, the substitution of life-like portraiture and clear, intelligible description, for philosophical comparison and analysis. Look abroad, too, to the schools of literary production which are rising on the Continent. In France, which up to the Revolution was singularly barren of historians, the new generation has applied itself to vigorous labour in the unoccupied field, and a school of writers has arisen which looks to Scott, principally, if not solely, as its teacher and master. The avowed ambition of Michelet is to write French history as Scott would have rendered it, in a series of romances. In the same spirit De Barante has written his *History of Burgundy*; and all the ingenuity displayed in Thierry's *History of the Norman Conquest* would have been lost to the world if the author's attention had not been rivetted by a single passage in *Ivanhoe*, wherein is delineated in a few bold lines the Saxon hind, Higg the son of Snell.

This notorious influence exerted by Scott on the whole productive intellect of our period, must necessarily give importance, as his vast celebrity must always give interest, to any inquiry like the present. To exhaust the subject would call for an effective definition of the province and offices of History, as well as a critical examination of Scott's merits and method. We will not even endeavour to answer these demands. It will be enough for us, if the few considerations which we throw out serve to clear the ideas of our readers respecting the real bearing of the question we propound, namely—Did History gain by the writings of Walter Scott?

We shall, perhaps, be pardoned for saying a few words regarding the sources from which Scott's mind derived its nourishment, and the artistic treatment, in conformity with which he developed the results of his mental experience. His intellectual capacities had, we think, this peculiarity, that their difference from those of men in general was not one of kind but of degree. He had a genuine love of the Beautiful— not, perhaps, of moral Beauty, but of that lower form which we denominate the picturesque,—a love which he possessed in common with many ordinary men. But the developement in Scott was enormous. He had strong prejudices, so strong, that it is sometimes hard to distinguish him from the fossil Tory of the October Club; though in no instance did his dislikes weaken his appreciation of the beauty and reasonableness, or, to speak more correctly, of the fitness and self-consistency, of his adversary's views. He was the most catholic admirer one can conceive. Witness his Balfours and Macbriars, who in the hands of a man equally prejudiced, and less singularly organised, would inevitably have become mere caricatures. And this acute relish for the Beautiful extended to immaterial objects, if indeed it was not especially whetted by them. To whatever thing there attached a chain of associations, however slight and meagre, and however imperceptible to most men, that thing was endeared to Scott. Of this sort is the *vertù* with which his house at Abbotsford is crowded; but, unlike most virtuosi, he prized nothing that was simply rare or curious, while all that bore the faintest relation to persons or events he loved as the apple of his eye. And this idiosyncrasy embraced all existences, which are rarely the subjects of antiquarian zeal, words, sentiments, and tunes. Like the Florentine academicians, who were said to mix disguised with the market-people for the purpose of collecting the *riboboli*, the rounded idiomatic sayings of the Tuscan peasantry, so of words, phrases, and turns of expression, indicative of the smallest peculiarity in the speaker or the class to which he belonged, Scott was an indefatigable collector and chronicler. Further, he was a subtle observer of human nature— as are many provincial attorneys. But here again his special singularity lay in degree. Indeed, his retentiveness of personal peculiarities seems almost to have amounted to disease. It was not that he had great power of looking into the deeper springs and sources of character—here certain individual deficiencies obstructed his vision—but looks, movements, singularities, and eccentricities of habit or manner he never forgot. And all this can easily be accounted for by the accidental circumstances of his life and education. His physical misfortune had from childhood made him a sedentary observer, and it had been his lot from his earliest years to reside alternately in Edinburgh, then intensely provincial, and consequently a mine of character, and on the Scottish border, a country where the very scantiness of surrounding objects contributes in a remarkable degree to give clearness and definiteness to the associations connected with them.

These, then, were the qualifications which Scott brought to the exercise of his art—common ones enough, but in him almost preternaturally developed. Against these available excellencies we must set various deficiencies, which, were his character as a Novelist only in question, it would be mere cavilling to mention. We allude to charges which have of late years been not unfrequently urged against him; as, for instance, that his perception of moral right was not extremely vivid —that his personal and peculiar ambitions marred the growth of many of the higher and finer aspirations—that his memory and imagination often, and especially as he grew an older man, were allowed to confuse each other—that he was not accurate, and that he was quite incapable of philosophical analysis or combination. But though his reflective powers were, comparatively speaking, weak, his perceptions and sympathies were pre-eminently strong; and when to all this is added the charm of his style, we need not wonder at the witchery he exercises over us, and indeed over the age. The unreflective reader he never tasks, the most cultivated critic he never disgusts; and then all is conveyed in language clear, flowing, and coherent, sometimes most racy and original. It is a free, bold, decided handling, which is and must be delightful, as long as men are men. The whole process is eminently what Carlyle has called 'intellectual shampooing'; and besides this, we must allow that his artistic method, when confined to its legitimate sphere, is almost perfect. What was this method, and how it has affected History, it is full time for us to inquire.

We conceive it will be admitted that Scott's treatment of a subject was very much as follows:—He drew on his own stores of observation for the characters he required; these characters, so obtained, he transferred bodily into the scene and action of the novel, generally unaltered,

sometimes slightly modified by an interchange of individual peculiarities: then he arrayed them in the costume necessary to perfect the
illusion, and arranged and disposed them according to his own
exquisite appreciation of grace and fitness. In thus stating the case,
we have included in the term *costume*, not only dress, but also language
and other adventitious appliances; for in the Waverley Novels the
trick of speech, borrowed from contemporary chronicles or ballads,
is as thoroughly adventitious as the buff-coat or the cuirass. The
propriety of this treatment is on most occasions unimpeachable. When
Scott depicted the Lowland Scotch and his scene was laid in comparatively modern times, the result of his method was full of natural
and artistic truth; for in his younger days real Jacobites were not
extinct: the Edinburgh lawyer, and the Lowland laird, were what they
had been in the beginning of the century; and at this very moment the
Scotch Presbyterian peasantry have altered surprisingly little from the
typical Cameronian and Covenanter. But then, when his rapid
exhaustion of old ground had forced him to change the field of his
labours, and he was tempted to thrust his characters farther back into
the past, he continued precisely the same process. Scott's early acquaintance, Janet Gordon, not only figures as Meg Merrilies, but also passes
into Norna of the Fitful Head, and beyond into the prophetess of
Front-de-Bœuf's castle; and the adventurous Scotchman, who is the
staple of his heroes, goes through the separate avatars of an advocate of
George the Second's reign, a cavalier of the Revolution, a courtier in
the time of James I, a Borderer of the reign of Henry VIII, and a
preux chevalier of the era of the Crusades. But we need not stay to discuss facts so notorious.

That a great and romantic effect was thus produced, is evident. There
is all the semblance of a genuine historical *tableau*; the elementary
characters are living, breathing men, and they offend us by no discrepancies of manner or costume. But is historical truth preserved?
We confidently answer that it is not, and that there is no surer way of
contravening the realities of History.

We know no more difficult branch of historical science than that
which professes to determine the action of an individual on his age,
and the reaction of his age on him. The investigation is infinitely complicated, since the character of its subject varies constantly with the
varying influences exerted on it: the man of this year is not necessarily
the man of last year, any more than the events of this year are those of
the last. The Lord-Protector Oliver is not the same with the Parlia-

mentary general, nor the Parliamentary general with Colonel Cromwell. Now if this is partially true of an individual life, it is certainly true of periods and generations. Each generation can only be the same with itself. Myriads of co-operating agencies—law—custom—literature—have joined to make it what it is, nor could the same result be obtained except under a perfect identity of conditions. Let us test the truth of this by looking to our own characters. Their growth has been determined by circumstances which only a miracle can enable us to recall and enumerate. Every book we read, every conversation we hold, modifies us in some way; and there must be some men whose characters, like coral islands, are built on the foregone labours of millions of their kind. Can we, then, by any effort of thought, suppose ourselves existing wholly in a period other than the present? Scott transported bodily the men of the nineteenth century into the fifteenth. Can *we* do the same with ourselves? We can easily imagine ourselves placed among all the *external* peculiarities of the feudal age. We can picture ourselves blessed by the priest or unhorsed by the knight with a vividness almost sufficient to rival truth; but no strain of the imagination can transform us into men, accepting all this in the light of common every day incident and accident; living continually under the influence of the universal Church, and looking on the iron circle of feudality as the unquestionable dispensation of Nature. It is just as impossible for the most imaginative among us to substitute for his own the sympathies and antipathies of a past age, as it was evidently then for the most resolute and advanced thinker to exhibit conclusions, tallying even distantly with the views we are in the habit of accepting as commonplaces. They can never come to us, and we can never return to them.

We are aware that it may be urged, in reply to these arguments, that, although we have not gained by Scott's treatment in the way of absolute truth, we are yet gainers by the removal of absolute error; and that though his tableaux do not give us the real men of the age they present, they have yet a sort of negative reality, in that they serve to weaken a besetting tendency to look on historical characters as mere names and abstractions. There is weight, no doubt, in this reasoning, and, so far as it goes, we gladly acquiesce in it; but we are not the less convinced that Scott engendered a large amount of new error to be set against that he removed. The Novelist will almost necessarily, in the spirit of his art, depict scenes and characters which, although for the sake of verisimilitude there must be in them some admixture of error, will yet, on the whole, be interesting and attractive. The consequence is the

introduction of a kind of rose-coloured medium which, by harmonis-
ing all objects, produces deception just as much as if it distorted them.
We are the more anxious to insist on this, because we are convinced
that what are called Young England views have originated in these
falsifications of history; and, indeed, the birth of these theories is in
itself sufficient to prove that no one can tamper innocently with historical truth. Representations, purely and avowedly imaginative, are
not without a peculiar danger of their own, and much more dangerous
are those but partially so. Fiction cannot border on reality without
creeping under its robe: indeed, men will do violence to themselves for
the purpose of investing the first with the dress of the last, in much the
same spirit as that in which the English yacht-voyagers to Copenhagen
have determined the position of Ophelia's grave, and of the pool in
which she drowned herself. And, after all, the advantages conferred
by Scott's treatment are but equivocal gain, if we are compelled to
accept with them intimate and substantial misrepresentations of historical periods. It was, no doubt, somewhat of an absurdity to see Garrick
acting Richard the Third in a court-suit and powdered wig. But we
should very dearly purchase our present attention to the proprieties of
theatrical costume, if we were compelled to retain Colley Cibber's
alterations in the text of the same play, in which the stilted rhetoric of
the eighteenth century jostles the racy eloquence of the Elizabethan
period, and 1750 and 1600 go hand-in-hand.

We said that we did not mean to hazard a definition of the historian's
province. We will, however, venture thus far, and assert that his office
is to note and comment on the *differences*, not the resemblances or the
peculiarities of successive ages. If the experience of the Past is to benefit
us at all, for doctrine, for example, or for reproof, it must be in virtue
of a power to make allowances and deductions for the discrepances
which hold between it and ourselves. Otherwise, each separate period
is insulated in time, and has no connexion with, or relation to the ages
which precede or follow it. Now for this branch of thought Scott was
peculiarly unfitted. Our readers may, perhaps, remember a celebrated
passage in Bacon, in which he distinguishes between *ingenia subtilia*
and *ingenia discursiva*, and then adds, '*utrumque ingenium facile labitur
in excessum, alterum prensando gradus rerum, alterum umbras*'.[1] To the
first class belonged the intellect of Scott. He loved to linger on the

---

[1] 'Distinguishes between the *acute mind* and the *discursive mind*, and then adds
"Both kinds easily err in excess, the one by catching at gradations, the other at
shadows".' *Novum Organum*, I, lv.

gradus rerum, on those small particulars, which, at some period in the mental experience of all, are full of interest and even of beauty. But to the last division we must emphatically assign the intellect of the man who possesses what is called in German the 'historical sense', and we know no better example of a writer so endowed, than David Hume. With some remarkable deficiencies, as for instance his incapacity for appreciating enthusiasm and religious faith, he had yet a distinct historical theory, and a full comprehension of national progress and social advance. He has in his day done more than any other man to show how the mere indications of one age become the sharply-defined characteristics of the next, and to demonstrate the fore-ordained aim and ultimate union and convergence of those innumerable, seemingly irreconcilable particulars which Scott and his school treat as distinct and isolated facts.

It is very difficult to take up a volume of Scott in anything like a spirit of critical examination. One cannot read him in cold blood. He sets all one's tastes and sympathies working at once to the dire distraction of the reason. Flooded by his humour, and exhilarated by his heartiness and freshness, one lingers in the company of his gloriously lifelike creations about as much disposed to question their title to the name they bear, as an opium-smoker to doubt the existence of his imaginary Houries. And here again Scott's admirable tact throws us at fault. We are never *taken aback* by a virtual paradox. Even in his delineations of single personages, where no more than an ordinary acquaintance with history at once convinces us that there is a misrepresentation somewhere, its exact nature is most difficult of detection. The dark side of a character, the remorseless cruelty of a Claverhouse, the mean-spirited selfishness of a Leicester, is always indicated—subdued, it is true, in tone, but still never wanting altogether. By this appearance of fairness, one's ideas on a broad question of right and wrong become strangely biassed in the teeth of oneself and one's convictions. There is a fallacy, certainly; it lies in the balance of motives; the writer has deceived us by his crafty adjustment of the scale; but not one reader in a hundred has the courage or the inclination to look farther than the conclusion of the process. And, if Scott can thus mislead us in cases where it was probably his deliberate intention to produce a certain and given effect, the danger of deception is much greater in instances where he himself sinned unknowingly and unconsciously against the truth, in his transpositions and translations of scenes and characters whose nature and peculiarities were due solely to the influences of his own age, upon the discordant world of the Past. Even more deceptive, as well as more untrustworthy, is the general result, when such methods are applied to the description of whole states of society and periods of history, with their complicated enginery of agency and consequence. We know but one way of keeping our eyes open. Let us not look to Scott, but to his imitators. Coleridge has somewhere said that pathology is the test of physiology. Examine things in their *diseased* form, and you will learn their true nature. Now we presume no one imagines Mr. James' novels to be real presentations of the past. If the eternal couple of knights, who open the tale by riding through impossible scenery at sunset, if the unnatural incident, the common-place morality, the dialogue forced into stilted quaintness, if all these, as brought out in the inimitable Barbazure, constitute a genuine historical picture, then is History something more uninstruct-ive than an old almanac. And yet detach a Waverley novel from its accidents, and the *caput mortuum* is a tale of Mr. James. Apart from Scott's taste, from his accuracy of detail, from his wit, from his humour, from his knowledge of human nature, these absurdities represent not unfairly those elements of his productions which bear directly on History.

God forbid that we should detract from the true fame of this great man. A veritable Nemesis would avenge so ungrateful a return for the hours of delight we owe to him. But we have distinctly said that the novelist, as such, is not the object of our strictures. We only lament that his method should have proved so fruitful of questionable con-sequences. In our opinion he might have adopted a different treatment without detriment to his peculiar excellences. He might have written always as he wrote occasionally, that is, he might have bestowed the additional pains necessary to give an artistic form to the materials with which he was so freely provided, without resorting to the deceptive illusion of a pseudo-historical garb: or perhaps he might have emulated the far more difficult achievement of describing the past as it really existed, and of illustrating, not creating it, by his acquaintance with the present: or he might at least have kept the subject and its accidental vehicle so far apart as partially to obviate all danger of misrepresenta-tion. This last appears to have been the method of Shakespeare, who almost takes pains to separate the characters introduced from the scene of introduction. The existing laws of the stage compelled him to transact his stage-action at Verona, Venice, Padua, Athens—anywhere but in Elizabethan England. But his Veronese Gentlemen belong to

Paul's and the Temple, Iago and Cassio smack somewhat of Alsatia, Dogberry and Verges are redolent of the Fleet, and some Stratford weaver certainly sat for the Athenian Bottom. Moreover, in the historical plays, in which nothing but the bare skeleton of fact is present, all historical consistency is systematically neglected. With Scott, on the contrary, there is a deliberate effort to identify the fictitious with the historical scene.

But we will not be tempted to mingle questions, which are in reality distinct. From taking Scott as our guide and instructor, we are learning to prefer to patient thought and candid investigation, an easily-induced attention to the imaginary graces and prettinesses of the past,—

> 'Le donne, i cavalier, l'ame, gli amori,
> Le cortesie, l'audaci imprese,'[1]

and the consequence is, that Mr. Smythe is likely to be the exponent of our opinions on History, Mr. Pugin of our views of Religion, and Lord John Manners of our statesmanship.

---

[1] 'Of dames, of knights, of arms, of love's delight,
Of courtesies, of high attempts I speak . . .'.
Ariosto's *Orlando Furioso*, I, i-ii, trans. Sir John Harington.

57. Walter Bagehot on Scott, *National Review*

1858

This essay first appeared as an unsigned review of various mid-nineteenth-century editions of the Waverley novels, *National Review* (April, 1858), vi, 444-72.

This is often considered one of the best of the Victorian essays on Scott.

It is not commonly on the generation which was contemporary with the production of great works of art that they exercise their most magical influence. Nor is it on the distant people whom we call posterity. Contemporaries bring to new books formed minds and stiffened creeds; posterity, if it regard them at all, looks at them as old subjects, worn-out topics, and hears a disputation on their merits with languid impartiality, like aged judges in a court of appeal. Even standard authors exercise but slender influence on the susceptible minds of a rising generation; they are become 'papa's books'; the walls of the library are adorned with their regular volumes; but no hand touches them. Their fame is itself half an obstacle to their popularity; a delicate fancy shrinks from employing so great a celebrity as the companion of an idle hour. The generation which is really most influenced by a work of genius is commonly that which is still young when the first controversy respecting its merits arises; with the eagerness of youth they read and re-read; their vanity is not unwilling to adjudicate: in the process their imagination is formed; the creations of the author range themselves in the memory; they become part of the substance of the very mind. The works of Sir Walter Scott can hardly be said to have gone through this exact process. Their immediate popularity was unbounded. No one—a few most captious critics apart—ever questioned their peculiar power. Still they are subject to a transition, which is in principle the same. At the time of their publication mature contemporaries read them with delight. Superficial the reading of grown men in some sort must ever be; it is only once in a lifetime that we can know the passionate reading of youth; men soon lose its eager learning power. But from peculiarities in their structure, which we shall try to indicate, the novels of Scott suffered less than almost any book of equal excellence from this inevitable superficiality of perusal. Their plain, and, so to say, cheerful merits, suit the occupied man of genial middle life. Their appreciation was to an unusual degree coincident with their popularity. The next generation, hearing the praises of their fathers in their earliest reading time, seized with avidity on the volumes; and there is much in very many of them which is admirably fitted for the delight of boyhood. A third generation has now risen into at least the commencement of literary life, which is quite removed from the unbounded enthusiasm with which the Scotch novels were originally received, and does not always share the still more eager partiality of those who, in the opening of their minds, first received the tradition of their excellence. New books have arisen to compete with these; new interests distract us from them. The time, therefore, is not perhaps unfavourable for a slight criticism of these celebrated fictions; and their continual republication without any criticism for many years seems almost to demand it.

There are two kinds of fiction which, though in common literature they may run very much into one another, are yet in reality distinguishable and separate. One of these, which we may call the *ubiquitous*, aims at describing the whole of human life in all its spheres, in all its aspects, with all its varied interests, aims, and objects. It searches through the whole life of man; his practical pursuits, his speculative attempts, his romantic youth, and his domestic age. It gives an entire feature of all these; or if there be any lineaments which it forbears to depict, they are only such as the inevitable repression of a regulated society excludes from the admitted province of literary art. Of this kind are the novels of Cervantes and Le Sage, and, to a certain extent, of Smollett or Fielding. In our own time, Mr. Dickens is an author whom nature intended to write to a certain extent with this aim. He should have given us *not* disjointed novels, with a vague attempt at a romantic plot, but sketches of diversified scenes, and the obvious life of varied mankind. The literary fates, however, if such beings there are, allotted otherwise. By a very terrible example of the way in which in this world great interests are postponed to little ones, the genius of authors is habitually sacrificed to the tastes of readers. In this age, the great readers of fiction are young people. The 'addiction' of these is to romance; and accordingly a kind of novel has become so familiar to us as almost to engross the name, which deals solely with the passion of love; and if it uses other parts of human life for the occasions of its art, it does so only cursorily and occasionally, and with a view of throwing into a stronger or more delicate light those sentimental parts of earthly affairs which are the special objects of delineation. All prolonged delineation of other parts of human life is considered 'dry', stupid, and distracts the mind of the youthful generation from the 'fantasies' which peculiarly charm it. Mr. Olmsted has a story of some deputation of the Indians; at which the American orator harangued the barbarian audience about the 'great spirit', and 'the land of their fathers', in the style of Mr. Cooper's novels; during a moment's pause in the great stream, an old Indian asked the deputation, 'Why does your chief speak thus to us? we did not wish great instruction or fine words; we desire brandy and tobacco.' No critic in a time of competition will speak uncourteously of any reader of either sex; but it is indisputable that the old kind of novel, full of 'great instruction' and varied pictures, does not afford to some young gentlemen and some young ladies either the peculiar stimulus or the peculiar solace which they desire.

The Waverley Novels were published at a time when the causes that thus limit the sphere of fiction were coming into operation, but when they had not yet become so omnipotent as they are now. Accordingly these novels every where bear marks of a state of transition. They are not devoted with any thing like the present exclusiveness to the sentimental part of human life. They describe great events, singular characters, strange accidents, strange states of society; they dwell with a peculiar interest—and as if for their own sake—on antiquarian details relating to a past society. Singular customs, social practices, even political institutions which existed once in Scotland, and even elsewhere, during the middle ages, are explained with a careful minuteness. At the same time the sentimental element assumes a great deal of prominence. The book is in fact, as well as in theory, a narrative of the feelings and fortunes of the hero and heroine. An attempt more or less successful has been made to insert an interesting love-story in each novel. Sir Walter was quite aware that the best delineation of the oddest characters, or the most quaint societies, or the strangest incidents, would not in general satisfy his readers. He has invariably attempted an account of youthful, sometimes of decidedly juvenile, feelings and actions. The difference between Sir Walter's novels and the specially romantic fictions of the present day is, that in the former the love-story is always, or nearly always, connected with some great event, or the fortunes of some great historical character, or the peculiar movements and incidents of some strange state of society; and that the author did not suppose or expect that his readers would be so absorbed in the sentimental aspect of human life as to be unable or unwilling to be interested in, or to attend to, any other. There is always a *locus in quo*, if the expression may be pardoned, in the Waverley Novels. The hero and heroine walk among the trees of the forest according to rule, but we are expected to take an interest in the forest as well as in them.

No novel, therefore, of Sir Walter Scott's can be considered to come exactly within the class which we have called the ubiquitous. None of them in any material degree attempts to deal with human affairs in all their spheres—to delineate as a whole the life of man. The canvas has a large background, in some cases too large either for artistic effect or the common reader's interest; but there are always real boundaries— Sir Walter had no *thesis* to maintain. Scarcely any writer will set himself to delineate the whole of human life, unless he has a doctrine concerning human life to put forth and inculcate. The effort is *doctrinaire*. Scott's imagination was strictly conservative. He could understand (with a few exceptions) any considerable movement of human life and action, and could always describe with easy freshness every thing which he did understand; but he was not obliged by stress of fanaticism to maintain a dogma concerning them, or to show their peculiar relation to the general sphere of life. He described vigorously and boldly the peculiar scene and society which in every novel he had selected as the theatre of romantic action. Partly from their fidelity to nature, and partly from a consistency in the artist's mode of representation, these pictures group themselves from the several novels in the imagination, and an habitual reader comes to think of and understand what is meant by 'Scott's world', but the writer had no such distinct object before him. No one novel was designed to be a delineation of the world as Scott viewed it. We have vivid and fragmentary histories; it is for the slow critic of after-times to piece together their teaching.

From this intermediate position of the Waverley Novels, or at any rate in exact accordance with its requirements, is the special characteristic for which they are most remarkable. We may call this in a brief phrase their *romantic sense*; and perhaps we cannot better illustrate it than by a quotation from the novel to which the series owes its most

usual name. It occurs in the description of the court-ball which Charles
Edward is described as giving at Holyrood House the night before his
march southward on his strange adventure. The striking interest of the
scene before him, and the peculiar position of his own sentimental
career, are described as influencing the mind of the hero. 'Under the
influence of these mixed sensations, and cheered at times by a smile of
intelligence and approbation from the Prince as he passed the group,
Waverley exerted his powers of fancy, animation and eloquence, and
attracted the general admiration of the company. The conversation
gradually assumed the line best qualified for the display of his talents
and acquisitions. The gaiety of the evening was exalted in character,
rather than checked, by the approaching dangers of the morrow. All
nerves were strung for the future, and prepared to enjoy the present.
This mood is highly favourable for the exercise of the powers of
imagination, for poetry, and for that eloquence which is allied to
poetry.' Neither 'eloquence' nor 'poetry' are the exact words with
which it would be appropriate to describe the fresh style of the
Waverley Novels; but the imagination of their author was stimulated
by a fancied mixture of sentiment and fact very much as he describes
Waverley's to have been by a real experience of the two at once. The
second volume of Waverley is one of the most striking illustrations of
this peculiarity. The character of Charles Edward, his adventurous
undertaking, his ancestral rights, the mixed selfishness and enthusiasm
of the Highland chiefs, the fidelity of their hereditary followers, their
striking and strange array, the contrast with the Baron of Bradwardine
and the Lowland gentry; the collision of the motley and half-appointed
host with the formed and finished English society, its passage by the
Cumberland mountains and the blue lake of Ullswater,—are unceasingly and without effort present to the mind of the writer, and
incite with their historical interest the susceptibility of his imagination.
But at the same time the mental struggle, or rather transition, in the
mind of Waverley,—for his mind was of the faint order which scarcely
struggles,—is never for an instant lost sight of. In the very midst of the
inroad and the conflict, the acquiescent placidity with which the hero
exchanges the service of the imperious for the appreciation of the
'nice' heroine, is kept before us, and the imagination of Scott wandered
without effort from the great scene of martial affairs to the natural
but rather unheroic sentiments of a young gentleman not very difficult
to please. There is no trace of effort in the transition, as is so common in
the inferior works of later copyists. Many historical novelists, especially

those who with care and pains have 'read up' their detail, are often evidently in a strait how to pass from their history to their sentiment. The fancy of Sir Walter could not help connecting the two. If he had given us the English side of the race to Derby, he would have described the Bank of England paying in sixpences, and also the loves of the cashier.

It is not unremarkable in connection with this the special characteristic of the 'Scotch novels', that their author began his literary life by collecting the old ballads of his native country. Ballad poetry is, in comparison at least with many other kinds of poetry, a sensible thing. It describes not only romantic events, but historical ones, incidents in which there is a form and body and consistence,—events which have a result. Such a poem as *Chevy Chace* we need not explain has its prosaic side. The latest historian of Greece has nowhere been more successful than in his attempt to derive from Homer, the greatest of ballad poets, a thorough and consistent account of the political working of the Homeric state of society. The early natural imagination of men seizes firmly on all which interests the minds and hearts of natural men. We find in its delineations the council as well as the marriage; the harsh conflict as well as the deep love-affair. Scott's own poetry is essentially a modernised edition of the traditional poems which his early youth was occupied in collecting. *The Lady of the Lake* is a sort of *boudoir* ballad, yet it contains its element of common sense and broad delineation. The exact position of Lowlander and Highlander would not be more aptly described in a set treatise than in the well-known lines:

[ll. 136-65 of Canto V of *The Lady of the Lake* are quoted]

We need not search the same poem for specimens of the romantic element, for the whole poem is full of them. The incident in which Ellen discovers who Fitz-James really is, is perhaps excessively romantic. At any rate the lines,—

> 'To him each lady's look was lent;
> On him each courteous eye was bent;
> Midst furs and silks and jewels sheen,
> He stood in simple Lincoln green,
> The centre of the glittering ring,
> And Snowdoun's knight is Scotland's king,'—

may be cited as very sufficient example of the sort of sentimental incident which is separable from extreme feeling. When Scott, according to his own half-jesting but half-serious expression, was 'beaten out of poetry' by Byron, he began to express in more pliable prose the same combination which his verse had been used to convey. As might have been expected, the sense became in the novels more free, vigorous, and flowing, because it is less cramped by the vehicle in which it is conveyed. The range of character which can be adequately delineated in narrative verse is much narrower than that which can be described in the combination of narrative with dramatic prose; and perhaps even the sentiment of the novels is manlier and freer; a delicate unreality hovers over *The Lady of the Lake*.

The sensible element, if we may so express it, of the Waverley Novels appears in various forms. One of the most striking is in the delineation of great political events and influential political institutions. We are not by any means about to contend that Scott is to be taken as an infallible or an impartial authority for the parts of history which he delineates. On the contrary, we believe all the world now agrees that there are many deductions to be made from, many exceptions to be taken to, the accuracy of his delineations. Still, whatever period or incident we take, we shall always find in the error a great, in one or two cases perhaps an extreme, mixture of the mental element which we term common sense. The strongest *un*sensible feeling in Scott was perhaps his Jacobitism, which crept out even in small incidents and recurring prejudice throughout the whole of his active career, and was, so to say, the emotional aspect of his habitual Toryism. Yet no one can have given a more sensible delineation, we might say a more statesmanlike analysis, of the various causes which led to the momentary success, and to the speedy ruin, of the enterprise of Charles Edward. Mr. Lockhart says, that notwithstanding Scott's imaginative readiness to exalt Scotland at the expense of England, no man would have been more willing to join in emphatic opposition to an anti-English party, if any such had presented itself with a practical object. Similarly his Jacobitism, though not without moments of real influence, passed away when his mind was directed to broad masses of fact and general conclusions of political reasoning. A similar observation may be made as to Scott's Toryism; although it is certain that there was an enthusiastic, and in the malicious sense, poetical element in Scott's Toryism, yet it quite as indisputably partook largely of two other elements, which are in common repute prosaic. He shared abundantly in the love of administration and organization, common to all men of great active powers. He liked to contemplate method at work and order in action. Every body hates to hear that the Duke of Wellington asked 'how the king's government was to be carried on'. No amount of warning wisdom will bear so fearful a repetition. Still he *did* say it, and Scott had a sympathizing foresight of the oracle before it was spoken. One element of his conservatism is his sympathy with the administrative arrangement, which is confused by the objections of a Whiggish opposition, and is liable to be altogether destroyed by uprisings of the populace. His biographer, while pointing out the strong contrast between Scott and the argumentative and parliamentary statesmen of his age, avows his opinion that in other times, and with sufficient opportunities, Scott's ability in managing men would have enabled him to 'play the part of Cecil or of Gondomar'. We may see how much an insensible enthusiasm for such abilities breaks out, not only in the description of hereditary monarchs, where the sentiment might be ascribed to a different origin, but also in the delineation of upstart rulers, who could have no hereditary sanctity in the eyes of any Tory. Roland Græme, in the *Abbot*, is well described as losing in the presence of the Regent Murray the natural impertinence of his disposition. 'He might have braved with indifference the presence of an earl merely distinguished by his belt and coronet; but he felt overawed in that of the soldier and statesman, the wielder of a nation's power, and the leader of her armies.' It is easy to perceive that the author shares the feeling of his hero by the evident pleasure with which he dwells on the regent's demeanour: 'He then turned slowly round toward Roland Græme, and the marks of gaiety, real or assumed, disappeared from his countenance as completely as the passing bubbles leave the dark mirror of a still profound lake into which the traveller has cast a stone; in the course of a minute his noble features had assumed their natural expression of melancholy gravity,' &c. In real life Scott used to say that he never remembered feeling abashed in any one's presence except the Duke of Wellington's. Like that of the hero of his novel, his imagination was very susceptible to the influence of great achievement, and prolonged success in wide-spreading affairs.

The view which Scott seems to have taken of democracy indicates exactly the same sort of application of a plain sense to the visible parts of the subject. His imagination was singularly penetrated with the strange varieties and motley composition of human life. The extraordinary multitude and striking contrast of the characters in his novels show this at once. And even more strikingly is the same habit of mind indicated by a tendency never to omit an opportunity of describing those varied crowds and assemblages which concentrate for a moment into a unity the scattered and unlike varieties of mankind. Thus, but a page or two before the passage which we alluded to in *The Abbot*, we find the following:

[a quotation from chapter 18 of *The Abbot* 'It was indeed' to 'generous bounty' is omitted]

As in the imagination of Shakespeare, so in that of Scott, the principal form and object were the structure—that is a hard word—the undulation and diversified composition of human society; the picture of this stood in the centre, and every thing else was accessory and secondary to it. The old 'rows of books', in which Scott so peculiarly delighted, were made to contribute their element to this varied imagination of humanity. From old family histories, odd memoirs, old law-trials, his fancy elicited new traits to add to the motley assemblage. His objection to democracy—an objection of which we can only appreciate the emphatic force, when we remember that his youth was contemporary with the first French Revolution, and the controversy as to the uniform and stereotyped rights of man—was, that it would sweep away this entire picture, level prince and peasant in a common *égalité*,—substitute a scientific rigidity for the irregular and picturesque growth of centuries,—replace an abounding and genial life by a symmetrical but lifeless mechanism. All the descriptions of society in the novels,—whether of feudal society, of modern Scotch society, or of English society,—are largely coloured by this feeling. It peeps out every where, and liberal critics have endeavoured to show that it was a narrow Toryism; but in reality it is a subtle compound of the natural instinct of the artist with the plain sagacity of the man of the world.

It would be tedious to show how clearly the same sagacity appears in his delineation of the various great events and movements in society which are described in the Scotch novels. There is scarcely one of them which does not bear it on its surface. Objections may, as we shall show, be urged to the delineation which Scott has given of the Puritan resistance and rebellions, yet scarcely any one will say there is not a worldly sense in it. On the contrary, the very objection is, that it is too worldly, and far too exclusively sensible.

The same thoroughly well-grounded sagacity and comprehensive appreciation of human life is shown in the treatment of what we may call *anomalous* characters. In general, monstrosity is no topic for art. Every one has known in real life characters which if, apart from much experience, he had found described in books, he would have thought unnatural and impossible. Scott, however, abounds in such characters. Meg Merrilies, Edie Ochiltree, Radcliffe, are more or less of that description. That of Meg Merrilies especially is as distorted and eccentric as any thing can be. Her appearance is described as making Mannering 'start'; and well it might: 'She was full six feet high, wore a man's greatcoat over the rest of her dress, had in her hand a goodly sloethorn cudgel, and in all points of equipment except the petticoats seemed rather masculine than feminine. Her dark elf-locks shot out like the snakes of the gorgon between an old-fashioned bonnet called a bongrace, heightening the singular effect of her strong and weather-beaten features, which they partly shadowed, while her eye had a wild roll that indicated something of insanity.' Her career in the tale corresponds with the strangeness of her exterior. 'Harlot, thief, witch, and gipsy', as she describes herself, the hero is preserved by her virtues; half-crazed as she is described to be, he owes his safety on more than one occasion to her skill in stratagem, and ability in managing those with whom she is connected, and who are most likely to be familiar with her weakness and to detect her craft. Yet on hardly any occasion is the natural reader conscious of this strangeness. Something is of course attributable to the skill of the artist; for no other power of mind could produce the effect, unless it were aided by the unconscious tact of detailed expression. But the fundamental explanation of this remarkable success is the distinctness with which Scott saw how such a character as Meg Merrilies arose and was produced out of the peculiar circumstances of gipsy life in the localities in which he has placed his scene. He has exhibited this to his readers not by lengthy or elaborate description, but by chosen incidents, short comments, and touches of which he scarcely foresaw the effect. This is the only way in which the fundamental objection to making eccentricity the subject of artistic treatment can be obviated. Monstrosity ceases to be such when we discern the laws of nature which evolve it: when a real science explains its phenomena, we find that it is in strict accordance with what we call the natural type, but that some rare adjunct or uncommon casualty has interfered and distorted a nature which is really the same, into a phenomenon which is altogether different. Just so with eccentricity in human character; it becomes a topic of literary art only when its identity with the ordinary principles of human nature is exhibited in the midst of, and, as it were, by means of, the superficial unlikeness. Such a skill, however, requires an easy careless familiarity with usual human life and common human conduct. A writer must have a sympathy with health before he can show us how, and where, and to what extent, that which is unhealthy deviates from it; and it is this consistent acquaintance with regular life which makes the irregular characters of Scott so happy a contrast to the uneasy distortions of less sagacious novelists.

A good deal of the same criticism may be applied to the delineation which Scott has given us of the *poor*. In truth, poverty is an anomaly to rich people. It is very difficult to make out why people who want dinner do not ring the bell. One half of the world, according to the saying, do not know how the other half lives. Accordingly, nothing is so rare in fiction as a good delineation of the poor. Though perpetually with us in reality, we rarely meet them in our reading. The requirements of the case present an unusual difficulty to artistic delineation. A good deal of the character of the poor is an unfit topic for continuous art, and yet we wish to have in our books a lifelike exhibition of the whole of that character. Mean manners and mean vices are unfit for prolonged delineation; the everyday pressure of narrow necessities is too petty a pain and too anxious a reality to be dwelt upon. We can bear the mere description of the *Parish Register*—

'But this poor farce has neither truth nor art
To please the fancy or to touch the heart.
Dark but not awful, dismal but yet mean,
With anxious bustle moves the cumbrous scene;
Presents no objects tender or profound,
But spreads its cold unmeaning gloom around;'—

but who could bear to have a long narrative of fortunes 'dismal but yet mean', with characters 'dark but not awful', and no objects 'tender or profound'. Mr. Dickens has in various parts of his writings been led by a sort of pre-Raphaelite *cultus* of reality into an error of this species. His poor people have taken to their poverty very thoroughly; they are poor talkers and poor livers, and in all ways poor people to read about. A whole array of writers have fallen into an opposite mistake. Wishing to preserve their delineations clear from the defects of meanness and vulgarity, they have attributed to the poor a fancied happiness and Arcadian simplicity. The conventional shepherd of ancient times was scarcely displeasing: that which is by every thing except express avowal removed from the sphere of reality does not annoy us by its deviations from reality; but the fictitious poor of sentimental novelists are brought almost into contact with real life, half claim to be copies of what actually exists at our very doors, are introduced in close proximity to characters moving in a higher rank, over whom no such ideal charm is diffused, and who are painted with as much truth as the writer's ability enables him to give. Accordingly, the contrast is evident and displeasing: the harsh outlines of poverty will not bear the artificial rose-tint; they are seen through it, like high cheek-bones through the delicate colours of artificial youth; we turn away with some disgust from the false elegance and undeceiving art; we prefer the rough poor of nature to the petted poor of the refining describer. Scott has most felicitously avoided both these errors. His poor people are never coarse and never vulgar; their lineaments have the rude traits which a life of conflict will inevitably leave on the minds and manners of those who are to lead it; their notions have the narrowness which is inseparable from a contracted experience; their knowledge is not more extended than their restricted means of attaining it would render possible. Almost alone among novelists Scott has given a thorough, minute, life-like description of poor persons, which is at the same time genial and pleasing. The reason seems to be, that the firm sagacity of his genius comprehended the industrial aspect of poor people's life thoroughly and comprehensively, his experience brought it before him easily and naturally, and his artist's mind and genial disposition enabled him to dwell on those features which would be most pleasing to the world in general. In fact, his own mind of itself and by its own nature dwelt on those very peculiarities. He could not remove his firm and instructed genius into the domain of Arcadian unreality, but he was equally unable to dwell principally, peculiarly, or consecutively, on those petty, vulgar, mean details in which such a writer as Crabbe lives and breathes. Hazlitt said that Crabbe described a poor man's cottage like a man who came to distrain for rent; he catalogued every trivial piece of furniture, defects and cracks and all. Scott describes it as a cheerful but most sensible landlord would describe a cottage on his property: he has a pleasure in it. No detail, or few details, in the life of the inmates escape his experienced and interested eye; but he dwells on those which do not displease him. He sympathises with their rough industry and plain joys and sorrows. He does not fatigue himself or excite their wondering smile by theoretical plans of impossible relief. He makes the best of the life which is given, and by a sanguine sympathy makes it still better. A hard life many characters in Scott seem to lead; but he appreciates, and makes his reader appreciate, the full value of natural feelings, plain thoughts, and applied sagacity.

His ideas of political economy are equally characteristic of his strong sense and genial mind. He was always sneering at Adam Smith, and telling many legends of that philosopher's absence of mind and inaptitude for the ordinary conduct of life. A contact with the Edinburgh logicians had, doubtless, not augmented his faith in the formal deductions of abstract economy; nevertheless, with the facts before him, he could give a very plain and satisfactory exposition of the genial consequences of old abuses, the distinct necessity for stern reform, and the delicate humanity requisite for introducing that reform temperately and with feeling:

[a quotation from chapter 6 of *Guy Mannering* 'Even so the Laird of Ellangowan' to ' "sax days of the week besides" ' is omitted]

Many other indications of the same healthy and natural sense, which gives so much of their characteristic charm to the Scotch novels, might be pointed out, if it were necessary to weary our readers by dwelling longer on a point we have already laboured so much; one more, however, demands notice because of its importance, and perhaps also because, from its somewhat less obvious character, it might escape otherwise without notice. There has been frequent controversy as to the penal code, if we may so call it, of fiction; that is, as to the apportionment of reward and punishment respectively to the good and evil personages therein delineated; and the practice of authors has been as various as the legislation of critics. One school abandons all thought on the matter, and declares that in the real life we see around us good people often fail, and wicked people continually prosper; and would deduce the precept, that it is unwise in an art which should hold the 'mirror up to nature', not to copy the uncertain and irregular distribution of its sanctions. Another school, with an exactness which savours at times of pedantry, apportions the success and the failure, the pain and the pleasure, of fictitious life to the moral qualities of those who are living in it—does not think at all, or but little, of every other quality in those characters, and does not at all care whether the penalty and reward are evolved in natural sequence from the circumstances and characters of the tale, or are owing to some monstrous accident far removed from all relation of cause or consequence to those facts and people. Both these classes of writers produce works which jar on the natural sense of common readers, and are at issue with the analytic criticism of the best critics. One school leaves an impression of an uncared-for world, in which there is no right and no wrong; the other, of a sort of Governesses' Institution of a world, where all praise and all blame, all good and all pain, are made to turn on special graces and petty offences, pesteringly spoken of and teasingly watched for. The manner of Scott is thoroughly different; you can scarcely lay down any novel of his without a strong feeling that the world in which the fiction has been laid, and in which your imagination has been moving, is one subject to *laws* of retribution which, though not apparent on a superficial glance, are yet in steady and consistent operation, and will be quite sure to work their due effect, if time is only given to them. Sagacious men know that this is in its best aspect the condition of life. Certain of the ungodly may, notwithstanding the Psalmist, flourish even through life like a green bay-tree; for providence, in external appearance (far differently from the real truth of things, as we may one day see it), works by a scheme of averages. Most people who ought to succeed, do succeed; most people who do fail, ought to fail. But there is no exact adjustment of 'mark' to merit; the competitive examination system appears to have an origin more recent than the creation of the world;—'on the whole', 'speaking generally', 'looking at life as a whole' are the words in which we must describe the providential adjustment of visible good and evil to visible goodness and badness. And when we look more closely, we see that these general results are the consequences of certain principles which work half unseen, and which are effectual in the main, though thwarted here and there. It is this comprehensive though inexact distribution of good and evil, which is suited to the novelist, and it is exactly this which Scott instinctively adopted. Taking a firm and genial view of the common facts of life,—seeing it as an experienced observer and tried man of action,—he could not help giving the representation of it which is insensibly borne in on the minds of such persons. He delineates it as a world moving according to laws which are always producing their effect, never *have* produced it; sometimes fall short a little; are always nearly successful. Good sense produces its effect, as well as good intention; ability is valuable as well as virtue. It is this peculiarity which gives to his works, more than any thing else, the life-likeness which distinguishes them; the average of the copy is struck on the same scale as that of reality; an unexplained, uncommented-on adjustment works in the one, just as a hidden imperceptible principle of apportionment operates in the other.

The romantic susceptibility of Scott's imagination is as obvious in his novels as his matter-of-fact sagacity. We can find much of it in the place in which we should naturally look first for it,—his treatment of his heroines. We are no indiscriminate admirers of these young ladies, and shall shortly try to show how much they are inferior as imaginative creations to similar creations of the very highest artists. But the mode in which the writer speaks of them every where indicates an imagination continually under the illusion which we term romance. A gentle tone of manly admiration pervades the whole delineation of their words and actions. If we look carefully at the narratives of some remarkable female novelists—it would be invidious to give the instances by name— we shall be struck at once with the absence of this; they do not half like their heroines. It would be satirical to say that they were jealous of them; but it is certain that they analyse the mode in which their charms produce their effects, and the minutiæ of their operation, much in the same way in which a slightly jealous lady examines the claims of the heroines of society. The same writers have invented the atrocious species of *plain* heroines. Possibly none of the frauds which are now so much the topic of common remark are so irritating as that to which the purchaser of a novel is a victim on finding that he has only to peruse a narrative of the conduct and sentiments of an ugly lady. 'Two-and-sixpence to know the heart which has high cheek-bones!' Was there ever such an imposition? Scott would have recoiled from such conception. Even Jeanie Deans, though no heroine, like Flora Macivor, is described as 'comely', and capable of looking almost pretty when required, and she has a compensating set-off in her sister, who is beautiful as well as unwise. Speaking generally, as is the necessity of criticism, Scott makes his heroines, at least by profession, attractive, and dwells on their attractiveness, though not with the wild ecstasy of insane youth, yet with the tempered and mellow admiration common to genial men of this world. Perhaps at times we are rather displeased at his explicitness, and disposed to hang back and carp at the admirable qualities displayed to us. But this is only a stronger evidence of the peculiarity which we speak of,—of the unconscious sentiments inseparable from Scott's imagination.

The same romantic tinge undeniably shows itself in Scott's pictures of the past. Many exceptions have been taken to the detail of mediæval life as it is described to us in *Ivanhoe*; but one merit will always remain to it, and will be enough to secure to it immense popularity. It describes the middle ages as we should have wished them to have been. We do not mean that the delineation satisfies those accomplished admirers of the old church system who fancy that they have found among the prelates and barons of the fourteenth century a close approximation to the theocracy which they would recommend for our adoption. On the contrary, the theological merits of the middle ages are not prominent in Scott's delineation. 'Dogma' was not in his way: a cheerful man of the world is not anxious for a precise definition of peculiar doctrines. The charm of *Ivanhoe* is addressed to a simpler sort of imagination,—to that kind of boyish fancy which idolises mediæval society as the 'fighting time'. Every boy has heard of tournaments, and has a firm persuasion that in an age of tournaments life was thoroughly well understood. A martial society, where men fought hand to hand on good horses with large lances, in peace for pleasure, and in war for business, seems the very ideal of perfection to a bold and simply fanciful boy. *Ivanhoe* spreads before him the full landscape of such a realm, with Richard Coeur-de-Lion, a black horse, and the passage of arms at Ashby. Of course he admires it, and thinks there was never such a writer, and will never more be such a world. And a mature critic will share his admiration, at least to the extent of admitting that nowhere else have the elements of a martial romance been so gorgeously accumulated without becoming oppressive; their fanciful charm been so powerfully delineated, and yet so constantly relieved by touches of vigorous sagacity. One single fact shows how great the romantic illusion is. The pressure of painful necessity is scarcely so great in this novel as in novels of the same writer in which the scene is laid in modern times. Much may be said in favour of the mediæval system as contradistinguished from existing society; much has been said. But no one can maintain that general comfort was as much diffused as it is now. A certain ease pervades the structure of later society. Our houses may not last so long, are not so picturesque, will leave no such ruins behind them; but they are warmed with hot water, have no draughts, and contain sofas instead of rushes. A slight daily unconscious luxury is hardly ever wanting to the dwellers in civilisation; like the gentle air of a genial climate, it is a perpetual minute enjoyment. The absence of this marks a rude barbaric time. We may avail ourselves of rough pleasures, stirring amusements, exciting actions, strange rumours; but life is hard and harsh. The cold air of the keen North may brace and invigorate, but it cannot soothe us. All sensible people know that the middle ages must have been very uncomfortable; there was a difficulty about 'good food;'—almost insuperable obstacles to the cultivation of nice detail and small enjoyment. No one knew the abstract facts on which this conclusion rests better than Scott; but his delineation gives no general idea of the result. A thoughtless reader rises with the impression that the middle ages had the same elements of happiness which we have at present, and that they had fighting besides. We do not assert that this tenet is explicitly taught; on the contrary, many facts are explained, and many customs elucidated from which a discriminating and deducing reader would infer the meanness of poverty and the harshness of barbarism. But these less imposing traits escape the rapid, and still more the boyish reader. His general impression is one of romance; and though, when roused, Scott was quite able to take a distinct view of the opposing facts, he liked his own mind to rest for the most part in the same pleasing illusion.

The same sort of historical romance is shown likewise in Scott's picture of remarkable historical characters. His Richard I is the traditional Richard, with traits heightened and ennobled in perfect conformity to the spirit of tradition. Some illustration of the same quality might be drawn from his delineations of the Puritan rebellions and the Cavalier enthusiasm. We might show that he ever dwells on the traits and incidents most attractive to a genial and spirited imagination. But the most remarkable instance of the power which romantic illusion exercised over him is his delineation of Mary Queen of Scots. He refused at one time of his life to write a biography of that princess 'because his opinion was contrary to his feeling'. He evidently considered her guilt to be clearly established, and thought, with a distinguished lawyer, that he should 'direct a jury to find her guilty'; but his fancy, like that of most of his countrymen, took a peculiar and special interest in the beautiful lady who, at any rate, had suffered so much and so fatally at the hands of a queen of England. He could not bring himself to dwell with nice accuracy on the evidence which substantiates her criminality, or on the still clearer indications of that unsound and over-crafty judgment, which was the fatal inheritance of the Stuart family, and which, in spite of advantages that scarcely any other family in the world has enjoyed, has made their name an historical byword for misfortune. The picture in *The Abbot*, one of the best historical pictures which Scott has given us, is principally the picture of the queen as the fond tradition of his countrymen exhibited her. Her entire innocence, it is true, is never alleged: but the enthusiasm of her followers is dwelt on with approving sympathy; their confidence is set forth at large; her influence over them is skilfully delineated; the fascination of charms chastened by misfortune is delicately indicated. We see a complete picture of the beautiful queen, of the suffering and sorrowful but yet not insensible woman. Scott could not, however, as a close study will show us, quite conceal the unfavourable nature of his fundamental opinion. In one remarkable passage the struggle of the judgment is even conspicuous, and in others the sagacity of the practised lawyer,— the thread of the attorney, as he used to call it,—in his nature, qualifies and modifies the sentiment hereditary in his countrymen, and congenial to himself.

This romantic imagination is a habit or power (as we may choose to call it) of mind which is almost essential to the highest success in the historical novel. The aim, at any rate the effect, of this class of works seems to be to deepen and confirm the received view of historical personages. A great and acute writer may from an accurate study of original documents discover that those impressions are erroneous, and by a process of elaborate argument substitute others which he deems more accurate. But this can only be effected by writing a regular history. The essence of the achievement is the proof. If Mr. Froude had put forward his view of Henry the Eighth's character in a professed novel, he would have been laughed at. It is only by a rigid adherence to attested facts and authentic documents, that a view so original could obtain even a hearing. We start back with a little anger from a representation which is avowedly imaginative, and which contradicts our impressions. We do not like to have our opinions disturbed by reasoning; but it is impertinent to attempt to disturb them by fancies. A writer of the historical novel is bound by the popular conception of his subject; and commonly it will be found that this popular impression is to some extent a romantic one. An element of exaggeration clings to the popular judgment: great vices are made greater, great virtues greater also; interesting incidents are made more interesting, softer legends more soft. The novelist who disregards this tendency will do so at the peril of his popularity. His business is to make attraction more attractive, and not to impair the pleasant pictures of ready-made romance by an attempt at grim reality.

We may therefore sum up the indications of this characteristic excellence of Scott's novels by saying, that more than any novelist he has given us fresh pictures of practical human society, with its cares and troubles, its excitements and its pleasures; that he has delineated more distinctly than any one else the framework in which this society inheres, and by the boundaries of which it is shaped and limited; that he has made more clear the way in which strange and eccentric characters grow out of that ordinary and usual system of life; that he has extended his view over several periods of society, and given an animated description of the external appearance of each, and a film representation of its social institutions; that he has shown very graphically what we may call the worldly laws of moral government; and that over all these he has spread the glow of sentiment natural to a manly mind, and an atmosphere of generosity congenial to a cheerful one. It is from the collective effect of these causes, and from the union of sense and sentiment which is the principle of them all, that Scott derives the peculiar healthiness which distinguishes him. There are no such books as his for the sick-room, or for freshening the painful intervals of a morbid mind. Mere sense is dull, mere sentiment unsubstantial; a sensation of genial healthiness is only given by what combines the solidity of the one and the brightening charm of the other.

Some guide to Scott's defects, or to the limitations of his genius, if we would employ a less ungenial and perhaps more correct expression, is to be discovered, as usual, from the consideration of his characteristic excellence. As it is his merit to give bold and animated pictures of this world, it is his defect to give but insufficient representations of qualities which this world does not exceedingly prize, —of such as do not thrust themselves very forward in it—of such as are in some sense above it. We may illustrate this in several ways.

One of the parts of human nature which are systematically omitted in Scott, is the searching and abstract intellect. This did not lie in his way. No man had a stronger sagacity, better adapted for the guidance of common men, and the conduct of common transactions. Few could hope to form a more correct opinion on things and subjects which were brought before him in actual life; no man had a more useful intellect. But on the other hand, as will be generally observed to be the case, no one was less inclined to that probing and seeking and anxious inquiry into things in general which is the necessity of some minds, and a sort of intellectual famine in their nature. He had no call to investigate the theory of the universe, and he would not have been able to comprehend those who did. Such a mind as Shelley's would have been entirely removed from his comprehension. He had no call to mix 'awful talk and asking looks' with his love of the visible scene. He could not have addressed the universe:

'I have watched
Thy shadow, and the darkness of thy steps;

And my heart ever gazes on the depth
Of thy deep mysteries. I have made my bed
In charnels or in coffins, where black death
Keeps records of the trophies won from thee,
Hoping to still these obstinate questionings
Of thee and thine, by forcing some lone ghost,
Thy messenger, to render up the tale
Of what we are.'

Such thoughts would have been to him 'thinking without an object', 'abstracted speculations', 'cobwebs of the unintelligible brain'. Above all minds his had the Baconian propensity to work upon 'stuff'. At first sight, it would not seem that this was a defect likely to be very hurtful to the works of a novelist. The labours of the searching and introspective intellect, however needful, absorbing, and in some degree delicious, to the seeker himself, are not in general very delightful to those who are not seeking. Genial men in middle life are commonly intolerant of that philosophising which their prototype in old times classed side by side with the lisping of youth. The theological novel, which was a few years ago so popular, and which is likely to have a recurring influence in times when men's belief is unsettled, and persons who cannot or will not read large treatises have thoughts in their minds and inquiries in their hearts, suggests to those who are accustomed to it the absence elsewhere of what is necessarily one of its most distinctive and prominent subjects. The desire to attain a belief, which has become one of the most familiar sentiments of heroes and heroines, would have seemed utterly incongruous to the plain sagacity of Scott, and also to his old-fashioned art. Creeds are *data* in his novels: people have different creeds, but each keeps his own. Some persons will think that this is not altogether amiss; nor do we particularly wish to take up the defence of the dogmatic novel. Nevertheless, it will strike those who are accustomed to the youthful generation of a cultivated time, that the passion of intellectual inquiry is one of the strongest impulses in many of them, and one of those which give the predominant colouring to the conversation and exterior mind of many more. And a novelist will not exercise the most potent influence over those subject to that passion if he entirely omit the delineation of it. Scott's works have only one merit in this relation: they are an excellent rest to those who have felt this passion, and have had something too much of it.

The same indisposition to the abstract exercises of the intellect shows itself in the reflective portions of Scott's novels, and perhaps contributes to their popularity with that immense majority of the world who strongly share in that same indisposition: it prevents, however, their having the most powerful intellectual influence on those who have at any time of their lives voluntarily submitted themselves to this acute and refining discipline. The reflections of a practised thinker have a peculiar charm, like the last touches of the accomplished artist. The cunning exactitude of the professional hand leaves a trace in the very language. A nice discrimination of thought makes men solicitous of the most apt expressions to diffuse their thoughts. Both words and meaning gain a metallic brilliancy, like the glittering precision of the pure Attic air. Scott's is a healthy and genial world of reflection, but it wants the charm of delicate exactitude.

The same limitation of Scott's genius shows itself in a very different portion of art—in his delineation of his heroines. The same blunt sagacity of imagination, which fitted him to excel in the rough description of obvious life, rather unfitted him for delineating the less substantial essence of the female character. The nice *minutiæ* of society, by means of which female novelists have been so successful in delineating their own sex, were rather too small for his robust and powerful mind. Perhaps, too, a certain unworldliness of *imagination* is necessary to enable men to comprehend or delineate that essence: unworldliness of *life* is no doubt not requisite; rather, perhaps, worldliness is necessary to the acquisition of a sufficient experience. But an absorption in the practical world does not seem favourable to a comprehension of any thing which does not precisely belong to it. Its interests are too engrossing; its excitements too keen; it modifies the fancy, and in the change unfits it for every thing else. Something, too, in Scott's character and history made it more difficult for him to give a representation of women than of men. Goethe used to say, that his idea of woman was not drawn from his experience, but that it came to him before experience, and that he explained his experience by a reference to it. And though this is a German, and not very happy, form of expression, yet it appears to indicate a very important distinction. Some efforts of the imagination are made so early in life, just as it were at the dawn of the conscious faculties, that we are never able to fancy ourselves as destitute of them. They are part of the mental constitution with which, so to speak, we awoke to existence. These are always far more firm, vivid, and definite, than any other images of our fancy, and we apply them, half unconsciously, to any facts and sentiments and actions which may occur to us later in life, whether arising from within or thrust upon us from the outward world. Goethe doubtless meant that the idea of the female character was to him one of these first elements of imagination; not a thing puzzled out, or which he remembered having conceived, but a part of the primitive conceptions which, being coeval with his memory, seemed inseparable from his consciousness. The descriptions of women likely to be given by this sort of imagination will probably be the best descriptions. A mind which would arrive at this idea of the female character by this process, and so early, would be one obviously of more than usual susceptibility. The early imagination does not commonly take this direction; it thinks most of horses and lances, tournaments and knights; only a mind with an unusual and instinctive tendency to this kind of thought, would be borne thither so early or so effectually. And even independently of this probable peculiarity of the individual, the primitive imagination in general is likely to be the most accurate which men can form; not, of course, of the external manifestations and detailed manners, but of the inner sentiment and characteristic feeling of women. The early imagination conceives what it does conceive very justly; fresh from the facts, stirred by the new aspect of things, undimmed by the daily passage of constantly forgotten images, not misled by the irregular analogies of a dislocated life,—the early mind sees what it does see with a spirit and an intentness never given to it again. A mind like Goethe's, of very strong imagination, aroused at the earliest age,—not of course by passions, but by an unusual strength in that undefined longing which is the prelude to our passions,—will form the best idea of the inmost female nature which masculine nature can form. The trace is evident in the characters of women formed by Goethe's imagination or Shakespeare's, and those formed by such an imagination as that of Scott. The latter seems so external. We have traits, features, manners; we know the heroine as she appeared in the street; in some degree we know how she talked, but we never know how she felt—least of all what she was: we always feel there is a world behind, unanalysed, unrepresented, which we cannot attain to. Such a character as Margaret in *Faust* is known to us to the very soul; so is Imogen; so is Ophelia. Edith Bellenden, Flora Macivor, Miss Wardour, are young ladies who, we are told, were good-looking, and well-dressed (according to the old fashion) and sensible; but we feel we know but very little of them, and they do not haunt our imaginations. The failure of Scott in this line of art is more conspicuous, because he had not in any remarkable degree the later experience of female detail, with which some minds have endeavoured to supply the want of the early essential imagination, and which Goethe possessed in addition to it. It was rather late, according to his biographer, before Scott set up for 'a squire of dames'; he was a 'lame young man, very enthusiastic about ballad poetry'; he was deeply in love with a young lady, supposed to be imaginatively represented by Flora Macivor, but he was unsuccessful. It would be over-ingenious to argue, from his failing in a single love-affair, that he had no peculiar interest in young ladies in general; but the whole description of his youth shows that young ladies exercised over him a rather more divided influence than is usual. Other pursuits intervened, much more than is common with persons of the imaginative temperament, and he never led the life of flirtation from which Goethe believed that he derived so much instruction. Scott's heroines, therefore, are, not unnaturally, faulty, since from a want of the very peculiar instinctive imagination he could not give us the essence of women, and from the habits of his life he could not delineate to us their detailed life with the appreciative accuracy of habitual experience. Jeanie Deans is probably the best of his heroines, and she is so because she is the least of a heroine. The plain matter-of-fact element in the peasant-girl's life and circumstances suited a robust imagination. There is little in the part of her character that is very finely described which is characteristically feminine. She is not a masculine, but she is an epicene heroine. Her love-affair with Butler, a single remarkable scene excepted, is rather commonplace than otherwise.

A similar criticism might be applied to Scott's heroes. Every one feels how commonplace they are—Waverley excepted, whose very vacillation gives him a sort of character. They have little personality. They are all of the same type;—excellent young men—rather strong—able to ride and climb and jump. They are always said to be sensible, and bear out the character by being not unwilling sometimes to talk platitudes. But we know nothing of their inner life. They are said to be in love; but we have no special account of their individual sentiments. People show their character in their love more than in any thing else. These young gentlemen all love in the same way—in the vague commonplace way of this world. We have no sketch or dramatic expression of the life within. Their souls are quite unknown to us. If there is an exception, it is Edgar Ravenswood. But if we look closely, we may observe that the notion which we obtain of his character, unusually broad as it is, is not a notion of him in his capacity of hero, but in his capacity of distressed peer. His proud poverty gives a distinctness which otherwise his lineaments would not have. We think little of his love; we think much of his narrow circumstances and compressed haughtiness.

The same exterior delineation of character shows itself in its treatment of men's religious nature. A novelist is scarcely, in the notion of ordinary readers, bound to deal with this at all; if he does, it will be one of his great difficulties to indicate it graphically, yet without dwelling on it. Men who purchase a novel do not wish a stone or a sermon. All lengthened reflections must be omitted; the whole armory of pulpit eloquence. But no delineation of human nature can be considered complete which omits to deal with man in relation to the questions which occupy him as man, with his convictions as to the theory of the universe and his own destiny; the human heart throbs on few subjects with a passion so intense, so peculiar, and so typical. From an artistic view, it is a blunder to omit an element which is so characteristic of human life, which contributes so much to its animation, and which is so picturesque. A reader of a more simple mind, little apt to indulge in such criticism, feels 'a want of depth', as he would speak, in delineations from which so large an element of his own most passionate and deepest nature is omitted. It can hardly be said that there is an omission of the religious nature in Scott. But at the same time there is no adequate delineation of it. If we refer to the facts of his life, and the view of his character which we collect from thence, we shall find that his religion was of a qualified and double sort. He was a genial man of the world, and had the easy faith in the kindly *Dieu des bons gens*[1] which is natural to such a person; and he had also a half-poetic principle of superstition in his nature, inclining him to believe in ghosts, legends, fairies, and elfs, which did not affect his daily life, or possibly his superficial belief, but was nevertheless very constantly present to his fancy, and affected, as is the constitution of human nature, by that frequency, the indefined, half-expressed, inexpressible feelings which are at the root of that belief. Superstition was a kind of Jacobitism in his religion; as a sort of absurd reliance on the hereditary principle modified insensibly his leanings in the practical world, so a belief in the existence of unevidenced, and often absurd, supernatural beings, qualifies his commonest speculations on the higher world. Both these elements may be thought to enter into the highest religion; there is a principle of cheerfulness which will justify in its measure a genial enjoyment, and also a principle of fear which those who think only of that enjoyment will deem superstition, and which will really become superstition in

[1] 'God of the good people', title of a song by Béranger.

the over-anxious and credulous acceptor of it. But in a true religion these two elements will be combined. The character of God images itself very imperfectly in any human soul; but in the highest it images itself as a whole; it leaves an abiding impression which will justify anxiety and allow of happiness. The highest aim of the religious novelist would be to show how this operates in human character; to exhibit in their curious modification our religious love, and also our religious fear. In the novels of Scott the two elements appear in a state of separation, as they did in his own mind. We have the superstition of the peasantry in *The Antiquary*, in *Guy Mannering*, every where almost; we have likewise a pervading tone of genial easy reflection characteristic of the man of the world who produced, and agreeable to the people of the world who read, these works. But we have no picture of the two in combination. We are scarcely led to think on the subject at all, so much do other subjects distract our interest; but if we do think, we are puzzled at the contrast. We do not know which is true, the uneasy belief of superstition, or the easy satisfaction of the world; we waver between the two, and have no suggestion even hinted to us of the possibility of a reconciliation. The character of the Puritans certainly did not in general embody such a reconciliation, but it might have been made by a sympathising artist the vehicle for a delineation of a struggle after it. The two elements of love and fear ranked side by side in their minds with an intensity which is rare even in minds that feel only one of them. The delineation of Scott is amusing, but superficial. He caught the ludicrous traits which tempt the mirthful imagination, but no other side of the character pleased him. The man of the world was displeased with their obstinate interfering zeal; their intensity of faith was an opposition force in the old Scotch polity, of which he liked to fancy the harmonious working. They were superstitious enough; but nobody likes other people's superstitions. Scott's were of a wholly different kind. He made no difficulty as to the observance of Christmas-day, and would have eaten potatoes without the faintest scruple, although their name does not occur in Scripture. Doubtless also his residence in the land of Puritanism did not incline him to give any thing except a satirical representation of that belief. You must not expect from a Dissenter a faithful appreciation of the creed from which he dissents. You cannot be impartial on the religion of the place in which you live; you may believe it, or you may dislike it; it crosses your path in too many forms for you to be able to look at it with equanimity. Scott had rather a rigid form of Puritanism forced upon him in his infancy; it is asking too much to expect him to be partial to it. The aspect of religion which Scott delineates best is that which appears in griefs, especially in the grief of strong characters. His strong *natural* nature felt the power of death. He has given us many pictures of rude and simple men subdued, if only for a moment, into devotion by its presence.

On the whole, and speaking roughly, these defects in the delineation which Scott has given us of human life are but two. He omits to give us a delineation of the soul. We have mind, manners, animation, but it is the stir of this world. We miss the consecrating power; and we miss it not only in its own peculiar sphere, which, from the difficulty of introducing the deepest elements into a novel, would have been scarcely matter for a harsh criticism, but in the place in which a novelist might most be expected to delineate it. There are perhaps such things as the love-affairs of immortal beings, but no one would learn it from Scott. His heroes and heroines are well dressed for this world, but not for another; there is nothing even in their love which is suitable for immortality. As has been noticed, Scott also omits any delineation of the abstract unworldly intellect. This too might not have been so severe a reproach, considering its undramatic, unanimated nature, if it had stood alone; but taken in connection with the omission which we have just spoken of, it is most important. As the union of sense and romance makes the world of Scott so characteristically agreeable,—a fascinating picture of this world in the light in which we like best to dwell in it, so the deficiency in the attenuated, striving intellect, as well as in the supernatural soul, gives to the 'world' of Scott the cumbrousness and temporality, in short, the materialism, which is characteristic of the world.

We have dwelt so much on what we think are the characteristic features of Scott's imaginative representations, that we have left ourselves no room to criticise the two most natural points of criticism in a novelist—plot and style. This is not, however, so important in Scott's case as it would commonly be. He used to say, 'It was of no use having a plot; you could not keep to it.' He modified and changed his thread of story from day to day,—sometimes even from bookselling reasons, and on the suggestion of others. An elaborate work of narrative art could not be produced in this way, every one will concede; the highest imagination, able to look far over the work, is necessary for that task. But the plots produced, so to say, by the pen of the writer as he passes over the events are likely to have a freshness and a suitableness to those events, which is not possessed by the inferior writers who make up a mechanical plot before they commence. The procedure of the highest genius doubtless is scarcely a procedure: the view of the whole story comes at once upon its imagination like the delicate end and the distinct beginning of some long vista. But all minds do not possess the highest mode of conception; and among lower modes, it is doubtless better to possess the vigorous fancy which creates each separate scene in succession as it goes, than the pedantic intellect which designs every thing long before it is wanted. There is a play in unconscious creation which no voluntary elaboration and preconceived fitting of distinct ideas can ever hope to produce. If the whole cannot be created by one bounding effort, it is better that each part should be created separately and in detail.

The style of Scott would deserve the highest praise if M. Thiers could establish his theory of narrative language. He maintains that an historian's language approaches perfection in proportion as it aptly communicates what is meant to be narrated without drawing any attention to itself. Scott's style fulfils this condition. Nobody rises from his works without a most vivid idea of what is related, and no one is able to quote a single phrase in which it has been narrated. We are inclined, however, to differ from the great French historian, and to oppose to him a theory derived from a very different writer. Coleridge used to maintain that all good poetry was untranslatable into words of the same language without injury to the sense: the meaning was, in his view, to be so inseparably intertwined even with the shades of the language, that the change of a single expression would make a difference in the accompanying feeling, if not in the bare signification: consequently, all good poetry must be remembered exactly,—to change a word is to modify the essence. Rigidly this theory can only be applied to a few kinds of poetry, or special passages in which the imagination is exerting itself to the utmost, and collecting from the whole range of associated language the very expressions which it requires. The highest excitation of feeling is necessary to this peculiar felicity of choice. In calmer moments the mind has either a less choice, or less acuteness of selective power. Accordingly, in prose it would be absurd to expect any such nicety. Still, on great occasions in imaginative fiction, there should be passages in which the words seem to cleave to the matter. The excitement is as great as in poetry. The words should become part of the sense. They should attract our attention, as this is necessary to impress them on the memory; but they should not in so doing distract attention from the meaning conveyed. On the contrary, it is their inseparability from their meaning which gives them their charm and their power. In truth, Scott's language, like his sense, was such as became a bold sagacious man of the world. He used the first sufficient words which came uppermost, and seems hardly to have been sensible, even in the works of others, of that exquisite accuracy and inexplicable appropriateness of which we have been speaking.

To analyse in detail the faults and merits of even a few of the greatest of the Waverley Novels would be impossible in the space at our command on the present occasion. We have only attempted a general account of a few main characteristics. Every critic must, however, regret to have to leave topics so tempting to remark as many of Scott's stories, and a yet greater number of his characters.

58. H. A. Taine on Scott

1863

An extract from the third volume of Taine's *Histoire de la littérature anglaise* (1863-4). The translator is H. Van Laun.

The Lady of the Lake, Marmion, The Lord of the Isles, The Fair Maid of Perth, Old Mortality, Ivanhoe, Quentin Durward, who does not know these names by heart? From Walter Scott we learned history. And yet is this history? All these pictures of a distant age are false. Costumes, scenery, externals alone are exact; actions, speech, sentiments, all the rest is civilized, embellished, arranged in modern guise. We might suspect it when looking at the character and life of the author; for what does he desire, and what do the guests, eager to hear him, demand? Is he a lover of truth as it is, foul and fierce; an inquisitive explorer, indifferent to contemporary applause, bent alone on defining the transformations of living nature? By no means. He is in history, as he is at Abbotsford, bent on arranging points of view and Gothic halls. The moon will come in well there between the towers; here is a nicely placed breastplate, the ray of light which it throws back is pleasant to see on these old hangings; suppose we took out the feudal garments from the wardrobe and invited the guests to a masquerade? The entertainment would be a fine one, in accordance with their reminiscences and their aristocratic principles. English lords, fresh from a bitter war against French democracy, ought to enter zealously into this commemoration of their ancestors. Moreover, there are ladies and young girls, and we must arrange the show, so as not to shock their severe morality and their delicate feelings, make them weep becomingly; not put on the stage overstrong passions, which they would not understand; on the contrary, select heroines to resemble them, always touching, but above all correct; young gentlemen, Evandale, Morton, Ivanhoe, irreproachably brought up, tender and grave, even slightly melancholic (it is the latest fashion), and worthy to lead them to the altar. Is there a man more suited than the author to compose such a spectacle? He is a good Protestant, a good husband, a good father, very moral, so decided a Tory that he carries off as a relic a glass from which the king has just drunk. In addition, he has neither talent nor leisure to reach the depths of his characters. He devotes himself to the exterior; he sees and describes forms and externals much more at length than inward feelings. Again, he treats his mind like a coal-mine, serviceable for quick working, and for the greatest possible gain: a volume in a month, sometimes in a fortnight even, and this volume is worth one thousand pounds. How should he discover, or how dare exhibit, the structure of barbarous souls? This structure is too difficult to discover, and too little pleasing to show. Every two centuries, amongst men, the proportion of images and ideas, the mainspring of passions, the degree of reflection, the species of inclinations, change. Who, without a long preliminary training, now understands and relishes Dante, Rabelais, and Rubens? And how, for instance, could these great Catholic and mystical dreams, these vast temerities, or these impurities of carnal art, find entrance into the head of this gentlemanly citizen? Walter Scott pauses on the threshold of the soul, and in the vestibule of history, selects in the Renaissance and the Middle Ages only the fit and agreeable, blots out plain spoken words, licentious sensuality, bestial ferocity. After all, his characters, to whatever age he transports them, are his neighbours, 'cannie' farmers, vain lairds, gloved gentlemen, young marriageable ladies, all more or less commonplace, that is, steady; by their education and character at a great distance from the voluptuous fools of the Restoration, or the heroic brutes and fierce beasts of the Middle Ages. As he has the greatest supply of rich costumes, and the most inexhaustible talent for scenic effect, he makes all his people get on very pleasantly, and composes tales which, in truth, have only the merit of fashion, though that fashion may last a hundred years yet.

That which he himself acted lasted for a shorter time. To sustain his princely hospitality and his feudal magnificence, he went into partnership with his printers; lord of the manor in public and merchant in private, he gave them his signature, without keeping a check over the use they made of it. Bankruptcy followed; at the age of fifty-five he was ruined, and one hundred and seventeen thousand pounds in debt. With admirable courage and uprightness he refused all favour, accepting nothing but time, set to work on the very day, wrote untiringly, in four years paid seventy thousand pounds, exhausted his brain so as to become paralytic, and to perish in the attempt. Neither in his conduct nor his literature did his feudal tastes succeed, and his manorial splendour was as fragile as his Gothic imaginations. He had relied on imitation, and we live by truth only; his glory is to be found elsewhere; there was something solid in his mind as well as in his writings. Beneath the lover of the Middle Ages we find, first the 'pawky' Scotchman, an attentive observer, whose sharpness became more intense by his familiarity with law; a good-natured man, easy and cheerful, as beseems the national character, so different from the English. One of his walking companions (Shortreed) said: 'Eh me, sic an endless fund o' humour and drollery as he had wi' him! Never ten yards but we were either laughing or roaring and singing. Wherever we stopped, how brawlie he suited himsel' to everybody! He aye did as the lave did; never made himsel' the great man, or took ony airs in the company.' Grown older and graver, he was none the less amiable, the most agreeable of hosts, so that one of his guests, a farmer, I think, said to his wife, when home, after having been at Abbotsford, 'Ailie, my woman, I'm ready for my bed . . . I wish I could sleep for a towmont, for there's only ae thing in this warld worth living for, and that's the Abbotsford hunt!'

In addition to a mind of this kind, he had all-discerning eyes, an all-retentive memory, a ceaseless studiousness which comprehended the whole of Scotland, and all classes of people; and we see his true talent arise, so agreeable, so abundant and so easy, made up of minute observation and gentle raillery, recalling at once Teniers and Addison. Doubtless he wrote badly, at times in the worst possible manner:[1] it is clear that he dictated, hardly re-read his writing, and readily fell into a pasty and emphatic style,—a style very common in the present times, and which we read day after day in prospectuses and newspapers. What is worse, he is terribly long and diffuse; his conversations and descriptions are interminable; he is determined, at all events, to fill three volumes. But he has given to Scotland a citizenship of literature—I mean to the whole of Scotland: scenery, monuments, houses, cottages, characters of every age and condition, from the baron to the fisherman, from the advocate to the beggar, from the lady to the fishwife. When we mention merely his name they crowd forward; who does not see them coming from every niche of memory? The Baron of Bradwardine, Dominie Sampson, Meg Merrilies, the antiquary, Edie Ochiltree, Jeanie Deans and her father,—innkeepers, shopkeepers, old wives, an entire people. What Scotch features are absent? Saving, patient, 'cannie', and of course 'pawky'; the poverty of the soil and the difficulty of existence has compelled them to be so: this is the specialty of the race. The same tenacity which they introduced into everyday affairs they have introduced into mental concerns,—studious readers and perusers of antiquities and controversies, poets also; legends spring up readily in a romantic land, amidst time-honoured wars and brigandism. In a land thus prepared, and in this gloomy clime, Presbyterianism sunk its sharp roots. Such was the real and modern world, lit up by the far-setting sun of chivalry, as Sir Walter Scott found it; like a painter who, passing from great show-pictures, finds interest and beauty in the ordinary houses of a paltry provincial town, or in a farm surrounded by beds of beetroots and turnips. A continuous archness throws its smile over these interior and *genre* pictures, so local and minute, and which, like the Flemish, indicate the rise of well-to-do citizens. Most of these good folk are comic. Our author makes fun of them, brings out their little deceits, parsimony, fooleries, vulgarity, and the hundred thousand ridiculous habits people always contract in a narrow sphere of life. A barber, in *The Antiquary*, moves heaven and earth about his wigs; if the French Revolution takes root everywhere, it was because the magistrates gave up this ornament. He cries out in a lamentable

---

[1] See the opening of *Ivanhoe*: 'Such being our chief scene, the date of our story refers to a period towards the end of the reign of Richard I, when his return from his long captivity had become an event rather wished than hoped for by his despairing subjects, who were in the meantime subjected to every species of subordinate oppression.' It is impossible to write in a heavier style [Taine].

voice: 'Haud a care, haud a care, Monkbarns! God's sake, haud a care!—Sir Arthur's drowned already, and an ye fa' over the cleugh too, there will be but ae wig left in the parish, and that's the minister's.' Mark how the author smiles, and without malice: the barber's candid selfishness is the effect of the man's calling, and does not repel us. Walter Scott is never bitter; he loves men from the bottom of his heart, excuses or tolerates them; does not chastise vices, but unmasks them, and that not rudely. His greatest pleasure is to pursue at length, not indeed a vice, but a hobby; the mania for odds and ends in an antiquary, the archaeological vanity of the Baron of Bradwardine, the aristocratic drivel of the Dowager Lady Bellenden,—that is, the amusing exaggeration of an allowable taste; and this without anger, because, on the whole, these ridiculous people are estimable, and even generous. Even in rogues like Dirk Hatteraick, in cut-throats like Bothwell, he allows some goodness. In no one, not even in Major Dalgetty, a professional murderer, a result of the thirty years' war, is the odious unveiled by the ridiculous. In this critical refinement and this benevolent philosophy, he resembles Addison.

He resembles him again by the purity and endurance of his moral principles. His amanuensis, Mr. Laidlaw, told him that he was doing great good by his attractive and noble tales, and that young people would no longer wish to look in the literary rubbish of the circulating libraries. When Walter Scott heard this, his eyes filled with tears: 'On his deathbed he said to his son-in-law: "Lockhart, I may have but a minute to speak to you. My dear, be a good man—be virtuous, be religious—be a good man. Nothing else will give you any comfort when you come to lie here." ' This was almost his last word. By this fundamental honesty and this broad humanity, he was the Homer of modern citizen life. Around and after him, the novel of manners, separated from the historical romance, has produced a whole literature, and preserved the character which he stamped upon it. Miss Austen, Miss Brontë, Mrs. Gaskell, George Eliot, Bulwer, Thackeray, Dickens, and many others, paint, especially or entirely in his style, contemporary life, as it is, unembellished, in all ranks, often amongst the people, more frequently still amongst the middle class. And the causes which made the historical novel come to naught, in Scott and others, made the novel of manners, by the same authors, succeed. These men were too minute copyists and too decided moralists, incapable of the great divinations and the wide sympathies which unlock the door of history; their imagination was too literal, and their judgment too unwavering. It is precisely by these faculties that they created a new species of novel, which multiplies to this day in thousands of offshoots, with such abundance, that men of talent in this branch of literature may be counted by hundreds, and that we can only compare them, for their original and national spirit, to the great age of Dutch painting. Realistic and moral, these are their two features. They are far removed from the great imagination which creates and transforms, as it appeared in the Renaissance or in the seventeenth century, in the heroic or noble ages. They renounce free invention; they narrow themselves to scrupulous exactness; they paint with infinite detail costumes and places, changing nothing; they mark little shades of language; they are not disgusted by vulgarities or platitudes. Their information is authentic and precise. In short, they write like citizens for fellow-citizens, that is, for well-ordered people, members of a profession, whose imagination does not soar high, and sees things through a magnifying glass, unable to relish anything in the way of a picture except interiors and make-believes. Ask a cook which picture she prefers in the Museum, and she will point to a kitchen, in which the stewpans are so well painted that a man is tempted to put soup and bread in them. Yet beyond this inclination, which is now European, Englishmen have a special craving, which with them is national and dates from the preceding century; they desire that the novel, like all other things, should contribute to their great work,—the amelioration of man and society. They ask from it the glorification of virtue, and the chastisement of vice. They send it into all the corners of civil society, and all the events of private history, in search of examples and expedients, to learn thence the means of remedying abuses, succouring miseries, avoiding temptations. They make of it an instrument of inquiry, education, and morality. A singular work, which has not its equal in all history, because in all history there has been no society like it, and which—of moderate attraction for lovers of the beautiful, admirable to lovers of the useful—offers, in the countless variety of its painting, and the invariable stability of its spirit, the picture of the only democracy which knows how to restrain, govern, and reform itself.

59. Henry James, *North American Review*

1864

Unsigned review of Nassau Senior's *Essays on Fiction* by Henry James, *North American Review* (October 1864), xcix, 580-7.

For Senior's criticism of Scott, see No. 29. James's opening section, which attacks Senior as a 'Half-critic', has been omitted.

He begins with Sir Walter Scott. The articles of which the paper on Scott is composed were written while the Waverley Novels were in their first editions. In our opinion this fact is their chief recommendation. It is interesting to learn the original effect of these remarkable books. It is pleasant to see their classical and time-honoured figures dealt with as the latest sensations of the year. In the year 1821, the authorship of the novels was still unavowed. But we may gather from several of Mr. Senior's remarks the general tendency of the public faith. The reviewer has several sly hits at the author of *Marmion*. He points out a dozen coincidences in the talent and treatment of the poet and the romancer. And he leaves the intelligent reader to draw his own conclusions. After a short preface he proceeds to the dismemberment of each of the novels, from *Rob Roy* downward. In retracing one by one these long-forgotten plots and counter-plots, we yield once more to something of the great master's charm. We are inclined to believe that this charm is proof against time. The popularity which Mr. Senior celebrated forty years ago has in no measure subsided. The only perceptible change in Sir Walter's reputation is indeed the inevitable lot of great writers. He has submitted to the somewhat attenuating ordeal of classification; he has become a standard author. He has been provided with a seat in our literature; and if his visible stature has been by just so much curtailed, we must remember that it is only the passing guests who remain standing. Mr. Senior is a great admirer of Sir Walter, as may be gathered from the fact that he devotes two hundred pages to him. And yet he has a keen eye for his defects; and these he correctly holds to be very numerous. Yet he still loves him in spite of his defects; which we think will be the permanent attitude of posterity.

Thirty years have elapsed since the publication of the last of the Waverley series. During thirty years it has been exposed to the public view. And meanwhile an immense deal has been accomplished in the department of fiction. A vast army has sprung up, both of producers and consumers. To the latter class a novel is no longer the imposing phenomenon it was in Sir Walter's time. It implies no very great talent; ingenuity is held to be the chief requisite for success. And indeed to write a readable novel is actually a task of so little apparent difficulty, that with many popular writers the matter is a constant trial of speed with the reading public. This was very much the case with Sir Walter. His facility in composition was almost as great as that of Mrs. Henry Wood, of modern repute. But it was the fashion among his critics to attribute this remarkable fact rather to his transcendent strength than to the vulgarity of his task. This was a wise conviction. Mrs. Wood writes three volumes in three months, to last three months. Sir Walter performed the same feat, and here, after the lapse of forty years, we still linger over those hasty pages. And we do it in the full cognizance of faults which even Mrs. Wood has avoided, of foibles for which she would blush. The public taste has been educated to a spirit of the finest discernment, the sternest exaction. No publisher would venture to offer *Ivanhoe* in the year 1864 as a novelty. The secrets of the novelist's craft have been laid bare; new contrivances have been invented; and as fast as the old machinery wears out, it is repaired by the clever artisans of the day. Our modern ingenuity works prodigies of which the great Wizard never dreamed. And besides ingenuity we have had plenty of genius. We have had Dickens and Thackeray. Twenty other famous writers are working in the midst of us. The authors of *Amyas Leigh*, of *The Cloister and the Hearth*, of *Romola*, have all overtaken the author of *Waverley* in his own walk. Sir Edward Bulwer has produced several historical tales, which, to use an expressive vulgarism, have 'gone down' very extensively. And yet old-fashioned, ponderous Sir Walter holds his own.

He was the inventor of a new style. We all know the immense advantage a craftsman derives from this fact. He was the first to sport a fashion which was eventually taken up. For many years he enjoyed the good fortune of a patentee. It is difficult for the present generation to appreciate the blessings of this fashion. But when we review the modes prevailing for twenty years before, we see almost as great a difference as a sudden transition from the Spenserian ruff to the Byronic collar. We may best express Scott's character by saying that, with one or two exceptions, he was the first English prose story-teller. He was the first fictitious writer who addressed the public from its own level, without any preoccupation of place. Richardson is classified simply by the matter of length. He is neither a romancer nor a story-teller: he is simply Richardson. The works of Fielding and Smollett are less monumental, yet we cannot help feeling that they too are writing for an age in which a single novel is meant to go a great way. And then these three writers are emphatically preachers and moralists. In the heart of their productions lurks a didactic *raison d'être*. Even Smollett—who at first sight appears to recount his heroes' adventures very much as Leporello in the opera rehearses the exploits of Don Juan—aims to instruct and to edify. To posterity one of the chief attractions of *Tom Jones* is the fact that its author was one of the masses, that he wrote from the midst of the working, suffering mortal throng. But we feel guilty in reading the book in any such disposition of mind. We feel guilty, indeed, in admitting the question of art or science into our considerations. The story is like a vast episode in a sermon preached by a grandly humorous divine; and however we may be entertained by the way, we must not forget that our ultimate duty is to be instructed. With the minister's week-day life we have no concern: for the present he is awful, impersonal Morality; and we shall incur his severest displeasure if we view him as Henry Fielding, Esq., as a rakish man of letters, or even as a figure in English literature. *Waverley* was the first novel which was self-forgetful. It proposed simply to amuse the reader, as an old English ballad amused him. It undertook to prove nothing but facts. It was the novel irresponsible.

We do not mean to say that Scott's great success was owing solely to this, the freshness of his method. This was, indeed, of great account, but it was as nothing compared with his own intellectual wealth. Before him no prose-writer had exhibited so vast and rich an imagination: it had not, indeed, been supposed that in prose the imaginative faculty was capable of such extended use. Since Shakespeare, no writer had created so immense a gallery of portraits, nor, on the whole, had any portraits been so lifelike. Men and women, for almost the first time out of poetry, were presented in their habits as they lived. The Waverley characters were all instinct with something of the poetic fire. To our present taste many of them may seem little better than lay-figures. But there are many kinds of lay-figures. A person who goes from the workshop of a carver of figure-heads for ships to an exhibition of wax-work, will find in the latter the very reflection of nature. And even when occasionally the waxen visages are somewhat inexpressive, he can console himself with the sight of unmistakable velvet and brocade and tartan. Scott went to his prose task with essentially the same spirit which he had brought to the composition of his poems. Between these two departments of his work the difference is very small. Portions of *Marmion* are very good prose; portions of *Old Mortality* are tolerable poetry. Scott was never a very deep, intense, poetic poet: his verse alone was unflagging. So when he attacked his prose characters with his habitual poetic inspiration, the harmony of style was hardly violated. It is a great peculiarity, and perhaps it is one of the charms of his historical tales, that history is dealt with in all poetic reverence. He is tender of the past: he knows that she is frail. He certainly knows it. Sir Walter could not have read so widely or so curiously as he did, without discovering a vast deal that was gross and ignoble in bygone times. But he excludes these elements as if he feared they would clash with his numbers. He has the same indifference to historic truth as an epic poet, without, in the novels, having the same excuse. We write historical tales differently now. We acknowledge the beauty and propriety of a certain poetic reticence. But we confine it to poetry. The task of the historical story-teller is, not to invest, but to divest the past. Tennyson's *Idyls of the King* are far more one-sided, if we may so express it, than anything of Scott's. But imagine what disclosures we should have if Mr. Charles Reade were to take it into his head to write a novel about King Arthur and his times.

Having come thus far, we are arrested by the sudden conviction that it is useless to dogmatize upon Scott; that it is almost ungrateful to criticize him. He, least of all, would have invited or sanctioned any curious investigation of his works. They were written without pretence: all that has been claimed for them has been claimed by others than their author. They are emphatically works of entertainment. As such let us cherish and preserve them. Say what we will, we should be very sorry to lose, and equally sorry to mend them. There are few of us but can become sentimental over the uncounted hours they have cost us. There are moments of high-strung sympathy with the spirit which is abroad when we might find them rather dull—in parts; but they are capital books to have read. Who would forego the companionship of all those shadowy figures which stand side by side in their morocco niches in yonder mahogany cathedral? What youth would willingly close his eyes upon that dazzling array of female forms,—so serried that he can hardly see where to choose,—Rebecca of York, Edith Plantagenet, Mary of Scotland, sweet Lucy Ashton? What maiden would consent to drop the dear acquaintance of Halbert Glendinning, of Wilfred of Ivanhoe, of Roland Græme and Henry Morton? Scott was a born story-teller: we can give him no higher praise. Surveying his works, his character, his method, as a whole, we can liken him to nothing better than to a strong and kindly elder brother, who gathers his juvenile public about him at eventide, and pours out a stream of wondrous improvisation. Who cannot remember an experience like this? On no occasion are the delights of fiction so intense. Fiction? These are the triumphs of fact. In the richness of his invention and memory, in the infinitude of his knowledge, in his improvidence for the future, in the skill with which he answers, or rather parries, sudden questions, in his low-voiced pathos and his resounding merriment, he is identical with the ideal fireside chronicler. And thoroughly to enjoy him, we must again become as credulous as children at twilight.

[a final short section in which James attacks Senior's remarks on Thackeray, Bulwer-Lytton, and Mrs. Stowe, is omitted]

60. Mrs. Oliphant to the defence, *Blackwood's Magazine*
1871

Excerpts from an unsigned article in a series, 'A Century of Great Poets', *Blackwood's Magazine* (August 1871), cx, 229-56.

The author of the article, Margaret Oliphant, was a novelist and literary historian.

This is the distinction of Scott's poetry: it is not profound, nor very lofty; it touches upon none of the deeper questions that agitate and confuse humanity. Its life and movement are on the surface, not veiled in mystery, or even haziness. The child enters into its meaning, while the oldest are stirred by it. It is simple and straightforward in its lyrical brightness. With a true sense at once of the power and of the limitations of his craft, the Minstrel puts nothing in his song which cannot be sung. And the very nature of the song forbids any over-vivacity of dramatic power, for the work is not a drama in which every man has to speak for himself, but a narrative proceeding from the lips of one. To compare this poetry with that of Wordsworth, for instance, would be a simple absurdity; it would be like comparing the Tay to the Thames. The well-trained, useful, majestic stream, which carries trade and wealth into the very bosom of the land, is as unlike as possible to the wayward child of the mountains, rushing against its rocks with wreaths and dashing clouds of spray, unfit to bear a boat for any steady progression, yet flowing on strongly, brightly, picturesquely, charming all eyes that look upon it, and delighting all hearts.

We do not of course mean this to apply to *The Lay of the Last Minstrel* only, but to its successors as well. In all these poems there is the same rapid, brilliant motion—the same animated variety of scenery and incident—the same warm, full tide of life.

Thus the greater artist had already begun to form and show himself within those early garments of poetry. This is, we think, the great distinction of *The Lady of the Lake*. His former poems have just enough humanity to interest the reader in the rapid course of the tale; but here the great Maker finds himself unable longer to refrain from putting character into his poetic creations. It was perhaps a dangerous experiment; for the art of the minstrel is too light, too swift, too essentially musical, to be weighted with such grave necessities of detail. In *Marmion* there is no character-painting. The great lord himself does and says nothing which can make us believe in the forged letters, or indeed which can help us to any insight into his probable proceedings one way or another. We accept him on the poet's showing in what character he pleases. Neither is De Wilton more distinct, nor the sweet conventional medieval figure of Clare. It is better for the poem that they should not be so; for it is a vivid narrative of events, not an inquiry into the secrets of human nature. And where was there ever found a broader landscape, or one more full of atmosphere and sunshine, than that great picture which opens upon the southern noble and his train as they approach Edinburgh? or where a more glowing and splendid sketch than that midnight scene at the Cross? or where such a battle-piece as that of Flodden? This is true minstrelsy, the song flung from rapid harp and voice, the strain of the primitive chronicler. The warm impulse of external life thrills through every line. There is no time nor place for details of individual humanity, nor for the deeper thoughts and emotions which clog and curb all instantaneous action. The minstrel cannot pause to disentangle that confused and confusing network. This is not his vocation in the world.

Thus the poems of Scott were but as the preface to his work. His real and enduring glory is in his novels—the fuller and greater drama which did not naturally with him shape itself into verse, and which was quite beyond the minstrel's sphere. There is a certain confusion here in words, which we trust may not involve our meaning to the reader's apprehension. Scott was a great poet—one of the greatest—but not in verse. In verse he is ever and at all times a minstrel, and nothing more. He is the modern representative of that most perennially popular of all characters, the bard who weaves into living song the exploits and the adventures of heroes. It is no mean band, for Homer stands at the head of it, supreme in the love and admiration of all the ages; but it is essentially different from the other schools of poetry which have flourished among us, and in more recent times. It does not admit of the great impersonations of the drama proper, and at the same time it forbids, as strictly as the true drama forbids, those explanations which are permitted to reflective and philosophical poetry. The impression it makes must be conveyed rapidly, without interruption to the song; the narrative must flow swift as a stream, vivid and direct to its end. The primitive passions, the motives known to all men, the great principles of life which all can comprehend and even divine, are the materials in which alone it ever works. The fact must never be lost sight of, that the tale is told by one voice, and that this one voice *sings*. The story has to be done at a hearing, or at two or three hearings, but must, by its nature, never be allowed to flag or become monotonous. Neither can it be permitted to be elaborate. Directness, simplicity, comprehensibleness, are absolute necessities to it. No one must pause to ask what does this or that mean. To thrill the listeners with a rapidly-succeeding variety of emotions—to hold them breathless in suspense for the *dénouement*—to carry them along with the hero through some rapid adventure—these are the minstrel's powers. If he lays his hand on the more complicated chords of existence, and tries to unravel the deeper mysteries, he forsakes his sphere. Hamlet and Lear are impossible to him, and so are the musings of Jacques, and even the delicious trifling of Rosalind. His is a hasty muse, with staff in hand and shoes on feet. He must be doing at all hazards. He must know how to relieve the strain upon his audience by a rapid change of subject, but never by a pause. Thus he stands apart among the ranks of the poets—a great artist in his way, the most popular perhaps of all—but never attaining to that highest sphere in which the crowned singers dwell.

This is Scott's position in what is called his poetry as distinct from his prose writings, and we think it is a mistaken love which claims a higher for him.

The curious breadth of Scott's character is apparent also in the fact that he has given us every possible kind of man and woman to add to the population of our world. Almost all other writers have been limited in this respect. In our own day, Dickens had his special kind of character which he could bring out to perfection—Thackeray his—and Lord Lytton his; but Scott, like Shakespeare, has a world of men under his belt. From Jenny Dennison, up to Rebecca the Jewess, what a range of variety; from Coeur-de-Lion to Dirk Hatteraick! and yet they are all so vivid that we might (as people say) shake hands with them. Every one of his figures is an individual study. They are not divided into classes, as is so usual even with novelists of genius, who have one stock old man whom they vary at their will, one humorous character, one grave one, with which they play all the changes possible in a circle so limited. Scott is entirely free from this. Baron Bradwardine and Jonathan Oldbuck are as little like each other as either is like Waverley or Fergus MacIvor; and the same may be said of every picture he has made. Except in the thankless *rôle* of hero, where it is very difficult to vary the no-character, he never repeats himself. Guy Mannering, Pleydell, and Dandie Dinmont are in no way to be confounded with the other soldiers, lawyers, or honest fellows in the series. Neither have we any counterpart or echo of Nicol Jarvie or of Andrew Fairservice. This notable expedient for saving trouble evidently had not occurred to him. Even his heroines, though they partake of the same disadvantages as the heroes, have a certain glimmer of identity. Rose and Lucy are not the same, neither are the sprightly Julia and Miss Wardour, though there is a certain resemblance between them. This wonderful variety cannot be better illustrated than by taking one class of characters as an example. There is Andrew Fairservice, Cuddie Headrigg, Ritchie Monyplies, all serving-men—all with a strong tendency to prudence and care of themselves, all quaintly attached to their masters, all full of native wit, and fertile in excuse and self-defence. They are all alike vivid and distinct, and are occasionally placed in very similar circumstances. But there is no resemblance between them. They are just as separate as if one had been a knight and another a baron. And then compare them with that wonderful picture of the old-world Major-domo, Caleb Balderstone. He is as distinct from them, in some respects as superior to them, as it is possible to conceive. It would be easy to go through the whole series, and prove from one group after another the manysidedness of the painter. There is not a child even whom he passes at a cotter's door, but becomes individual to him. He notes every similarity, every feature they have in common with others, and then he makes them different. There is no more to be said. If we knew how he did it, we too ourselves could do it—but at least we can perceive the fact. They are like the people we meet—alike in a thousand things, exactly alike in none. This is another point of resemblance between the broad and expansive nature of our great novelist and that of Shakespeare. He too, and above all who have ever tried, painted all mankind —not a few typical figures disturbed by doubts of their own identity, and followed about by a little crowd of shadows, but a host of individuals. In the same way from prince to bedesman, from the ewe-milker to the lady of romance—Scott is able for all. He looks on the world with eyes of sunshiny daylight, not with spectacles coloured by his own theories or other people's. He is indeed troubled by no theories which can warp his cheerful unfailing eyesight. What he sees and feels, what he has laid up and noted unconsciously in the long bright days of silence and obscure existence, he brings forth now with an instinctive fidelity. Though he is called the *Great Unknown*, people find him out everywhere by chance words he says, by the stories he tells—by the current, as it were, of his mind. At all times he is true to nature and recollection, and brings forth out of his treasures things new and old— things always genial, large, and true. We cannot, after reflection (barring always the heroes), bring to our mind a single instance of repetition. His smaller figures and his great are alike distinct: every new novel has a new standing-ground, a new succession of groups, an individuality distinctive to itself. The reader has but to cast his eye upon all the works of imagination he knows, except Shakespeare and Scott, and he will easily perceive how rare and remarkable this distinction is.

Scott's first novel was published in 1814, and by the year 1818 his genius had attained one of its distinct climaxes and culminating-points in *The Heart of Midlothian*. Between these two dates, *Waverley*, *Guy Mannering*, *The Antiquary*, *The Black Dwarf*, *Old Mortality*, and *Rob Roy*, had been published. Of these *The Black Dwarf* is the only[1] weak spot; all the others show the full fervour and power of his first and freshest inspiration. It is difficult to distinguish where all are so much above criticism; but there can be no question that, among so many remarkable works, *The Heart of Midlothian* separates itself, prince or rather princess among equals. Here is the humblest, commonest tale of deception and betrayal, a story in its beginning like one of those that abound in all literature. There is the pretty, vain, foolish girl gone astray, the 'villain' who deceived her, the father and sister broken-hearted with shame, the unhappy young heroine's life spoilt, and ruined

---

[1] This weakness was discovered before its publication by William Blackwood, the founder and first Editor of this Magazine, and pointed out by him with the courage and clear-sightedness which distinguished him—a bold act, which roused Scott into a most unusual outburst of petulance, almost the only one recorded of him; though it is evident that he soon adopted the opinion which had irritated him [Mrs. Oliphant].

like that of a trodden-down flower; nothing, alas! can be more ordinary than the tale. Put to it but its usual moral conclusion, the only one possible to the sentimentalist, the 'only act' which the 'lovely woman' who has 'stooped to folly' can find 'her guilt to cover', and the moralist has no more well-worn subject; but the touch of Scott's hand changed all. 'Had this story been conducted by a common hand,' says a judicious anonymous correspondent quoted in Lockhart's *Life*, 'Effie would have attracted all our concern and sympathy—Jeanie only cold approbation: whereas Jeanie, without youth, beauty, genius, warm passions, or any other novel-perfection, is here our object from beginning to end.' Jeanie Deans, to our thinking, is the cream and perfection of Scott's work. She is tenfold more, because in all ordinary circumstances she would be so much less interesting to us than a score of beautiful Rowenas, than even Flora or Rebecca. She is a piece of actual fact, real as the gentle landscape in which she is first enclosed, true as her kine that browse upon the slope—and yet she is the highest ideal that Scott has ever attained. A creature absolutely pure, absolutely truthful, yet of a tenderness, a forbearance, and long-suffering beyond the power of man, willing to die rather than lie, but resolute that the truth her nature has forced her to speak shall not be used for harm if her very life can prevent it. And this flower of human nature expands and blooms out, its slow sweet blossom opening before our eyes without one moment's departure from the homely guise, the homely language, even the matter-of-fact channel in which her thoughts run by nature. She is never made anything different from what it is natural that the daughter of David Deans, cowfeeder at St. Leonards, should be. In all her many adventures she is always the same simple, straightforward, untiring, one-idea-ed woman; simple, but strong not weak in her simplicity, firm in her gentleness, resisting all unnecessary explanations with a sensible decision, at which the clever, bold, unscrupulous villain of the piece stands aghast. He has not the courage to keep his secrets, he who has courage to break hearts and prisons; but Jeanie has the courage. There is not one scene in which this high valour of the heart, this absolute goodness, fails her; nor is there one in which she departs ever so little from the lowliness of her beginning. She is as little daunted by the Duke and the Queen as she is by the other difficulties which she has met and surmounted with that tremulous timidity of courage which belongs to nerves highly strung; nay, she has even a certain modest pleasure in the society of these potentates, her simple soul meeting them with awe, yet with absolute frankness; making no commonplace attempt at equality. Nothing but the beautiful unison of a soul so firm and true with the circumstances and habits appropriate to her class, could have brought out the whole of Jeanie's virtues. Nor do her dangers, or the fame and success she has won, make for a moment that effect upon her which such experiences would make upon the temperament to which a desire of 'bettering itself'—in one way as noble a desire as it is possible to entertain—is the chief of human motives. That desire has been the parent of many fine deeds, but its introduction would have desecrated Jeanie. With a higher and nobler art, the poet has perceived that the time which has been so important to her is, after all, but a little interval in her life, and that it has no power to upset the sweet balance of her nature, or whisper into her sound and healthful brain any extravagant wishes. The accidental and temporary pass away, the perennial and natural remain. Jeanie is greater than rank or gain could make her in the noble simplicity of her nature; and the elevation which is the natural reward of virtue in every fairy tale would be puerile and unworthy of her—false to every principle of art as well as nature. The pretty Perdita becomes a princess by every rule of romance, even when she is not an anonymous king's daughter to begin with; but Jeanie is above any such primitive reward. She is herself always, which is greater than any princess; and there never was a more exquisite touch than that in which, after her outburst of poetic eloquence to the Queen—eloquence to which she is stimulated by the very climax of love and anxiety—she sinks serene into herself, and contemplates Richmond Hill as 'braw rich feeding for the cows', the innocent dumb friends of her simple and unchanging soul. This is the true moderation of genius. An inferior writer would have kept Jeanie up at the poetic pitch, and lost her in an attempt to prove the elevating influence of high emotion—an elevation which in that case would have been as poor as it was artificial, and devoid of all true insight. Scott knew better; his humble maiden of the fields never ceases for a moment to be the best and highest thing he could make her—herself.

It is with a mingling of surprise and amusement that we read in the letter we have just quoted a contemporary's bold criticism upon the construction of this tale. When we think of it, we entirely agree with what is said, and have felt it all our life, though it has been a kind of irreverence to think of saying it. 'The latter part of the fourth volume unavoidably flags,' says this bold critic, whom we suppose by the style to be a woman. 'After Jeanie is happily settled at Rosneath, we have no more to wish for.' This is quite true. The post-scriptal part of the story is unnecessary and uncalled for. We do not much care to know what became of Effie, nor have we any interest to speak of in her abandoned child. We are perfectly contented to part with them all, after the hurried farewell between the sisters, and when the minister's wife has been settled in homely dignity upon her beautiful peninsula. We cannot even make out very clearly for what object this postscript is added on. It does not help, but rather mars, the tale; it is huddled up and ended in a hurry, and no necessity of either art or nature demands its introduction.

61. Leslie Stephen: hours in a library with Scott, *Cornhill Magazine*

1871

An unsigned article, 'Some Words About Sir Walter Scott', *Cornhill Magazine* (September 1871), xxiv, 278-93.

This article is the third in a series, 'Hours in a Library', by Sir Leslie Stephen.

Various enthusiastic persons have recently been celebrating the centenary of Sir W. Scott's birth. Some people may possibly inquire whether there is any particular reason for remembering a man at the distance of precisely one hundred years from his first appearance in the world. Would not a more appropriate epoch be at the expiration of a similar period from the appearance of *The Lay of the Last Minstrel*, or of *Waverley*? And that suggests the further question whether the celebration, if postponed to the year 1905 or 1914, would produce any vivid enthusiasm. The doubt would have seemed profane a very few years ago; and yet we may already, perhaps, find some reason for suspecting that the great 'Wizard' has lost some of his magic power, and that the warmth of our first love is departed. How many of those ladies and gentlemen who recently appeared in costume at the Waverley Ball were able to draw upon the stores of their memory, and how many were forced to cram for the occasion? A question, perhaps, not to be asked; but certainly one not to be answered with too much confidence by those who reflect upon the stock of information generally at the disposal of a well-educated English man or woman. We have heard it said—in private, be it understood, for such utterances do not so easily find their way into print, and least of all do they intrude into the speeches of centenary orators—that Scott is dull. People whisper dark hints of their hesitating allegiance to literary monarchs before the voice of rebellion swells into open expression. Yet even a muttered discontent sounds strange to middle-aged persons, who, in their schoolboy days, could spout the Death of Marmion or the Description of Melrose Abbey, till wise elders checked their undue excitement, or who followed with breathless interest the heroics of Meg Merrilies, and felt for the gallant Locksley almost as warm an enthusiasm as for the immortal Shaw the Lifeguardsman. Perhaps even the fame of that hero is growing dim. We don't talk about the Battle of Waterloo so much as formerly, and should rather blush to quote the 'Up, Guards, and at them', even if historical criticism had not ruined that with so many other fine phrases. And yet, to couple the name of Scott with dulness sounds profane, especially when one remembers the kind of literature which is bought with avidity at railway bookstalls, and, for some mysterious reason, supposed to be amusing. If Scott is to be called dull, what reputation is to be pronounced safe? Will our descendants yawn portentously over the *Pickwick Papers*, wonder how anybody could have been amused by the humours of Dick Swiveller, and even find fault with Mrs. Gamp? Greater revolutions have taken place in the popular taste. One literary dynasty succeeds another with strange rapidity; and the number of writers who enjoy what we are pleased to call immortality is singularly small. How many English authors between Shakespeare and Scott are still alive, in the sense of being familiar, not merely to students, but to the ordinary bulk of conventionally 'educated persons'? Not so long ago an author took for his motto a passage from one of Pope's most famous poems, which was known by heart to all our grandfathers. Amongst a large circle of highly intelligent readers scarcely one could trace it to its origin. A few fragments of Pope have fixed themselves in our stock of generally-known quotations, and he is far less dead than most of our great reputations; but, in spite of his vivacity and his brilliance, the bulk of his writings has retired from our tables to our bookshelves. How many people can now read *Clarissa Harlowe* which so many great authorities have pronounced to be the masterpiece of English fiction? Would any large minority of first-class men be ready to stand an examination in *Tom Jones* or *Tristram Shandy*? But our scepticism is, perhaps, leading us upon dangerous ground. It is enough to say that, if the charge of dulness merely means that the same change is passing over Scott which has already dimmed the glory of Fielding and Richardson and Pope, and almost every eminent writer in the language, it may be admitted without offence. It means merely that he has lost that gloss of novelty which alone induces those people to read whose reading is habitually conducted at a gallop. Nobody can kill an hour in an express train who has been dead for twenty-five years. The question, however, must be asked whether the decay of interest in Scott does not mean something more than this. The lapse of time must, in all cases, corrode some of the alloy with which the pure metal of all, even of the very first writers, is inevitably mixed. That Scott adulterated his writings with inferior materials, and in some cases beat out his gold uncommonly thin, cannot be denied. But when time has done its worst, will there be some permanent residue to delight a distant posterity, or will his whole work gradually crumble into fragments? Will some of his best performances stand out like a cathedral amongst ruined hovels, or will they all sink into the dust together, and the outlines of what once charmed the world be traced only by Dryasdust and historians of literature? It is a painful task to examine such questions impartially. This probing a great reputation and doubting whether we can come to anything solid at the bottom, is specially painful in regard to Scott. For he has, at least, this merit, that he is one of those rare natures for whom we feel not merely admiration but affection. We cherish the fame of Byron or Pope or Swift, in spite of, not on account of, their personal characters; if we satisfied ourselves that their literary reputations were founded on the sand, we might partly console ourselves with the thought that we were only depriving bad men of a title to genius. But for Scott most men feel in even stronger measure that kind of warm fraternal regard which Macaulay and Thackeray expressed for the amiable, but, perhaps, rather cold-blooded, Addison. The manliness and the sweetness of the man's nature predispose us to return the most favourable verdict in our power. And we may add that Scott is one of the last great English writers whose influence extended beyond his island, and gave a stimulus to the development of European thought. We cannot afford to surrender our faith in one to whom, whatever his permanent merits, we must trace so much that is characteristic of the mind of the nineteenth century. Whilst, finally, if we have any Scotch blood in our veins, we must be more or less than men to turn a deaf ear to the promptings of patriotism. When Shakspeare's fame decays everywhere else, the inhabitants of Stratford-on-Avon, if it still exist, should still revere their tutelary saint; and the old town of Edinburgh should tremble in its foundations when a sacrilegious hand is laid upon the glory of Scott.

Let us, however, take courage, and, with such impartiality as we may possess, endeavour to sift the wheat from the chaff. And, by way of following a safe guide, let us dwell for a little on the judgment pronounced upon Scott by one whose name should never be mentioned without profound respect, and who has a special claim to be heard in this case. Mr. Carlyle is both a man of genius and a Scotchman. His own writings show in every line that he comes of the same strong Protestant race from which Scott received his best qualities. 'The Scotch national character,' says Mr. Carlyle himself, 'originates in many circumstances. First of all, the Saxon stuff there was to work on; but next, and beyond all else except that, in the Presbyterian gospel of John Knox. It seems a good national character, and, on some sides, not so good. Let Scott thank John Knox, for he owed him much, little as he dreamed of debt in that quarter! No Scotchman of his time was more entirely Scotch than Walter Scott: the good and the not so good, which all Scotchmen inherit, ran through every fibre of him.' Nothing more true; and yet the words would be even more strikingly appropriate if for Walter Scott we substitute Thomas Carlyle. Even *Sartor Resartus* loses perceptibly unless it is read with a broad Scotch accent. And to this source of sympathy we might add others. Who in this generation could rival Scott's talent for the picturesque, unless it be Mr. Carlyle? Who has done so much to apply the lesson which Scott, as he says, first taught us—that the 'bygone ages of the world were actually filled by living men, not by protocols, state-papers, controversies, and abstractions of men'? If Scott would in old days—we still quote his critic—have harried cattle in Tynedale or cracked crowns in Redswire, would not Mr. Carlyle have thundered from the pulpit of John Knox his own gospel, only in slightly altered phraseology—that shams should not live but die, and that men should do what work lies nearest to their hands, as in the presence of the eternities and the infinite silences?

That last parallel reminds us that if there are points of similarity, there are contrasts both wide and deep. The rugged old apostle had probably a very low opinion of moss-troopers, and Mr. Carlyle has a message to deliver to his fellow-creatures, which is not quite according to Scott. And thus we see throughout his interesting essay a kind of struggle between two opposite tendencies—a genuine liking for the man, tempered by a sense that Scott dealt rather too much in those same shams to pass muster with a stern moral censor. Nobody can touch Scott's character more finely. There is a perfect little anecdote told in charming Carlylese which every reader must remember: how there was a 'little Blenheim cocker' of singular sensibility and sagacity; how the said cocker would at times fall into musings like those of a Wertherean poet, and lived in perpetual fear of strangers, regarding them all as potentially dog-stealers; how the dog was, nevertheless, endowed with 'most amazing moral tact', and specially hated the genus *quack* and, above all, that of *acrid-quack*. 'These,' says Mr. Carlyle, 'though never so clear-starched, bland-smiling, and beneficent, he absolutely would have no trade with. Their very sugar-cake was unavailing. He said with emphasis, as clearly as barking could say it, "Acrid-quack, avaunt!"' But once, when 'a tall, irregular, busy-looking man came halting by', that wise, nervous little dog ran towards him, and began 'fawning, frisking, licking at the feet' of Sir Walter Scott. No reader of reviews could have done better, says Mr. Carlyle; and, indeed, that canine testimonial was worth having. We prefer that little anecdote, told with a humour which reminds us oddly of Lamb, even to Lockhart's account of the pig which had a romantic affection for the author of *Waverley*. Its relater at least perceived and loved that unaffected benevolence, which invested even Scott's bodily presence with a kind of natural aroma, perceptible, as it would appear, to very far-away cousins. But Mr. Carlyle is on his guard, and though his sympathy flows kindly enough, it is rather harshly intercepted by his sterner mood. He cannot, indeed, but warm to Scott at the end. After touching on the sad scene of Scott's closing years, at once ennobled and embittered by that last desperate struggle to clear off the burden of debt, he concludes with genuine feeling. 'It can be said of

Scott, when he departed he took a man's life along with him. No sounder piece of British manhood was put together in that eighteenth century of time. Alas, his fine Scotch face, with its shaggy honesty, sagacity, and goodness, when we saw it latterly on the Edinburgh streets, was all worn with care, the joy all fled from it, ploughed deep with labour and sorrow. We shall never forget it—we shall never see it again. Adieu, Sir Walter, pride of all Scotchmen; take our proud and sad farewell.'

And now it is time to turn to the failings which, in Mr. Carlyle's opinion, mar this pride of all Scotchmen, and make his permanent reputation doubtful. The faults upon which he dwells are, of course, those which are more or less acknowledged by all sound critics. Scott, says Mr. Carlyle, had no great gospel to deliver; he had nothing of the martyr about him; he slew no monsters and stirred no deep emotions. He did not believe in anything, and did not even disbelieve in anything: he was content to take the world as it came—the false and the true mixed indistinguishably together. One Ram-dass, a Hindoo, 'who set up for god-head lately', being asked what he meant to do with the sins of mankind, replied that 'he had fire enough in his belly to burn up all the sins in the world'. Ram-dass had 'some spice of sense in him.' Now, of fire of that kind we can detect few sparks in Scott. He was a thoroughly healthy, sound, vigorous Scotchman, with an eye for the main chance, but not much of an eye for the eternities. And that unfortunate commercial element, which caused the misery of his life, was equally mischievous to his work. He cared for no results of his working but such as could be seen by the eye, and, in one sense or other, 'handled, looked at, and buttoned into the breeches'-pocket'. He regarded literature rather as a trade than an art; and literature, unless it is a very poor affair, should have higher aims than that of 'harmlessly amusing indolent, languid men'. Scott would not afford the time or the trouble to go to the root of the matter, and is content to amuse us with mere contrasts of costume, which will lose their interest when the swallow-tail is as obsolete as the buff-coat. And then he fell into the modern sin of extempore writing, and deluged the world with the first hasty overflowings of his mind, instead of straining and refining it till he could bestow the pure essence upon us. In short, his career is summed up in the phrase that it was 'writing impromptu novels to buy farms with'—a melancholy end, truly, for a man of rare genius. Nothing is sadder than to hear of such a man 'writing himself out'; and it is pitiable, indeed, that Scott should be the example of that fate which rises most naturally to our minds. 'Something very perfect in its kind,' says Mr. Carlyle, 'might have come from Scott, nor was it a low kind— nay, who knows how high, with studious self-concentration, he might have gone: what wealth nature implanted in him, which his circumstances, most unkind while seeming to be kindest, had never impelled him to unfold?'

There is undoubtedly some truth in the severer criticisms to which some more kindly sentences are a pleasant relief; and there is something too which most persons will be apt to consider as rather harsher than necessary. Is not the moral preacher intruding a little too much on the province of the literary critic? In fact we fancy that, in the midst of these energetic remarks, Mr. Carlyle is conscious of certain half-expressed doubts. The name of Shakespeare occurs several times in the course of his remarks, and suggests to us that we can hardly condemn Scott whilst acquitting the greatest name in our literature. Scott, it seems, wrote for money; he coined his brains into cash to buy farms. Well, and did not Shakespeare do pretty much the same? As Mr. Carlyle himself puts it, 'beyond drawing audiences to the Globe Theatre, Shakespeare contemplated no result in those plays of his.' Shakespeare, as Pope puts it,

> 'Whom you and every playhouse bill
> Style the divine, the matchless, what you will,
> For gain, not glory, wing'd his roving flight,
> And grew immortal in his own despite.'

To write for money was once held to be disgraceful; and Byron, as we know, taunted Scott, because his publishers combined

> 'To yield their muse just half-a-crown a line;'

whilst Scott seems half to admit that his conduct required justification, and urges that he sacrificed to literature very fair chances in his original profession. Many people might, perhaps, be disposed to take a bolder line of defence. Cut out of English fiction all that which has owed its birth more or less to a desire of earning money honourably, and the residue would be painfully small. The truth, indeed, seems to be simple. No good work is done when the one impelling motive is the desire of making a little money; but some of the best work that has ever been done, has been indirectly due to the impecuniosity of the labourers. When a man is empty he makes a very poor job of it, in straining colourless trash from his hardbound brains; but when his mind is full to bursting he may still require the spur of a moderate craving for cash to induce him to take the decisive plunge. Scott illustrates both cases. The melancholy drudgery of his later years was forced from him in spite of nature; but nobody ever wrote more spontaneously than Scott when he was composing his early poems and novels. If the precedent of Shakspeare is good for anything, it is good for this. Shakspeare, it may be, had a more moderate ambition; but there seems to be no reason why the desire of a good house at Stratford should be intrinsically nobler than the desire of a fine estate at Abbotsford. But then, it is urged, Scott allowed himself to write with preposterous haste. And Shakspeare, who never blotted a line? What is the great difference between them? Mr. Carlyle feels that here too Scott has at least a very good precedent to allege; but he endeavours to establish a distinction. It was right, he says, for Shakspeare to write rapidly, 'being ready to do it. And herein truly lies the secret of the matter; such swiftness of writing, after due energy of preparation, is, doubtless, the right method; the hot furnace having long worked and simmered, let the pure gold flow out at one gush.' Could there be a better description of Scott in his earlier years? He published his first poem of any pretensions at thirty-four, an age which Shelley and Keats never reached, and which Byron only passed by two years. *Waverley* came out when he was forty-three—most of our modern novelists have written themselves out long before they arrive at that respectable period of life. From a child he had been accumulating the knowledge and the thoughts that at last found expression in his work. He had been a teller of stories before he was well in breeches; and had worked hard till middle life in accumulating vast stores of picturesque imagery. The delightful notes to all his books give us some impression of the fulness of mind which poured forth a boundless torrent of anecdote to the guests at Abbotsford. We only repine at the prodigality of the harvest when we forget the long process of culture by which it was produced. And, more than this, when we look at the peculiar characteristics of Scott's style—that easy flow of narrative never heightening into epigram, but always full of a charm of freshness and fancy most difficult to analyze— we may well doubt whether much labour would have improved or injured him. No man ever depended more on the perfectly spontaneous flow of his narratives. Mr. Carlyle quotes Schiller against him, amongst other and greater names. We need not attempt to compare the two men; but do not Schiller's tragedies smell rather painfully of the lamp? Does not the professor of aesthetics pierce a little too distinctly through the exterior of the poet? And, for one example, are not Schiller's excellent but remarkably platitudinous peasants in *William Tell* miserably colourless alongside of Scott's rough border dalesmen, racy of speech, and redolent of their native soil in every word and gesture? To every man his method according to his talent. Scott is the most perfectly delightful of story-tellers, and it is the very essence of story-telling that it should not follow prescribed canons of criticism, but be as natural as the talk by firesides, and, it is to be feared, over many gallons of whisky-toddy, of which it is, in fact, the refined essence. Scott skims off the cream of his varied stores of popular tradition and antiquarian learning with strange facility; but he had tramped through many a long day's march, and pored over innumerable ballads and forgotten writers before he had anything to skim. Had he not—if we may use the word without offence—been cramming all his life, and practising the art of story-telling every day he lived? Probably the most striking incidents of his books are in reality mere modifications of anecdotes which he had rehearsed a hundred times before, just disguised enough to fit into his story. Who can read, for example, the wondrous legend of the blind piper in *Redgauntlet* without seeing that it bears all the marks of long elaboration as clearly as one of those discourses of Whitfield, which, by constant repetition, became marvels of dramatic art? He was an impromptu composer, in the sense that when his anecdotes once reached paper, they flowed rapidly, and were little corrected; but the correction must have been substantially done in many cases long before they appeared in the state of 'copy'.

Let us, however, pursue the indictment a little further. Scott did not believe in anything in particular. Yet once more, did Shakspeare? There is surely a poetry of doubt as well as a poetry of conviction, or what shall we say to *Hamlet*? Appearing in such an age as the end of the last and the beginning of this century, Scott could but share the intellectual atmosphere in which he was born, and at that day, whatever we may think of this, few people had any strong faith to boast of. Why should not a poet stand aside from the chaos of conflicting opinions, so far as he was able to extricate himself from the unutterable confusion around them, and show us what was beautiful in the world as he saw it, without striving to combine the office of prophet with his more congenial occupation? Some such answer might be worked out; but we begin to feel a certain hesitation as to the soundness of our argument. Mr. Carlyle did not mean to urge so feeble a criticism as that Scott had no very uncompromising belief in the Thirty-nine Articles;

for that is a weakness which he would share with many undeniably good writers. The criticism points to a different and more unfortunate deficiency. 'While Shakspeare works from the heart outwards, Scott,' says Mr. Carlyle, 'works from the skin inwards, never getting near the heart of men.' The books are addressed entirely to the every-day mind. They have nothing to do with emotions or principles, beyond those of the ordinary country gentleman; and, we may add, of the country gentleman with his digestion in good order, and his hereditary gout still in the distant future. The more inspiring thoughts, the deeper passions, are altogether beyond his range. If in his width of sympathy, and his vivid perception of character within certain limits, he reminds us of Shakspeare, we can find no analogy in his writings to the passion of *Romeo and Juliet,* or to the intellectual agony of *Hamlet.* The charge, we see, is not really that Scott lacks faith, but that he never appeals, one way or the other, to the faculties which make faith a vital necessity to some natures, or lead to a desperate revolt against established faiths in others. If Byron and Scott could have been combined; if the energetic passions of the one could have been joined to the healthy nature and quick sympathies of the other, we might have seen another Shakspeare in the nineteenth century. As it is, both of them are maimed and imperfect on different sides. It is, in fact, remarkable how Scott fails when he attempts a flight into the regions where he is less at home than in his ordinary style. Take, for instance, a passage from *Rob Roy,* where our dear friend, the Baillie, Nicol Jarvie, is taken prisoner by Rob Roy's amiable wife, and appeals to her feelings of kinship. ' "I dinna ken," said the undaunted Baillie, "if the kindred has ever been weel redd out to you yet, cousin—but it's kenned, and can be proved. My mother, Elspeth Macfarlane (otherwise MacGregor), was the wife of my father, Denison Nicol Jarvie (peace be with them baith), and Elspeth was the daughter of Farlane Macfarlane (or MacGregor), at the shieling of Loch Sloy. Now this Farlane Macfarlane (or Mac-Gregor), as his surviving daughter, Maggy Macfarlane, wha married Duncan Macnab of Stuckavrallachan, can testify, stood as near to your gudeman, Robin MacGregor, as in the fourth degree of kindred, fur—"

'The virago lopped the genealogical tree by demanding haughtily, If a stream of rushing water acknowledged any relation with the portion withdrawn from it for the mean domestic uses of those who dwelt on its banks?'

What are we to say to this? That the Baillie is as real a human being as ever lived—as the present Lord Mayor, or Mr. Edmond Beales, or

Dandie Dinmont, or Sir Walter himself; and that Mrs. MacGregor has obviously just stepped off the boards of a minor theatre, devoted to the melodrama. As long as Scott keeps to his strong ground, his figures are as good flesh and blood as ever walked in the Salt-market of Glasgow; when once he tries his heroics, he manufactures his characters from the materials used by the frequenters of masked balls. There are, indeed, occasions, on which his genius does not so signally desert him. Balfour of Burley may rub shoulders against genuine Covenanters, and west-country Whigs without betraying his fictitious origin. The Master of Ravenswood attitudinizes a little too much with his Spanish cloak and his slouched hat; but we feel really sorry for him when he disappears in the Kelpie's Flow. And when Scott has to do with his own peasants, with the thoroughbred Presbyterian Scotchman, he can bring real tragic events from his homely materials. Douce Davie Deans, dis-tracted between his religious principles and his desire of saving his daughter's life, and seeking relief even in the midst of his agonies, by that admirable burst of spiritual pride: 'Though I will neither exalt myself nor pull down others, I wish that every man and woman in this land had kept the true testimony and the middle and straight path, as it were on the ridge of a hill, where wind and water steals, avoiding right-hand snares and extremes, and left-hand way-slidings, as well as Johnny Dodds of Farthy's acre and ae man mair that shall be name-less'—Davie, we say, is as admirable a figure as ever appeared in fiction. It is a pity that he was mixed up with the conventional mad-woman, Madge Wildfire, and that a story most touching in its native simplicity, was twisted and tortured into needless intricacy. These pathetic passages, with others that might be mentioned, imply after all a rather narrow compass of feeling. The religious exaltation of Balfour, or the religious pigheadedness of Davie Deans, are pictures-quely described; but they are given from the point of view of the kindly humorist, rather than of one who can sympathize with the sublimity of an intense faith in a homely exterior. And though many good judges hold *The Bride of Lammermoor* to be Scott's best perform-ance, in virtue of the loftier passions which animate the chief actors in the tragedy, we are, after all, called upon to sympathize rather with the gentleman of good family who can't ask his friends to dinner without an unworthy device to hide his poverty, than with the passion-ate lover whose mistress has her heart broken. Surely this is the vulgarest side of the story. Scott, in short, fails unmistakeably in pure passion of all kinds; and for that reason his heroes are for the most part mere wooden blocks to hang a story on. Cranstoun in *The Lay of the Last Minstrel*, Graeme in *The Lady of the Lake*, or Wilton in *Marmion*, are all unspeakable bores. Waverley himself, and Lovel in *The Antiquary*, and Vanbeest Brown in *Guy Mannering*, and Harry Morton in *Old Mortality*, and, in short, the whole series of Scott's pattern young men, are all chips of the same block. It is quite painful to observe how much pains he takes with them; they can all run, and ride, and fight, and make pretty speeches, and express the most becoming sentiments; but somehow they all partake of one fault, the same which was charged against the otherwise incomparable horse, namely, that they are dead. There is not a spark of vitality in the whole party. They are like the five brothers Osbaldistone, who were mixtures in different proportions of sot, gamekeeper, horse-jockey, bully, and fool. We must indeed substitute some more complimentary qualities, yet, with the exception of sot and bully, it must be confessed that these qualities appear more or less conspicuously even in these patterns of their sex. And we must confess that this is a considerable drawback from Scott's novels. To take the passion out of a novel is something like taking the sunlight out of a landscape; and to condemn all the heroes to be utterly commonplace is to remove the centre of interest in a manner detrimental to the best intents of the story. When Thackeray endeavoured to restore Rebecca to her rightful place in *Ivanhoe*, he was only doing what is more or less desirable in all the series. We long to dismount these insipid creatures from the pride of place, and to supplant them by some of the admirable characters who are doomed to play subsidiary parts. And yet we may fairly assert that after many deductions there remains a whole gallery of portraits which could have been drawn by none but a master. If Scott has contributed no great characters, like Hamlet, or Don Quixote, or Mephistopheles, to the world of fiction, he is the undisputed parent of a whole population full of enduring vitality, and, if rising to no ideal standard, yet reflecting with unrivalled clearness the characteristics of some of the strongest and sturdiest of the races of man.

If, indeed, Scott, feeling instinctively that lofty passion was out of his reach, had confined himself to the ordinary daylight of common sense and common nature, he would have perhaps left more enduring work, though he would have produced a less marked impression at the time. Unluckily, or luckily,—who shall say which?—he took to that 'buff-jerkin' business of which Mr. Carlyle speaks so contemptuously, and fairly carried away the hearts of his contemporaries by a lavish display of mediæval upholstery. Lockhart tells us that Scott could not bear the commonplace daubings of walls with uniform coats of white, blue, and grey. All the roofs at Abbotsford 'were, in appearance at least, of carved oak, relieved by coats-of-arms duly blazoned at the intersections of beams, and resting on cornices, to the eye, of the same material, but composed of casts in plaster of Paris, after the foliage, the flowers, the grotesque monsters and dwarfs, and sometimes the beautiful heads of nuns and confessors, on which he had doated from infancy among the cloisters of Melrose Abbey.' That anecdote, recounted by the admiring Lockhart, gives the true secret of all Scott's failures. The plaster looks as well as the carved oak—for a time; but the day speedily comes when the sham crumbles into ashes, and Scott's knights and nobles, like his carved cornices, became dust in the next generation. It is hard to say it, and yet we fear it must be admitted that the whole of those historical novels, which once charmed all men, and for which we have still a lingering affection, are rapidly converting themselves into mere debris of plaster of Paris. Even our dear *Ivanhoe* is on the high-road to ruin; it is vanishing as fast as one of Sir Joshua's most carelessly painted pictures; and perhaps we ought not to regret it. Sir F. Palgrave says somewhere that 'historical novels are mortal enemies to history', and we shall venture to add that they are mortal enemies to fiction. There may be an exception or two, but as a rule the task is simply impracticable. The novelist is bound to come so near to the facts that we feel the unreality of his portraits. Either the novel becomes pure cram, a dictionary of antiquities dissolved in a 'thin solution of romance, or, which is generally more refreshing, it takes leave of accuracy altogether and simply takes the plot and the costume from history, but allows us to feel that genuine moderns are masquerading in the dress of a bygone century. Even in the last case, it generally results in a kind of dance in fetters and a comparative breakdown under self-imposed obligations. *Ivanhoe* and *Kenilworth* and *Quentin Durward* and the rest are of course bare blank impossibilities. No such people ever lived and talked on this planet; fragments of genuine history and fragments of genuine character may be embedded in the plaster of Paris, but there is no solidity or permanence in the workmanship. The love of these conventional heroes unluckily sank very deeply into Scott's mind. His puritans are generally better than his cavaliers, though he loved the cavaliers best in theory, just so far as in the puritans he was really painting from the life around him and only transporting modern Scotchmen into antiquated surroundings.

The evil extends beyond the purely historical romances. Scott, for example, invented the modern Highlander. It is to him more than to anybody else that we owe the strange perversion of facts which induces a good Lowland Scot to fancy himself more nearly allied to the semi-barbarous wearers of the tartan than to his English blood-relations. This fashion of talking twaddle about claymores and targets and kilts reached its height, as Macaulay remarks, in the marvellous performance of our venerated ruler, George IV. That monarch, he observes, 'thought that he could not give a more striking proof of his respect for the usages which had prevailed in Scotland before the Union than by disguising himself in what, before the Union, was considered by nine Scotchmen out of ten as the dress of a thief'. The passage recalls one of the most tragi-comic passages in Scott's life. When we think of the great poet appropriating the wine-glass in which his sacred Majesty had drank his first draught in Scotland, and carelessly sitting down upon it afterwards, we can only say, in the words of Pope,—

'Who would not laugh if such a man there be?
Who would not weep if—Waverley—were he?'

That the sturdiest piece of manhood in the British Islands should lower himself to that wretched bit of mock loyalty amounts almost to a national misfortune. The same might be illustrated by a picture at one of the interesting portrait exhibitions. There, in South Kensington, was hung up for the admiration of all men, a representation of George IV, which it was simply impossible to contemplate without exploding in a laugh. It portrayed a stalwart highlander in full costume, some seven or eight feet high, as far as could be judged, and with the most tremendous muscular development. Above its shoulders rose a black cylindrical column, which was, in fact, the stock with which our ancestors used to encourage an attack of apoplexy. Above this again appeared the red puffy cheeks of the first gentleman in Europe, suggestive of innumerable bottles of port and burgundy at Carlton House. And the whole structure was surmounted by a bonnet with waving plumes. Anything more grotesque and more significant of the taste of the epoch could hardly be invented. And Scott was chiefly responsible for disguising that elderly London debauchee in the costume of a wild Gaelic cattle-stealer, and was apparently insensible of the gross absurdity. We are told that an air of burlesque was thrown over the proceedings at Holyrood by the apparition of a true London alderman in the same costume as his master. We could almost hope that by some strange blunder, Wilkie had painted the alderman instead of the monarch. Alas! the evidence is too strong; and such as we have seen was the earthy idol before whom Scott delighted to bow his manly head. Let us pass by with a passing lamentation that so great and good a man should have encouraged the miserable British tendency for explaining unselfish loyalty by gross snobbishness and fancying that it is the genuine article. This miserable taint of unreality threatens Scott's genius more than any other defect; and so far Mr. Carlyle's verdict can hardly be disputed. Already we have lost our love of buff jerkins and other scraps from mediæval museums, and Scott is suffering from having preferred working in stucco to carving in marble. The mediævalism of this day is perhaps deficient in any real vitality; yet we have got some way in advance of Strawberry Hill and Abbotsford and the carpenter's father of fifty years back. There is, however, something still to be said. *Ivanhoe* cannot be given up without some reluctance. The vivacity of the description—the delight with which Scott throws himself into the pursuit of his knicknacks and antiquarian rubbish, has something contagious about it. *Ivanhoe*, let it be granted, is no longer a work for men, but it still is, or still ought to be, delightful reading for boys. The ordinary boy, indeed, when he reads anything, seems to choose descriptions of the cricket-matches and boat-races in which his soul most delights. But there must still be some unsophisticated youths who can relish *Robinson Crusoe* and the *Arabian Nights* and other favourites of our own childhood, and such at least should pore over the 'Gentle and free passage of arms at Ashby', admire those incredible feats with the long-bow which would have enabled Robin Hood to meet successfully a modern volunteer armed with the Martini-Henry, and follow the terrific head-breaking of Frond-de-Bœuf, Bois-Guilbert, the holy clerk of Copmanshurst, and the *Noir Fainéant*, even to the time when, for no particular reason beyond the exigencies of the story, the Templar suddenly falls from his horse, and is discovered, to our no small surprise, to be 'unscathed by the lance of the enemy', and to have died a victim to the violence of his own contending passions. But if *Ivanhoe* has rightly descended from the library to the schoolroom, we should not be ungrateful to Scott for wasting his splendid talents on what we can hardly call by a loftier name than most amusing nonsense. We could not, without venturing into boundless fields of controversy, decide upon the good and the evil results of that romanticism of which Scott was the great English founder. This much may perhaps be safely said: a reaction from the eighteenth-century spirit of indiscriminating contempt for our past history, and specially for the 'Dark Ages', was necessary and right. At a time when the public taste was too ill educated to distinguish between tinsel and genuine gold, it could only be attracted by that fast-failing material which Scott offered for its acceptance. Had he taken a loftier tone he might have amused people more in the twentieth century, but he would have produced a smaller immediate effect on his own. Why should not a man stir a love of art by producing daubs when neither he nor his audience are capable of appreciating masterpieces? May we not at times accept with gratitude the sacrifice made by a genius which condescends to provide us with the only food that we can digest, as well as the sacrifice of temporary fame made by the man who works for our great grandchildren? It is a difficult problem, and one which we need not attempt to solve. Certainly, however, we must set against it that Scott contributed more than most people to that prevalent delusion of our times, that there is a hopeless divergence between the beautiful and the useful; that we cannot keep up historical associations except at the price of injuring our own generation, or do good now without making a clean sweep of all that appeals to the imagination. In so doing, he played into the hands of the purely obstructive people, who would not only live in a picturesque ruin, but build modern ruins to be like it; the end of which is, of course, that which they most dread, a final revolution by catastrophe, instead of a continuous development.

Scott, however, understood, and nobody has better illustrated by example, the true mode of connecting past and present. Mr. Palgrave, whose love of Scott's poetry is, perhaps, rather stronger than we can generally follow, observes in the notes to the *Golden Treasury* that the songs about Brignall banks and Rosabelle exemplify 'the peculiar skill with which Scott employs proper names'; nor, he adds, 'is there a surer sign of high poetical genius'. The last remark might possibly be disputed; if Milton possessed the same talent, so did Lord Macaulay, whose ballads, admirable as they are, are not first-rate poetry; but the conclusion to which the remark points is one which is illustrated by each of these cases. The secret of the power is simply this, that a man whose mind is full of historical associations somehow communicates to us something of the sentiment which they awake in himself. Scott, as all who saw him tell us, could never see an old tower, or a bank, or the rush of a stream without instantly recalling a boundless collection of appropriate anecdotes. He might be quoted as a case in point by those who would explain all poetical imagination by the power of associating ideas. He is the poet of association. A proper name acts upon him like a charm. It calls up the past days, the heroes of the '41, or the skirmish of Drumclog, or the old Covenanting times, by a spontaneous and inexplicable magic. When the barest natural object is taken into his imagination, all manner of past fancies and legends crystallize around it at once.

Though it is more difficult to explain how the same glow which ennobled them to him is conveyed to his readers, the process somehow takes place. We catch the enthusiasm. A word, which strikes us as a bare abstraction in the report of the Censor General, say, or in a collection of poor-law returns, gains an entirely new significance when he touches it in the most casual manner. A kind of mellowing atmosphere surrounds all objects in his pages, and tinges them with poetical hues; and difficult as it is to analyze the means by which his power is exercised, though we may guess at its sources, this is the secret of Scott's most successful writing. Thus, for example, we have always fancied that the second title of *Waverley*—*'Tis Sixty Years Since'*,—indicates precisely the distance of time at which a romantic novelist should place himself from his creations. They are just far enough from us to have acquired a certain picturesque colouring, which conceals the vulgarity, and yet leaves them living and intelligible beings. His best stories might be all described as *Tales of My Grandfather*. They have the charm of anecdotes told to the narrator by some old man who had himself been part of what he describes. Some people, who condemn the sham knights and nobles and the mediæval upholstery of Scott's novels, have, by a natural reaction, taken a rather different view. There is a story of a dozen connoisseurs in the Waverley Novels, who agreed that each should separately write down the name of his favourite story, when it appeared that each had, without concert, mentioned *St. Ronan's Well*. It has, indeed, the merit of representing modern life, and therefore giving no scope for the sham romantic. But the public is surely a wiser critic than any clique of connoisseurs; and, in this instance especially, we suspect that it is right. The ladies and gentlemen at the hotel are rather out of Scott's peculiar line, and excellent as Meg Dodds and the retired nabobs may be, they are scarcely equal to some of the old men and women in his less prosaic novels. If we were to give a list of the novels which to us appear to have the best chance of immortality, we should mention *Waverley*, *The Antiquary*, *Guy Mannering*, *Old Mortality*, and *The Bride of Lammermoor*. Some of the others—especially

The Heart of Mid-Lothian—contain passages equal to the best of these; but those we have noticed seem to be less defaced by Scott's inferior style, and they all of them depend, for their deep interest, upon the scenery and society with which he had been familiar in his early days, more or less harmonized by removal to what we may call, in a different sense from the common one, the twilight of history; that period, namely, from which the broad glare of the present has departed, and which we can yet dimly observe without making use of the dark-lantern of ancient historians, and accepting the guidance of Dryasdust. Dandie Dinmont, though a contemporary of Scott's youth, represented a fast perishing phase of society; and Balfour of Burley, though his day was past, had yet left his mantle with many spiritual descendants who were scarcely less familiar. Between the times so fixed Scott seems to exhibit his genuine power; and within these limits we should find it hard to name any second, or indeed any third.

When naturalists wish to preserve a skeleton, they bury an animal in an anthill and dig him up after many days with all the perishable matter fairly eaten away. That is the process which great men have to undergo. A vast multitude of insignificant, unknown, and unconscious critics destroy what has no genuine power of resistance and leave the remainder for posterity. Much disappears in every case, and it is a question, perhaps, whether the firmer parts of Scott's reputation will be sufficiently coherent to resist after the removal of the rubbish. We must admit that even his best work is of more or less mixed value, and that the test will be a severe one. Yet we hope, and chiefly for one reason, which remains to be expressed. Every great novelist describes many characters from the outside: but as a rule, even the greatest—and, with Mr. Carlyle's leave, we will add even Shakespeare—describes only one from the inside: and that, we need not say, is himself. We must add, indeed, to make the statement accurate, that every man is really a highly complex personage, and, like Mrs. Malaprop's Cerberus, is at least three gentlemen in one. His varying moods, or the different stages of developement through which he passes, may supply us with what we take to be different men, as Goethe utilized all the successive phases of his life, or as, to speak more conjecturally, Shakespeare in his cups was Falstaff, and Shakespeare melancholy was Hamlet. Not to work this out at length, or to supply the necessary qualifications, we may surely say that Scott has painted a full-length portrait of himself; and that no more loveable or in some respects more powerful nature was ever revealed to us. Scott, indeed, setting up as the landed proprietor at Abbotsford and solacing himself with painted plaster of Paris instead of carved oak, does not strike us any more than he does Mr. Carlyle, as a very noble phenomenon. To test Scott we may set aside such performances as *Ivanhoe, Kenilworth Castle, The Monastery,* and other stucco-work of a highly crumbling and unstable tendency. But luckily for us, we have also the Scott who must have been the most charming of all conceivable companions; the Scott who was idolized even by a judicious pig; the Scott, who, unlike the irritable race of literary magnates in general, never lost a friend, and whose presence diffused an equable glow of kindly feeling to the farthest limits of the social system which gravitated round him. He was not precisely brilliant; nobody, we know, ever wrote so many sentences and left so few that have fixed themselves upon us as established commonplaces; beyond that unlucky phrase about 'my name being Macgregor and my foot being on my native heath'—which is not a very admirable sentiment—we do not at present remember a single gem of this kind. Landor, if we remember rightly, said that in the whole of Scott's poetry there was only one good line, that, namely, in the poem about Helvellyn referring to the dog of the lost man—

'When the wind waved his garments, how oft didst thou start!'

To judge either of poetry or prose on such principles is obviously unfair. Scott is not one of the coruscating geniuses, throwing out epigrams at every turn, and sparkling with good things. But the poetry, which was first admired to excess and then rejected with undue contempt, is now beginning to find its due level. It is not poetry of the first order. It is not the poetry of deep meditation or of rapt enthusiasm. Much that was once admired has now become rather offensive than otherwise. And yet it has a charm, which becomes more sensible the more familiar we grow, the charm of unaffected and spontaneous love of nature; but not only is it perfectly in harmony with the nature which Scott loved so well, but it is still the best interpreter of the sound healthy love of wild scenery. Wordsworth, no doubt, goes deeper; and Byron is more vigorous; and Shelley more ethereal. But it is, and will remain, a good thing to have a breath from the Cheviots brought straight into London streets, as Scott alone can do it. When Washington Irving visited Scott, they had an amicable dispute as to the scenery: Irving, as became an American, complaining of the absence of forests; Scott declaring his love for 'his honest grey hills', and saying that if he did not see the heather once a year he thought he should die. Everybody who has refreshed himself with mountain and moor this summer should feel how much we owe, and how much more we are likely to owe in future, to the man who first inoculated us with his own enthusiasm, and who is still the best interpreter of the 'honest grey hills'. Scott's poetical faculty may, perhaps, be more felt in his prose than his verse. The fact need not be decided; but as we read the best of his novels we feel ourselves transported to the 'distant Cheviots blue'; mixing with the sturdy dalesmen, and the tough indomitable puritans of his native land; for their sakes we can forgive the exploded feudalism and the faded romance which he attempted in vain, as such an attempt must always be vain, to galvanize into life. The pleasure of that healthy open-air life, with that manly companion, is not likely to diminish; and Scott as its exponent may still retain a hold upon our affections which would have been long ago forfeited if he had depended entirely on his romantic nonsense. We are rather in the habit of talking about a healthy animalism, and try most elaborately to be simple and manly; indeed, we have endeavoured to prove that the cultivation of our muscles is an essential part of the Christian religion. When we turn from our modern professors in that line, who affect a total absence of affectation, to Scott's Dandie Dinmonts and Edie Ochiltrees, we see the difference between the sham and the reality, and fancy that Scott may still have a lesson or two to preach to this generation. Those to come must take care of themselves.

62. A centenary view—Scott's characters, *Athenaeum*

1871

An unsigned article in *Athenaeum*, 7 January 1871, 7–9.

The article is ostensibly a review of several editions of Scott's works. The author of the review was possibly John Doran, a miscellaneous writer and editor (see *Notes & Queries* (27 April 1889), 7th Series, vii, 324).

' 'Tis sixty years since' the author of *Waverley* took the first step towards realizing the dream of his life by becoming a landed proprietor. In 1811 he bought the first instalment of Abbotsford. This fact may properly be placed at the head of an article on Sir Walter Scott, since it is well known that all his literary fame and all the pleasure which he derived from literature were as nothing in his eyes compared with the position of a Scotch country gentleman and a kinsman of the Bold Buccleuch. It is clear from the language of Mr. Lockhart that he lived in two worlds in a more literal sense than is commonly attached to that expression: and that underneath the law and the literature, the field sports and the woodcraft in which he was apparently absorbed, lay another existence, unsuspected by the world at large, which he passed in company with the creatures of his own imagination, among the scenes and events of past ages, under the shadow

'of great old houses
And fights fought long ago,'

with which he sympathized so completely that it might almost at times have seemed doubtful to him which was the reality and which the illusion. There can hardly be a question but that when he described the habits of Edward Waverley he was thinking of his own. The beautiful passage at the conclusion of the fourth chapter, in which the hero's propensity to brood over the old family legends till they gradually became instinct with life, and Crusader and Cavalier started from their long sleep, to re-enact their parts before his eyes, must have been a reflex of the mental habit to which we owe Hugo de Lacy, Albert Lee, Peveril of the Peak, Lord Evandale, Tressilian, and a host of others, which make the 'Waverley Novels' like an historical picture gallery.

This habit of mind told upon Scott in two ways. The artificial world in which he lived, though it could supply him with everything necessary to the conduct of a romantic drama, was inevitably deficient in studies of character; and accordingly we find that what may be termed the psychological element of the novels is their weakest point. But if to this extent Scott's life among the dead was a hindrance to him, the loss was far more than atoned for by the simplicity which it imparted to his writings. By simplicity we do not mean that healthiness and purity of tone which play over them like a sea-breeze, and have always been appreciated; but a total absence of self-consciousness, of straining at effect, of a syllable which would seem to insinuate that the author was above his readers, or imagined himself to be engaged in anything very wonderful or splendid. The strength of his belief in what he undertook to paint made him paint it with exquisite fidelity. His indifference to the literary result saved him from errors which are usually the fruits of vanity. The Waverley Novels remind one more of a sensible, well-bred gentleman detailing the scenes of his youth to a few chosen friends after dinner, than of the professed *littérateur*, with himself and the public before his eyes. In no other writer of fiction with whom we are acquainted is the author so completely sunk in the man, as it is in Sir Walter Scott, and though, were this the result of affectation, nothing could be more offensive, where it is perfectly natural and undesigned nothing can be more delightful. Those who look on Walter Scott as a man wrapped up in his literary successes and gloating over his great secret will never understand his books. We are not sure that his literary character was regarded even by himself with unmixed satisfaction. But most assuredly he considered it as wholly subordinate to his position as a Scotch Laird, which he made himself by the purchase of Abbotsford.

It will be a hundred years ago next August since this wonderful man was born into the world to exercise an influence literary, social, and political not inferior in the aggregate to that of Shakspeare. Shakspeare's influence was almost exclusively literary, and in this of course he was even to Sir Walter Scott as the sun is to the moon. But Scott's influence in another sphere was greater than Shakspeare's by as much as Shakspeare's in that sphere was greater than his: and the hundredth anniversary of his birthday well deserves the honour with which it is proposed to celebrate it. Our own contribution to the stream of homage shall be in the shape of a bird's-eye view of the new world which he discovered, and the commemoration of one or two features in the landscape which, though not unknown to criticism, have scarcely, in our judgment, received adequate consideration.

We have said that in the Waverley Novels the psychological element is the weakest point, and of this defect nobody was more conscious than the author. But he knew how wretched was the result when this kind of writing was attempted in the absence of peculiar talents for it, and he wisely abstained from a field in which he recognized living superiors. He says of *Granby*, 'It is well written but over-laboured—too much attempt to put the reader exactly up to the thoughts and sentiments of the parties. The women do this better'—citing Misses Edgeworth, Ferrier, and Austen; and again of Miss Austen in particular, 'That young lady had a talent for describing the involvements and feelings and characters of ordinary life which is to me the most wonderful I ever met with. The big bow-wow strain I can do myself, like any now going; but the exquisite touch which renders ordinary common-place things and characters interesting from the truth of the description and the sentiment, is denied to me.' It is by no means improbable that the publication of *Sense and Sensibility*, in 1811, *Pride and Prejudice*, in 1813, and *Mansfield Park*, in 1814, may have had a great effect upon the character of the Waverley Novels, and have determined Scott to avoid all rivalry with the mistress of that 'exquisite touch' which he felt that Nature had denied to him. And we are the more confirmed in this conjecture because in *Waverley*, the only one of his novels which was written before the appearance of Miss Austen, there is evidence that Scott was not yet fully aware of his own comparative weakness, and that in the character of Waverley he was attempting to do what he afterwards reprobated, namely, 'to put the reader exactly up to the thoughts and sentiments of the parties'. Miss Austen showed him how much better she could do it; and henceforth he seems to have abandoned, if he ever entertained, the idea of making the delineation of human nature for its own sake, unaccompanied by circumstances of a striking or uncommon character, the subject of his labours. Yet, after all, Scott's weakness even in this respect would have been the strength of an inferior artist; for the character of Colonel Mannering, which is his nearest approach to Miss Austen, shows that Nature had been less unkind to him than he supposed. But there is no reason to believe that he laboured at this character for its own sake, as there is some reason to believe he had laboured at Waverley, or beheld in its development the main object of his work. Even in Waverley he must have felt how quickly the idea with which he started was swept away and forgotten in the rush and roar of the great romance which followed. But whatever the mixture of motives by which he was actuated, the great fact that 'the women do this better' was probably among those which deterred him from seeking popularity as a novelist of character. Had he lived till the present day, he could have had only the more reason to think as he did upon the subject; and would have recognized another specimen of feminine superiority not unequal to his favourite, in the authoress of *Adam Bede*.

But though he did not excel in the exhibition of those delicate and nameless traits by which commonplace characters are distinguished from each other, while to all but the eye of genius there seems no more difference between them than between the sheep in a flock which only the shepherd knows apart, he has few superiors in the portraiture of either types of character, generic traits, that is, which distinguish a whole class, or of individual peculiarities where these are strongly marked. His gentlemen and ladies, his soldiers and barons, his lawyers, farmers and humourists, his beggars and his butlers, his villains and his witches, are all perfect *of their kind*. And perhaps we may be doing some service to the rising generation by exhibiting one or two examples of this in some detail.

Were we to search literature for the complete embodiment of all those qualities which constitute our idea of a gentleman, where could we find anything superior to Lord Evandale in *Old Mortality*, to Damian Lacy in *The Betrothed*, to Tressilian in *Kenilworth*, and last, but not least, to that most interesting of all his heroes, the Master of Ravenswood? For a gentleman, be it remembered, is no more a perfect moral character than anybody else. Certain great and good qualities he must possess: but these may, or may not, be mingled with others which are weak or bad. But the two first upon our list seem almost faultless. We do not envy the man who can read without rising of the throat, either the death of Lord Evandale, or the interview between Damian and his uncle in the Castle prison. In each case, however, we see but the consummation of what everything in their lives had been pointing to—self-sacrifice, generosity, fidelity, fearlessness, tenderness. Bright and gay and gallant, they were earnest and devoted, pure and constant. In them strength of character was not hardened to severity, as in Ravenswood, nor was gentleness allied to weakness, as in Tressilian. Knights and gentlemen *sans peur et sans reproche*,[1] it were well if they were better known than we fear they are to the youth of England. Tressilian too easily allowed himself to be crushed by the blow which fell upon him. But a man may be a gentleman without being a hero. Ravenswood's noble nature was prematurely warped by adversity, as a man's physical beauty may be tarnished by exposure to rough weather. But a man may be a gentleman without being a saint. And such was the character of Ravenswood, perched like an eagle on his solitary crag, to swoop down with desolation in his wings upon the plains below.

If, secondly, we turn to Scott's young ladies, where shall we find among the heroines of modern fiction one equal to Alice Bridgnorth, or Alice Lee, or Catharine Seyton, or Diana Vernon? Innocence and fun, love and duty, passionate yearnings and patient self-control, are the characteristics more or less of them all. It has long been clear to us that the demure Miss Lee was far from adverse to a flirtation with Louis Kerneguy, though too proud to accept a lover in Charles Stuart. She was no prude,—most likely found Woodstock very dull,—and the Page was a godsend. It is in drawing girls of snow-white modesty and delicacy, without imparting to the character the faintest tinge of prudery or 'slowness', that Scott is peculiarly successful. Catharine Seyton and Diana Vernon speak for themselves. What a kiss that must have been, worth a king's ransom, which Catharine gave Roland at parting, on that sorrowful May morning, when she stood with her royal mistress on the shores of the Solway Firth, and looked her last on Scotland for many a long day! But, after all, we think the Queenship of his heroines must be allowed to lie between Die Vernon and Alice Bridgnorth. They both show with how much common sense, self-control, and sense of duty, the most ardent passion is consistent, and represent, we should think, with exact fidelity, Scott's ideal of womanhood. The scene between Julian Peveril and Alice in the Isle of Man, where he tries to persuade her to elope with him, is one of the finest which Scott ever drew. The vain struggle of the girl to disguise her love: the half-consent which, for a single moment, it extorts from her: with the sudden recovery of her self-command and the re-assertion of her pride: show indeed an 'exquisite touch', which Miss Austen herself might have envied. Many of Scott's heroines are colourless, like Isabella

[1] Without fear or reproach.

Wardour, Rowena, Mary Avenel; others are merely soft, warm lovable pets, like Rose Bradwardine, Lucy Bertram, Lucy Ashton, and we might add, perhaps, Amy Robsart: but all are thorough ladies: all are girls whose natures would have recoiled with a shiver from the modern idea of 'fastness'. We do not know whether we ought to make an exception in the case of Julia Mannering, in whom at times there is something bordering on pertness: but we feel that the remark is hypercritical. Scott's young ladies then as a class are simply well-bred unaffected English girls, with nothing of the Goody Two-Shoes about them: high-spirited and high-principled, capable of warm and lasting attachments, but wholly free from maudlin sentimentalism. Scott evidently laid great stress on the virtue of constancy. The length of time which his lovers are obliged to wait is a feature in his novels. Alice Bridgnorth must have waited several years; Alice Lee from the outbreak of the Civil War till after the Battle of Worcester,—some seven or eight years; Catharine Seyton nearly as long; while Edith Bellenden nursed a seemingly hopeless passion near a dozen years before she met with her reward. At least her attachment to Morton began before the Battle of Bothwell Brigg, and she was not married till after the Battle of Killiecrankie.

We have dwelt at some length on these points because an impression is abroad that in characters of the above class Scott is apt to be insipid. This opinion must have been propagated in the first instance by persons of defective sympathy, and accepted by the public without reflection. His heroines, with one or two exceptions, are not indeed the kind of girls who take one by storm; still less are they powdered, painted, and bewigged, in the style complained of by the 'French Lady' in *The Times*. But they grow on us by degrees, like their prototypes in real life; both their characters and their persons being full of a quiet beauty, which, like that of Hero,

'Sweetly creeps
Into our study of imagination,'

and retains possession of the field against all comers.

The supreme merit of Scott's humorous characters has been so universally admitted that little now remains to be said about them. We do not know, however, whether it has been noticed that in Scott we have no exaggeration either in the way of grotesqueness like Smollett, or caricature like Dickens; for as a humourist he is to be classed rather with these two than with Thackeray and Fielding. But the odd characters whom Scott introduces to our notice are peculiarly easy and natural; and in the portraiture of these he displays quite as much delicacy of touch as the ladies to whom he thought himself inferior. Commodore Trunnion and Sam Weller would have seemed strange to every one who knew them. But not so Jonathan Oldbuck, or Nicol Jarvie, or Dugald Dalgetty, or even the Baron of Bradwardine. Just as we see individuals in real life whose sayings and doings teem with an unconscious humour which many people neither see, nor seeing would appreciate; so we imagine that to his ordinary acquaintances Oldbuck was only the caustic scholar, Nicol Jarvie the shrewd, conceited old trader, and Dugald Dalgetty the pedantic mercenary; that is, comparatively commonplace personages. Scott has done for them what Miss Austen and Miss Evans have done for characters still more commonplace—brought their humours to light for our delectation, and kept each idiosyncrasy distinct with the rarest power of discrimination. We doubt if there is anything to be found out of Shakspeare equal to the dialogue in *The Antiquary*; especially in the scenes between Oldbuck and Dousterswivel, Miss Grizzel and Hector M'Intyre.

A class of characters in which Scott has not been equally successful are his villains. The best of them, no doubt, is Glossin, for we are not including men like Balfour of Burley or Dirk Hatteraick in the list. The scheming, intriguing, Iago style of villain is what we mean, such as Glossin, Rashleigh Osbaldistone, Richard Varney and Christian. Glossin is drawn with boldness and freedom; and we have no fault to find with him, except that we have never been quite able to understand the full extent of the wrong which he did to Ellangowan. But Rashleigh and Varney are too much laboured, and while the latter shows no originality, the former is made too little of. Scott seems to have begun by meaning him to be much more prominent. But Frank could have been got into the Highlands without such a roundabout device as Rashleigh's embezzlement; and his villany towards Miss Vernon is no part of the story. Frank somewhere boasts that he had rescued Miss Vernon from his toils; but he had done nothing of the kind—she had rescued herself long before he set eyes upon her. On the whole, then, Rashleigh plays no part in the plot at all commensurate with the importance assigned to him at the outset. Nor can we think of any other novel besides *Guy Mannering* in which he has succeeded better. He is thought to have failed even more in his fops and *petits-maîtres*, such as Buckingham, Dalgarno, Sir Percy Shafton, Lord Etherington, and others. We hardly know why. But even if he has, there are so few of them in his novels that they form no serious detraction from the merit of the whole.

Scott's treatment of historical personages cannot well be separated from his treatment of history; and it will probably be a long time before the controversies which this has provoked are consigned to obscurity. Our own opinion is, that Sir Walter's reputation will gain instead of losing by the continuance of it; and that people will eventually be taught that in treating such things as an artist, it was impossible he should be bound by the same rigid laws as an historian. A writer of romance must be romantic; and Scott took the materials which each party possessed for that purpose as they came to hand. If Stuarts, Cavaliers and Jacobites had more of them than Puritans and Whigs, that was not Sir Walter Scott's fault. A losing cause, just for the very reason that it is so often entwined with much that is ancient and venerable, is more likely to be the picturesque cause. And men are not less satisfied with the comforts of a good modern house because they have just seen the ruins of Glastonbury Abbey. And the word 'picturesque' may be applied to sentiments and ideas as well as to material objects: some are more suitable than others to the painter's art, and it does not at all follow that they are sure to be those which are the most entitled to our homage.

It may be said, of course, that this is no sufficient justification of Sir Walter Scott; that the facts of history are too precious to be treated in this manner; and that to pervert the judgment of a whole generation with regard to great principles, and the character, conduct and motives of their ancestors, is a crime not to be atoned for by the production of a brilliant novel. We should be disposed to say, that this is a question of degree; and that the degree in which Scott has really offended against history is so trifling as to take him altogether out of the category of such persons. In the case of Mary, Queen of Scots, he lets his own serious opinion be seen very plainly; and we have always admired the extraordinary skill which he has shown in conveying this impression to the reader without in the least injuring the effect which it was his object, as an artist, to produce. Nearly the same thing may be said of his treatment of the entire question from the days of Queen Mary down to those of Prince Charles Edward. In *Peveril of the Peak*, in *Old Mortality*, in *Rob Roy*, and in *Waverley*, he never disguises his conviction that the Stuart cause was practically the wrong one. The champions of the Puritans, if they want truth, must not object to the whole truth; and Scott good humouredly laughs at their acknowledged peculiarities, as he does at those of the Cavaliers. Mause Headrigg is hardly more ridiculous than Roger Wildrake. Bothwell is certainly more repulsive than Balfour of Burley, and gets the worst of the quarrel. Scott's most charming heroine was a Puritan, and two of his heroes, distinguished both in love and in war, were Rebels. In all his appeals to the imagination there is always an audible 'aside', which is for the benefit of the reason. Nor do we honestly believe that the sympathies with romantic misfortune, which he evokes and sustains with so much power, are ever in real danger of corrupting our historical judgment.

The royal and noble persons whom he has introduced in his historical fictions are probably painted very much as they appeared to the majority of their contemporaries, who had no very strong bias. His Queen Elizabeth is much what we should suppose her to have seemed, whether we take Mr. Froude's or any other estimate of her character. The fascinations of her rival cannot very easily be exaggerated. Charles the Second repays the hospitality of Sir Henry Lee by attempting the ruin of his daughter; and nothing worse was ever said of him; and he lounges through his palace at Whitehall with all the easy grace, good-natured affability, and ready wit, which are his traditional characteristics. Nobody has ever asserted that the picture of Prince Charles Edward was too favourable. Charles of Burgundy and Louis the Eleventh, Richard and John of England, are inevitably rather more of lay figures.

We have hitherto addressed ourselves only to those points in the Waverley Novels which have at different times, and by various critics, been challenged. A few parting words must be given to those in which all agree. We are informed by the booksellers that the novels which sell most readily in the cheap modern editions are those of which the scenes are laid in England—*Kenilworth* and *The Fortunes of Nigel*, *Woodstock* and *Ivanhoe*; and that of the Scotch ones, the popular favourites are *Waverley*, *The Abbot*, and *The Bride of Lammermoor*;— *Guy Mannering: Rob Roy*, *The Antiquary*, *Old Mortality*, *The Heart of Mid-Lothian*, &c., being rarely asked for. This was not the verdict of Scott's contemporaries; for though *Waverley* and *Kenilworth* were always in the front, *Guy Mannering* and *Old Mortality* were thought to be the foremost; but it probably indicates as just a conception of his genius. The fact we have quoted shows a marked preference for those in which there is a strong tragic element. Four out of the seven we have quoted possess it in a high degree. And if *The Antiquary*, where it also fills a large space, has sunk, *The Fortunes of Nigel* and *The Bride of Lammermoor* have risen in public estimation. It is possible that the opening chapter of *The Antiquary* may have deterred many readers from pursuing that inimitable story till the full beauty of the contrast between Glenallan Castle, wrapped in solemn and mysterious gloom, and the cheerful, bright, middle-class life of comfortable Monkbarns breaks upon them. *The Bride of Lammermoor* carries no such weight. The story begins at once; from first to last are we oppressed by that lurid and sultry atmosphere charged to bursting with such elements of misery. A sense of impending doom is over us throughout; nor can the absurdities of Caleb Balderstone chase from our minds for an instant the fortunes of the fated lovers. *The Bride of Lammermoor* is a complete tragedy, far superior both in design and execution to *Kenilworth*, because our interest is never divided, and the action is never broken. But it is in the character of Ravenswood himself that the grandeur of the tale consists. We know not whether it has ever been observed before that this is the only effort which Scott ever made in the Byronic style. Lockhart calls this novel the 'purest and most powerful of the tragedies which Scott ever wrote', and De Quincey saw in it his nearest approach to Shakspeare. Its rise in public favour must therefore be regarded as a hopeful sign of the times. Scott, then, as a consummate tragedian, is a character to which we may say that universal consent has been given. A second point is one that we might not have thought it necessary to allude to but for certain social phenomena of the present age at which we have already glanced: we mean the masculine simplicity of his mind in all cases where vice is in question. Would any lady put *The Heart of Mid-Lothian* out of her daughter's reach? or would any gentleman dread the effect of the Baron of Bradwardine's example on his son? In this respect there is another curious resemblance between Scott and Dickens. The remarkable fact that no one, even at the present day, sees any harm in the whole Pickwick Club getting drunk, not once only, but habitually, has already been noticed by a distinguished critic. And no one has ever charged the *Pickwick Papers* with any tendency to promote excess. The story of *Little Em'ly* is equally free from all taint, not only of prurience, but even coarseness. In the character of Hetty Sorrel, Miss Evans has shown how closely she could tread in these footsteps; but there is a nameless something even there—a taint of animalism—which makes it inferior.

Something like a re-action set in against Sir Walter Scott between thirty and forty years ago. The warlike and conservative age which had received with rapture his pictures in which feudalism and loyalty were the main sources of interest was passing away, and the age so well described by Burke was coming in its stead. But that too, having done its work, is disappearing, and with its departure is reviving that cordial sympathy with Sir W. Scott which succeeding centuries will only confirm and enlarge. From the revival of letters to the present day it is questionable whether anything will, in the judgment of posterity, be found worthier to rank after Shakspeare's dramas and Milton's epics than the Waverley Novels.

63. A late centenary view, *London Quarterly*

1872

An extract from an unsigned review of editions of Scott's poems and novels and of several biographies, *London Quarterly* (April 1872), xxxviii, 35-59.

The art so exquisitely practised by Jane Austen, within strait enough intellectual limits, and without any deep perceptions of human passion or any wide knowledge of the human heart—the art of making ordinary people in ordinary circumstances intensely interesting, reached its noblest height in George Eliot's *Sad Fortunes of the Rev. Amos Barton*,[1] wherein absolute simplicity of character and event is seen through the wide intellectuality and profound soul-lore of a strong spirit and a great artist. But this art, 'denied', as Scott said, to him, will never countervail, for the uses of our youths and maidens, at all events, the art which was *not* denied to Scott. Such work as Jane Austen's and George Eliot's will grow in use and influence, and will probably reach lower and lower down the grades of society as education spreads itself; but such work cannot displace the simple healthful interest in lives of

[1] *Scenes of Clerical Life* [reviewer].

adventure, and all young people feel gratified in reading the Waverley Novels, unencumbered as those books are by any didactic or other purpose ulterior to the original nature of romance; and so we cannot regret that it was 'denied' to Scott to do what others have done so well, while it was permitted to him to do so magnificently what no one else has yet approached him in.

But if Scott was unable to render the commonplace in character and event vitally interesting by the 'exquisite touch' we have referred to, neither did he obtain a factitious interest by cynical raids on human weaknesses, or gross exaggeration of human peculiarities; and thus he kept clear of the pitfalls that have since snared Thackeray on the one hand, and Dickens on the other. Thackeray's supreme power to chisel a statuesque story, as in *Esmond*, we might not find amiss in some of Scott's looser tales, any more than an infusion of Scott's largeness of heart might well be coveted as an antidote for the cynic obliquity of gaze that led to much that is not admirable in Thackeray. But from Dickens we covet not a single quality for his great predecessor, who, with a more exquisite humour, never became coarse, and with an equal power to draw remarkable persons, never produced a single character that can fairly be stigmatised as a caricature. The nearest approach to a caricature that the Waverley portrait gallery affords is, perhaps, Dominie Sampson; and he certainly stops short of being that hollow embodiment of ridiculous traits that he would have been if Dickens had had the making of him. Awkward, eccentric, and ludicrous, and rendered often doubly so under the sprightly satirical flashes of Miss Julia Mannering, he is yet kept thoroughly real and true to his humanity by that noble, simple devotedness to his patron and his patron's memory and race: we can never find it in our hearts to laugh at his straining to his breast the brawny young Scot whom he persistently designates as 'little Harry Bertram;' and everything about his inner being is so thoroughly worthy of respect, that his uncouth sayings and doings are overlooked with a smile, even when there is no sufficient pathos to carry the reader above smiling point, as he is carried at the recognition between the Dominie and Harry Bertram. Similarly, the crazy litigant in *Redgauntlet*, poor Peter Peebles, plaintiff in 'the great cause of Peebles against Plainstanes', remains true to his appointed part of pursuing a hopelessly burdened cause, from one year to another, through poverty, and distress, and madness, firmly enthusiastic as to the rectitude and importance of his plea; and this is not managed by the endless cumulation of ridiculous incidents and distorted scraps of laughable speech, but by that fluent *insouciant* speaking and acting to the point, in every circumstance of the fiction, that distinguishes Scott's personages, in all ranks and relations of life, from the laboriously worked up creatures of Dickens's brain.

For a popular and at the same time healthful beguiler of the leisure hours, Scott lacked no single quality, and as far transcended the much admired caricaturist just named in these particulars as he did in the weighty consideration of quality of art. First among Scott's qualifications for popularity, we may note that he possessed the power to make an action deeply interesting without any of those factitious complications resorted to by later and feebler hands; and so much was this the case that he frequently, with the greatest *naïveté*, allowed his mystery or coil, the unravelling of which furnished the ostensible interest of the plot, to be quite transparent to the reader long before being professedly cleared up. It is delightful to note how, when a disguise is no longer necessary, he calmly assumes that the reader saw through it all the time, and does not even take the trouble to invent any particular clearing up of the circumstances for his benefit. We take no whit less interest in the establishment of the identity of Harry Bertram and Lord Geraldin because there are no particular points at which those lost heirs are discovered by the reader under their disguises of Vanbeest Brown and Lovell; and yet there have been but few workers in fiction who could afford to let us so much into the secret of their heroes' aliases as Scott did with these and such-like characters.

But beside this power to keep up the interest in a genuine and straightforward manner, we find in the Waverley Novels an intimate acquaintance with the manners and customs of all kinds of people in all kinds of places and periods, that is astonishing in a high degree, notwithstanding the circumstances of education and growing up that fostered the artist's taste in that direction; and works in fiction representing social phases are naturally and properly popular when they have other good qualities. Those works now under consideration command popularity in a special degree as novels of manners (to use a somewhat inadequate expression), because, though the author's conception of an ideal social state was evidently and unquestionably Feudalism, he maintains in the most pointed manner the respect of the higher classes to the lower classes as well as the converse bearing of the lower to the higher. In those novels, particularly, which deal with Scottish and Border life, the conception of the value and importance of the 'dependent' classes is strongly and clearly set forth; and those Scottish tales are beyond a question the best of the series taken all round, whether we judge them on the ground of what the writer drew directly from the life of the persons among whom he moved with his keen observation and prodigious memory, or of what he reconstructed from hints thrown off by some old person whom he encountered, or of what he filled in mainly by the power of his rich imagination. Most of them also, though clearly novels of manners, rise to the higher importance of what it has generally been deemed Scott's peculiar glory to have constituted, historic romance—inasmuch as whether he depicted the actors in the gradually lessening struggle between Jacobitism and Hanoverianism, or those who were pitted against each other as Cavaliers and Roundheads, or the heroes of the old Crusading times, he always endeavoured to give us faithfully the real bent and purpose of national movements, as well as the mere manners and customs of the people. And he was generally pretty successful, though it must be admitted that the *Tales of the Crusaders* are infinitely less vigorous than such works as *Old Mortality*, *Peveril of the Peak*, and the three tales representing three generations of Scotch society,—*Waverley*, *Guy Mannering*, and *The Antiquary*, which tales taken all in all are probably the most completely excellent of Sir Walter's voluminous works in poetry, romance, history, biography, criticism, and translation from foreign tongues.

The importance which Scott gave in his romances to persons occupying a subordinate rank in life is subject sufficient for an elaborate critical study: it is not only that his books teem with masterly portraits, from the rough occasional sketch to the finished picture, taken from the yeomanry, peasantry, domestic and vagrant classes; not only that these are touched with a profound respect for their common humanity with the artist, such as is good for this Dickens-worshipping age to contemplate and set beside the irreverent travesties of human nature known as Chadband, Uriah Heep, Pecksniff, and so on; but beside and beyond all this, we have numerous instances of the very best workmanship in a book being bestowed on one of these characters of what, to Scott's feudal mind, was a distinctly inferior rank, and several instances in which one of them is made of vital importance in the development of the story. Meg Merrilies, Edie Ochiltree, Elspeth of the Craigburnfoot, Cristal Nixon (with his insidious emissary, Little Benjie), poor daft Davie Gellatly, are but a few examples of a goodly company of graphically and powerfully drawn characters outside the pale of gentility; and two of these, Meg Merrilies and Edie Ochiltree, are among the most complete and remarkable characters created by

Scott or any other man. Indeed, Meg Merrilies is far more the heroine of *Guy Mannering* than either of the young ladies of the book is, and than the Colonel or any other male character is the hero; and Edie Ochiltree is superior even to the delightful 'Antiquary' himself; while both Gipsy Meg and Gaberlunzie Edie, as well as the other 'minor persons' named above, and a great number in other books, are so far instrumental in carrying on the respective actions that it would be utter ruin to the tales to drop those persons out.

The venerable sneerer, Thomas Carlyle, whose celebrated essay on Scott seems to have been written with a sincere desire to repress the caustic, cynical, often farcical tone that is natural to him, remarked, with much truth, that the characters of the great novelist seemed to have been modelled from the clothes inwards, instead of from the heart outwards, as in the case of Shakespeare's characters. This keen sword-sweep was probably meant to shear away more laurels from the brow of Sir Walter than posterity will consent to have taken from him, even on so respectable a dictum; for though it may be perfectly clear that the descriptive method of Scott commenced with the exteriors of his personages, it is by no means clear that that was a very important inversion of the Shakespearean order of things, unless it could be shown that the novelist never arrived at the heart after all in his progress inwards. That he did get to the heart sometimes even Mr. Carlyle will not, we imagine, deny; and considering the nobility of heart discernible in such personages as Meg Merrilies and Edie Ochiltree, Mr. Oldbuck of Monkbarns, and the Baron of Bradwardine, Jeanie Deans and Dominie Sampson, we need not mind admitting that even they were created 'from the clothes inwards'. Indeed, the characters of Scott are just as good as they could possibly be, within the limits of his apparent knowledge of the human heart and the motives of men and women: his *method* of creation is first-rate, although what he describes as a rule indicates that he was more concerned with the surface of human nature than he was with its depths.

64. Gladstone on *The Bride of Lammermoor*
1870s [?]

An extract from Sydney Colvin's *Memories and Notes of Persons and Places* (N.Y., 1921).

In this passage Colvin reports on a conversation with William Ewart Gladstone, the British statesman, which occurred sometime after 1873, the date of their first meeting.

The best talk about literature in which I can remember Mr. Gladstone taking a leading part turned on the nature and elements of tragedy, and on the difference between themes inherently tragic and those which owed their tragic character mainly to their treatment. Some examples from Greek and Elizabethan drama having been discussed, Mr. Gladstone presently, in his most earnest and arresting manner, affirmed that in his judgment no theme was either more tragic in itself or more heightened in effect by its treatment than that of Scott's *Bride of Lammermoor*. He insisted on the circumstances of the deadly hereditary hate, fresher and better grounded than that of Montagues and Capulets, between the houses of Ravenswood and Ashton, and on the sense of such fixed implacable hate foredooming to disaster what might under other stars have been the reconciling loves of Edgar and Lucy. He dwelt on the heightening of all the actions and passions by the romantic gloom of the scenery amid which the tale unfolds itself, and by the grim staves of legendary prophecy represented as current in the minds of the common people and creating from the first an atmosphere of dire expectancy and awe. He reminded us how such prophetic saws and staves are not only ever on the lips of the hateful warlock, Elsie Gourlay, but how they darken with tragic foreknowledge even that almost incomparable, almost fully Shakespearean, comic and pathetic creation of the old steward Caleb Balderstone; and he dilated on the terrible intensity of the scene of the mad bride-murderess on her wedding night, and on the foretold but not less thrilling climax of the disappearance of the last heir of Ravenswood in the Kelpie's Flow. None of those present was disposed to contest on general grounds the claim thus made for Scott's masterpiece, I least of all; and the further talk, to which Mr. Gladstone listened attentively but did not, if I remember aright, contribute much, turned on certain doubts and reservations to be made in regard to it; as for instance, whether some of the incidents, such as those of the wild bull and the crash of lightning on Wolfe's Crag in the opening chapters, did not push romantic coincidence to the point of melodrama, and whether the Master himself is not a character partaking as much of the externally and conventionally melodramatic as of the truly tragic. And how, we all agreed in wondering, could the magician in his carelessness possibly have allowed himself to introduce, as he does, the finely conceived incident of the apparition to the Master beside the Mermaid's well of the spirit of old Alice at the moment of her death with an apology to the rationalist and sceptical which robs it of half its effect?

65. R. L. Stevenson on Scott's place in literary history, *Cornhill Magazine*

1874

Excerpts from an unsigned article entitled 'Victor Hugo's Romances', *Cornhill Magazine* (August 1874), xxx, 179-94. The author is Robert Louis Stevenson.

When we compare the novels of Walter Scott with those of the man of genius who preceded him and whom he delighted to honour as a master in the art—I mean Henry Fielding—we shall be somewhat puzzled, at the first moment, to explain the difference that there is between these two. Fielding has as much human science; has a far firmer hold upon the tiller of his story; has a keen sense of character, which he draws (and Scott often does so too) in a rather abstract and academical manner; and finally, is quite as humorous and quite as good-humoured as the great Scotchman. With all these points of resemblance between the men, it is astonishing that their work should be so different. The fact is, that the English novel was looking one way and seeking one set of effects in the hands of Fielding; and in the hands of Scott it was looking eagerly in all ways and searching for all the effects that by any possibility it could utilise. The difference between these two men marks a great enfranchisement. With Scott the Romantic movement, the movement of an extended curiosity and an enfranchised imagination has begun. This is a trite thing to say; but trite things are often very indefinitely comprehended: and this enfranchisement, in as far as it regards the technical change that came over modern prose romance, has never perhaps been explained with any clearness.

This touches the difference between Fielding and Scott. In the work of the latter, true to his character of a modern and a romantic, we become suddenly conscious of the background. Fielding, on the other hand, although he had recognised that the novel was nothing else than an epic in prose, wrote in the spirit not of the epic, but of the drama. This is not, of course, to say that the drama was in any way incapable of a regeneration similar in kind to that of which I am now speaking with regard to the novel. The notorious contrary fact is sufficient to guard the reader against such a misconstruction. All that is meant is, that Fielding remained ignorant of certain capabilities which the novel possesses over the drama; or, at least, neglected and did not develope them. To the end he continued to see things as a playwright sees them. The world with which he dealt, the world he had realised for himself and sought to realise and set before his readers, was a world of exclusively human interest. As for landscape he was content to underline stage directions, as it might be done in a play-book: Tom and Molly retire into a practicable wood. As for nationality and public sentiment it is curious enough to think that *Tom Jones* is laid in the year forty-five, and that the only use he makes of the rebellion is to throw a troop of soldiers into his hero's way. It is most really important, however, to notice the change which has been introduced into the conception of character by the beginning of the romantic movement and the consequent introduction into fiction of a vast amount of new material.

Fielding tells us as much as he thought necessary to account for the actions of his creatures; he thought that each of these actions could be decomposed on the spot into a few simple personal elements, as we decompose a force in a question of perfectly abstract dynamics. The larger motives are all unknown to him; he had not understood that the configuration of the landscape or the fashion of the times could be for anything in a story; and so, naturally and rightly, he said nothing about them. But Scott's instinct, the instinct of the man of an age profoundly different, taught him otherwise; and, in his work, the individual characters begin to occupy a comparatively small proportion of that canvas on which armies manœuvre, and great hills pile themselves upon each other's shoulders. Fielding's characters were always great to the full stature of a perfectly arbitrary will. Already in Scott we begin to have a sense of the subtle influences that moderate and qualify a man's personality; that personality is no longer thrown out in unnatural isolation, but is resumed into its place in the constitution of things.

It is this change in the manner of regarding men and their actions first exhibited in romance, that has since renewed and vivified history. For art precedes philosophy and even science. People must have noticed things and interested themselves in them before they begin to debate upon their causes or influence. And it is in this way that art is the pioneer of knowledge; those predilections of the artist he knows not why, those irrational acceptations and recognitions, reclaim, out of the world that we have not yet realised, ever another and another corner; and after the facts have been thus vividly brought before us and have had time to settle and arrange themselves in our minds, some day there will be found the man of science to stand up and give the explanation. Scott took an interest in many things in which Fielding took none; and for this reason, and no other, he introduced them into his romances. If he had been told what would be the nature of the movement that he was so lightly initiating, he would have been very incredulous and not a little scandalised. At the time when he wrote the real drift of this new manner of pleasing people in fiction was not yet apparent; and, even now, it is only by looking at the romances of Victor Hugo that we are enabled to form any proper judgment in the matter. These books are not only descended by ordinary generation from the Waverley novels, but it is in them chiefly that we shall find the revolutionary tradition of Scott carried farther; that we shall find Scott himself, in so far as regards his conception of prose fiction and its purposes, surpassed in his own spirit, instead of tamely followed. We have here, as I said before, a line of literary tendency produced, and by this production definitely separated from others. When we come to Hugo, we see that the deviation, which seemed slight enough and not very serious between Scott and Fielding, is indeed such a great gulph in thought and sentiment as only successive generations can pass over; and it is but natural that one of the great advances that Hugo has made upon Scott is an advance in self-consciousness. Both men follow the same road; but where the one went blindly and carelessly, the other advances with all deliberation and forethought. There never was artist much more unconscious than Scott; and there have been not many more conscious than Hugo.

66. George Brandes: morality as drawback

1875

An extract from a chapter on Scott in *Naturalism in England*, volume iv of *Main Currents in Nineteenth Century Literature* by George Brandes, the Danish critic.

Previous to the section given below, Brandes called Scott 'one of the greatest character portrayers in all literature'.

When we look back from the vantage-ground of our own day on the second, the prose, period of Scott's authorship, we find it impossible to see the long series of the Waverley Novels in the same light in which they appeared to his contemporaries. We understand the satisfaction which lay in the certainty that they would never give offence, that they might always be welcomed gladly, not only as gifted, but as perfectly moral works. This particular qualification is, however, exactly what makes them less attractive to us. There is no exaggeration in declaring it to be a law in the modern literature of every country, that an author *must* cause offence to at least one generation of his contemporaries, and be considered immoral by it, if he is not to seem tiresome and narrow-minded to readers of the period immediately succeeding his own. To us the defects of Scott's novels are very plain. They give pleasure by their excellent character-drawing and the liveliness of their dialogue, but they do not satisfy the reason, do not appeal very strongly to the feelings, do not even arouse any great degree of curiosity. They are soulful, but idealess. We feel that Scott, as a patriotic author, was determined to keep up the interest in Scotland which Macpherson and Burns had awakened in the reading public; therefore he writes in such a manner as to estrange not even the most narrow-minded reader. Himself denied the sensual organisation of the artist, he is so discreet in his treatment of the relations between the sexes that there is next to no description of erotic situations. And, the moral to be conveyed seeming of greater importance to him than art, he represents past ages with such a toning down of all the coarse elements that historic truth suffers terribly. The species of fiction which Scott introduced, and which indicated a distinct step in advance of the older novel, is now in its turn antiquated; the literary critics of every country lean to the opinion that the historical novel, with all its merits, is a bastard species—now it is so hampered with historical material that the poetic development of the story is rendered impossible, again it is so free in its paraphrase of history that the real and the fictitious elements produce a very discordant whole. In the third volume of *The Heart of Midlothian* (Chap. x), for example, the manner in which imaginary speeches are mixed up with the historical utterances of the Duke of Argyle, distinctly offends the critical taste. It becomes, moreover, increasingly evident how different the general impression conveyed by Scott's pictures of past times is from the essential character of these far-off days, an unvarnished representation of which, supposing it to be understood at all, would certainly fail to awaken sympathy. His *Tales of the Crusaders* are circulating-library novels, which describe the wonder-lands and the romantic, adventurous deeds of the Crusades with almost as little regard to reality as Tasso's *Gerusalemme Liberata*; but which do not display anything like the Italian's poetic talent, or his artistically conscientious attention to style.

How could it be otherwise in the case of an author like Scott, who wrote without ever re-reading, much less correcting, a page, who had not the gift of conciseness, and who made no serious demands on himself in the matter of composition? He demands still less of his readers, as far as attention and quick apprehension are concerned. He repeats himself and allows his characters to repeat themselves, puts in his word in the middle of the story, points out and explains. Not satisfied with showing the temperament and character of his personages by their mode of action, he makes them, when necessary, give account of themselves in such phrases as: 'I am speaking with calmness, though it is contrary to my character'; or in speeches in which the speaker draws the moral lesson from his own wicked actions, in the case the reader should by any chance miss it and be tempted to imitation. (Read, for example, George Staunton's whole confession to Jeanie Deans, a model of bad style and false psychology.) With such serious faults as these in the details, it is of little avail that the plots of the best novels are excellent, leading up naturally to dramatic crises, one or more as the case may be. A book which is to retain its fame for centuries must not only be poetically planned, but artistically elaborated in every detail—a task for which Scott, from the moment he began to write in prose, never left himself time. Even the most dramatic scene he ever wrote—the splendid and powerfully affecting trial-scene in *The Heart of Midlothian*, in which Jeanie, with a bleeding heart, but with noble devotion to the truth, gives witness against her own sister—loses half of its effect from the careless prolixity of the style. We learn from Moore's *Memoirs* that the main theme of the book—the story of the young girl who refuses to give witness in court in favour of her sister, and afterwards undertakes the long journey to beg a pardon for her—is a true story, which was communicated to Scott in an anonymous letter. He has evidently had the keenest perception of the moral beauty of the incident, but very little of its essentially dramatic character. If he had possessed only half the amount of talent that he had, along with double the amount of culture and instinct of self-criticism, he would doubtless have made less stir in the world, but he would have produced works of greater and more enduring value.[1]

---

[1] He does not seem to have had any understanding of plastic art. Desiring to give an impression of the old Puritan in *The Heart of Midlothian*, he evolves the following artistically impossible fabulous creature: 'The whole formed a picture, of which the lights might have been given by Rembrandt, but the outline would have required the force and vigour of Michael Angelo' [Brandes].

67. R. H. Hutton: Scott as man of letters

1878

Extracts from Richard H. Hutton, *Sir Walter Scott* (1878), published in the 'English Men of Letters' series, so many of the volumes of which have become classics in their own right.

The first two sections of the text below are on the poems; later sections discuss the novels.

If we ask ourselves to what this vast popularity of Scott's poems, and especially of the earlier of them (for, as often happens, he was better remunerated for his later and much inferior poems than for his earlier and more brilliant productions) is due, I think the answer must be for the most part, the high romantic glow and extraordinary romantic simplicity of the poetical elements they contained. Take the old harper of *The Lay*, a figure which arrested the attention of Pitt during even that last most anxious year of his anxious life, the year of Ulm and Austerlitz. The lines in which Scott describes the old man's embarrassment when first urged to play, produced on Pitt, according to his own account, 'an effect which I might have expected in painting, but could never have fancied capable of being given in poetry'.
Every one knows the lines to which Pitt refers:—

> 'The humble boon was soon obtain'd;
> The aged minstrel audience gain'd.
> But, when he reach'd the room of state,
> Where she with all her ladies sate,
> Perchance he wish'd his boon denied;
> For, when to tune the harp he tried,
> His trembling hand had lost the ease
> Which marks security to please;
> And scenes long past, of joy and pain,
> Came wildering o'er his aged brain,—
> He tried to tune his harp in vain!

481

The pitying Duchess praised its chime,
And gave him heart, and gave him time,
Till every string's according glee
Was blended into harmony.
And then, he said, he would full fain
He could recall an ancient strain
He never thought to sing again.
It was not framed for village churls,
But for high dames and mighty earls;
He'd play'd it to King Charles the Good,
When he kept Court at Holyrood;
And much he wish'd, yet fear'd, to try
The long-forgotten melody.
Amid the strings his fingers stray'd,
And an uncertain warbling made,
And oft he shook his hoary head.
But when he caught the measure wild
The old man raised his face, and smiled;
And lighten'd up his faded eye,
With all a poet's ecstasy!
In varying cadence, soft or strong,
He swept the sounding chords along;
The present scene, the future lot,
His toils, his wants, were all forgot;
Cold diffidence and age's frost
In the full tide of song were lost;
Each blank in faithless memory void
The poet's glowing thought supplied;
And, while his harp responsive rung,
'Twas thus the latest minstrel sung.
  *   *   *   *   *
Here paused the harp; and with its swell
The master's fire and courage fell;
Dejectedly and low he bow'd,
And, gazing timid on the crowd,
He seem'd to seek in every eye
If they approved his minstrelsy;
And, diffident of present praise,
Somewhat he spoke of former days,
And how old age, and wandering long,
Had done his hand and harp some wrong.'

These lines hardly illustrate, I think, the particular form of Mr. Pitt's criticism, for a quick succession of fine shades of feeling of this kind

482

could never have been delineated in a painting, or indeed in a series of paintings, at all, while they *are* so given in the poem. But the praise itself, if not its exact form, is amply deserved. The singular depth of the romantic glow in this passage, and its equally singular simplicity,— a simplicity which makes it intelligible to every one,—are conspicuous to every reader. It is not what is called classical poetry, for there is no severe outline,—no sculptured completeness and repose,—no satisfying wholeness of effect to the eye of the mind,—no embodiment of a great action. The poet gives us a breath, a ripple of alternating fear and hope in the heart of an old man, and that is all. He catches an emotion that had its roots deep in the past, and that is striving onward towards something in the future;—he traces the wistfulness and self-distrust with which age seeks to recover the feelings of youth,—the delight with which it greets them when they come,—the hesitation and diffidence with which it recalls them as they pass away, and questions the triumph it has just won,—and he paints all this without subtlety, without complexity, but with a swiftness such as few poets ever surpassed. Generally, however, Scott prefers action itself for his subject, to any feeling however active in its bent. The cases in which he makes a study of any mood of feeling, as he does of this harper's feeling, are comparatively rare. Deloraine's night-ride to Melrose is a good deal more in Scott's ordinary way, than this study of the old harper's wistful mood. But whatever his subject, his treatment of it is the same. His lines are always strongly drawn; his handling is always simple: and his subject always romantic. But though romantic, it is simple almost to bareness,—one of the great causes both of his popularity, and of that deficiency in his poetry of which so many of his admirers become conscious when they compare him with other and richer poets. Scott used to say that in poetry Byron 'bet' him; and no doubt that in which chiefly as a poet he 'bet' him, was in the variety, the richness, the lustre of his effects. A certain ruggedness and bareness was of the essence of Scott's idealism and romance. It was so in relation to scenery. He told Washington Irving that he loved the very nakedness of the Border country. 'It has something,' he said, 'bold and stern and solitary about it. When I have been for some time in the rich scenery about Edinburgh, which is like ornamented garden-land, I begin to wish myself back again among my honest grey hills, and if I did not see the heather at least once a year, *I think I should die.*' Now, the bareness which Scott so loved in his native scenery, there is in all his romantic elements of feeling. It is while he is bold and stern, that he is at his highest ideal point. Directly he begins to attempt rich or pretty subjects, as in parts of *The Lady of the Lake*, and a good deal of *The Lord of the Isles*, and still more in *The Bridal of Triermain*, his charm disappears. It is in painting those moods and exploits, in relation to which Scott shares most completely the feelings of ordinary men, but experiences them with far greater strength and purity than ordinary men, that he triumphs as a poet. Mr. Lockhart tells us that some of Scott's senses were decidedly 'blunt' and one seems to recognize this in the simplicity of his romantic effects. 'It is a fact,' he says, 'which some philosophers may think worth setting down, that Scott's organization, as to more than one of the senses, was the reverse of exquisite. He had very little of what musicians call an ear; his smell was hardly more delicate. I have seen him stare about, quite unconscious of the cause, when his whole company betrayed their uneasiness at the approach of an overkept haunch of venison; and neither by the nose nor the palate could he distinguish corked wine from sound. He could never tell Madeira from sherry,—nay, an Oriental friend having sent him a butt of *sheeraz*, when he remembered the circumstance some time afterwards and called for a bottle to have Sir John Malcolm's opinion of its quality, it turned out that his butler, mistaking the label, had already served up half the bin as *sherry*. Port he considered as physic . . . . in truth he liked no wines except sparkling champagne and claret; but even as to the last he was no connoisseur, and sincerely preferred a tumbler of whisky-toddy to the most precious "liquid-ruby" that ever flowed in the cup of a prince.'

However, Scott's eye was very keen:—'*It was commonly him,*' as his little son once said, '*that saw the hare sitting.*' And his perception of colour was very delicate as well as his mere sight. As Mr. Ruskin has pointed out, his landscape painting is almost all done by the lucid use of colour. Nevertheless this bluntness of organization in relation to the less important senses, no doubt contributed something to the singleness and simplicity of the deeper and more vital of Scott's romantic impressions; at least there is good reason to suppose that delicate and complicated susceptibilities do at least diminish the chance of living a strong and concentrated life—do risk the frittering away of feeling on the mere backwaters of sensations, even if they do not directly tend towards artificial and indirect forms of character. Scott's romance is like his native scenery,—bold, bare and rugged, with a swift deep stream of strong pure feeling running through it. There is plenty of colour in his pictures, as there is on the Scotch hills when the heather is out. And so too there is plenty of intensity in his romantic situations;

but it is the intensity of simple, natural, unsophisticated, hardy, and manly characters. But as for subtleties and fine shades of feeling in his poems, or anything like the manifold harmonies of the richer arts, they are not to be found, or, if such complicated shading is to be found—and it is perhaps attempted in some faint measure in *The Bridal of Triermain*, the poem in which Scott tried to pass himself off for Erskine,—it is only at the expense of the higher qualities of his romantic poetry, that even in this small measure it is supplied. Again, there is no rich music in his verse. It is its rapid onset, its hurrying strength, which so fixes it in the mind.

It was not till 1808, three years after the publication of *The Lay*, that *Marmion*, Scott's greatest poem, was published. But I may as well say what seems necessary of that and his other poems, while I am on the subject of his poetry. *Marmion* has all the advantage over *The Lay of the Last Minstrel* that a coherent story told with force and fulness, and concerned with the same class of subjects as *The Lay*, must have over a confused and ill-managed legend, the only original purpose of which was to serve as the opportunity for a picture of Border life and strife. Scott's poems have sometimes been depreciated as mere *novelettes* in verse, and I think that some of them may be more or less liable to this criticism. For instance, *The Lady of the Lake*, with the exception of two or three brilliant passages, has always seemed to me more of a versified *novelette*,—without the higher and broader characteristics of Scott's prose novels—than of a poem. I suppose what one expects from a poem as distinguished from a romance—even though the poem incorporates a story—is that it should not rest for its chief interest on the mere development of the story; but rather that the narrative should be quite subordinate to that insight into the deeper side of life and manners, in expressing which poetry has so great an advantage over prose. Of *The Lay* and *Marmion* this is true; less true of *The Lady of the Lake*: and still less of *Rokeby*, or *The Lord of the Isles*, and this is why *The Lay* and *Marmion* seem so much superior as poems to the others. They lean less on the interest of mere incident, more on that of romantic feeling and the great social and historic features of the day.

And *Marmion* registers the high-water mark of Scott's poetical power, not only in relation to the painting of war, but in relation to the painting of nature. Critics from the beginning onwards have complained of the six introductory epistles, as breaking the unity of the story. But I cannot see that the remark has weight. No poem is written for those who read it as they do a novel—merely to follow the interest of the story; or if any poem be written for such readers, it deserves to die. On such a principle—which treats a poem as a mere novel and nothing else,—you might object to Homer that he interrupts the battle so often to dwell on the origin of the heroes who are waging it; or to Byron that he deserts Childe Harold to meditate on the rapture of solitude. To my mind the ease and frankness of these confessions of the author's recollections give a picture of his life and character while writing *Marmion*, which adds greatly to its attraction as a poem. You have a picture at once not only of the scenery, but of the mind in which that scenery is mirrored, and are brought back frankly, at fit intervals, from the one to the other, in the mode best adapted to help you to appreciate the relation of the poet to the poem. At least if Milton's various interruptions of a much more ambitious theme, to muse upon his own qualifications or disqualifications for the task he had attempted, be not artistic mistakes—and I never heard of any one who thought them so—I cannot see any reason why Scott's periodic recurrence to his own personal history should be artistic mistakes either. If Scott's reverie was less lofty than Milton's, so also was his story. It seems to me as fitting to describe the relation between the poet and his theme in the one case as in the other. What can be more truly a part of *Marmion*, as a poem, though not as a story, than that introduction to the first canto in which Scott expresses his passionate sympathy with the high national feeling of the moment, in his tribute to Pitt and Fox, and then re-proaches himself for attempting so great a subject and returns to what he calls his 'rude-legend', the very essence of which was, however, a passionate appeal to the spirit of national independence? What can be more germane to the poem than the delineation of the strength the poet had derived from musing in the bare and rugged solitudes of St. Mary's Lake, in the introduction to the second canto? Or than the striking autobiographical study of his own infancy which I have before extracted from the introduction to the third? It seems to me that *Marmion* without these introductions would be like the hills which border Yarrow, without the stream and lake in which they are reflected.

Never at all events in any later poem was Scott's touch as a mere painter so terse and strong. What a picture of a Scotch winter is given in these few lines:—

'The sheep before the pinching heaven
To shelter'd dale and down are driven,

486

> Where yet some faded herbage pines,
> And yet a watery sunbeam shines:
> In meek despondency they eye
> The wither'd sward and wintry sky,
> And from beneath their summer hill
> Stray sadly by Glenkinnon's rill.'

Again, if Scott is ever Homeric (which I cannot think he often is, in spite of Sir Francis Doyle's able criticism,—he is too short, too sharp, and too eagerly bent on his rugged way, for a poet who is always delighting to find loopholes, even in battle, from which to look out upon the great story of human nature), he is certainly nearest to it in such a passage as this:—

[Canto V, lines 128-35 of *Marmion* are quoted]

In hardly any of Scott's poetry do we find much of what is called the *curiosa felicitas* of expression,—the magic use of *words*, as distinguished from the mere general effect of vigour, purity, and concentration of purpose. But in *Marmion* occasionally we do find such a use. Take this description, for instance, of the Scotch tents near Edinburgh:—

> 'A thousand did I say? I ween
> Thousands on thousands there were seen,
> That chequer'd all the heath between
>   The streamlet and the town;
> In crossing ranks extending far,
> Forming a camp irregular;
> Oft giving way where still there stood
> Some relics of the old oak wood,
> That darkly huge did intervene,
> *And tamed the glaring white with green;*
> In these extended lines there lay
> A martial kingdom's vast array.'

The line I have italicized seems to me to have more of the poet's special magic of expression than is at all usual with Scott. The conception of the peaceful green oakwood *taming* the glaring white of the tented field, is as fine an idea as it is in relation to the effect of the mere colour on the eye. Judge Scott's poetry by whatever test you will—whether it be a test of that which is peculiar to it, its glow of national feeling, its martial ardour, its swift and rugged simplicity, or whether it be a test of that which is common to it with most other poetry, its attraction for all romantic excitements, its special feeling for the pomp and circumstance of war, its love of light and colour—and tested either way, *Marmion* will remain his finest poem. The battle of Flodden Field touches his highest point in its expression of stern patriotic feeling, in its passionate love of daring, and in the force and swiftness of its movement, no less than in the brilliancy of its romantic interests, the charm of its pictures-que detail, and the glow of its scenic colouring. No poet ever equalled Scott in the description of wild and simple scenes and the expression of wild and simple feelings. But I have said enough now of his poetry, in which, good as it is, Scott's genius did not reach its highest point. The hurried tramp of his somewhat monotonous metre, is apt to weary the ears of men who do not find their sufficient happiness, as he did, in dreaming of the wild and daring enterprises of his loved Border-land. The very quality in his verse which makes it seize so powerfully on the imaginations of plain, bold, adventurous men, often makes it hammer fatiguingly against the brain of those who need the relief of a wider horizon and a richer world.

There is more than one novelist of the present day who has far surpassed Scott in the number of his tales, and one at least of very high repute, who has, I believe, produced more even within the same time. But though to our larger experience, Scott's achievement, in respect of mere fertility, is by no means the miracle which it once seemed, I do not think one of his successors can compare with him for a moment in the ease and truth with which he painted, not merely the life of his own time and country—seldom indeed that of precisely his own time—but that of days long past, and often too of scenes far distant. The most powerful of all his stories, *Old Mortality*, was the story of a period more than a century and a quarter before he wrote; and others,—which though inferior to this in force, are nevertheless, when compared with the so-called historical romances of any other English writer, what sunlight is to moonlight, if you can say as much for the latter as to admit even that comparison,—go back to the period of the Tudors, that is, two centuries and a half. *Quentin Durward*, which is all but amongst the best, runs back farther still, far into the previous century, while *Ivanhoe* and *The Talisman*, though not among the greatest of Scott's works, carry us back more than five hundred years. The new class of extempore novel writers, though more considerable than, sixty years ago, any one could have expected ever to see it, is still limited, and on any high level of merit will probably always be limited, to the delineation of the times of which the narrator has personal experience. Scott seemed to have had something very like personal experience of a few centuries at least, judging by the ease and freshness with which he poured out his stories of these centuries, and though no one can pretend that even he could describe the period of the Tudors as Miss Austen described the country parsons and squires of George the Third's reign, or as Mr. Trollope describes the politicians and hunting-men of Queen Victoria's, it is nevertheless the evidence of a greater imagination to make us live so familiarly as Scott does amidst the political and religious controversies of two or three centuries' duration, to be the actual witnesses, as it were, of Margaret of Anjou's throes of vain ambition, and Mary Stuart's fascinating remorse, and Elizabeth's domineering and jealous balancings of noble against noble, of James the First's shrewd pedantries, and the Regent Murray's large fore-thought, of the politic craft of Argyle, the courtly ruthlessness of Claverhouse, and the high-bred clemency of Monmouth, than to reflect in countless modifications the freaks, figures, and fashions of our own time.

The most striking feature of Scott's romances is that, for the most part, they are pivoted on public rather than mere private interests and passions. With but few exceptions—(*The Antiquary*, *St. Ronan's Well*, and *Guy Mannering* are the most important)—Scott's novels give us an imaginative view, not of mere individuals, but of individuals as they are affected by the public strifes and social divisions of the age. And this it is which gives his books so large an interest for old and young, soldiers and statesmen, the world of society and the recluse, alike. You can hardly read any novel of Scott's and not become better aware what public life and political issues mean. And yet there is no artifi-ciality, no elaborate attitudinizing before the antique mirrors of the past, like Bulwer's, no dressing out of clothes-horses like G. P. R. James. The boldness and freshness of the present are carried back into the past, and you see Papists and Puritans, Cavaliers and Roundheads, Jews, Jacobites, and freebooters, preachers, schoolmasters, mercenary soldiers, gipsies, and beggars, all living the sort of life which the reader feels that in their circumstances and under the same conditions of time and place and parentage, he might have lived too. Indeed, no man can read Scott without being more of a public man, whereas the ordinary novel tends to make its readers rather less of one than before.

Next, though most of these stories are rightly called romances, no one can avoid observing that they give that side of life which is unromantic, quite as vigorously as the romantic side. This was not true of Scott's poems, which only expressed one-half of his nature, and were almost pure romances. But in the novels the business of life is even better portrayed than its sentiments. Mr. Bagehot, one of the ablest of Scott's critics, has pointed out this admirably in his essay on *The Waverley Novels*. 'Many historical novelists,' he says, 'especially those who with care and pains have read up the detail, are often evidently in a strait how to pass from their history to their sentiment. The fancy of Sir Walter could not help connecting the two. If he had given us the English side of the race to Derby, *he would have described the Bank of England paying in sixpences, and also the loves of the cashier.*' No one who knows the novels well can question this. Fergus MacIvor's ways and means, his careful arrangements for receiving subsidies in black mail, are as carefully recorded as his lavish highland hospitalities; and when he sends his silver cup to the Gaelic bard who chaunts his greatness, the faithful historian does not forget to let us know that the cup is his last, and that he is hard-pressed for the generosities of the future. So too the habitual thievishness of the highlanders is pressed upon us quite as vividly as their gallantry and superstitions. And so careful is Sir Walter to paint the petty pedantries of the Scotch traditional conservatism, that he will not spare even Charles Edward—of whom he draws so graceful a picture—the humiliation of submitting to old Bradwardine's 'solemn act of homage', but makes him go through the absurd ceremony of placing his foot on a cushion to have its brogue unlatched by the dry old enthusiast of heraldic lore. Indeed it was because Scott so much enjoyed the contrast between the high sentiment of life and its dry and often absurd detail, that his imagination found so much freer a vent in the historical romance, than it ever found in the romantic poem. Yet he clearly needed the romantic excitement of picturesque scenes and historical interests, too. I do not think he would ever have gained any brilliant success in the narrower region of the domestic novel. He said himself, in expressing his admiration of Miss Austen, 'The big bow-wow strain I can do myself, like any now going, but the exquisite touch which renders ordinary commonplace things and characters interesting, from the truth of the description and the sentiment, is denied to me.' Indeed he tried it to some extent in *St. Ronan's Well*, and so far as he tried it, I think he failed. Scott needed a certain largeness of type, a strongly-marked class-life, and, where it was possible, a free, out-of-doors life, for his delineations. No one could paint beggars and gipsies, and wandering fiddlers, and mercenary soldiers, and peasants and farmers and lawyers, and magistrates, and preachers, and courtiers, and statesmen, and best of all perhaps queens and kings, with anything like his ability. But when it came to describing the small differences of manner, differences not due to external habits, so much as to internal sentiment or education, or mere domestic circumstance, he was beyond his proper field. In the sketch of the St. Ronan's Spa and the company at the *table-d'hôte*, he is of course somewhere near the mark,—he was too able a man to fall far short of success in anything he really gave to the world; but it is not interesting. Miss Austen would have made Lady Penelope Penfeather a hundred times as amusing. We turn to Meg Dods and Touchwood, and Cargill, and Captain Jekyl, and Sir Bingo Binks, and to Clara Mowbray,—i.e. to the lives really moulded by large and specific causes, for enjoyment, and leave the small gossip of the company at the Wells as, relatively at least, a failure. And it is well for all the world that it was so. The domestic novel, when really of the highest kind, is no doubt a perfect work of art, and an unfailing source of amusement; but it has nothing of the tonic influence, the large instructiveness, the stimulating intellectual air, of Scott's historic tales. Even when Scott is farthest from reality—as in *Ivanhoe* or *The Monastery*—he makes you open your eyes to all sorts of historical conditions to which you would otherwise be blind. The domestic novel, even when its art is perfect, gives little but pleasure at the best; at the worst it is simply scandal idealized.

Scott often confessed his contempt for his own heroes. He said of Edward Waverley, for instance, that he was 'a sneaking piece of imbecility', and that 'if he had married Flora, she would have set him up upon the chimney-piece as Count Borowlaski's wife used to do with him. I am a bad hand at depicting a hero, properly so called, and have an unfortunate propensity for the dubious characters of borderers, buccaneers, highland robbers, and all others of a Robin-Hood description.' In another letter he says, 'My rogue always, in despite of me, turns out my hero.' And it seems very likely that in most of the situations Scott describes so well, his own course would have been that of his wilder impulses, and not that of his reason. Assuredly he would never have stopped hesitating on the line between opposite courses as his Waverleys, his Mortons, his Osbaldistones do. Whenever he was really involved in a party strife, he flung prudence and impartiality to the winds, and went in like the hearty partisan which his strong impulses made of him. But granting this, I do not agree with his condemnation of all his own colourless heroes. However much they differed in nature from Scott himself, the even balance of their reason against their sympathies is certainly well conceived, is in itself natural, and is an admirable expedient for effecting that which was probably its real use to Scott,—the affording an opportunity for the delineation of all the pros and cons of the case, so that the characters on both sides of the struggle should be properly understood. Scott's imagination was clearly far wider—was far more permeated with the fixed air of sound judgment—than his practical impulses. He needed a machinery for displaying his insight into both sides of a public quarrel, and his colourless heroes gave him the instrument he needed. Both in Morton's case (in *Old Mortality*), and in Waverley's, the hesitation is certainly well described. Indeed in relation to the controversy between Covenanters and Royalists, while his political and martial prepossessions went with Claverhouse, his reason and educated moral feeling certainly were clearly identified with Morton.

It is, however, obviously true that Scott's heroes are mostly created for the sake of the facility they give in delineating the other characters, and not the other characters for the sake of the heroes. They are the imaginative neutral ground, as it were, on which opposing influences are brought to play; and what Scott best loved to paint was those who, whether by nature, by inheritance, or by choice, had become unique and characteristic types of one-sided feeling, not those who were merely in process of growth, and had not ranged themselves at all. Mr. Carlyle, who, as I have said before, places Scott's romances far below their real level, maintains that these great types of his are drawn from the outside, and not made actually to live. 'His Bailie Jarvies, Dinmonts, Dalgettys (for their name is legion), do look and talk like what they give themselves out for; they are, if not *created* and made poetically alive, yet deceptively *enacted* as a good player might do them. What more is wanted, then? For the reader lying on a sofa, nothing more; yet for another sort of reader much. It were a long chapter to unfold the difference in drawing a character between a Scott and a Shakespeare or Goethe. Yet it is a difference literally immense; they are of a different species; the value of the one is not to be counted in the coin of the other. We might say in a short word, which covers a long matter, that your Shakespeare fashions his characters from the heart outwards; your Scott fashions them from the skin inwards, never getting near the heart of them. The one set become living men and women; the other amount to little more than mechanical cases, deceptively painted automatons.' And then he goes on to contrast Fenella in *Peveril of the Peak* with Goethe's Mignon. Mr. Carlyle could hardly have chosen a less fair comparison. If Goethe is to be judged by his women, let Scott be judged by his men. So judged, I think Scott will, as a painter of character—of course, I am not now speaking of him as a poet,—come out far above Goethe. Excepting the hero of his first drama (Götz of the iron hand), which by the way was so much in Scott's line that his first essay in poetry was to translate it—not very well—I doubt if Goethe was ever successful with his pictures of men. *Wilhelm Meister* is, as Niebuhr truly said, 'a ménagerie of tame animals'. Doubtless Goethe's women—certainly his women of culture—are more truly and inwardly conceived and created than Scott's. Except Jeanie Deans and Madge Wildfire, and perhaps Lucy Ashton, Scott's women are apt to be uninteresting, either pink and white toys, or hardish women of the world. But then no one can compare the men of the two writers, and not see Scott's vast pre-eminence on that side.

I think the deficiency of his pictures of women, odd as it seems to say so, should be greatly attributed to his natural chivalry. His conception of women of his own or a higher class was always too romantic. He hardly ventured, as it were, in his tenderness for them, to look deeply into their little weaknesses and intricacies of character. With women of an inferior class, he had not this feeling. Nothing can be more perfect than the manner in which he blends the dairy-woman and woman of business in Jeanie Deans, with the lover and the sister. But once make a woman beautiful, or in any way an object of homage to him, and Scott bowed so low before the image of her, that he could not go deep into her heart. He could no more have analysed such a woman, as Thackeray analysed Lady Castlewood, or Amelia, or Becky, or as George Eliot analysed Rosamond Vincy, than he could have vivisected Camp or Maida. To some extent, therefore, Scott's pictures of women remain something in the style of the miniatures of the last age—bright and beautiful beings without any special character in them. He was dazzled by a fair heroine. He could not take them up into his imagination as real beings as he did men. But then how living are his men, whether coarse or noble! What a picture, for instance, is that in *A Legend of Montrose* of the conceited, pragmatic, but prompt and dauntless soldier of fortune, rejecting Argyle's attempts to tamper with him, in the dungeon at Inverary, suddenly throwing himself on the disguised Duke so soon as he detects him by his voice, and wresting from him the means of his own liberation! Who could read that scene and say for a moment that Dalgetty is painted 'from the skin inwards'? It was just Scott himself breathing his own life through the habits of a good specimen of the mercenary soldier—realizing where the spirit of hire would end, and the sense of honour would begin—and preferring, even in a dungeon, the audacious policy of a sudden attack to that of crafty negotiation. What a picture (and a very different one) again is that in *Redgauntlet* of Peter Peebles, the mad litigant, with face emaciated by poverty and anxiety, and rendered wild by 'an insane lightness about the eyes', dashing into the English magistrate's court for a warrant against his fugitive counsel. Or, to take a third instance, as different as possible from either, how powerfully conceived is the situation in *Old Mortality*, where Balfour of Burley, in his fanatic fury at the defeat of his plan for a new rebellion, pushes the oak-tree, which connects his wild retreat with the outer world, into the stream, and tries to slay Morton for opposing him. In such scenes and a hundred others—for these are mere random examples—Scott undoubtedly painted his masculine figures from as deep and inward a conception of the character of the situation as Goethe ever attained, even in drawing Mignon, or Klärchen, or Gretchen. The distinction has no real existence. Goethe's pictures of women were no doubt the intuitions of genius; and so are Scott's of men—and here and there of his women too. Professional women he can always paint with power. Meg Dods, the innkeeper, Meg Merrilies, the gipsy, Mause Headrigg, the Covenanter, Elspeth, the old fishwife in *The Antiquary*, and the old crones employed to nurse and watch, and lay out the corpse, in *The Bride of Lammermoor*, are all in their way impressive figures.

And even in relation to women of a rank more fascinating to Scott, and whose inner character was perhaps on that account, less familiar to his imagination, grant him but a few hints from history, and he draws a picture which, for vividness and brilliancy, may almost compare with Shakespeare's own studies in English history. Had Shakespeare painted the scene in *The Abbot*, in which Mary Stuart commands one of her Mary's in waiting to tell her at what bridal she last danced, and Mary Fleming blurts out the reference to the marriage of Sebastian at Holyrood, would any one hesitate to regard it as a stroke of genius worthy of the great dramatist? This picture of the Queen's mind suddenly thrown off its balance, and betraying, in the agony of the moment, the fear and remorse which every association with Darnley conjured up, is painted 'from the heart outwards', not 'from the skin inwards', if ever there were such a painting in the world. Scott hardly ever failed in painting kings or peasants, queens or peasant-women. There was something in the well-marked type of both to catch his imagination, which can always hit off the grander features of royalty, and the homelier features of laborious humility. Is there any sketch traced in lines of more sweeping grandeur and more impressive force than the following of Mary Stuart's lucid interval of remorse—lucid compared with her ordinary mood, though it was of a remorse that was almost delirious—which breaks in upon her hour of fascinating condescension?—

[a quotation from chapter 31 '"Are they not"' to '"alone-away-away!"' of *The Abbot* is omitted]

And equally fine is the scene in *Kenilworth* in which Elizabeth undertakes the reconciliation of the haughty rivals, Sussex and Leicester, unaware that in the course of the audience she herself will have to bear a great strain on her self command, both in her feelings as a queen and her feelings as a lover. Her grand rebukes to both, her ill-concealed preference for Leicester, her whispered ridicule of Sussex, the impulses of tenderness which she stifles, the flashes of resentment to which she gives way, the triumph of policy over private feeling, her imperious impatience when she is baffled, her jealousy as she grows suspicious of a personal rival, her gratified pride and vanity when the suspicion is exchanged for the clear evidence, as she supposes, of Leicester's love, and her peremptory conclusion of the audience, bring before the mind a series of pictures far more vivid and impressive than the greatest of historical painters could fix on canvas, even at the cost of the labour of years. Even more brilliant, though not so sustained and difficult an effort of genius, is the later scene in the same story, in which Elizabeth drags the unhappy Countess of Leicester from her concealment in one of the grottoes of Kenilworth Castle, and strides off with her, in a fit of vindictive humiliation and Amazonian fury, to confront her with her husband. But this last scene no doubt is more in Scott's way. He can always paint women in their more masculine moods. Where he frequently fails is in the attempt to indicate the finer shades of women's nature. In Amy Robsart herself, for example, he is by no means generally successful, though in an early scene her childish delight in the various orders and decorations of her husband is painted with much freshness and delicacy. But wherever, as in the case of queens, Scott can get a telling hint from actual history, he can always so use it as to make history itself seem dim to the equivalent for it which he gives us.

And yet, as every one knows, Scott was excessively free in his manipulations of history for the purposes of romance. In *Kenilworth* he represents Shakespeare's plays as already in the mouths of courtiers and statesmen, though he lays the scene in the eighteenth year of Elizabeth, when Shakespeare was hardly old enough to rob an orchard. In *Woodstock*, on the contrary, he insists, if you compare Sir Henry Lee's dates with the facts, that Shakespeare died twenty years at least before he actually died. The historical basis, again, of *Woodstock* and of *Redgauntlet* is thoroughly untrustworthy, and about all the minuter details of history,—unless so far as they were characteristic of the age,— I do not suppose that Scott in his romances ever troubled himself at all. And yet few historians—not even Scott himself when he exchanged romance for history—ever drew the great figures of history with so powerful a hand. In writing history and biography Scott has little or no advantage over very inferior men. His pictures of Swift, of Dryden, of Napoleon, are in no way very vivid. It is only where he is working from the pure imagination,—though imagination stirred by historic study,—that he paints a picture which follows us about, as if with living eyes, instead of creating for us a mere series of lines and colours. Indeed, whether Scott draws truly or falsely, he draws with such genius that his pictures of Richard and Saladin, of Louis XI and Charles the Bold, of Margaret of Anjou and René of Provence, of Mary Stuart and Elizabeth Tudor, of Sussex and of Leicester, of James and Charles and Buckingham, of the two Dukes of Argyle—the Argyle of the time of the revolution, and the Argyle of George II,—of Queen Caroline, of Claverhouse, and Monmouth, and of Rob Roy, will live in English literature beside Shakespeare's pictures—probably less faithful if more imaginative—of John and Richard and the later Henries, and all the great figures by whom they were surrounded. No historical portrait that we possess will take precedence—as a mere portrait—of Scott's brilliant study of James I in *The Fortunes of Nigel*. Take this illustration for instance, where George Heriot the goldsmith (Jingling Geordie, as the king familiarly calls him) has just been speaking of Lord Huntinglen, as 'a man of the old rough world that will drink and swear':—

[a quotation from chapter 32 ' "O Geordie!" ' to ' "to cast that up to him?" ' of *The Fortunes of Nigel* is omitted]

Assuredly there is no undue favouring of Stuarts in such a picture as that.

Scott's humour is, I think, of very different qualities in relation to different subjects. Certainly he was at times capable of considerable heaviness of hand,—of the Scotch 'wut' which has been so irreverently treated by English critics. His rather elaborate jocular introductions, under the name of Jedediah Cleishbotham, are clearly laborious at times. And even his own letters to his daughter-in-law, which Mr. Lockhart seems to regard as models of tender playfulness and pleasantry, seem to me decidedly elephantine. Not unfrequently, too, his stereotyped jokes weary. Dalgetty bores you almost as much as he would do in real life,—which is a great fault in art. Bradwardine becomes a nuisance, and as for Sir Piercie Shafton, he is beyond endurance. Like some other Scotchmen of genius, Scott twanged away at any effective chord till it more than lost its expressiveness. But in dry humour, and in that higher humour which skilfully blends the ludicrous and the pathetic, so that it is hardly possible to separate between smiles and tears, Scott is a master. His canny innkeeper, who, having sent away all the pease-meal to the camp of the Covenanters, and all the oatmeal (with deep professions of duty) to the castle and its cavaliers, in compliance with the requisitions sent to him on each side, admits with a sigh to his daughter that 'they maun gar wheat flour serve themsels for a blink',— his firm of solicitors, Greenhorn and Grinderson, whose senior partner writes respectfully to clients in prosperity, and whose junior partner writes familiarly to those in adversity,—his arbitrary nabob who asks how the devil any one should be able to mix spices so well 'as one who has been where they grow';—his little ragamuffin who indignantly denies that he has broken his promise not to gamble away his sixpences at pitch-and-toss because he has gambled them away at 'neevie-neevie-nick-nack',—and similar figures abound in his tales,— are all creations which make one laugh inwardly as we read. But he has a much higher humour still, that inimitable power of shading off ignorance into knowledge and simplicity into wisdom, which makes his picture of Jeanie Deans, for instance, so humorous as well as so affecting. When Jeanie reunites her father to her husband by reminding the former how it would sometimes happen that 'twa precious saints might pu' sundrywise like twa cows riving at the same hayband', she gives us an admirable instance of Scott's higher humour. Or take Jeanie Deans's letter to her father communicating to him the pardon of his daughter and her own interview with the Queen:—

[Jeanie Deans's complete letter to her father is omitted]

This contains an example of Scott's rather heavy jocularity as well as giving us a fine illustration of his highest and deepest and sunniest humour. Coming where it does, the joke inserted about the Board of Agriculture is rather like the gambol of a rhinoceros trying to imitate the curvettings of a thoroughbred horse.

Some of the finest touches of his humour are no doubt much heightened by his perfect command of the genius as well as the dialect of a peasantry, in whom a true culture of mind and sometimes also of heart is found in the closest possible contact with the humblest pursuits and the quaintest enthusiasm for them. But Scott, with all his turn for irony—and Mr. Lockhart says that even on his death-bed he used towards his children the same sort of good-humoured irony to which he had always accustomed them in his life—certainly never gives us any example of that highest irony which is found so frequently in Shakespeare, which touches the paradoxes of the spiritual life of the children of earth, and which reached its highest point in Isaiah. Now and then in his latest diaries—the diaries written in his deep affliction— he comes near the edge of it. Once, for instance, he says, 'What a strange scene if the surge of conversation could suddenly ebb like the tide, and show us the state of people's real minds!

> "No eyes the rocks discover
> Which lurk beneath the deep."

Life could not be endured were it seen in reality.' But this is not irony, only the sort of meditation which, in a mind inclined to thrust deep into the secrets of life's paradoxes, is apt to lead to irony. Scott, however, does not thrust deep in this direction. He met the cold steel which inflicts the deepest interior wounds, like a soldier, and never seems to have meditated on the higher paradoxes of life till reason reeled. The irony of Hamlet is far from Scott. His imagination was essentially one of distinct embodiment. He never even seemed so much as to contemplate that sundering of substance and form, that rending away of outward garments, that unclothing of the soul, in order that it might be more effectually clothed upon, which is at the heart of anything that may be called spiritual irony. The constant abiding of his mind within the well-defined forms of some one or other of the conditions of outward life and manners, among the scores of different spheres of human habit, was, no doubt, one of the secrets of his genius; but it was also its greatest limitation.

68. Julia Wedgwood: 'the romantic reaction', *Contemporary Review*

1878

A review of R. H. Hutton's *Sir Walter Scott* in the 'English Men of Letters' series (see No. 67), *Contemporary Review* (October 1878), xxxiii, 514-39.

The reviewer is Frances Julia Wedgwood, a miscellaneous writer of the period. The title of the review is 'Sir Walter Scott and the Romantic Reaction'.

Is a strong attraction for a particular writer an advantage or a disadvantage in the attempt at an appreciation of his genius? Could the answer be received as disinterested, we would boldly avow the first view as our own. A strong literary partiality may disqualify the student of literature for any proportionate estimate of the particular mind which has fascinated him, but we cannot but consider it an adequate compensation for all limitation in critical power, that it lights up for him what is actually there. However, any expansion of this view would be a most unbecoming as well as impolitic prelude to a literary attempt of which it is the main justification. We will not provoke sceptics to question our vantage-ground by a preliminary *éloge* of its strength. We will rather frankly admit that whatever critical advantage lies in an impartial position must be at once disclaimed here. The beginning of our century was one of those wonderful literary eras which stand out like glowing Alpine peaks in any review of history; and we do not advance for our poet the claim that in that group to which its splendour is owing his figure is predominant. But could we, for our own part, recall one of those who made the time what it was, the poet who should be summoned back to a world he was not loath to quit should be Walter Scott. Doubtless we might revive a better man and a better poet in Wordsworth, a far keener genius in Byron, a deeper thinker in Coleridge, a more subtle spirit in Shelley. Yet in none of these do we find that indescribable delightfulness of nature which mingles like a perfume with the utterance of genius, blending our admiration for the creation and the creator, and making us doubt whether we love the writer for the sake of his work, or the work because it recalls the writer. Perhaps it is not thus that we feel towards absolutely the first-rate creations of genius. A dramatic genius, if perfect, is self-effacing. But, this concession made, we would ask if the sense of contact with a robust and spirited nature, distinct with absolute simplicity, and graceful in its frank modesty—if this is not to be taken into account in judging of works which would stand high on their own merits? Of how many men of genius could you say what nobody, we suppose, would deny of Scott? How many modest men of genius has the world known? How many, of whom you could say that they were emphatically *men*? No one would have had so much excuse for the failings of genius, for no genius ever before met with such universal recognition and such solid recompense. And yet he—the most lionized of men—never, so far as we can see, allowed a taint of vanity or egotism to mar the genial frankness of his attitude to all the world. There are, no doubt, many men of genius of whose personality we do not gain a sufficiently distinct glimpse to discern either the presence or absence of modesty, but to feel at once that a man is pre-eminent in intellect, and that he is modest, is a literary experience belonging, we should say, almost exclusively to the readers of Sir Walter Scott.[1]

'That may have been an important fact to his friends and dependents,' the reader may perhaps object, 'but it is nothing to those who know him only through his books.' This seems to us a delusion. The thing that showed itself in Scott's character as kindness to the insignificant and the lowly,—exaggeration of the powers of others, and depreciation of his own,—showed itself in his intellect as that perfect simplicity which is one of the finest characteristics of his genius. It is simplicity which gives his style both its rapidity and its pathos. He moves unencumbered by his own personality. We cannot say this of any of his great contemporaries. We are not denying that in some respects their interest for us depends upon the fact that we cannot say it. Their pictures of nature and of life are often made more interesting by the presence of an interesting personality. Still this particular charm is his

[1] 'Not being endowed with the talents of Burns or Chatterton,' he begins his autobiography, 'I have been delivered also from their temptations.' It is impossible to suspect him of affectation, even were affectation probable in a fragment of self-description, only to be read after the writer's death [Wedgwood].

more than theirs. To find Scott's peer in simplicity we must go to the kings of the poetic world, and set him by the side of Shakespeare and Homer. We need hardly add that it is only in this single quality we make such a claim for him, but in this we make it fearlessly. The simplicity of the poet is as perfect as was the modesty of the man.

We dwell at length upon this quality in Scott because, in the charming little volume which has called forth these remarks, *pride* is singled out as the distinguishing note of his character. Not standing on the level of our poet, we must not imitate him in saying that 'we do not write for that dull elf' who imagines any distinction of contrast between pride and modesty; but we will venture to assert that they are much more often found together than apart. The man who is modest on his strong side is generally proud on his weak side. Take the first reserved, manly, sensitive person you meet, and it is a chance which of the two words you will be inclined to use in describing him. The sense of personal honour and that reticence which guards it may be expressed almost equally by either; and if self-suppression does not imply a low estimate of self, it always resembles and sometimes produces it. In the case of Sir Walter Scott, the two things, we believe, were mutually cause and effect.

In saying that Scott was singularly free from the faults of genius, we do not mean that he was faultless. He had great faults as a man, and these, like his great virtues, coloured his genius and leave their trace on his works. Of the worldliness in his character we think Mr. Hutton speaks too mildly. It seems the main aspect that attracted the notice of Scott's great countryman and impressed itself on the only attempt at an appreciation of the Northern singer by an equal, if not a superior. From Carlyle's review of Scott we should suppose him to be a mere manufacturer of well-paid literary luxuries for the fashionable and indolent,—a varnisher of antique trash made, according to the facetious tale, to sell,—a mere lover of the world's high places and clever earner of the needful means of winning them. Such an estimate, proceeding from such a man, is a cruel blow to a great reputation, and it is no small part of the satisfaction we have had in the little book before us (which we have with utter astonishment seen criticized as repeating the estimate against which we welcome it as a protest) that it indicates a return in general feeling from the most exaggerated reaction commemorated in that review. But to protest against any injustice with effect we must recognize the fibre of truth, apart from which injustice has no coherence. Scott's was, we have said, eminently a manly nature.

Everything about him is manly, whether we take that word in its nobler or in its more conventional sense. And the more manly a character is, the more handles the world finds in it. Courage, decision, spirit, self-control, are qualities which all men appreciate. They are the instruments of successful action; the ladders by which the high places of the world are scaled. To be richly endowed with all that worldly men most prize and honour, and yet to be 'unspotted by the world', is not impossible; but we must never expect to be able to say as much of one to whose other difficulties were added the tremendous temptations of genius. For while the manly nature supplies the soil where worldliness will grow, we may be very sure that the domain of genius is not unvisited by the winged seed, so swift to settle, so inconceivably hard to uproot. It is not less tempting to the son of a solicitor to become a baronet, a laird, and the founder of a family, because he is also a man of genius. When men of genius are indifferent to these things, they are more indifferent than other men. Wordsworth would have cared nothing for them, and so would Mr. Carlyle himself. On the other hand, when a man of genius does care for them, he cares more than most do. There is more imagination to reflect every object of desire; there is a greater variety of intellectual channels, and these deeper and wider, for all satisfaction to fill. Mr. Carlyle speaks of Scott's 'vulgar worldliness' as if he had been a citizen of London aspiring to move from the east to the west, to see his name in the *Morning Post* at the tail of a list of dukes, to eat French cookery off gold plate, and have his wife's horses noted in the park. It is not just thus to confuse different shades even of what is contemptible. Worldliness it was, no doubt, to find his stimulant to literary activity in the hope of founding a line of Scotts of Abbotsford, but it was not exactly the same thing as if he had made it an object of ambition to live in Grosvenor Square. One great Scotchman might, in judging another, have made more allowance for what was national in his weakness. He whose nature vibrated to the touch of the past, may he not be judged more lightly for greed, if we must call it so, that reaches forward to the future? If his genius was steeped in images of grandeur, and the clans of Scotland were to find in him a singer who has made their dialect and their manners familiar to many generations, may he not find some excuse for having tried to set up his tawdry imitation of the antique Scottish home he has made familiar and dear to us all? It is easy to sneer at his stucco panellings, his scraps of armour and antique furniture, his bran-new castle, redolent of upholsterers' bills. The same imagination that revived a buried past invested all these things with the dignity of a distant future. Edgar Quinet has imagined Homer creating the *Iliad* from some fragment of half-buried masonry, revealing to him a half-buried past to be peopled by his genius. The Cyclopean ruin, according to the brilliant Frenchman, gave the hint which a great genius, helped by vague tradition, developed into the tale of Troy divine. That seems to us a transplantation of modern growth to the soil of antiquity; but something like it was true of the poet who has some few but striking characteristics in common with Homer. And though it is a long way from a hoary ruin recording in its scars the tale of a fierce and stormy past to the bran-new trumpery of Abbotsford, still between the spirit that loves the one and creates the other there is the connection that exists between any right and healthful feeling and its distortion. If Scott could have been content with his position in the world of imagination and thought, if he had craved no tangible, material expression of his link to the far-away, he would not only have been a greater man, he would have been a far happier, a far more prosperous man. Ah! how paltry, how impotent, appear the objects of worldly ambition when they are seen with the reverted eye! But we must not allow this discernment, overwhelming as it is, to blind us to the ready alliance of these allurements with what is excellent. All that was good in Scott allied itself with the desire to be a holder of Scottish land. His genial hospitality, his sympathy alike with high and low, his love of the careless, free, open-air life, and his intense feeling for nature—all, in short, that gives charm to his writing, arrayed itself on the same side as vulgar ambition. Few of us are capable of measuring the danger of that alliance. Few can estimate the promise of the Tempter when he whispers, 'All these things will I give thee if thou wilt fall down and worship me.' Only once in the world's history, we believe, was that promise heard, adequately comprehended, and entirely rejected.

Carlyle's harsh estimate, we must remember, was written before he had seen the last touching volume of Lockhart's life of his father-in-law. That noble and pathetic struggle with disease and poverty could not, we think, leave the severest condemnation unsoftened towards him who 'still with the throttling hands of Death at strife', struggled to pay off a load of debt, and broke down under the gigantic effort. But the judgment, to which the unswerving desire is as the successful achievement, set a seal of acceptance on his patient struggle. To Scott, in the mental weakness of incipient brain disease, was granted by a merciful Heaven the delusion that the hard work was over and the load of debt paid. We almost feel as if we ought to share this delusion; or, at least, in reviewing those years of solitude, of dreary, desolate effort, of the occupation which from a delight had become a torment, the enchanter's rod turned to a scourge, the only words that express our sense of a great spiritual victory are 'He hath received at the Lord's hand the double (*i.e.*, according to the true reading, the adequate punishment) for all his sins.'

We cannot trust ourselves to dwell on those last years of one whose nature seemed formed for joy. But it is a weak shrinking. He was spared the awful fate of impunity. He was granted the privilege accorded by Heaven to its favoured sons, of expiating, all that was weak and unworthy by painful struggle—of exhibiting, side by side, the fugitive nature of those things for which he had striven and the enduring reality of that which he had gained almost unsought. High and low brought their tribute to his death-bed alike. 'Do you know where he is lying, sir?' asked a poor man of Allan Cunningham when Scott lay dying, as if there were only one 'he' in London; and the vessel which bore him to a milder clime, too late to revive his exhausted frame, was supplied by a Government to which he was hostile. 'The glory dies not, and the pain is past.'

We ought not, perhaps, to wonder that the temptations of worldliness should fail of their due allowance from one who has never shown any capacity for feeling them. But when we turn from Mr. Carlyle's judgment of the intellectual status of his great countryman, we own ourselves as little satisfied as with his moral judgment. An intelligent Frenchman or German wishing to gain some knowledge of English literature, and studying for that purpose the *Miscellanies* of our great critic, would, we imagine, come to the conclusion that it was mere waste of time for any one who wished to disentangle only what is permanent from what calls itself literature, to make himself acquainted with Scott. 'It was not,' our investigating foreigner might conclude, as he closed the article Mr. Carlyle wrote for the *Westminster Review*,— 'it was evidently not an outburst of any original or spontaneous genius which attracted so much attention. Scott translated Götz von Berlichingen, and, finding that pictures of mediæval life were attractive, went on copying cleverly what he had studied, and giving the English world unlimited doses of Götz and water, which rapidly became weaker and weaker. If his clever seasoning and the thirst of the time supplied an eager demand for the manufacture during his lifetime, it would clearly be a waste of time to taste it now.' This imaginary decision embodies an honest attempt to put the effect of Carlyle's article into a few words, and we would ask any one who even glances at reviews, if it would not be an enormous mistake? There are a great many writers much deeper and more subtle than Scott whom a student of English literature might neglect with far less loss. It is dangerous, perhaps, to bring a comparison into one's own time, but we should venture to say that, from this point of view—not that of the lover of poetry, but that of the student of poetry as the interpreter of English life—a reader had much better leave the works of Tennyson unread, than those of Scott. The flower may be far more exquisite, but the plant is not in the same degree a characteristic of the soil. We do not imagine the future historian of the Victorian age will turn much to any contemporary poet to illustrate the reign which forms his subject. He may extract Tennyson's ode on the death of the Duke of Wellington, which rather illustrates the past than the present, and there may be one or two other pieces which would come in well enough to give a picturesque touch to some part of his narrative, but his treatment of the literary part of his subject will be curiously separate from the rest; and in the case of one who, according to our own view, is the greatest English poet of the last generation, the historian will look in vain for any point of contact whatever with the political and practical life of commonplace men. This is remarkably untrue of all the great English poets whose youth was contemporary with the French Revolution, and we do not think it would be so untrue of any as of Walter Scott. It was not that his allusions to contemporary events are particularly interesting. For our own part we can never get through the *Vision of Don Roderick*; and the monody on the death of Pitt and Fox, which seemed the most exquisite poetry in the world when read by a child about halfway between the present date and that of its being written, reveals, on a mature re-perusal, a good deal that we must confess to be somewhat trite. No, it is not his allusions to the men and events of the day that make Scott an interpreter of the life of his day. It is his sympathy for a past suddenly become remote; it is the part of his nature that vibrated to an order of things doomed, indeed, everywhere to perish by more or less gradual decay, but which the great crash of the French Revolution banished with a sudden clamour of hatred and outcry that attracted the attention of the world, and, breaking up all other lines of division, arrayed the nations in hostile ranks according to the fears or the hopes roused by the new-born democracy of France.

[a short passage on Sir James Mackintosh is omitted]

The great movement of which the French Revolution forms the political summit has many sides, and an attempt to appreciate the genius of Scott demands a hasty glance at each. It implies—although in connection with that great event we can hardly say it exhibits—a new interest in individual life, a new respect for idiosyncrasy, and a minute and delicate appreciation for shades of character, both national and personal. Its tendency to develop sympathy with the lowly and obscure, though in reality only a part of the first-mentioned influence, is far more obvious, and is indeed but the literary side of modern democracy. On the other hand, a large part of its influence, and that which most concerns a critic of Sir Walter Scott, is to be traced in the reaction in favour of all that democracy undervalues and obliterates. The feudal past was never loved as it was just before France for ever cast away all traces of feudalism. And finally—for a summary of such a movement crowded into such a space must be confined to these bare hints—it exhibits a peculiar love and reverence for nature, in every sense of that vague word, most obviously in the simple outward sense in which alone a critic of Scott need consider it, but also in other shades of meaning more disputable and subtle, though probably, if their import were well weighed, not less valid. However, we have nothing to do with the last, and only mention that aspect of the movement because these other shades of meaning are so important that, even when they are not relevant, it is impossible to approach the subject without naming them.

Scott shows some trace of almost all these tendencies. But if we had to condense into a single phrase the part of this mighty movement embodied in his genius, we should say that that genius was animated by the sympathy with chivalry that was created by its death-blow. Such a summary omits so much that it must throw some undue importance on what it selects; we seem to pass over Scott as what he was so eminently, the painter of nature, and even to deny what he was not less eminently, the painter of humble life. Still we believe it states the most important thing about him. We must always be very careful not to confuse the spirit which admires a particular character with that character itself. Very often they are exactly opposite. The love of chivalry was, in Scott's mind, a love of the past. Of course it was quite unlike any feeling men could have known while that past was present. Nothing is more unlike the feeling of childhood than the feeling with which we revisit the scenes of childhood. Nothing is so unlike the spirit of the men who built castle or abbey as the spirit which delights to trace and restore their ruins. 'I have never,' says Scott himself, 'been able to gain a good idea of a battle from a soldier;' and we have heard of a soldier who professed himself quite unable to recognize anything describing his own experience in the despatches recording an engagement in which he had taken part. The spirit that moves men to action is not the spirit that enables them to review action. No doubt Scott would have made a noble knight, a noble soldier. But then he would not have been the Walter Scott we know. If he could have *lived* his ideal he would not have *written* it. His genius, we may say, would not in that case have existed.

The description given above might perhaps be objected to on chronological grounds; we may be thought to antedate the feeling of which we make Scott the representative. We may be reminded that he was a staunch opponent of the triumphant Washington when he had scarcely ceased to find his dearest playfellows in the lambs on his grandfather's farm; and if the enthusiasm of the young politician should be set aside as worthless (which for our part we should not allow), there is plenty of indication throughout Scott's youth[1] of the strong bent of his sympathies, while as yet the floods had not descended or the waves beat, and the house that was soon to fall with a mighty crash seemed founded on a rock. But we must never think of that or any other great event in history as something unpreluded through years when our ear marks no announcing chord; a finer organ or a more attentive listener would be prepared for the crash of sound—harmonious or discordant according to our sympathies—which announces a new movement in the great symphony of the ages. Chesterfield's celebrated prophecy dates from the middle of the century which closed with its fulfilment, and the assertion that in 1753 'all the symptoms I have ever met with in history previous to great changes and revolutions exist and increase in France' is one of many proofs that the eighteenth century was above all a preparation for the French Revolution. Throughout all that period men were unconsciously ranging themselves for a great conflict. More or less we fix every one's position by the question— Did he advance or did he resist the principles of the Revolution? It is true many, in our own country perhaps most, of those who had prepared the enemy's march, were startled when they found themselves fighting by his side. Gibbon, for instance, was one of those whose

[1] He was born in 1771 [Wedgwood].

influence we should describe as making the rough places plain for the invader, yet when he came the spirit of democracy was 'the blackest demon of hell'. Now this same mighty influence that bid men work for a great breach with the past told on the generations who felt it, in heightening an affection for the past that was thus to be cast off. We shall often find in history and in our own individual lives that there seems to have been a spirit of foreboding in the air; we knew not why the moments were precious till in looking back we see the coming death or estrangement mark off that time as something the years were not to repeat for us. Something of this spirit seems to us to have moulded the genius of Scott. He hardly lived really to *see* the French Revolution, for we should say that only our own generation have reached a point whence they may look back and discern the clear outline against the sky. He lived amid its stir and throb; he knew not how profoundly, how permanently it was to influence the modern world, but unconsciously he turned with the tenderness of farewell to that great system of things it was to sweep away, and, like a painter in a foreign land, where he knows his sojourn will be short, he flung with hasty hand its lineaments on his glowing canvas. We may be told that all he cared for was to see his pictures framed and glazed at the most advantageous position in the dealer's shop. True, in a sense— in a very important sense. But still it is also true that he painted a past made dearer to him by its unlikeness to the spirit of all around him which stirred his forebodings and opposed his taste.

[a passage on the evolution of the taste for the medieval is omitted]

It was only ten years later that he began his translations from the German, which certainly gave the first suggestion to his genius, and revealed to him his destined *rôle* in the great literary movement of his day. Nevertheless we should say that Byron's name for him, 'the Ariosto of the North', was a truer indication of the real affinities of his genius than the fact that he was a translator from 'the elegant author of *The Sorrows of Werther*'. Götz von Berlichingen may be the spiritual father of Quentin Durward and his allies, but we could have spared them and still kept the best of Scott. Sometimes we are even tempted to doubt whether it was not a misfortune that his first essay tempted him on to foreign soil, and to suspect that his work would have been more enduring if his genius had been confined to the soil where it flourished best—that of his native land. However, his German phase was significant as an indication of the place German literature was to take in the coming age. At the end of the last century a paper read by the author of the *Man of Feeling* (1788) revealed to the literary world of Edinburgh, says Scott, 'the existence of works of genius in a language cognate with English, and still more closely approaching Lowland Scotch.' We have known an old Scotch lady, ignorant of German, who declared, after a visit to Germany, that she found no difficulty whatever in making herself understood; and whether she flattered herself or not, there is no doubt that a German would guess at the meaning of Scotch much more successfully than at that of English, while the intellectual differences between the inhabitants of the northern and southern half of our nation draw the Scotch near the Germans in other respects than that of language. The discovery of German literature formed, indeed, a sort of second Renaissance; and in 1792 a class was formed, consisting of Scott and several of his friends, for the prosecution of this 'new learning'. Scott's interest in German life had been awakened some years before: his assistant in his vain but persistent attempts to acquire some power over the pencil was a Prussian Jew whose father had been a commissary, 'or perhaps a spy', in the armies of Frederick the Great, and young Scott heard from his drawing-master many a picturesque tale of the great general's battles, far more valuable to him than the precepts of his art had they been ever so successful. He now turned with ardour, if not with industry, to the acquirement of this new lore, and it needed the classic severity of taste of his friend Erskine (well known to all readers of *Marmion*) to hold him back from the 'extravagances' of the literature which charmed him, for so it impressed the minds that were moulded on the great writers of Rome. Mrs. Barbauld has the honour to have first applied the match to this well-arranged pile, and her credit is the greater that her reading at Dugald Stewart's, in 1795, which was the origin of his first essay, was only made known to him at second-hand by a friend who had formed one of the audience, and whose account fired him with an eagerness that knew no pause till he acquired a copy of the original German ballad from which she had read William Taylor's translation—Burger's *Lenore*. Thus originated his first attempt at published verse. The fact that a great part of the edition of Scott's translation of Burger's ballads was consigned to the trunkmaker is less important as an index of the taste of the day than that which was partly its cause—that many translations of the same poem appeared at the same time. And Scott, undaunted by the failure, and encouraged by the sympathy of many whose sympathy was worth more than the applause of the public,—his rival, William Taylor of Norwich, among them,—pursued his way, and his translation of Götz von Berlichingen (1799) was an event of no small importance as a landmark in the history of literature, although the ridicule then showered by the genius of Canning on the German drama helped to consign the translation itself to oblivion.

The avowal that Carlyle's view of Goethe's influence on Scott has some of the exaggeration natural to one who has done more to make German literature known to us than any other writer now alive would excuse any critic of Scott from an attempt even to give a name to the most prominent characteristics of that literature; and in the present writer such an attempt would be presumptuous as well as irrelevant. So far as Scott presents any marked characteristics of the German mind, it is only because they are also the characteristics of the Scotch mind, or indeed of the whole Teutonic race, of which we are ourselves a branch. However, in any study of the movement we are tracing, these broader differences are of great importance, and a word may be given to them in passing.

Will it be thought fanciful if we fix on a trifling distinction of dialect noted by Tacitus between his race and ours as a type of their radical divergence? 'They do not reckon by days, as we do, but by nights, for they consider that night leads on the day.' The sense of mystery, of awe, of all that is awakened and typified in that nightly plunge of our planet into the shadow which reveals a heaven strewn with glittering worlds, where daylight shows a mere background for vagrant clouds—this we believe is the element that is wanting to the most characteristic thought of Rome (we are not, it must be remembered, including the literature from which Rome borrowed), and is predominant in the most characteristic thought of the Gothic world. Its expression, in the architecture which bears that name, is an unquestionable utterance of the spirit we would here indicate—the round and the pointed arch, side by side, expressing severally the feeling that returns to earth, and aspires to heaven—the contrasted genius of the people whose most characteristic remains are to be found in the road, the aqueduct, and the triumphal arch, and in the castle and the abbey. And the genius of one to whom hoary castle and ruined abbey were the most appropriate material, and who has set them against the imperishable background of blended poetic and historic feeling, is coloured throughout by that sense of mystery which nowhere emerges into prominence in his writing. Scott's genius was rooted in a firm belief in the invisible—not a very deep belief perhaps, but one that came very near some of his thoughts, and insensibly affects them all. He was above all a Scotchman, and Scotland is not more the 'land of the mountain and the flood' than she is of stern faith and intense belief in a whole unseen universe. We cannot say that either of these things is manifested in the writings of this best known of Scotchmen; the faith is conventional—the belief in the world of thought is concealed by the luxuriant overgrowth of a rich and vivid interest in the world of sense. But they know little of the nature of faith who deem that its indirect influence is worthless. As well might you suppose that before sunrise or after sunset the sky would show no purple or golden hues, no hope or memory of the hidden orb. The dimness of a passing cloud, that seems rather to efface the shadows than the lights on the landscape, is not more distinct from the blackness of a cloudy midnight than unconscious faith from disbelief in the invisible. The God of our fathers grants His faithful servants the inestimable privilege of bequeathing the influence apart from the possession of their faith, and the children of those who have died for the right to worship Him, though they ignore and deny Him, yet remain in a sense His witnesses. Scott had not much definite faith of any kind. His picture of the Scotch Covenanters has been censured for irreverence, quite unjustly in our opinion; and we regard his picture of the torture and death of one of them as his finest contribution to the history of his country. Still he had but little sympathy with the religious fervour which marks that history, on whichever side it was displayed, and in his horror of 'enthusiasm' he is a true son of the eighteenth century. Nevertheless, the genius of Scott could have grown only out of the soil of a rich and deep faith. The feudalism he loved was at once softened and animated by its loyalty to the Church, which enlisted all the sympathy of his taste as much as it alienated the sympathy of his reason; and that loyalty to a fallen house, which will ever be associated with his pictures of the last struggles for its restoration, borrows a softer lustre from the rays of that earlier feeling, sunk below the horizon, and never again probably to shine upon the path of history.

[a short passage on Scott's influence on a poem by Macaulay is omitted]

He once gave this as his reason against undertaking a history of Queen Mary,—and it is a very valid reason against undertaking the history of any period,—that judgment and sympathy are on different sides, but we think it an advantage for a *dramatic* view of the past. A

Fergus Mac Ivor, endowed with Scott's genius, could not have given forth an equally vivid and brilliant picture of the struggle in which he was ready to fight and die. We do not say that such a picture would not have a very vivid interest—it would form the most valuable material alike for the historian or the dramatic writer. But it would not be a work of art.

It is the balance of genius and good sense—the harmony of a cool shrewdness of intellect and a glowing fervour of imagination, which gives Scott's picture of the death of feudalism its peculiar mellowness and force. In speaking of the death of feudalism we include, indeed we specially have in mind, the fall of the Stuarts. It would be a very narrow and superficial survey of history which should confine the limits of the phase of society which, for want of a better name, we sum up in that word, within those ages which bear its name. The middle ages are the feudal ages, but we are yet living in the late twilight of feudalism. Those only can refuse to recognize the influence of its fading light whose eyes, turned from the west to the east, like the watchers in a northern summer, discern the approach of a new day. The evening of every age in history is, indeed, like that of which our poet wrote in the graceful verses which he sent to the Duke of Buccleuch from his voyage in the Hebrides, that

> 'Morning weaves
> Her chaplet with the hues that Twilight leaves.'

The east is radiant before the west is dark, and those who watch the growing light will generally be blind to any other. Nevertheless, we suppose it would be generally granted that in England the feudal past is still a mighty influence which no one could ignore without a complete misunderstanding of even the political life of our country. It is waning fast, no doubt; it may be that to our children it will have become an influence to be thrown out of account. But it fades slowly, and its twilight is yet clear around us. The fall of the Stuarts marks a great era in its decay. It ends the stage of unreasoning loyalty; from henceforth the throne is no indefeasible inheritance, but a position imposing duties as well as conferring rights; and the terrible emphasis with which France repeats the lesson has deafened us to its first utterance in our own country. It is the interval between the English and French Revolution which appears to us to exhibit best the outline of Scott's historic sympathy, against the background of his judgment. With the French Revolution he had no sympathy whatever. With the

English Revolution he had a partial sympathy; he was compelled to approve it by the dictates of his excellent sense. But the element of taste and feeling, predominant in the second act of the great drama, was latent thus early, and from the first his dramatic sympathies array themselves on the side which judgment condemns. Thus the double feeling supplies the place of impartiality, and art has the mellowing atmosphere it needs.

In the foregoing attempt to set forth Scott's position as a representative of historic life and feeling, we have already indicated the most marked traits of his genius. But it remains to make some more direct attempt in this direction, an attempt, however, which we gladly find almost superseded by the little volume which has suggested the present attempt. Mr. Hutton's appreciation of Scott as a poet seems to us full of subtle insight and balanced judgment, and an elaborate criticism on our own part would to a considerable extent repeat his, which is especially welcome to us, we must repeat, as a protest against the injustice of one whose very injustice we note with reverence. Mr. Carlyle, in the article to which we have made frequent reference, imputes to the writings of Scott an intellectual poverty which, from his point of view, is undeniable. 'The sick heart,' he says, 'will find no healing here; the darkly struggling heart no guidance; the heroic that is in all men no divine awakening voice.' We do not think the judgment even quite true; and even where it is true, it is unjust. One who holds the key that lets the weary spirit out of its dungeon of petty cares and gnawing anxieties into a sunny garden, is not devoid of healing influence. Others, no doubt, have taught us more,—others have implanted germs of deeper conviction, of finer speculation, of a far more pregnant and powerful range of thought. But in certain moments we feel as if even these things could not make up to us for that sense of transplantation to another soil,—for the tear that starts at sorrows not our own, and yet grants our own the wonderful relief of a half-transmuted expression, and makes us question whether the relief lies in what that rush of emotion helps us to remember or to forget:—

$$\Pi\alpha\tau\rho\sigma\kappa\lambda\sigma\upsilon\ \pi\rho\sigma\phi\alpha\sigma\iota\upsilon,\ \sigma\phi\omega\upsilon\ \delta'\ \alpha\dot{\upsilon}\tau\omega\upsilon\ \kappa\eta\delta\epsilon\ \dot{\epsilon}\kappa\alpha\sigma\tau\eta.$$[1]

And if the perplexed spirit finds no counsel in Scott's healthy and simple pages, how many a one has gone back to the perplexities of life

---

[1] ['. . . and with her, did th' other ladies moan] Patroclus' fortunes in pretext, but in sad truth their own.' *Iliad*, XIX, 302, trans. George Chapman.

with a fresher eye, because that rapid, simple, vivid narrative has woven a temporary curtain between those problems and the eyes that are weary of poring over them? The troubles of this life, after an hour with Scott, are what they were. The riddle of the painful earth is as far as ever from being solved; we have found no rushlight even to throw its ray upon the gloom. But we have been far away, and everything looks different. And there is no question that if his peculiar gifts are worth less than valuable thought, they are also rarer. That broad objective painting, that clear representation of simple feelings, that rapid movement, that sense of life and stir, which we find everywhere in the best writing of Scott, we find almost nowhere in the literature of our own day.

We would say the same of his pathos. The literature of the day— even the best literature of the day—seems to us greatly wanting in this quality. Its poverty in this respect is closely connected with its wealth in that which we have just quoted. Pathos is inseparable from reserve, it is felt in its highest measure in the presence of a dumb suffering, and the triumph of genius is to paint this dumb suffering in few words, and make the reader feel as he feels in the presence of one who represses tears, to convey a perception of emotions only half clothed in words, or rather of words which are, as Sir Fitzjames Stephen has finely said, 'like the signs of prisoners to each other',— faint suggestions beyond which lies a world of secret meaning, intelligible to him who has the key. We suppose this was what Pitt meant when he said that 'he should not have conceived it possible that this sort of feeling'—*i.e.*, the description of the Last Minstrel as, with feeble and uncertain fingers he attempts the Lay—'could have been expressed in words'. If it were not a disrespectful way of speaking of a great man's utterance, we should say it was about the worst criticism ever made in a very few words on a fine passage; for it implies that 'this sort of feeling' might be expressed by either painting or music, and it seems to us that the Minstrel's emotions are equally unsuited to both. We give the well-known lines, that the reader may, if he please, side with Pitt against us.

[the first forty-one lines of a passage from Scott's *Lay of the Last Minstrel* quoted by Hutton (No. 67), reprinted on pages 481-2 above, are omitted here]

What Pitt meant, probably, that this sort of feeling could not be expressed by *his* words, is profoundly true. Pathos is so inaccessible to no man as to the orator. How can he who is nothing when he is not emphatic understand the power of him who is nothing when he is emphatic? The same person might as well undertake to beat the drum and touch the harp as to stir the passion of the crowd and rouse the emotions that respond only to some delicate touch that we forget in the rush of feeling that it excites, knowing not if the sudden tear starts from some fountain hidden in the shadows of memory, or is evoked by the simple image set before us. It was some dim perception in the great orator, probably, of a power of words new to him and unattainable by him, that found vent in a remark which, however inappropriate absolutely, is full of interest on his lips, and points out the true aspect of the poet to the man of eloquence. And we recall with satisfaction how the tribute was repaid, how the poet brought his laurel wreath to the freshly closed tomb, and sang, in verse, which though we have admitted its sentiment to be somewhat trite, will yet, we believe, last as long as the fame of the statesman it celebrates; of the new Palinurus, whose dying hand never slackened on the rudder when the storm was highest, and the rocks were just ahead. Neither poet nor orator knew of the tribute each paid to each, but they were kindred souls, and their fame, we believe, will be coæval.

Mr. Hutton's criticism on the passage which moved the admiration of Pitt seems to us so full of truth and beauty that we will allow ourselves to quote it, as a comment on this illustrious admiration:—

[a quotation from Hutton (No. 67), reprinted on page 483 above ('The singular depth . . .' to '. . . poets ever surpassed') is omitted here]

It is the last word which conveys our own feeling of the essential quality of Scott's style. Perhaps the reader will think it a poor thing to say of any poet that he moves more quickly than others. If what is said of pathos be true, he must allow, however, that almost the most characteristic gift of the poet depends on this capacity, or is at least closely connected with it. The pathetic writer must have quitted a point almost as soon as you are aware that he has touched it. It is very dangerous to quote passages for their pathos; like the lesser stars, this quality is apt to become invisible under direct attention—indeed, the sense of being taken unawares is almost an element in it. But the following passage, descriptive of the commonplace perils and hardships in the life of the lowly, seems to us to unite this quality in no common degree with so many others characteristic of Scott's genius, being one of the few, moreover, in which we trace a reminiscence of Burns, that we will venture to insert it:—

[introduction to Canto IV, ll. 55-97 of *Marmion* are quoted]

We would venture to say of these lines that if any one finds them uninteresting he need never read a line of Scott's poetry again. The interest of Scott's narrative (wanting here, it is true) is hardly large enough to rouse any one who finds no merit in the broad, simple, vigorous painting of his passage—the sense of the characteristic aspects of nature given with a word, the sympathy with what is common, the firm touch as with a rapid sweep of his brush he paints the winter sunset, the cottage whence the shepherd is summoned forth by the pitiless storm, the storm itself, the cottage window gradually hid by it, and then the lonely death at that very cottage door, and the dumb companion's vain efforts to wake his master from the last sleep. Think how many words a poet of our day might use in painting a snowstorm, and note how our poet, in describing it as 'dark above, and white below', gives with two mere touches of colour the characteristic which everybody recognizes as specially belonging to falling snow, but which only a poet could have thus at once caught and said this and no more. It is the painter's eye, turned to subjects unsuitable for the painter's art. But the picturesque power is the least interest in this passage to our mind. We hardly know a greater debt of gratitude to the masters of song than that incurred by those who are made to feel, from the poet's point of view, the dim voiceless sorrows in which there is nothing poetic. The sorrows, not of warrior or bard, of fair lady or gentle knight, but of rude clod-hoppers hardly more intelligent than the four-footed companions who share their cares and perils,—the hardships of the life that is associated in the minds of the genteel world with Dresden china figures and Arcadian inanities,—these things brought home to the mind in simple homely verse like that we have quoted, cannot, we think, so far as they influence the reader at all, fail to make him better. He *feels* for the moment that hardship and peril, rare visitors at his door, are the inmates of the poor man's house. He realizes, not oppressively but through the mellowing aspect of poetry, that the majority of the world are born to struggle and privation; and if when the impression passes from the mind it leaves no trace upon the heart, then the reader must be one whose heart is unfitted to respond to the sorrows of those obscure lives which constitute the most important division of humanity.

The feeling is the more striking in Scott because it is essentially opposed to the spirit of chivalry with which he had so vivid a sympathy. The absence of all trace of pity for the worst sufferers from the wars which occupy the page of Froissart has been noted as a striking characteristic of his time, for there is no need to suppose any special hardness in the chronicler to account for it. The spirit of chivalry, on its harsher side, was never more adequately condemned than by Scott, in the very romance which has made the manners of chivalry familiar to us. 'What is it, valiant knight' (*i.e.*, the glory of chivalry), asks the heroic Jewess of Ivanhoe,—'what is it save an offering of sacrifice to a demon of vainglory, and a passing through the fire to Moloch? What remains to you as the prize of all the blood you have spilled—of all the travail and pain you have endured —of all the tears which your deeds have caused, when death hath broken the strong man's spear, and overtaken the speed of his war-horse?'

'What remains?' cried Ivanhoe: 'Glory, maiden, glory! which gilds our sepulchre and embalms our name.'

'Glory?' continued Rebecca: 'Alas! is the rusted mail which hangs as a hatchment over the champion's dim and mouldering tomb—is the defaced sculpture of the inscription which the ignorant monk can hardly read to the inquiring pilgrim—are these sufficient rewards for the sacrifice of every kindly affection, for a life spent miserably that ye may make others miserable? Or is there such virtue in the rude rhymes of a wandering bard, that domestic love, kindly affection, peace and happiness, are so wildly bartered, to become the hero of those ballads which vagabond minstrels sing to drunken churls over their evening ale?'

The whole character of Rebecca seems to us an illustration of what we have said of the current of his sympathies towards the weak and the oppressed. Doubtless, a large part of his nature sided with the paltry hero at whose unfeeling behest Rebecca exposes herself to the shafts of an invading band at the window of the chamber where Ivanhoe lies wounded. But the insight into the cruelty and hardness of the social order he paints so brilliantly seems to us to indicate a wonderful width and range of sympathy. This is what we mean by his setting the chivalric ideal on a modern background. When Shakespeare paints a Jew, he borrows the spirit of his persecutors, and his Jewess is held up to admiration for robbing her father and deserting his faith. Scott lets the Jewess shine forth in spotless purity against her Christian persecutors, and gives, in his finest female creation,[1] a voice to a race down-trodden for ages.

[a short passage on Robert Browning is omitted]

Scott's sympathy with what is common constitutes at once a striking characteristic of his genius and the most loveable element in his character. 'Vulgar, my dear,' he once remonstrated with his daughter Anne, who had applied the epithet to something which did not deserve it, 'do you know the meaning of vulgar? It means only common, and when you have lived to my years you will thank God that nothing worth caring most for is uncommon.' The remark is one of the very few which remain as an adequate expression of the man. It came from the core of his hearty, simple, genial nature; it expressed that width of unfastidious sympathy which, while it leaves its stamp on every work of his genius, is even more felt in the records which put the reader, as much as mere records can do, in contact with himself. Width of sympathy is, in fact, in the moral world what dramatic power is in the intellectual. Scott's range is not, like Shakespeare's, impartial. It has certain lacunæ; it has also certain definite preferences. He cannot paint those of his own class effectively; he must look up, or look down, to be at his best; and though, even on the level of common-place genteel life, it appears to us that his pictures are redeemed from mediocrity by occasional reflections of his own magnanimous character, still no doubt it is in the extremes of social life that he is at his best. What we would now dwell upon is, that of these extremes the most effective is the lowest. The Scotch peasant owes his literary existence to Scott's portrait. We must allow that it is the Scotch peasant under a certain rather artificial aspect—it is the *feudal* attitude of the poor which strongly interests him. What Caleb Balderstone would be, apart from his paltry master, we do not gain much help from his creator to imagine. But to speak of this as a limitation of Scott's sympathies is simply to say that he should not have allowed them to be captivated by a feudal ideal. It would be almost as unfair to say that Shakespeare shows a narrowness of sympathy because, while he has painted many men in other attitudes than in relation to women, he has never painted any woman except in relation to a man. The relation of contrast will always, we believe, remain the most poetic and the most picturesque in which any character can be represented. And perhaps, when the peculiar sense of bond between the lowly born and the highly born,

---

[1] It must be remembered that Jeanie Deans is hardly a creation [Wedgwood].

which Scott delighted to paint, has faded into remoteness, it will be more distinctly seen than it is now that some excellences can only be thus developed. We do not, indeed, allow that Scott has no power of drawing peasant life except in this attitude: the picture of Jeanie Deans is enough to save his advocate from such a concession; but though a most striking exception, we should still call this noble picture, regarded from this point, an exception to the ordinary course of his dramatic sympathy. He is in this respect the complement of Wordsworth, and we own that, while Scott's ideal is no doubt the much less original conception of peasant life, we do not find it the least interesting of the two.

His pictures of royalty, on the other hand, seem to us to bear in a peculiar manner the stamp of his swift, simple, outward genius. There is no elaborate pomp of description, yet the reader is always made to confront in imagination some stately and dignified presence; we feel that something in Scott's nature readily vibrated to the summons that demanded the respect of a subject, yet retaining his manliness and balance at the same time. No doubt he had in this respect eminently the *défaut de sa qualité*. His attitude towards George IV is not the most pleasing part of his career, and we are glad to think of that tumbler in his coat pocket, honoured by having touched the lips of that illustrious monarch, which his loyal subject begged, pocketed, forgot, and sat down upon, startling the poet Crabbe by his sudden rebound from his uneasy seat. We should gladly have hung up what remained of the fragile treasure by the side of Murray of Broughton's saucer,—the cup belonging to which was destroyed in a nobler manner by Scott's father, when it had through Mrs. Scott's officiousness conveyed a cup of tea to the renegade,—as a vestige of two different kinds of loyalty. And well would the broken glass, at all events, have symbolized the brittle nature of all that was associated with Scott's intercourse with George IV. But we have said enough of his weaknesses.

No creation of his art interests us quite so much as the revelations of himself with which that art supplies us. Even his description of nature, —the most valuable part of his poetry, and that in which he is eminently a representative of the movement we have connected with his name,— seems to us most interesting when it blends itself with what Mr. Ruskin so happily calls his 'far away Æolian note'—a touch of senti- ment always simple, sometimes what might be called commonplace, but commonplace only because the feelings represented are so common, not because the allusion is borrowed. The feeling is always slight and

expressed as shortly as possible, yet it appears to us to set his bright
objective pictures on a wonderfully effective background of pensive
colouring, while it often contains what seems the reflection of his
own conscience on his genius. As for instance:

> 'It seemed some mountain rent and riven,
> A channel for the stream had given,
> So high the cliffs of limestone grey
> Hung beetling o'er the torrent's way,
> Yielding, along their rugged base,
> A flinty footpath's niggard space,
> Where he, who winds 'twixt rock and wave,
> May hear the headlong torrent rave, ...
> Till foam-globes on her eddies ride,
> Thick as the schemes of human pride
> That down life's current drive amain,
> As frail, as frothy, and as vain!'

This sense of the fugitiveness of all things earthly is impressed with a
peculiar vividness on all Scott's poetry. It is difficult to find anything
in the circumstances of his life, at the time his poetry was written, to
explain this sense of insecurity and change; at least it is only in a single
case that we can trace any actual cause for it; and though this one deep
and enduring feeling seems to us to have been not sufficiently allowed
for in any review of his life, yet a healthy nature does not allow any
single feeling, however deep and strong, to colour its whole being.
Scott's early love was not, however, obliterated by any adequate
domestic companionship, and some pathetic verses[1] (pathetic at least
in their circumstances), in the feeble handwriting of his last years, but
not his own composition, and known to have been much admired by
this young lady, remained after his death associated with her initials,
to witness to the undying love which seems to have been the source of
a wonderfully enduring pain, but perhaps also of that deeper tone
never wanting to his poetry, and giving it, to our mind, its special
charm. It often happens, we believe, that a nature of much sensibility
associates with some painful memory many feelings which are not
caused by it, and unawares lets some event become a symbol of

[1] They were addressed 'To Time', and believed to have been the composition
of the object of his affection. They are a specimen of the slight conventional style
of eighty years ago, and, though not actually written by the person to whom they
were attributed, are an evidence of a certain power, both of mind and character,
in their possible author [Wedgwood].

temptations and sorrows with which it has no direct connection. We could almost fancy that the fair young girl whom he remembered so tenderly in his old age (and to whom his thoughts seem to have recurred after his wife's death almost with a sense of freedom) symbolized for him higher, purer aims, and that he regretted in her some ideal to which his whole life had been faithless. It is in the poem where he attempted to paint her[1] that we also find many of the lines which seem dictated by the spirit of self-reproach. We could fancy that the spirit of warning and guidance which most of us can trace in some form or other, in looking back at our lives, sometimes threw the shadow of his own temptations on the canvas that glowed with his creative power. It might have been his guardian angel who bid him write,

[canto I, ll. 707-26 of *Rokeby* are quoted]

Trite moralizing, the reader may decide, whose palate, accustomed to the highly seasoned speculation of our own day, finds insipidity in what is simple. To such a mood the grandest thoughts of antiquity would appear trite if they were not veiled in a learned language, and hallowed by the respectful attention of ages. This first of the Romanticists (first at least in fame) may take his place by the side of many a classic writer for the purity and simplicity of the thought which seems poor at first, and enriches itself with the growing experience of life, so that it expands to take in a part of all that we most vividly remember and hope.

That note of dissatisfaction is what we most gladly remember, as we bid him farewell. Whatever in his career was worldly and disappointing, he did not sink so low as to be satisfied with it. He felt the emptiness and poverty of the things he grasped at. Such at least was the utterance of his truest self—such we will also believe (though from a proud, reserved nature there could hardly be evidence of it) was the conviction that lay deeper even than the sense of their loss, and blended with the sense of things eternal that showed clearer as his brittle follies were swept away.

[1] We suppose that she must have been the lady 'long since dead' whom he described as the original of the colourless Matilda [Wedgwood].

69. Ruskin: 'Fiction—Fair and Foul', *Nineteenth Century*

1880

An article by John Ruskin, *Nineteenth Century* (June 1880), vii, 941-62.

The introductory section, which discusses the effects of the filth and corruption of modern life on fiction, is here omitted.

In the work of the great masters death is always either heroic, deserved, or quiet and natural (unless their purpose be totally and deeply tragic, when collateral meaner death is permitted, like that of Polonius or Roderigo). In *Old Mortality*, four of the deaths, Bothwell's, Ensign Grahame's, Macbriar's, and Evandale's, are magnificently heroic; Burley's and Oliphant's long deserved, and swift; the troopers', met in the discharge of their military duty, and the old miser's, as gentle as the passing of a cloud, and almost beautiful in its last words of—now unselfish—care.

' "Ailie" (he aye ca'd me Ailie, we were auld acquaintance,) "Ailie, take ye care and haud the gear weel thegither; for the name of Morton of Milnwood's gane out like the last sough of an auld sang." And sae he fell out o' ae dwam into another, and ne'er spak a word mair, unless it were something we cou'dna mak out, about a dipped candle being gude eneugh to see to dee wi'. He cou'd ne'er bide to see a moulded ane, and there was ane, by ill luck, on the table.'

In *Guy Mannering*, the murder, though unpremeditated, of a single person, (himself not entirely innocent, but at least by heartlessness in a cruel function earning his fate,) is avenged to the uttermost on all the men conscious of the crime; Mr. Bertram's death, like that of his wife, brief in pain, and each told in the space of half-a-dozen lines; and that of the heroine of the tale, self-devoted, heroic in the highest, and happy.

Nor is it ever to be forgotten, in the comparison of Scott's with inferior work, that his own splendid powers were, even in early life, tainted, and in his latter years destroyed, by modern conditions of commercial excitement, then first, but rapidly, developing themselves. There are parts even in his best novels coloured to meet tastes which he despised; and many pages written in his later ones to lengthen his article for the indiscriminate market.

But there was one weakness of which his healthy mind remained incapable to the last. In modern stories prepared for more refined or fastidious audiences than those of Dickens, the funereal excitement is obtained, for the most part, not by the infliction of violent or disgusting death; but in the suspense, the pathos, and the more or less by all felt, and recognised, mortal phenomena of the sick-room. The temptation, to weak writers, of this order of subject is especially great, because the study of it from the living—or dying—model is so easy, and to many has been the most impressive part of their own personal experience; while, if the description be given even with mediocre accuracy, a very large section of readers will admire its truth, and cherish its melancholy. Few authors of second or third rate genius can either record or invent a probable conversation in ordinary life; but few, on the other hand, are so destitute of observant faculty as to be unable to chronicle the broken syllables and languid movements of an invalid. The easily rendered, and too surely recognised, image of familiar suffering is felt at once to be real where all else has been false; and the historian of the gestures of fever and words of delirium can count on the applause of a gratified audience as surely as the dramatist who introduces on the stage of his flagging action a carriage that can be driven or a fountain that will flow. But the masters of strong imagination disdain such work, and those of deep sensibility shrink from it.[1] Only under conditions of personal weakness, presently to be noted, would Scott comply with the cravings of his lower audience in scenes of terror like the death of Front-de-Bœuf. But he never once withdrew the sacred curtain of the sick-chamber, nor permitted the disgrace of wanton tears round the humiliation of strength, or the wreck of beauty.

No exception to this law of reverence will be found in the scenes in Cœur de Lion's illness introductory to the principal incident in

---

[1] Nell, in the *Old Curiosity Shop*, was simply killed for the market, as a butcher kills a lamb (see Forster's *Life*), and Paul was written under the same conditions of illness which affected Scott—a part of the ominous palsies, grasping alike author and subject, both in *Dombey* and *Little Dorrit* [Ruskin].

the *Talisman*. An inferior writer would have made the king charge in imagination at the head of his chivalry, or wander in dreams by the brooks of Aquitaine; but Scott allows us to learn no more startling symptoms of the king's malady than that he was restless and impatient, and could not wear his armour. Nor is any bodily weakness, or crisis of danger, permitted to disturb for any instant the royalty of intelligence and heart in which he examines, trusts and obeys the physician whom his attendants fear.

Yet the choice of the main subject in this story and its companion— the trial, to a point of utter torture, of knightly faith, and several passages in the conduct of both, more especially the exaggerated scenes in the House of Baldringham, and hermitage of Engedi, are signs of the gradual decline in force of intellect and soul which those who love Scott best have done him the worst injustice in their endeavours to disguise or deny. The mean anxieties, moral humiliations, and mercilessly demanded brain-toil, which killed him, show their sepulchral grasp for many and many a year before their final victory; and the states of more or less dulled, distorted, and polluted imagination which culminate in *Castle Dangerous*, cast a Stygian hue over *St. Ronan's Well*, *The Fair Maid of Perth*, and *Anne of Geierstein*, which lowers them, the first altogether, the other two at frequent intervals, into fellowship with the normal disease which festers throughout the whole body of our lower fictitious literature.

Fictitious! I use the ambiguous word deliberately; for it is impossible to distinguish in these tales of the prison-house how far their vice and gloom are thrown into their manufacture only to meet a vile demand, and how far they are an integral condition of thought in the minds of men trained from their youth up in the knowledge of Londinian and Parisian misery. The speciality of the plague is a delight in the exposition of the relations between guilt and decrepitude; and I call the results of it literature 'of the prison-house', because the thwarted habits of body and mind, which are the punishment of reckless crowding in cities, become, in the issue of that punishment, frightful subjects of exclusive interest to themselves; and the art of fiction in which they finally delight is only the more studied arrangement and illustration, by coloured firelights, of the daily bulletins of their own wretchedness, in the prison calendar, the police news, and the hospital report.

[a long section discussing particular examples of corruption displayed in modern fiction is omitted]

It is to say little for the types of youth and maid which alone Scott felt it a joy to imagine, or thought it honourable to portray, that they act and feel in a sphere where they are never for an instant liable to any of the weaknesses which disturb the calm, or shake the resolution, of chastity and courage in a modern novel. Scott lived in a country and time, when, from highest to lowest, but chiefly in that dignified and nobly severe[1] middle class to which he himself belonged, a habit of serene and stainless thought was as natural to the people as their mountain air. Women like Rose Bradwardine and Ailie Dinmont were the grace and guard of almost every household (God be praised that the race of them is not yet extinct, for all that Mall or Boulevard can do), and it has perhaps escaped the notice of even attentive readers that the comparatively uninteresting character of Sir Walter's heroes had always been studied among a class of youths who were simply incapable of doing anything seriously wrong; and could only be embarrassed by the consequences of their levity or imprudence.

But there is another difference in the woof of a Waverley novel from the cobweb of a modern one, which depends on Scott's larger view of human life. Marriage is by no means, in his conception of man and woman, the most important business of their existence;[2] nor love the only reward to be proposed to their virtue or exertion. It is not in his reading of the laws of Providence a necessity that virtue should, either by love or any other external blessing, be rewarded at all;[3] and marriage is in all cases thought of as a constituent of the happiness of life, but not as its only interest, still less its only aim. And upon analysing with some care the motives of his principal stories, we shall often find that the love in them is merely a light by which the sterner features of character are to be irradiated, and that the marriage of the hero is as subordinate to the main bent of the story as Henry the Fifth's courtship of Katherine is to the battle of Agincourt. Nay, the fortunes of the person who is nominally the subject of the tale are often little more than a background on which grander figures are to

[1] Scott's father was habitually ascetic. 'I have heard his son tell that it was common with him, if any one observed that the soup was good, to taste it again, and say, "Yes—it is too good, bairns," and dash a tumbler of cold water into his plate.'—Lockhart's *Life* (Black, Edinburgh, 1869), vol. i, p. 312. In other places I refer to this book in the simple form of 'L' [Ruskin].

[2] A young lady sang to me, just before I copied out this page for press, a Miss Somebody's 'great song', 'Live, and Love, and Die'. Had it been written for nothing better than silkworms, it should at least have added—Spin [Ruskin].

[3] See passage of introduction to *Ivanhoe*, wisely quoted in L. vi. 106 [Ruskin].

be drawn, and deeper fates forth-shadowed. The judgments between the faith and chivalry of Scotland at Drumclog and Bothwell bridge owe little of their interest in the mind of a sensible reader to the fact that the captain of the Popinjay is carried a prisoner to one battle, and returns a prisoner from the other: and Scott himself, while he watches the white sail that bears Queen Mary for the last time from her native land, very nearly forgets to finish his novel, or to tell us—and with small sense of any consolation to be had out of that minor circumstance, —that 'Roland and Catherine were united, spite of their differing faiths'.

Neither let it be thought for an instant that the slight, and sometimes scornful, glance with which Scott passes over scenes which a novelist of our own day would have analysed with the airs of a philosopher, and painted with the curiosity of a gossip, indicate any absence in his heart of sympathy with the great and sacred elements of personal happiness. An era like ours, which has with diligence and ostentation swept its heart clear of all the passions once known as loyalty, patriotism, and piety, necessarily magnifies the apparent force of the one remaining sentiment which sighs through the barren chambers, or clings inextricably round the chasms of ruin; nor can it but regard with awe the unconquerable spirit which still tempts or betrays the sagacities of selfishness into error or frenzy which is believed to be love.

That Scott was never himself, in the sense of the phrase as employed by lovers of the Parisian school, 'ivre d'amour', may be admitted without prejudice to his sensibility,[1] and that he never knew 'l'amor che move 'l sol e l'altre stelle', was the chief, though unrecognised, calamity of his deeply chequered life.[2] But the reader of honour and feeling will not therefore suppose that the love which Miss Vernon sacrifices, stooping for an instant from her horse, is of less noble stamp, or less enduring faith, than that which troubles and degrades the whole existence of Consuelo; or that the affection of Jeanie Deans for the companion of her childhood, drawn like a field of soft blue heaven beyond the cloudy wrack of her sorrow, is less fully in possession of her soul than the hesitating and self-reproachful impulses under which a modern heroine forgets herself in a boat, or compromises herself in the cool of the evening.

I do not wish to return over the waste ground we have traversed,

[1] See below [note 1, p. 530], on the conclusion of *Woodstock* [Ruskin].

[2] 'The Love that moves the sun and the other stars.' Dante's *Paradiso*, XXXIII, 145.

comparing, point by point, Scott's manner with those of Bermondsey and the Faubourgs; but it may be, perhaps, interesting at this moment to examine, with illustration from those Waverley novels which have so lately retracted the attention of a fair and gentle public, the universal conditions of 'style', rightly so called, which are in all ages, and above all local currents or wavering tides of temporary manners, pillars of what is for ever strong, and models of what is for ever fair.

But I must first define, and that within strict horizon, the works of Scott, in which his perfect mind may be known, and his chosen ways understood.

His great works of prose fiction, excepting only the first half-volume of *Waverley*, were all written in twelve years, 1814-26 (of his own age forty-three to fifty-five), the actual time employed in their composition being not more than a couple of months out of each year: and during that time only the morning hours and spare minutes during the professional day. 'Though the first volume of *Waverley* was begun long ago, and actually lost for a time, yet the other two were begun and finished between the 4th of June and the 1st of July, during all which I attended my duty in court, and proceeded without loss of time or hindrance of business.'

Few of the maxims for the enforcement of which, in *Modern Painters*, long ago, I got the general character of a lover of paradox, are more singular, or more sure, than the statement, apparently so encouraging to the idle, that if a great thing can be done at all, it can be done easily. But it is in that kind of ease with which a tree blossoms after long years of gathered strength, and all Scott's great writings were the recreations of a mind confirmed in dutiful labour, and rich with organic gathering of boundless resource.

Omitting from our count the two minor and ill-finished sketches of *The Black Dwarf* and *Legend of Montrose*, and, for a reason presently to be noticed, the unhappy *St. Ronan's*, the memorable romances of Scott are eighteen, falling into three distinct groups, containing six each.

The first group is distinguished from the other two by characters of strength and felicity which never more appeared after Scott was struck down by his terrific illness in 1819. It includes *Waverley*, *Guy Mannering*, *The Antiquary*, *Rob Roy*, *Old Mortality*, and *The Heart of Midlothian*.

The composition of these occupied the mornings of his happiest days, between the ages of 43 and 48. On the 8th April, 1819 (he was

48 on the preceding 15th August) he began for the first time to dictate—being unable for the exertion of writing—*The Bride of Lammermoor,* 'the affectionate Laidlaw beseeching him to stop dictating, when his audible suffering filled every pause. "Nay, Willie," he answered, "only see that the doors are fast. I would fain keep all the cry as well as all the wool to ourselves; but as for giving over work, that can only be when I am in woollen." ' From this time forward the brightness of joy and sincerity of inevitable humour, which perfected the imagery of the earlier novels, are wholly absent, except in the two short intervals of health unaccountably restored, in which he wrote *Redgauntlet* and *Nigel.*

It is strange, but only a part of the general simplicity of Scott's genius, that these revivals of earlier power were unconscious, and that the time of extreme weakness in which he wrote *St. Ronan's Well,* was that in which he first asserted his own restoration.

It is also a deeply interesting characteristic of his noble nature that he never gains anything by sickness; the whole man breathes or faints as one creature: the ache that stiffens a limb chills his heart, and every pang of the stomach paralyses the brain. It is not so with inferior minds, in the workings of which it is often impossible to distinguish native from narcotic fancy, and the throbs of conscience from those of indigestion. Whether in exaltation or languor, the colours of mind are always morbid, which gleam on the sea for *The Ancient Mariner,* and through the casements on *St. Agnes' Eve;* but Scott is at once blinded and stultified by sickness; never has a fit of the cramp without spoiling a chapter, and is perhaps the only author of vivid imagination who never wrote a foolish word but when he was ill.

It remains only to be noticed on this point that any strong natural excitement, affecting the deeper springs of his heart, would at once restore his intellectual powers in all their fulness, and that, far towards their sunset: but that the strong will on which he prided himself, though it could trample upon pain, silence grief, and compel industry, never could warm his imagination, or clear the judgment in his darker hours.

I believe that this power of the heart over the intellect is common to all great men: but what the special character of emotion was, that alone could lift Scott above the power of death, I am about to ask the reader, in a little while, to observe with joyful care.

The first series of romances then, above named, are all that exhibit the emphasis of his unharmed faculties. The second group, composed in the three years subsequent to illness all but mortal, bear every one of them more or less the seal of it.

They consist of the *Bride of Lammermoor, Ivanhoe, The Monastery, The Abbot, Kenilworth*, and the *Pirate*.[1] The marks of broken health on all these are essentially twofold—prevailing melancholy, and fantastic improbability. Three of the tales are agonisingly tragic, *The Abbot* scarcely less so in its main event, and *Ivanhoe* deeply wounded through all its bright panoply; while even in that most powerful of the series, the impossible archeries and axestrokes, the incredibly opportune appearances of Locksley, the death of Ulrica, and the resuscitation of Athelstane, are partly boyish, partly feverish. Caleb in the *Bride*, Triptolemus and Halcro in *The Pirate*, are all laborious, and the first incongruous; half a volume of *The Abbot* is spent in extremely dull detail of Roland's relations with his fellow-servants and his mistress, which have nothing whatever to do with the future story; and the lady of Avenel herself disappears after the first volume, 'like a snaw-wreath when it's thaw, Jeanie'. The public has for itself pronounced on *The Monastery*, though as much too harshly as it has foolishly praised the horrors of *Ravenswood* and the nonsense of *Ivanhoe*; because the modern public finds in the torture and adventure of these, the kind of excitement which it seeks at an opera, while it has no sympathy whatever with the pastoral happiness of Glendearg, or with the lingering simplicities of superstition which give historical likelihood to the legend of the White Lady.

But both this despised tale and its sequel have Scott's heart in them. The first was begun to refresh himself in the intervals of artificial labour on *Ivanhoe*. 'It was a relief,' he said, 'to interlay the scenery most familiar to me[2] with the strange world for which I had to draw so much on imagination.'[3] Through all the closing scenes of the second

---

[1] 'One other such novel, and there's an end; but who can last for ever? who ever lasted so long?'—Sydney Smith (of the *Pirate*) to Jeffrey, December 30, 1821. (*Letters*, vol. ii, p. 223) [Ruskin].

[2] L. vi, p. 188. Compare the description of Fairy Dean, vii. 192 [Ruskin].

[3] All, alas! were now in a great measure so written. *Ivanhoe, The Monastery, The Abbot*, and *Kenilworth* were all published between December 1819 and January 1821, Constable & Co. giving five thousand guineas for the remaining copyright of them, Scott clearing ten thousand before the bargain was completed; and before the *Fortunes of Nigel* issued from the press Scott had exchanged instruments and received his bookseller's bills for no less than four 'works of fiction', not one of them otherwise described in the deeds of agreement, to be produced in unbroken succession, *each of them to fill up at least three volumes, but with proper saving clauses as to increase of copy money in case any of them should run to four*; and

he is raised to his own true level by his love for the queen. And within the code of Scott's work to which I am about to appeal for illustration of his essential powers, I accept *The Monastery* and *Abbot*, and reject from it the remaining four of this group.

The last series contains two quite noble ones, *Redgauntlet* and *Nigel*; two of very high value, *Durward* and *Woodstock*; the slovenly and diffuse *Peveril*, written for the trade; the sickly *Tales of the Crusaders* and the entirely broken and diseased *St. Ronan's Well*. This last I throw out of count altogether, and of the rest, accept only the four first named as sound work; so that the list of the novels in which I propose to examine his methods and ideal standards, reduces itself to these following twelve (named in order of production): *Waverley, Guy Mannering, The Antiquary, Rob Roy, Old Mortality, The Heart of Midlothian, The Monastery,* the *Abbot, The Fortunes of Nigel, Quentin Durward,* and *Woodstock.*[1]

It is, however, too late to enter on my subject in this article, which I may fitly close by pointing out some of the merely verbal characteristics of his style, illustrative in little ways of the questions we have been examining, and chiefly of the one which may be most embarrassing to many readers, the difference, namely, between character and disease.

One quite distinctive charm in the Waverleys is their modified use of the Scottish dialect; but it has not generally been observed, either by their imitators, or the authors of different taste who have written for a later public, that there is a difference between the dialect of a language, and its corruption.

A dialect is formed in any district where there are persons of intelligence enough to use the language itself in all its fineness and force, but under the particular conditions of life, climate, and temper, which introduce words peculiar to the scenery, forms of word and idioms of sentence peculiar to the race, and pronunciations indicative of their character and disposition.

Thus 'burn' (of a streamlet) is a word possible only in a country

---

within two years all this anticipation had been wiped off by *Peveril of the Peak, Quentin Durward, St. Ronan's Well,* and *Red Gauntlet* [Ruskin].

[1] *Woodstock* was finished 26th March 1826. He knew then of his ruin; and wrote in bitterness, but not in weakness. The closing pages are the most beautiful of the book. But a month afterwards Lady Scott died; and he never wrote glad word more [Ruskin].

where there are brightly running waters, 'lassie', a word possible only where girls are as free as the rivulets, and 'auld', a form of the southern 'old', adopted by a race of finer musical ear than the English.

On the contrary, mere deteriorations, of coarse, stridulent, and, in the ordinary sense of the phrase, 'broad' forms of utterance, are not dialects at all, having nothing dialectic in them, and all phrases developed in states of rude employment, and restricted intercourse, are injurious to the tone and narrowing to the power of the language they affect. Mere breadth of accent does not spoil a dialect as long as the speakers are men of varied idea and good intelligence; but the moment the life is contracted by mining, millwork, or any oppressive and monotonous labour, the accents and phrases become debased. It is part of the popular folly of the day to find pleasure in trying to write and spell these abortive, crippled, and more or less brutal forms of human speech.

Abortive, crippled, or brutal, are however not necessarily 'corrupted' dialects. Corrupt language is that gathered by ignorance, invented by vice, misused by insensibility, or minced and mouthed by affectation, especially in the attempt to deal with words of which only half the meaning is understood, or half the sound heard. Mrs. Gamp's 'aperiently so'—and the 'underminded' with primal sense of undermine, of—I forget which gossip, in *The Mill on the Floss*, are master- and mistress-pieces in this latter kind. Mrs. Malaprop's 'allegories on the banks of the Nile' are in a somewhat higher order of mistake: Mrs. Tabitha Bramble's ignorance is vulgarised by her selfishness, and Winifred Jenkins' by her conceit. The 'wot' of Noah Claypole, and the other degradations of cockneyism (Sam Weller and his father are in nothing more admirable than in the power of heart and sense that can purify even these); the 'trewth' of Mr. Chadband, and 'natur' of Mr. Squeers, are examples of the corruption of words by insensibility: the use of the word 'bloody' in modern low English is a deeper corruption, not altering the form of the word, but defiling the thought in it.

Thus much being understood, I shall proceed to examine thoroughly a fragment of Scott's Lowland Scottish dialect; not choosing it of the most beautiful kind; on the contrary, it shall be a piece reaching as low down as he ever allows Scotch to go—it is perhaps the only unfair patriotism in him, that if ever he wants a word or two of really villanous slang, he gives it in English or Dutch—not Scotch.

I had intended in the close of this paper to analyse and compare the characters of Andrew Fairservice and Richie Moniplies, for examples, the former of innate evil, unaffected by external influences, and undiseased, but distinct from natural goodness as a nettle is distinct from balm or lavender; and the latter of innate goodness, contracted and pinched by circumstance, but still undiseased, as an oak-leaf crisped by frost, not by the worm. This, with much else in my mind, I must put off; but the careful study of one sentence of Andrew's will give us a good deal to think of.

I take his account of the rescue of Glasgow Cathedral at the time of the Reformation.

'Ah! it's a brave kirk—nane o' yere whigmaleeries and curliewurlies and opensteek hems about it—a' solid, weel-jointed mason-wark, that will stand as lang as the warld, keep hands and gunpowder aff it. It had amaist a doun-come lang syne at the Reformation, when they pu'd doun the kirks of St. Andrews and Perth, and thereawa', to cleanse them o' Papery, and idolatry, and image-worship, and surplices, and sic-like rags o' the muckle hure that sitteth on seven hills, as if ane wasna braid eneugh for her auld hinder end. Sae the commons o' Renfrew, and o' the Barony, and the Gorbals, and a' about, they behoved to come into Glasgow ae fair morning, to try their hand on purging the High Kirk o' Popish nicknackets. But the townsmen o' Glasgow, they were feared their auld edifice might slip the girths in gaun through siccan rough physic, sae they rang the common bell, and assembled the train-bands wi' took o' drum. By good luck, the worthy James Rabat was Dean o' Guild that year—(and a gude mason he was himsell, made him the keener to keep up the auld bigging), and the trades assembled, and offered downright battle to the commons, rather than their kirk should coup the crans, as others had done elsewhere. It wasna for luve o' Paperie—na, na!—nane could ever say that o' the trades o' Glasgow—Sae they sune came to an agreement to take a' the idolatrous statues of sants (sorrow be on them!) out o' their neuks—And sae the bits o' stane idols were broken in pieces by Scripture warrant, and flung into the Molendinar burn, and the auld kirk stood as crouse as a cat when the flaes are kaimed aff her, and a'body was alike pleased. And I hae heard wise folk say, that if the same had been done in ilka kirk in Scotland, the Reform wad just hae been as pure as it is e'en now, and we wad hae mair Christian-like kirks; for I hae been sae lang in England, that naething will drived out o' my head, that the dog-kennel at Osbaldistone-Hall is better than mony a house o' God in Scotland.'

Now this sentence is in the first place a piece of Scottish history of quite inestimable and concentrated value. Andrew's temperament is the type of a vast class of Scottish—shall we call it *'sow*-thistlian'— mind, which necessarily takes the view of either Pope or saint that the thistle in Lebanon took of the cedar or lilies in Lebanon; and the entire force of the passions which, in the Scottish revolution, foretold and forearmed the French one, is told in this one paragraph; the coarseness of it, observe, being admitted, not for the sake of the laugh, any more than an onion in broth merely for its flavour, but for the meat of it; the inherent constancy of that coarseness being a fact in this order of mind, and an essential part of the history to be told.

Secondly, observe that this speech, in the religious passion of it, such as there may be, is entirely sincere. Andrew is a thief, a liar, a coward, and, in the Fair service from which he takes his name, a hypocrite; but in the form of prejudice, which is all that his mind is capable of in the place of religion, he is entirely sincere. He does not in the least pretend detestation of image worship to please his master, or any one else; he honestly scorns the 'carnal morality[1] as dowd and fusionless as rue-leaves at Yule' of the sermon in the upper cathedral; and when wrapt in critical attention to the 'real savour o' doctrine' in the crypt, so completely forgets the hypocrisy of his fair service as to return his master's attempt to disturb him with hard punches of the elbow.

Thirdly. He is a man of no mean sagacity, quite up to the average standard of Scottish common sense, not a low one; and, though incapable of understanding any manner of lofty thought or passion, is a shrewd measurer of weaknesses, and not without a spark or two of kindly feeling. See first his sketch of his master's character to Mr. Hammorgaw, beginning: 'He's no a'thegither sae void o' sense, neither'; and then the close of the dialogue: 'But the lad's no a bad lad after a', and he needs some carefu' body to look after him.'

Fourthly. He is a good workman; knows his own business well, and can judge of other craft, if sound, or otherwise.

All these four qualities of him must be known before we can understand this single speech. Keeping them in mind, I take it up, word by word.

You observe, in the outset, Scott makes no attempt whatever to indicate accents or modes of pronunciation by changed spelling, unless the word becomes a quite definitely new, and scarcely writeable one. The Scottish way of pronouncing 'James', for instance, is entirely peculiar, and extremely pleasant to the ear. But it is so, just because it does *not* change the word into Jeems, nor into Jims, nor into Jawms. A modern writer of dialects would think it amusing to use one or

[1] Compare Mr. Spurgeon's not unfrequent orations on the same subject [Ruskin].

other of these ugly spellings. But Scott writes the name in pure English, knowing that a Scots reader will speak it rightly, and an English one be wise in letting it alone. On the other hand he writes 'weel' for 'well', because that word is complete in its change, and may be very closely expressed by the double *e*. The ambiguous '*u*'s' in 'gude' and 'sune' are admitted, because far liker the sound than the double *o* would be, and that in 'hure', for grace' sake, to soften the word;—so also 'flaes' for 'fleas'. 'Mony' for 'many' is again positively right in sound, and 'neuk' differs from our 'nook' in sense, and is not the same word at all, as we shall presently see.

Secondly, observe, not a word is corrupted in any indecent haste, slowness, slovenliness, or incapacity of pronunciation. There is no lisping, drawling, slobbering, or snuffling: the speech is as clear as a bell and as keen as an arrow: and its elisions and contractions are either melodious, ('na', for 'not',—'pu'd', for 'pulled',) or as normal as in a Latin verse. The long words are delivered without the slightest bungling; and 'bigging' finished to its last *g*.

I take the important words now in their places.

Brave. The old English sense of the word in 'to go brave' retained, expressing Andrew's sincere and respectful admiration. Had he meant to insinuate a hint of the church's being too fine, he would have said 'braw'.

Kirk. This is of course just as pure and unprovincial a word as 'Kirche', or 'église'.

Whigmaleerie. I cannot get at the root of this word, but it is one showing that the speaker is not bound by classic rules, but will use any syllables that enrich his meaning. 'Nipperty-tipperty' (of his master's 'poetry-nonsense') is another word of the same class. 'Curlieurlie' is of course just as pure as Shakespeare's 'Hurly-burly'. But see first suggestion of the idea to Scott at Blair-Adam (L. vi. 264).

Opensteek hems. More description, or better, of the later Gothic cannot be put into four syllables. 'Steek', melodious for stitch, has a combined sense of closing or fastening. And note that the later Gothic, being precisely what Scott knew best (in Melrose) and liked best, it is, here as elsewhere, quite as much himself[1] as Frank, that he is laughing at, when he laughs *with* Andrew, whose 'opensteek hems' are only a ruder metaphor for his own 'willow-wreaths changed to stone'.

---

[1] There are three definite and intentional portraits of himself, in the novels, each giving a separate part of himself: Mr. Oldbuck, Frank Osbaldistone, and Alan Fairford [Ruskin].

Gunpowther. '-Ther' is a lingering vestige of the French '-dre'.

Syne. One of the melodious and mysterious Scottish words which have partly the sound of wind and stream in them, and partly the range of softened idea which is like a distance of blue hills over border land ('far in the distant Cheviot's blue'). Perhaps even the least sympathetic 'Englisher' might recognise this, if he heard 'Old Long Since' vocally substituted for the Scottish words to the air. I do not know the root; but the word's proper meaning is not 'since', but before or after an interval of some duration, 'as weel sune as syne'. 'But first on Sawnie gies a ca', Syne, bauldly in she enters.'

Behoved (to come). A rich word, with peculiar idiom, always used more or less ironically of anything done under a partly mistaken and partly pretended notion of duty.

Siccan. Far prettier, and fuller in meaning than 'such'. It contains an added sense of wonder; and means properly 'so great' or 'so unusual'.

Took (o' drum). Classical 'tuck' from Italian 'toccata', the preluding 'touch' or flourish, on any instrument (but see Johnson under word 'tucket', quoting *Othello*). The deeper Scottish vowels are used here to mark the deeper sound of the bass drum, as in more solemn warning.

Bigging. The only word in all the sentence of which the Scottish form is less melodious than the English, 'and what for no', seeing that Scottish architecture is mostly little beyond Bessie Bell's and Mary Gray's? 'They biggit a bow're by yon burnside, and theekit it ow're wi rashes.' But it is pure Anglo-Saxon in roots; see glossary to Fairbairn's edition of the Douglas *Virgil*, 1710.

Coup. Another of the much-embracing words; short for 'upset', but with a sense of awkwardness as the inherent cause of fall; compare Richie Moniplies (also for sense of 'behoved'): 'Ae auld hirplin deevil of a potter behoved just to step in my way, and offer me a pig (earthen pot—etym. dub.), as he said "just to put my Scotch ointment in;" and I gave him a push, as but natural, and the tottering deevil coupit owre amang his own pigs, and damaged a score of them.' So also Dandie Dinmont in the postchaise: ' 'Od! I hope they'll no coup us.'

The Crans. Idiomatic; root unknown to me, but it means in this use, full, total, and without recovery.

Molendinar. From 'molendinum', the grinding-place. I do not know if actually the local name,[1] or Scott's invention. Compare Sir Piercie's

---

[1] Andrew knows Latin, and might have coined the word in his conceit; but, writing to a kind friend in Glasgow, I find the brook was called 'Molyndona' even before the building of the Sub-dean Mill in 1446. See also account of the

'Molinaras'. But at all events used here with bye-sense of degradation of the formerly idle saints to grind at the mill.

Crouse. Courageous, softened with a sense of comfort.

Ilka. Again a word with azure distance, including the whole sense of 'each' and 'every'. The reader must carefully and reverently distinguish these comprehensive words, which gather two or more perfectly understood meanings into one *chord* of meaning, and are harmonies more than words, from the above-noted blunders between two half-hit meanings, struck as a bad piano-player strikes the edge of another note. In English we have fewer of these combined thoughts; so that Shakespeare rather plays with the distinct lights of his words, than melts them into one. So again Bishop Douglas spells, and doubtless spoke, the word 'rose', differently, according to his purpose; if as the chief or governing ruler of flowers, 'rois', but if only in her own beauty, rose.

Christian-like. The sense of the decency and order proper to Christianity is stronger in Scotland than in any other country, and the word 'Christian' more distinctly opposed to 'beast'. Hence the back-handed cut at the English for their over-pious care of dogs.

I am a little surprised myself at the length to which this examination of one small piece of Sir Walter's first-rate work has carried us, but here I must end for this time, trusting, if the Editor of the *Nineteenth Century* permit me, yet to trespass, perhaps more than once, on his readers' patience; but, at all events, to examine in a following paper the technical characteristics of Scott's own style, both in prose and verse, together with Byron's, as opposed to our fashionably recent dialects and rhythms; the essential virtues of language, in both the masters of the old school, hinging ultimately, little as it might be thought, on certain unalterable views of theirs concerning the code called 'of the Ten Commandments', wholly at variance with the dogmas of automatic morality which, summed again by the witches' line, 'Fair is foul, and foul is fair', hover through the fog and filthy air of our prosperous England.

---

locality in Mr. George's admirable volume, *Old Glasgow*, pp. 129, 149, &c. The Protestantism of Glasgow, since throwing that powder of saints into her brook Kidron, has presented it with other pious offerings; and my friend goes on to say that the brook, once famed for the purity of its waters (much used for bleaching), 'has for nearly a hundred years been a crawling stream of loathsomeness. It is now bricked over, and a carriage-way made on the top of it; underneath the foul mess still passes through the heart of the city, till it falls into the Clyde close to the harbour' [Ruskin].

70. Twain: Scott as warmonger
1883

Excerpt from chapter 46 of Mark Twain, *Life on the Mississippi* (1883).

Immediately before the passage selected, Twain praises the French Revolution and Napoleon for 'permanent services to liberty, humanity, and progress'.

Then comes Sir Walter Scott with his enchantments, and by his single might checks this wave of progress, and even turns it back; sets the world in love with dreams and phantoms; with decayed and swinish forms of religion; with decayed and degraded systems of government; with the sillinesses and emptinesses, sham grandeurs, sham gauds, and sham chivalries of a brainless and worthless long-vanished society. He did measureless harm; more real and lasting harm, perhaps, than any other individual that ever wrote. Most of the world has now outlived good part of these harms, though by no means all of them; but in our South they flourish pretty forcefully still. Not so forcefully as half a generation ago, perhaps, but still forcefully. There, the genuine and wholesome civilization of the nineteenth century is curiously confused and commingled with the Walter Scott Middle-Age sham civilization, and so you have practical commonsense, progressive ideas, and progressive works, mixed up with the duel, the inflated speech, and the jejune romanticism of an absurd past that is dead, and out of charity ought to be buried. But for the Sir Walter disease, the character of the Southerner—or Southron, according to Sir Walter's starchier way of phrasing it—would be wholly modern, in place of modern and mediæval mixed, and the South would be fully a generation further advanced than it is. It was Sir Walter that made every gentleman in the South a major or a colonel, or a general or a judge, before the war; and it was he, also, that made these gentlemen value these bogus decorations. For it was he that created rank and caste down there, and also reverence for rank and caste, and pride and pleasure in them. Enough is laid on slavery, without fathering upon it these creations and contributions of Sir Walter.

Sir Walter had so large a hand in making Southern character, as it existed before the war, that he is in great measure responsible for the war. It seems a little harsh toward a dead man to say that we never should have had any war but for Sir Walter; and yet something of a plausible argument might, perhaps, be made in support of that wild proposition. The Southerner of the American Revolution owned slaves; so did the Southerner of the Civil War; but the former resembles the latter as an Englishman resembles a Frenchman. The change of character can be traced rather more easily to Sir Walter's influence than to that of any other thing or person.

One may observe, by one or two signs, how deeply that influence penetrated, and how strongly it holds. If one take up a Northern or Southern literary periodical of forty or fifty years ago, he will find it filled with wordy, windy, flowery 'eloquence', romanticism, sentimentality—all imitated from Sir Walter, and sufficiently badly done, too—innocent travesties of his style and methods, in fact. This sort of literature being the fashion in both sections of the country, there was opportunity for the fairest competition; and as a consequence, the South was able to show as many well-known literary names, proportioned to population, as the North could.

But a change has come, and there is no opportunity now for a fair competition between North and South. For the North has thrown out that old inflated style, whereas the Southern writer still clings to it— clings to it and has a restricted market for his wares, as a consequence. There is as much literary talent in the South, now, as ever there was, of course; but its work can gain but slight currency under present conditions; the authors write for the past, not the present; they use obsolete forms and a dead language. But when a Southerner of genius writes modern English, his book goes upon crutches no longer, but upon wings; and they carry it swiftly all about America and England, and through the great English reprint publishing houses of Germany— as witness the experience of Mr. Cable and 'Uncle Remus', two of the very few Southern authors who do not write in the Southern style. Instead of three or four widely-known literary names, the South ought to have a dozen or two—and will have them when Sir Walter's time is out.

A curious exemplification of the power of a single book for good or harm is shown in the effects wrought by *Don Quixote* and those wrought by *Ivanhoe*. The first swept the world's admiration for the mediæval chivalry-silliness out of existence; and the other restored it. As far as our South is concerned, the good work done by Cervantes is pretty nearly a dead letter, so effectually has Scott's pernicious work undermined it.

This list is intended to comprise and supplement the lists of contemporary reviews contained in James C. Corson's *A Bibliography of Sir Walter Scott* (Edinburgh, 1943).

The novels are listed in order of publication, the reviews in order of appearance (the actual dates of publication of the *Quarterly Review* are taken from H. and H. C. Shine, *The Quarterly Review Under Gifford* (Chapel Hill, N.C., 1949)). Attributions of authorship, given in parentheses when known or suspected (indicated by '?'), are taken mostly from standard sources: for the *Quarterly*, Shine, as cited above; for the *Edinburgh Review*, Walter E. Houghton, ed., *The Wellesley Index to Victorian Periodicals* (London and Toronto, 1966); for *Blackwood's Magazine*, Alan L. Strout, *A Bibliography of Articles in Blackwood's Magazine* (Lubbock, Texas, 1959); for the *Monthly Review*, B. C. Nangle, *The Monthly Review* (Oxford, 1955). The attributions for the *London Magazine* are taken from T. R. Hughes' unpublished dissertation, 'The London Magazine' (Oxford University, 1931); and those for the *Eclectic Review* are taken from marked copies in the London Library. Other attributions are from Corson's bibliography, cited above.

Asterisks by page numbers indicate misnumbering.

Abbreviations used

AjR	*Antijacobin Review and Magazine* (1798-1821)
AugR	*Augustine Review* (1815-16)
LaBA	*La Belle Assemblée* (1806-32)
BC	*British Critic* (1793-1826)
BLM	*British Lady's Magazine* (1815-18)
BM	*Blackwood's Edinburgh Magazine* (1817-)
BR	*British Review* (1811-25)
Champ	*Champion* (1814-22)
CO	*Christian Observer* (1802-74)

CR	*Critical Review* (1756-1817)
EcR	*Eclectic Review* (1805-68)
EdM	*Edinburgh Magazine* (1817-26)
EM	*European Magazine and London Review* (1782-1826)
ER	*Edinburgh Review* (1802-1929)
Exam	*Examiner* (1808-81)
GM	*Gentleman's Magazine* (1731-1868)
LC	*Literary Chronicle and Weekly Review* (1819-29)
LG	*Literary Gazette* (1817-62)
LitMus	*Literary Museum* (1822-24)
LitReg	*Literary Register* (1822-23)
LJGM	*Literary Journal, and General Miscellany* (1818-19)
LM	*London Magazine* (1820-29)
Gold's LM	*London Magazine; and Monthly Critical and Dramatic Review* (1820-21)
LMM	*Lady's Monthly Museum* (1798-1828)
LS	*Literary Speculum* (1821-23)
LSB	*Literary Sketch-Book* (1823-24)
LSMS	*Literary and Statistical Magazine for Scotland* (1817-22)
MC	*Monthly Censor* (1822-23)
MM	*Monthly Magazine* (1796-1825)
MinMag	*Miniature Magazine* (1818-1820)
MR	*Monthly Review* (1749-1845)
NAR	*North American Review* (1815-1940)
NEM	*New European Magazine* (1822-24)
NER	*New Edinburgh Review* (1821-23)
NMM	*New Monthly Magazine* (1814-36)
QR	*Quarterly Review* (1809-)
Scot	*Scotsman* (1817-)
SM	*Scots Magazine* (1739-1817)
TI	*Theatrical Inquisitor* (1812-21)
UR	*Universal Review* (1824-25)
WestR	*Western Review* (1819-21)
WR	*Westminster Review* (1824-1914)

Waverley (1814)

SM, LXXVI (July 1814), 524-33; QR, XI (July 1814), 354-77 [pub. between 2 July and 30 July] (J. W. Croker); *Champ*, 24 July 1814, 238-9 (J. Scott); BC, II 2s (Aug. 1814), 189-211; *AjR*, LXVII (Sept. 1814), 217-47*; NMM, II (Sept. 1814), 156; *Scourge*, VIII (Oct. 1814), 291-8; ER, XXIV (Nov. 1814), 208-43 (F. Jeffrey); MR, LXXV (Nov. 1814),

275-89 (J. Merivale); *CR*, I 5s (March 1815), 288-83*; *The Port Folio*, V 3s (April 1815), 326-33; *ER*, XXXIII (Jan. 1820), 1-54 (F. Jeffrey); *GM*, LXXXV-i, 538.

Guy Mannering (1815)

QR, XII (Jan. 1815), 501-9 [pub. by 14 Jan. 1815] (J. W. Croker); *BC*, III 2s (April 1815), 399-409; *NMM*, III (April 1815), 256; *Champ*, 9 April 1815, 118; *BLM*, I (May 1815), 355-8; *MR*. LXXVII 2s (May 1815), 85-94; *AjR*, XLVIII (June 1815), 544-50; *CR*, I 5s (June 1815), 600-3; *AugR*, I (July 1815), 228-33; *SM*, LXXVII (Aug. 1815), 608-14; *NAR*, I (Sept. 1815), 403-36; *Port Folio*, II 4s (Aug. 1816), 159-78; *ER*, XXXIII (Jan. 1820), 1-54 (F. Jeffrey).

The Antiquary (1816)

SM, LXXVIII (May 1816), 365-73; *BC*, V 2s (June 1816), 633-57; *GM*, LXXXVI-i (June 1816), 521-3; *NMM*, V (June 1816), 444; *AjR*, L (July 1816), 625-32; *QR*, XV (April 1816), 125-39 [pub. Aug. 1816] (J. W. Croker); *AugR*, III (Aug. 1816), 155-77; *BLM*, IV (Aug. 1816) 103-5; *EM*, LXX (Sept. 1816), 248-50; *MR*, LXXXII (Jan. 1817), 38-52; *ER*, XXXIII (Jan. 1820), 1-54 (F. Jeffrey).

Tales of My Landlord: *The Black Dwarf* and *Old Mortality* (1816)

SM, LXXVIII (Dec. 1816), 928-34; *CR*, IV 5s (Dec. 1816), 614-25; *BC*, VII 2s (Jan. 1817), 73-97; *Edinburgh Christian Instructor*, XIV (Jan. 1817), 41-73, (Feb. 1817), 100-140, (Mar. 1817), 170-201 (Thomas M'Crie); *MM*, XLII (1 Jan. 1817), 546; *NMM*, VI (Jan. 1817), 533-4; *BLM*, V (Feb. 1817), 94-101; *BR*, IX (Feb. 1817), 184-204; *ER*, XXVIII (March 1817), 193-259 (F. Jeffrey); *QR*, XVI (Jan. 1817), 430-80 [pub. April 1817] (W. Scott, W. Erskine, and W. Gifford); *EcR*, VII 2s (April 1817), 309-36 (J. Conder); *MR*, LXXXII 2s (April 1817), 383-91; *NAR*, V (July 1817), 257-86 (J. G. Palfrey); *The Port Folio*, IV 4s (Nov. 1817), 400-408; *ER*, XXXIII (Jan. 1820), 1-54 (F. Jeffrey).

Rob Roy (1818)

AjR, LIII (Jan. 1818), 417-31; *EdM*, II 2s (Jan. 1818), 41-50, (Feb. 1818), 148-53 (R. Morehead); *TI*, XII (Jan. 1818), 36-40; *Scot*, 3 Jan. 1818, 7; *LG*, 17 Jan 1818, 34-6; *BR*, XI (Feb. 1818), 192-255; *EM*, LXXIII (Feb. 1818), 137-9; *ER*, XXIX (Feb. 1818), 403-32 (F. Jeffrey); *LSMS*, II (Feb. 1818), 45-60; *MM*, XLV (1 Feb. 1818), 63; *GM*, LXXXVIII-i, (March 1818), 243; *MR*, LXXXV (March 1818), 261-75; *Analectic Magazine*, II (April 1818), 273-311; *BC*, IX 2s (May 1818), 528-40; *NAR*, VII (July 1818), 149-84 (E. T. Channing); *ER*, XXXIII (Jan. 1820), 1-54 (F. Jeffrey); *QR*, XXVI (Oct. 1821), 109-28 [pub. Dec. 1821] (N. W. Senior).

Tales of My Landlord, Second Series: *The Heart of Midlothian* (1818)

BM, III (Aug. 1818), 567-74; *EdM*, III (Aug. 1818), 107-17; *LSMS*, II (Aug. 1818), 314-22; *Scot*, 1 Aug 1818, 247; *LG*, 8 Aug. 1818, 497-500; *LJGM*, 8 Aug. 1818, 304-6, 15 Aug. 1818, 324-7; *Edinburgh Advertiser*, 14 Aug. 1818, 100; *BC*, X 2s (Sept. 1818), 246-60; *MM*, XLVI (1 Sept. 1818), 158; *NMM*, X (Oct. 1818), 250; *AjR*, LV (Nov. 1818), 212-18; *BR*, XII (Nov. 1818), 396-406; *GM*, LXXXVIII-ii (Nov. 1818), 426-9; *MR*, LXXXVII (Dec. 1818), 356-70; *Green Man*, 26 Dec. 1818, 68-9; *EcR*, XII 2s (Nov. 1819),

422-52 (J. Conder); *ER*, XXXIII (Jan. 1820), 1-54 (F. Jeffrey); *QR*, XXVI (Oct. 1821), 109-48 [pub. Dec. 1821] (N. W. Senior).

Tales of My Landlord, Third Series: *The Bride of Lammermoor* and *A Legend of Montrose* (1819)

BM, V (June 1819), 340-53; *EdM*, IV 2s (June 1819), 547-54, V 2s (July 1819), 38-45; *LC*, 26 June 1819, 81-6, 3 July 1819, 101-4; *LG*, 26 June 1819, 401-5, 3 July 1819, 419-23; *Scot*, 26 June 1819, 207; *MinMag*, III (July 1819), 85-93 [*Bride of Lammermoor*]; *MM*, XLVII (1 July 1819), 539; *AjR*, LVI (Aug. 1819), 507-14; *BR*, XIV (Aug. 1819), 233-47; *MR*, LXXXIX 2s (Aug. 1819), 387-403; *NER*, II (Aug. 1819), 160-84; *NMM*, XII (Aug. 1819), 67-73; *MinMag*, III (Sept. 1819), 184-93 [*Legend of Montrose*]; *EcR*, XII 2s (Nov. 1819), 422-52 (J. Conder); *LG*, 18 Dec. 1819, 802-6; *ER*, XXXIII (Jan. 1820), 1-54 (F. Jeffrey); *LC*, 9 Dec. 1820, 784; *QR*, XXVI (Oct. 1821), 109-48 [pub. Dec. 1821] (N. W. Senior).

Ivanhoe (1820)

BM, VI (Dec. 1819), 262-72; *LG*, 25 Dec. 1819, 817-23; *Scot*, 25 Dec. 1819, 414; *EdM*, VI 2s (Jan. 1820), 7-16 (R. Morehead); *ER*, XXXIII (Jan. 1820), 1-54 (F. Jeffrey); Gold's *LM*, I (Jan. 1820), 79-84, (Feb. 1820), 154-71; *LM*, I (Jan. 1820), 79-84 (J. Scott); *MR*, XCI (Jan. 1820), 71-89; *NMM*, XIII (Jan. 1820), 73-82; *LC*, 1 Jan. 1820, 1-4, 8 Jan. 1820, 21-4; *Champ*, 9 Jan. 1820, 27-8, 15 Jan. 1820, 42-4; *LMM*, XI 3s (Feb. 1820), 97-101; *MM*, XLIX (Feb. 1820), 71; *NER*, III (Feb. 1820), 163-99; *WestR*, II (May 1820), 204-24; *BR*, XV (June 1820), 393-454; *EcR*, XIII 2s (June 1820), 526-40; *QR*, XXVI (Oct. 1821), 109-49 [pub. Dec. 1821] (N. W. Senior).

The Monastery (1820)

BM, VI (March 1820), 692-704; *EdM*, VI 2s (March 1820), 254-56, (April 1820), 297-304; *LG*, 25 March 1820, 193-200; *Scot*, 25 March 1820, 101; *AjR*, LVIII (April 1820), 174-83; *EM*, LXXVII (April 1820), 344-7; Gold's *LM*, I (April 1820), 414-22, (May, 1820), 506-14; *GM*, XC-i (April 1820), 334-6; *LC*, 1 April 1820, 209-14; *MR*, XCI 2s (April 1820), 404-26; *NMM*, XIII (April 1820), 486-7; *LM*, I (May 1820), 565-8 (J. Scott); *LMM*, XI 3s (May 1820), 273-80; *MM*, XLIX (1 May 1820), 354-5; *BR*, XV (June 1820), 393-454; *WestR*, II (July 1820), 341-54; *EcR*, XIV 2s (Oct. 1820), 244-53; *NER*, IV (Dec. 1820), 691-717; *The Port Folio*, IX (1820), 337-8; *QR*, XXVI (Oct. 1821), 109-48 [pub. Dec. 1821] (N. W. Senior).

The Abbot (1820)

AjR, LIX (Sept. 1820), 49-66; *BM*, VII (Sept. 1820), 665-7 (J. G. Lockhart); *EdM*, VII 2s (Sept. 1820), 248-56; *EM*, LXXVIII (Sept. 1820), 241-6; *MR*, XCIII (Sept. 1820), 67-83; *LG*, 2 Sept. 1820, 561-9; *LC*, 9 Sept. 1820, 577-85; *Scot*, 9 Sept. 1820, 295; *EcR*, XIV 2s (Oct. 1820), 254-68; Gold's *LM*, II (Oct. 1820), 414-16, (Nov. 1820), 493-503; *LM*, II (Oct. 1820), 427-37 (J. Scott); *LMM*, XII 3s (Oct. 1820), 213-15; *NMM*, XIV (Oct. 1820), 421-30; *MM*, L (1 Oct. 1820), 266-7; *GM*, XC-ii (Nov. 1820), 433-6; *NER*, IV (Dec. 1820), 691-717; *The Port Folio*, X (Dec. 1820), 370-87; *WestR*, III (Dec. 1820), 255-60; *QR*, XXVI (Oct. 1821), 109-48 [pub. Dec. 1821] (N. W. Senior).

Kenilworth (1821)

BM, VIII (Jan. 1821), 435-42; *EdM*, VIII 2s (Jan. 1821), 10-16 (R. Morehead); *EM*, LXXIX (Jan. 1821), 53-61; *Scot*, 13 Jan. 1821, 15, 20 Jan. 1821, 22; *LG*, 20 Jan. 1821, 33-40; *LC*, 20 Jan. 1821, 33-37, 27 Jan. 1821, 52-7; *Dublin Inquisitor*, I (Feb. 1821), 138-50; *LM*, III (Feb. 1821), 188-200 (J. Scott); *MR*, XCIV (Feb. 1821), 146-61; *NMM*, I (Feb. 1821), 243-9; *BR*, XVII (March 1821), 216-29; *Gold's LM*, III (March 1821), 291-4; *GM*, XCI-i (March 1821), 246-52; *MM*, LI (March 1821), 167; *NER*, V (March 1821), 324-53; *The Port Folio*, XI (March 1821), 161-93; *Exam*, 11 March 1821, 156-7; *WestR*, IV (April 1821), 154-76; *QR*, XXVI (Oct. 1821), 109-48 [pub. Dec. 1821] (N. W. Senior).

The Pirate (officially published 1822; actually published Dec. 1821)

BM, X (Dec. 1821), 712-28 (J. G. Lockhart?); *EdM*, IX 2s (Dec. 1821), 535-54; *GM*, XCI-ii (Dec. 1821), 541-2, (supp. Feb. 1822), 607-13; *LG*, 22 Dec. 1821, 801-8; *Scot*, 29 Dec. 1821, 414; *Exam*, 30 Dec. 1821, 826-7; *BC*, XVII 2s (Jan. 1822), 93-109; *EM*, LXXXI (Jan. 1822), 45-57; *LM*, V (Jan. 1822), 80-90 (W. Hazlitt); *MR*, XCVII (Jan. 1822), 69-83; *NER*, II (Jan. 1822), 196-213; *QR*, XXVI (Jan. 1822), 454-74 [pub. March 1822] (N. W. Senior); *LC*, 5 Jan. 1822, 1-6, 12 Jan. 1822, 19-22; *LMM*, XV 3s (Feb. 1822), 98-102; *MM*, LIII (Feb. 1822), 65; *CO*, XXII (March 1822), 157-72, (April 1822), 237-50; *LSMS*, III (March 1822), 88-96.

The Fortunes of Nigel (1822)

EdM, X 2s (May 1822), 563*-9; *BM*, XI (June 1822), 734-5 (William Howison?); *EM* LXXXI (June 1822), 543-9; *ER*, XXXVII (June 1822), 204-25 (F. Jeffrey); *LMM*, XVI 3s (June 1822), 42, (Aug. 1822), 98-101; *MC*, I (June 1822), 216-24; *MR*, XCVIII (June 1822), 169-84; *LC*, 1 June 1822, 337-43; *LG*, 1 June 1822, 335-8, 8 June 1822, 355-8; *LitMus*, 1 June 1822, 81-3, 8 June 1822, 97-9, 15 June 1822, 117-19; *Exam*, 2 June 1822, 345-6; *General Weekly Reporter*, 2 June 1822, 345-52, 9 June 1822, 377-83; *GM*, XCII-ii (July 1822), 52-4; *MM*, LIII (July 1822), 548-9; *NMM*, IV (July 1822), 77-81; *EcR*, XVIII 2s (Aug. 1822), 163-70; *QR*, XXVII (July 1822), 337-64 [pub. Oct. 1822] (N. W. Senior); *LS*, II, 124-31.

Peveril of the Peak (1822)

EcR, XVIII 2s (Aug. 1822), 163-70; *EdM*, XII 2s (Jan. 1823), 54-60; *GM*, XCIII-i (Jan, 1823), 48-50; *Edinburgh University Journal*, 8 Jan. 1823, 38-44; *LG*, 18 Jan. 1823, 33-9. 25 Jan. 1823, 53-4; *LitMus*, 18 Jan. 1823, 44-5, 25 Jan. 1823, 49-54, 1 Feb. 1823, 67-70, 8 Feb. 1823, 83-7; *LitReg*, 25 Jan. 1823, 49-50; 1 Feb. 1823, 68-71; *LC*, 25 Jan. 1823, 49-54, 1 Feb. 1823, 70-3; *EM*, LXXXIII (Feb. 1823), 169-74; *LaBA*, XXVII (Feb. 1823), 91-4; *LM*, VIII (Feb. 1823), 205-10 (W. Hazlitt); *MM*, LV (Feb. 1823), 62, (March 1823), 166-7; *MR*, C 2s (Feb. 1823), 187-206; *NEM*, II (Feb. 1823), 152-8; *Exam*, Feb. 9 1823, 89-92; *BC*, XIX 2s (March 1823), 259-73; *British Magazine*, I (March 1823), 19-33; *NMM*, VII (March 1823), 273-8; *EcR*, XX 2s (July 1823), 36-46; *QR*, XXXV (March 1827), 518-66 (J. Heraud).

Quentin Durward (1823)

BC, XIX 2s (May 1823), 535-51; *EdM*, XII 2s (May 1823), 529-37; *GM*, XCIII-i (May 1823), 448-9; *NEM*, II (May 1823), 453-61; *LitMus*, 3 May 1823, 273-80, 17 May 1823,

309-11, 24 May 1823, 327-9; *LitReg*, 10 May 1823, 289-94, 17 May 1823, 308-12; *LG*, 10 May 1823, 297-8, 17 May 1823, 305-11; *Edinburgh Literary Gazette*, 17 May 1823, 237-40; *Scot*, 21 May 1823, 321; *LC*, 24 May 1823, 321-4, 7 June 1823, 362-3; *British Magazine*, I (June 1823), 159-75; *EM*, LXXXIII (June 1823), 544-6; *Knight's Quarterly Magazine*, I (June 1823), 200-14 (John Tell [pseud.?]); *MM*, LV (June 1823), 449; *MR*, CI 2s (June 1823) 187-202; *Exam*, 1 June 1823, 363; *EcR*, XX 2s (July 1823), 36-46; *LaBA*, XXVIII (July 1823), 32-3; *La Muse Francaise*, I (July 1823), (V. M. Hugo); *LMM*, XVIII 3s (July 1823), 31-40; *NMM*, VIII (July 1823), 82-7; *MM*, LVI (1 Sept. 1823), 118-22; *NMM*, IX (1 Sept. 1823), 416; *QR*, XXXV (March 1827), 518-66 (J. Heraud).

St. Ronan's Well (1824)

EdM, XIII 2s (Dec. 1823), 738-43; *GM*, XCIII-ii (Dec. 1823), 537-40; *LC*, 27 Dec. 1823, 820-4, 3 Jan. 1824, 1-3, 10 Jan. 1824, 24; *LG*, 27 Dec. 1823, 817-18, 3 Jan. 1824, 6; *LitMus*, 27 Dec. 1823, 817-19, 3 Jan. 1824, 7-9; *Scot*, 3 Dec. 1823, 833; *BC*, XXI 2s (Jan. 1824), 16-26; *Knight's Quarterly Magazine*, II (Jan. 1824), 238; *MR*, CIII (Jan. 1824), 61-75; *NEM*, IV (Jan. 1824), 54-61; *Exam*, 4 Jan. 1824, 2-3; *LSB*, 10 Jan. 1824, 337-41; *LaBA*, XXIX (Feb. 1824), 76-7; *LMM*, XIX 3s (Feb. 1824), 98-100, (March) 153-5; *MM*, LVII (Feb. 1824), 64; *Cambridge Quarterly Review*, I (March 1824), 99-136; *UR*, I (May 1824), 334-9; *QR*, XXXV (March 1827), 518-66 (J. Heraud).

Redgauntlet (1824)

NMM, XI 2s (May 1824), 93-6; *EdM*, XIV 2s (June 1824), 641-7; *GM*, XCIV-i (June 1824), 538-43; *MR*, CIV (June 1824), 198-209; *NEM*, IV (June 1824), 536-45; *Scot*, 16 June 1824, 377; *LC*, 19 June 1824, 385-92; *LG*, 19 June 1824, 385-90; *LaBA*, XXX (July 1824), 32-3; *LM*, X (July 1824), 69-78 (W. Hazlitt?); *LMM*, XX 3s (July 1824), 45; *Monthly Critical Gazette*, I (July 1824), 171-5; *Philomathic Journal*, I (July 1824), 235-9; *NMM*, XI (July 1824) 93-6; *UR*, I (July 1824), 514-20; *WR*, II (July 1824), 179-94; *Exam*, 11 July 1824, 441; *BC*, XXII 2s (Aug. 1824), 185-92; *Metropolitan Literary Journal*, I (Aug. 1824), 341-3; *United States Literary Gazette*, 15 Aug. 1824, 134-6; *The Port Folio*, XVIII 4s (Sept. 1824), 197-202; *QR*, XXXV (March 1827), 518-66 (J. Heraud).

Tales of the Crusaders: *The Betrothed* and *The Talisman* (1825)

EdM, XVI 2s (June 1825), 641-6; *MR*, CVII (June 1825), 160-74; *LC*, 25 June 1825, 401-8, 2 July 1825, 420-3; *LG*, 25 June 1825, 401-5, 2 July 1825, 420-2; *Scot*, 22 June 1825, 393; *Dublin and London Magazine*, I (July 1825), 223-8; *Dumfries Monthly Magazine*, I (July 1825), 80-8; *GM*, XCV-ii (July 1825), 40-4; *NMM*, XIV 2s (July 1825), 27-32; *MM*, LIX (1 July 1825), 551-2; *Exam*, 3 July 1825, 416-17; *LM*, VII (Aug. 1825), 766-73; *LM*, II 2s (Aug. 1825), 593-9; *Repository of Arts*, VI 3s (1 Aug. 1825), 102-13 (signed: Reginald Hildebrande); *United States Literary Gazette*, 1 Sept. 1825, 401-6; *QR*, XXXV (March 1827), 518-66 (J. Heraud).

Woodstock (1826)

WR, V (April 1826), 399-457; *LC*, 29 April 1826, 257-66, 6 May 1826, 278-80; *LG*, 29 April 1826, 257-60, 6 May 1826, 276-8, 13 May 1826, 295-6; *EdM*, XVIII 2s (May 1826), 542-7; *GM*, XCVI-i (May 1826), 434-7; *MR*, II 3s (May 1826), 73-96; *Panoramic Miscellany*, 31 May 1826, 673, 30 June 1826, 811-12; *Dublin and London Magazine*, II (June 1826), 264-71; *EcR*, XXV 2s (June 1826), 542-5; *LM*, V 2s (June 1826), 173-81; *MM*, I 2s

(June 1826), 626-7; *NMM*, XVIII 2s (1 June 1826), 230-1; *Repository of Arts*, VII 3s (1 June 1826), 341-50 (R. Hildebrand); *QR*, XXV (March 1827), 518-66 (J. Heraud).

Chronicles of the Canongate: *Two Drovers, The Highland Widow,* and *The Surgeon's Daughter* (1827)

London Weekly Review, 20 Oct. 1827, 305-10, 3 Nov. 1827, 340-3; *LG*, 27 Oct. 1827, 689-94, 3 Nov. 1827, 709-12; *BM*, XXII (Nov. 1827), 556-70 (J. Wilson); *GM*, XCVII-ii (Nov. 1827), 439-45; *LM*, IX 2s (Nov. 1827), 341-60, 409-25; *LC*, 3 Nov. 1827, 689-92; *Scot*, 3 Nov. 1827, 697; *Exam*, 4 Nov. 1827, 689-91; *LMM*, XXVI 3s (Dec. 1827), 336-7; *MM*, IV 2s (Dec. 1827), 645-7; *NMM*, XXI 2s (1 Dec. 1827), 510-2; *LMM*, XXVII (June 1828), 343.

Chronicles of the Canongate, Second Series: *The Fair Maid of Perth* (1828)

Le Globe, 10 May 1828, 395-6; *LC*, 17 May 1828, 305-8, 24 May 1828, 325-6; *LG*, 17 May 1828, 305-9; *London Weekly Review*, 17 May 1828, 305-8; *Athenaeum*, 21 May 1828, 466-9; *GM*, XCVIII-i (June 1828), 531-2; *LMM*, XXVII 3s (June 1828), 343; *Exam*, 1 June 1828, 359; *Le Globe*, 25 June 1828, 500-2; *Repository of Arts*, XII 3s (1 July 1828), 35-51 (signed: Reginald Hildebrande); *L'Indicatore Genovese*, 12 July 1828, 34 (Giuseppe Mazzini); *Southern Review*, II (Aug. 1828), 216-63.

Anne of Geierstein (1829)

New Scots Magazine, I (May 1829), 393-5; *Revue de Paris*, II (May 1829), 248-50; *LG*, 9 May 1829, 297-300, 16 May 1829, 313-16; *Edinburgh Literary Gazette*, 16 May 1829, 2-4, 30 May 1829, 41-2; *Edinburgh Literary Journal*, 16 May 1829, 367-71; *GM*, XCIX-i (June 1829), 520-4; *LMM*, I 5s (June 1829), 343-5; *MR*, XI 3s (June 1829), 288-301; *Athenaeum*, 3 June 1829, 337-40; *Exam*, 14 June 1829, 370-1; *WR*, XI (July 1829), 211-28; *Le Globe*, 15 Aug. 1829, 514-16; *Southern Review*, IV (Nov. 1829), 498-522.

Tales of My Landlord, Fourth Series: *Count Robert of Paris* and *Castle Dangerous* (1832)

Border Magazine, I (Dec. 1831), 90-3; *GM*, CI-ii, (Dec. 1831), 531-4; *Athenaeum*, 3 Dec. 1831, 777-80, 10 Dec. 1831, 796-7; *Edinburgh Literary Journal*, 3 Dec. 1831, 317-21; *LG*, 3 Dec. 1831, 770-2; *MM*, XII 2s (Jan. 1832), 118-20; *MR*, I 5s (Jan. 1832), 65-71; *Fraser's Magazine*, V (Feb. 1832), 6-19 (Bulwer-Lytton).

Select Bibliography

This select, annotated bibliography includes lists of criticisms of
Scott and studies of his reputation.

CORSON, J. C., *A Bibliography of Sir Walter Scott* (London, 1943): the
standard bibliography of Scott, it contains listings of many of the
contemporary reviews given in the Appendix.

CRUSE, AMY, *An Englishman and His Books in the Early Nineteenth
Century* (London, 1930): contains a chapter on Scott's contemporary
reputation, especially as found in letters and memoirs of the time;
eminently readable but of no scholarly value.

HAYDEN, J. O., *The Romantic Reviewers* 1802-24 (Chicago and London,
1969): a section on the contemporary reception of Scott's poetry and
miscellaneous prose works supplements Hillhouse's study of the
reception of the novels; also a source of information on the English
reviewing periodicals of the early nineteenth century.

HILLHOUSE, J. T., *The Waverley Novels and Their Critics* (Minneapolis,
1936): the most important source of information on the reputation
of Scott's novels down to the early 1930s.

HILLHOUSE, J. T. (revised by A. Welsh), 'Sir Walter Scott', in *The
English Romantic Poets and Essayists*, ed. by C. W. and L. H. Houtchens
(New York, 1966): an annotated bibliography condensing the
material in Hillhouse's study and supplementing it with information
on the reputation of the poetry and with additional material to date
of publication.

Select Index

Rather than list the contents in the usual single alphabetical scheme, I have divided the references as follows: I Periodicals in which Scott's works have been criticized. II Critics. III Authors compared with Scott. IV References to Scott's works, where there is significant comment.

I

An index of periodicals from which criticism of Scott has been taken or about which pertinent comment is made.

II

An index of critics, both public and informal.

III

An index of authors compared by critics to Scott.

IV

An index of Scott's works with entries where significant comment was made.

SELECT INDEX

The Lord of the Isles, No. 13; early
reception 6; 202, 211, 214, 339, 484,
485

Marmion, No. 2; publication and early
reception 3, 6; 199, 200, 201, 205,
210, 211, 213, 338, 343, 430, 433,
485, 486, 487, 488, 516
The Minstrelsy of the Scottish Border,
early reception 6; 353
The Monastery, Nos. 22, 25, 29, 50;
publication 3; early reception 12;
13, 183, 195-6, 201, 214, 262, 333,
343-4, 457, 491

Old Mortality, Nos. 16, 17, 50;
publication and early reception 3,
9; 152, 167, 179, 181, 182, 201, 204,
208, 212, 214, 262, 275, 285, 309,
317, 342-3, 376, 386, 415, 422, 430,
436, 455, 488

Paul's Letters to His Kinsfolk, 327
Peveril of the Peak, Nos. 22, 24c, 50;
early reception 13; 14, 286, 344
The Pirate, Nos. 22, 30; early
reception 13; 13, 274, 333

Quentin Durward, No. 34; early
reception 13; 286, 319

Redgauntlet, early reception 13; 376,
447, 470-1, 496
Rob Roy, Nos. 19, 20, 29; publication
and early reception 3, 10; 210-11,
275, 286, 308, 436, 448-9, 465, 532-6
Rokeby, No. 5; early reception 6;
209, 211, 214, 252, 339, 343, 485

St. Ronan's Well, No. 22; early
reception 13; 13, 284, 374, 490, 491

Tales of the Crusaders, 472, 479
The Talisman, early reception 13

The Vision of Don Roderick, 66, 505

Waverley, Nos. 6, 7, 8, 9; publication
and early reception 3, 8; 86, 89, 98,
101, 104, 115, 150, 204, 205, 209,
210, 211, 213, 214, 222, 228, 247,
250, 254, 262, 275, 285, 308, 327,
361, 365, 398, 415, 416, 429, 436,
455, 461
Woodstock, No. 36; early reception
13; 13, 14, 496